THE COURT OF QUEEN'S BENCH OF MANITOBA, 1870–1950: A BIOGRAPHICAL HISTORY

PATRONS OF THE SOCIETY

Blake, Cassels & Graydon LLP

Gowlings

McCarthy Tétrault LLP

Osler, Hoskin & Harcourt LLP

Paliare Roland Rosenberg Rothstein LLP

Torkin Manes Cohen Arbus LLP

Torys LLP

WeirFoulds LLP

The Osgoode Society is supported by a grant from
The Law Foundation of Ontario

THE LAW
FOUNDATION
OF ONTARIO

The Society also thanks The Law Society of Upper Canada
for its continuing support.

The Court of Queen's Bench of Manitoba
1870–1950

A Biographical History

DALE BRAWN

Published for The Osgoode Society for Canadian Legal History by
University of Toronto Press
Toronto Buffalo London

Printed in Canada

ISBN-13: 978-0-8020-9225-0
ISBN-10: 0-8020-9225-X

Printed on acid-free paper

Library and Archives Canada Cataloguing in Publication

Brawn, Dale, 1948–
The Court of Queen's Bench of Manitoba, 1870–1950 : a biographical history / Dale Brawn.

Includes bibliographical references and index.
ISBN-13: 978-0-8020-9225-0
ISBN-10: 0-8020-9225-X

1. Manitoba. Court of Queen's Bench – Biography. 2. Judges – Manitoba – Biography. 3. Manitoba. Court of Queen's Bench – History. 4. Courts – Manitoba – History. I. Osgoode Society for Canadian Legal History. II. Title

KE396.M3B73 2006 347.7127'0234 C2006-904167-9 KF345.Z9.A1B73 2006

University of Toronto Press acknowledges the financial assistance to its publishing program of the Canada Council for the Arts and the Ontario Arts Council.

University of Toronto Press acknowledges the financial support for its publishing activities of the Government of Canada through the Book Publishing Industry Development Program (BPIDP).

This book is dedicated to Doug Hay,
without whose inspiration, guidance, and
constant encouragement it would never have become a reality.

Contents

Foreword

THE OSGOODE SOCIETY FOR CANADIAN LEGAL HISTORY

In this meticulously researched and engaging collective account of the Manitoba Court of Queen's Bench judiciary, Professor Donald Brawn presents a unique biographical history of a provincial bench. This study also doubles as a history of the court itself. It shows the close connections in the early days between the Ontario bar and the judges of the new province, and highlights the political nature of the judicial appointment process, in the period prior to 1950. But it also suggests that in addition to political and legal ability, many lawyers became judges because they, more than others, had made themselves known in the communities in which they practised. These biographies of the first thirty-three men appointed to the Court of Queen's Bench highlight ways in which the members of the legal elite shared remarkably similar views and modes of thinking. The collective biography approach also allows an intimate look at personalities ranging from prime ministers to senior government officials to practising lawyers.

The purpose of The Osgoode Society for Canadian Legal History is to encourage research and writing in the history of Canadian law. The Society, which was incorporated in 1979 and is registered as a charity, was founded at the initiative of the Honourable R. Roy McMurtry, a former attorney general for Ontario, now chief justice of Ontario, and officials of the Law Society of Upper Canada. Its efforts to stimulate the study of legal history in Canada include a research-support program, a graduate student research-assistance program, and work in the fields of oral history and legal archives. The Society publishes volumes of interest to its members that contribute to legal-historical scholarship in Canada, including studies of the courts, the judiciary, and the legal profession, biographies, collections of documents, studies in criminology and penology, accounts of significant trials, and work in the social and economic history of the law.

Until earlier this year the editor-in-chief of the Osgoode Society for Canadian Legal History was Professor Peter Oliver, who had served in that role since 1979. Professor Oliver passed away in May 2006, but not before he worked extensively with the authors of our 2006 books; he is primarily responsible for seeing them through from inception to publication, as he was for all of the other 63 books published during his tenure of more than a quarter of a century. The Society is much indebted to him for all his contributions.

The annual report and information about membership may be obtained by writing: The Osgoode Society for Canadian Legal History, Osgoode Hall, 130 Queen Street West, Toronto, Ontario M5H 2N6. Telephone: 416-947-3321. E-mail: mmacfarl@lsuc.on.ca. Website: Osgoodesociety.ca

R. Roy McMurtry
President

Jim Phillips
Interim Editor-in-Chief

Acknowledgments

More than ten years ago I met for the first time my doctoral supervisor at Osgoode Hall Law School, Doug Hay. Early in our relationship he recommended that until a different methodology suggested itself I should organize my research around the biographies of the judges whose lives I was examining. This book grew out of that suggestion and Doug's continuing interest in my research.

Early encouragement was also offered by Harry Arthurs and the late Peter Oliver, both of whom patiently waded through a very preliminary draft of the manuscript and offered a number of helpful suggestions. I am particularly indebted to Peter, without whose support and stewardship this work would never have become a reality.

Two other individuals deserve special mention. DeLloyd Guth of the Faculty of Law of the University of Manitoba was ever ready to offer his help and to read drafts of each chapter as they were written. His passion for the legal history of Manitoba, and the individuals and institutions who are part of that history, was an inspiration. So too were the efforts of my brother Gary, who on numerous occasions put aside a busy law practice to keep the project on track.

Special thanks go to Wesley Pue of the Faculty of Law of the University of British Columbia, and to Professor Susan Glover of the Department of English at Laurentian University, both of whom took a particular interest in this history, and to my colleagues in the Department of Law and Justice at Laurentian.

I am also indebted to Jim Phillips and Marilyn MacFarlane of the Osgoode Society, who were incredibly thoughtful during what for the Society and the friends of Peter Oliver was a very difficult time; to the two anonymous readers of this manuscript for their helpful comments; and to the Manitoba Law Foundation for its grant to the Canadian Legal History Project, Faculty of Law, University of Manitoba, in support of publication.

THE COURT OF QUEEN'S BENCH OF MANITOBA, 1870–1950: A BIOGRAPHICAL HISTORY

Introduction

This collection of thirty-three biographies is at the same time a history of Canada and the development of a Canadian national identity and a history of Manitoba's Court of Queen's Bench. It explores the relationships that the province's first judges had with the societies in which they worked and socialized; and although these were ordinary men more concerned with practical realities than idealism, their biographies allow for the construction of a theory of 'lawyering' that integrates the study of a single bench into a much larger historical framework.

A theme running through the work is that judicial appointments represented the culmination of an on-going process of socialization. Understanding how lawyers were socialized is important because it helps us to understand how courts functioned and ought to function, and explains why judges occupied a middle ground legally, socially, and politically. As these biographies suggest, lawyers were socialized through a broad range of experiences not exclusively confined to courtrooms and law offices. Transmitting attitudes and values to law students during their time under articles and through legal education were the first and most formal methods,[1] but the process was often much less obvious. Social interactions with other practitioners, for instance, and membership in the same churches, clubs, and sports teams were additional mechanisms by which professional bonds were cemented. Such involvements served the dual function of enhancing and confirming a lawyer's professional status while simultaneously providing visible evidence that judicial aspirants had been appropriately socialized through their association with senior members of the bar. 'Being together allowed lawyers to size each other up. Their personalities and foibles and, therefore, their reliability could be measured.'[2] Law society and bar gatherings also served to reinforce traditions and values, and as Justice J.F. Bain noted in his speech to a 1892 bar dinner, such occasions were important for the 'fostering and promotion of a proper *esprit de corps*.'[3] More formal shapers of opinions and vehicles of socialization were professional journals, which in the 1880s became an important forum for disseminating the views of senior counsel.[4]

A second theme is that developing a close relationship with someone connected to the political, social, and legal establishments of the province, and of the nation, has been a key criterion in the judicial appointment process. Law is an intensely social calling, requiring the nurturing of contacts, the most important of whom are mentors. Although mentors played a particularly significant role in ensuring the proper socialization of young lawyers, the extent of their influence is difficult to measure because only glimpses of such relationships can be found in the private correspondence of members of the bar. What is clear, however, is that Manitoba's first judges each had a close relationship with at least one mentor whose influence could not be ignored by the federal political party in power, and that by the end of the nineteenth century advising and promoting the careers of others was a significant feature of Manitoba's professional culture.[5]

The last theme is that between 1885 and the 1920s the Manitoba bar transformed itself. The first lawyers appointed to the Court of Queen's Bench were part of a group who sought to build the province in the likeness of Ontario, where most had lived and worked before emigrating west. After 1885, however, the influence these individuals exerted on the legal profession was challenged by men raised and educated in Manitoba. Their vision was not from Ontario, but of something they considered newer and better; and the individuals they wanted on the bench were those who shared a uniquely western Canadian set of beliefs and values.

Understanding judges and judicial benches is important for a number of reasons. Judges are members of the public service elite and, along with politicians and senior bureaucrats, they are part of a most exclusive club in Canada. Its members are decision-makers and arbiters of state power in the same way that members of the corporate elite are decision-makers for the private sector. Knowing how and why judges acted as they did in the past gives us useful insights into how modern benches function. In contrast to administrative studies heavily grounded in statistics, historical studies allow us to identify patterns and to put into perspective the influences of eccentric and conventional judges, who may be important in so small a profession. Once identified, the roles of such factors as religion, education, family background, and politics can be measured. Historical data, specifically biographical, often offers the only way that such influences can be understood, because there is usually a lack of similar contemporary data available for synthetic and systemic studies.

Collective biographies are particularly important to an understanding of how benches function, and they stand in sharp contrast to sociological and political science judicial studies, where the emphasis is on identifying and predicting voting patterns. One of the best examples of a collective biography is R.F.V. Heuston's two-volume *Lives of the Lord Chancellors*.[6] Both depict England's Lord Chancellors in their legal, political, and personal lives. In *Law and Politics: The House of Lords as a Judicial Body, 1800–1976* Robert Stevens uses biographical data but moves away from traditional biography to examine the judicial role of the House of Lords in terms of the policy and legal doctrine it developed.[7] Daniel Duman's *The Judicial Bench in England 1727–1875, The Reshaping of a Professional Elite* is an exhaustive study of the lives of English judges and another leading study of the English bench.[8]

Although collection studies have been used by Canadian academics for some time, there yet remains relatively few. Among the earliest is David Read's *The Lives of the Judges of Upper Canada and Ontario*.[9] His thirty-one individual biographies grew out of a series of articles commissioned by *The Magazine of Western History*, published in Cleveland, Ohio. A work that would have predated Read's had it been published during the lifetime of its original author is *The Judges of New Brunswick and Their Times*.[10] Joseph Lawrence was the founding president of the New Brunswick Historical Society, and the inspiration for his collection of biographies was his inaugural address 'The First Courts, and Early Judges of New Brunswick,' delivered in 1874.[11] He was still working on the first draft of his book when he died eighteen years later. Finally published in 1983, it consists of the biographies of the twenty judges appointed to the bench of New Brunswick between 1784 and 1867. The collective biography of the bench of Lower Canada stands somewhere between *The Lives of the Judges of Upper Canada and Ontario* and *The Judges of New Brunswick*. Published in 1925, A.W. Patrick Buchanan's

The Bench and Bar of Lower Canada Down to 1850 provides brief biographical sketches of the province's early chief justice, selected puisnes, and a handful of members of the bar.[12]

One of the first and still rare examinations of a Canadian bench is William John Klein's doctoral thesis, *Judicial Recruitment in Manitoba, Ontario, and Quebec 1905–1970*.[13] His study is a quantitative analysis of the careers of judges appointed by the federal government in the provinces of Manitoba, Ontario, and Quebec between 1905 and 1970. Using data generated by law lists and parliamentary guides and information garnered from the Canadian Bar Association and provincial law societies, he looks at the appointment process, political activities, and career mobility of his seven hundred and forty-nine subjects and the law firms with which they were associated. A recent study is Robert Fraser's *Provincial Justice: Upper Canadian Legal Portraits from the Dictionary of Canadian Biography*.[14] The work presents a more complete picture of its subjects than earlier collection studies, but its aim is descriptive rather than analytical, and its focus the individual lives and times of those connected to the law, not the examination of a bench.

Canadian court studies, as opposed to biographical histories, that provide a valuable insight into the judiciary of this country include *A Progression of Judges: A History of the Supreme Court of British Columbia*,[15] Ian Bushnell's *The Captive Court: A Study of the Supreme Court of Canada*[16] and *The Federal Court of Canada, A History, 1875–1992*,[17] James Snell and Frederick Vaughan's *The Supreme Court of Canada, History of the Institution*,[18] and Paul Weiler's *In the Last Resort: A Critical Study of the Supreme Court of Canada*.[19]

The 1969 examination of the Supreme Court of Canada by George Adams and Paul J. Cavalluzzo [20] and Clara Greco's 'The Superior Court Judiciary of Nova Scotia, 1754–1900: A Collective Biography'[21] are two of the earliest Canadian biographical studies. The usefulness of the first, however, is limited by its methodology, or lack thereof. As noted by the authors, the purpose of the paper was merely the collection of data. 'Nowhere has biographical information on the members of the Supreme Court of Canada been collected and categorized in an orderly fashion ... [T]his study does not attempt to relate the biographical data to the decision-making process.'[22] Greco's study, by contrast, is both useful and methodologically sound. Although her analysis is limited by a lack of information about many of her subjects, she uses the data available to discuss ages and judicial tenure, birthplace, social status, religion, education, legal training and practice, political activities, family patronage networks, and judicial income. In *Lords of the Western Bench: A Biographical History of the Supreme and District Courts of Alberta, 1876-1990*[23] Louis Knafla and Richard Klumpenhouwer describe the lives of their subjects in one or two paragraphs, commenting on educational background, dates of call and appointment, legal experience, and the organizations with which individuals were associated.

The most recent Canadian collective biography is R. Blake Brown and Susan Jones's examination of the lives of the ninety men and women appointed to the Supreme Court of Nova Scotia during the twentieth century.[24] Their article builds on Greco's work and they too examine the background of members of the bench, paying particular attention to birthplace, social status, religion, education, ethnicity, legal practice, and political career. One of their significant findings is that beginning in the twentieth century there was a declining emphasis on privileged background and an increasing inclination by federal governments to reward individuals, including those 'with more humble social backgrounds,' who through hard work and the 'careful development of political connections' came to the attention of those responsible for making judicial appointments. A second important conclusion was that by the middle of the twentieth century the route to the Nova Scotia bench had changed and the appointment of retired politicians gave way to the appointment of those whose political involvement was behind the scenes, a change that 'had the benefit of hiding the political nature of judicial selection from most of the public.'[25]

The suggestion by the authors of *Lords of the Western Bench* that the Canadian prairies have no tradition of judicial biography is not accurate.[26] Manitoba, for example, has a long and impressive history of such studies. One of the first was published in 1887 as *A Political Manual of the Province of Manitoba and the North-west Territories*.[27] John Palmerston Robertson's work, however, is not original, and the judicial biographies it contains owe much to those in Henry J. Morgan's 1878 legal directory.[28] Both are written in the style of contemporary biographical dictionaries, as is *Lords of the Western Bench*. But apart from Robertson's early efforts, there are a number of articles and books about members of Manitoba's judiciary, each of which offers an often fascinating insight into their subjects.[29] To date, however, Manitoba has benefited from two exceptional studies of the legal profession, both of which are heavily biographical. Dale and Lee Gibson's *Substantial Justice: Law and Lawyers in Manitoba 1670–1970* is a history of the province's lawyers and legal institutions organized chronologically around themes like the Bench,

Lawyers' Organizations, Legal Education, Personalities, Police, and the Law Society.[30] They examined forces that shaped Manitoba's legal profession and tell us much about the conditions under which the profession first worked, and then recreated itself. In *'These Legal Gentlemen': Lawyers in Manitoba: 1839–1900* [31] Richard Willie uses a collective biography of the late-nineteenth-century Manitoba bar to measure the rate at which the province's legal profession matured and its members became integrated in the wider social and political community.

The history of Manitoba's Court of Queen's Bench merits particular attention for a number of reasons. First, its relative youth and small size required between 1870 and 1950 the appointment of only thirty-three men to the province's highest trial court. This made possible very detailed investigation of their backgrounds. Such research allows historians to look beyond family, law, and politics, the source of much of the data generated by other studies, to examine the extent to which individual lawyers were socialized by the practice of law, and the consequences of such socializing influences for the legal profession as a coherent group.

A huge amount of primary and secondary data, both biographical and statistical, survives for the study of Manitoba's Queen's Bench. The province's archives contain the professional and personal files of a number of judges, and they reveal much of the philosophy and beliefs of both the individuals and those with whom they shared the bench. The papers of justices like Ralph Maybank, J.T. Thorson, and Arnold Campbell are rich in material relating to the judicial selection process. Their opinions of other lawyers and judges, and their discussions of the significance of religion, ethnicity, geography, legal experience, and politics as criteria for appointment are some of the most intimate in Canadian legal history, and are particularly relevant because many involved federal and Manitoba cabinet ministers who ended their careers on the bench.

A third reason to study Manitoba's Queen's Bench is because of the role its members played in nation-building during an unusual period of social, economic, and political changes. Courts were particularly important in frontier societies like that of Manitoba because of the need to furnish a body of law for a variety of institutions. Judicial decisions legitimated economic relationships and rules for social order, defining the course of future development. Manitoba's first judges parachuted into the province to participate in building a newer and greater Canada west of Ontario. They saw themselves as agents of improvement, and were determined to create an environment conducive to rapid and sustained growth. They became an essential part of John A. Macdonald's National Policy because of their role in ensuring that peace, order, and good government prevailed in a potentially violent frontier, and that growth took place within the confines of law.

Finally, an examination of the history of the Court of Queen's Bench of Manitoba is important because of the leading role that Manitoba lawyers played in the professionalization of the Canadian bar.[32] According to Wes Pue, historians have not yet recognized that the most influential and creative force behind this process was Manitoba's legal profession.[33] He suggests, for instance, that the Code of Ethics adopted by the Canadian Bar Association was essentially the 'transformative vision' of professionalism of many of the men who went to the Manitoba bench, and it was their Manitoba Law School that for a time became the model for legal education in Canada.[34]

Although Manitoba entered Confederation in 1870, the history of its Court of Queen's Bench can be traced back to 2 May 1670, when Charles II affixed the Great Seal of England to the royal charter of the Governor and Company of Adventurers of England trading into Hudson's Bay.[35] In doing so he gave to the Hudson's Bay Company complete commercial and legal control over what is now Manitoba and the prairie provinces. According to the Charter, the law applicable to the territory was to be that of England and such laws enacted by the Company that were both reasonable and not contrary to the law of Great Britain. For the next one hundred and forty-five years the administration of justice in north-western North America, or Rupert's Land as it came to be known, was rudimentary at best. Crimes committed by Aboriginals against other Aboriginals were left to Aboriginal customary processes. Serious crimes were either dealt with by the local Hudson's Bay governor and his council, or an accused was supposed to be tried in England.

In 1803 the parliament of Great Britain passed the *Canada Jurisdiction Act*, which established for the first time a framework for the administration of justice in the lands under Company control.[36] According to the *Act*, the courts of Lower Canada had authority to hear criminal matters originating in Rupert's Land, or they could assign that authority on a case-by-case basis to the courts of Upper Canada. Less serious matters were to be heard by magistrates, who were to be appointed by the governor of Lower Canada. The major shortcoming of the *Canada Jurisdiction Act*, however, was that it did not explicitly state whether its provisions amended the judicial authority granted to the Hudson's Bay

Company in 1670. Commercial rivals of the Company argued that it no longer had the authority to administer justice in Rupert's Land. The Company, on the other hand, maintained that the *Act* had no application to the north-west, since it was intended to deal with crimes committed in 'Indian territories' not already under the governance of a recognizable authority.

In 1809 Thomas Douglas, Earl of Selkirk, wanted a legal opinion on the issue before he would agree to establish the first European settlement in Rupert's Land. He was advised that notwithstanding the provisions of the *Canada Jurisdiction Act*, the Hudson's Bay Company did indeed possess legislative and judicial authority over the north-west and those who resided therein.[37] Two years later Lord Selkirk purchased just under two hundred thousand acres of land around the junction of the Red and Assiniboine Rivers in what is now Manitoba. He referred to the area as the Red River Settlement, and within a year he sent to Canada the first of the 'Selkirk settlers.' From a legal perspective, however, Selkirk's purchase did not change a thing in the north-west. The Hudson's Bay Company may have sold some of its vast land holdings, but it retained the right to both govern and administer justice in the territory. The Selkirk colony's first manager was made a local governor by the Company and was advised that he could not exercise judicial authority in the settlement until he had appointed a council to assist him. In 1814 the council was finally appointed, and a year later the Hudson's Bay Company published the *Code of Penal Laws for Rupert's Land*.[38] Despite the fact that the code purported to deal with offences punishable by the laws of England, in reality it dealt only with offences against the Company, or company employees.

Between 1815 and 1821, when the Hudson's Bay Company merged with the North West Company, doubt persisted about whether the HBC had the authority to administer a legal system in Rupert's Land. In response to these concerns, the Company advised its North American governor to avoid the issue by persuading those with civil complaints to submit their disputes to arbitration by their neighbours. Those who refused to do so should have their disputes heard by a panel of four or five lay judges, who should be assisted by a jury of five or more. In a community that numbered in the hundreds, the proposal would have had the effect of keeping serious disputes to a minimum, but more important it would also have saved the Company from having to defend formally its right to administer justice in the Red River Settlement.

In 1821 Britain passed a statute that confirmed that the 1803 *Canada*

Jurisdiction Act applied to all of the territory under the control of the Hudson's Bay Company and that the British government had authority to establish courts and appoint judges in the west.[39] The jurisdiction of these courts, however, was to be limited to non-capital criminal offences and minor civil claims. A year after that act passed, Britain announced that it was not going to give effect to it and that it had no intention of establishing a court system in Rupert's Land. It also reaffirmed that the Hudson's Bay Company was responsible for the administration of justice in its territories. In 1822 a new governor was appointed to administer the affairs of the Red River Settlement. Unlike the instructions given his predecessors, however, this governor's mandate explicitly included the exercise of judicial authority. But although the administration of justice in the colony gradually became more systematic and effective, by the time Lord Selkirk's heirs transferred their control over the Red River Settlement back to the Hudson's Bay Company in 1835, the settlement's population numbered four thousand and it was clear to all that a more sophisticated legal system had to be put into place.

One change instituted following the re-transfer was dividing the settlement, now known as Assiniboia, into four judicial districts. A magistrate was assigned to each and was required to hold court every three months. These courts, referred to interchangeably as either 'Petty' or 'Petty Sessions,' were authorized to hear minor criminal and civil matters. A General Quarterly Court, precursor to the present Court of Queen's Bench, was created to hear more serious cases and appeals from Petty Sessions Courts. The Quarterly Court comprised the four Petty Sessions magistrates, the governor, and members of the Council of Assiniboia. Almost immediately it adopted the use of juries to decide questions of fact.[40]

In 1837 the number of judicial districts was reduced from four to three, and the number of magistrates (also known as justices of the peace) in each district increased to two. The more senior of the two was referred to as president. Other important changes included the requirement that Petty Sessions Courts be presided over by a panel of not less than three magistrates, one of whom had to be from a district other than the one in which the court sat. The composition of the Quarterly Court was also altered. Members of the Council of Assiniboia were no longer allowed to play a judicial role in the affairs of the settlement, thus separating executive office from judicial. In future, the court was to be presided over by at least four magistrates and the governor, or, in the absence of the governor, by the company's principal officer. The minimum monetary value of civil disputes heard by the Quarterly Court was also increased, and the purchase of law books and magistrates' manuals authorized for each judicial district.

In 1839 the Hudson's Bay Company again reorganized the judicial administration of Assiniboia. For the first time the colony was served by a legally trained judge, referred to as a recorder. One of his duties was sitting on the panel of Quarterly Court magistrates. The first recorder of Rupert's Land was Adam Thom. His disregard for court rules, which on at least one occasion saw him acting as counsel, witness, and judge in the same proceeding, resulted in his removal in 1851.[41] Instead of leaving the settlement, however, he stayed on as clerk of the court and legal adviser to the Company, and agreed to assist in the preparation of a report on the state of the law in Assiniboia. His findings took the form of a consolidated code of regulations, which was adopted by the Company in 1852. The most significant change suggested by Thom dealt with the date English law was deemed to have been received in the colony. Before 1852 the law applicable to the colony was the law that existed in England on the date Charles II granted to the Hudson's Bay Company its charter. In his report, however, Thom noted that it was difficult to determine the state of the law in 1670, since there were few legal texts in the colony. He suggested that the applicable law be that which was in force in England on 20 June 1837, the date Queen Victoria ascended the throne.

Also included in the 1852 consolidation were regulations dealing with marriage licences, customs duties, the administration of justice, and the use of printed legal forms. To ensure that the colony's residents could make themselves aware of these changes, copies of new laws were posted throughout the settlement, given to public officials and prominent citizens, and nailed to the doors of churches. Some of the laws adopted were well in advance of those in use in England. Among them was the right of an accused to testify in his or her own defence, and the right of a judge to apportion damages in contributory negligence cases.[42]

Between 1852 and Manitoba's entry into Confederation the judicial system in Assiniboia remained largely unchanged. Lay magistrates continued to preside over the colony's three Petty Sessions Courts, and their jurisdiction was enlarged to include the supervision of public works and the right to hear matters in private homes. Two changes, however, significantly affected the way justice was administered. The first had to do with the Quarterly Court. Although it continued to hear serious matters after 1862, the colony's governor no longer sat with the court, and five years later neither did lay magistrates. For all intents and purposes the court was presided over by Assiniboia's only trained lawyer, the recorder. The second had to do with the date English law was deemed to have been received in the colony. As of 1864 the laws applicable to the colony were those currently in force in England.

Two years before Manitoba became Canada's fifth province, Great Britain passed a statute that had a direct impact on justices of the peace in the territory. The 1868 *Rupert's Land Act*[43] provided that, until Canada's parliament determined otherwise, the authority and jurisdiction of all magistrates and justices of the peace within the colony were to continue in effect. The law, which described the jurisdiction of Canadian justices of the peace, was enacted the following year, when justices were given the authority to hear summary conviction and other matters specifically authorized by statute.[44] Actions were to be heard by a single justice of the peace unless the act that set out the offence provided otherwise. In such cases hearings were to be presided over by two or more justices.[45] The *Act* also provided that superior court judges and magistrates each had the power to do alone what would otherwise have to be done by two or more justices of the peace.[46]

That Manitoba's early justices of the peace lacked legal training was virtually guaranteed because the statute that provided for their appointment excluded lawyers from filling the office.[47] The only qualifications were that they had to be among the most competent persons residing in the area over which they had jurisdiction, and that they had to possess real property having a net value of at least five hundred dollars. Besides lawyers, those disqualified from acting as a justice of the peace included sheriffs and coroners.

In the years leading up to 1870 the biggest challenge to the administration of justice in Assiniboia was less black-letter law than political and social frustration. In anticipation of acquiring control of the Red River Settlement the government of Canada had sent into the colony a group of surveyors. These men were charged with preparing land descriptions so that newly arrived immigrants would be able to obtain title to their own pieces of the prairies. Unfortunately, the government did not consult those already residing in the colony. The resentment and uncertainty caused by the arrival of the surveyors led to an armed uprising and creation of a provisional government. As a consequence, the Council of Assiniboia ceased to exercise its authority as of October

1869, although both the Quarterly Court and Petty Sessions Courts continued to function for another two months. That they did not continue longer had less to do with the wishes of the colony's residents than with the proclamation by William McDougall, the region's governor-to-be, that as of 1 December legal authority over the settlement would be officially transferred to the government of Canada. In truth, such was not the case. Ottawa had not yet finalized arrangements with the Hudson's Bay Company to take over the colony. As a result of the confusion caused by McDougall's premature proclamation, settlement residents believed that the courts established by the Hudson's Bay Company no longer had the authority to administer justice in the colony. In the absence of courts established by Canada, the provisional government of Louis Riel created a new structure to be used until Canada assumed formal control of the settlement.

The new judicial system resembled the one that had been in place for thirty years. The main differences had more to do with form than substance. Five Petty Sessions Court districts were created, rather than the three that existed before 1869, and for the first time a distinction was made between magistrates and justices of the peace. Almost all of the judges who had held office during the administration of the Hudson's Bay Company were to be reappointed, and the colony's former sheriff was nominated Chief Justice of the new Supreme Court. Armed resistance to the provisional government prevented implementation of the new court structure, however. As a consequence, when Manitoba officially became a province the court system put into place by its former owner ceased to exist, but nothing had officially taken its place. The General Quarterly Court was scheduled to sit in June, but did not; and although a chief justice was sworn in, he never took office. Minor legal matters continued to be dealt with by Petty Sessions Courts, however, and they sat until the August 1870 arrival of British and Canadian troops led by Colonel Garnet Wolseley, at which point Riel's provisional government effectively ceased functioning.

Before Manitoba's entry into Confederation the terms justice of the peace and magistrate were used interchangeably. Manitoba magistrates, however, have always occupied a slightly higher rung on the judicial ladder than justices. Their authority was originally limited to property offences where the value of the affected property did not exceed ten dollars, cases of assault, hindering a government official in the performance of his duties, and keeping or being an inmate in a bawdy house.[48] Magistrates had the authority to try each of these cases summarily (i.e., without a jury), provided that an accused consented to their doing so. When that consent was withheld, the presiding magistrate lost his jurisdiction.

The first reference to a Manitoba magistrate or police court occurred in 1872. The same act that changed the name of the province's Supreme Court to the Court of Queen's Bench made the justices of the new court *ex officio* stipendiary magistrates throughout the province. It also directed that one of their number attend at the police station in Winnipeg to hear all cases that would otherwise be heard by two or more justices of the peace.[49] Shortly after the 1874 incorporation of the City of Winnipeg, the docket of its police court had become so crowded that it was necessary to hold sessions on a daily basis. For the next two years it was not unusual for the court to be presided over by the city's mayor, or by one or more of its aldermen, in their capacity as *ex officio* justices of the peace. When their authority was reduced to hearing offences against municipal by-laws,[50] a justice of the Court of Queen's Bench was forced to preside in his capacity as stipendiary magistrate.

The District of Assiniboia's Petty Sessions Courts would have ranked somewhere between police and county courts. In 1872, however, they were replaced by county courts.[51] The new courts were initially presided over by a Queen's Bench judge and held in each of the province's counties six times a year. The jurisdiction of county courts was limited to debt actions not exceeding one hundred dollars and petty assaults where damages claimed did not exceed twenty-five dollars. At its first meeting each year the county court opened as a court of sessions, and all of the justices of the peace and members of the grand jury for the county were required to attend. By law the court was required to deal first with its judicial agenda before conducting the municipal business of the county.

In 1875 the Manitoba legislature redefined the judicial responsibilities of lay justices.[52] They were now to have jurisdiction in all matters relating to municipal by-laws and in the exercise of their authority they were to proceed summarily. The effect of this enactment was to narrow the role played by these judicial officers to that of enforcing municipal by-laws. Sixteen years later the province set a limit on even this role by mandating that justices had the power to hear cases arising under municipal by-laws only in the absence of a police magistrate.[53]

By 1879 the jurisdiction of county courts had expanded to include actions involving gambling debts, liquor consumed in saloons, actions for ejectment, actions in which the validity of a will was disputed, actions for malicious prosecution, libel, slander, criminal conversation, seduction, and breach of marriage. In addition, county court judges could hear tort and replevin cases where the value of the object did not exceed one hundred dollars.[54]

In 1881 the government of Manitoba implemented a number of legal reforms. One was aimed at reducing the workload of Superior Court justices, in part by transferring responsibility for probate matters to a Surrogate Court, to be established in every judicial district. Each was to be presided over by the senior county court judge.[55] Although the Court of Queen's Bench retained nominal jurisdiction over estates of the deceased, for all intents and purposes the new court exercised its powers without interference from above. As a result, it alone decided all matters relating to granting or revoking the probate of wills and letters of administration.

A second reform divided Manitoba into three judicial districts and authorized the appointment of a county court judge for each.[56] Immediately after their appointment all powers and responsibilities of judges of the Court of Queen's Bench, sitting as justices of the county courts, were transferred to the new appointees. The province's first county court judge was appointed to the Central Judicial District in August 1882. A second was appointed to the Western Judicial District later the same month; and Winnipeg, as the administrative centre of the Eastern Judicial District, received its first judge a year later. Even before these judges were appointed, however, the provincial government expanded the jurisdiction of their court by creating in each judicial district a County Court Judges' Criminal Court. The new body was a court of record for the trial, without jury, of persons charged under the federal *Speedy Trials Act*.[57] In 1887 the jurisdiction of the court was enlarged to allow judges to hear appeals from orders of justices of the peace and magistrates.[58]

As a superior court of record Manitoba's Court of Queen's Bench had since its inception exercised the power and authority possessed by English courts of common law at Westminster and the court of Chancery.[59] Thus, the judges of the Queen's Bench had original authority over civil and criminal matters, including actions in law and equity.[60] In 1886, however, the provincial government decided to lay to rest a long-standing concern of the province's legal profession. The issue was the distinction between judges sitting as a court of equity and sitting as a court of law. In England and several Canadian provinces, one court system dealt with questions of law, while another dealt with issues of fairness or equity. In Manitoba Queen's Bench was a single court, with two divisions, each governed by different rules. Lawyers were required to use different procedures, depending upon whether they were making an argument in law or equity.

The distinction between the two branches of the court can be traced back to the Middle Ages. Plaintiffs regularly complained that the common law had become so fixed by tradition that it either gave them no remedy, when it should have done, or it gave judgment to their opponent, when he did not deserve one. Litigants increasingly began petitioning the royal chancellor for relief based not on law but on fairness. While common-law judges had no discretion to rewrite bad law, or interpret a case beyond what the law required, the chancellor's right to intervene on behalf of a litigant was unfettered. Among the issues with which his court, referred to as Chancery, began dealing were the specific performance of contracts, trusts, and the foreclosure of mortgages. Although the court of Chancery was originally established, in part at least, to correct the harshness of the common law, by the eighteenth century it too had become bound by a plethora of rules and procedures.

By the middle of the nineteenth century a movement to fuse the two courts was well under way. One of the first significant steps in that direction was the *Common Law Procedure Act* of 1854. It established that defendants at law could, in certain circumstances, use equitable defences. Twenty-one years later judicial fusion was complete. English courts of law and equity became distinct divisions of a single system. Queen's Bench justices could entertain equitable defences and grant equitable remedies, and courts of equity could consider questions of law and award damages.

When Manitoba's Court of Queen's Bench was established in 1870 it was, for reasons of economy, not given two separate court systems. Instead, Queen's Bench was one court, with two divisions or sides. In 1886 the procedural differences between law and equity were eliminated.[61] Two clauses in the amending act are particularly significant:

> 7. [In] any action on the common law side of the court, the court or a judge thereof, according to the circumstances of the case, may at the trial or any other stage of the action or other proceeding, pronounce such judgment, or make such order or decree as the equitable rights of the parties respectively require.
>
> ...
>
> 9. The said court in any suit or other proceeding instituted on the equity side thereof shall have jurisdiction in all matters which would be

> cognizable in a court of law and may grant therein to any person all such relief and remedies as he may be entitled to.

Although these amendments allowed Queen's Bench justices to grant equitable remedies in common law actions, and vice versa, fusion remained incomplete. If questions of equity or law were raised in actions commenced on the opposite side of the court, a judge still had to transfer the entire action to one side or the other, whichever was more appropriate.[62] The distinction between the two systems, and the need to transfer an action from one division of the court to another, was not abolished until 1895.[63]

A significant change affecting the structure of the Court of Queen's Bench was effected in 1906. So many members of the court had become ill from overwork that one of their number felt compelled to write the minister of justice to complain.[64] The provincial and federal governments responded by establishing a Court of Appeal. The new body was made up of four judges, two elevated from the Queen's Bench and two appointed directly from the bar.

The appellate jurisdiction of the Court of Queen's Bench had been spelled out in 1871, when the court was created. Originally only appeals from judgments of justices of the peace and a Court of Petty Sessions lay with the Riel government's Supreme Court;[65] but when those courts were replaced by county courts, appeals from the new courts could also be heard.[66] In 1874 the legislature directed that a panel of not less than two judges was to hear appeals three times a year.[67] Six years thereafter the Court of Queen's Bench was given the authority to hear appeals out of term;[68] and three years later a judge was allowed to hear his own appeal, provided that the panel considering the matter was made up of four justices, rather than the customary three.[69]

In the 1880s two changes substantially affected the Queen's Bench appeal process in Manitoba. First, the provincial legislature passed an act that allowed appeals from convictions and orders of justices of the peace to be heard in the county court of the district in which the conviction or order appealed from was made.[70] Second, *The County Courts Act* was amended to distinguish between appeals of law and appeals of fact.[71] An appeal from a decision of a county court judge now lay to the Court of Queen's Bench, regardless of the value of the claim, but only if it involved a question of law, or a mixed question of law and fact. The following year jurisdiction over appeals from summary convictions was transferred from Queen's Bench to the County Court.[72]

The appellate work of Queen's Bench justices was considerably reduced when judges of that court, sitting alone, could no longer reserve a case, or any part of a case, for consideration of the court sitting as a whole.[73] Before 1895 a judge had the right to refer to the full court any matter that, in his opinion, should be considered by the court *en banc*. These references consumed much of the court's time. The following year the number of appeals heard by the Court of Queen's Bench was further reduced by an amendment to *The County Court Act* that introduced a two-tiered system for appeals from decisions of county court judges.[74] Those involving actions with a monetary value of less than fifty dollars were to be heard by a single Queen's Bench justice, while those whose values exceeded fifty dollars were to be heard by the entire court.

The most significant change to the appellate function of the Court of Queen's Bench, however, was brought about in 1906 by creation of the province's Court of Appeal.[75] The statute that established the court provided that

> There shall be, and is hereby created, a Court of Appeal for Manitoba, to be called 'The Court of Appeal,' which shall consist of a Chief Justice, who, as long as the present Chief Justice of the Court of King's Bench continues to hold such office, shall be styled 'The Chief Justice of Appeal,' and three other judges, to be called Judges of Appeal, and the said Court shall sit at the City of Winnipeg, and each of the said Judges shall have all the jurisdiction, both civil and criminal, possessed by any Judge of the Court of King's Bench, under any statute of Canada or of this Province.[76]

Furthermore:

> The Chief Justice of Appeal and the other Judges of Appeal shall also be ex-officio Judges of the Court of King's Bench and may, in addition to their duties as Judges of the Court of Appeal, preside over any trials of civil or criminal cases in the Court of King's Bench to be tried before a Judge with a jury, and over any trials at bar, and over the trials of any election petitions, and any of them may also hold sittings of the County Court Judge's Criminal Court for the trial of criminal matters and proceedings to be heard, tried and disposed of by a single Judge without a

> jury, and for all purposes of any such trial shall have all the powers, rights, privileges and immunities of a Judge of the Court of King's Bench.[77]

When *The King's Bench Act* was amended to remove the right of its justices to hear appeals, the change was evident in what was not said, rather than what was. Before 1906 the court was described as having both original and appellate powers.[78] After 1906 it was described as possessing only an original jurisdiction,[79] and with that jurisdictional change the Court of Queen's Bench of Manitoba as it is currently constituted came into existence.

1

The Red River Settlement Becomes a Province, 1872

Although Manitoba became Canada's fifth province on 15 July 1870, the province's colonial era did not end until a month later. The expedition under the command of Colonel Wolseley, sent by the three-year-old government of Canada to put an end to the provisional government of Louis Riel, trudged through a heavy rain in ankle-deep mud through the north-west gate of Fort Garry, as Riel vanished into the rain through the south-east gateway.[1] The settlement into which Wolseley and his men marched was a pastoral community of stone residences and white farmhouses, 'with here and there a windmill.' Buffalo trails were so well used that as late as 1873 it was possible to walk where buffaloes had meandered along the banks of the Red and Assiniboine rivers.[2] In short, it was a community with 'no bank, no insurance office, no lawyers, only one doctor, no City Council, only one policeman, no taxes – nothing but freedom,' and whose citizens were 'tolerably virtuous and unmistakably happy.'[3]

The structure of Manitoba society changed almost overnight following the creation of the province, primarily because of the elimination of the buffalo. By 1870 there had been no buffalo in the Red River Settlement for years and few anywhere on the prairies. Those Metis who continued to rely on hunting were forced to spend increasingly longer periods of time away from their river-front farms in pursuit of their prey. After Manitoba became a province these hunters and gatherers were required to apply to a governmental official for title to their land.

The problem for most residents was that beginning in 1871 Ontario immigrants began to stake their claims, ignoring the signs of Metis occupation. Because many Metis lived in the province only a few weeks per year, their claims for land they had occupied for years were routinely denied. Over 90 per cent of Metis claims were rejected. As a result, by 1880 Manitoba had ceased to be a Metis community, and the number of Roman Catholics living in the province had shrunk from one-half of the population in 1870 to about one-eighth.[4]

The *Manitoba Act*, according to which the land belonging to the Hudson's Bay Company was transferred to Canada, was enacted by Parliament on 12 May 1870.[5] That transfer was confirmed by a British order-in-council six weeks later, and on 15 July 1870 Manitoba became the nation's fifth province, despite being only 130 miles wide and 100 miles long. The *Manitoba Act* provided for establishment of a Supreme Court, which was to exercise both original (trial) and appellate (appeal) jurisdictions. Until operational, however, such authority was exercised by the existing General Quarterly Court created in the 1830s by the Hudson's Bay Company. The Act also replaced the old Petty Courts of Assiniboia with five Courts of Petty Sessions, one for each of the counties of Provencher, Selkirk, and Lisgar, and two for the county of Marquette. Each court was staffed with a president, one or more justices of the peace, a clerk, and a bailiff.[6]

Francis G. Johnson was hired by the federal government to supervise the interim judicial system as head of the General Quarterly Court. He was a logical choice, since he had been the second recorder (chief judicial officer) of the General Quarterly Court under the Company. After leaving the Red River Settlement in 1858, however, Johnson was appointed a judge of the Quebec Superior Court. As a consequence, he had to take a leave of absence to administer justice in the new province. With the return of Johnson, Manitoba's lieutenant-governor felt confident that things could return to normal, and so issued a proclamation on 6 October 1870 confirming that there was no longer any excuse for citizens of the new province to take the law into their own hands.[7] A little over a month later Judge Johnson made a similar declaration, warning that 'if there be any unruly spirits here who imagine that the law ... is to be over-ridden they will find, to their cost, that they are mistaken.'[8]

When Manitoba entered Confederation, it did so without the benefit of an established government. Adams Archibald, the province's first lieutenant-governor, immediately ordered that a census be taken, a necessary precursor to dividing the province into twenty-four electoral districts. The taking of a census would also enable him to allocate the 1,400,000 acres of land promised to the families of half-breed residents by the *Manitoba Act*. Once the census was completed, Archibald called an election for 28 December 1870. Before the elected legislative assembly sat for the first time, however, he selected four members from the legislature and one from the appointed Legislative Council to form his cabinet. When the session was finally called to order, the setting was anything but regal. Many of the new members 'appeared in rough suits, coats open, no vest, collar or tie, but with brightly coloured flannel shirts and around the waist the gay coloured sash worn on the prairies.'[9]

Before 1870 no law or regulation prevented someone who wanted to practise law in Manitoba from doing so, regardless of whether he had any legal training or education. That changed in 1871, however, when the province's first government enacted a statute restricting the right to practise to three categories of individuals: those who had no qualifications in law but who could satisfy the government that they deserved the right; those who had completed a five-year apprenticeship and passed an examination set by the province's chief justice; and lawyers who had been admitted to the practice of law either elsewhere in Canada or in Great Britain after serving an appropriate apprenticeship.

The first two lawyers admitted in Manitoba examined the next seven applicants, two of whom were to become the first practitioners from the provincial bar to be appointed to the Queen's Bench.[10] Admissions to practice were made by the Lieutenant-Governor in Council until 19 December 1871, when the recently formed Bar Society of Manitoba took over that responsibility.[11] None of the first lawyers admitted, however, impressed the province's lieutenant-governor. In a letter written to Prime Minister John A. Macdonald in February 1872, Archibald said that none of the ten admitted to date had much of a professional reputation. 'Of the whole ten there are not over four who know enough law to draw the commonest contract, and probably the aggregate fortunes of the whole bunch would not exceed $500.00.'[12]

In 1872 the federal government changed the name of the Supreme Court of Manitoba, before it was even formally constituted, to the Court of Queen's Bench. At the same time it established a system of County Courts, to be presided over by justices of the Queen's Bench, to replace the Courts of Petty Sessions. In addition to sitting on these two courts, justices of the Court of Queen's Bench were also required to act as police magistrates.

Between 1870 and the summer of 1872 the federal government refused to appoint anyone to the bench of Manitoba and, as a result, Judge Johnson continued to preside over sessions of the General Quarterly Court. In May 1872 Johnson returned to Quebec and Prime Minister John A. Macdonald made Alexander Morris, a former member of his cabinet, the first judge and first Chief Justice of Manitoba. Macdonald did not, however, appoint puisne justices to assist him. As a consequence, when the court opened for the first time on 8 October 1872 Morris sat alone. One of the most significant of his early rulings was that the procedure to be followed in the Court of Queen's Bench was to be that of English common law rather than French civil law, despite the fact that a majority of the province's first lawyers were from Quebec. 'Fortunately, the legislature here adopted English practice and English law, and I have quietly enforced both, and *have carried with me the French bar*.'[13]

ALEXANDER MORRIS

With the benefit of hindsight it is hard to imagine anyone better suited to becoming Manitoba's first judge than Alexander Morris. Raised in wealth and influence, but imbued with a hatred of racial and religious intolerances, he preached the gospel of western expansion long before that refrain became popular in post-Confederation Canada. He was also unique in that history presented him with a chance to create reality out of not just one vision, but two. Although he arrived in Manitoba as the province's first judge, he stayed on to become the region's second lieutenant-governor. In carrying out the responsibilities associated with both roles, he refused to be corrupted by the stereotypes and prejudices with which he dealt on a daily basis. His ability to broker compromise, exhibited when he negotiated the settlement that persuaded George Brown and John A. Macdonald to put aside personal antipathy and political differences in favour of a larger vision, figured significantly in the settlement of the West.

Morris was born into a prominent Scottish family of Welsh origin. His grandfather Alexander Morris left Kilmarnock, County Ayr, for Paisley, in County Renfrew, Scotland in the seventeenth century.[14] Despite the wealth and the status he earned as a manufacturer, Alexander left Paisley for Canada in 1801[15] at the relatively advanced age of forty-nine. All four children born to him and to Janet Long, his much-travelled wife, were born in Scotland.[16] The second of the four was the father of Alexander.

Alexander Morris (1826–89). Chief justice of the Court of Queen's Bench 1872. Morris was the first judge appointed to the bench in Manitoba and the province's first chief justice. Before his appointment he was better known as a politician than as a lawyer, and played a role in brokering the compromise between political opponents John A. Macdonald and George Brown that resulted in the creation of Canada. (Provincial Archives of Manitoba)

Although William Morris, like his brothers and sister, was brought up in comfort, things changed four years after they arrived in Canada. After initial success in the Montreal–Scotland import and export business, William Sr suffered a series of financial reverses, including the loss of an uninsured cargo ship. William Jr was in Scotland when he learned of the disaster to his family's fortune. By the time the twenty-year-old and his brother Alexander returned to Canada in the fall of 1806, their father had retired from Montreal to a farm near Brockville, Ontario (then known as Elizabethtown, Upper Canada). Determined to pay off his debts and rebuild the family fortune, the two opened a store in their adopted home, where they functioned as middlemen between the large merchant houses of Montreal and the natives, loggers, and settlers who surrounded them.

In 1816 William Jr opened a store in the newly established military settlement of Perth. During the time it took another store to prosper he slept on a buffalo robe behind a birch-bark counter.[17] His efforts paid off. Within a few years he was the town's largest merchant and one of its biggest landowners. Remembering how quickly their father had lost his money, William and his brother refused to overextend themselves, or to invest too much money in any one area. The two soon acquired a small fortune, and William took a portion of his share and bought land throughout Upper Canada. Part of the money he earned from speculating in real estate he reinvested in more real estate, and part he invested in the province's growing banking industry. Although his cautious approach to business did not prevent him from making mistakes, most notably his investment in the Tay Navigation Company, diversification was a philosophy he never relinquished. He retained an active interest in his Perth store until shortly before his death in 1858, and he left an estate of more than thirty-seven thousand pounds.

Although William Morris was widely regarded as one of Perth's most successful businessmen, he was better known as the man who led the British charge in the battle of Ogdensburg during the War of 1812. On the strength of his considerable reputation he was an easy winner in the region's first general election. From 1820 until he was appointed to the Legislative Council of Upper Canada he was a popular and influential member of the House of Assembly. Although his religious convictions and attitude towards education kept him from joining the ruling elite, he was widely regarded as an able parliamentarian, a shrewd tactician, and one of the hardest working members of the legislature.[18] William Morris was also a devout Scots nationalist who believed that the Church of Scotland was the foundation upon which Scottish society rested. He regarded Scotland as the equal of England in every way and felt that Scottish Canadians had a key role to play in building the infrastructure of their adopted homeland. The passion with which he adhered to these beliefs made him popular among Presbyterians, but alienated him from most of the Anglican-dominated House of Assembly for Upper Canada. His estrangement from the ruling elite became complete in 1823 when he introduced a bill demanding that the Church of Scotland be recognized and funded as one of the British empire's two national churches. For the next seventeen years William almost single-handed led the battle to protect the rights of Scottish Presbyterians. His task was made considerably more difficult by the fact that Upper Canadian Presbyterians could not agree on a single doctrine and were scattered throughout the province in unorganized groups. By 1831, however, his efforts paid off, arguably too well. Instead of coalescing in a single synod, Presbyterians formed two. The United Presbyterian Synod represented a number of congregations in Upper Canada, while the much larger Synod of the Presbyterian Church of Canada became the voice of the majority of churches in Upper and Lower Canada.

William became involved in education in 1822 when, as a member of Perth's Court of Quarter Sessions, he was responsible for supervising the community's grammar school. That experience tweaked his interest in education, and by the end of the decade he was widely recognized as an authority on the state of schools throughout Upper Canada.[19] He believed that the cornerstone of any prosperous society was a comprehensive system of free, state-controlled, publicly funded schools. Although the system he advocated included both common and grammar schools in each district, he was opposed to creating a provincial university, primarily because he believed that it would be used to advance the power of the Anglican church. When it became clear that a university was going to be established in Upper Canada, regardless of his concerns, he argued that it should at least be non-sectarian. When that argument failed, and Bishop Strachan succeeded in assuming control of King's College (now the University of Toronto), Morris changed course. He conceded that if his church was to avoid being shut out of the education system altogether, it would have to establish its own university. By 1840 he had prepared a draft charter for a Presbyterian college, complete with faculties of arts and science. He suggested that it be located in Kingston and, to give it at least a semblance of equality with the Anglican college in Toronto, that it be called Queen's. When a royal charter was granted the following year William became the first chairman of the college's board of trustees.

By 1837 Morris was popularly regarded as one of Canada's three leading churchmen. Although he possessed considerably less influence than the Church of England's John Strachan or the Methodist's Egerton Ryerson, he was nonetheless regarded as the voice of Presbyterians. His status was enhanced when the Synod of the Presbyterian Church of Canada, in connection with the Church of Scotland, asked him to petition the English government on its behalf for official recognition and funding. Although he was initially rebuffed in his efforts, the British government agreed to recognize the Church if Morris could persuade the two Canadian synods to put aside their differences and unite as a single body. That union came about in 1840, but the government waffled on its commitment. Although it officially recognized the Presbyterian church, the funding awarded it was one half of that granted to the Church of England.

The experience he gained working with members of the clergy had a profound impact on William. He came to regard clergymen as lazy and inefficient, with a pronounced thirst for power,[20] and he regularly complained of their incompetence and secretiveness.[21] And although Alexander was to start a children's religious magazine, the *Juvenile Presbyterian*, become the church's Superintendent of Sunday Schools, an elder of the St Andrews congregation, and a member of both the Presbytery and the Synod, he shared his father's opinions of the clergy and his opposition to sectarian education.

When Upper and Lower Canada were united in 1841, William was appointed to the newly created Legislative Council. He stepped down two years later amid infighting over the issue of patronage, but in 1844 was asked to join the Draper administration as receiver general. He agreed, and eventually became president of the Executive Council. The government fell in 1848 and Morris retired from politics, but before that happened he persuaded a political protégé to take over as receiver general. John A. Macdonald returned the favour twenty years later when he invited William's son to enter his cabinet.

James Morris, the younger brother of William, also had considerable success in politics. He represented the constituency of Leeds in the Legislative Assembly and later became a member, and then speaker, of the Legislative Council. He is now best remembered by the town named after him, Morrisburg, Ontario. But James and William were not the only relatives of Alexander to achieve political success. The uncle of Alexander's wife was Philip VanKoughnet, a wealthy and much respected son of United Empire Loyalist parents. Born in Lunenburg,

Nova Scotia, to a family of wealthy landowners, he immigrated to Upper Canada while a youth and fought in both the War of 1812 and the rebellion of 1837–8. In the latter conflict he was a lieutenant-colonel and commanded a battalion of militia against a group of American invaders at the battle of the Windmill. VanKoughnet was elected to the assembly of Upper Canada for the riding of Stormont and Russell in 1816 and remained in the assembly until 1828. He returned to politics in 1830, before leaving again in 1834. Twenty-three years later a second comeback failed. Although a wealthy merchant and landowner, he was considered a secondary member of Upper Canada's 'family compact.' After he left the assembly he spent five years in the Legislative Council and was chair of the Canadian Board of Government Arbitrators when he died in 1873.

Alexander Morris received his early education in Perth. When he graduated from the Perth Grammar School in 1840 he was fifteen and one of the oldest students in the district. He immediately left for Scotland, where he spent the next two years studying at Madras College in St Andrews and at the University of Glasgow. At Madras he took first prize in Latin and second in Greek. In 1842 he entered university, and earned fourth prize in logic. The following year Morris returned to Canada, settling in Montreal, where he studied French and joined the commission agency of Thorne & Heward. Three years later, at his father's urging, he left the world of commerce to become a clerk in the Perth law office of Daniel McMartin. At the time McMartin was one of Canada's most senior lawyers, but his relationship with Morris did not last long.[22] Almost immediately after the two signed a five-year articling agreement, the indenture was assigned to a Kingston lawyer thirteen years McMartin's junior.

Morris divided his time in Kingston between the law office of John A. Macdonald and Queen's College, where he was a student in the faculty of arts. Poor health soon forced him to abandon both pursuits, and Canada's future prime minister acknowledged Morris's presence with a perfunctory handwritten note: 'I certify the above named Alexander Morris served for nine months in my office under the above written Articles of Apprenticeship. – beginning on the 10th Nov 1847.'[23] The registrar of Queen's, however, was more enthusiastic. He issued a certificate dated 6 January 1849 in which he certified that 'Mr. Alexander Morris, Student in the Faculty of Arts, during the Session 1847–48, attended the Mathematical, Natural Philosophy, Logic & Rhetoric Classes, so long as the state of his health would permit, that he conducted himself entirely to my satisfaction, and gave many pleasing proofs of ability & diligence.'[24]

After leaving Kingston, Morris returned to Montreal. There he entered the law office of the attorney general of Canada East, William Badgley, and John Joseph Caldwell Abbott, a future father of Confederation. Most of the work he did while under articles was on behalf of the firm's commercial clients. Chief among them was Hugh Allan, one of the country's largest shipping tycoons. Other clients included Montreal's largest hardware businesses, a large drug plant, and several rail companies. But Morris worked on more than legal files. As attorney general, Badgley was responsible for administering the province's criminal laws, and Morris helped him revise the province's eight-hundred-article *Criminal Code*. It was an experience that likely served him well years later, when he drafted the first rules of Manitoba's Court of Queen's Bench.

While under articles Morris entered McGill College as a law student. In so doing he reduced his time under articles from five to three years, and because the three-year Bachelor of Civil Law program required him to spend one year in Arts, a year before he received his B.C.L. he also received the institution's first arts degree (1849). Any pressure he felt at having to divide his time between a law office and a law school was likely reduced by the fact that the school's only professor, Badgley, operated it out of a bank located next to his office. There Morris, like his twenty-one fellow students, studied legal history, Roman, international, criminal, and commercial law, and, if they chose, French customs. Two degrees, however, did not satisfy his thirst for knowledge. In 1852 he received a Master of Arts degree, and ten years later became one of the first McGill students to earn a doctorate in law. In an eight-page summary of his academic career, written following his return from Manitoba, Morris noted only that by 1852 he had taken three degrees, and had 'done much to serve Law Faculty.'[25] Actually, he did more than merely serve the faculty of law. The year he received his M.A. his classmates elected him a 'Fellow in Arts.' In 1856 he became a member of the college's board of governors, and two years after that he was appointed a trustee of Queen's College. In 1883 he was elected the board's chair.

Eighteen fifty-one was a watershed year for Alexander Morris. First, it was the year he married Margaret Cline, a daughter of Cornwall's William Cline. Morris and his wife were to have eleven children, the youngest of whom was Edmund Montague Morris, who studied art in

New York and Paris and was elected an associate of the Royal Canadian Academy. His paintings of Aboriginals made him famous, and some of his works are in the National Gallery of Canada.[26]

In 1851 as well Morris was called to the bar of Upper Canada. Although John Ross, the province's attorney general, offered him a partnership, he declined and returned to Montreal.[27] There he presented proof of his membership in the Law Society of Upper Canada, passed an exam, and was admitted to the bar of Lower Canada. Soon after trying to establish a practice on his own he abandoned the effort and joined the firm of Frederick William Torrance. The Torrance family was one of Montreal's most influential, economically and socially.[28] Frederick's grandfather made a fortune in the grocery, liquor, and tea-importing business, and by 1851 the family was the fourth largest private landowner on the island of Montreal. Their other investments included the Montreal Towboat Company, the Montreal and Quebec Steamboat Company, and railroads like the Champlain and Saint Lawrence. But the Torrance influence extended well beyond Lower Canada. Frederick's brother was married to a daughter of Cornelius Vanderbilt, Frederick's brother-in-law was Alexander Tilloch Galt, and the family's commercial partners included the Molsons and Allans.

Frederick Torrance was called to the bar three years before Morris. After articling in the law office of his grandfather, Duncan Fisher, and Fisher's partner, Attorney-General James Smith, he immediately set about building a commercial practice based on the management of his family's business interests. By 1851 it was flourishing. The bulk of the work done by Torrance and Morris consisted of preparing partnership agreements, corporate charters, agreements of sale and bills of lading and probating estates. When not actually drafting documents, they consulted clients, prepared letters of opinion, and structured enterprises.[29] Their practice was typical of other large Montreal and Toronto law firms. Besides the two of them, it consisted of one or two junior lawyers, a law student, a clerk, and a bookkeeper. It also made regular use of a local land surveyor and frequently joint-ventured legal work with other firms.

As a young lawyer Morris frequently used literary gatherings to advance his social and political interests. He was twenty-three and a vice-president of the Mercantile Library Association of Montreal when he delivered his first lecture. His topic was 'The North American Indian, Their Origin, Present Conditions and Oratory.' Four years later he published an academic article on the railway consolidation acts of

Canada; and his 1855 essay *Canada and Her Resources* won second prize in an international literary contest. But the work that best expressed his political beliefs arose out a series of lectures he gave in Montreal. All were delivered to the Mercantile Library Association and were immensely popular. The attention they attracted likely earned Morris a cabinet seat in Macdonald's first ministry. In 1858 three thousand copies of his essay *Nova Britannia; or, British North America, Its Extent and Future* were sold within ten days. Morris used it to predict the federation of Great Britain's remaining North American colonies and the construction of a network of rail lines across Canada. He also warned his readers that when Confederation became a reality, the country's first leaders would be wise to take into account the legal rights and social needs of Aboriginals. The essay predated by months the speech given by Alexander Tilloch Galt, widely regarded as the first call for a confederation of the provinces. Among the sentiments expressed in *Nova Britannia* is Morris's belief that

> This great country cannot long remain unoccupied and if we do not proceed to settle it, the Americans will appropriate it as they did the Oregon. Without entering upon the question of the alleged vices in the Charter by which the powerful Company holds its possessions, and the mode of adjudicating thereon, there are certain measures which should at once be adopted. A means of communication by road and water, for summer and winter use, should be opened between Lake Superior and the Red River Settlement ... Should such a 'Paradise of Fertility' as this remain locked up? Will the gathering of a few peltries more or less compensate for the withdrawal of such a region from the industry of our race?[30]

Morris used a second 1858 lecture, 'The Hudson's Bay and Pacific Territories,' to voice his strong opposition to allowing the Hudson's Bay Company to control the north-west. He argued that Rupert's Land and the rest of the west rightfully belonged to Canada, not the Hudson's Bay Company.

The first of the three books published by Morris was *The Railway Clauses Consolidation Acts of Canada*.[31] Its introduction contains *An Act to consolidate and regulate the General Clauses relating to Railways*, assented to in 1851, and *An Act in addition to the General Railway Clauses Consolidation Act*, assented to two years later. The second half is a twenty-six-page alphabetical index, which is the rationale behind the work. Throughout, Morris offers no analysis or comments. He merely divides the statutes contained in the first part of the book into ninety-two headings and several hundred sub-headings.

The Judicature Acts of Lower Canada[32] is an even smaller effort. It contains only an alphabetical index to the *Judicature Act*, which was not otherwise described in the forty-nine-page book. The index did, however, contain one hundred and nine separate headings, compared to the ninety-two of his earlier work.

Morris published his last book, *The Treaties of Canada with the Indians of Manitoba and the North-West Territories, including the negotiations on which they are based, and other information relating thereto*,[33] three years after he left Manitoba. It is not altogether dissimilar to his analytical indices, although in its introduction and several of its chapters he provided a historical background to Canada's treaty-making process, discussed the Sioux and 'half-breeds,' and speculated about the future of Canada's original inhabitants. That Morris was deeply moved by the plight of the Indians was evident. During treaty negotiations he tried to learn as much as he could about their culture, history, traditions, and way of life. And it was the fruits of these labours that he wanted to share with his readers.

> It is the design of the present work to tell the story of these treaties, to preserve, as far as practicable, a record of the negotiations on which they were based, and to present to the many in the Dominion and elsewhere, who take a deep interest in these sons of the forest and the plain, a view of their habits of thought and speech, as thereby presented, and to suggest the possibility, nay, the certainty, of a hopeful future for them.[34]

Although Morris was more plodding compiler than historian, he was also one of the first to speak publicly of a Canada stretching from sea to sea.

Morris left Montreal in 1861 to pursue a political career in Upper Canada and was replaced in the Torrance firm by his younger brother, John Lang Morris. Although he did not have in Perth the same success he experienced in Montreal, he and his former partner eventually both ended their legal careers on the bench. The first of Morris's two Ontario partners was John Deacon, Jr. While it was not known whether Deacon became the firm's senior partner because he was called to the bar two years before Morris, or because he had established a practice in Perth before his partner arrived, it was known that the partnership did not last. By 1870 Deacon & Morris had become Morris & Radenhurst, and

William Horatio Radenhurst was the firm's junior partner. Neither practice flourished, however, probably because Morris devoted most of his time to politics, the Presbyterian church, and managing his personal business interests. Those included investments in iron ore, canals, and railways. Morris also took a leading role in the founding of the Bedford Navigation Company, and sat on several boards, including that of the Commercial Bank of Canada. In Manitoba he was also to pursue a variety of commercial interests. He bought hundreds of acres of land in and around Winnipeg, invested in a number of land companies, and built the 'Morris Block' in what is now the heart of downtown Winnipeg. Following his return to Ontario he sat on numerous boards. Among them were Toronto General Trusts, North American Life, and the Imperial Bank of Canada.

Biographers have traditionally regarded Alexander's 1861 victory in Lanark South as his first venture into politics. In reality his involvement started a few years earlier. Morris suggested that his first political battle occurred between 1853 and 1855, when he '[r]an for Renfrew as a candidate, unsuccessfully against two local candidates, but polled 196 votes.'[35] That defeat did little to discourage him. Three years before he was elected in his father's old constituency, Morris noted that he was invited to run in South Lanark with certainty of election, but declined on account of having to care for a bedridden member of his family.[36] He was seldom completely out of the eye of the public, however, and returned to Lanark later the same year to give an address to the North Lanark Agricultural Society.

His inclination to explore the political landscape before venturing into a political battle suggested that Morris was stretching the truth when, following his 1861 victory as a Liberal-Conservative, he said that 'the people brought me out without my knowledge and returned me by a majority of upwards of four hundred so that my sphere of influence is widening. I was very reluctant to accept but as it was my father's Country ... [I] could not say no.'[37] That Alexander was perceived as a worthy successor to his father was evident in a song sung at his victory celebration.

> [He] has been an honest man,
> In virtue he has shone,
> The Father's virtue we ha'e seen
> Reflected in the Son.[38]

Morris played a useful, though not a leading, role in the legislature of Upper Canada. His non-confrontational approach made him friends on both sides of the chamber. That came in handy in June 1864, when the defeat of the Taché-Macdonald government on a vote of non-confidence precipitated one of the most serious political crises in pre-Confederation Canada. The government fell amid charges that Alexander Tilloch Galt had illegally paid $100,000 to the Grand Trunk Railway for property located in Montreal. Following its defeat, the government asked the governor general to dissolve the House. Monck agreed to do so, but first wanted the government to at least consider forming a coalition ministry. Such a ministry would necessarily include the leader of the Reformers, George Brown. Brown had been outspoken in his support of a federation of the provinces of British North America and in opposition to the government. Although his personal antipathy towards Macdonald made him reluctant to enter the provincial cabinet, he agreed to meet with Morris to discuss what he would expect should he change his mind. Morris was the ideal middleman. He was someone with whom Brown had always gotten along well, and he shared the newspaperman's belief in confederation and annexation of the west. Macdonald's relationship with Morris was even closer.

During a drive in the country, Brown gave his companion permission to tell Macdonald that he would enter a coalition government if it agreed to support the idea of a federation. Morris took the offer to his former Kingston mentor. When Brown and Macdonald next entered the assembly, Macdonald announced the agreement. What followed was pandemonium.

> The House, wearied of piecemeal and sterile politics, wearied of prolonged crisis, rose cheering, and leaders and backbenchers alike stumbled into the aisles and poured onto the floor. The leaders shook hands and clapped shoulders; with a spring the little Bleu member for Montcalm, Joseph Dufresne, embraced the tall Brown and hung from the neck of the embarrassed giant. The tension of years of frustration broke in the frantic rejoicing.[39]

Two years before Canada became a nation D'Arcy McGee, one of the fathers of Confederation, stood in the House of Assembly to pay tribute to Morris and his ground-breaking 1858 essay:

> There is another little book to which I must refer. It is a pamphlet which met with extraordinary success, entitled Nova Britannia, by my honourable friend the Member for South Lanark; and as he has been one of the principal agents in bringing into existence this present government, which is now carrying out the idea embodied in his book, I trust he will forgive me if I take the opportunity, although he is here present, of reading a single sentence to show how far he was in advance of, and how true to the coming event we are now considering. Says Mr. Morris, 'The dealing with the destinies of a future Britannic Empire, the shaping its course, the laying its foundations broad and deep, and the erecting thereon a noble superstructure are indeed duties that will nerve the arms and give power and enthusiasm to all true patriots. The very magnitude of the interests involved will I doubt not, elevate many among us above the demands of sectionalism, with issues so momentous, and to originate a national line of commercial and general policy adapted to the exigencies of our position.'[40]

Morris continued to represent South Lanark after Confederation, and on 16 November 1869 entered the cabinet as minister of inland revenue. He succeeded William Pearce Howland and in due course was himself succeeded by Wilfrid Laurier. While in cabinet he introduced two reform bills, one abolishing public executions and the other requiring the municipal registration of births, marriages, and deaths. Morris remained in government until 1 July 1872, when failing health and finances persuaded him to retire.[41]

When Morris left federal politics in 1872 he felt comfortable enough in his relationship with the prime minister to ask for the job he wanted, a seat on the Manitoba bench. A year earlier he told Macdonald, 'If I must retire, I would like you to send me to Manitoba as Judge. The work would be light & though an exile, the country has a future & I could be of use.'[42] Macdonald agreed. Morris resigned from both the Privy Council and the cabinet, and twenty days later he was sworn in as Chief Justice of Manitoba.[43] He arrived in the province on 13 August. What he found was a village that a year earlier had a population of just over two hundred. Still dominated by the presence of the Hudson's Bay Company and the fifteen-foot walls of its headquarters, Winnipeg was already a rapidly growing service community. While many of its merchants continued to supply the fur trade, an increasing number were switching the focus of their businesses to agriculture. By the time Morris arrived farms ran for miles along the Red, Assiniboine, and Seine rivers, a stage coach route connected Winnipeg to Pembina, a telegraph line had been built, and the city had a bank, school, three colleges, grist mill, several churches and regular steamboat service.

Immediately upon arrival Morris began travelling throughout his adopted home, revising and confirming federal electoral lists. What he found, however, was distressing. In a community lacking a constabulary, violence was a common occurrence. During the September federal election so many riots broke out that he advised Ottawa of the immediate need for a police force. Much of the lawlessness that prevailed was part of the aftermath of the Riel uprising. Physical confrontations between Metis and Ontario immigrants were common and often spilled over into his court. On one occasion a French-Canadian lawyer who had prosecuted a group of English-Canadian rioters was nearly beaten to death, and on another Morris had to rush to the jail to prevent a group of rowdies from releasing a man arrested for assaulting members of Louis Riel's family.

The first sitting of the Queen's Bench was held on 8 October 1872. Morris wanted to hold it earlier, when he could open both it and the County Court, but the provincial attorney general refused to make the latter courts operational until Ottawa appointed the two remaining Queen's Bench justices. When the wrangling between the two levels of government continued into the fall, Morris was forced to open the Queen's Bench sitting alone. Among the first to appear before him was a man who a year later became Winnipeg's first mayor. Frank Cornish was a unique character. While a mayor in Ontario he once prosecuted himself for driving a carriage while impaired, obtained a conviction, levied a fine, and then reduced it on the grounds of previous good conduct.[44]

Unlike Cornish, most of the lawyers who practised in Manitoba in 1872 came from Quebec. This presented Morris with a problem when it came time to promulgate a set of rules to be followed by his court. Although English practices had traditionally been used by Hudson's Bay Company recorders, a majority of the lawyers who now practised in the province were trained in the French civil law system. It was up to the new chief justice to decide which system was to prevail. When he announced his decision on 14 October, the six rules he adopted all dealt with common-law matters. Morris succeeded in avoiding controversy by pointing out that he was simply following the lead of the provincial legislature. 'Fortunately, the legislature here adopted English practice and English law, and I have quietly enforced both, and have carried with me the French bar.'[45]

That Morris was able to bring order to the region had much to do with his ability to broker compromise and with his refusal to show favouritism. 'I determined from the hour I entered the province, to know no parties in it, & have steadily maintained that position.'[46] The conciliatory attitude he adopted was evident in his charge to the province's first grand jury. Embedded in words he knew would be historically significant were imperialist sentiments he had harboured since an 1849 meeting of the British American League, and to which he later gave voice in *Nova Britannia*:

> The establishment of social institutions, the laying the foundation of law and order, are always eras in the history of a new country; and respect for the laws, and due and orderly regard for the requirements of civil power, are prominent characteristics of the races who are under British supremacy. Such respect I look forward to in Manitoba, and in discharging the functions I am called upon to exercise, it shall be my anxious desire to know neither race, creed nor party, but to administer the laws without fear, favour, or partiality .... There is, beyond question, and I am enabled to speak from an extended observation of various sections of Manitoba, a brilliant future before British North-western America. As an agricultural country, it must take the highest rank. But, to secure that rapid development which its advantages entitled it to, and to attract that great influx of population which its natural resources fit it for, there must be stability in the institutions of the country, and there must be confidence that British law and justice will be found in full and entire force.
>
> I trust that, henceforth, British subjects in this Province will remember that free men are freest when they yield a ready obedience to the law; and that men of all classes in the land will resolve to work out the destiny of the Province, by the use of the free institutions of the country, without resort to acts of violence, which only bring discredit on those who commit them, and discredit on the fair fame of the British Empire.[47]

Unfortunately, the pressure of administering law in a province lacking even a courthouse proved too much for a man whose health was always fragile. In November Morris told the prime minister that he might have to step down. Imagine, he wrote, 'a courtroom packed with people, one day so cold that I have to have a robe over my knees and a refreshing blast whistling past me, and afterwards stifling with the heat.'[48] Three weeks later he resigned as chief justice, and on 2 December was sworn in as Manitoba's second lieutenant-governor. In that capacity Morris was responsible for administering Indian and crown lands, acting as the prime minister's eyes and ears, and supervising the administration of the province. It was this responsibility that preoccupied him for much of the next two years.

In 1872 Manitoba was ostensibly governed by a twenty-four-person assembly, split evenly along linguistic lines, and a seven-member Legislative Council, or Upper House. Responsible government had not yet become a reality, however, and the lieutenant-governor picked his own cabinet and had a veto power over all legislation. Few of the members of the legislature had any political experience, and most were as unsophisticated and as colourful as their constituents.[49] Morris wanted to introduce responsible government as soon as he could for both philosophical and political reasons. Growing up in a political family and spending ten years in the Ontario legislature had fostered in him a deep conviction that no society could mature and prosper until its members governed themselves. In addition, the prime minister wanted him to reform Manitoba's system of government before the anticipated flood of Ontario immigrants arrived. When the ministry of Henry Joseph Clarke resigned in the summer of 1874, Morris asked Marc-Amable Girard to accept the premiership. His insistence that the new premier pick his own cabinet signalled the arrival of responsible government, a process completed two years later when the Upper House was abolished.

These changes allowed Morris to turn his attention to something of which he had long dreamed: opening the west to settlement. For almost twenty years Morris had argued that the 'time has come when the claims of humanity and the interests of the British Empire, require that all portions of this vast empire which are adapted for settlement should be laid open to the industrious emigrant.'[50] His pre-Confederation dream became the political platform of the prime minister, and Morris's vision of colonies on either coast connected by a railway and a telegraph laid the groundwork for Macdonald's national policy. When Morris became lieutenant-governor, however, he did not want to build simply a western version of Ontario; he wanted to create an even better society. But before he could do so he realized that he would have to deal with the region's inhabitants.

In 1871 his predecessor had signed two treaties with the natives of southern Manitoba, thereby opening that area to settlement. By the time Morris negotiated the North-West Angle Treaty, or Treaty No. 3, conditions had deteriorated. Dwindling buffalo herds and the lack of a police force increasingly led to violent confrontations between Indians and Metis on the one hand, and American whisky traders on the other. Disease, a scarcity of food, and the existence of a state of war between the Cree and the Blackfoot made things even worse. Morris urged the federal government to come up with a solution.

> Prompt steps necessary when season permits for enforcement of law in North West; we have Police Force and small Battalion; Privy Council have not yet fully realized the magnitude of the task; force now here is inadequate; steps have not been taken hitherto with a view to enforcement; Grandin informed me a half breed murdered his wife and walks unpunished; last year a party of Americans shot 30 Indians; American outlaws have fortified posts in our territory and carry on illicit trade; there are no less than six forts of United States traders ... [and] the difficulties Canada has assumed have never been fully appreciated by Government or People.[51]

The shooting to which Morris referred occurred in May, 1873 and it dealt a serious blow to the government's hope for a peaceful settlement of the west. The savagery of the attack, during which one victim was clubbed to death and beheaded, shocked and outraged Morris. His request for a western police force finally fell on receptive ears. On 23 May the act bringing into being the North West Mounted Police was passed and a contingent of men and horses immediately dispatched. The peace the police brought to the west allowed Morris to concentrate on what he seemed to enjoy most, treaty making. The first one he negotiated was with the Ojibwas of the Lake of the Woods region, and it became the model upon which future treaties were based. He, along with Joseph Alfred Norbert Provencher, Simon James Dawson, and a group of Metis, convinced the Ojibwa that the offer presented to them was much improved over what they had been offered previously. That such was the case was largely because Morris had been able to persuade the government to accept responsibility for educating its new charges, and to recognize the rights possessed by natives since the *Royal Proclamation of 1763*. He believed that if Ottawa was sincere in its desire to negotiate treaties in advance of settlement it had to recognize the Aboriginal rights of natives. Then, in return for accepting a relinquishment of those rights, the federal government had to guarantee natives the right to hunt and to fish on unsettled land. He also suggested that by settling natives on reserves in the area in which they traditionally hunted they would feel less alienated from their land, and the violence and hardship associated with the American system of forced removals could be avoided.[52]

Implicit in Morris's approach to treaty making was the belief that it was in the best interests of natives to be assimilated into mainstream society. By recognizing the authority of Aboriginal leaders he hoped to create a network of peaceful Indian communities throughout the west. Over time they would become surrounded by immigrants, and they would eventually become assimilated. Morris also believed that education would 'civilize' natives and that agriculture would make them more settled. Notwithstanding these lofty sentiments, however, he was not above cajoling native leaders, first through pomp and pageantry, and if that did not work, threats.

His carriage was usually preceded by a marching band and surrounded by a detachment of North West Mounted Police as Morris made his way across the prairies from one native encampment to another. Attired in cocked hat, gold braid, and lace, he was typically met with festivities appropriate for such an auspicious occasion. Colourfully painted warriors repeatedly fired their rifles as they raced their horses around the assembly, and others danced and chanted to the beat of drums, waving their brightly hued blankets in the air. And while this was going on, the main participants sat and smoked.[53] Morris was invariably impressed on such occasions. Describing negotiations that took place at Fort Carlton, he noted:

> On my arrival I found that the ground had been most judiciously chosen, being elevated, and with abundance of trees, hay marshes and small lakes. The spot which the Indians had left for my council tent overlooked the whole. The view was very beautiful: the hills and the trees in the distance, and in the foreground, the meadow land being dotted with clumps of wood, with the Indian tents here and there to the number of two hundred.[54]

One of the chiefs with whom he negotiated at Fort Carlton became notorious during Riel's 1884–5 rebellion. Poundmaker was both handsome and articulate, with his hair parted in the middle and braids interwoven with brass wire. To Morris he declared, 'This is our land, it isn't a piece of pemmican to be cut off and given in little pieces back to us. It is ours and we will take what we want.'[55] Sensing that the timing was not right to make demands, Morris adjourned the negotiating session to let tempers cool. When the meeting resumed he addressed less contentious matters. Their resolution led to a settlement of yet other issues, and by the time that they too were resolved support among natives for Poundmaker's confrontational approach to sovereignty had evaporated, and the treaty was signed.

Morris's refusal to engage in partisan arguments and name calling was also evident during the trial of Ambroise Lepine, who was convicted and sentenced to hang for his role in the execution of Thomas Scott. The animosity that lingered over Scott's 1869 execution had become as much a political as a legal problem four years later, when Frank Cornish swore out a private warrant charging Riel and Lepine with murder. Although Morris refused to treat the affair as anything other than a criminal trial, he was aware of the dangers it posed, and he advised Prime Minister Macdonald that 'Cornish's motive can be love of mischief but may be prompted by Ontario opposition with whom he is in contact to embarrass you ... [So] we are between two fires – fanatic English Orangemen, and excitable half-breeds and French.'[56]

Unfortunately, Morris was not only caught between two fires, but was hemmed in by a third as well. The double-barrelled threat posed by American lawbreakers and invading Fenians required him to exercise all the diplomacy he could muster. In a report to the government he noted that he 'was under strongest pressure to have prisoners released on bail; was opposed as we are exposed to constant eruptions of American desperadoes; matter was likely to lead to serious trouble and possible Fenian invasion ... British, American and, under pressure, Canadian wished release on bail – tantamount to an absolute failure of justice.'[57] Morris's refusal to be drawn into either controversy served to defuse the tensions that existed in what was still a frontier community.

The lawlessness that remained even after the arrival of the North West Mounted Police strengthened Morris's belief in the need to establish an efficient justice system. He complained that 'justice in a country of such vast distances cannot be administered except at enormous public cost and great private inconvenience if all criminals are to be brought here [Winnipeg] for trial; stipendiary magistrates should be appointed as asked for by N.W. Council and only grave crimes sent here for trial.'[58] A year later he voiced the same concern in a letter to the prime minister. 'Expense of bringing criminals & witnesses here is so great that it is necessary to devise a more effective system.'[59]

Despite the pressure attached to being a head of state, Morris still had time to speculate in real estate. He, like his father and other politicians of his era, viewed nation building through an economic prism. Few saw a conflict in acquiring wealth by exploiting the country they were helping to create. William Morris, for example, was one of six directors of the Grand Trunk Railway who were members of cabinet when the bill creating the company was introduced. And Alexander was quick to take personal advantage of the boom in Manitoba real estate when he was lieutenant-governor. In doing so he was not alone. Few could resist the lure of easy money. One of the largest investors was A.W. Ross, a Winnipeg Member of Parliament. 'I was considered very foolish when I purchased property on Main Street near the station at $75 a foot. But people looked at it through different spectacles when I sold shortly afterwards at $400 a foot. The choice lots on Main Street which I then purchased for $400 are now worth $1,500 a foot.'[60] Lots that Morris purchased for $50 were resold for five times that amount, and his purchase of twenty-five acres from an estate was described as one of the best investments in the city's brief history. Bought for $15,000, it was worth ten times as much.[61] And although many easterners were under the mistaken impression that the boom was restricted to Winnipeg property, Morris was not. He invested heavily throughout the province, both in land and in land companies, and even speculated on lots in Edmonton, Alberta. There was a downside to his activities, however. By the time his term as lieutenant-governor ended he and more than one-half the members of the provincial legislature were deeply in debt to the Hudson's Bay Company.

Much of the public criticism levelled at Morris was based on the belief of many Manitobans that his administration had connived in the dispossession of a majority of the province's Metis population. Rumours that he was complicit in the lawlessness associated with the sale of their allotments swirled during his 1878 election loss to Donald Smith, when his response was weak and unconvincing.

Alexander witnessed first hand his father's struggle to keep religion out of education, and when he became Lieutenant-Governor of Manitoba he had a unique opportunity to apply what he had learned. Even though the population of Winnipeg was less than three hundred, Morris was determined to establish a university.[62] To avoid the kind of denominational squabbling that existed in Ontario he decided to create a single secular university. In 1872 Manitoba had three colleges – St John's, Manitoba, and St Boniface. Although the staff of all three doubted the need for a university in a largely uninhabited prairie wilderness, the main opposition to establishing a secular university came from the Catholic church. It insisted that even if St Boniface were to become part of such a body, it would still have to retain its own autonomy. That stumbling block was removed when the boards of all three colleges agreed to federation similar to the format adopted by the University of London. When the provincial government expressed its own misgivings, Morris exerted his influence as head of state, and it grudgingly came on side. In the end, the University of Manitoba was forced on a reluctant government and a lukewarm citizenry because of the passion of one man.[63]

Two years before Morris returned to Ontario the federal government gave the North-West Territories its own lieutenant-governor and made it independent of Manitoba. From that time forward he grew increasingly disinterested in his job. 'My sphere here, has lost its attraction, by the proposed cutting off, of the North West. I wish I had been left to complete my work there, during the remainder of my term of two years. However I have settled the Indian policy & the work will go on. Now that I am in health, I am weary of the loneliness & want of companionship here, & to my family, it is an exile.'[64]

The city from which Morris and his daughter departed on 2 December 1877 was much different from the one he had first seen five years earlier. Not only had its population and business community grown and the fur trade given way to agriculture, the city had matured both physically and culturally. Its streets were graded and widened, a hospital and city hall built, a sewer system installed, and its banks and merchants serviced the entire west. York boats and canoes had been replaced by steamers, schooners, and tugs, many carrying cargoes produced in the province. The city even had its first private club, along with dramatic, literary, and philharmonic societies. Morris could take personal satisfaction for having introduced responsible government, establishing a provincial university, and for initiating the peaceful settlement of the west.

When his tenure as lieutenant-governor ended in December, Morris returned to Perth. Within eight months, with both his health and his finances restored, he was anxious to re-enter the political arena. He sounded out Bishop Taché of St Boniface about his chances of being elected in the federal riding of Marquette, and on 2 August 1878 he returned to Winnipeg. He lost the Marquette nomination to Joseph O'Connell Ryan and immediately turned his attention to the Selkirk riding,[65] where Donald Smith had already been chosen by the Liberals.

John Norquay, a future premier of the province, and Alexander Logan, a prominent local businessman, both had withdrawn from the Conservative race. Norquay formally introduced Morris to the nomination meeting, and with that introduction 'the first shot was fired of a campaign which for partizan exhibition, and extreme political recriminations, had certainly in Manitoba never been equalled.'[66] Years later a witness to the Smith-Morris battle described it as a contest between a political traitor and an old woman.

> [In] Winnipeg the campaign was conducted with such cheerful indifference to temperate expression of opinion, that on most occasions the meetings called by either of the principals culminated in pronounced 'whoop-ups.' This, however, was all in keeping with the character with which we are credited, and which we are always anxious to sustain, viz: that of being a very *live* people.[67]

Morris lost the September election by ten votes.[68] Although he won five of ten wards, including three in Winnipeg, he could not overcome the accusation that he was a carpetbagger who had used his position as lieutenant-governor to restore his fortune. Despite the charges, and his ineffective and evasive speaking style, Morris might still have become the member for Selkirk had it not been for some political skullduggery. Because of 'informalities' in the return of ballot boxes, Mr Justice McKeagney of the Queen's Bench ordered that a recount be held on 3 October 1878. Before it took place, however, Smith also asked for a recount, claiming that two ballots that should have been credited to him were not. A second Queen's Bench judge then ordered that Smith's recount take place the day before the date set by McKeagney. When Morris showed up to witness the recount he was informed by the returning officer that, following the recount held a day earlier, all of the ballots had been forwarded to Ottawa and Smith officially declared elected.[69]

Within weeks of his return to Ontario Morris was again on the campaign trail. After Matthew Crooks Cameron resigned his provincial seat to go to the bench, Morris ran in the resulting by-election and on 21 December 1878 he became the member for Toronto East. His victory in the general election held the following year, when he defeated Oliver Mowat by fifty-seven votes, was particularly satisfying to Morris because Mowat not only was the Premier of Ontario but had shared space with Morris when the two were law clerks in Kingston. Morris served in the legislature as opposition house leader until his health problems resurfaced, and in 1886 he did not seek re-election. Suffering from 'hereditary rheumatism of the head' and other ailments, he left Ontario for England, where he sought treatment.

Alexander Morris died at 9:00 a.m. on 28 October 1889 at the age of sixty-three. He had been confined to bed the preceding six weeks after contracting a malaria-like illness while vacationing at his estate in Ontario's Muskoka region. At his bedside were his wife, four daughters, four sons, his brother John, and two attending physicians. His funeral was held several days later. As dozens of horse-drawn carriages pulled up to the family home on Jarvis Street, spectators stood in a chilling autumn rain to watch the nation's political and business leaders gather to honour one of their own. As Morris's family watched in silence, one after the other of the assembled mourners laid a floral wreath on his plain black coffin. From Jarvis the cortege proceeded to Old St Andrew's Church. Between the singing of 'Rock of Ages' and the Dead March, Principal Caven of Queen's read a portion of the 90th Psalm and the fifteenth chapter of Corinthians. After the intense silence that followed the reading, the service ended. With two of his sons on either side, the coffin of the first justice of Manitoba's Court of Queen's Bench was carried to a hearse. From there it was taken to Mount Pleasant cemetery, where he was laid in the family plot.

Ten years after his death the *Manitoba Free Press* suggested that Morris 'held a position in the history of the west similar to that of Governor Simcoe in Ontario. They had the pioneers work to do, laying the foundations and establishing law and order.'[70] But perhaps his most fitting tribute was paid five years before he died. In an exchange of letters between two of his sons, the elder wrote the younger: 'Father never failed to make a friend of everyone he met, and his success in life was in no small measure due to this. You inherit a good name. Make the best of it.'[71]

2

A Time of Controversy, 1872–1878

The year after Manitoba became a province Winnipeg's population of 241 made it the nation's 62nd largest community, and by the end of 1871 it had grown to a town of more than 900 buildings. Of this number, 400 were houses, 127 were occupied by manufacturers and merchants, and the balance were used as hotels, saloons, boarding houses, and office buildings.[1]

Despite the crudeness of many of its structures, however, there was no doubt that Winnipeg was established by businessmen for business purposes. The community's natural leaders were members of the city's commercial and social elites, and prominent in both groups were members of the bar. These men were pragmatic individuals who saw themselves as agents of improvement and few had much regard to the plight of others, perhaps a not surprising observation about a community described in the 1870s as one of the two most evil places in Canada.[2]

A lack of transportation facilities meant that in its infancy Winnipeg was effectively isolated from the rest of the country. Those making their way to the province, much like the Wolseley Expedition of 1870, had the option of an overland route via Lake of the Woods, a northern route by water through Hudson's Bay and Lake Winnipeg, or travelling by rail to Minnesota and then north by either ox-cart or flat boat. Wolseley's trip west by way of Lake of Woods took a gruelling ninety-six days.[3] The hardships associated with the trek from eastern Canada to the prairies, however, did not discourage some. Between 1870 and 1880 a total of 72,600 Canadian-born citizens migrated west. Of that number two-thirds settled in one of the northern United States, with the balance settling in Manitoba.[4] During the same decade the Canadian government successfully recruited hundreds of Russian Mennonites and impoverished Icelanders directly to Manitoba.

Between the first sitting of Queen's Bench in October 1872 and its second sitting three months later, two puisne justices were appointed to the court and its chief justice resigned. When he announced the appointment of Alexander Morris, Prime Minister Macdonald had said that the remaining seats on the court would go to lawyers from Quebec and the Maritimes. True to his word, the prime minister's next appointments went to James Charles McKeagney, a fifty-seven-year-old political veteran and probate judge from Cape Breton, and Louis Betournay, the law partner of Macdonald's colleague, George-Étienne Cartier.[5] Shortly before the appointments were announced, however, Manitoba's first lieutenant-governor left the province and Morris told the prime minister that he would like to be offered the post. It was, he said, an offer that he would regard as a compliment, but that he would decline on the basis of his failing health. In December 1872 the offer was made and accepted. When the second sitting of the Queen's Bench was called on 7 January 1873 it was presided over by McKeagney and Betournay, with Morris looking on as Manitoba's newly appointed lieutenant-governor. A month later the two justices sat with five panels of magistrates as judges of the province's first county courts. Between February and November 1873, McKeagney and Betournay kept their regular Queen's Bench term and worked their way through a backlog of criminal cases by sitting during three more terms (June, September, and November) in addition to exercising their responsibilities as magistrates and judges of the province's county courts.[6]

On 11 March 1874 Edmund Burke Wood was appointed Chief Justice of Manitoba, bringing the Queen's Bench to its full complement of three justices. Wood, like Morris and McKeagney, was an experienced political veteran and one of the most dynamic chief justices to preside over a Manitoba bench. With a booming voice and only one arm, the fifty-seven-year-old brought to the province a large reputation and considerable notoriety. Few, however, doubted his abilities as a jurist. Two of his first judgments discussed at some length the duties of justices of the peace and were published by the provincial government for the guidance of justices. 'Both judgments demonstrated that Wood was a painstaking lawyer, a sound logician, and a lucid writer.'[7]

Unlike the history of western settlement in the United States, the history of the Canadian prairies was non-violent, with one exception. In

May of 1873 a gang of wolf hunters camped outside one of a handful of trading posts that dotted the west. These posts were crude affairs, consisting of two or three shacks surrounded by a log palisade about ten feet in height, around which bands of Cree and Assiniboine and white hunters spent days drinking and trading goods. Shortly after arriving at one of them, located at Cypress Hills, in what is now southern Saskatchewan, the wolfers entered the camp of a group of Assiniboines, accusing them of stealing a horse. By the time the confrontation ended twenty Indians had been killed and one victim clubbed to death, with his severed head jammed on a pole outside the post. Three wolf hunters were charged with murder and tried in Winnipeg in 1876. Although they were acquitted, when the details of the massacre were made public the federal government almost immediately dispatched the North West Mounted Police to keep the peace on the prairies.[8] In actuality the process of sending the force west was already in hand, since the Canadian government had for some time regarded the Indians of the west as a potential threat to immigration. [9]

By 1874 Winnipeg was beginning to look like the commercial metropolis it was to become, with two and one half miles of sidewalks and a mile of graded streets. Included in the city's business community were four dry-goods, four hardware, five book, and nineteen general stores, two watchmaker shops, two banks, four livery stables, three pharmacies, six paint shops, nine blacksmiths, two barber shops, four harness and four carriage makers, one marble works, four printing offices, four furniture shops, four auctioneers, three tobacconists, three photographers, four furriers, six bakeries, a telegraph office, three milliners, two flour and feed stores, three butcher shops, eleven lawyers and eight physicians, one soda manufacturer, three saw and two planing mills, three brick yards, and two tailors.[10]

Winnipeg's first chief of police was appointed in 1874. Described as 'the greatest rowdy in Winnipeg at the time' the chief was dismissed a year later after he was arrested by his own lieutenant during a raid on 'a den in the western portion of the city.'[11] The extent to which law had still not yet made its way beyond Winnipeg was made evident in a strongly worded communique sent to the provincial government from a grand jury empanelled in 1875 to investigate a murder in the Portage la Prairie area.

> Yesterday a barbarous murder was committed in our midst, on the public road in broad day, and today the Sheriff was forced to call upon almost every ablebodied man in the settlement to aid him in the arrest of seven

> Indians charged with the said murder. When arrested, the Sheriff had no proper place to put them in to secure them, and no appliances, not even a set of handcuffs, and the prisoners had to be guarded entirely by inhabitants who volunteered for that purpose. In consequence of a number of us being called on to serve on this jury, the guards were so few in number that the prisoners by a united effort over-powered them and escaped, and now cannot be found. This is certainly a state of affairs that calls loudly for amendment and we now urge upon the provincial Government the necessity of stationing some small force of police or military here, and providing a secure place of imprisonment.[12]

In 1876 the structure of the Manitoba legislature underwent a profound change, when a mounting financial crisis forced the government to abolish the Legislative Council, or Upper House. Its seven members had been appointed for life and equipped with powers similar to those possessed by members of the Canadian Senate. But modernizing the structure of the legislature did nothing to change the idiosyncrasies of some of its members, including the premier. When the Public Accounts Committee censured the government for financial laxness, the premier became incensed. He was, he told the house, 'prepared to censure himself when necessary but censure from the opposition he would not stand. He thought he knew as well as most people when he went astray and was not going to submit to the indignity of having it thrown up to him by his opponents when he had already condemned himself.'[13] The city's first mayor was equally prepared to condemn himself. Sitting one morning as a police magistrate, he announced to those assembled that he was charging himself for being disorderly as a result of his conduct the previous evening. He then stood, stepped away from his magisterial chair, and in a submissive tone entered a plea of guilty. Resuming his seat, he fined himself five dollars.[14]

In 1877 the legislature passed an act merging the province's three religious colleges (the Roman Catholic St Boniface College, the Church of England's St John's College, and Manitoba College, affiliated with the Presbyterian church) into a single non-sectarian body to be known as the University of Manitoba. The three original schools did, however, retain the power to grant degrees in theology. That same year the legislature also passed a new school act, under which a Board of Education was established, consisting of twelve Protestants and nine Catholics. Each section had its own Superintendent, and two sections of land in each township were set aside for school purposes. When the new act became law the government immediately increased its education grant from $10,000 to $18,000 per year, or 14.4 per cent of the province's annual budget.[15]

The principal of Queen's University was one of many easterners struck by the changes in Winnipeg during the 1870s. Although the city's growth, he wrote, was nothing short of phenomenal, the thing that first struck a visitor was 'that incongruous blending of the new and the old, of barbarism jostling against civilization, that distinguishes every corner of Winnipeg and every phase of its life. Specimens of almost extinct savage and semi-savage nationalities gaze at steam-boats and steam-mills and all the appliances of modern life with eyes that dream of far different scenes that were yesterday but have vanished forever.'[16] Also standing on Winnipeg street corners by this time were immigrants from England, Ireland, Scotland, Iceland, the United States, Norway, and Wales, and those described by contemporaries as Canadians, Frenchmen, Negroes, and Mennonites. Prominent among these groups was at least one transplanted Nova Scotian.[17]

JAMES CHARLES McKEAGNEY

Few individuals in the history of the Manitoba judiciary went to the bench better prepared to excel than James Charles McKeagney. A practising lawyer with thirty-five years' experience, a politician elected to both senior levels of government, and a judge in Nova Scotia (probate and vice-admiralty), he had spent nearly a lifetime getting ready. Yet when he died Manitoba newspapers barely mentioned his passing.

McKeagney was born in County Tyrone, Ireland, in 1815. His family had immigrated to Northern Ireland from Scotland following the battle of Culloden, during which the Scottish Highlander army of Charles Edward Stuart was crushed by the Duke of Cumberland.[18] They arrived in Cape Breton when he was seven, two years after the island officially became part of Nova Scotia. In immigrating to North America the McKeagneys joined thousands of Catholics who fled Ireland in the 1820s to avoid the hardships they faced under English rule. This influx was principally made up of tradesmen and farmers who, though poor, were not destitute. Most made the trip believing the stories told them by ship captains and land agents, who described Canada as a land of plenty. Between 1815 and 1838 more than thirteen thousand Irish immigrants arrived in Nova Scotia. Most settled in or around established communities, rather than on farms. Many, like the McKeagneys, ended up in the Irish parish of Sydney, Cape Breton,[19] which comprised all of the eastern coast of the island. There they joined a settlement made up of fellow immigrants, as well as disbanded soldiers and descendants of American Loyalists.

Although Patrick McKeagney and his wife Catherine McCarney may have come to Nova Scotia for many of the same reasons as other Irish immigrants, they also had the added incentive that one of their sons was already living there. James's older brothers Henry and Patrick both became Roman Catholic priests, as did their cousin Michael.[20] The first to arrive in Canada was Henry, who received tonsure at Quebec in June 1821 and was ordained four months later. After spending a year in charge of St Patrick's church he was transferred to Cape Breton.[21] By 1836 the church was regularly receiving complaints about Henry's conduct. He had not only lost the confidence of his parishioners, he had become a source of considerable irritation to Sydney's civil authorities as well. After ignoring a number of questioning letters from the church for four years, McKeagney was finally suspended. He spent the ensuing sixteen years embroiled in disputes with both the church and the civil tribunal of Halifax. When he died in 1856 only one person, apart from the presiding priest and his brother James, came to pay his respects.

The second of the two McKeagney 'Fathers' made a good impression when he arrived in Cape Breton in December 1832. Patrick's appealing appearance, polished speaking manner, good humour, and amiability were noticed even by priests in other parishes. Twenty-two years later, however, he too was forced out of the ministry:

> His ministry had been far from satisfactory. He acknowledged the fact and decided to make a public act of reparation for it ... After his last Mass at Cheticamp he said that he hated the place but loved its fine people, and he asked them publicly to forgive him. They knew how eccentric he was, but they loved him for his unaffected friendliness to all and for his devotion to the sick, and they were moved to tears by his great act of humility.[22]

Michael was the third McKeagney to serve as a priest in Nova Scotia. He studied theology for three years in Ireland before arriving in Nova Scotia in 1829. Unlike Henry and Patrick, however, he ministered without controversy and died in the service of his parishioners, by whom he was much loved.[23]

The Cape Breton in which James McKeagney and his family settled in 1822 was a frontier community only beginning to establish a rudimentary industrial base. While much of its population was made up of immigrants from Scotland, Ireland, and the eastern seaboard of the United States, it also included a significant number of Micmacs and blacks. But towns like Sydney were growing, both in population and economically, as coal mines began complementing the traditional fishing industry. With growth came increased stability, and with stability a desire to know what was going on elsewhere. Still, the McKeagneys had been living on the island for ten years before the first newspaper appeared in Sydney, and until shortly before their arrival there were only one hundred sixty miles of highway in the entire province. The few stage coaches in operation were driven by men who carried up to six passengers and the mail, and who routinely stopped to shoot partridges for food.

When it was time for the McKeagneys to send James to school they could send him to a school in either Sydney or Arichat. He, however, attended neither. The same influence that would dominate his political career played a key role in determining where he received his education. After Cape Breton became part of Nova Scotia, a grammar school had been established at Sydney. The school did not operate continuously, however, because of a shortage of both teachers and students. What teachers were available were either Anglican or Presbyterian clergymen. The tiny community of Baddeck had a grammar school that operated even less often. It opened only when one of the island's few itinerant teachers arrived for a few days' stay. But because the community was largely Irish Catholic, McKeagney went there.[24] Among the subjects he studied were English, grammar, Latin, Greek, the use of globes, orthography, and mathematics.

By the time McKeagney left Baddeck for McQueen's Academy in Halifax, academies were no longer denominational institutions devoted to preparing young men for the ministry. Largely financed by government grants, many had begun teaching everything but theology.[25] Others, like the short-lived Sydney Academy, on whose board McKeagney's uncle Henry sat, were run by lay persons and representatives from each of the churches in the area. But whether an academy was denominational or secular, until the *Test Act* was abolished in 1827 no Catholic law student could be admitted to the provincial bar unless he agreed to receive the Lord's Supper in the Anglican rite, took the State Oaths, and renounced his belief in the Mass, Transubstantiation, and the intercession of the Mother of God.[26] But faith aside, the study of law in Nova

Scotia was a daunting task when the seventeen-year-old McKeagney took articles in 1832:

> A half-hours inspection of a large law library is almost enough to deter any young person from embracing such a profession; and even the nerves of those who have been inured to pouring over black letter, and law-French, and, worse than that, law-Latin, will sometimes twitch with involuntary shrinking from the barbarous aspect of these Sibylline leaves. The motley and tasteless jargon, the obsolete dialect, the antiquated questions and rules, the puzzling contractions of the early Gothic type, and the mouldering dust, that unite in presenting impediments to the enquirer, seem to throw an impenetrable veil over the original features of our jurisprudence.[27]

Before he was admitted to the bar of Nova Scotia as a student-at-law, however, McKeagney had to locate a lawyer with whom he was able to negotiate an acceptable fee for the years of instruction he was about to receive. The normal fee was one hundred and five pounds, although many principals charged nothing.[28] Once the question of a fee was decided, McKeagney had to satisfy the requirements of the 1811 act passed by the provincial legislature 'for the better regulation of Attorneys, Solicitors and Proctors practising in the courts of Law and Equity in this Province.'[29] It mandated that he be examined by a judge of the Supreme Court, and produce evidence that he was possessed of a satisfactory education and appropriate 'habits.' Because he lacked a university degree, the act also required him to serve five years in the office of an attorney instead of four. Among the questions James was likely to be asked during his examination for admission were 'What English Baron was the King-Maker in the War of the Roses?'and 'Where are the Fiji Islands and to whom do they belong?'[30]

Although he was not obligated to take specific courses, since there was no faculty to provide them, McKeagney was expected to possess a thorough knowledge of the English language and to be familiar with Latin and French, as well as the writings of Cicero, Chatham, Walpole, Fox, Burke, Curran, and Erskine. Among the books he was to read while under articles were *Blackstone's Commentaries*, *Phillips on Evidence*, *Maddox on Chancery*, *Jones on Bailment*, *Coke on Littleton*, *Roberts on Wills*, *Holt on Shipping*, and *Brown's Civil and Admiralty Law*.[31] It is likely, however, that he spent his time copying forms, creating indexed digests out of the law found in whatever books his principal possessed, and attending court, 'all in the hope of learning an arcane discipline by a method that might amount to little more than osmosis.'[32] On the other hand, it was also possible he spent his time in idleness: 'If his barrister happened to be a very busy one the chances were that he would have very little time indeed to give to his student, and if per contra it was a man who was blessed with ample leisure, well then, the chances were that his leisure was due to the fact that he was not fit for anything better than to sit and twiddle his thumbs, so that in either case ... the student had a rather poor chance.'[33]

At the end of his articles McKeagney was required to prove he was at least twenty-one years of age, and to be examined by a judge and two barristers. He passed the examination, and on 31 October 1837 he was admitted as an attorney. A year later he was called as a barrister.[34] The Sydney in which he set up practice, however, was nothing like the Halifax where he had attended school. Sydney was a community of few houses and a population of about five hundred, the souls of whom were safeguarded by Episcopal, Catholic, and Methodist clergy, and whose bodies were protected by a garrison of one company of regulars.[35]

In 1838 Nova Scotia had a population of 177,000, of whom slightly more than 30,000 lived in Cape Breton. The provincial bar numbered 107, including seven who practised in Cape Breton. McKeagney joined the four who lived in Sydney. Between his call and appointment to the bench, the province's legal community was remarkably stable. An average of seven lawyers entered each year, and no more than seven practised in Cape Breton, including four in Sydney.[36] The legal system in which they worked was rudimentary, even for a frontier community. Depending on when an offence was alleged to have been committed, an accused could spend six months or more in jail before being brought before a judge. Even the consequences of engaging in improper non-criminal conduct could be devastating for those involved. An example involved the adultery of a Cape Breton woman. 'Kaulbach obtained a divorce from his wife Margaret in consequence of improper conduct on her part, no alternative therefore was left her but to proceed to some foreign land, where she would be unknown, and earn herself a living.'[37]

Apart from the few divorces heard on the island, there were three reasons why the services of a lawyer were not likely in much demand. First, Nova Scotia communities were extremely clannish over religion and culture, and residents seldom called upon outsiders to service their needs.[38] Second, disputes were usually trivial. During one twelve-month period, for instance, the most serious action heard involved keeping a vicious dog.[39] And lastly, a significant number of differences were settled through a kind of collective retribution. Because rural Cape Breton was so isolated, over time most towns developed a tradition of community censure, initially used when relations between two families had deteriorated to the point of violence. By the time McKeagney received his call, however, virtually every dispute involving land went to arbitration. By 1855 the procedure was also popular in Ontario, where the 'feeling in favor of arbitration as an inexpensive and satisfactory mode of settling long disputed accounts, and differences having their origin in family quarrels, is every year becoming stronger.'[40] Unfortunately for members of the bar, these procedures seldom required the services of a lawyer.

When he started practising, McKeagney likely harboured no illusions that he could survive solely on what he earned as a lawyer. 'No lawyer coming to the bar ... could hope for the income of a gentleman by virtue of professional competence alone. In the pattern of the first Loyalist generation, a 'genteel independency' was possible only for those who could supplement ordinary professional fees with income from public office.'[41] McKeagney did this in two ways: through politics and appointments to the provincial civil service.

In taking an active interest in politics while he waited for his practice to flourish McKeagney adopted a course of action that had for years been the norm for Protestant lawyers in Nova Scotia. That he and other Catholics could do so, however, was something new. Before Cape Breton was reunited with the mainland in 1820, restrictive laws passed by the provincial legislature barred Catholics from owning land, thereby disqualifying them from holding office as either elected politicians or appointed civil servants. But by the time of union, things had begun to change. The lobbying efforts of the Catholic Association began showing results as more and more Irish immigrants arrived in the province. One product of its work was the Repeal Movement. When the newly annexed Cape Breton was given the right to elect two members to Nova Scotia's House of Assembly, a combination of the movement's influence and his family's wealth ensured that Laurence Kavanagh Jr was one of them. This presented the government with a dilemma. Roman Catholics were legally barred from taking a seat in a British legislature, but the Kavanaghs were the province's most influential and powerful merchant family. In 1823 the provincial legislature settled on a compromise. By a special royal prerogative extended only to him, Kavanagh was allowed to take his seat in the assembly without taking the oath of office, with its offensive references to the Catholic doctrine of Holy Communion. Four years after he entered the Nova Scotia legislature, and six years before anyone of his faith sat in the British House of Commons,[42] Kavanagh and other Irish residents of Nova Scotia presented to the government their first ever political petition, asking the Crown to remove from all oaths of office the declaration against Transubstantiation. The government acceded to their request, and on 17 April 1827 Nova Scotia repealed the anti-Catholic *Test Act*. Two years later Great Britain followed suit.

Shortly after receiving his call, McKeagney embarked on what was to be a remarkably successful political career, thanks to the efforts of his brothers and the Catholic church. Patrick, for example, took such an active part in his brother's first election campaign that he was reprimanded by the priest of an adjoining parish and ultimately transferred out of the area. His activities, however, paled in comparison to Henry's. Even before James became a politician his oldest brother had been active on behalf of Catholic candidates. In 1832 his candidate was Sydney's Richard Smith. When one hundred and fifty Smith opponents came into Henry's parish armed with sticks, and surrounded the house in which voting was to take place, Henry led a mob against them. The confrontation turned violent, and he was the first to fall. The violence escalated until fifteen hundred armed Smith supporters surrounded two thousand equally equipped opponents. Father McKeagney finally realized things had gotten out of control, and rushed through the mob, imploring everyone not to fire. His counsel prevailed and the crowd gradually dispersed.[43]

When the 1840 provincial election was called James, who was only twenty-five years old, decided to run as a Reformer in Richmond, one of the four counties of Cape Breton. He won the seat previously held by Kavanagh, but he was not a resident of the county, and the election was declared void. His residency status became the main issue in the by-election held the following July, and he was defeated by local lawyer William Clarke Delaney.

James McKeagney obtained his first appointment, as registrar of probate and surrogate in the Court of Vice-Admiralty for Cape Breton county, between his 1841 election win and subsequent disqualification and his victory two years later. He relinquished both positions in 1849, when he was made a judge of probate.[44] In that capacity he had the authority to determine the validity of wills and grant administration of estates where no will existed. Proceedings before him were usually conducted by way of petition, but where someone filed an objection, or caveat, a judge of probate had the authority to compel the appearance of a party by citation. So, for example, where a widow or next of kin of a deceased delayed or refused to administer an estate, a judge of probate could cite the reluctant administrator, and transfer that individual's rights to someone else. As a probate judge McKeagney was required to maintain two sets of records, described as 'will books' and 'estate papers.' The former were indexed and bound ledgers into which individual wills were transcribed on the date they were filed with the court. The latter consisted of files containing copies of all documentation used to support an application. The job of a probate judge was to ensure these records were kept up to date and that, within thirty days of the death of a testator, an executor brought the deceased's will to the registry office of the county in which the deceased had resided. A judge was thus technically expected to know who had died within his jurisdiction and when that death occurred.[45] The reality was something different, however, since relatively few Nova Scotians died with a will, and the law did not require heirs to seek court approval before settling the affairs of a deceased. Courts of probate were, therefore, not used by large numbers of people.[46]

Such was not the case for the Court of Vice-Admiralty. In the 1840s, although there was only one judge of vice-admiralty in Nova Scotia, he had the authority to appoint a number of surrogates, who held court in any convenient place within their jurisdiction. As a surrogate, McKeagney heard disputes involving part-owners of ships, seamen's wages, salvage, the sale of cargo, and damage resulting from collisions at sea. In times of peace, most admiralty suits were commenced against vessels or the goods they carried. During a war, however, judges of vice-admiralty sat as a prize court, deciding who received the ships and cargoes captured from an enemy.

When McKeagney entered politics balloting, like everything else about elections, was very public. On the day voting was to take place the county sheriff made himself available at the most convenient place in the district. There, some time between ten and twelve in the morning, he read the election writ and swore in two electoral assistants. That done, an elector moved the nomination of his candidate, another seconded it, and the candidate gave a speech in which he outlined his fitness for office. The procedure was repeated until every candidate was given a chance to speak. When the speeches ended, voting began.

In larger counties the sheriff and his clerks went from poll to poll, often over the course of several days. After the last elector publicly made his vote known, voting officially ended and ballots were tabulated.[47]

This was the procedure McKeagney followed in 1843 when he was elected in Inverness, the county immediately adjacent to and northwest of Richmond. His fellow assemblyman was William Young, who became speaker of the House when it convened in February 1844. Three years later the legislature was dissolved and another general election called. McKeagney was not elected, but became member for Sydney Township when Edmund Dodd resigned to go to the bench. He held the seat for four years before being defeated by the senior member of the local bar, Donald McQueen. That loss was avenged in 1855, when for the last time James was elected to the oldest legislative body in Canada.[48]

During McKeagney's first two campaigns Nova Scotia was administered by a lieutenant-governor and a twelve-member executive council. Although councillors officially acted only in an advisory capacity, in reality the role they played was substantially more important. They served in what was as a combination of provincial cabinet and colonial version of the British House of Lords. The men appointed to it, therefore, were usually highly regarded. It is unlikely, however, that that could be said about McKeagney. He was a member of a provincial administration for only six months and most contemporary references to him were disparaging.[49]

Nova Scotia politics in the 1840s and 1850s was not a pastime pursued by the faint of heart. Elections were a time of celebration throughout the province, but particularly so in Cape Breton. One of McKeagney's contemporaries kept a diary in which he recorded some of the events that occurred during a typical election rally. His observations make it clear that politics was something about which everyone had an opinion:

> This is 'nomination day,' early in the morning the flags of both parties were to be seen floating from the different places in Town. About 9 O'clock the Conservative party with Banners and music marched out to meet the party on their way from Bridgewater; soon the two parties met and marched into town in good order, displaying a large number of flags and accompanied with a goodly number of musicians ... About midnight Dr. Chas. Tupper, the 'great gun' of the Conservative party arrived here; for the purpose of counteracting the hostile impressions the Arch-Demagogue and great Radical Howe, may have made on the voters

> of this County against the Conservative party. Dr. Tupper will follow Howe through the County, and falsify many of the misstatements and infamous lies that Howe is spreading broad cast among the people, in order to induce them to vote for the radicals, so that party may be enabled to retain power and further injure the County by their mis-management, and incapacity to conduct the public affairs of the province.[50]

The role religion played in Cape Breton elections cannot be overstated, nor was it restricted to the efforts of the Catholic church:

> Contrary to all expectations the radical Candidates gained the election, but to the discredit of the County be it said it was through means most despicable and shameful that they were enabled to succeed. Every means was resorted to by these men to gain their ends, bribery was practised to a fearful extent, and last though not least those professing to be Ministers of the Gospel lent in every way a helping hand; these Ministers, mainly of the Free Presbyterian Church, Lutheran Church, and Methodist Church, preached daily and nightly sermons from their pulpits, and not alone this but canvassed their people and urged upon them the necessity of voting for the Radicals, their conduct has been most shameful and a disgrace to their profession.[51]

Apart from sitting as a judge of probate and vice-admiralty, McKeagney received at least four other appointments during his career at the bar. They included membership on the Land Board and Board of School Commissioners for Cape Breton county, appointment as harbour master for the port of Sydney, and provincial Inspector of Mines.[52] This last appointment proved to be the most controversial of his career. When the government announced in the spring of 1859 that McKeagney was going to become inspector of mines, the ensuing House debate went on longer, and was more heated, than the discussion over railway construction. Members were well aware of McKeagney's constant search for patronage, which many believed he received as a sop to the province's politically well-connected Catholic minority. They became incensed, however, when as inspector of mines he was awarded an office that did not legally exist, and for which he had no qualifications even if it had. Regardless, he occupied the position from 9 December 1859 until it was abolished in 1862.[53]

The other provincial appointment McKeagney received attracted much less attention than those that preceded it, probably because its focus was military rather than political, and those who held it were paid in status rather than money. Between 1855 and 1860 the government encouraged communities throughout the province to establish their own volunteer militia units, each of which was to be attached to a company of regular militia. By 1860 thirty such units, including nine regiments in Cape Breton, had received official recognition. The 2nd was placed under the command of McKeagney. He was made a lieutenant-colonel, and given six officers, two majors and four captains. Each volunteer was responsible for maintaining a musket, a bayonet, a box sufficient to hold eighteen cartridges, and whatever else might be used in a military campaign. To ensure that these items were accounted for, militiamen were required to provide the government with a five-pound bond and a surety. Anyone who used his musket for 'fowling' or private purposes, or failed to attend a muster, was liable to a fine, and those called to active service were selected by ballot.[54]

Although there is no evidence that McKeagney's regiment saw action, the threat posed to Nova Scotia by Fenian raiders and deserters from the American civil war was real.

While religious considerations did not influence McKeagney's decision to retire from provincial politics in 1859, or his entry into the federal realm nine years later, it was a factor during his last campaign. By the time Canada became a nation he had been out of politics for eight years, and before his 1867 acclamation he gave an undertaking to his local bishop that he would support confederation. McKeagney also privately guaranteed the prime minister that he would support the government in return for a seat on the bench of the North-West Territories. Both Macdonald and Sir Charles Tupper, the senior member from Nova Scotia, agreed to the demand. Before the promise was acted upon, however, McKeagney was asked to perform one last favour for the Catholic church. In the 1872 election three candidates were contesting two Nova Scotia seats. There was no doubt that one would go to the Conservative candidate, and it was likely that the other would go to Hector McLeod, a supporter of the opposition Liberal party. Both he and the third candidate, independent Newton McKay, were Protestants. The Church was anxious that McKay win, since he had made it known that if elected he would support Macdonald's Conservative government. To facilitate McKay's victory, the Church asked McKeagney to run, in the belief that he would win the vote of Liberal Catholics while leaving untouched the non-Catholic votes of the staunchly Protestant McKay. The stratagem worked. Both McKay and the Conservative were elected. In a post-election letter to Tupper, McKeagney made it clear that his heart was never really in the campaign, and that he had not forgotten the promise of a judicial appointment.

> Up to the last hour I had not made up my mind to go into the nomination, but finding the field occupied by Mr. McLeod, a Grit candidate, and fearing that Mr. McKay, the nominee of the Protestant party friendly to the government, might be defeated by McLeod if I did not colesce with him at the polls, I was advised to do so, and I went into the contest rather to strengthen McKay, than to secure my own success, which in view of the understanding I had with Sir John and yourself, I regarded as of no importance.[55]

It was hardly surprising that McKeagney expected to receive the appointment promised him. Throughout his career he had sought and received one appointment after another, and was widely regarded as 'an unending searcher after patronage.'[56] Such searches were not uncommon in mid-nineteenth-century Nova Scotia, however, when a lawyer's income and status were often directly related to the offices he held.

By 1872 McKeagney had devoted 60 per cent of his life to public service, and he sought one last appointment. His age and lack of professional reputation, however, appeared to have influenced Macdonald and Tupper to renege on their promise. When it became apparent that their attitude towards him had changed, McKeagney reminded the government of its promise to him, and of the gratitude Nova Scotia's 80,000 Catholics would feel should one of their own be sent to the bench. And then he played his ace, asking for the help of the Archbishop of Halifax. Thomas Louis Connolly, like McKeagney, was born in Ireland early in the nineteenth century. He entered the Capuchin novitiate at sixteen, went to Rome when he was eighteen, and came to Halifax in 1842 as secretary to the city's bishop. Within seventeen years he was Metropolitan of the Maritimes. His zeal for good works made him a favourite of Pope Pius IX, while his political acumen and close friendship with politicians like Macdonald, Tupper, and Thomas D'Arcy McGee gave him an influence well beyond the Church and Nova Scotia. McKeagney was among those who had frequently benefited from his patronage, and in 1872 he asked his patron for a last favour. Whether because of Connolly's influence, a remembered promise, or even the intervention of Joseph Howe, McKeagney was appointed to the Court of Queen's Bench of Manitoba on 7 October 1872.

Prime Minister Macdonald was perhaps exaggerating a little when, referring to the ability of his most recent judicial appointee, he informed Alexander Morris that 'I understand that he is a pretty fair lawyer and will help you to dispose of all the small business of the Courts.'[57] To have said less would have contradicted his undertaking that no amount of political pressure would induce him to appoint an incompetent judge.[58] The assessment of McKeagney's abilities by two Manitoba contemporaries was likely more accurate. Two months after he arrived in the province one described him as, at best, a friendly, good-natured, and conscientious non-entity, and at worse, an old woman lacking even the ability to scold.[59] The other referred to him as an honest old man possessed of mediocre ability and little law.[60]

While McKeagney may have looked forward to the security of his $3999 salary, he did not likely enjoy the controversy in which he immediately became embroiled. Early in 1872 the Manitoba legislature, made up of an equal number of French- and English-speaking members, passed an act that prohibited anyone from sitting on a superior court bench 'unless such person is able to speak both the English and French languages.'[61] When McKeagney was appointed he assured the prime minister that he could understand French. The fact that he lied, or at least exaggerated, quickly became apparent. One of the first cases he heard was a jury trial involving a dispute over a promissory note. The jury consisted of an equal number of French- and English-speaking jurors. At the end of the case McKeagney addressed the jury in English, and instructed the Prothonotary to address it in French. Counsel for the defence promptly objected on the grounds that McKeagney's inability to speak French disqualified him from sitting. Although the dispute ended when Manitoba's Executive Council agreed that the provincial law requiring judges to be bilingual was an unconstitutional restriction of Ottawa's authority under section 96 of the *British North America Act* to appoint judges, the incident did nothing to enhance McKeagney's already weak reputation.[62]

The most infamous case with which McKeagney was involved was that of Lord Gordon Gordon. The Scotsman, whose real name was Hubert Campbell Smith, was one of the most successful fraud artists in the province's history. He started his career in crime in 1868 in Scotland and over the ensuing four years passed himself off as the Hon. Mr Herbert Hamilton, Lord Glencairn, George Gordon, George Herbert Gordon, John Herbert Charles Gordon, and Lord Gordon Gordon. During the two years preceding his appearance before

McKeagney he convinced those with whom he had contact that he owned property throughout England, and that he was about to inherit the title of Glencairn, along with a fortune. He even persuaded a firm of London solicitors to guarantee his various business accounts. By the time he left Scotland for the United States, he had accumulated thousands of pounds' worth of debts, including five thousand he owed his lawyers.

In 1871 he turned up in Minneapolis, Minnesota. Within weeks he had convinced members of the city's social and business elites that he was the Scottish nobleman Lord Gordon Gordon. He was fawned over at both private and public functions, and when he indicated an interest in buying land on which to settle some of his Scottish employees, the Northern Pacific Railway immediately organized a hunting party in the hopes of persuading him to purchase one of its holdings. Within days Gordon was part of a caravan consisting of forty horses, twelve men to pitch tents, a French chef, a contingent of black waiters decked out in linen aprons and white silk gloves, and two covered wagons full of guns and fishing tackle. Meals were served on silver and china, and the guest of honour was provided with fourteen changes of clothes. By the time the group returned to Minneapolis the railway was out of pocket more than forty-five thousand dollars. Before the Northern Pacific discovered that it had wasted its money, Gordon left for New York City. It was his good luck to make the trip on the same train as one of those whom he had impressed in Minnesota. Through her he was introduced to the famous Jay Gould, a wealthy American businessman who was fighting for control of the Erie Railroad. Gordon seized the opportunity and told the financier he personally owned thirty million dollars worth of Erie stock and controlled another twenty million through friends. That much stock was sufficient to guarantee Gould victory in his battle with the Vanderbilts for control of the railway company. In return for Gordon's promise of support he lodged with the Scotsman, as a token of good faith, 600 shares of Erie stock, nearly 2000 shares in companies affiliated with Erie, 4722 shares in the Oil Creek and Allegheny Railroad, and more than $180,000 in cash and bonds.

Two weeks later Gould learned that Gordon had begun selling the Oil Creek and Allegheny stock, and had him arrested and charged with fraud. During his trial, held two months later, Gordon discovered that the New York police were looking into his background. He promptly fled to Toronto and from there to Winnipeg. He lived quietly on the outskirts of the city from October 1872 until the following summer, when he was recognized by one of the men he swindled in Minneapolis. Within days two American detectives arrived with a warrant for his arrest. They faced a dilemma, however, when they learned that their warrant was not valid in Canada. Since they knew Gordon would never return to the United States willingly, they decided to kidnap him. The kidnappers, with Gordon in hand, were arrested at the U.S. border and returned to Winnipeg.

The news that citizens of the United States were being held without bail in a foreign jail inflamed American feelings of nationalism, and by the time the kidnappers appeared before McKeagney emotions had risen to the point that legal arguments often turned into shouting matches between the province's attorney general and counsel for the defence. Someone eventually suggested that it would be in everyone's best interest if the prisoners pled guilty and were sentenced to no more than a day in jail, which they had already served. Both Prime Minister Macdonald and the governor of Minnesota agreed with the proposal, and McKeagney promptly imposed a sentence of twenty-four hours' incarceration on the accused.

While the affair ended in embarrassment for McKeagney, it ended in tragedy for Gordon. Before he could leave the province for British Columbia, he was again recognized, this time by Attorney General Clarke. He was immediately arrested and charged with a variety of offences. Gordon sued Clarke, and the dispute dragged on until a new warrant was issued in Toronto – this time supported by evidence of the fraud committed in Scotland more than four years earlier – and served on Gordon by a Toronto detective. After packing his bag in anticipation of accompanying the detective to Ontario, Gordon received permission to return to his room to get a warmer coat. Instead, grabbing a pistol from a nightstand, he fatally shot himself in the head.[63]

McKeagney's career on the Manitoba bench started out poorly and never got better. He continually allowed himself to be browbeaten, and was widely regarded as incompetent. In short, he was a poor judge because he had been a weak lawyer. Years spent in politics did nothing to prepare him for the bench, and were it not for his connections to the Church, the political establishment, and the family of his first wife it is unlikely that he would have had even that career. When he married Eliza Henry in 1842, McKeagney became a member of one of Cape Breton's wealthiest families. Patriarch Robert Nesbit Henry had the good fortune to marry a well-to-do widow four years after emigrating from Ireland. A combination of her property and his hard work meant that by the time his daughter married McKeagney Henry was in a strong position to advance the career of his son-in-law. Robert Henry was not only one of the island's most successful farmers, and active in the formation of organizations like the Antigonish Agricultural Society, he was a successful merchant, district postmaster, school trustee, justice of the peace, clerk to the Board of School Commissioners, and captain of a company of militia.

Although McKeagney's wife died after only nine years of marriage, by then her brother William Henry was also in a position to advance McKeagney's career. Like his brother-in-law, William was a lawyer, a politician, and a lieutenant-colonel in the militia. Unlike him, however, he had earned an outstanding reputation at the bar, as mayor of Halifax, and as a father of Confederation. And unlike the comments that followed McKeagney to the bench, those surrounding Henry's appointment to the Supreme Court of Canada were complimentary.[64]

McKeagney died on 14 September 1879 while vacationing with his second wife in St Andrew's, New Brunswick. The report of his passing was mentioned briefly by the *Manitoba Free Press*, and a cursory summary of his career published two days later.[65]

LOUIS BETOURNAY

The third judge appointed to the Court of Queen's Bench of Manitoba, Louis Betournay, was born on 13 November 1825 in the Longueuil parish of St-Lambert de Chambly, Lower Canada. His great-grandfather had been a captain with the Carignan-Salières regiment,[66] while his father died without having made a name for himself, three and one-half months before the birth of his son.[67] Louis Betournay studied at Montreal College before entering the law office of Joseph-Ubalde Beaudry. Like his pupil, Beaudry was a graduate of Montreal College, and during the time Betournay clerked for him he was a Montreal city councillor.[68] Beaudry ended his career as a justice of the province's Superior Court.

Following his call to the bar of Canada East in 1849, Betournay practised briefly in St-Lambert before returning to Montreal, where he practised on his own until 1862. He then entered the office of George-Étienne Cartier, whose influence was directly responsible for his appointment to the Manitoba bench.

By the time Betournay joined the partnership the firm's clients in-

Louis Betournay (1825–79), puisne judge (1872–9). Betournay was the first of several judges appointed to Queen's Bench who owed his appointment to the influence of a political mentor rather than to his ability as a lawyer. A number of his contemporaries attributed Betournay's sudden death to the guilt he was said to have suffered for his part in the scandal associated with a recount of votes in the 1878 federal election in which Donald Smith defeated Alexander Morris by ten votes in the riding of Selkirk. (Provincial Archives of Manitoba)

cluded the Catholic church, the French government, shipping and mining companies, and the Grand Trunk Railway.

In one of the last political acts of his life, Cartier asked John A. Macdonald to appoint Betournay to the bench of Manitoba. Despite working in the office of a father of Confederation, and serving as a Montreal alderman for two years, Betournay had done nothing to distinguish himself. In a letter to Alexander Morris the best that a clearly unimpressed prime minister could say of his appointee was that he was 'a very nice gentlemanlike fellow.'[69] Although Betournay was appointed on 31 October 1872, he did not leave Montreal for his new home until the middle of December. During the ten-day trip west he was accompanied by Louis Frasse de Plainval, one of the most colourful men of his era.

Before becoming Manitoba's second chief of police de Plainval was forced to flee his native France, where he had been a member of the nobility, after a duelling incident in which one man was killed and another wounded. In New York he became an opera singer, but soon grew bored and emigrated to Montreal. When General Wolseley's troops marched out to deal with what remained of the Riel uprising, he joined them. Soon after he arrived in Manitoba he was made second-in-command of the province's police force, and in 1872 became its chief. Six months after Betournay arrived in Canada's newest province, however, the enigmatic Frenchman left under what can only be described as mysterious circumstances. Seriously in debt to a number of Winnipeg creditors, de Plainval hired a horse and buggy for what he said was a trip east. Instead, he headed straight for the United States. His plans went awry when concerned creditors had him held at the border until he was able to make arrangements for payment of his debts.[70]

Almost immediately upon going to the bench Betournay, like McKeagney before him, was caught up in controversy. When he and McKeagney convened the second sitting of the province's highest court in January 1873 one of the first cases to be heard involved Ambroise Lepine, the man charged with murdering Thomas Scott during the Red River disturbance of 1869–70. Lepine's counsel argued that the court had no jurisdiction to try his client, since it was a superior court of Canada and when Scott was murdered Manitoba was not yet part of the Dominion. With counsel on both sides raising their voices and making threatening gestures, Betournay adjourned the court. His lack of knowledge of English law and procedure, combined with a lack of courtroom experience, made it difficult for him to maintain order. The

Manitoba Gazette complained that on one occasion things got so out of control that the dignity of both bench and bar were placed at risk. 'We sincerely hope that in future our courts may be kept free from any such unseemly proceeding, and that any person, no matter what his position, shall be taught that respect which is due a British Court of Justice, and that any infringement of its dignity will be punished promptly, and with the full force of the law.' And in case anyone failed to understand where the real problem lay, the paper went on to note that '[h]ad such proceeding taken place before Dominion Judges that we [know] of the offenders would not have escaped with immunity, but would have been severely taught a lesson of respect both to themselves, the Bench, and the Bar of which they are supposed to be representatives.'[71]

Two years later Betournay made judicial history when he heard the first extradition case to come before a Manitoba court. Abner Getz was an American citizen living in Manitoba who was charged with committing a robbery at Bismarck, North Dakota. It was subsequently discovered that he was also a deserter from the United States Army, and that the robbery charge was an attempt to avoid a costly and time-consuming formal extradition hearing.[72]

During his seven years on the bench Betournay failed to win either the affection or admiration of the bar, despite having made a good first impression on Chief Justice Morris, whose law books he borrowed in an effort to become acquainted with English common law. Betournay, wrote Morris, 'is sharp and will get on by and by.'[73] Unfortunately, that did not prove to be the case. He and McKeagney were described by a contemporary as 'the two pinpricks,' and Betournay as 'anxious to do right – well disposed in every way but not up to law.'[74] In addition to his ability, Betournay's integrity was also called into question. When he was appointed to head a commission charged with investigating allegations of corruption levied against Selkirk Member of Parliament Donald Smith, Manitobans complained of what they perceived to be his obvious bias. One prominent Winnipegger wrote a scathing indictment to the prime minister:

> Judge Betournay whose conduct of the inquiry is a matter of scandal here is indebted to Donald A. Smith to the extent of nearly $16,000.00, secured nominally on real estate & chattels; on the former $10,280, on the latter $5,237.50. Betournay is only assessed at $5,000.00. I agreed with them that it was a flagrant indecency that a Judge having such pecuniary relations

> with Donald A. Smith should preside over an inquiry which might issue in Mr. Smith's losing his seat for Selkirk.[75]

Betournay's luck was no better outside court. Ten days after arriving in Winnipeg he was involved in a road accident, and a few months later was found lying unconscious in the street after being run over by a horse while on his way to a day of shooting in one of the city's outlying suburbs.[76] Three months before his death he suffered an even greater indignity when he was attacked by his own bull mastiff dog.[77]

Betournay died just before midnight on 31 October 1879. He was fifty-four, the same age at which his father passed away. The official cause of his death was dropsy. Four days later his funeral was held. The procession proceeded from his home in Winnipeg to the banks of the Red River, where a path had been broken through the ice. As the boat carrying his casket made its way to St Boniface, pallbearers and mourners walked silently across the ice beside it. From the boat four men carried Betournay's remains to the cathedral, accompanied along the way by Joseph Royal, J.A.N. Provencher, Joseph Dubuc, Gilbert McMicken, J.H. McTavish, A.A.C. LaRivière, and robed members of the province's bar. Amid the sounds of toiling bells and the strains of the 'Funeral March,' the procession, joined by the clergy of St Boniface, walked solemnly past windows and galleries draped in black. At the front of the cathedral's centre aisle the coffin was placed on a high catafalque. There, surrounded by candles and covered in black velvet upon which his robes of office had been placed, the casket looked down on those in attendance. Throughout the mass the sounds of the church choir, consisting of three sopranos, three bass, four tenors, and a pianist and violincello, paid homage to the dead judge. When the ceremony ended the doors of the cathedral swung open, and Archbishop Taché, preceded by a cross-bearer, acolytes, and selected clergy, walked slowly towards the coffin. Clouds of incense filled the church as holy water was sprinkled over the casket. With that the service ended, and the body of Betournay was borne to its final resting place.[78]

Betournay was survived by his wife and six of his children. Friends remembered him as an urbane gentleman, possessed of a fine library and a deep passion for both books and horses.[79] The *Manitoba Free Press* described him as a genial man with a high sense of probity.[80] In actuality he was one of a number of judges who were not competent either before or after their appointments. [81]

EDMUND BURKE WOOD

Before becoming Manitoba's second chief justice, Edmund Burke Wood was regarded as one of the country's outstanding lawyers and foremost orators. He also headed the largest and most lucrative practice west of Toronto, was simultaneously a member of both senior levels of government, and served as a bencher of the Law Society of Upper Canada. A true renaissance man, Wood was charismatic, mathematical in his deductions, intelligent, widely read, possessed of an encyclopaedic knowledge of Canadian history, a close reasoner, and genial and witty in private. On the bench he was very much a man of his time and place. Yet he died in ignominy, ridiculed by the Supreme Court of Canada, under investigation by a special committee of the House of Commons, regarded as venal and an opportunist, and one of whom the best that could be said was that his work was useful.

The first contact that Wood's family had with North America occurred during the American Revolution, when his grandfather fought as a British army officer. His father emigrated to the United States from Ireland at the beginning of the nineteenth century, and to Canada following the War of 1812. He settled briefly in Drummondville before moving to the County of Wentworth, where he became a well-to-do farmer. Edmund was born on 13 February 1820 near Fort Erie, in Welland County, the fourth son of Samuel and Charlotte. He was still at home in 1840 when he blew off his left arm in a hunting accident. That ended his career in farming and prompted his return to the district school that he had largely ignored while growing up. After graduating Wood earned a teaching certificate, and for just over two years divided his time between teaching and ministering in the local Methodist church. By the mid-1840s, however, he gave up both positions to enrol in Ohio's Oberlin College, from which he graduated in 1848 with a Bachelor of Arts degree.[82] The following year Wood became a member of the Law Society of Upper Canada and one of three clerks articling with Hamiltonians Samuel Black Freeman and Stephen James Jones. In 1850 his articles were assigned to Archibald Gilkinson, and he moved to Brantford. The influence that two of these men had on his career was enormous. Through Jones Wood became clerk of the Brant county court, deputy clerk of the crown, and secretary-treasurer of the Board of Public School Trustees. Through Gilkinson's influence he became solicitor for the Buffalo and Lake Huron Railway, and as their representative

Edmund Burke Wood (1820–82). Chief justice of the Court of Queen's Bench 1874–82. Wood was an exceptionally talented lawyer but was best known as one of Canada's most controversial politicians. He was accused by many of being a puppet of Ontario railway interests. By the time he was appointed to the Manitoba bench, Wood's political influence had waned and years of hard drinking had left him in failing health. He died from the effects of a stroke as parliament was debating whether to remove him from the bench because of alleged wrongdoing. (Brant County Museum)

quickly gained a prominent place within the legal profession and political arena.[83]

Wood was admitted to the bar of Upper Canada as a solicitor on 21 November 1853, and a year later received his call. Faced with the choice of continuing as clerk and deputy clerk in Brant County or practising law full time, he resigned his civic offices to work with Gilkinson. The firm's largest client was the Buffalo and Lake Huron Railway. Gilkinson left law shortly after Wood joined his practice and his junior partner replaced him as solicitor for the newly reorganized rail company, acting as both corporate counsel and principal promoter. By 1863 Wood had an income of ten thousand dollars a year and the largest practice west of Toronto. When Canada West entered Confederation, the legal fees paid by the amalgamated Grand Trunk and Buffalo railways exceeded twenty-thousand dollars a year, a significant portion of which went to Wood.

That he had the opportunity of working for railway interests was largely due to political pressure exerted on Canada West's Baldwin government in 1850. Before then the cost of obtaining a railway charter was almost as expensive as building the line itself. Things changed for a few months following passage of an amendment to the *Plank Road Act*, which allowed communities like Brantford to build rail lines without parliamentary approval. The only company brought into existence before the law was repealed was the Buffalo and Brantford Railway. It was funded by the town of Brantford and city of Buffalo, which purchased, respectively, $100,000 and $70,000 of its stock. Additional funding was provided by a $500,000 loan from England's Baring Brothers. Gilkinson was the company's first secretary and legal counsel.

On 13 January 1854 the first trains to arrive in Brantford were met with loud cheers and a firing of the town's cannon. That evening railway officials were honoured with fireworks, a grand ball, and music supplied by a Cotillion band and the Brantford Philharmonic. Within a year, however, much had changed. On four occasions thugs hired by competitors attempted to derail trains by removing rails or jamming switches. The expense of meeting these threats, coupled with the cost of extending the line from Brantford to Goderich, virtually bankrupted the once prospering company. Matters were made worse when unpaid labourers began tearing up what tracks had already been laid. By 1856, when the company was reorganized as the Buffalo and Lake Huron Railway, it had spent over $3 million on construction and equipment but had built just eighty-four miles of track.[84]

His association with railway interests provided Wood with more than money. It gave him the opportunity to hone his already considerable skills as a litigator and raised his profile inside and outside the profession. Citizens of Brantford regularly watched him square off against legal heavyweights like Edward Blake, B.B. Osler, Matthew Crooks Cameron, and Dalton McCarthy, all of whom had national reputations. A witness to one battle noted that '[k]een argument and cross examination were punctuated with many brilliant interchanges and the jury addresses were of a memorable description.'[85] Typical of Wood's ability to sway a jury was his summation on behalf of a native charged with manslaughter:

> He first dilated upon man's inhumanity to man, and especially the inhumanity of white men to the red men, and as he warmed up to this, he really felt the wrongs himself, and his indignation knew no bounds, and his deep, sombre, full-toned voice pealed forth like a great organ. The Court House was filled with Indians, who were there to stand by their brother, and as they listened to Wood paint in graphic language their wrongs, it was with difficulty they could be restrained from scalping the entire jury, and were very probably persuaded from doing so by the assurance that Wood would be sure to get High Flyer off, which sure enough he did ... The Indians ever afterwards banked on 'Big Thunder' to pull them through any difficulties they got into, until he left Brantford for Manitoba.[86]

The case that solidified his already considerable reputation, however, involved the defence of two men charged with murdering a local mail carrier. It is illustrative of how quickly justice was meted out in mid-nineteenth-century Ontario, and how a reputation could be earned even in a losing cause. On 15 April 1859 the body of Lancelot Adams was found on a road less than two miles outside Brantford. He had been shot in the head, and the mail he carried the seven miles between Paris and Brantford had been stolen. Two days later a local labourer confessed that he and two friends had committed the crime. His trial was deferred to allow him to give evidence against his companions. Two weeks after the murder two of the mail carrier's killers were tried and sentenced to hang, and a month later the sentence was carried out. Within fifty-three days a man had been murdered, his assailants arrested, a coroner's jury assembled, a trial held, and a sentence executed. Wood was one of the few to gain from the process, having 'evinced much talent and tact in the defence.'[87] Notwithstanding his success at the criminal bar, however, Wood spent most of his time as a civil litigator. Between 1866 and 1873 the *Upper Canada Queen's Bench Reports* described sixteen cases with which he was involved, including an equal number of trials and appeals. He acted for a plaintiff four times and respondent twelve. At each level he was unsuccessful only once, giving him a 'winning' record of 88 per cent. One half of his clients were railway companies. On their behalf he was successful all but once, and on that occasion the court of appeal expressed its regret at having to rule against him.[88]

From 1856 until 1858 Wood practised with Peter Ball Long, a former owner of the *Brantford Herald*. Although Long was a solicitor, and possessed of a much lower profile than his partner, he still found time to serve a term as town councillor. After his association with Long ended Wood spent the rest of his career practising alone. In the mid-1860s, however, he took John Charles Dent into his office as a student. Dent left after receiving his call, and went on to earn an international reputation as a journalist, author, and historian.

Just as Wood's success in law was inextricably linked with the work he did for rail interests, so too was his success in politics. When he first ran for public office, his aim was to extend his personal influence and promote the interests of his clients. From the beginning to the end of what was to be an illustrious career, he pursued both with equal vigour.

Wood's first foray into politics occurred in 1858, when he was an active supporter of Reform incumbent Herbert Biggar in his campaign against Reverend William Ryerson. Five years later he was the candidate, and he defeated Ryerson by more than five hundred votes. His success, however, probably had as much to do with Ryerson's unpopularity over his support of separate schools than with his own appeal. But Wood was not a man who could be easily overlooked. Huge physically, with a large head, solid jaw, and a projecting under lip, when not speaking he held his mouth firmly shut beneath dark, deep-set eyes and shaggy brows.

Through years spent in courtrooms Wood developed into an extraordinary public speaker. Combining a remarkable command of language with a deep, rich, full-toned voice, his speeches flashed with wit and literary allusion. And each was delivered with an energy and enthusiasm that seldom failed to carry conviction.[89] As a fourteen-year-old Sir John Willison had stood on a rough platform outside a village tavern and watched Wood perform:

> I gazed at the bulky figure on the platform, I noticed that he had lost one arm, that his dusty white vest was buttoned unevenly so that one side hung below the other, and that in the teeth of the shouting he was indomitably calm and unperturbed ... His voice thundered out over the cross-roads. His words came with stormy fluency. There was tremendous volume and vigour. The conquest was complete. He had not gone far before there was tumultuous cheering. He seemed to sway the crowd as he would.[90]

That ability came in handy in 1867. When Wood agreed to join the 'Patent Combination' of Ontario premier John Sandfield Macdonald he incurred the wrath of the Reform party, for whom he had become principal spokesperson. Before entering cabinet as the province's first treasurer, however, the law required that his appointment be confirmed in a re-election. He lost the Reform nomination to Biggar, and when he sought the federal nomination, he lost it too. Both losses can be attributed to his decision to enter that Macdonald government, and to his close connection to the Grand Trunk Railway. Losing the two nominations incensed Wood. Since the law allowed him to sit in the provincial legislature and the House of Commons simultaneously, he decided to run both provincially and federally. By the time he gave his first campaign speech, however, sentiment in Brantford was running strongly against him. When he rose to speak, his Town Hall audience began shouting threats. Against the advice of his few supporters, he decided to stay, and amid the hissing and booing he, with considerable deliberation, climbed onto a table and shouted:

> 'Serpents may hiss and devils in hell may shout, but damn you, I am going to have a hearing.' This could be heard, clear and distinct, in all parts of the hall, above all the din. Many were so struck by the great physical courage displayed by him that they subsided to hear what he had to say in his defence, and he soon had a splendid hearing ... illustrating the old adage that men will follow great men much quicker than they will follow principles.[91]

Wood's victory was complete. With the considerable help 'of a number of Methodists & friends,' he became the member for Brant South in both Houses.[92] The new provincial treasurer immediately clashed with his premier. The former's reformist background stood in stark contrast to the conservatism of the latter. Often his fights with the Conservative establishment extended to the federal wing of the party. Wood was leader of a group of maverick federal backbenchers who opposed improving the terms under which Nova Scotia entered Confederation. As provincial treasurer, however, he was a staunch defender of the financial interests of Ontario, and his rhetoric during post-Confederation discussions between Ontario and Quebec echoed the sectionalist tone of pre-1867 politics.

Sandfield Macdonald joked that the only thing which kept his cabinet together was the fact that three of its five members were physically challenged. 'What a curious lot we are, a sort of one-horse concern; here is Wood with but one arm, Cameron with one foot, and I with one lung.'[93] Ultimately, even that was not enough. After the 1871 provincial election the government was left with only a slim majority in the legislature, although Wood had won in South Brant, this time as a Liberal-Coalitionist, defeating a well-known Brantford miller. His tenure in the Sandfield Macdonald cabinet, however, soon came to an end. When the House convened in December, the Blake Liberals introduced a motion of non-confidence. Although it carried by seven votes, Macdonald refused to resign. Edward Blake, provincial Liberal leader, had been negotiating Wood's return to the party for some time. After losing three successive votes, the government was on the brink of collapse, and Blake desperately tried to persuade Wood that the time was right for him to return to his roots. Wood was not against making the move, but wanted some assurance he would be offered a position in a Liberal government. It was a guarantee he did not get. Still, on 16 December he resigned from the government. Three days later it fell,[94] and Blake became the province's second premier. In one of his first acts as Macdonald's successor, Sir Matthew Crooks Cameron, a true blue Tory, sought to establish an inquiry into possible improprieties associated with Wood's resignation. Although the motion was defeated, Wood's support within the Liberal party had been irreparably damaged by his association with the Conservatives, and he was not offered a seat in Blake's cabinet.

Following his resignation from the Sandfield Macdonald government Wood sat in the legislature as a private member. In 1872 dual representation was abolished, and he resigned his seat in the provincial house. After first refusing to run in that year's federal election he changed his mind and won a by-election in West Durham, called when Edward Blake decided to sit as the federal member for South Bruce. Although re-elected in the 1874 general election, Wood's passion for politics seems to have dissipated. Notwithstanding that his booming voice was often heard during the Pacific Railway scandal debates, when the Conservative government of John A. Macdonald finally fell, incumbent Liberal prime minister Alexander Mackenzie remembered the role Wood played in the provincial administration of Sandfield Macdonald and refused to offer him a cabinet portfolio.

Although contemporaries regarded Wood's political philosophy as genuinely held, his entry into the Macdonald cabinet brought to the surface suspicions that his shift from Reformist to Conservative ranks was prompted more by economic self-interest than political conviction. Few doubted that he left the Liberal party primarily because of his close business and professional ties to the railway. They were right. Wood's decision represented an attempt to enlarge personal influence and power, and had nothing to do with principle:

> Since his economic interests were perceived to be dependent upon securing the co-operation of government [on behalf of the Buffalo and Lake Huron and Grand Trunk railways], Wood preferred power to either principle or party ... That [he] joined and remained a member of the Combination for four years was evidence not only of his pragmatism during a relatively fluid situation between 1867 and 1871, but also of the importance of personal economic interests in determining party support.[95]

By the spring of 1874 Wood's excesses were finally catching up to him. The cost of building and maintaining a palatial home in Brantford, combined with his heavy drinking and the collapse from neglect of his law practice, brought him to edge of bankruptcy. Although he had been effective during the Pacific Railway debates, he was unable to win the trust of Mackenzie, who regarded Wood's appointment to the bench in Manitoba as the solution to two problems. It got rid of someone in whom the Liberals no longer had confidence, but owed a debt, and it sent to the bench someone who could bring order out of the chaos that existed under Betournay and McKeagney. Wood regarded the $5000 a year salary he would receive as his economic salvation. His appointment as chief justice was made on 11 March 1874. Although initially intending to leave for Manitoba in early May, a case of measles contracted while vacationing in St Catharines delayed his departure by a month. On his arrival in Winnipeg he was immediately called to the provincial bar (a requirement of Manitoba law), and on 20 June heard his first case. Ironically, it was the most infamous of his career.

When neither the provincial nor federal government made any attempt to bring Louis Riel, Ambroise Lepine, or any of the other Metis leaders to trial for the March 1870 murder of Thomas Scott, a local ultra-Protestant swore out an information on his own, and a warrant for Lepine's arrest was issued. On 23 September 1873 he was brought before Betournay and Justice of the Peace Gilbert McMicken for a preliminary hearing. Lepine's counsel argued that a Manitoba court had no jurisdiction to try the case since, according to the *Imperial Act* of 1821, all murders committed in the North-West were to be tried in either Upper or Lower Canada. In 1841 jurisdiction had been transferred to the courts of the united provinces of Canada; but when the Canadian nation came into being in 1867 the act of 1841 was repealed, and *The Rupert's Land Act* was passed the following year. It provided that on a date to be established Canada would become responsible for the administration of justice in the North-West. The order-in-council fixing that date was not passed until June 1870, several months after Scott's execution. When the *Manitoba Act* was passed it expressly provided that its application was not to be retroactive. As a consequence, Manitoba courts did not receive jurisdiction over cases of murder until 1871. Lepine's argument was that the alleged murder of Thomas Scott fell between the jurisdictional cracks, and no Manitoba court had the authority to hear his case.

At Lepine's preliminary hearing Betournay decided it was premature to rule on the issue of jurisdiction, and after a five-day hearing committed Lepine to trial. Two months later it was McKeagney's turn. During the regular Court of Queen's Bench assizes he held that a true bill for murder had been made by a grand jury and ordered that the case be heard the following February. When the trial got under way Lepine's lawyer again raised the defence of want of jurisdiction. McKeagney decided that he was neither competent nor justified in deciding such an important issue and adjourned the matter until a chief justice was appointed.

With Wood's appointment the issue of jurisdiction was finally argued, and he immediately handed down his decision. After tracing the judicial history of the North-West from 1670 to the date of the Lepine hearing, he held that he had jurisdiction to hear the case. The trial itself, however, did not get under way until the following October. The court sat for eleven days before returning a guilty verdict after two and one-half hours of deliberation. On 28 October Lepine was sentenced to be hanged. Four days before he was to die, however, Governor General

Dufferin commuted his sentence to two years in prison and forfeiture of his civil rights. William Farmer, the man who started the whole process, received $2000 from the reward offered for the arrest and conviction of Scott's killers.[96]

Wood's next case had the potential to be just as controversial as his first. The accused, André Nault, had been in charge of the firing squad that executed Scott. This time, however, the jury could not reach a unanimous verdict, and Nault was discharged.

Although soon enmeshed in a series of controversies that were to plague him throughout his tenure on the bench, Wood made a strong first impression. Referring to his recent arrival, a contemporary suggested 'from that day till now, a more perfect and comprehensive administration of justice has prevailed.'[97] In an editorial commenting on his performance during the Lepine trial, the *Manitoba Free Press* was effusive in its praise: 'Chief Justice Wood marshalled legal fact and fact, and in one of the ablest charges, if not the ablest, ever given to a jury in Canada, expounded the law clearly, powerfully and exhaustively, so that a child might have understood him ... Chief Justice Wood is one of the ablest, if not the ablest, constitutional lawyers in the Dominion.'[98]

The comments of the man Wood replaced, while generally positive, proved prophetic. Morris noted that while there was no doubt that the new chief justice had the ability to be an excellent judge, he appeared to find it difficult to put aside old biases and confine himself to the bench.[99] The first to publicly criticize his behaviour was the same newspaper that only three months earlier had sung his praises:

> Few men immediately upon their elevation to the Bench gained the general very great respect that Chief Justice Wood did. But it is undeniable that he has not altogether retained that confidence which was so suddenly reposed in him. It being well known, that prior to his appointment he was a very enthusiastic politician, his conduct may have been watched rather more closely than it otherwise would have been; and it is equally possible that conclusions have been arrived at, which would not have been under ordinary circumstances. Be these things as they may, however, the fact is as we have stated; and there is a strong disposition to believe that the Chief Justice is not altogether superior to political bias. It is very unfortunate that such should be the case.[100]

One of the things that called into question Wood's impartiality was his relationship with Dr John Schultz, a controversial Member of Parliament and leader of the Protestant faction during the Red River disturbance. Within two months of his arrival in the province, Wood borrowed from Schultz just under six thousand dollars. News of the loan soon became public and a matter of concern to the federal government. That a Manitoba judge would allow himself to become indebted to one of the province's leading businessmen upset Prime Minister Mackenzie, and he asked Chief Justice Morris to find out if the rumours were true. 'I was informed that Judge Wood had allowed himself to get deeply in debt to Mr. Schultz. I hope this is not true as I would not doubt that person had purposely intended to lay the Judge under obligations to him. It is a delicate subject to touch but I would like to know if you heard this.'[101] Morris was quick to respond:

> As to the Chief, I fear he is in deep water. I know he had no means when he came here. He then bought from Schultz a lot and unfinished house, which the latter was to finish for him, but eventually Wood took it into his own hands and completed it. It must have cost him $7,000 or $ 8,000 and unless his brothers helped him, which I doubt, I fear the popular impression is too true, that he is heavily indebted to Schultz.[102]

Wood's actions during and after a trial involving Schultz did nothing to dispel the rumours about the nature of his relationship with the politician. During a Court of Revision, Schultz testified that a number of natives had returned the annuities paid to them by the government, thereby gaining the right to vote. It turned out that this was not the case, and he was charged with perjury. His trial attracted a considerable amount of attention, as did Wood's conduct. After the charges were dismissed the *Free Press* accused the chief justice of acting more as counsel for the defence than as a dispassionate judge.[103] When Wood read the editorial he immediately cited the paper's editor for contempt and fined him $200. His actions so enraged those attending the hearing, however, that within minutes a collection was taken and the fine paid.

By the end of 1875 Wood's economic dependency on Schultz was accepted as fact even in Ottawa, and the prime minister was worried about the possible political fallout. '[W]hat I feared about Wood getting into debt has happened; have had his letters outlining his poverty and appealing for assistance; his foolish extravagance will lead government and himself into serious difficulty; there must be some change in respect to him; I fear his course has already interfered with efficient discharge of his duties.'[104]

Wood's indiscretions and tendency towards partisanship had an immediate and decided impact on how others perceived the Manitoba judiciary. The *Free Press* frequently rebuked him for his intemperate speeches. For example, after reporting on his comments at a St Andrew's dinner, the paper noted, 'It is Chief Justice Wood's privilege to *believe* that a certain political party would fan the embers of strife in respect of language, etc; but it is not his privilege to *publicly express* this belief ... neither does he act wisely in administering public "withering rebukes" to any political party or faction.'[105] After commenting on the inappropriateness of a judge giving a public speech critical of the government, the paper made fun of his street-corner oratory, noting that by his language he managed to 'wound the feelings of at least half his immense audience.'[106]

Wood gave the *Free Press* even more ammunition when it became known that he had written a number of editorials for another newspaper. Instead of admitting what everyone knew to be true, he denied responsibility. The *Free Press* belittled his response, suggesting that if he were not guilty he should sue, which it said he would never do out of fear of being proven a liar.[107]

Wood also gave his critics ample reason to question his ethics, if not his honesty. Some accused him of pressuring Betournay into favouring railway magnate Donald Smith during the 1879 Smith-Morris recount, suggesting that it was regret over his actions that caused Betournay's premature death. A friend of Morris wrote the lieutenant-governor about what was being said of the chief justice. '[M]any are of opinion Betournay's action guided by Wood in recount and regret by him after hastened his death.'[108]

Manitoba's first court reporter, William Perkins, frequently appeared in courts presided over by Wood. He was also a friend of Nathaniel Hagel, a prominent Winnipeg lawyer, and witnessed a confrontation between the two. Wanting to speak with the chief justice prior to a trial that was about to get under way, Hagel decided to wait in Wood's chambers. Looking down, he noticed on the judge's desk a written judgment in the case that he was about to argue. He also noticed that Wood's decision had gone against his client. When court opened Hagel immediately rose and informed Wood that he wished to make a motion to impeach. When asked to explain himself the clearly irritated lawyer said, 'If your Lordship will read that document which you had in your hand when you came into Court and which now lies before you, it will be apparent to all in this Court what I mean.' Wood jumped to his feet, grabbed the document, and as he left the courtroom shouted over his shoulder, 'Impeach and be damned.' In due course Wood returned, and when Hagel's case was heard, decided in favour of Hagel's client.[109]

Wood made things even more difficult for himself by deliberately antagonizing his predecessor. In a despatch to the federal secretary of state, lieutenant-governor Morris made it clear that his relationship with the chief justice was strained at best:

> With respect to 'Report of Chief Justice Wood respecting Claims to reward for apprehension of murderers of Thomas Scott' published by Leg. Ass. of Ontario, Wood has made statements about me which are utterly unfounded and unjust ... [H]e has deliberately written a statement he knew to be untrue ... [T]he animus in Wood's remark on the face of the John A. Macdonald government and the influence upon Morris is a clue to the motives which have actuated him in going beyond the bounds of his Commission.[110]

It is likely that at least some of Wood's unusual behaviour, both on and off the bench, can be attributed to his drinking problem. Within months of his arrival in Manitoba the amount of alcohol he consumed was the topic of considerable conversation, primarily because he did much of his drinking in public. In January 1877 provincial officials sent a formal complaint to Ottawa, and before long a legislative committee was established to investigate charges that Wood became so intoxicated on his way to preside over the County Court of Marquette that court had to be adjourned for the day. Although the federal government accepted Wood's denials, and no formal action was taken, he continued to drink.[111]

Wood was persistent in his efforts to antagonize the press, federal officials, members of the bar, and the lieutenant-governor. In 1879 he added the provincial cabinet to the list. After submitting to the government a draft *County Courts Act*, he had it published without authority, adding a title and introduction. He called his creation 'A complete Code of Law, Practice and Procedure in County Courts, designed to make every man his own lawyer.' Its introduction is part description of an unusual court system, and part a thinly veiled attack:

> The vast importance to business men, and to the public in general, of a simple, plain expeditious and inexpensive mode of collecting debts, of seeking redress for wrongs and of testing rights, has induced the publica-

> tion of the 'County Courts Act' in its present form, separate from the General Statutes of the Province ... The Act as a whole, is a complete code of law, practice and procedure ... and so plain and simple is it in its provisions, that anyone of the most ordinary understanding cannot fail in the conduct and management of his litigation in these courts. By this Act, the County Courts are made just what they ought to be, the people's and the poor man's Courts; in which there is little room and less use for professional gentlemen, but in which every man may with propriety and advantage, be his own lawyer, 'without having a fool for a client' ... The public will expect, and no doubt will not be disappointed in its anticipation, that the judges, and especially the government, which has, with doubtful propriety, retained in its own hands the appointment of clerks and bailiffs, will see to it, that the provisions of the Act are administered and carried out with the same completeness, and in the same spirit as that in which they have been conceived and formulated.[112]

When provincial government officials became aware of the content of Wood's preface, they demanded that every volume of the act be returned to the binders, that the pages containing the preface be removed, and that the books be rebound.

Another controversy that raged during Wood's tenure on the bench was his alleged involvement in the lawlessness associated with the administration of Metis land claims. When the federal government purchased the North-West Territories from the Hudson's Bay Company in 1869, it extinguished most of the company's land rights in the west. By treaty it attempted to do the same to natives. Most inhabitants of the Red River Settlement, however, were neither employees of the Hudson's Bay Company nor treaty Indians but, for the most part, a mixture of the two. Following Manitoba's entry into Confederation the federal government agreed to distribute 1.4 million acres of land, on a per capita basis, among the Metis who were residing in the settlement when it became part of Canada. Between 1873 and 1884, however, the *Manitoba Act* was amended eleven times, and the number of Metis entitled to share in the distribution reduced from ten thousand to six thousand. This was done by restricting the allotment of 140-acre parcels to Metis children, and giving heads of families scrip, or an entitlement to land, rather than land itself.

Once governmental officials started distributing land, scrip speculators began buying them up, often for a fraction of their value. Before parcels owned by children could be transferred, however, the transactions had to be approved by a judge of the Queen's Bench. Hundreds of such sales were approved, even though the court knew its actions deprived children of their birthright. The obvious inequities associated with the procedure upset many, and much of their indignation was directed at Wood. His grandson worked in the office of one of the province's largest speculators, and his son was employed by the law firm that prepared many of the applications. Approximately 75 per cent of infant lands changed hands by being funnelled through the courts to speculators.[113] The evidence implicating Wood in wrong-doing was so convincing that on 28 October 1881 the provincial government established a commission to inquire into the sale of infant lands. Wood testified at the enquiry, but died before the government could act on its findings.

Ironically, the most critical comment about Wood made by a fellow judge was not the result of something Wood said on the bench, but of something he said as a litigant. It was even more ironic that the case that gave rise to those comments involved his former benefactor, John Schultz. Between 1874 and 1879 Wood's debt to Schultz was assigned twice, first by Schultz to Duncan Macarthur, and then by Macarthur to the Manitoba and North-West Land Company. Few, if any, payments were made. When the last assignee threatened to foreclose, Wood denied liability and sued Schultz for an accounting. Two years later the dispute ended up in the Supreme Court of Canada, where Chief Justice Ritchie was unequivocal in his condemnation of Wood. He criticized the evidence Wood gave at trial and noted that he had been allowed 'to make most objectionable statements, and statements he knew not to be evidence, to use most intemperate language, and generally to give his evidence and act in a most unbecoming manner, wholly inconsistent with the due and proper administration of justice.'[114] He concluded by suggesting that Wood had shown himself to be deluded, negligent, and reckless.

But despite becoming embroiled in one controversy after another, Wood was a judge of above-average ability. His decisions were usually thoughtful and reasoned, often settled important questions of law, and gave both impetus and direction to the way the province's legal system evolved. In *Boultbee* v. *Shore*, for example, he brought about a change that did not occur in Ontario for several years. In that case he determined that the Court of Queen's Bench in Manitoba, unlike the courts of its eastern neighbour, had jurisdiction to grant any relief, whether common law or equitable, no matter in what form an action was brought:

> The Judicature Act of 1873 is not in force in this Province, but we have in force – in so far as the jurisdiction of the Court of Queen's Bench is concerned, the only and sole Superior Court in this province – what is equivalent to that Act as to merging and fusing in this Court all common law, equity and probate jurisdiction of the several Courts of law, equity and probate as they were and existed in England on 15th July, 1870 ... It is not a court having mere equity jurisdiction, nor a court having mere common law jurisdiction, so as in fact to form two distinct courts, under one name, having separate and independent jurisdiction of law and equity, as distinct systems of jurisprudence, but one court, combining and blending within itself, as one court, equity, common law, probate and every other jurisdiction possessed and exercised by all or any of the superior courts of law, equity and probate in England on 15th July, 1870.[115]

That Wood took an active part in the trials over which he presided was evident in his jury charges. One such case involved a Jewish labourer assaulted by an anti-Semitic thug. The trial attracted a considerable amount of attention, largely because of its religious and cultural undertones. In his summation he spoke at length of the historical role of the Jewish people, and of the 'senseless and unmeaning persecution of that people by Christian communities,' moving a Jewish author to comment that, by his address, 'Chief Justice Wood had set the record straight that justice would be done to all comers, regardless of origin.'[116]

By 1881, however, it had become clear to many members of Manitoba's legal profession that Wood's drinking habits and arbitrary ways were bringing the administration of justice in the province into disrepute. Four Wood protagonists, including Henry Clarke, W. Boyle, Justice of the Peace T.J. Bradley, and J.E. Cooper, prepared a petition in which they alleged that the chief justice had been guilty of no less than twelve misdemeanours. They included:

> i. changing the dates on certain documents and records and thereby procuring the illegal outlawry of Louis Riel;
> ii. illegally and corruptly preparing a list of half-breeds who were enemies of Ambroise Lepine to serve on the jury which tried him for the murder of Thomas Scott;
> iii. being so notoriously partial, dishonest and unjust in his judgments so as to have lost the confidence of the people of Manitoba;
> iv. taking an active part in politics, and continually introducing into his

charges to the grand jury contentious local and Dominion political issues;

v. declaring that he had no confidence in the oath of French-Canadians;

vi. evident and notorious partiality in favor of certain members of the bar, including his own near relatives;

vii. giving legal advice to individuals before they appeared in his court as litigants;

viii. using abusive language towards both suitors and members of the bar in open court, and displaying such uncontrollable temper and bursts of passion while on the bench as to disgust all parties who were so unfortunate as to be compelled to submit to his abuse;

ix. habitually taking the unsworn statements of persons on the streets or at his home in preference to the sworn testimony of witnesses in court;

x. showing partiality towards his son and nephew in the case of Hogan v. Manning et al and preventing an appeal from his decision by refusing to allow the court reporter to take notes of the proceeding;

xi. hearing the case of McAdams v. McDonald at 11:00 p.m. and ordering the assets of the defendant seized, all within three hours of the defendant being served with the plaintiff's claim;

xii. degrading the administration of justice by gross exhibitions of intemperance while travelling on circuit.[117]

On 4 March 1881 the petition was presented to the House of Commons by Joseph Royal. The following Monday it was ordered read and received, and on Thursday a copy was introduced in the Senate. The Toronto *Globe* immediately leapt to Wood's defence, suggesting that Clarke's notorious character made it wrong to call into question the integrity of a judge of Wood's stature 'merely because he has some personal eccentricities and a somewhat fervent manner.'[118] The *Manitoba Free Press* was also outspoken, both in its defence of the embattled jurist and in its attack on Clarke, alleging that the petition was Clarke's revenge for Wood deciding against him in a case in which Clarke was held to have acted inappropriately by naming himself sole devisee in a will signed by a client of unsound mind. After calling the petition's charges baseless in fact and false in spirit, the *Free Press* wrote glowingly of the respect the community continued to hold for its chief justice.[119]

On 20 March a second petition, signed by Edward Elliott, W. Gibbens, and W.F. McCready, was presented to Parliament. The three brought to the attention of members the fact that an investigation into the way

Wood administered justice in Manitoba had been undertaken, and its evidence showed the chief justice had misconducted himself. The petition concluded by asking the House to inquire into the truth of the allegations contained in the commission's report. Two days later Schultz moved that both petitions be referred to a joint committee of the Commons and Senate. Before the committee could begin holding hearings, however, Wood died.

In the months leading up to his death, Wood was a pathetic figure on the bench. A serious stroke suffered in October 1880 had left him partially paralysed. He was nearly deaf, and his incoherent speech made it difficult for him to be understood by others. Health problems, however, did not appear to have affected his mind. A judgment Wood handed down just days before his death was described as both lucid and exhaustive.[120]

On the morning of Saturday, 7 October 1882, the sixty-three-year-old chief justice called his court to order, and with only a break for lunch he sat throughout the day. At four o'clock Wood announced that he was inclined to dismiss the action he was trying, but agreed with the plaintiff's request for an adjournment instead:

> He then appeared to sit in meditation, leaning on his staff, and with his head hung down. Thinking he was exhausted, some of those present asked him if they should assist him down the steps, but he made no reply. It was then found that he was completely helpless from an attack of paralysis. He was supported till a cab was called and was then carried down to the street in his judicial chair ... The stricken man was placed in a cab and taken to his home ... [where] he lay in an unconscious state until about eight o'clock when the weary heart ceased to beat.[121]

That Wood died prematurely did not come as a surprise to his family. Before he left Brantford in 1874 he was suffering from what his doctors referred to as *ataxie locomotrice progressive*. While the disease did not affect a sufferer's mind, it interfered with his ability to walk and usually induced paralysis and death.[122]

The poverty in which Wood died made the years remaining to his widow difficult ones. Jane Augusta Marter was the younger of two daughters born to a prominent Brantford medical doctor. Raised in comfort, she continued to enjoy a luxurious lifestyle following her 1855 marriage to Wood. Her sister also married well, becoming the wife of the local registrar of the High Court of Justice, and a brother went on to become a respected member of the Ontario legislature.[123] The lack of a pension income following his death, however, forced Wood's widow to depend on whatever assistance could be provided by her two daughters and four sons, one of whom had followed his father into law. Edmund Marter Wood was born at Brantford, educated at Upper Canada College, and came west with his family in 1874. After articling with Bain & Blanchard he became the first law student trained in law in Manitoba to be called to the provincial bar. He immediately joined his cousin S.C. Biggs in what became one of Winipeg's most lucrative law practices. The two practised together until 1887, although for four years most of Wood's time was devoted to his role as solicitor for the city of Winnipeg. He resigned that position on 1 September 1884, when the city's finance committee announced that it was going to conduct an investigation into the way in which money was handled by his department. A week later the mayor accused him of embezzling $15,000 of the city's money and issued an order for his arrest. Before it could be executed, he fled. On 9 September Alderman George Fisher was arrested and charged with conspiring with Wood to defraud the city of $2500. When all the facts were known, the charges against Fisher were dismissed and he sued the city for false imprisonment. While Wood had mismanaged some of the funds with which he had been entrusted, his actions were not criminal. He remained in St Paul, Minnesota, for eighteen months before returning to Manitoba, where he was disbarred for non-payment of fees.

In a frontier community, the importance of the role played by judges cannot be overemphasized. Their decisions influenced what institutions survived and how they evolved. That judgments were often not grounded on law was less important than that they be perceived as just. To stick to the strict letter of the law, a judge ran the risk of undermining the confidence settlers had in institutions that lacked familiarity or tradition. Edmund Burke Wood recognized this. Many of his important decisions were questionable law, but each settled important issues. For example, when he arrived in Manitoba, the province was in a state of near chaos. The sparks of mistrust that accompanied the province's entry into Confederation had been fanned into flames of hatred as more and more English Protestants settled in what had previously been a French-Catholic community. Scott had become a martyr, and Riel and Lepine symbols of a past the new majority wanted exorcised. Had Wood held that he had no jurisdiction to try Lepine for Scott's murder, he would have been following the law. By holding otherwise, he put an end to further social unrest. Although eminent lawyers like J. Hillyard Cameron, D'Arcy Boulton, and Justice J.H. Gray publicly denounced his decision as wrong in law, it was upheld, probably not because it was right, but because it was necessary.

In *Farmer* v. *Livingston* Wood again handed down a decision grounded on community values rather than law.[124] It was overturned, and an injustice perpetrated, not strictly because it was bad law but because, had it stood, it would have impaired the federal government's ability to settle the west in an organized fashion. In that case, Farmer obtained legal title to a quarter section of land on the basis that he intended to occupy and improve it. In reality he was a speculator and had already taken possession of a homestead forty miles away. Livingstone, noticing the land was unoccupied, filed an application for title with the local Dominion land agent. He then paid the required fee and went into possession. Although Farmer knew what had transpired, he did nothing until after Livingstone had built a house and cultivated the land. He then filed a suit to have the defendant ejected. When the action came before him for trial, Wood held that the issue involved a principle of law and natural justice too obvious for doubt, and that Farmer had obtained his title by fraud and deception. Fairness, he said, dictated that the plaintiff's action against Livingstone should fail. Wood's decision, however, was overturned by the Supreme Court of Canada, which decided that regardless of whether a title was issued in error or through fraud, it gave the holder the legal right to remove anyone already in possession. For any other judge this may well have settled the issue, but not for Wood. He issued an order preventing Farmer from taking action on his judgment, effectively overruling the Supreme Court. When an appeal of this order reached it, the court condemned Wood's actions in no uncertain terms and again ruled in favour of Farmer.

What Wood tried to do in *Farmer* v. *Livingston* was not dissimilar to what he succeeded in doing in the Lepine case. Although the results were very different, in both instances he felt compelled to make rather than follow law because local circumstances required that he do so. In *Boultbee* v. *Shore* he did the same and, as with Lepine, his decision was allowed to stand, notwithstanding that it was based on the same rationale that had been rejected in the *Farmer* case. The issue in *Boultbee* was whether the Manitoba Court of Queen's Bench was a court both of law and of equity, or whether it was one or the other. If Wood decided it was both, the system put in place in 1870 would remain; if he decided the Court could sit as either, but not both, the system would become substantially more expensive to operate. In a province with little money, that would have had disastrous consequences. The decision he made was the necessary one, and it was allowed to stand for that reason.

Throughout his career Edmund Burke Wood was often selfish, self-serving, headstrong, and irresponsible. His actions were censured by the legislatures of Ontario and Manitoba, the House of Commons, and the Law Society of Upper Canada, which ordered him removed as a bencher for missing three successive meetings.[125] He earned a well-deserved reputation for opportunism, venality, and drunkenness. Few of his accomplishments have endured, and the praise that followed his death was muted. Some even suggested that the speeches for which he earlier became famous gave an impression of learning greater than he possessed.[126] But Wood was more than the sum of his shortcomings. He brought to Manitoba a sense of legal order, and it was because he was an autocrat that he was able to control the ambitions and egos of the men entrusted with the province's stewardship. In politics he may have been a historical event, but in law he was an influence.

3

The End of an Era, 1879–1884

In the fall of 1879 Justice McKeagney died while vacationing in New Brunswick. Betournay died a month later. For the second and last time in its history Manitoba's Court of Queen's Bench was staffed by a single judge. Two weeks after Betournay's death, however, one of the vacancies was filled when thirty-eight-year-old Joseph Dubuc went to the bench 'at the peak of a brilliant forensic and political career.'[1] A young lawyer from St Catharines, Ontario, followed him less than a year later. According to correspondence between the federal minister of justice, who opposed the latter appointment, and the prime minister, James Andrews Miller 'had been causing difficulty on the federal political scene for John A. Macdonald, and to get Miller out of the way Macdonald decided to place him on the Manitoba bench.'[2] Miller was older than Dubuc when appointed to the bench, but Miller's appointment was criticized by the *Canada Law Journal* on the grounds of his youth, although the journal did not question his professional ability.[3]

When McKeagney and Betournay went to the Queen's Bench, Manitoba was treated as a single judicial district. The year they died that changed when the provincial government divided the province into the Eastern district, centred at Winnipeg, and the Western district sitting at Portage la Prairie.[4] By 1881 the population of Manitoba had doubled to nearly 100,000 and the federal government increased the size of the province by extending its boundaries north to include most of Lake Winnipeg and Lake Winnipegosis and west to the present

Manitoba-Saskatchewan boundary.[5] The provincial government acknowledged its enlarged jurisdiction by passing two statutes that had a direct impact on the administration of justice in the region. It created a third judicial district, centred in Brandon, to be known as the Western district (Portage became the judicial centre of the Central district) and the provincial government shifted the responsibility for probate matters from the Queen's Bench to a newly created Surrogate Court.[6] By 1882 the growth of both the province and its legal profession had attracted the attention of the *Canada Law Journal*, which suggested that Winnipeg 'has more lawyers to the square acre than any other place on the face of the earth.'[7]

When Miller threatened to resign in May 1882 unless he received an increase in his salary, leading members of the provincial bar seized on the opportunity to pass a resolution demanding that future judicial appointments go to Manitoba lawyers. 'Whereas the bar of this province has attained the size and importance which justifies the appointment of judges for this province from amongst its members, therefore the bar in meeting requests the government when vacancies hereafter occur to endeavour to secure for that position some efficient member of our bar before appointing judges from the bar of another province.'[8]

Five months after Miller issued his ultimatum to the federal government, Wood suffered a stroke and died. When Miller was not elevated to replace Wood as chief justice he resigned. The new chief justice was Lewis Wallbridge, Speaker of the House during the debates that preceded Confederation and, like Morris, a political crony of Prime Minister Macdonald. Replacing Miller as puisne justice of the court was Thomas Wardlaw Taylor, the Master in Ordinary in Ontario.[9]

Although by 1883 justices of the Court of Queen's Bench were no longer regularly presiding over sittings of the province's county courts, and their workload was reduced when the federal government gave county courts jurisdiction over speedy criminal trials,[10] they were still 'hopelessly overworked.'[11] In 1881, for instance, 735 court writs were issued. The next year that increased to 2874, and in 1883 to just under 6000.[12] The federal government eventually recognized that the justices of the Queen's Bench needed help, and in 1884 added a fourth judge to the court. The extent to which the justices continued to be overworked, however, became glaringly apparent when, within six months of going to the bench, Robert Smith died from exhaustion. Mr Justice Dubuc narrowly avoided a similar fate when he was temporarily forced off the bench earlier in 1884. Smith's successor was Albert Clements Killam, a brilliant young Ontario-trained lawyer who had been practising in Manitoba since 1879 and had 'earned an enviable reputation for professional excellence and personal integrity.'[13]

A source of considerable frustration to the Manitoba bar was the fact its overworked judges were paid $1000 a year less than their Ontario counterparts. While that disparity was regarded by members of the provincial bar as unfair, the editor of the *Manitoba Law Journal* suggested, tongue firmly in cheek, that the difference in salary was a mixed blessing. It was, he said, 'extremely unfair to our judges, although the bar cannot but be pleased with the arrangement if the result is that the political candidates strive for the Ontario Bench and leave the Manitoba for the hard working and able devotees of the profession.'[14]

One reason that the Manitoba judiciary was so busy was because of a massive influx of immigrants in search of land and wealth. During the first two years of the 1880s Winnipeg experienced the largest boom in its history, increasing the city's population from 241 in 1871 to 7985 ten years later, making it the seventeenth largest city in Canada. 'Location of the Canadian Pacific Railway's western yards and service shops in Winnipeg was probably the greatest single factor in prompting this buying and building fever.'[15] Hotels and saloons sprang up so quickly that some were equipped with only canvas roofs and all were full to overflowing. Fuelling the boom was a huge trade in illegal liquor, some of which was shipped out of the city concealed in barrels of oatmeal, beans, and coal oil. Rural distribution was typically by canoe in the summer and dog train in the winter, with liquor selling at $3.00 a bottle or $15.00 a gallon.[16]

Although by the end of 1882 the expansion bubble had burst, it left behind a permanent infrastructure of streets, railways, stores, and warehouses that solidified Winnipeg's status as the educational, administrative, economic, and judicial centre of western Canada. And of course this commercial boom and bust kept the province's lawyers busy. Prominent among their number was one of the most distinguished Francophone judges in the history of Manitoba, and the first practising member of the local bar to go to the bench.

JOSEPH DUBUC

Joseph Dubuc was born in the Lower Canada community of Ste-Martine on Boxing Day 1840. His father's Norman ancestors had started farming in the St Lawrence Valley in 1682, but by the nineteenth century possessed considerably more status than money. Dubuc spent two years in school before economic necessity dictated that he help on the family farm. He laboured there for ten years, but by the time he turned eighteen it was evident that there would be no money to establish him on a farm of his own. Seeking a job and the opportunity to learn English, he left for the United States. Within a year he was disillusioned and homesick, but instead of returning to the family farm he became a student in the Christian Brothers' Commercial School in Beauharnois, Lower Canada. His tuition was waived on the understanding that his non-school time would be spent devoted to religious contemplation and study. While there his devotion to the Church attracted the attention of several members of the clergy, who succeeded in having him enrolled in Montreal College. The regime enforced by the Sulpicians was one in which Dubuc excelled. Dressed in a uniform of navy pants, a coat extending to his knees, and a round cap, he studied Latin, Greek, French, English, mathematics, philosophy, physics, chemistry, astronomy, and botany. Examinations were frequent, religious studies mandatory, and contact with the outside world virtually forbidden.[17]

For five years Dubuc's entire life was lived within a four-storey building surrounded by a high stone wall. Sports were banned, baths limited to once a week, and every activity carried out under the supervision of black-robed priests. The experience had a profound affect on Dubuc. He not only became a daily communicant with an intense love of the Church, he met two classmates who were to figure prominently in his future. One was the future Bishop Conaty, who administered his last rites in a Los Angeles hotel fifty-six years later. The other was Louis Riel, the father of Manitoba, whose fate was eventually to rest in Dubuc's hands.

Dubuc completed his studies with the Sulpicians in 1866 and immediately entered law school, rejecting the highly partisan Institut Canadien in favour of the more neutral English and Protestant alternative, McGill University. That choice was made at the same time as he was considering what political party to join. The decision was not an easy one, and like so many things in nineteenth-century Quebec, it was imbued with religious overtones. It was understood that young French-Canadians were expected to become involved in politics as a means of protecting and enlarging the influence of the Church, and the party of the Church was the Conservatives. But Dubuc's enthusiasm for reform had grown during his years at college, and his inclination was to join the Liberals.

After agonizing over the decision, however, he could not go against his faith.

At McGill Dubuc started writing articles for local newspapers, always submitting them under a pseudonym. He later worked for the Montreal paper *La Minerve*, where he reported, wrote, edited, and translated short articles.[18] In 1869 he graduated with a Bachelor of Civil Law degree, and passed his bar examination with 'great distinction.' From September until he left for Manitoba the following spring he practised law in Montreal with another recent graduate, Eustache Prud'homme. Neither prospered. When Riel wrote suggesting that the west could offer him both money and excitement, Dubuc was tempted. Four months later he was persuaded to meet the Reverend Joseph-Noel Ritchot, then pastor of a Catholic mission at St Norbert, in what is now south Winnipeg. Officially, the priest had been sent east by Bishop Taché to discuss with the federal government the terms of Manitoba's entry into Confederation. Unofficially, his mission was to secure for the Metis an infusion of educated leaders who could counter the growing influence of what had become a flood of Ontario Protestants. Taché had for some time been sending Metis youth to be educated in Montreal, but there were never enough such youths, and he was anxious to secure new blood from Quebec.

Even before Dubuc met Ritchot at the archbishop's palace in Montreal, Riel had inculcated in him a concern for the French-speaking population of Manitoba. The desire to help his friend administer to their needs, combined with a failing law practice, were powerful incentives to move. Times were tough, and Dubuc was not optimistic about making a living in Montreal. 'To the Quebec lawyer [the future offered] no pleasant prospect of ease and competence in the decline of life ... His life path is monotonous, shadeless, arid, dusty.'[19] He had also met someone he wanted to marry, and at thirty he felt it was time to settle down. After a fifteen-day journey by rail, steamer, and cart, Ritchot, Dubuc, and Charles Champagne, a young law student, arrived in St Boniface a month before Manitoba entered Confederation.[20] The settlement's population consisted of 558 Indians, 5757 French-speaking Metis, 4083 English-speaking Metis, and 1565 whites. Of that number, 6247 were Catholic.[21] It was out of concern for them that immediately upon his arrival Dubuc began writing a series of articles for *La Minerve*. His reasoned and even-handed description of Riel and the Metis did much to sway Quebec public opinion in favour of the two Catholic brethren. It also had an influence in Ontario, where readers of the *Globe* read

Joseph Dubuc (1840–1914). Puisne judge 1879–1903, chief justice of King's Bench 1903–9. Members of the Dubuc family had resided in the Ste-Martine region near Montreal since the seventeenth century. A friend and Montreal classmate of Louis Riel, Dubuc emigrated to Manitoba hoping to earn enough money to marry and raise a family. He and Marian Anna Henault (standing beside him in this 1883 photograph) were the parents of five sons and five daughters. (Provincial Archives of Manitoba)

translations of articles published in *La Minerve, L'Opinion Publique, L'Ordre, Le Courier d'Ottawa,* and *La Gazette d'Outaouais.* The articles were popular and served to lessen the impact of the anti-French and anti-Catholic writings of Charles Mair, an Ontario journalist and poet who emigrated to Manitoba in 1869.[22]

In the years immediately following his arrival in Manitoba Dubuc was very much under the influence of Archbishop Taché. Apart from his relationship with Riel, his association with the churchman was the most important of his life. Their friendship began in 1870 and lasted until the archbishop's death twenty-four years later. Alexandre-Antonin Taché was born in 1823 in Rivière-du-Loup, Lower Canada. His family had for decades resided there, and his uncle, Sir Étienne-Paschal Taché, had three times formed a government with Sir John A. Macdonald. Taché was educated at the College of St Hyacinthe and the Seminary of Montreal, and in 1844 became a novice in the Oblate order. A year later he was sent to the Red River Settlement, where he was ordained by Bishop Provencher, the mission's founder. Taché remained in Manitoba for the rest of his life. He was only twenty-eight when he became co-adjutor bishop and thirty when Provencher died and he became bishop of St Boniface. For the last twenty-three years of his life he was archbishop and metropolitan of his mission.

Even before the disturbances of 1869 Taché had urged the government of Canada to take seriously the grievances of the Metis as it negotiated the purchase of the Red River Settlement. The government ignored his entreaties, just as it was to do a year later when Taché sought an amnesty for Riel and the other leaders of the uprising. The close relationship Taché maintained with Dubuc did much to raise the latter's profile within the province's legal community, and to solidify Dubuc's status in the eyes of the Metis.[23] That he had a position to solidify, however, was because of his friendship with Louis Riel.

Although Dubuc had always been a supporter of the Metis, it was not until the collapse of the Provisional Government and Riel's flight from the province that he assumed a position of prominence. In October 1870 Riel asked his former classmate to lead the Metis in his absence, suggesting that he had already won their confidence.[24] Dubuc refused. He realized that he was still an outsider and that most Franco-Manitobans still yearned for the return of Riel. But he agreed that if he would not lead the Metis, he would at least speak on their behalf, and for the next forty-four years he did precisely that.

Until he was called to the Manitoba bar, necessity forced Dubuc to spend much of his time working for Francis Godschall Johnson. Johnson was the second of the Red River Settlement's four recorders, all of whom obtained their appointment and authority from the Hudson's Bay Company. Johnson presided over the pre-Confederation courts of Manitoba from 1854 to 1858 before returning to Montreal. Although born in England, he was fluently bilingual, and by the time he was appointed to the Superior Court for the District of Montreal he was a leader of the Quebec bar. In 1870 Sir George Cartier persuaded him to accept a year's secondment in his former home, giving the government more time to appoint the province's first chief justice. The choice was welcomed by almost everyone, including Lieutenant-Governor Adams Archibald. 'Nobody could better do the duty than Judge Johnson. His courteous and kind manners – not less than his proficiency in the two languages – his knowledge of the law – and his acquaintance with the country, point him out as peculiarly fitted for a position requiring a union of these qualities.'[25]

Johnson's appointment was ultimately extended to a second year. While wintering in eastern Canada in 1871 he even agreed to serve as Archibald's replacement. But accusations of double, and even triple, 'dipping' forced the government to cancel his commission before he officially assumed his additional duties. He learned the news while on his way back to Manitoba early in 1872 and agreed to hold only a single session of the Quarterly Court before returning to Montreal. Johnson was generally well liked by the Metis, and his sense of humour and fondness for food and drink made him an agreeable person to be around. His relationship with the straight-laced Dubuc, however, was not a good one. Dubuc found the judge's vanity and temper insufferable.[26] Their relationship ended in June 1871 when Dubuc was called to the bar.

Almost immediately he entered into partnership with Joseph Royal, another of Taché's recruits. The realities of the day required both men to spend a considerable amount of time in court while they built their practice. Over time, however, they shifted their focus to corporate and commercial work.[27] The firm eventually became Dubuc, Royal, LaRivière & Bernier, and for several years the four, in conjunction with Archbishop Taché, supervised the legal and political affairs of most of the French-speaking residents of Manitoba.[28] Although the partnership maintained offices in both Winnipeg and St Boniface, aside from Taché and the Church, the bulk of its clients were Metis. Working for them did not generate much in the way of fees, however, since before 1870 Taché had done the work gratuitously. Still, Dubuc did sufficiently well that within two years he was able to leave his room at the archbishop's residence and move into a duplex he co-owned with Alphonse Alfred Clement LaRivière.

Despite a quiet and unassuming manner, Dubuc gained a reputation as an able and articulate lawyer. He was widely regarded as 'fair and honest, and never subtle or endeavouring to get an unfair advantage.'[29] Even those opposed to him on political or religious grounds regarded him as extremely conscientious, and non-confrontational, one who 'favoured the settlement of civil law suits out of court, not hesitating to sacrifice the fees accruing from a trial if he could bring about an understanding between the parties involved.'[30] The one occasion when no compromise was possible, however, was the trial of Ambrose Lepine. After the Metis leader was arrested and charged with Thomas Scott's murder, Dubuc was elected secretary of a mass meeting held to protest the action. In an article published shortly thereafter, he alleged that the arrest was not only unjust, but was politically motivated.[31] Dubuc was given a chance to prove his allegations when Lepine made his first appearance. He and Royal acted as co-counsel, and to ensure that reports of what they said would appear in both English- and French-language newspapers, Dubuc addressed the court in French and his partner in English. The constitutional argument the two advanced was the first made in a Manitoba court. Although many regarded Wood's ruling against their position as wrong in law,[32] by the time the ruling was made the question was moot, at least from Dubuc's point of view. In 1874 he became the Attorney General of Manitoba, and took no further part in Lepine's defence.

That may have been just as well. Issues of language and religion were almost always inherent in cases heard in the early 1870s, and violence often accompanied an unfavourable decision. One example occurred in 1872, when Dubuc, acting for the Crown, questioned a group of English Protestants about acts of election vandalism they had witnessed. Despite receiving little cooperation from those he questioned, he knew who was involved in the vandalism and named them in a bill submitted to the grand jury. Although the charges were not proceeded with, as he was leaving the courthouse Dubuc was assaulted, knocked unconscious, and beaten so badly he was permanently blinded in one eye. His assailant, John Ingram, fled to the United States, eventually returning to become Winnipeg's chief of police.

While work he did on behalf of Archbishop Taché and the Catholic church provided Dubuc with some income, it alone was not sufficient to sustain him, his wife Marie-Anne Henault, whom he married shortly after arriving in Manitoba, and a growing family. As a consequence he took on two other responsibilities. In 1872 he became Superintendent of Catholic Schools for the province. For his six hundred dollar a year salary he supervised a seven-member board and twenty schools,[33] introduced changes in curriculum, and monitored the performance of teachers. In addition, Dubuc for several years travelled throughout the North-west as a justice of the peace.

It is perhaps ironic that his only attempt to make money outside either law or politics came about after Dubuc went to the bench. Although his large and growing family required that he earn a substantial income, he had no personal interest in money and recognized that he had little talent outside his chosen fields. The real estate boom of 1882 was too tempting to resist, however, and he invested in a variety of properties. That he had the resources to make investments of upwards of $35,000 suggests that he had prospered at law. That he lost all that he invested is indicative of something else.

In the spring of 1871 Dubuc and Royal, also a former journalist, started a French-language paper they called *Le Metis*. Through it they attempted to build a bridge between the French-Canadian populations of Manitoba and Quebec. They also used the paper to criticize laws that undermined the legal, political, or cultural position of the Metis. Laws allowing Ontario immigrants to take over land occupied by Metis were of particular concern to Dubuc and Royal, and the two urged Metis voters to support candidates sympathetic to their cause.[34] Dubuc also encouraged Riel to run for a seat in the House of Commons, despite knowing that in doing so he was going against the wishes of Taché, who felt Riel's return from exile was premature. Ultimately Riel did return and was twice elected in Provencher. When it became clear, however, that he would not be allowed to take his seat, he gave up politics and went into exile. Riel's extremism eventually disillusioned the pragmatic Dubuc, however, and by 1875 the two had become estranged. Riel's bitterness towards his former comrade is evident in a poem he wrote about him that summer:

> What gall you have!
> Betrayed Metis are dying.
> You serve their hated tyrants.
> Deep in your shameless soul you say:
> 'I do for them
> What any other coward would.'[35]

Two things lay at the heart of the differences between the two men. Dubuc had not been born and raised in the Red River Settlement and his aim was preservation of French and Catholic culture, rather than a way of life. Riel, by contrast, wanted to preserve a homeland in which the Metis could continue in the ways of their ancestors. Dubuc was also an insider who believed that the most effective way of protecting the rights of the Metis was through participation in the electoral process and even governmental commissions.

After Manitoba entered Confederation, the federal government conducted a census and enacted a number of regulations that governed the distribution of land to the Metis. Almost immediately, however, problems arose. Many had to do with land used by the Metis to grow hay, known as the 'outer two miles.' Incoming settlers regarded such land as open for settlement, since it was unoccupied. Riel's position had always been that it was important to keep settlers off these lands, by force if necessary. Dubuc argued in favour of allowing settlement, but on a fair and equitable basis. To convince the Metis that he was right, he travelled throughout the French parishes, settling whatever disputes he could and generally acting as a moderating influence. He also drew up a series of petitions, demanding that the land problem be resolved as soon as possible. His work paid off. On 30 October 1873 he and John Bain were appointed commissioners to investigate the complaints of the Metis and to award compensation in cases of wrong-doing. In recognition of the uniqueness of their way of life, and the importance of their hay lands, Dubuc recommended that the Metis receive an extra allotment if they did not receive adequate compensation for the loss of their outer two miles.[36] Even that was not enough for Riel, however, who criticized Dubuc's participation in the commission and accused him of pursuing his own self-interest at the expense of the Metis.

In 1875 Taché encouraged Dubuc, Royal, A.A.C. LaRivière, and Thomas Spence to form La Société Manitobaine de Colonisation as a patriotic society with one aim: increasing the number of French Catholics emigrating to the province. A lack of money meant that they had to proceed cautiously, and their first efforts were limited to asking newspapers in Quebec and the United States to reprint articles extolling the virtues of Manitoba. Within a year, however, a trickle of immigrants started arriving. Some came from eastern Canada, and others from the New England seaboard. While the trickle never became a flood, the number of newcomers grew substantially over the next few years, likely because of the efforts of Taché's brother, the deputy minister of agriculture. Because of him and a handful of other French Canadians in Ottawa, the federal government supported efforts to divert westward the stream of Canadian emigrants flowing into the United States.

Efforts to attract to Manitoba settlers from Quebec, however, were hampered by two realities. One was the fact that French Canadians considered the St Lawrence Valley their traditional home, and to most emigrating was tantamount to exile. The second was the fact that it was much easier for those leaving the province to head south, to the factories of New England, than to the unsettled west. Matters were made worse by a handful of settlers who tried and failed to put down roots in the Red River Settlement and returned to tell of the hardships they faced. Failure bred a lack of enthusiasm, and by the time Dubuc started the Colonisation Society he and his co-founders were fighting an uphill battle. Despite the fact that between 1875 and 1880 the Society persuaded more than fifteen thousand French Canadians to settle in Manitoba, as a percentage of the province's total population the number of Franco-Manitobans grew by only 52 per cent, compared to 687 per cent for English Protestants. Ten years later things were even worse, and only 8 per cent of Manitoba's population was French Canadian.[37]

While Dubuc played a number of important roles in the early history of Manitoba, none offered him the same exposure as politics. He was in the province for just over six months when the first provincial election was held. During a period of great turbulence and charged emotions the constituencies of Baie St Paul and St François Xavier West were bastions of calm. Dubuc was elected by acclamation in the former, Royal in the latter. In the rest of the province the election was a heated contest between two groups. One was made up of English-speaking Ontario immigrants known as 'Canadians,' although during the election they referred to themselves as 'loyalists.' The other group were moderates who called themselves the 'government party.' The Canadians were opposed to an amnesty for Riel and to granting French Canadians the same rights as those possessed by English residents. During the election 'loyalists' demanded that those who supported Riel during the uprising of 1869–70 be punished. The moderates, on the other hand, supported the conciliatory approach adopted by Lieutenant-Governor Adams Archibald.

Because Manitoba had no experience with parliamentary institutions before joining Canada, Archibald and his successor were, in effect, the province's government. Excluded from those appointed to advise him were both supporters of ultra-Protestant agitator John Schultz and the leaders of Riel's provisional government. Instead, the astute Archibald named to his council a more or less equal mix of moderate French Catholics and English Protestants.

Despite the emotions generated during the 1870 election the legislature opened in March 1871. Dubuc gave the body's first address. In replying to the Speech from the Throne he spoke in both English and French, publicly placing himself in the camp of those who believed in the concept of duality. In the context of the times this meant that he supported both linguistic and religious equality, a stand not popular with extremists on either side of the legislature. During the ensuing session the balance that Archibald had hoped to achieve by dividing electoral districts equally between English- and French-speaking residents was often overturned as alliances formed, broke apart, and reformed. The position of moderates like Dubuc was made particularly difficult because of two realities. First, the cohesiveness associated with membership in a political party was not present, since political parties as such did not yet exist. And second, differences among French-speaking members were often used by their English counterparts for their own political advantage. The delicate balance that existed when the legislature convened quickly eroded as differences between French-Canadian and Metis members and French Catholic and Irish Catholic members broke into the open.

In the legislature Dubuc quickly established himself as one the most effective advocates of Metis rights and as the unofficial spokesperson for the Catholic church. One of the first petitions presented to the House was his bill to incorporate the Roman Catholic bishop of St Boniface.[38] In fact, most of the private-members bills he introduced dealt with Church interests, like the incorporation of St Boniface College. He was, however, also actively involved in drafting many of the other bills introduced in the legislature. An example was *The School Act* of 1871, which established a provincial board of education. If this kind of legislative work was strenuous, it at least attracted the attention of the public. On committees, however, lawyer-legislators laboured in private, unseen by potential clients. It was a climate in which Dubuc excelled. Ever the pragmatist, he recognized that a politician was more likely to compromise outside of the eyes of constituents than in public. He therefore took an active part in committee meetings, sitting on those that dealt with statutory amendments, public accounts, education, agriculture, immigration, and libraries.[39]

The tensions that threatened to explode during the provincial election of 1870 were still evident during the federal election held two years later. Unfortunately for Dubuc, one of the more potentially serious acts of violence involved him. As returning officer for the constituency of Marquette, he was responsible for counting ballots and declaring a winner. When the contest ended, the sitting member and his opponent were tied. Since he had no authority to cast a deciding vote, he declared both men elected. For his efforts, supporters of the candidates chased him all the way to Baie St Paul.[40]

The legislative session that opened in 1874 propelled Dubuc into the political spotlight. When Manitoba's attorney general introduced a bill extending the franchise to newly arrived Ontario immigrants, he was attempting to destroy the political equilibrium created when the legislature's twenty-four seats were divided equally between English Protestant and French Catholic residents. Dubuc opposed the bill, which would have given more seats to English Protestants, and moved a motion of non-confidence in which he confirmed his support for the government, but condemned the actions of the attorney general. In the end the government was forced to resign and a new administration formed under the leadership of Dubuc's ally, Marc-Amable Girard. Dubuc entered the cabinet as the new attorney general, although his tenure lasted less than six months. When two members of Girard's government resigned, the premier was forced to call an election. Dubuc ran in St Norbert against its sitting member, a close friend of Riel. He won by a margin of fifty-one to thirty-one votes, and in 1876 he became speaker of the house in the government of former provincial treasurer, R.A. Davis. Three years later Dubuc left provincial politics to run federally in the constituency of Provencher.

Provencher runs south along both sides of the Red River from Winnipeg to the United States border. Its first member was elected in 1871, but the following year the seat was awarded to George Étienne Cartier after he was defeated in Quebec. When Cartier died in 1873, Louis Riel became Provencher's third representative. Despite not being allowed to sit in the House of Commons, Riel retained the seat in the 1874 general election. Although expelled in April by a resolution of parliament, he was re-elected by acclamation six months later. After being expelled yet again Riel resigned and the seat was won by A.G.B. Bannatyne in the ensuing special election. By 1878 Provencher was the most densely populated French-Canadian constituency in Manitoba. Although Bannatyne spoke French, and was a friend of Riel's, his constituents wanted a member who was one of their own. When Dubuc was asked to run he followed his usual course of action, and turned to Taché for advice. In the election that followed his opponent was an Irish Catholic and an avowed enemy of the archbishop. During the campaign he and Dubuc travelled in Red River carts throughout the constituency, stopping every evening to engage in a public debate that often lasted until three o'clock in the morning. On voting day, however, there was neither a debate nor a vote. Dubuc's opponent failed to appear and Dubuc was elected by acclamation.

In the year he spent in Ottawa, away from family and without the income generated by his law practice, Dubuc continued to take an active role in Manitoba politics. In 1879, for example, he was asked to mediate a settlement in the dispute between Premier Norquay and Dubuc's former partner, Joseph Royal. His efforts failed when Royal refused to compromise on his insistence that the French language continue to be used in the provincial legislature. After Royal resigned, Norquay turned to Dubuc and offered him a choice of whatever portfolio he wanted. Although tempted, Dubuc refused the offer, perhaps because he saw a more attractive opportunity on the horizon.

Even before Betournay's untimely death his failing health made it obvious that there would soon be two Queen's Bench vacancies to fill (McKeagney died in September 1879). Dubuc's name was among those mentioned most often as a candidate for one of the seats. He felt uncomfortable with such discussions, based as they were on the supposition that Betournay would soon be dead; and he refused to indicate whether he would accept an appointment should one be offered. His reluctance was not shared by Royal, who actively solicited the job. A week after Betournay died, however, Dubuc was summoned to a meeting with Taché. He was advised that the archbishop had recommended to the prime minister that Dubuc be given the recently vacated francophone seat on the Queen's Bench. When Macdonald's telegram arrived a few days later, the job was his, subject to satisfying the prime minister's concern about who would replace him as member for Provencher. Dubuc's response was immediate. 'I accept readily. Provencher will elect a Conservative, probably Royal.'[41] That he accepted Macdonald's offer so quickly was likely out of economic necessity. By 1878 he had little, if any, money. In the preceding four years he and his wife had become the parents of four children and they were also supporting at least one in-law.[42] Things had become so tight for Dubuc that while living in Ottawa his friend Joseph Tassé, a local Member of Parliament, provided him with free food and lodging. And on his return to Manitoba he had to borrow the money necessary to build a store on the corner of his property, which he hoped would earn him an income of $30 a month.[43]

Dubuc's appointment went virtually unnoticed in the English press. Before it became official the *Manitoba Free Press* referred to it as likely, and after it became a reality said only that '[t]he ceremony of swearing in the Hon. Joseph Dubuc as one of the puisne judges of Manitoba, took place yesterday, the oath of office being administered by Chief Justice Wood.'[44] The *Canada Law Journal* was even less enthused: 'There is the most urgent necessity for the appointment of a strong judge to the vacancy still remaining on the Manitoba Bench ... The recent appointment (Mr. Debuc), though giving high character and integrity to the bench, does not do much, we understand, to its judicial ability.'[45]

Whether or not these comments were prompted by the same anti-French bias evident in the pages of the *Free Press*, they were likely quite accurate. The new justice was a man of substantial principle and commitment to the cause of the Church and the Metis, but by his own admission was never comfortable at the bar. Despite his shortcomings, on 13 November 1879 Dubuc became the fifth judge appointed to Manitoba's Court of Queen's Bench. Not surprisingly, his tenure, unlike that of his predecessors, was marked by an absence of scandal. His personal sense of integrity immediately brought him into conflict with Wood. He was disturbed by the chief justice's willingness to either overlook, or even take part in, abuses associated with the sale of Metis lands. Within a year he asked the government to establish a public inquiry, and he was a willing witness a few months later when it held its first hearings. Although Dubuc was not alone in being offended by what had become the wholesale dispossession of thousands of Metis, a majority of the legal profession had little sympathy with his position. Heber Archibald was a Law Society bencher in 1881 when he testified that 'it was the opinion of nine out of ten members of the profession that it was an improvident grant to the Half Breeds – in the first place – that it would bring them more harm than good – and that the sooner the whole of these lands was settled the better.'[46]

Dubuc had always been a hard worker, and that continued to be the case while he was on the bench. At first keeping long hours was necessary because Wood's increasingly frequent bouts of drinking prevented him from sitting. Later it became a habit that lasted until overwork made Dubuc ill, resulting in a period of enforced bed rest. Ironically, the long hours Dubuc was forced to put in made him the focus of criticism. In 1885 the *Manitoba Law Journal* suggested that his decision in *Maddill* v. *Kelly* was ill-considered, probably because '[j]udges under the pressure of work are too apt to decline an analysis of a large mass of evidence for the purpose of ascertaining whether or not the verdict is consonant with it.'[47]

While Dubuc wrote few, if any, path-breaking decisions, he did not hesitate to use his position on the bench to protect the rights of the Metis. One of the first occasions in which he did so involved the trial of Maxime Lepine, who had been charged with assault; and although obviously guilty, a jury refused to convict him. Wood was offended by the verdict, which he suspected resulted from a refusal on the part of Metis members of the jury to convict one of their own. The chief justice promptly empanelled a second, this time anglophone, jury, which quickly convicted Lepine. Dubuc regarded Wood's actions as an attempt to encroach on the right of an accused to be tried by a jury composed of an equal number of Metis and non-Metis. When the petition charging Wood with misconduct was presented to the House of Commons a year after Lepine's trial, one of the allegations it contained was that the chief justice had knowingly misconducted himself during the hearing. In preparing the petition, 'Dubuc played a discreet but important role.'[48]

While not a gifted judge, Dubuc was at least competent. In many cases he was asked to decide issues never previously considered. In others he was forced to determine when a law was received in the province, and whether or in what way English procedure had application.[49] His judgments were thoughtful but, like the man, lacked colour or the sweeping phrase destined to be remembered. The two cases with which Dubuc was most closely associated, however, both involved causes with which he had been identified while at the bar. In one he played no role, but in the other he wrote what was arguably the most passionate and persuasive judgment of his career. Not surprisingly, the first involved Louis Riel. The relationship between the two men had once been exceptionally close, and the deeply sensitive Riel was determined that nothing should come between them.

> I received your kind letter and I begin with what preoccupies me most. Have I hurt your feelings? It seems to me that it was understood between us, by our friendship and in every other way, that neither you nor I was responsible for the difficult circumstances in which we found ourselves. Consequently, it was also understood that our intellects and hearts were

> in perfect accord, that we would never reproach each other, nor even think of a rebuke.[50]

By 1885, however, Dubuc had not only become estranged from his friend, he had become one of his harshest critics. Riel's extremism and religious eccentricities offended him, and he felt Riel's actions were undermining the efforts he and others were making on behalf of the Metis. When the appeal from Riel's conviction and sentence came before the Manitoba Court of Queen's Bench, he was placed in a dilemma. If he sat on the case, and the appeal was successful, his past relationship with the appellant would create the impression of bias. Should he not sit, an anglophone bench would likely dismiss the appeal, and a man Dubuc believed insane would be hanged. In the end he refused to sit, and headed east to what he said was a reunion of Montreal College alumni. Riel lost his appeal and his life.

The other case occurred as a result of the flood of Ontario immigrants that swept into Manitoba in the 1880s. The rapid increase in the number of Protestants in the province meant that French Canadians were receiving more from school taxes than their numbers indicated they warranted. Influenced by the rhetoric of Dalton McCarthy and his Ontario-based Equal Rights Association, Manitoba's attorney general vowed to correct the imbalance by abolishing the province's dual school system and the official use of the French language. When the government of Thomas Greenway introduced legislation to do just that, Archbishop Taché responded by assembling his closest advisers for a strategy session. Among them was Dubuc. He had been intimately involved in efforts to protect the education rights of French Catholics in Manitoba, and it was his *Education Act*, passed in 1871, that established the system that Greenway now wanted to abolish. In addition, as a Member of Parliament he had returned to the province to thwart an earlier attempt to limit the official use of French. In short, Dubuc regarded the proposed legislation as an attack on everything he stood for.

He advised Taché that the school bill was unconstitutional and in direct contradiction of section 22 of *The Manitoba Act*, which said that no law could prejudicially affect the right to denominational schools that any group possessed 'by law or practice' when Manitoba became a province. In other words, Catholics had the right to receive continued public funding of their schools. Taché decided to test the law in court. A Winnipeg doctor whose three children attended St Mary's Parochial School refused to pay his school taxes on the basis that the Greenway legislation was unconstitutional. His argument was rejected at trial and an appeal was heard by a panel of three Queen's Bench judges, one of whom was Dubuc. In his judgment Dubuc suggested that the case turned on what parliament intended when it inserted section 22 into *The Manitoba Act*. He argued that the words 'by law or practice' could only refer to both Protestant and Catholic public schools, since only they existed in 1870, and therefore the funding of both was guaranteed. Although Dubuc's position was not shared by either Chief Justice Thomas Wardlaw Taylor or fellow puisne John Farquhar Bain, the Supreme Court of Canada was of a different mind. In a unanimous decision it adopted Dubuc's reasoning and the 1890 school act was held to be *ultra vires*. The Judicial Committee of the Privy Council, however, restored the judgment of the Manitoba Court of Appeal. It decided that, as long as the act did not ban parochial schools or force students to attend public schools, the province had the jurisdiction to pass the Greenway legislation.

The case went back to both the Supreme Court of Canada and the Privy Council one more time before the federal and provincial governments negotiated a settlement. Dubuc's reaction to the stance taken by the Greenway government exposed his intellectual Achilles heel. He felt that the legislation was solely a product of bigotry on the part of provincial Liberals. His papers suggest that after years of fighting to protect the rights of French Catholics he had developed a deep-seated suspicion of anglophones and had grossly underestimated the social and political complexity of the issue.[51]

The closeness with which Dubuc was identified with the Catholic church and the debate over education and language rights was likely responsible for his twice being passed over for promotion. In 1887 Thomas Wardlaw Taylor, who had been sitting for only four years, was elevated to the chief justiceship ahead of Dubuc. The appointment was not popular in some quarters. James A.M. Aikins, the founder of one of the province's first large law firms, expressed no opinion of the relative merit of the two men, but he warned the prime minister that the 'Taylor appointment over Dubuc has raised the ire of the St. Boniface people.'[52] Dubuc was passed over again in 1899 when Albert Clements Killam, a future member of the Supreme Court of Canada, was made chief justice. In 1903, however, his turn finally came, and he was sworn in with the kind of simplicity with which he was always associated.[53] The ceremony took place in the judge's consulting room. The clerk of the court produced Dubuc's patent of office and presented it to the new

Chief Justice Joseph Dubuc. This picture was taken in 1903, the year Dubuc became chief justice of the Court of King's Bench. Although Dubuc was an able and well-respected lawyer and a competent judge, he was twice passed over before being appointed the province's chief justice, in part because of his close association with the Catholic church. In 1906 the Manitoba Court of Appeal came into being, and its senior judge became both the court's and the province's chief justice. (Provincial Archives of Manitoba)

chief justice. The oath of allegiance to his Majesty King Edward VII was then administered by Mr Justice Richards, and Dubuc swore his oath of office, thirty-four years after General Wolseley and his troops had marched into Fort Garry.[54]

When Manitoba's Court of Appeal was established in 1906 its chief judge became the chief justice of the province, with one proviso. The title 'Chief Justice of Manitoba' would belong to Dubuc until his retirement, which occurred on 15 November 1909. Three years later he was made a Knight of St Michael and St George by King George V, and in 1913 Parliament passed an act conferring on him the title 'Honourable.'

Dubuc and his wife and daughter were vacationing in Los Angeles in January 1914 when he suddenly took ill. The first indication that he was in distress occurred just before six o'clock in the morning, when he complained of a feeling of suffocation. His wife and daughter immediately summoned medical assistance, but by the afternoon those assembled feared the worse. The Right Reverend Bishop Conaty, a friend since youth, was summoned and immediately delivered the last rites. Dubuc died of heart failure at 6:30 p.m. on Wednesday, 7 January 1914. The body of the former chief justice arrived in Winnipeg a week later. Amid much pageantry, the province and city paid their respects. A funeral cortege consisting of more than one hundred carriages formed up at the home of his daughter, where his body had lain in a plain black coffin. Walking behind the hearse as it made its way down Edmonton Street were the premier, lieutenant-governor, members of the judiciary, and city dignitaries. At Water Street the procession stopped and the mourners entered their respective carriages. The cortege then proceeded slowly to St Boniface Cathedral, where it was met by Archbishop Langevin. As a full choir chanted from the gallery, Dubuc's casket was carried solemnly down the cathedral's centre aisle to a lofty catafalque. Waiting were priests resplendent in robes of gold, a choir of boys dressed in lace surplices, and monsignors clothed in deep purple. Lighted candles and the perfume of incense poured out in a thin haze from slowly swinging censers, and the brilliantly lit altar stood in marked contrast to the brown and black robes of the nuns.[55]

Apart from the church, the institution with which Dubuc was most closely associated was the University of Manitoba. He was one of the school's founders and served on its council from 1877 until 1888, when he became vice-chancellor, a position that he held for the next twenty-five years. Dubuc was the first practising member of the Manitoba bar to go to the bench. He was a good though not exceptional judge. A hard worker, intellectually gifted, and possessed of a quick, analytical mind, he was also hen-pecked and much influenced by both his wife and the archbishop of St Boniface. His legacy, however, was that he endured and fought a tireless battle on behalf of his church and culture. He was present for the birth of Manitoba, sat in its first legislature, and was a father of the bar. More importantly, he restored to the bench a sense of decency and integrity that had waned under Wood.[56]

JAMES ANDREWS MILLER

James Andrews Miller is one of only two justices of the Queen's Bench to resign from the judiciary to enter politics. He was born on 29 July 1839 in Galt, Upper Canada. His father was admitted as an attorney in 1834, called the following year, and practised in Galt (now Cambridge, Ontario). Following his death his widow joined their son in St Catharines, Ontario.[57] Miller had received his early schooling in Galt, Simcoe, and Toronto. He was considered a clever student and academically gifted.[58] In 1859 he graduated from the University of Toronto's Trinity College with a Bachelor of Arts degree, with honours in classics and mathematics. He then articled with Richard Miller, of St Catharines. After receiving his call he practised with his mentor briefly before returning to Trinity to earn a Bachelor of Civil Law degree. In 1873 the same institution awarded him a Doctorate of Civil Law and he returned to his former practice in St Catharines. Richard and James Miller were not related. Richard was twenty-one years older than his junior and, although raised in Niagara, spent his entire career in St Catharines. Admitted as an attorney in 1840 and called six years later, he practised first with George Boomer; and after Boomer left to join Skeffington Connor in Toronto, Miller and John H. Conolly became partners. Conolly was a solicitor, rather than a barrister, and by the time James Miller joined the firm Conolly had left both the practice and law.

In the twenty-three years he practised law before becoming associated with James Miller, Richard Miller had built a substantial reputation and a lucrative practice. According to his contemporaries, he was 'well known here, there and everywhere, throughout the Province, for his legal lore, court quality, special pleadings, successful suits, and collecting habits.'[59] Despite the latter's professional success, however, James was forced to supplement his income by becoming an agent of the North British and Mercantile Fire and Insurance Company. His relationship with the company continued for the next ten years, by which time he was regarded as a litigator of regional prominence. In the 1860s making a living solely from the practice of law may well have been difficult. In 1865, for example, St Catharines was served by nine law firms, six of which were solo practitioners, the remaining three being two-person partnerships. Still, James Miller was the only lawyer to advertise himself as something other than a barrister. For more than half his career he described himself as 'Barrister, Agent.'

Miller & Miller was an unusually stable firm. The first change in its composition did not occur until 1876, when Robert Gregory Cox joined. That year the city of 10,000 was served by twelve firms, including four single practitioners, six partnerships, and one three-person practice, a crown attorney, and a clerk of the peace. When Miller departed for Manitoba he was replaced by H. Yale and the firm became Miller, Cox and Yale.

During his seventeen years at the Ontario bar, James Miller spent a considerable amount of time in court. Between 1864 and 1879 forty-two cases in which he was counsel were reported in either the *Upper Canada Queen's Bench Reports* or the *Canada Law Journal*. On average three cases a year were reported and, with one exception, in no year more than five. That exception was his last year in practice, when he appeared as counsel in eleven cases. Miller was as likely to be counsel at trial as on appeal, a pattern that did not change over the course of his career. He usually acted for plaintiffs, 70 per cent of whom were individuals, and won twice as often as he lost. His win-loss ratio was the same regardless of whether he acted for a plaintiff or a defendant, or whether the action involved a trial or an appeal, with one exception. He was successful on all four occasions when his client was a corporation. Usually, however, his clients were individuals. One quarter of his cases involved debt actions, 20 per cent municipal disputes, and five insurance claims.

Miller had a solid local reputation. The cases of no other St Catharines lawyer were reported as often, and he frequently appeared in courts throughout his geographic region. His high professional profile no doubt helped him win election as a bencher of the Law Society of Upper Canada, and gave him sufficient clout to extract from the government its promise that, if he agreed to go to the Manitoba bench, he would be a puisne justice only temporarily.[60] When Prime Minister Macdonald first approached him about becoming a judge, Miller was reluctant to leave his lucrative practice. Only after being assured that he would succeed Wood as chief justice did he accept, and on 28 October 1880

Miller became the sixth judge appointed to the Court of Queen's Bench of Manitoba.[61]

His appointment, however, did not please everyone. An Ontario lawyer complained to his local newspaper that it was a piece of 'perfidy,' that he had been given to understand that the Manitoba position was to be his.[62] The editors of the *Canada Law Journal* were even more upset. Although they conceded that Miller was a good lawyer, with shrewd common sense, they thought the forty-one year old was too young:

> [T]here are many older men in the profession quite as qualified, who were more entitled to preferment. It is said that it is well to have men as generals in the army who have still a good share of youthful vigour and dash, but the same reasons do not apply to judicial appointments. Vigour of mind of course is necessary, as also a fair share of bodily strength, but the wisdom of age and experience had also been considered worthy of consideration in such matters.[63]

The *Manitoba Free Press* was equally put off by the appointment, but like its Ontario counterparts acknowledged Miller's 'high' reputation as both a lawyer and a man. They suggested, however, that if the only criteria for the job were being a lawyer and a Conservative, the position should have been offered to the province's attorney general, since he at least knew the local laws and 'conditions of human life.'[64]

Two weeks after being informed that the appointment was his Miller arrived in Winnipeg. His conduct on the bench, and constant demands, did not long go unnoticed. Eighteen months after taking up his seat he threatened to resign if he did not receive an increase in salary. Although he did not carry out his threat, the Manitoba bar supported his demand for improved salaries for the local judges.[65] If that did not make Miller's position a little uncomfortable, a series of charges contained in letters published by the *Manitoba Free Press* did. Rumours that he was pressuring the federal government to force Wood to resign circulated from the moment Miller arrived in Manitoba. The controversy came to a head in October 1881. Edmund Marter Wood, a son of the chief justice, made a number of accusations against him which the *Free Press* published in the form of a letter to the editor. Wood accused Miller of secretly campaigning to have his father forced off the bench, failing to attend a trial, and listening at the key-hole of his servants' rooms and using what he heard against them in a criminal proceeding. Miller sued for libel, and both Wood and the *Free Press* were forced to apologize.[66]

But criticism of Miller was not limited to Winnipeg papers. The *London Advertiser* argued that his ambitions were undermining the integrity of the judiciary:

> There has been a difficulty in the way of putting Mr. Miller in the first place. That difficulty is Chief Justice Wood. Mr. Wood won't resign, nor will he consent to be superannuated. All sorts of charges have been made against him to get him out of the road; so far they have broken down. The last one, it is said, has been instigated by Mr. Miller himself ... It is a bad business to promise a Chief Justiceship that is not vacant, to worry and slander the occupant to get him out of the way; to offer his place to a brother judge upon condition that he can drive him from the Bench. This is not Nihilism, but it is worse. It is making the highest judicial office the reward of political Thuggism.[67]

If this controversy was not embarrassing enough, another was to follow. When Miller noticed a man forcing a woman into a cab he demanded that the man stop and threatened to have him arrested. Unimpressed, the assailant turned from the woman to her putative protector and hit him. What caused Miller embarrassment was not the assault, but finding out that he had interrupted an argument between one of the city's most notorious prostitutes and her employer.[68]

It quickly became obvious to Miller, even before Wood died, that the federal government had no intention of making him chief justice. He reacted by submitting his resignation, effective at the end of 1882. Whether he did so to pressure Ottawa into making the appointment, or because he had been offered the portfolio of attorney general in the provincial cabinet, was not known. His resignation, however, was accepted. In his diary future Queen's Bench justice Thomas Wardlaw Taylor noted that Toronto newspapers discussed both the passing of Wood and those who might replace him. Probably because he too was rumoured to be in line for a seat on the Manitoba bench, he found the articles of great interest:

> Who will now be Chief Justice? It is understood, that Miller, the junior puisne judge, has a letter from Sir John Macdonald, promising him the position in the event of Wood's death or resignation. There have been a great many, recent rumours, however, seriously affecting Miller's charac-

James Andrews Miller (1839–86). Puisne judge 1880–2. Miller was an ambitious and highly successful lawyer from St Catharines, Ontario. According to Miller, Prime Minister John A. Macdonald promised to make him chief justice of Manitoba's Queen's Bench as soon as Wood either retired or was removed from office. When the promised appointment was not forthcoming Miller submitted his resignation. Four years later the rotund former justice fell to his death while walking up a hotel staircase. (Provincial Archives of Manitoba)

> ter, and his conduct as a judge, which may prevent the promise being carried out. Then there are stories as to Wood's judicial conduct ... Miller has, for some time, been pressing the Government to inquire into this, and have Wood removed. Lately, thinking to force the Government, he is said to have sent to Ottawa his own resignation, to take effect on 31 December next. I suppose, he thinks, that rather than lose his services, they will displease Wood. If the position is not given to Miller, the appointment will, in all probability, be a political one.[69]

Eight days after Miller's resignation was accepted, Taylor made another entry. 'No doubt Sir John, clever man that he is, accepted it so soon as he heard of Wood's death. By doing so, before Miller could withdraw it, he got himself out of the awkward position created by his letter to Miller. Cannot understand, how a man like Sir John ever wrote it.'[70] A day after writing that passage Taylor made a third entry:

> Today, George Morphy showed me a letter, he has received from his nephew, Edward Morphy, in Winnipeg. It seems, Miller was showing the letter from Sir John to boon companions at the Club and in saloons. The words in it are, 'Thunder Wood will not last long, and if he drops off in our time, you shall be Chief Justice.' From Morphy's letter, I learn, that there was some opposition to my name being suggested to the Government, but from only four men.[71]

After leaving the bench Miller remained in Winnipeg to practise law and was immediately embroiled in yet another controversy. On 2 January the Law Society had held a special meeting to consider his application for admission and agreed to admit him 'on payment of the usual fees' of $150. The following month Miller signed the rolls, but refused to pay the required fee. In October 1884 his name was struck from the register. He appealed the actions of the Law Society, and his appeal was heard the following year. Presiding over the panel of judges who heard it was the man who got the job Miller so badly wanted, Chief Justice Lewis Wallbridge. Miller represented himself at the hearing, and argued that the act which created the Law Society authorized it to admit to the bar three classes of persons: lawyers who had been called to the bar of another province, lawyers who had been called to the bar of England, Ireland, or Scotland, and attorneys in good standing who were practising law in Manitoba at the time the act was passed. Miller contended that he was none of the three. He was admitted as a lawyer, he said, under section 5 of a federal statute that provided 'that any judge of a superior court of the Dominion of Canada who may have been superannuated or resigned, shall be entitled to be admitted to the bar and to practise as an attorney without examination or other formality.'[72] Since that section did not prescribe a fee, he argued that none was payable. Wallbridge and Dubuc agreed, Taylor dissented, and Miller was re-admitted.[73]

The *Winnipeg Sun* suggested that when Miller left the bench he made 'the mistake of his life, for while his legal attainments qualified him for the bench, his disposition was such as to unfit him to a very large extent for active politics.'[74] Miller was not an accomplished public speaker and came across as arrogant. But despite his shortcomings, he was an experienced politician. In Ontario he had been president of the Lincoln County Conservative constituency association for many years, and in 1877 ran unsuccessfully in a federal by-election. His platform style, however, was plodding, lawyer-like, and tedious, and most of his speeches consisted of a recitation of evidence taken at public hearings. It was not what the people of Lincoln County wanted, and he lost.[75] Things were no different in Manitoba. When Premier Norquay offered him a seat in his cabinet, Miller accepted. He ran in the constituency of Rockwood, located slightly north and west of Winnipeg, in the general election held less than a month after he left the bench. He was not a good campaigner and audiences did not like his arrogance. The *Free Press* suggested that while Miller might possess a gigantic intellect, 'he does not always have it with him.'[76] Even worse, he was boring. In a prairie community, where campaigns were part carnival and part revival meeting, he made the mistake, 'natural to all professional men, of supposing that an audience should be interested with the technicalities of their profession ... [A]lthough it might have been very acceptable in a court-room, [this tendency] was altogether out of place in a political meeting. The audience became wearied.'[77]

Although he lost by 270 to 75, Miller was given a second chance. Voting in Rat Portage, now Kenora, had been postponed pending settlement of a jurisdictional dispute between the provinces of Ontario and Manitoba. Norquay wanted the former judge in his cabinet and called an election even before the dispute was settled. Miller won handily, and on 6 September 1883 was sworn in as attorney general. During his year in office he filed the last of a series of legal actions he used to attack those who he believed had wronged him. A more prudent politician might have done otherwise. While Miller was still on the bench his cousin, visiting in the city, was arrested for stealing $400 from a drinking companion. At the police station he informed the arresting officer of his relationship to Miller and asked to see him. Miller attended, made arrangements for the accused to be released on bail, and asked the chief of police to have the matter dropped. This the chief did. Two years later the arresting officer related his version of events to a reporter for the *Winnipeg Daily Sun* and shortly thereafter a story appeared in the paper. Miller promptly obtained a court order requiring the paper's owner, who happened to be the nephew of former Chief Justice Woods to appear to answer a charge of criminal libel. It did Miller's reputation no good to have the three justices hearing the case dismiss his claim on the basis that the facts contained in the article were very likely true.[78]

Less than a year after he became attorney general of Manitoba, Miller's political career came to an abrupt end. Two months after he entered the Norquay cabinet Miller was invited by Ontario premier Oliver Mowat to a meeting to discuss the Manitoba-Ontario border dispute. Although the Rat Portage area, which included Miller's constituency of Varennes, had always been considered part of Manitoba, Mowat argued that it should now become part of the Lake of the Woods district, which was already part of Ontario. At the Toronto meeting Miller was clearly out of his element, and the 'outcome of their negotiations was an agreement so one-sided that it is doubtful if even Mowat himself could have anticipated such a coup.'[79] And if that was not humiliating enough, Miller allowed the premier to dictate the exact wording of the reference to be submitted to the Privy Council. The result was foreordained. Miller lost the reference and his seat. He was forced to resign, and on 11 December 1884 he left the Manitoba legislature. When the province introduced a new system of land holding the following year (the Torrens system), Miller became the province's first registrar general. He still occupied that office when he died, two years later.

Miller left no legal legacy. Like Dubuc, he was a capable judge, but unlike the former chief justice he regarded the bench as little more than a stepping stone. Remembered more for his personality than his ability, he was a self-confident, arrogant, overbearing individual who seldom hesitated to give others the benefit of his opinion – qualities that did not prevent him from carving out a successful career at the bar. And while a lawyer he also reaped the benefit of marrying into wealth and influence. His father-in-law was one of the most successful and respected businessmen in St Catharines. In 1842 he established the first flour mill in the Niagara District and before long was one of the region's largest shipbuilders.

Along with a large ego Miller had a huge body. He enjoyed much of what life had to offer, and his propensity for over-indulging ultimately contributed to his premature death. Shortly before he died he had sold his household effects and moved into the McKenzie Hotel. Almost immediately he began supervising its staff, with whom he was both blunt and impulsive. The incident that brought about his demise occurred while he ascended the hotel's steep main stairway; as he climbed on his way to prepare for dinner his foot slipped, and he fell over the first floor bannister:

> Mrs. Scarth saw him and notified some hotel attendants, who soon had him conveyed to his room. Dr. Blanchard was summoned and examined the patient, announcing that several ribs were broken, and some slight internal injuries received. All that night Mr. Miller was in a bad state and several doctors were by his bedside. He suffered greatly and was so sore that he could not bear anyone to touch his injured parts. During the following days he was quite ill and very frequently delirious. When his attendants spoke to him however, he was quite sensible and talked quite frequently. He seemed to have a presentment that his end was near, for on one or two occasions he expressed the opinion that he would not recover. Although the public had no idea anything serious was wrong, his immediate attendants knew it was likely to go hard with him, and when questioned the doctor usually shook his head warningly, although he saw no immediate cause of apprehension. Quite a number of his friends visited him yesterday, and to some he spoke at intervals. He was not, however, feeling bright, and often lapsed into a delirious condition. His doctor remained by his bedside as much as possible. About one o'clock this morning he sank into a sleep in which he remained for a couple of hours, when the doctor observing that his pulse was growing very weak, sought to awaken him. He had very great difficulty doing so, and when the patient did awaken, he only opened his eyes partially and stared blankly and vacantly around not recognizing anyone, the glaze of death upon his orbs, and when the poor man again lapsed into unconsciousness, or heavy sleep, the doctor announced that the end was very near, and a few friends in the hotel, including Mr. Miller's devoted and sorrowing wife, were admitted to the chamber of death to see the lamp of life slowly extinguished ... The watchers had not long to wait. With his fingers on the pulse of the dying man, the doctor from time to time announced how near of approach was the death valley. The minutes dragged slowly along, the breathing of the sleeper, who began in life the longsleep of death, merging unconsciously from the former into the latter, grew fainter

> and fainter, and came at longer intervals. There was a slight gurgle in the throat, a tremor shot through the once powerful frame, the doctor sighed and dropped the wrist, and all knew that judge Miller was dead.[80]

It was 1 November 1886.

LEWIS WALLBRIDGE

If Manitoba can be said to have had an 'aristocrat' numbered among its judiciary it would undoubtedly have been Lewis Wallbridge. The province's third chief justice was born in Belleville, Upper Canada, on 27 November 1816 to a family that had been prominent for more than two centuries.

When Henry Wallbridge was driven from his ancestral home in Dorsetshire, England, because of his support for the Duke of Monmouth in his ill-fated rebellion against King James II, he fled to North America. There he and his family settled in the colony of Connecticut, and in 1690 he and his wife became the father of William. Over time William's children dispersed throughout the colonies, including Saratoga, New York, and it was there that the grandfather of Lewis was raised.

The American War of Independence caused a great rift in the Wallbridge family. Some fought with the colonial army led by Washington, others with the British. Lewis's grandfather Elijah was a loyalist, and in one engagement led a successful attack on a military prison. When the war ended Elijah returned to the Saratoga area, where he grew wealthy in business. In 1800 his brother persuaded him to look at an area rich in game in the Upper Canada Bay of Quinte region near the mouth of the Moira River. Two years later Elijah bought two thousand acres there, and by 1812 he had established his three sons and two of his three daughters on separate 300-acre farms. Whether they received help from the family's slaves was uncertain, but it was known they came to Canada with them.[81] The houses of the various members of the Wallbridge family were the first in the area, and the log cabin of Asa Wallbridge, Elijah's brother, was the first built in Belleville.

When Asa died the father of Lewis bought his house, expanded it, and became a gentleman farmer and full-time lumber merchant and trader. He and Mary Everett had a family of five boys and two girls. Four of their sons, including Lewis, became lawyers.[82] The relative affluence of his parents meant that Lewis received the best education available. He spent his early schooling in Montreal, studying under the well-known Dr Benjamin Workman. In 1831 he entered Upper Canada College, then one of the province's most exclusive preparatory schools. Two years later he became a student-at-law of Robert Baldwin. Although still in his thirties when Wallbridge entered his office, Baldwin was already well known throughout the Canadas. He was elected to the Legislative Assembly when he was twenty-five, and appointed to the Executive Council at thirty-two. Shortly after Wallbridge became his student Baldwin was made solicitor general for Upper Canada, and in 1841 attorney general for Canada West. He later headed a number of administrations, often with Louis-Hippolyte Lafontaine, and was instrumental in persuading Britain to grant the colony responsible government.[83]

Admission to Baldwin's office as an articled clerk was considered a privilege, and parents frequently paid one hundred and twenty pounds or more for the honour. The three-storey office housing the firm, located on King Street West in downtown Toronto, was occupied for many years by both Baldwin and by William Warren Baldwin, his lawyer-doctor-politician father. On the ground floor the desks of students surrounded a central reception area, and a staircase led up to the second floor, which housed a library and the offices of the partners. Among the firm's alumni were numerous judges and an assortment of illustrious non-judges, including the Hon. James A. Lougheed of Calgary.[84]

Wallbridge was called to the bar of Upper Canada in 1839 and immediately established his own firm in Belleville. He practised alone for twenty years, until his brother Adam received his call. They were partners for a decade and a half before the firm of Wallbridge & Brother was dissolved. The two ended their careers as solo practitioners. The Belleville in which Wallbridge set up his practice was a community of two hundred homes and a population of more than 1700. It contained a courthouse, six churches, an equal number of taverns, an iron foundry, five schools (three for girls and two for boys), three saddle factories, a watchmaker, ten shoemakers, seven tailors, three butchers, three breweries, a distillery, two brickyards, and a variety of other manufacturing concerns. In addition, the existence of the Moira River flowing through its heart made it a port of entry and encouraged the establishment of a number of flour, paper, and sawmills, together with six warehouses. Among the town's corps of professionals were six physicians, four lawyers, and two pharmacists. Until the 1850s travel was by stagecoach, carriage, or wagon. Roads were few and often impassable. The exception was the route from Belleville to Trenton, which was planked.[85]

Wallbridge's practice flourished from the beginning, in no small part because people were 'suing each other like the devil.'[86] He was soon considered one of the district's leading lawyers, and although he gained a reputation as a highly competent criminal counsel, the focus of his practice was civil litigation. In many communities this meant arguing cases in a tavern, often the only building large enough to house the court. On such occasions the presiding judge paid from his own pocket the cost of fuel and candles, and sat without even a desk through long days in small rooms dense with smoke, crowded nearly to the point of suffocation. Impatient litigants were forced to divide their attention between proceedings in the court and activities in the bar. As often as not, by the time a case was called both litigants and witnesses were either absent or too drunk to testify.

Wallbridge's growing reputation helped him win election in 1855 as a bencher of the Law Society of Upper Canada and, a year later, appointment as Queen's Counsel. His professional status was enhanced even further in 1857 when he became a lecturer in law at Osgoode Hall. Two years later he and William Buell Richards, the future first chief justice of the Supreme Court of Canada, became the Law Society's first salaried instructors. In the 1860s he supplemented that income with what he earned as an examiner in the Victoria University Law School.[87] When Wallbridge worked for the Law Society as a lecturer, classes were held most weekday mornings, consisting of two hours a week instruction in each of two subjects. Among them were bills of exchange, contracts, pleading, promissory notes, criminal law, torts, and partnership. In addition to formal lectures, students participated in informal moot courts, where they were observed by instructors carefully watching for any breach of etiquette. This emphasis on form was very important, and students were reprimanded if they failed to exhibit the expected 'principles and habits' of barristers.[88]

Although he likely welcomed the money he earned as a lecturer and examiner, Wallbridge continued to maintain an active litigation practice. Forty-one actions and appeals with which he was involved were reported. They indicated that 60 per cent of his work involved appeals, that two-thirds of the time he acted for plaintiffs, and that he lost more often than he won. He was just as likely to appear in a regional as in a local court, and 20 per cent of his cases involved estates, compared to a third involving real property (referred to by the *Canada Law Journal* as his speciality).[89]

Success at the bar, his election as a bencher, and the visibility he gained as a Law Society lecturer gave Wallbridge the profile and confidence to enter politics. He fought his first campaign in 1854, when he ran as a moderate Reformer against a 'Clear Grit' follower of the *Globe*'s George Brown. Although he lost in Hastings South his first time out, he was successful three years later. This time he campaigned as a Conservative and an advocate of representation by population, settling the west, and withdrawing government aid to the Grand Trunk Railway. As a rookie legislator he became increasingly moderate and soon developed a close relationship with John A. Macdonald. His attitude towards other parliamentarians, however, was less friendly. He referred to many as babblers, because of their propensity for long-winded, theoretical speeches. Wallbridge was re-elected in 1861, and despite his initial ambivalence towards John Sandfield Macdonald, entered the Macdonald–Antoine-Aimé Dorion ministry two years later as solicitor general for Canada West. That summer he won re-election on a platform of liberal capitalism and support for prohibition. When the legislature was recalled he was elected House speaker, despite accusations that he was an anti-Catholic francophobe. He remained speaker of the legislature through the joint administrations of Sir Étienne-Paschal Taché and John A. Macdonald. Joining him in the legislature at that time were future Manitoba lieutenant-governors James Cox Aikins and Joseph Cauchon, and future chief justices Alexander Morris and Edmund Burke Wood.

Wallbridge presided over the House during the heated debates that preceded Confederation and was the last speaker of the Province of Canada:

> [It] was during this period that the future political stability of not only the two provinces but also the country as a whole was debated. At the beginning of the third session, a motion was put forward which requested that the Assembly write an address regarding the proposed Confederation of the provinces for submission to the Imperial government. From this one routine parliamentary procedure came the test of Wallbridge's abilities as Speaker: the Confederation debates. The ensuing arguments for and against this address tested not only the limits of his patience but also of his knowledge of parliamentary procedure. Wallbridge was forced

to rule no fewer than five times during the debates on points of privilege, or order and of procedure.[90]

In 1867 Wallbridge decided not to seek a seat in the country's first parliament, probably because the campaign would have pitted him against his brother, Thomas Cambridge Wallbridge, who sat in the pre-Confederation legislature as the Liberal member for Hastings North and now opposed Confederation. An attempt to re-enter the political arena eleven years later failed, despite Lewis's being an overwhelming favourite. His liberal leanings alienated both Catholics and anti-reform Conservatives, and their support turned the tide in favour of Colonel James Brown, a Liberal who had won the three previous contests as a Conservative.[91] After his defeat Wallbridge resumed his legal career. He also continued to sit on the board of the Bank of Upper Canada and the senate of Albert College, a Belleville preparatory school, and to take an active part in the affairs of the Church of England. By 1880 he was reputed to possess the largest and most lucrative legal practice in the Belleville area. Time previously spent in politics was now devoted to farming and his duties as second vice-president of the provincial Bee-keepers' Association.

Wallbridge was likely aware of the judicial opening in Manitoba, since Miller's aggressive campaigning for the job of chief justice of the province had captured the attention of the Ontario bar. After Wood died on 7 October 1882 and Miller's resignation was accepted, attention shifted to John O'Connor, who was a member of John A. Macdonald's cabinet and, according to the *Globe*, was offered the appointment on 10 October; 'though as a matter of form, he has asked time for consideration there is no doubt that he will accept the position. He is a man utterly unfit by habits and disposition to fill the office – having neither the legal knowledge nor the personal dignity requisite to enable him to do so with credit. His appointment is an outrage to the province.'[92] O'Connor ultimately turned the position down and focus briefly shifted to Dalton McCarthy, a leader of the Ontario bar and member of the House of Commons. When he too declined the offer Macdonald appointed Wallbridge, despite his family's connection to the Liberal party. 'He will be a good judge,' Macdonald suggested. 'It is so seldom one can indulge one's personal feelings with due consideration for public interests.' One of the prime minister's few concerns about Wallbridge's fitness for office was his teeth. He could not contemplate the prospect of the future chief justice delivering judgments through a mouthful of black, decaying stumps. Mackenzie Bowell, a member of the federal cabinet from Wallbridge's hometown, was given the task of persuading him to get a set of false teeth, a task Bowell described as of 'gnashing importance.'[93]

A more serious concern of Macdonald's was Wallbridge's age. In 1882 he was sixty-six, an age when most of his contemporaries were either dead or retired. The prime minister overcame his misgivings, however, and in December made his former ally Manitoba's chief justice. The *Canada Law Journal* predicted the appointment would meet the approval of the province's legal profession, despite the bar's desire for someone with more equity experience. 'But though they are disappointed in this, they will have in Mr. Wallbridge a sound lawyer and one of large experience in all branches of the law, most genial and courteous in his manner, and personally everything that the most fastidious could wish.'[94]

Wallbridge was an ideal judicial complement to Dubuc. Both had been competent, if colourless lawyers, and both led unblemished personal lives. Their judgments reflected a sincere, plodding, and unemotional approach to law. The main difference between the two was that Wallbridge did not share Dubuc's concern with protecting the rights of French Catholics, and Dubuc did not share the chief justice's antipathy for provincial legislation that put obstacles in the way of free access to the courts. One such statute was passed a year after Wallbridge went to the bench. The legislation prevented litigants from filing a statement of claim against a railway without first complying with a plethora of formalities he regarded as an intrusion on the sanctity of the common law. Shortly after the act was passed a Winnipeg lawyer asked Wallbridge to dismiss a claim against a railway on the ground that the action did not comply with the precise wording of the statute. As soon as arguments ended, the angry chief justice addressed the counsel for the plaintiff:

> I regret I will have to abide by the Act and decide against your client. My duty compels me to give force to this outrageous legislation, which is a disgrace to the statute book and to those who enacted it. But when I discover something which is beyond anything in the heavens above, or in the earth beneath, or in the waters under the earth, I thereupon fall down and worship it, which I do this statute.[95]

As he stopped talking, Wallbridge pushed back his glasses and threw a bound copy of the legislation over the head of the court clerk.

In 1886 he became embroiled in the only real controversy of his judicial career. As head of a provincial royal commission he was charged with investigating whether Premier John Norquay had made an illegal profit through his connection to a parcel of land bought by the government. His report, exonerating the premier, did not receive the overwhelming endorsement of the general public.

In the ten days before his death Wallbridge was in great physical discomfort, although he continued to hold court. On 12 October 1887, however, he became so ill during a hearing that he went home to bed. His doctor was immediately called and informed Wallbridge's niece and nephew, who had been taking care of him, that their uncle would not recover. Seven days later Wallbridge was told his time had just about run out and was asked if he wanted to see his minister. The chief justice declined, informing those present that he was already at peace with the world. Just after midnight on 20 October, Wallbridge died.[96] The following morning the body of the former chief justice was transported to the court's Queen's Bench room, where it lay in state from one to four o'clock. The room, like his chair and bench, was adorned in black. The rosewood coffin was covered with four floral arrangements and surrounded by a military honour guard from the School of Mounted Infantry. After the Metropolitan of Rupert's Land read the Church of England funeral service, those in attendance filed by the open casket. It was then sealed, taken out of the building, and loaded into a hearse. From the courthouse the funeral procession made its way past city hall to the railway station, and Wallbridge started his last trip home.

Lewis Wallbridge died unmarried, leaving an estate consisting of little more than his personal effects. As a judge he was remembered as highly competent, amiable, generous, urbane, and unfailingly polite. His main shortcoming was a tendency to appear almost undignified in his determination not to disappoint litigants, or to hurt feelings. Whatever his faults, he was the ideal person to follow Wood as chief justice. He restored to the bench the confidence of both the bar and the citizens of Manitoba, and his simplicity and lack of guile were ideal antidotes to the machinations and excesses of Miller. In short, his strength lay in what he was not, rather than in what he was.

THOMAS WARDLAW TAYLOR

No judge elevated to the Manitoba bench was by disposition and training better prepared for the appointment than Thomas Wardlaw Taylor.

His writing and work in Ontario's Court of Chancery brought him to the attention of the profession, and so large was his reputation that the bar of Manitoba actually petitioned Ottawa to have him appointed to its bench.

Taylor was born on 25 March 1833 in the manse of the East United Secession Church in Auchtermuchty, Scotland, one of the smallest of the royal burghs of Fifeshire. His father John, the church's minister, obtained his medical licence a year before he was ordained. Thomas's mother, Marion Antill Wardlaw, was the youngest daughter of John Wardlaw, a banker resident in Dalkeith. The Wardlaws were an ancient Scottish family of considerable prominence. During the Middle Ages Cardinal Walter Wardlaw was bishop of Glasgow and secretary of state to David II. Henry Wardlaw was bishop of St Andrews, primate of Scotland, and tutor to James I, and his daughter a maid of honour to Mary, Queen of Scots.[97]

Taylor's early schooling was taken at home, first with his mother and latterly with his father. Almost his entire youth was spent without companionship. Lessons were unstructured, with neither student nor teacher attempting to formulate any scheme for a complete education. Eventually Taylor studied only those topics that interested him, which in turn cultivated the belief that he should get his own way as of right. 'Apart from his father's teaching, Tom can have known no discipline of any kind. It is possible that there were moments, when he obeyed the voice of authority ... But there is no report of such. Instead, every anecdote of his childhood proves, that he usually followed the devices and desires of his own heart. Even in infancy, it was so.'[98]

Notwithstanding the drawbacks of his early education Taylor became an enthusiastic student. 'I began Macaulay's *History* one forenoon, read all day, all night, all the next day, and finished early in the morning. During all that time, I never slept, so intense was my interest in the book.'[99] At fifteen he entered the University of Edinburgh. For a one-pound, one-shilling fee he received a card of registration and, for an additional three guineas per class, entitlement to attend any lecture he wanted. Classes in Greek and Latin, attended by as many as two hundred students, took up most of his mornings, while the afternoons were split between studying geometry and working in the office of a solicitor. Time in school was time his employer demanded he make up, and he was forced to return to work most evenings until nearly 10:00 p.m.

Taylor did sufficiently well at university that he decided to sit the special examination required to obtain a Bachelor of Arts degree. In the

Scotland of his youth few university students received a degree at the conclusion of their studies, since it was of no practical or professional benefit. Those entering one of the professions needed only a university education, not a degree. To study medicine or law a student had only to show that he had attended university lectures and passed the ensuing examinations. To receive a degree, students were required to take an additional examination. Only in England did law students receive credit for passing the exam. In that country the rare student who possessed a degree was entitled to be called to the bar after an additional three years of apprenticeship, instead of the usual five.

Taylor was an above-average student, with a second in Latin and mathematics and a first in Greek. Despite his accomplishments, he had expected to do better. 'When I look back upon it, and think of the great privileges and opportunities I had – of what I might have done – of how little I did – what great improvement I should have made, and how much time was wasted – I feel humiliated.'[100]

The year that Taylor graduated from Edinburgh the United Presbyterian Church in Canada asked the Scottish synod to provide it with a professor of theology. Taylor's father was nominated, and on 1 June 1852 the family departed for Canada aboard the steamship *Glasgow*. On his arrival Taylor left his family in Toronto and settled on a farm. By 1854, however, he had a change of heart. Farming 'disgusted me very much,' and in October he abandoned his homestead to study law in Toronto.[101] Before Taylor's application to become a student-at-law was accepted, however, he had to prove that he possessed a knowledge of English, Latin, Greek, algebra, geometry, philosophy, rhetoric, and history. This he did, and on 13 February 1855 he became a member of the Law Society of Upper Canada. A month later he entered into a three-year articling agreement with Sechar Brough. Brough was a partner in the Chancery firm of Brough & Robinson, his partner being John Beverley Robinson, the second son of the chief justice of the Court of Queen's Bench. The common-law side of the Brough-Robinson partnership was known as Robinson & Robinson, and consisted of brothers James Lukin, John Beverley, and Christopher Robinson.

In 1858 Taylor completed his articles, was called to the bar, and married Jessie Cameron. The two met when Jessie and her father, a Delaware physician, attended the same Toronto church as Taylor. She died after five years of marriage, leaving her husband a single father of three, the youngest of whom was four months old. Taylor allowed his wife's mother to take the couple's two youngest children to Wilmington, while he kept the three-and-a-half-year-old daughter he had named after his beloved mother, Marion.

From 1858 until 1866 Taylor twice practised on his own and six times was a member of a partnership.[102] After leaving Brough he joined Strong & Matheson, one of the most successful and influential firms in the country. Its senior member was Sir Samuel Henry Strong, a close friend and legal adviser to John A. Macdonald. Strong eventually became chief justice of the Supreme Court of Canada and a member of the Judicial Committee of the Privy Council. Taylor was with the Strong firm for a year when the temperamental Strong suddenly, and for no apparent reason, dissolved the partnership. Taylor and Matheson stayed together for about eleven months before Taylor accused his partner of neglecting the firm's business and he terminated their partnership. He then practised alone until 1862, when he joined the firm headed by Member of Parliament Skeffington Connor. Their association lasted only a few months before Connor was elevated to the Court of Queen's Bench. Six months later Taylor took as partner his former student George Martin Rae. Within twelve months they too went their separate ways, and Taylor joined William Vynne Bacon, an English-trained solicitor. A year to the day later Bacon died of pneumonia and Taylor was again on his own. Thereafter he practised in association, rather than in partnership, with James E. McMurray. The two exchanged work so that one could specialize in the common law and the other in equity.

Taylor was sensitive about having been in so many partnerships. Throughout his career at the bar he was saddled with an unduly sensitive nature and an explosive, almost uncontrollable temper. Seldom satisfied with the effort of others, he had difficulty coping with the petty irritations of everyday practice. Even he was forced to admit that he was badly suited to the practice of law.[103]

In 1864 Taylor married for the second time. Margaret Vallance was attending the Ontario Normal School, located directly across the street from Taylor's home. She noticed him right away. He was, she said,

> handsome, very erect and tall, with flowing Dundreary whiskers, straight, regular features, firmly set mouth, and piercing, dark eyes. For his dress, what with shiny, high hat, cravat precisely tied, Prince Albert, with skirts flaring in the latest cut, tight, lavender-gray trousers, and ivory-headed cane, he was a veritable fashion plate. And as for his air, it was not so much one of superiority, or command, or unapproachable dignity, as it was a serenely unconscious suggestion of all three.[104]

Two years later Taylor was hired by the government of Ontario to examine all existing Chancery accounts, and to make recommendations for the implementation of a new system of record keeping. When that work was done he became the province's first Judges' Secretary. As such he heard all but a few of the chambers motions previously heard by a judge, and he oversaw the preparation of court orders and decrees. His conscientiousness caught the eye of both the profession and the press. In an editorial the *Globe* noted that

> [t]he judges of this Court have hitherto been required to devote a large portion of time each day to the hearing and consideration of matters of practice or routine while sitting in Chambers. The suitors who seek relief in equity are becoming more numerous every day, and the number of places at which sittings of the Court are held is much increased, and it has been rendered plain that either an additional judge or a deputy of some kind was required to assist in Chamber business. It is, therefore, no matter of surprise that the judges have called to their aid the services of Mr. T. W. Taylor, a barrister distinguished for his intimate knowledge of the rules and practice of the Court of Chancery. Mr. Taylor has entered upon his duties this week, and, in his capacity of Judges' Secretary, sits in Chambers and hears all matters not requiring the direct attention of a judge. He is to all appearances a Chambers Judge, although all orders issue with the approbation of the Chancellor, or one of the Vice-Chancellors, as before. We understand that the profession are unanimous in expressing their approval of the election of Mr. Taylor for this office.[105]

While judges' secretary Taylor also became a referee under the Ontario *Quieting Titles Act*. The act had been passed to bring some order into the province's system of landholding, under which real property was routinely transferred from person to person without the formality of registration. As a result purchasers often had to deal with competing claims when they tried to register their deeds, and many had no way of ridding themselves of the often fraudulent claims of fictitious mortgage holders. The *Quieting Titles Act* was passed to remedy this problem. It provided that titles of claimants were to be investigated by two referees, who were to determine the validity and priority of competing claims. In 1869 Taylor replaced Alexander Leith, one of the two original referees. His first year investigating claims provided him with sufficient knowledge that he published a monograph on the subject. *The Investigation of Titles to Estates in Fee Simple* was received favourably in both Canada and England.[106]

Despite being generally well regarded by the legal community, Taylor was subjected to some withering criticism by the Toronto *Telegraph*. In April 1870 a letter it published attacked all the officers of Ontario courts, but none more viciously than him:

> Next came the official tail [*sic*] of B.H. & Co, Chancery Reformers &c. I refer to the Secretary, the Accountant, and the Clerk of Records. The last named is lazy, the next snuffy, wheezy and stupid, and the third narrow-minded, vain, grasping and treacherous ... He pockets fees as Secretary, fees as Referee of Titles, fees as General Utility, and wanders about in Osgoode Hall jeering over this man's shoulder, and into that man's office to see what everybody is doing, and how they are doing it. The Clerk of the Crown can be approached without dropping on one knee, but this whipper-snapper of a clerk, whose private practice was insufficient to feed him, assumes the air of a judge, and from behind a fine table nods with all the gravity of the olympian at the much astonished youths, who sit gaping at this embodiment of Chancery practice. It is impossible to know when one may safely venture within the Secretary's clutches. Since he has been given the reins, applications have been so hedged with technical requirements, and there is such a propensity to strain out motes, that the pockets of suitors and the tempers of solicitors are sorely tried. Chancery Chambers have been converted into a mousetrap. Great ingenuity is manifested in discovering undotted I's and uncrossed T's. This tendency to nose out the technicalities of bygone times and graft them on the practice of the present day, seems to me very absurd. It swells bills of costs to alarming proportions, and brings the Court into disrepute. While the judges are doing all they can to give a tinge of common sense to the practice, their Secretary seems to be doing all he can to neutralize their efforts. While the policy of our duty is to simplify practice, to do away with splitting hairs about matters which do not affect the points at issue in the case, the Secretary bristles with objections and exhibits wonderful industry in thwarting applications. While the Courts of Common Law are giving up that small-minded lore for technicalities, and devoting their attention to the merits of cases brought before them, the Court of Chancery appears to be rolling itself up in the cast off rags of its rivals. Unfortunately the judges have appointed (illegally too) a young man as Secretary, who has as his distinguishing characteristics a mania for enforcing effete rules and the old round-about method of getting at what is wanted. The Court is complained of as an expensive nuisance. Suitors are beginning to find out that a great deal of their money is wasted in settling points of practice which have nothing to do with the merits of cases ... The

> truth is, a mistake was made, when Chancery Chambers practice was placed under the control of a person, other than one having the ability and breadth of view of a judge. The Government should not give up to anybody the right of appointment to positions; such as that occupied by the Secretary. It is now admitted that the Secretary has not a judicial mind. Certainly the more experienced practitioners advise, that applications of importance should be made before one of the Judges. If so, he is totally unfit for the position of Master.[107]

In 1871 the Ontario government announced a restructuring of the province's courts. As part of that process the office of Master of the Court was changed to Master in Ordinary. Despite Premier John Sandfield Macdonald's promise that Taylor would receive the appointment, it went to Alexander Boyd, while Taylor became the province's first Referee in Chambers. It was a change without a difference. He retained his old office, but under a new name. During the twenty-two months that he was referee he made 3816 orders, from which 38 appeals were taken. Of these, nine were allowed, four varied, one compromised, and twenty-four dismissed.[108]

In 1872 Boyd resigned as Master in Ordinary and Oliver Mowat, the new premier and a close friend, offered Taylor the job. On 16 December Thomas Wardlaw Taylor became Master in Ordinary to the Court of Chancery for Ontario, a position he held for the next ten years. When members of the Manitoba bar petitioned the federal government to appoint an equity lawyer to fill the vacancy created by Miller's resignation, Taylor's knowledge of the principles of equity jurisprudence and the practice of the Court of Chancery made him the obvious choice.[109] Even before he gained a solid reputation as an official in Chancery, however, Taylor had come to the attention of Ontario's legal profession. In the 1860s he wrote three books, and in the succeeding eleven years four more. All were critically acclaimed and one used as a text by the Law Society of Upper Canada.

Taylor's first effort was *Orders of the Court of Chancery for Upper Canada*, written as a practical guide to the legal profession.[110] Its usefulness lay primarily in the brief comments that followed every Chancery order. Although the comments are relatively few in number, they referred to leading cases and served as helpful procedural guidelines to lawyers not experienced in the Courts of Chancery. For example, section three of the act allowed a defendant to move for dismissal when a plaintiff delayed a suit unreasonably. Taylor offered practical observa-

Thomas Wardlaw Taylor (1833–1917). Puisne justice 1883–7, and chief justice 1887–99. Taylor was widely respected for his intellect, his prodigious capacity for hard work, and his knowledge of the law. He was the author or co-author of seven books, one of which was used by the Law Society of Upper Canada as a textbook. Taylor's vanity and explosive temper, however, made him hard to get along with and may explain his being involved with eight partnerships during his first eight years at the bar. Even he admitted that he was badly suited for the practice of law. (Provincial Archives of Manitoba)

tions about how the section operated: 'An injunction does not prevent a defendant from moving to dismiss for want of prosecution ... The court may grant the plaintiff further time, but it is usual to do so only on terms as to the future conduct of the suit. On moving to dismiss the registrar's certificate, must not merely shew what proceedings have been taken, it must state that no further proceedings have been had.'[111]

Five years after this publication Taylor teamed up with his law partner Rae to write *General Orders of the Court of Chancery*.[112] Although little more than a thirty-eight-page addendum to his earlier work, it considerably improved it with a table of contents and table of cases.[113] The most original of Taylor's books, however, and the most highly regarded by the profession, was *The Investigation of Titles to Estates in Fee Simple*,[114] published in 1869 as a guide to the province's *Quieting Titles Act*, passed four years earlier. Taylor wrote the book for members of the profession who were confused about how the new procedures worked. 'From the loose system which has prevailed, and to which they have been accustomed, they are comparatively ignorant of the practice of conveyancers, and as to the evidence which they ought to require, and are entitled to call for when examining a title.'[115] Although he regularly used cases to illustrate his arguments, the book was a historical treatment of real property law. Its usefulness lay primarily in its author's simple, almost conversational, style of writing:

> In this country the question of title by possession, as against a paper title, often presents peculiar features, and is not always a matter of easy solution. Thus the question has sometimes arisen whether the occupation of part of a lot of land will give title by possession to the whole. The present current of authority seems to be, that such a possession will confer title only to the part actually occupied.[116]

In *Commentaries on Equity Jurisprudence Founded on Story* (1875) Taylor used *Story*, a popular contemporary U.S. legal text as a template to discuss the law of equity.[117] The structure of the book, however, was weak and his style repetitive. In his chapter on equity jurisprudence, for example, he began virtually every paragraph with phrases like 'Another maxim is,' 'Another maxim of no small extent is,' 'It is also a maxim that,' and 'Another maxim of general use is.'[118]

The only book Taylor wrote that did not focus on law and the legal profession was *The Public Statutes Relating to the Presbyterian Church in Canada* (1879),[119] which contained a series of unannotated statutes, by-laws, and regulations of the Presbyterian Church. In the first part of the book he reproduced, without comment, the public provincial statutes relating to the amalgamation of the Canada Presbyterian Church, the Presbyterian Church of Canada in connection with the Church of Scotland, the Church of the Maritime Provinces in connection with the Church of Scotland, and the Presbyterian Church of the Lower Provinces. In part 2 he described, again without comment or analysis, the statutes that established Queen's College at Kingston, Knox College in Toronto, Morin College in the City of Quebec, Presbyterian College in Montreal, and Manitoba College in Winnipeg.

The last of Taylor's six legal texts was co-written with someone very much his professional and intellectual equal. John Skirving Ewart was one of Canada's most talented constitutional lawyers, and in his own right wrote a number of highly acclaimed treatises. He and Taylor published *The Judicature Act and Rules 1881* while both were solidifying their already considerable reputations in Toronto,[120] although shortly after it was published both emigrated to Manitoba. The book was designed to introduce lawyers to changes in laws affecting Ontario's courts of law and equity. In an eleven-page preface the authors discussed how the new *Judicature Act* removed the distinction between the two courts and tied that discussion to an analysis of how courts in Ontario differed from those in Great Britain. Throughout the book Taylor and Ewart offered an extended analysis of the law and made suggestions about how the new act could be used effectively. Taylor's remaining book was an historical sketch of Toronto's Saint James Square Presbyterian Congregation.

The circumstances under which Taylor was sworn on 30 January 1883 were considerably less formal than those with which he became familiar as a court officer in Ontario. Winnipeg's courthouse had been sold during the real estate boom of 1882 and a new one was not yet finished. His first trials were held in a ten-by-ten-foot room in a small wooden framed house. He sat in the poorly lit and badly ventilated 'court' eight hours a day, six days a week. When not there Taylor spent his time in his hotel room, writing judgments. But what bothered him more than personal discomfort was the lack of respect lawyers showed his court, and it was not something he allowed to continue. 'The first intimation of the changed order was quiet, but dramatic. The Attorney General, young and very Western, entered the room, and he was smoking a cigar. Five minutes later, he was seated in an office down stairs, writing a letter of apology, and the offence was never repeated.'[121]

Taylor's first assize consisted of 14 criminal prosecutions, 166 jury trials, and 268 non-jury actions. By sitting until nearly midnight several evenings per week he was able to complete both the jury trials and the entire civil list in three months.

The most historically significant action involving Taylor was the appeal from Louis Riel's 1885 conviction for treason. Riel had been tried by a stipendiary magistrate and jury in Regina in July, and sentenced to death. An appeal came before the Manitoba Court of Queen's Bench on 3 September and lasted three days. Court adjourned on a Saturday afternoon and the participants were informed that a decision would be handed down the following Wednesday. Taylor spent the rest of Saturday reading the evidence and began writing his judgment after breakfast Monday. He finished two days later. Between Saturday afternoon and Wednesday morning he ate only three meals, and the day before the court announced it had dismissed the appeal he slept for only two hours. In denying Riel's leave to appeal the Privy Council would single out Taylor's judgment for praise, noting that he had showed 'a learning, patience and ability in arriving at the conclusion not to set aside the judgment of the Magistrate, which left nothing to add.'[122]

One of his more unpopular decisions involved a colourful Portage la Prairie butcher named Fant. Even before he appeared before Taylor, Fant had achieved a remarkable degree of notoriety. The former Sunday School superintendent became the stuff of legend when he volunteered to lead a search for the man who stole a horse belonging to the local sheriff. When Fant turned up at the home of the sheriff, ready to track down the culprit, the sheriff noted that the animal Fant was riding bore a remarkable resemblance to his stolen horse. For the next two days the sheriff rode in a posse led by a man riding a horse the sheriff was increasingly convinced was his own. When he could contain himself no longer he arrested Fant, who was eventually convicted of the theft and sentenced to Stony Mountain penitentiary. Three months after his release, however, the butcher resumed his old habits. As Winnipeg's chief of police attempted to arrest him, Fant shot him twice and fled into the United States. He was arrested, extradited, and charged with attempted murder. During the trial Taylor learned that, when the police chief attempted to arrest the accused, he did not have in his possession an arrest warrant. The law at the time stated that a person who killed a police constable while that constable was attempting to make a lawful arrest was guilty of murder. If the constable was only wounded, an accused was to be charged with attempted murder. But someone who killed a policeman who was trying to make an arrest without a warrant could only be charged with manslaughter. According to Taylor, this meant Fant had to be acquitted. Since he had only wounded the sheriff, rather than killed him, the most that he could be charged with was attempted manslaughter and there was no such charge. Because the accused was extradited to face a charge of attempted murder, he could not be tried for anything else.[123]

Taylor sat as a puisne trial judge for only four years before he became the province's chief justice in 1887. He retired twelve years later.[124] During his tenure on the bench he sat on two commissions, and a third following his retirement. In 1886 the federal government appointed him a commissioner to investigate the conduct of a Calgary stipendiary magistrate, and nine years later he chaired a royal commission established to enquire into the management of the University of Toronto. While retired he also sat on a commission to revise and update the statutes of Ontario.

During his seventeen years as a judge, 539 of Taylor's decisions were reported and only one reversed by the Privy Council.[125] Yet despite the high regard others had of Taylor, his father was quick to criticize:

> '[I]t is well that your judgments are generally sustained ... I observe, however, that you sometimes say "assent" for "consent." We assent to a proposition. We consent to a proposal ... I am anxious that you shd. be quite exact, and therefore return you part of the report with a remark of two. The first sentence I have marked at the side, is incomplete, and there shd. have been only a comma where I have placed one. The second sentence marked is complete, but you have appended to it a participial clause, which shd. have been separated only by a comma as I have indicated. As a general rule, judgments shd. be expressed in short, simple sentences.' Taylor's response was to note that 'I am giving judgment, not producing literature.'[126]

Taylor took considerable pride in his ability to influence a jury, and regarded himself as the only judge in Manitoba who could persuade a jury of farmers to return a verdict in favour of the much despised Canadian Pacific Railway. On one such occasion a juror was nearly killed by an angry crowd of farmers. The juror saved himself by laying the blame on Taylor. 'He told us to find for the Railway.'[127] In another case, the defendant was a well-known politician. The testimony of the plaintiff and the politician conflicted, leaving the jury to conclude that one or the other was lying. Taylor initially asked the jury to decide which of the two they believed, but as the jurors filed out of the courtroom he wondered aloud whether it would be of any assistance to members of the jury if he told them what he personally believed. Before the jurors could respond he answered his own question. 'I do not believe one word that the defendant, or any of his witnesses, has spoken.'[128]

Taylor was a strict legal formalist and believed that his role in the judicial process was to find the law, not dispense justice. When it was suggested that his duty should be to do what was morally right, he disagreed. 'I am here to dispose of this case, according to the law. Whether that is, or is not, justice, is a question for the Legislature to determine.'[129] His only duty, he said, was 'to interpret it exactly.'[130]

Although Thomas Wardlaw Taylor was a forceful, strong-willed, arrogant, irascible, and dynamic individual who influenced by intimidation, he was also one of the most important judges in the history of Manitoba. He was intellectually gifted, professionally knowledgeable, ethical, and determined to remake the profession in the image of the Ontario bar. He did just that. Taylor was knighted by Queen Victoria in 1897, two years before he retired and moved to Hamilton. There he conducted Sunday church services, promoted the city's home for women, and headed Hamilton's anti-gambling Citizen's League. While retired he was twice commissioned to sit as judge *pro tempore* of the Exchequer Court of Canada. A chill he picked up while attending a Sunday service at St Paul's Presbyterian Church developed into pneumonia, and he died at home on 2 March 1917.[131]

ROBERT SMITH

The second last puisne judge appointed during the tenure of Chief Justice Wallbridge was born in Loweswater, in the Lake District of England, on 19 June 1839. The Smith family had been large landowners in the County of Cumberland for several generations before Robert's grandfather improved the family's fortunes considerably by marrying an heiress. The couple had two children, one of whom died unmarried. The other was Robert's father Thomas, who also married well, to the daughter of a prominent captain in the British navy.[132]

Robert was one of seven children, all but one of whom emigrated to Ontario in 1857. Two became physicians, two lawyers, one a banker, and both sisters married railway executives.[133] Family wealth provided

Robert with the kind of education expected of a gentleman. His first years were spent in London's St John's Foundation School, and at seventeen he entered college in Cambridge. He was in his second year when the Smith family departed for Canada. Almost immediately upon his arrival Robert became a student in the Toronto law office of Edward, Jonas and Clarkson Jones. While finishing his articles with Edward, and Samuel Blake, he enrolled in the law department of the University of Toronto. In 1861 he graduated with a law degree, and as class medalist received his call to the bar. He immediately moved to Stratford, where his family had settled while Robert was studying in Toronto, to start his own firm. He practised alone for five years before he was joined by his brother James. F.W. Patterson was admitted to the firm in 1878, and when Patterson left two years later he was replaced by F.W. Gearing. The partnership persisted after Robert went to the bench, but dissolved in 1886 when James returned to England.

Smith prospered as a lawyer. Among his clients were many of the area's largest municipal and business concerns, including the Stratford and Huron Railway Company, the Town of Stratford, the County of Perth, and the Merchant's Bank. Protecting their interests frequently took him into local courts, and twenty cases and appeals in which he appeared as counsel were reported in the *Canada Law Journal* and the *Upper Canada Queen's Bench Reports*. They indicated that as a litigator he acted for corporate clients 75 per cent of the time, almost always as defendant, and that he was unsuccessful only five times. Several of the cases in which Smith was counsel became leading precedents in both Ontario and Manitoba. In *Canty* v. *Clark* the court accepted his argument that if a building contract contained a term specifying that work must be completed to the satisfaction of a named engineer, it was a condition precedent to a contractor's right to sue that the engineer must be satisfied.[134] In another case he successfully prosecuted employees of the Great Western Railway Company who tore up tracks belonging to his client. Opposing him were two of the province's leading lawyers, John Idington and M.C. Cameron, both of whom went on to have outstanding careers on the bench.[135]

Smith earned the respect of his contemporaries with his keen, logical mind and their affection with his unfailing politeness. A local paper was referring to both when it discussed his courtroom manner. '[At] one time persuading the doubting, at another confirming the hesitating and, while courteous to his opponent, allowing no opportunity to slip in order that he might pierce the armour of his antagonist.'[136] The

Robert Smith (1839–85). Puisne judge June 1884–January 1885. A lawyer from Stratford, Ontario, Smith came to Manitoba with a penchant for hard work and a weak physique, a deadly combination. He died after sitting on the bench for six months. The ever polite Smith was once described as one of the best lawyers west of Toronto, and quickly won both the respect and affection of the Manitoba bar. (Provincial Archives of Manitoba)

Manitoba Law Journal regarded Smith as a gentleman, and the *Canada Law Journal* described him as one of the best lawyers west of Toronto.[137]

On 15 June 1863 Smith married the daughter of Read Burritt, who was both a two-term member of the provincial legislature and the first county court judge of the County of Perth.[138] Smith and Charlotte Annie had six children, the survivors being Leonard, Margaret Annie, Edward Bewley, and Walter David. Charlotte died in 1875, leaving her thirty-six-year-old husband a widower and father of four.

While living in Stratford may not have made Smith a good lawyer, it was an environment that provided him with the opportunity to excel. Located on the Avon River at the junction of four municipalities, the town was the commercial and cultural hub of one of the most fertile and populous districts in Ontario. In 1870 Stratford's population was over four thousand, and by the time Smith departed for Manitoba, it had more than doubled. Much of the respect Smith earned had little to do with law. His involvement with Stratford's school system made him one of the community's most influential citizens. In the 1870s and 1880s school trustees were important people. They dictated what teachers taught, where they lived, and how they conducted their private lives. And for fifteen years Smith was the town's most influential trustee, first as chairman of the Joint School Board and then as chair of the Collegiate Institute Board. He had stewardship over a high school, central school, and five ward schools, and at least some influence over the community's two Catholic separate schools.[139] Smith was also active in other aspects of public life. He was a member of St James Anglican Church and delegate to its diocesan synod, and sat on the congregation's building committee. In addition, he was a lieutenant in No. 2 Company of the 28th Regiment (Perth Infantry), organized in 1866, seeing duty at Stratford, Chatham, Windsor, and Thorold.

In 1876, a year after the death of his first wife, Smith married Robina Lizars, the older daughter of Daniel Home Lizars, who succeeded Read Burritt as judge of the County Court of Perth. The Lizarses were among Stratford's most prominent families. Before going to the bench Daniel had been crown attorney for the county and one of its leading churchmen. Land he donated was used to build Home Memorial Church, named in memory of a son who died after catching influenza while sleighing in Montreal.[140]

Despite possessing fragile health, or perhaps because of it, Smith seemed to go out of his way to participate in activities that were both dangerous and strenuous. Apart from the militia he was a member of the Victoria Fire Company, one of the founders of the County of Perth Rifle Association, and an enthusiastic duck hunter and cricketer. Not all of his efforts were altruistic or sporting. Both he and his father speculated in local real estate, and during the Manitoba real estate boom of 1883, he bought at least one piece of property 120 miles west of Winnipeg. A Stratford newspaper was not exaggerating when it said of Smith: 'In every scheme for the advancement of the interests of the town, he took a part and spared neither time nor labor in advocating measures fraught with benefit to its inhabitants.'[141]

Although a Conservative, and an active participant in the political process, Smith retained the respect of Reformers. Few doubted the accuracy of the suggestion that '[i]t is an open secret that had he chosen at any time since Confederation to accept the party nomination of North Perth, he would have been elected without any difficulty.'[142] His near 'superhuman' exertions during the 1882 election increased an already considerable debt owed him by local Conservatives, not least of which was owed by S.R. Hesson, the Conservative Member of Parliament for North Perth. In November Hesson wrote the prime minister on Smith's behalf:

> The resignation of Judge Squires of Huron leaves a vacancy on the Bench. At the urgent request of your warmest and best friends here, I write you on behalf of Robert Smith, Q.C. of this place once again asking you to cause that he may be appointed to the vacant Judgeship of Huron. Our friends are united in saying that no legal gentleman in all the West is more deserving of this appointment than our faithful hard working friend who never confined his usefulness to one Riding or County but was ever willing to go where duty to his party called him.[143]

The letter suggested that before November 1882 a movement was already under way to have Smith appointed to the bench, a career move predicated on the belief that what remained of his health would be better preserved if he were a judge rather than a lawyer. When offered the position of deputy county court judge, he accepted, notwithstanding that he had both a political and a professional right to expect a more prestigious appointment. Although Smith was gazetted as the Deputy Judge of the County Court of Perth on 14 June 1884, before his appointment became official negotiations to send Smith to the bench in Manitoba heated up. The federal minister of justice had earlier written a letter to Smith offering him the seat, but when pressure was exerted on the prime minister to appoint Albert Clements Killam, a prominent Winnipeg lawyer, he held it back:

> [I had] written to Smith of Stratford offering him the Manitoba Judgeship but had not mailed the letter. I will keep it back until I have seen you. Smith is not only recommended by Adam Wilson but by Christopher Robinson and others as an excellent lawyer and they much need such a man in Manitoba. Hesson and other friends have pressed him. I think he should be preferred to the other [A.C. Killam].[144]

Within days of the minister of justice's letter to the prime minister Smith's appointment was announced, and on 26 August 1884 he was sworn into office by Chief Justice Wallbridge. His gentle manner and considerable knowledge of the law were both immediately apparent and, from beginning to end of his six-month tenure, he was regarded as able and conscientious. That did not mean, however, that his decisions were above criticism. When he held that orders-in-council could be proven by publication in the same volume as provincial statutes, he was taken to task by the *Manitoba Law Journal*, which suggested that Smith got it wrong. Publication was never intended as a means of proof, but as a statement of the procedure for proving.[145]

What evidence exists of the few judgments handed down by Smith suggests he wrote without pretension, but with a literary flair. Referring to trading companies, he said, 'No doubt, amidst the turmoil and haste of the commercial world in which they strive for existence and profit, it is absolutely necessary that they should act promptly.'[146] And he was not unaware of the impact his decisions would have on societal and political goals. 'It must not be forgotten also, that it is of interest to a community, such as ours, that as much land should be brought and kept under cultivation as possible.'[147] He also believed that in a frontier community, legal technicalities must sometimes be ignored. As businesses grew in the west, '[t]hey must, in many cases, enter into arrangements and conclude bargains with the utmost speed and at a distance from the head office in order to protect their property, or avert a loss, or gain a profit ... where it would be highly inconvenient to require the use of a seal.'[148]

Although Smith's brother, a physician and fellow resident of Stratford, suggested a move west would be beneficial to Robert's health, that did not prove to be the case. The docket he faced was one of the heaviest in the province's history, and he was forced to sit without a break for days on end, sustaining himself as best he could with stimulants. In the end, weakened from the effects of tuberculosis, he could not handle the strain. On 7 December 1884 he was forced to bed, and when his condition did not improve, he was transferred to the Winnipeg General Hospital. Margaret Annie put on hold her studies at St John's Ladies College to look after her father, and for a while he seemed to rally. A friend even telegraphed his brother James, reporting that Robert looked better than he had previously and that his health seemed to have improved. Early in January, however, Smith's condition worsened, and his wife was sent for. Delayed by a blizzard in Chicago, she arrived on the morning of 20 January to learn that her husband had died the previous day.

After agreeing to allow his body to lie briefly in state at the court house, Robina returned with it to the train station, and the two returned to Stratford. Smith was buried in one of the largest funerals ever held in the community. Just after 3:00 p.m. the procession, with the 28th Battalion Band leading the way, moved from the home of James Smith to St James' Church, and from there to the Avondale cemetery. His body was buried in the family plot next to that of his first wife.[149]

Smith left his family economically comfortable, though not wealthy. Two policies of life insurance were intended to provide for each of his two families, and everything else was to be sold and distributed in like manner. His investments included shares in the Stratford & Huron Railway Co., the Stratford Gas Company, and the British Mortgage Loan Company of Ontario. Guardianship of the younger children of his first marriage was given to James and one of his brothers-in-law.[150]

Robert and Robina Smith were the parents of two sons. Bruce Longworth became a bank manager and a member of the board of the Royal Trust Company, while his brother had an even more distinguished career. Robert Home Smith graduated from the University of Toronto before articling in the offices of George Gordon McPherson and John Idington, who became a justice of the Supreme Court of Canada. After practising briefly with the Honourable J.J. Foy he left private practice to spend twelve years as legal counsel to the National Trust Company, and ended his career as one of the country's leading real estate developers. His best-known project involved the development of a large residential site on the Humber River in west Toronto. Although politically active on behalf of the Conservative party, Home Smith never ran in an election, despite being offered a seat in the cabinet of Robert Borden. By the time he died at fifty-eight he had been a long-serving chair of the Toronto Harbour Commission, a member of the Ottawa Planning Commission, the Dominion Good Roads Commission, the board of the University of Toronto, and the boards of the Toronto Land Corporation, Algoma Central & Hudson Bay Railroad, Lake Superior Corporation, and Huronian Mining and Finance Company. He was also a member of the country's most exclusive clubs, including the York, Toronto, National, Albany, and Lambton Golf Clubs.[151]

Following the death of her husband Robina moved into the Lizars family home, located two doors away, where she and her sister Kathleen raised her two sons. Kathleen Macfarlane Lizars was named after her father's law partner and was a woman of exceptional talent. Educated in Toronto and Scotland, she spent three years as private secretary to her uncle John Robson while he was premier of British Columbia. When his term of office ended in 1892 she returned to Stratford. Four years later Kathleen and Robina published the first of their three highly successful books, *In the Days of the Canada Company*, a biography of John Galt and an anecdotal history of the Canada Company.[152] Despite a somewhat overblown writing style, not unusual for the late Victorian era, and little attempt to hide the author's biases, the book was a fascinating social commentary. It became a best-seller and received favourable reviews in newspapers throughout England and North America.

In 1897 the Lizars published their second book, *Humours of '37 Grave, Gay and Grime: Rebellion Times in the Canadas.* Although their style was again a little flamboyant, it was obvious that the two enjoyed poking fun at conventional histories. 'Like lichens on rocks, myths have grown about that time; but myth is worth preserving for the sake of the germ of truth which gave it birth. Historians sometimes tell the truth, not always the whole truth, certainly never anything but the truth, and nothing is to be despised which gives a peep at the life as it really was.'[153]

The cynicism embedded in their second book was even more apparent in their third. *Committed to His Charge, A Canadian Chronicle*, although written in the style of a romantic novel, was pure social commentary.[154] Set in the imaginary community of Slowford, a thinly veiled reference to Stratford, the book overflowed with caricatures of real people. Singled out for particular attention was Mrs Stuart, one of the few residents seemingly aware that a world existed beyond the town's boundaries.

> She read the current literature of a light kind, and, with her boy, had a passing idea of each month's reviews, of the personal and political gossip of the outside world. Above all, she had an inkling that Slowford was not the centre of the universe ... In a sense she despised the persons whom circumstances had placed socially above her; but she was very human, and often longed for what she despised but could not have ... Mrs. Stuart saw nothing of the thresholds of her fellows. She would not know those whom she could, and the other members of that mysterious Inquisition called Canadian Society had decided that she could not know those whom she would.[155]

Praise for *Committed to His Charge* was universally positive. The *Globe* reviewed it twice, first noting that it 'is now exciting so much attention in England, where it has already been published,'[156] and then applauding its abundant humour and fine character studies. The *Canadian Churchman* referred to the sisters as Canada's Jane Austen, while *The Westminister* likened them to Ellen Thorneycroft Fowler. 'There is the same tendency to epigram, the same keen and sympathetic outlook on human life, and may we say the same curious aberration of vision with regard to some of its departments.'[157]

While Kathleen went on to write *The Valley of the Humber*[158] by herself, Robina devoted her time to her children and her music. She was firm-willed and took her responsibilities as a single mother seriously. When Robert Home wanted to become an architect she refused to allow it and insisted that he follow his father and grandfather into law.[159] Robina was also an accomplished musician. For twenty-seven years she was her church's organist, a well-known music teacher and pianist, and for a time a member of the executive of the Ontario Music Teachers' Association. Robina died in Niagara-on-the-Lake on 26 August 1918. She, Kathleen, and Robert Home are buried in a family plot in Toronto's Parklawn Cemetery.

Although he did not live long enough to establish a legacy of judgments, Robert Smith was regarded as one of the finest individuals to sit on a Manitoba bench. He had a precise, logical, and subtle mind, and enjoyed talking about the law. John Ewart expressed the view of the entire profession when he referred to Smith as one of the finest men who ever adorned the bench.

4

The Manitoba Bar Comes of Age, 1885–1907

The years separating the appointment of Albert Killam to Manitoba's Court of Queen's Bench in 1885 and that of William Egerton Perdue eighteen years later marked a watershed in the province's history. Most of the first lawyers to practise in Manitoba had either retired or died, and the professionalization of the provincial bar was largely complete. While the growth of the profession had slowed from the heady days of the preceding decade, the province's lawyers finally succeeded in consolidating both their position in, and visions of, Manitoba.

An indicator that the Manitoba legal profession had finally come into its own by the end of the nineteenth century was the growing demand that the province's superior court justices be appointed from the local bar. In 1884 the *Manitoba Law Journal* suggested that 'it is humiliating to be (in effect) told that out of our whole bar there is not one fit to be a judge, that Manitobans are less advanced than the natives of India, from among whom her judges are now frequently appointed.'[1] The *Manitoba Free Press* was equally outspoken. The time has come, it suggested,

> when Manitoba's own men should be selected for appointments in this Province. It is nothing short of an insult to our people to pass them over time after time in favor of outsiders. The Manitoba bar is as well organized and as respectable as that of any other Province. It includes not a few men who, in ability, learning and all that is held to constitute a claim to legal preferment, will compare favorably with the best of their Eastern

> brethren. Why should these be passed over? Why should Manitoba be treated in a manner to which no other Province would submit?[2]

Although not the first, Killam's was one of the few Manitoba judicial appointments that was not the result of considerations of either patronage or political expediency. More important, it was an implicit acknowledgment that the bar of a province barely fifteen years old was sufficiently mature that at least one of its members could be entrusted with the responsibility of helping to shape the future of a country still searching for a national identity. Killam's elevation also changed the criteria for future appointments. From 1885 onwards the Manitoba bench became the exclusive preserve of Manitoba lawyers, a change that brought no complaints from the eastern bar. As the *Canada Law Times* pointed out, 'Mr. Killam though educated in Ontario belongs to the Manitoba family of lawyers and is a credit to both Provinces.'[3]

Between 1885 and 1903 the face of both Winnipeg and the province of Manitoba underwent a dramatic transformation. From a frontier community of 19,000 residents Winnipeg had grown to a city of more than 56,000, geographically divided by the Red and Assiniboine Rivers and the tracks of the Canadian Pacific Railway.[4] The division was both physical and cultural. The wealthy and members of the upper class resided on large lots situated on wide, well-treed streets that ran along the Assiniboine River in the city's south end. To the west the middle class lived in modest houses on narrower lots, while eastern European and working-class British immigrants resided north of the CPR yards. For Winnipeggers, 'the unequal distribution of wealth was a fact of life.'[5]

Rural Manitoba had undergone a similar if somewhat less dramatic change than that experienced by the province's capital. The small treed bluffs that had previously dotted the prairies had given way to ploughed fields and protective cottonwood shelter belts designed to shield both human and animal occupants from biting northern winds. By 1886 the old way of life in Manitoba was gone, and what less than two decades earlier had been a Metis community subsisting on the vestiges of the fur and buffalo trades had become a British-Ontarian province whose engine of steady if unspectacular growth was Winnipeg's 400 retail merchants and 80 wholesale concerns.[6] Just as the shape of Manitoba's landscape had undergone a dramatic transformation by the turn of the century, so too had the way in which the province's citizens thought of themselves. There had grown in the minds of most a provincial consciousness, although changes in the way things were done were more often the result of large farms and a small population than unhappiness with tradition.

With the establishment of the Winnipeg Grain Exchange in 1887, Manitobans increasingly came to regard Winnipeg not just as their provincial capital but as the metropolis of the west. It was, however, a feeling that was seriously challenged between 1885 and 1896. Immigration slowed from 60,000 in 1882 to 21,000 five years later, and it was not unusual for settlers to give up their holdings in Manitoba in favour of emigration to the prairies of the United States. For those who remained the times were difficult. Below-average rainfall and mounting municipal debts were but two of the hardships experienced by Manitobans. By the mid-1890s, however, things had begun to change. After a decade of stagnation the province enjoyed a period of spectacular growth. A drop in railway rates coincidental with bumper crops and an increase in the demand for western wheat and cattle brought an economic windfall to farmers. In addition, efforts by the federal government to attract European immigrants were starting to pay off, and Manitoba began benefiting from one 'of the great population movements of history.'[7] This wave of settlers differed from that which flooded Manitoba in the late 1870s, however, and making their first sustained appearance were Swedes, Hungarians, Danes, Norwegians, and Icelanders.

What W.L. Morton referred to as 'the Red River era in Manitoban politics' lasted from the province's entry into Confederation until the provincial election of 1886.[8] Before Thomas Greenway, a former Ontario Liberal Member of Parliament, arrived in Manitoba, government was based on the joint participation of French and English politicians in a communal representative system. Although there had always been opposition members in the legislature, the province lacked the kind of party organization seen in eastern Canada. Beginning in 1882, however, Greenway became the unofficial leader of a growing number of highly partisan legislators who regarded themselves as 'provincial righters' in the mould of Ontario's premier Oliver Mowat.

When John Norquay resigned as premier in December 1887, he was succeeded by one of his ministers, D.C. Harrison of Minnedosa. After losing two by-elections the Harrison administration also resigned, and on 18 January 1888 Greenway became the premier of Manitoba. Almost immediately he introduced a bill calling for the redistribution of the province into thirty-eight electoral districts. Although the bill gave residents of the newly settled regions of the province seats in the legislature, it did away with the old concept of communal representation. In the June general election only five opposition members were elected, marking 'the triumph of Ontario over Quebec.'[9]

Between the fall of the Norquay administration and his own defeat eleven years later, Greenway worked to refashion the bicultural province whose government he had inherited into one reflecting the British-Ontario heritage of most of its citizens. First, he abolished the official use of French in the legislature, provincial courts, and civil service, then followed that with a bill doing away with the province's dual school system. The public funding of French and English schools had been both a financial and political fact of life since Manitoba entered Confederation; but the new premier argued that a change was necessary because, although a minority of the population, Catholics were receiving proportionately more by way of school grants than were Protestants. After the Judicial Committee of the Privy Council upheld Greenway's public school legislation in 1892, a group of Manitoba Roman Catholics appealed the premier's decision to the Governor-General-in-Council. Their right to do so was challenged, and the dispute once again reached the Judicial Committee, which decided in favour of the plaintiffs. The federal Conservatives then intervened by exercising Ottawa's constitutional right to demand that the Manitoba school legislation be repealed. Greenway refused. Although the 1896 federal election brought the Liberals and Wilfrid Laurier to power, and the federal and provincial governments quickly reached a political compromise over the schools issue, the political damage to Greenway was fatal. In 1896 Manitoba Conservatives elected as their leader the youthful and dynamic Rodmond P. Roblin. Sensing that the only thing likely to prevent his party from winning the next provincial election was a better-known leader, Roblin stepped aside in favour of Hugh John Macdonald, the son of the country's first prime minister. The move worked, and in 1899 the Conservatives took office. Prominent among their number were several lawyers.

The formation by Manitoba Liberals of the province's first permanent party organization in 1885 offered a new avenue for members of the bar to showcase their 'abilities in the appropriate organizations which were political in organization and aims.'[10] As the biographies of the judges described in this book illustrate, practising law and running for elective office were complementary pursuits for many practitioners. In the 1893 provincial election, for instance, eight of the forty men elected to the legislature were lawyers, prompting the editor of the *Western Law Times* to lament that the results compared unfavourably with those of parliamentary elections, where lawyers typically represented one-quarter of those elected.[11] The election of even a single member of the bar, however, was too many in the opinion of one reader of the *Manitoba Free Press*. Lawyers, the writer argued, were occupationally unfit for elective office because their commitment to the doctrine of precedent contributed to the passage of bad laws, and their pursuit of government patronage kept them aloof from the concerns of regular Canadians.[12]

By 1895 a decade of depression had given way to a period of economic growth and prosperity, and for Manitoba lawyers the 'the essential aspects associated with professional life were in place.'[13] Ten years earlier the University of Manitoba had established a three-year reading course leading to a law degree, and in 1890 new rules were put in place to clarify and tighten the expectation the profession had of students-at-law. A year later a series of formal lectures were introduced by the Law Society in response to demands of the newly formed Law Students Society, and on the literary side the *Manitoba Law Reports* became the first legal journal of its kind published in western Canada. In 1890 the *Western Law Times* succeeded the now defunct *Manitoba Law Reports* and provided lawyers with reports on cases, news of the profession, and legal articles.[14] Among changes in the law that significantly affected members of the bar was the right of lawyers to charge clients a contingency fee, something that could be done nowhere else in the British Commonwealth;[15] and for the first time permanent police magistrates staffed municipal benches, although it was not until 1902 that the court was fully staffed by men with legal training.

Restructuring police courts, however, did little to lessen the workload of the Queen's Bench judges. Following the death of Lewis Wallbridge on 20 October 1887, the work of the court barely slowed. Two days later he was replaced as chief justice by Thomas Wardlaw Taylor, and the vacancy created on the bench was filled by John Farquhar Bain, the second practising member of the provincial bar to be appointed to the judiciary. In 1899 Taylor retired, Killam was made the province's chief justice, and Albert Elswood Richards filled the puisne vacancy created by Killam's elevation. When Killam went to the Supreme Court of Canada in 1903, Dubuc, in his twenty-fourth year on the bench, became chief justice. Filling the empty seat created by Killam's departure was William Egerton Perdue, another of the bar's leading lights.

By 1905, however, the justices of the Court of King's Bench were still severely overworked, a situation made worse in May of that year by the death of Bain (who was replaced in August by Thomas Graham Mathers) and the physical infirmity of Dubuc and Perdue. One of the reasons for the on-going health problems experienced by members of the King's Bench was the extra burden placed on them by virtue of the fact that they formed both a trial and an appellate court. In the latter capacity they heard not only appeals from cases tried in Manitoba, but also from those heard in the North-West Territories, which became the provinces of Saskatchewan and Alberta in 1905. Part of the problem was alleviated in 1906, however, when the federal government established the Manitoba Court of Appeal. Of the four judges appointed to the new court, two were elevated from King's Bench: Richards and Perdue. That same year Daniel Alexander Macdonald, a lawyer practising in Portage la Prairie but originally from Charlottetown, filled one of the two King's Bench vacancies created by the elevation of Richards and Perdue.

Court data suggest that Manitoba justices were certainly kept busy both before and after the creation of the Court of Appeal. Between 1903, the year after the province created a fourth judicial district,[16] and 1909, 8815 statements of claim were filed in Winnipeg's Court of King's Bench (1259 per year) and the Court of Appeal heard 548 appeals. The main reason Manitoba superior courts were kept so busy was because of the increase in the population of its capital. In 1901 more than 42,000 people resided in Winnipeg, making it the country's sixth largest city.[17]

Until at least the end of the first decade of the twentieth century Manitoba lawyers continually expressed frustration about the understaffing of their provincial benches. In a 1908 letter published in the *Manitoba Free Press* a reader pointed out that 1794 Statements of Claim were filed in the King's Bench that year, just 130 fewer than were filed in Toronto. Yet, said the author, 'In Toronto they have five times the number of clerks and court officials that we have in Winnipeg and twelve supreme court trial judges to our three.'[18]

Although by 1907 vestiges of the eastern Canadian values of the profession's first comers still remained, Manitoba lawyers were now being trained at home and their sense of their profession and their province was no longer derivative. The province's bar had come of age.

ALBERT CLEMENTS KILLAM

Albert Clements Killam was born into a family of wealth and privilege at Yarmouth, Nova Scotia, on 18 September 1849. His paternal ancestors left Yorkshire, England, for Massachusetts in 1637, and 130 years later his great-great-grandfather completed the journey when he emigrated from Wenham to Yarmouth. Killam's grandfather, Thomas, was a prominent merchant, shipowner, and Member of Parliament. He was only thirty-seven when he built his first ship, a 92-ton schooner christened *Sophia*. From 1839 until 1865 he constructed, commissioned, or bought outright between one and six vessels a year. During that period, twenty-five of the sixty ships he owned were lost at sea. Thomas's main business interest was developing a trade network between North America and Great Britain; and to that end his companies shipped a variety of commodities, including fishing supplies, iron, cordage, coal, wheat, and flour.

In 1847 Thomas Killam was elected to the Nova Scotia legislature as a Reformer. He quickly became a member of a number of committees, including the influential public accounts committee. Throughout his career in provincial politics he opposed governmental involvement in the economic development of Nova Scotia, and in 1853 played a leading role in helping the opposition Tories thwart Joseph Howe's attempt to build a publicly funded railway. Differences with Howe and other members of the Reform ministry eventually caused Killam's estrangement from the rest of his party, and in 1855 he won re-election to the legislature as a Conservative. In the mid-1860s he opposed party leader Charles Tupper's desire that Nova Scotia join in creating a new country out of what remained of British North America, and with Joseph Howe established an anti-confederate league to protest Confederation. When the *British North America Act* of 1867 made Canada a reality, however, Killam was elected in the nation's first federal election. Joining the member for Yarmouth were eighteen other Nova Scotians, including Tupper and Howe. After attending the first session of Canada's parliament Killam returned to Nova Scotia, where he became part of a movement to take Nova Scotia out of Confederation. He refused to return to the nation's capital thereafter, believing that by resuming his place in parliament he would be acknowledging the reality of Confederation. Killam died in Digby, Nova Scotia, while the political storm caused by the repeal movement still raged on. The one Halifax paper to mention his passing referred to him only in the context of his defective education, poor grammar, and strong prejudices.[19]

In 1869 Albert's uncle succeeded Thomas Killam as Member of Parliament for Yarmouth. Like the majority of his family, Frank was a shipowner and merchant, and member of the firm Killam Brothers. He was re-elected in 1872, 1874, and 1878, but left politics four years later following his first election defeat. One of his sons followed Albert to western Canada, although Lawrence made his name in academics and business rather than law. From 1914 to 1921 he was a professor of mechanical engineering at the University of British Columbia, and five years later became president and general manager of the British Columbia Pulp and Paper Company. He remained in that position until 1950.

George Killam, Albert's father, acquired a sizeable fortune in his own right. Between 1852 and 1865 he owned twenty-five vessels and was a major shareholder in a variety of Nova Scotia companies, including the Yarmouth Marine Insurance Association, the Acadian Insurance Company, Yarmouth Gas-Light Company, and the Yarmouth Steam-Navigation Company. Like his father, George was actively involved in the affairs of his community. He was a co-founder of the Mountain Cemetery, the Yarmouth Seminary, and the Hiram Freemason Lodge, which he organized in 1848, and for two terms he was a Yarmouth municipal councillor. In addition to being a shipowner, George was a sea captain, and in 1855 he commanded the *Eastern State*, the pride of his family's fleet.[20]

Albert Killam attended elementary and high school in Yarmouth before enrolling at the University of Toronto. In 1872 he graduated with a Bachelor of Arts degree, the silver medal in mathematics and modern languages, and the Prince of Wales medal. After leaving university he became a student-at-law in the Toronto offices of Crooks, Kingsmill & Cattanach. Adam Crooks was called to the bar of Canada West in 1851. Nicol Kingsmill and Alexander Cattanach joined his practice in 1864, and Wellington Francis eight years later. When Killam entered his office Crooks had just begun what was to be a twelve-year career in politics. During the Liberal administration of Oliver Mowat he served as Ontario's attorney general, provincial treasurer, and finally, the province's first minister of education.[21]

Killam left the Crooks firm after two years to finish his articles with Charles Horne, a lawyer in Windsor, who had been born in the West Indies and was called to the bar in 1862. After Killam received his call in 1877 the two practised together until Killam left for Manitoba. He became a member of the Law Society of Manitoba in February 1879 and immediately joined the Winnipeg partnership of William Henry Ross and Arthur Wellington Ross. The following year W.H. Ross died and his place was taken by Alex Haggart.[22] The Ross, Killam & Haggart firm was one of the most successful in Manitoba, and its success was largely due to the real estate dealings of its senior partner. Arthur Ross emigrated from Ontario in 1877, five months before he was to have received his call. As a result, before he could be admitted in Manitoba he was required to obtain passage of a special act of the provincial legislature. Once called he immediately began speculating in real estate, and by 1882 had acquired the eighth most valuable block of real estate holdings in Winnipeg. Whether he acquired his fortune honestly, however, was called into question by the federal government, which accused him of bribing an employee of the Dominion lands branch to obtain advance information about what lands were about to come onto the market.

The Ross firm attempted to take advantage of Killam's family contacts by circulating in Nova Scotia pamphlets advising prospective immigrants to contact the firm before buying land in the west. Questions about the likely success of their efforts became moot when the real estate boom collapsed in 1883. Arthur Ross was ruined overnight. To recover his wealth, and the firm's influence, Ross shifted his focus to politics. Running on an anti–Canadian Pacific Railway platform, he won the federal riding of Lisgar. Two years later, still in debt, he underwent a remarkable transformation and became a key defender of the CPR. He published copies of one of his speeches and circulated them throughout Nova Scotia as an inducement to potential immigrants to buy land in Manitoba. Before the year was out Ross was hired by the CPR to manage construction of its Vancouver terminus. The information he obtained while working for the railway there allowed him to restore his lost wealth, again through speculating in real estate.[23]

Despite devoting much of his time to politics Arthur Ross was an active solicitor who spent most of his in-office time focusing on real estate sales and money lending. Alexander Haggart, too, was a solicitor. Although a much less dynamic individual than either of the Ross brothers, he acquired most of his considerable influence as a bencher and, after the Ross, Killam & Haggart firm dissolved, as a municipal politician. In 1912 he followed Killam to the bench when he was appointed to the provincial Court of Appeal.

Almost immediately on his arrival in Manitoba Killam became a leading member of the Winnipeg bar, and in 1881 a Law Society examiner. A year later he became a bencher, and three years after that Queen's Counsel. He sat on various committees of the Law Society, and while on the bench lectured law students on equity and jurisprudence.

Although Killam's family had long been prominent in politics, it was an enthusiasm he did not share until he became incensed at the federal government's decision to disallow provincial railway legislation. Despite being a life-long Liberal, when he ran in the 1883 provincial election he did so as a Provincial Rights candidate. He easily defeated his Winnipeg South opponent, Charles Richard Tuttle, a colourful local newspaperman, and his election was overwhelmingly welcomed by the local press. It can, said the *Free Press*, 'only be viewed in one light. It is the clear and distinct declaration of the electors of this city in favor of public probity and private worth' and 'the most satisfactory evidence that the electors of Winnipeg are fully alive to the importance of a judicious exercise of the franchise.'[24] Although he made no lasting impression in the legislature, in his two years there Killam was, after party leader Thomas Greenway, the leading figure on the opposition bench.

In 1884 Killam became the senior partner in Killam, Richards, Brophy & Darby. Like Haggart, Richards also became a judge. In both his own and the Ross firm, Killam was a litigator of considerable talent and dominated the provincial bar. In the only year cases were reported before he became a judge, his name appeared as counsel of record sixteen times. His record, however, did not reflect his dominance. He lost as often as he won, was just as likely to represent a plaintiff as a defendant, and usually litigated debt actions.

Killam was thirty-six when he was appointed on 3 February 1885 to the Queen's Bench vacancy created by the sudden death of Robert Smith. His elevation, however, was far from a straight-forward judicial appointment. After James Miller's Rat Portage constituency officially became part of Ontario and he was forced to relinquish his seat, Premier John Norquay wanted to make C.E. Hamilton the province's attorney general. Hamilton was a member of Aikins, Culver & Hamilton, one of the city's largest and most prestigious firms, and had just been elected mayor of Winnipeg. The problem was that he needed a seat in the legislature. Norquay's solution was to persuade John A. Macdonald to appoint Killam to the bench, thereby making his seat in the legislature available to Hamilton.[25] After the deal was consummated the Manitoba premier became increasingly frustrated when the anticipated announcement was delayed. He demanded to know why the appointment had not been made. 'Delay in appointment Killam causing dissension in our ranks. Matter gone so far cannot recede. Answer requested.'[26] Regardless of what part Norquay played in it, the appointment was

Albert Clements Killam (1849–1908). Puisne judge 1885–99, chief justice of the Court of Queen's Bench 1899–1903, justice of the Supreme Court of Canada 1903–5, chair of the federal Board of Railway Commissioners. Killam is regarded as one of the most able jurists in the history of Manitoba, and was the first justice from western Canada to be appointed to the Supreme Court of Canada. He was not reluctant to break new legal ground, and while a member of Queen's Bench often challenged his colleagues to overrule him if they did not agree with his judicial activism. (Provincial Archives of Manitoba)

universally applauded, in part because of the outstanding qualities Killam brought to the bench, and in part because the appointment went to a member of the local bar:

> [We] should not and must not be asked to submit to the bestowal of all our public gifts on Eastern friends of the Government. Manitoba has attained her majority, and must no longer be treated as an infant. She will not submit to treatment which the weakest of her elder sisters would resent. In the matter of our judiciary we have of late felt with more than ordinary bitterness the discrimination of which we have been victims. Our local bar is able and well trained. It is graced by men who would do credit to the bench of any Canadian Court. That these should be passed over time after time in favor of outsiders not a whit more capable than they, was fast becoming intolerable.[27]

The most controversial trial over which Killam presided was the Manitoba Schools case. Although ultimately making its way to the Privy Council, it was grounded on one of the first acts passed by the first Manitoba legislature. In 1870 the province created a board of education that reflected the fact that its population was made up of an equal number of Protestants and Catholics. Two sections were formed, one Catholic and the other Protestant. Twenty-four school districts also came into being. Of these, twelve were under the control of the Catholic board and twelve under the control of the Protestant board. Provincial funding was divided equally between the two sections. Among the first members of the Catholic board was future Manitoba chief justice Joseph Dubuc; and John Norquay was a prominent member of the Protestant board. Between 1870 and 1878, however, Manitoba underwent a profound change. Most of those settling in the province had come from Ontario, and they were both Protestant and English-speaking. By 1878 the proportion of Franco-Manitobans fell from one-half to one-third, and a year later a flood of new immigrants reduced it to one-sixth. It was clear that a change in school funding was needed, and so the legislature changed the financing scheme established in 1870 and began funding sections of the school board in proportion to the number of Protestant and Catholic children who resided in districts where schools existed.

After the Riel Rebellion of 1885 the movement to end the funding of Catholic schools picked up steam. It became a full-blown political controversy in 1889 when Ontario ultra-Protestant, Dalton McCarthy spoke at an Orange Order banquet in Portage la Prairie. He urged his audience to pressure the Manitoba government into abolishing the funding of Catholic schools. In the audience was Attorney General Joseph Martin. He promptly announced his support for McCarthy's proposal, and told those in attendance that he would no longer sign official documents written in French. Within two months the *Manitoba Gazette* was published in one rather than the usual two languages, and in 1890 the government introduced an education bill that denied funding to any public school providing religious instruction. Because the Catholic church refused to allow its members to educate their children in schools that did not offer religious instruction, the new law would force Catholics taxpayers to support schools to which they could not send their children.

Dr J.K. Barrett was a Catholic taxpayer who resided in Winnipeg. He sued the provincial government on behalf of all Manitoba Catholics, arguing that the provincial education act was invalid because it was not within the power of the province to deprive Catholics of their schools. When the Barrett case came before him, Killam was asked to decide on the constitutionality of the legislation. On 21 November 1890 he denied Barrett's application and held that the statute was within the jurisdiction of the provincial legislature. His decision was reversed by the Supreme Court of Canada, but restored by the judicial committee of the Privy Council.

Other important cases with which Killam was involved included *The Queen* v. *Riel, Gibbons* v. *Metcalfe,* and *C.P.R.* v. *Cornwallis.*[28] In *Gibbons* Killam held that the Winnipeg grain exchange was not a combination in restraint of trade, and in 1885 he joined a unanimous bench in dismissing Riel's appeal.

Killam was one of the most committed judicial activists in the history of the Manitoba bench. Although he paid lip service to the notion of precedent ('In a case, exactly similar ... I should feel bound to come to the same conclusion'),[29] he went out of his way to raise hypotheticals not considered by counsel and to make rulings he challenged his colleagues to overturn.[30] Typical of his approach was *McKenzie* v. *Fletcher,*[31] where he noted, 'There is a further point which I merely suggest, as it does not seem to have occurred to the parties.'[32] These types of comments served two purposes: they allowed him to focus argument on the area of law that he considered most relevant, thereby allowing him to make new law; and they allowed him to point out to counsel the weakness of their performance. In *Winnipeg and Hudson's Bay Co.* v. *Mann,*[33] despite the fact that all four counsel were leaders of the bar, he suggested that 'there are some questions which have not been fully discussed before me. It appears to have been almost assumed upon all hands that the bill is sufficient upon this part of the case.' Killam then showed that such was not the case, and pointed out what the real issue was. 'I desire to deal with this question merely for the purpose of this application, as no argument upon the point has been addressed to me.'[34]

When counsel did not fully appreciate the point of law on which Killam wanted them to focus, Killam was not reluctant to take control. In an estate action, for example, he listened to the argument of the plaintiff with great patience, then 'I intimated to counsel for the parties my opinion ... I then suggested to counsel to consider who would have been obliged to bear the loss if the stock had turned out a very unprofitable instead of a very profitable investment.' And it was on this last point that he based his decision.[35] Perhaps because of the role he played in advancing arguments not raised by counsel, he often suggested his decisions should be challenged in a higher court. 'I hope that the question itself or the result of the present suit, may be considered by the parties to be of sufficient importance to induce them to take the opinion of a court of final resort upon the point.'[36]

Although Killam had the reputation of being polite to members of the junior bar, such was not always the case with senior counsel, litigants, and the provincial legislature. He found the attitude of one defendant so offensive, for instance, that he said, '[I]f I had the power, I would not merely deprive him of costs, but also make him pay at least the costs [of] the plaintiff.'[37] In a criminal action he was equally critical of the Crown. 'I trust that, upon the application to quash the conviction, it may be shown that the proceedings were not conducted in as arbitrary a manner as just now appears.'[38] And in comments applauded by the editors of the *Western Law Times* as 'vigorous and impressive,' he illustrated in what ways the provincial *County Court Act* was deficient:

> I trust that the next session of the Legislature will not pass without an amendment of the practice relating to appeals from the County Courts ... It is a disgrace to the administration of justice that so much time should be wasted in the courts in the consideration of such objections as we have so frequently been obliged to give effect to in respect of these appeals and some other applications to the court. I hope that some more elastic practice will be provided, which will leave to someone some discretion in this matter.[39]

The judgment that arguably best illustrated why Killam had so much influence over other members of the bench involved a mortgage action. Because it dealt with the purchase of an equity of redemption, it permitted him to discuss the famous case of *Boultbee* v. *Shore*,[40] in which Chief Justice Wood had held that in Manitoba there had been a fusion of law and equity. Until the issue was revisited by Killam, Wood's decision was accepted as the law. Killam started out as he usually did when criticizing the decision of another judge, then proceeded to show why the case was bad law. 'I have the greatest respect for the learning and ability of that great judge,' but in his opinion Wood's judgment not only went too far, it totally ignored the fact that courts of law and courts of equity had existed for centuries. 'The only purpose that I can conceive the two systems to be intended to serve was that which they formerly served - to administer the two systems of law separately.'[41]

On 15 April 1899 Killam succeeded Thomas Wardlaw Taylor as the province's chief justice. At the time Isaac Campbell was one of the most senior lawyers in the province, and one of the most respected. When offered the vacant chief justiceship by Prime Minister Laurier he suggested that it go instead to Killam, since he knew more law.[42] Even before that appointment was made, however, Killam was being touted for a seat on the Supreme Court of Canada. In 1895 the *Western Law Times* discussed at some length his outstanding performance on the Manitoba bench and suggested that, if the government were finally to appoint a westerner to the country's highest court, he was the ideal candidate.[43]

Between 1895 and 1903 the *Western Law Times* continued to promote both Killam's appointment to the Supreme Court and the concept of regional representation on it. The main critic of the idea was the *Canada Law Journal*, which warned that '[t]his miserable political necessity of appointing men to the Bench because they represent some sect or section has been, and will be, disastrous to the best interests of the Dominion.'[44] Despite the opposition of the *Canada Law Journal*, however, members of the western bar were becoming increasingly strident in their demands that one of their own be appointed to the Court. They passed resolutions, raised the issue in the House of Commons, and undertook an intense lobbying effort. And the man who most wanted to occupy the first western seat on the court was Killam. On 8 August 1903 Ottawa agreed, and the appointment met with approval from almost the entire Canadian bar:

> We congratulate the Dominion Government upon its recent appointment to the Supreme Court Bench. From the time that Mr. Albert Clement Killam, K.C., a pronounced politician of the Reform stripe, was chosen by Sir John A. Macdonald to fill a vacancy in the Manitoba Bench, the wisdom of the selection then made has been shewn. Mr. Justice Killam's reputation as a lawyer has grown with his years and he has proved to be a most painstaking, able and impartial judge. It is not inappropriate that the best of our judges in the West, transplanted from the extreme East, should succeed the most able jurist of our premier Province in the position he held in the highest court of the Dominion. His removal will be a great loss to Manitoba, but a gain to the country at large.[45]

Killam's tenure on the Supreme Court of Canada lasted only two years. In 1903 the federal government was under considerable pressure from organizations like the Toronto Board of Trade, the Canadian Manufacturers' Association, the Cattle Dealers' Association, and the United Fruit Growers' Association to create a railway commission with the authority to adjust and control freight rates. In March the federal government succumbed to the pressure, and introduced an amendment to the federal *Railway Act*. It abolished the Railway Committee of the Privy Council, established a three-person Board of Railway Commissioners, and gave the new body the power to regulate rates and control both the operation and equipment of trains. Because there would be no appeals from Board decisions on questions of fact, the government agreed that the chairman of the Commission would be someone acceptable to Canadian rail companies.[46]

Two months after the government's amendment became law Andrew George Blair resigned as minister of railways and canals in a dispute over Laurier's decision to support the Grand Trunk Railway's proposal to become a national rail line. To limit the political fallout from his resignation the prime minister made him the Board of Railway Commissioners' first chair. Less than a year later, however, he resigned. The dilemma for the government was twofold. It had to find a replacement acceptable to both railways and to rail users, and it had to find someone sufficiently conservative to be counted on to proceed with caution through what were still considered uncharted waters.

In choosing Killam as the Board's second chair, the government hoped to deflect western criticism over freight rates and grain handling. Killam's rationale for accepting the position, on the other hand, was unclear, although it likely had something to do with money. The $10,000 a year he would receive as chairman of the railway commission was a substantial increase over what he received as a justice of the Supreme Court of Canada. Before accepting the post, however, he demanded the same kind of job security that he had as a judge. To accommodate Killam, Laurier was forced to amend the *Railway Act* to provide that when a superior court judge was appointed chairman of the commission, he could not be removed except by motion of both the Senate and House of Commons. Satisfied, Killam presided over his first meeting on 6 February 1905.

In his first year on the Board, the commission issued over a thousand orders and heard 353 cases. The workload proved overwhelming. Killam was only fifty-eight when he died of pneumonia on 1 March 1908.[47] Although his official duties required him to reside in Ottawa for much of the year, Killam had continued to maintain his principal residence in Manitoba. His body was transported back to Winnipeg in the private railway car *Arcadis*, and he was buried in St John's Cemetery next to the grave of his daughter. Killam's funeral procession left the family residence on Roslyn Road shortly after half past two and proceeded in solemn order down Osborne Street to All Saints' Church. A majority of those in attendance followed the funeral cortege on foot. Among that group were most members of Winnipeg's bar, a large number of the city's leading citizens, Mayor Harvey, several aldermen, members of the provincial cabinet, and, leading the cortege, officers of the Law Society of Manitoba. When the procession arrived at the doors of the church it was met by His Grace Archbishop Matheson, who read the Anglican service for the burial of the dead. After the ceremony Killam's body was removed from the church while the 'Dead March' was played. The procession then reformed on Broadway Avenue, and the late chief justice was conveyed down Main Street to the cemetery.

Killam was eulogized as a judge of above-average ability in both local and national newspapers:

> With his wide knowledge of the law, his great industry, his untiring patience, and his large endowment of what is termed the judicial temperament, he was, during the twenty years that he was on the bench, one of the greatest judges of the Dominion, and his successive promotions into wider spheres of influence were the natural result of his ever-growing reputation as a jurist.[48]

Albert Killam's reputation within the Manitoba legal community had always been high, in part because of his wide knowledge of the law, a prodigious work ethic, and his untiring patience with younger lawyers. Few members of the bar or bench possessed his scrupulously judicial temperament. His decisions, with sentences often more than fourteen or fifteen lines in length, were clear, convincing, and usually upheld on appeal. As an individual he was dignified, unassuming, charming, and unfailingly kind.

JOHN FARQUHAR BAIN

John Farquhar Bain was the eldest of eight children born to the Reverend William and Annie Bain. William was a native of Nairn, Scotland, and emigrated to Canada in 1838. After a short career in teaching he entered Queen's College as a theological student. A year after he graduated he took up what became a thirty-five-year pastorate at St Andrew's Church in Perth, Ontario.[49] Two of the reverend's four sons became lawyers, one became a physician, and the fourth was a Toronto executive. One daughter lived for much of her adult life with John, a second lived with another brother, one died in infancy, and nothing is known about the fourth.

John Bain graduated from Queen's University with a Bachelor of Arts degree before becoming a student-at-law. Although he was one of nine students to pass his examinations and be called to the bar in Hilary Term 1870, because he did not finish in the top two he was required to take both a written and an oral exam. Bain practised in Perth for less than a year before emigrating to Manitoba. He arrived in June 1871 to become one of the first lawyers called to the provincial bar. Before the provincial legislature passed *An Act to Regulate Admission to the Study and Practice of Law in Manitoba*[50] the previous May, anyone could call himself a lawyer, and practise as such. Bain was the seventh lawyer called to the bar of Manitoba, although he was only the fifth with legal training. He was, according to a contemporary, 'the best lawyer of them all.'[51] The *Manitoban*'s assessment of his abilities, however, was coupled with something less than enthusiasm for lawyers generally: 'Seeing that lawyers are a necessary evil and that the righting of wrongs is to a great extent in their hands, we cannot but feel the great advantage of having gentlemen like Mr. Bain, who has passed through his legal course with marked ability, and who brings with him the highest possible recommendation.'[52]

In 1873 Bain and Dubuc were appointed commissioners charged with settling Metis land claims. Their recommendations were in the main adopted by the federal government, and the exposure the two gained did much to solidify their reputations as leaders of the local bar. If any further exposure was needed, Bain got it from the infamous Lord Gordon Gordon case. In July 1874, Marshall & Son, a firm of Scottish jewellers defrauded by Gordon, learned that was living just outside Winnipeg. They immediately obtained two warrants for his arrest, one charging him with obtaining goods under false pretenses, and the other with bringing stolen goods into Canada. The firm's Canadian agents hired Bain to assist a private constable sent to arrest Gordon, to ensure that the apprehension was carried out legally. Just before midnight one day before the arrest was to take place, Bain was at home when two men hired to help the constable arrived at his residence. He suggested that Gordon be apprehended late the following evening, making it difficult for him to obtain the services of a lawyer before being whisked out of the province. The next morning Bain examined the warrants for Gordon's arrest and had them endorsed by a local justice of the peace. Bain, the constable, and the two private police officers then waited until almost ten o'clock in the evening before confronting the fugitive. The public inquiry held following Gordon's arrest and suicide made everyone involved in the escapade a celebrity.

Most of the work that Bain did in the years immediately following his arrival in Manitoba was far less exciting than capturing criminals. He quickly became solicitor of record for companies like the Central Railway Company of Manitoba, the North-West Railway Company of Manitoba, and the North-West Company. In 1873 Bain and Sedley Blanchard formed one of the first and most successful legal partnerships in Manitoba's early history. Blanchard was a native of Truro, Nova Scotia, and had been called to the bar there in 1871. He came west as the private secretary of Lieutenant-Governor Adams Archibald, a fellow Nova Scotian, and as clerk of the Executive Council. When he and Bain became partners they made a formidable pair. Both were competent, personable, and ambitious. It was their good fortune to meet just as the province was embarking on a ten-year period of almost unrestrained growth. It was even more their good fortune, however, that the engine of that growth was their client, the Hudson's Bay Company.

Although Bain did some work for the company, most was done by his partner, who often acted in the dual capacity of lawyer and agent. For example, when the HBC wanted to build a bridge across the Assiniboine River, it realized that if it became known that it was behind the scheme, the costs associated with the project would immediately rise. As a result, when the Assiniboine Bridge Company was incorporated in 1879 Blanchard held the company's shares in his own name. Similarly, when the company-owned Winnipeg and Western Transportation Company was created, Blanchard was one of the incorporators.[53]

But even if such involvement brought sizeable legal fees into Bain & Blanchard, they paled in comparison to what could be earned speculating in real estate. After the land department of the Hudson's Bay Company was organized in 1872 the company began selling off much of the property it acquired when Manitoba became a province. Sales started slowly, however, and over the next seven years generated revenues of only $100,000. That changed in 1881. During a twelve-month period the company sold 62,400 acres of land for just under half a million dollars. The province was undergoing a full-scale land boom, and with less than one in four purchasers settling on the land they bought, speculation became an integral part of business life. Firms like Bain & Blanchard provided an important service to out-of-province investors. Their knowledge of the market, coupled with an understanding of the law and local personalities, ensured that speculators would get what they paid for.

It was a heady time for members of Manitoba's young bar. Many 'built their practices employing the same basic strategies which were designed to respond to the rapidly changing needs of an agricultural-mercantile-service economy. Until the land boom was finished, lawyers advertised conveyancing services, the availability of money to loan on mortgages and real estate agency services.'[54] Competition among lawyers for a share in the thousands being spent on legal fees was fierce. When one expatriate Ontario solicitor persuaded a Hamilton loan company to transfer its business to his firm, the company's current lawyer refused to hand over his work-in-progress. Before long other lawyers were trying to persuade the lender to make yet another change.[55]

By the time the boom ended in 1884, Blanchard was not only the Hudson's Bay Company's lawyer, but one of its largest customers. Within a month, lots he purchased in Regina for $3600 increased in value to over $100,000. His client was not impressed, however, and was even less impressed with his purchase of a large block of land in

Winnipeg. As the 1882–3 boom was nearing its end Blanchard and two associates agreed to pay the HBC $280,000 for a parcel of land located just outside the city's business core. Each partner paid to the company $18,000 as his share of the deposit, but even before their purchase was complete the three resold a portion for $275,000. Although they eventually lost most of their profit on other speculative ventures, the partners remained obligated to the Hudson's Bay Company for the unpaid balance. The fact that their own lawyer made such a huge profit at their expense upset company directors, and they instructed their Winnipeg agent to change solicitors. To make matters worse, Blanchard no longer had any money, and he was unable to pay his share of the remaining debt. Although the company was owed nearly one million dollars by dozens of failed speculators, it was Blanchard's debt that caused most concern. The company's local agent was Blanchard's friend, and he tried to deflect the outrage of the directors:

> In regard to Mr. Blanchard, – he is in possession of a considerable amount of property, at present unsalable, but no cash, – to proceed against him would simply result in obtaining a judgment, which would result in nothing. All the property he owns has been bought, as is the case generally throughout this Country, one time, and subject to a mortgage for the balance of the purchase money. In a great many cases at present the properties could not be sold for the amount of the mortgage.[56]

By 1885, however, Hudson's Bay Company directors felt they had been victimized enough. Not only were they paying their lawyers over $15,000 a year in fees, but Blanchard had left them with more than a quarter million dollars in bad debts. The following spring they replaced Bain & Blanchard with the firm headed by the prime minister's son.

Despite the embarrassment caused Bain by the land dealings of his partner, the partnership flourished, in part because of the efforts of the firm's junior partner. William Redford Mulock was born in Ontario, educated at Queen's University, and practised for ten years with the prestigious Toronto firm of Blake, Kerr, Lash & Cassels. His father, like Bain's, was a clergyman, and Mulock took an active part in the Canadian Bible Society, the missionary efforts of the Anglican church, and the Manitoba temperance movement; and he worked on campaigns to raise funds for the blind and to rehabilitate criminals.

By 1883, aside from Mulock, Bain, and Blanchard the firm included E.D. Carey, Howard Morphy, and William Egerton Perdue. Of all his associates, however, Bain probably appeared in the court the least often. Only five of his cases were reported, and he was on the losing side in four. When not in his office, he devoted much of his time to the affairs of the Law Society. He was one of nine benchers mentioned in the statute incorporating the society, and when the organization met for the first time in the spring of 1877 he became its first treasurer. He continued as such for three years before becoming president. From 1881 until Blanchard's death in 1886 he was often out of the province attempting to recover his health, and he did not resume his involvement with the society until he was asked to complete the term of his late partner. Other bodies with which Bain was involved included Manitoba College, on whose board he served for many years, the St Andrew's Society, the Manitoba Club, and the Winnipeg General Hospital.

These extra-legal activities were typical of attempts by Manitoba's first lawyers to attract both public attention and clients. The most successful of the Bain partners at doing so was Blanchard. When he died in 1886 from the effects of typhoid fever, the entire Winnipeg business community closed for his funeral. Attending were local members of the Law Society, St George's Society, St Andrew's Society, the Manitoba Rifle Association, and the city's elected council, of which he had been a member. The funeral procession of the man described as one of the bar's brightest ornaments and most useful members was over a mile long. It included more than 150 vehicles.[57]

Although Bain kept the firm intact following his partner's death, it was dissolved when he went to the bench on 15 November 1887. The first suggestion that Bain might be appointed appeared in the *Montreal Herald*, and was indicative of how both the Manitoba bar and the press reacted when the appointment became official:

> There is a vacancy on the Manitoba bench, and it is much to be hoped that it may be offered to Mr. J. F. Bain. That gentleman is the senior partner of the oldest legal firm in Manitoba; a firm that has stood among the first in the profession in the Province since its establishment. Mr. Bain enjoys the confidence of the Bar and of the Province generally, both on account of ability and character. There was a time when the Bar of Manitoba could not be relied upon to supply material for the bench, but that day is passed, and the appointment of Mr. Bain would meet with the approval of everybody.[58]

Although Bain was never the focus of judicial controversy, many of his cases were the subject of intense public interest. One example was the first he tried. Thomas Newton appeared before Bain on 14 March 1888, charged with murdering John Henry Ingo during a dispute over a dog. The last time anyone had been convicted of murder in Manitoba was in 1883; and the last hanging was in 1877. Newton was found guilty and Bain's first verdict was a sentence of death. It was not carried out, however. Instead of being hanged, Newton was released from jail and banished. Bain's next murder case was even more controversial than his first, although the role he played was much different. In 1889 a Chicago grand jury charged an Illinois man with murdering a prominent local physician. Before the accused could be arrested he fled the jurisdiction. A short time later Winnipeg's chief of police noticed someone matching the description of the fugitive waiting to board a train and arrested him. Extradition proceedings were immediately begun, and the following month the prisoner appeared in front of Bain. Counsel for the accused murderer argued that the warrant for his client's arrest was invalid, since it was based on depositions taken in a foreign court in the absence of the accused. Bain disagreed, and his decision was upheld when the matter was re-heard by the full court. The accused was returned to Chicago, where he was tried and convicted.

Another prosecution heard in 1889, although of little interest to the general public, involved an issue of considerable importance to the legal profession. Six years earlier a Portage la Prairie lawyer had defrauded two clients out of money, and the Law Society obtained an order demanding that he show cause why he should not be disbarred. The issue at trial was in what capacity the funds had been received by the lawyer, and whether misconduct as a solicitor meant a lawyer could be prevented from practising as a barrister. The issue was more easily settled in England, where a lawyer could be either a barrister or a solicitor, but not both. In Manitoba a court had the power to disbar a lawyer acting in his capacity as a barrister, but it was not settled law whether it could also disbar a lawyer for misconduct committed while acting as a solicitor. Bain believed it could not do so, arguing that 'it would be unduly straining the meaning of the provision which is essentially a penal one, to hold that it gives us power to strike a member off both rolls, when he has been shown to have misconducted himself in the discharge of his duties in one branch of the profession only.' Aware that his decision was bound to be the subject of considerable debate, Bain agreed it was absurd to strike a lawyer off the rolls of solicitors but allow him to continue to practise 'in the higher and more honorable position of a barrister.' But, he pointed out, such an anomaly was for the legislature to correct, not the court.[59]

Throughout most of his adult life Bain suffered from health problems, and in the years preceding Blanchard's death spent most of his time outside the country. On at least one of those occasions he recuperated in India. In 1903 he went underwent a tumour operation in England and while recovering stayed at the home of Lord Strathcona at Knobworth. He died nineteen months later while a patient at Montreal's Royal Victoria Hospital. His funeral was held in Perth, where he was interred.

Bain was a member of one of the strongest benches in Manitoba history. And although not of the calibre of Taylor and many of his successors, he was cordial, pleasant to be around, and respected.

ALBERT ELSWOOD RICHARDS

Albert Elswood Richards was born on 10 July 1848 into a family of prominent lawyers, judges, and politicians. One of his uncles was the first chief justice of the Supreme Court of Canada, another the Lieutenant-Governor of British Columbia, his father was Commissioner of Crown Lands for Ontario and Treasurer of the Law Society of Upper Canada, and one of his sons a justice of the Manitoba Court of Appeal.[60]

Both of Richards's parents came from wealthy and influential Brockville families. His grandfather, William Buell, became a hero of the Battle of Cryseler's Farm during the War of 1812, when he and eight hundred members of the local militia defeated a force of almost six thousand Americans. His fourth daughter married Stephen Richards, Albert's father, who happened to be a business associate of Buell's.

The Richards family had multiple connections to members of Canada's political and legal establishments. Among the most connected was William Buell Richards, who in 1848 ran as a Reformer in Leeds, defeating Ogle Robert Gowan.[61] His close friendship with Robert Baldwin secured his position within the Reform party, and following his re-election he became Attorney General of Upper Canada in the Hincks-Morin administration.

Albert Norton Richards, the younger of Albert Elswood's uncles, was called to the bar of Upper Canada in 1848 and practised at Brockville. In the 1850s he became a prominent member of the South Leeds Reform establishment, and in 1863 its member in the provincial assembly. He was solicitor general under Sandfield Macdonald from 26 December until the end of January 1864, when he was defeated in the by-election called to confirm his appointment. In 1869 he left Ontario to serve as attorney general for the North-West Territories, accompanying would-be governor William McDougall during his ill-fated attempt to establish a federal mandate in the Red River Settlement. When Manitoba entered Confederation, Richards's appointment as attorney general was rescinded, and he returned to Ontario. Three years later he ran as a Liberal in the federal constituency of Leeds South and sat in the House of Commons for two years. He did not contest his seat in the subsequent general election and gave up his law practice to emigrate to British Columbia. For several years he acted as the federal government's west coast legal agent, and in 1876 became the province's lieutenant-governor. When his five-year term expired he became a Victoria police magistrate.

Albert Elswood Richards's only personal involvement in the political process occurred in 1896, when he was elected to represent Ward One on Winnipeg's city council. When his term expired he retired from municipal politics and was appointed to the city's board of licence commissioners. Following the death of R.W. Jameson in 1897 he became the board's chair.

The most famous and influential member of the Richards family arguably was someone who had nothing to do with either law or politics. Frances Elswood Richards was the daughter of Albert Norton Richards, and a well-known artist and musician. After earning a reputation in New York, London, and Paris she returned to Canada, and in 1881 was made an associate of the Royal Academy of Art and director of the Ottawa Art School. The following year she began what became a close friendship with the Irish poet and dramatist Oscar Wilde. Her portrait of him sparked his comment 'What a tragic thing it is, this portrait will never grow old and I shall,' and became the inspiration for his famous novel *The Picture of Dorion Gray*.[62]

Richards's father and uncles were all professionally prominent, although William Buell Richards achieved the greatest professional acclaim. After receiving his call in 1837 he practised briefly with George Malloch before joining the law firm of his uncle, Andrew Norton Buell. In 1853 he was appointed to the Court of Common Pleas and ten years later became its chief justice. Although not considered brilliant he was widely regarded as a judge of unusual common sense. Few of his decisions were overturned; and that, together with his keen sense of humour, earned him the respect and affection of his peers. In 1868 both factors probably played a part in influencing his appointment as chief justice of Ontario's Court of Queen's Bench. One of the most famous cases over which he presided was the trial of the assassin of Thomas D'Arcy McGee. Another involved the trial of a number of political associates of John A. Macdonald. Their conviction for campaign bribery forced the prime minister to give up his seat and run in a by-election.

In 1871 William Richards was active in discussions about the feasibility of establishing a Canadian supreme court. When Prime Minister Alexander Mackenzie brought the court into being four years later Richards became its first chief justice. Also appointed was William Alexander Henry, James McKeagney's brother-in-law. During much of his term on the court William Richards was a spokesman for those who believed that it should be completely separate from the legislative arm of the federal government. He was knighted in 1877, and subsequently appointed deputy governor general of Canada.

Albert Elswood Richards was educated at Toronto's prestigious Upper Canada College and at the University of Toronto. He was determined if not gifted academically. In his second year at Toronto he was in the bottom third in four of five courses, and in his final year, despite a first in chemistry and a second in mathematics, was also in the bottom third. He graduated with a Bachelor of Arts in 1870 and earned a Master's degree the following year. He then became a student-at-law, where he was again a relatively poor student. In his third year he received 144 out of a possible 240 marks, and stood fourteenth in a class of seventeen. Last was Thomas Mayne Daly, a future mayor of Brandon and Canada's first juvenile court judge.

Richards received his call on 13 February 1874 and returned to Brockville from Toronto to become county crown attorney and clerk of the peace for Leeds and Grenville. Within a year, however, he and Christopher Finlay Fraser, who had been a lawyer in the office of Albert Norton Richards, became partners. Three years later they were joined by Edward J. Reynolds, and the firm became Fraser, Richards & Reynolds. After the partnership dissolved in 1881 Richards practised alone for twelve months before emigrating to Manitoba. His application for admission to the provincial bar was accepted on condition that he article for a year; and on 23 May 1882 he agreed to spend that time under the supervision of Sedley Blanchard. After receiving his call Richards practised alone until joined by C.W. Bradshaw. The firm remained intact until Richards went to the bench. Neither partner was an experienced litigator and that was especially true of Richards. Between 1885 and 1895 only six cases in which he was counsel were reported. In five he acted for a corporate client, and in five he acted on an appeal. His expertise as solicitor did not go unnoticed, however, and the *Toronto Star Weekly* suggested that he was one of Manitoba's most prominent corporate counsel. Despite lacking a reputation as a barrister, Richards earned the respect of the bar. Between 1883 and 1899 he twice served as Law Society treasurer, twice as secretary, and his record for continuous service as bencher was unusual, especially among small-firm members of convocation.

On 1 May 1899 Albert Richards followed in the footsteps of his illustrious uncle when he was appointed a puisne judge of Manitoba's Court of Queen's Bench. Although regarded as a competent judge, Richards was not above making it clear to a jury where his sentiments lay. Before he became a Winnipeg police magistrate, Robert Blackwood Graham was one of many to complain about Richards's pro-defence bias. Referring to a trial involving Robert Andrew Bonnar, one of the province's most illustrious defence counsel, Graham suggested that Richards's 'charge was even a better address for the defence than was Bonnar's. He magnified the weaknesses of the Crown's case and minimised those of the defence. He reversed the process with regard to the strong points in each.'[63]

While on the bench Richards was a member of two royal commissions. In 1901, filling a vacancy created by the sudden death of Judge Edmond Sinclair, he was charged with investigating the shipping and transportation of grain by railway companies in Manitoba and the North-West Territories. He subsequently played a key role in drafting the first federal *Grain Act*. Two years later he was charged with determining whether a number of lumber companies had combined in restraint of trade.

When Manitoba established a Court of Appeal in 1906 Richards became one of its first four justices. He was still a member of that court and only sixty-nine when he died of cancer on 27 May 1917. After Killam and Dubuc he was Manitoba's third-longest-serving superior court judge.[64]

WILLIAM EDGERTON PERDUE

William Edgerton Perdue was the thirteenth judge appointed to Manitoba's Court of Queen's Bench. The families of both of his parents had roots in Ireland, where one of his maternal ancestors, Sir Julius

Caesar, was a judge during the reign of King James I. Perdue's mother emigrated from Ireland with the rest of her family in 1810, twenty-two years before his father was to do so. Michael Perdue and Margaret Caesar were the parents of four sons and one daughter. William was the only who did not farm.[65]

When Michael, his four brothers, and a sister settled west of Toronto in what is now Brampton, they were one of the area's few non-Aboriginals.[66] As the community grew, so too did Michael's prominence. For most of his adult life he was either a councillor or the reeve of his municipality, and between 1866 and 1877 he served as justice of the peace. His farming interests included raising and showing Devon and Hereford cattle, and for a time he was president of the Brampton Exhibition.

William Egerton Perdue was born on the Second Line East, Lot 26, Chinguacousy, Peel County, Canada West, on 20 June 1850. He was a good student, and instead of playing during recess like the rest of his classmates typically stayed inside, reading in the school library. He was not excused from his responsibilities on the family farm, however, and in 1867 he won prizes for showing Devon, Hereford, Calloway, and Angus cattle at the Provincial Exhibition in Kingston.[67]

The first school attended by William was a log structure containing a single desk, around which students sat on benches. From there he graduated to the Brampton High School, where his classmates included Sir James Albert Manning Aikins and Sir Thomas White, the latter of whom became a prominent Member of Parliament. Perdue's high school education was interrupted briefly when he left school to apprentice as a grocer. During that period he worked in the election campaign of a local lawyer and the experience encouraged him to finish his education. While in high school his poetry was sufficiently mature that a local newspaper published excerpts. After leaving Brampton he attended the University of Toronto, where he usually ranked in the top third of his class. In 1873 he graduated with a Bachelor of Arts degree and first-class honours in the classics. For the next two and a half years Perdue was headmaster of his former high school. He and an assistant taught fifty students, for which Perdue received a salary of between three and four hundred dollars a year. When his school inspector suggested that he had a brighter future in law than teaching, Perdue agreed and returned to Toronto.[68]

After studying in several law offices Perdue completed his articles with Macdonald, Macdonald & Marsh, the Toronto firm headed by

John A. Macdonald, the Conservative prime minister. At the same time, he was hired as a legal reporter by the country's leading Liberal, the *Globe*'s George Brown. This irascible newspaperman hired Perdue primarily because, in his letter of application, the future judge went to great lengths to explain what he could do for the paper. According to Brown, Perdue 'understood better than the others who applied [for the job] exactly what it is I want, and you make better suggestions of your own than any of the others.' The offer of employment, at $15 a week, was temporarily withdrawn when Brown learned that his new reporter was articling with his political enemy. As he threw down his pen and turned away, the publisher wanted to know what Perdue had to say for himself:

> Mr. Brown, I hope to be called to the bar before many months are over, and then to enter upon the practise [*sic*] of my profession. I intend to devote myself to my clients interest to the best of my ability and to be faithful in serving them. If you do me the honor, sir, to appoint me Osgoode Hall reporter for the *Globe*, I will consider the *Globe* my first client, and I will hold it to be my duty that I must give the *Globe* faithful loyal service.[69]

Perdue was called to the bar in 1879, and with Frederick Wright immediately established the firm of Perdue & Wright. Within months, however, Perdue left to practise with Dennis Ambrose O'Sullivan. Their partnership persisted until the spring of 1882, when Perdue met Heber Archibald. What the prominent Winnipeg lawyer had to say about the west excited him, and before the year was out Perdue moved to Winnipeg, where he immediately became a junior in Bain, Blanchard & Mulock. When the firm dissolved five years later he spent almost four years practising on his own. Between 1890 and 1900 he was senior to Thomas Robinson in Perdue & Robinson, and during his last three years at the bar practised with S.J. Rothwell. The two were still partners when Perdue went to the bench in August 1903. Contemporaries described him as a successful lawyer with a 'splendid' practice.[70]

Even before he left Ontario Perdue realized that to succeed in the practice of law it was necessary to attract the attention of others. One way he did that was as a case reporter for the Law Society of Upper Canada and as editor of volume eight of the *Ontario Practice Reports*. His use of writing as a means of becoming noticed persisted, and within weeks of his arrival in Manitoba the *Canada Law Journal* published his

'Fusion of Law and Equity in Manitoba.' The article was a brief analysis of Chief Justice Wood's decision in *Boultbee* v. *Shore*.[71] Although the extent to which Perdue's conclusions were misguided was made clear in Justice Killam's indictment of the judgment, his article was among the first authored by a member of the Manitoba bar.

Another way Perdue came to the attention of his peers was through the short-lived Winnipeg Legal Club. Its aims included promoting the study of the law, cultivating public speaking, and the writing of essays on topics of interest to the profession. That the club was noticed by lawyers is born out by the fact one-third of the local bar became members. The *Manitoba Law Journal* also gave it a ringing endorsement:

> We believe that the refining influence of such clubs extends both to the intellect and the manner; that the tone and standard insensibly adopted is almost always that of the most cultivated member and sometimes reaches even a higher plane. All that young men, as a rule, require for their education in polite demeanour is the presence of a proper ideal during action – extended, of course, over a period sufficiently long to closely associate the one with the other.[72]

Perdue was one of the club's founders and its first president. A year after it was established he was asked to be a Law Society examiner. His relationship with the Society changed three years later when he was elected a bencher. An association with one of the province's premier law firms no doubt influenced his first election; but in 1888 he was practising alone, and his subsequent success likely had more to do with his reputation than any other factor. In the 1898 elections forty-one lawyers received votes, and Perdue was tied for first with perennial top vote-getter Isaac Campbell. Perdue's total surpassed those of the acknowledged leaders of the bar, including a future chief justice, the son of the prime minister, the senior partner in the province's largest law firm, and a future justice of the Court of Appeal.[73]

Perdue was a bencher from 1888 until he went to the King's Bench in 1903. During that period he spent six years as Law Society treasurer (1892–8) and three as president (1898–1901). Although his involvement with clubs and the Law Society unquestionably attracted attention within the profession he was more widely known as a litigator of exceptional competence. Between 1884 and 1899 fifty-six of his cases were reported, no doubt a small fraction of the number with which he was involved. Nevertheless the data reveal that two-thirds of the time he appeared in the Queen's Bench, that he won a third more often than he lost, that he was just as likely to represent a corporation as an individual, and that he acted for a plaintiff as often as he did for a defendant. In short, Perdue was prepared to act for whomever had the resources to retain him, and in doing so won the respect of the judges before whom he appeared. Chief Justice Taylor's comment that Perdue was very 'able' was an accurate assessment.[74]

Three years after arriving in Winnipeg Perdue married Mary Fairbanks Macdonnell, the fourth daughter of a prominent Whitby lawyer. The two were the parents of a daughter and three sons, one of whom was killed in the battle of Courcellete during the First World War. Another son articled in Manitoba with a future justice of the Supreme Court of Canada.[75] Although a life-long enthusiast of shooting and fishing, Perdue's chief hobby was reading. His main literary interests were history and poetry, but he worked hard to keep up with the most recent developments in politics and business. He was reputed to be one of the first to argue publicly in favour of using the natural resources of Manitoba as the foundation on which to build the province's industrial base. Socially, he spent much of his leisure time in two of the province's most exclusive clubs, the Manitoba and St Charles Country Clubs. Perdue was an active member of the congregation of Holy Trinity Anglican Church, in addition to being involved in politics. Although he never sought elective office personally, he often chaired political meetings and campaigned on behalf of Liberal candidates in several elections.

Perdue was appointed to the Court of King's Bench on 25 August 1903. Two weeks later he was honoured at a banquet sponsored by members of the Winnipeg bar. Welcoming the new justice to the bench was John Ewart. The well-known barrister was an out-spoken nationalist and earned an international reputation for his appearances before the Supreme Court of Canada and the Privy Council. Instead of paying tribute to the guest of honour Ewart embarked on a bitter attack on the judiciary. He accused judges of engaging in acts that gave rise to doubts about their impartiality and, without referring directly to Perdue, said judges were increasingly viewed by the public as being in the pocket of politicians and corporations. 'I am firmly convinced that the recent Governmental practice of giving jobs to judges [is] subversive of the usefulness of the Bench, because it is destructive of the popular belief in its impartiality and integrity.'[76] Ewart then drew the audience's attention to two recent controversies involving members of the judiciary. 'Two of the very best and purest-minded of the Ontario judges are believed by probably scores of thousands of people to have been influenced by circumstances not found in the evidence.' Furthermore:

> In Dawson City, at the present moment, a judge, who, till yesterday, was a strong political partisan, is inquiring into matters in controversy between the political parties. And can we be surprised that his rulings are being telegraphed to the Opposition at Ottawa to be there discussed and denounced? While Mr. Justice Britton's salary runs at the usual rate, he is presented by his political friend with the finest holiday trip that the continent can afford and a bonus of $2,000. His judicial usefulness in every case of political complexion is forever gone.[77]

As Perdue and his fellow judges sat in silence Ewart turned his attention to the man who until a few weeks earlier had been a practitioner. He warned of the temptations to come:

> My Lord, now that you are Mr. Justice Perdue, you will be approached by the railway companies, and will be offered free transportation over their lines of railway. It is my belief that you will refuse all such degrading offers. If it be asked whether I think that Government jobs and railway passes influence judges, I reply that human nature is weak; that motive and mental influence work subtly, and their operations are much more easily discerned by onlookers than by the one affected; that such things usually do produce a frame of mind favorable to the donors, and that I myself, with all my innate and trained respect (reverence, I would almost say), for the Bench, cannot sometimes restrain the thought that elevation to the Bench is not equivalent to inoculation against the feelings of gratitude for past favors or pleasing anticipations of those to come.[78]

Ewart continued his harangue by suggesting that there was little to distinguish between members of the judiciary accepting appointments to royal commissions and accepting gifts from corporations:

> My Lord, it is a fact of some sinister significance that the political parties, the Governments and their Oppositions, have in these later days become the most frequent of litigants, and that the practice which I am venturing to condemn has grown up and expanded synchronously with the development of that condition. My Lord, I see no justification for the employment of judges in matters outside their office and not covered by their salaries in the assertion that it is the Governments of the day that are the

William Egerton Perdue (1850–1933). Puisne judge of the Court of King's Bench 1903–6, judge of the Manitoba Court of Appeal 1906–18, chief justice of Manitoba 1918–29. Perdue was unfailingly polite on the bench, and was respected for his learning and patience. He was one of the province's most literate jurists. While he was in high school his poems were regularly published in Brampton newspapers, and within weeks of his call to the bar of Manitoba he published an article in the *Canada Law Journal*. He was one of the founders and the first president of the Winnipeg Legal Club, an organization dedicated to the publication of essays on legal topics. (Provincial Archives of Manitoba)

> employers and paymasters. The 'Government of the day' is but an euphemistic alternative for the name of some particular politician, representing some political party ... If from the Government of the day, whose members are deeply interested in much litigation, why not from the Canadian Pacific Railway, or the Hudson's Bay Company? Would it be sufficient reply to such employment to say that the judges were too pure and too little human to be affected by such engagements and if, my Lord, judges may accept free transportation from the railway companies and be unaffected, why may they not also accept a cask of wine from Mr. Galt, a bale of silk from Mr. Stobart, or a bag of flour from the Ogilvie Milling Company.[79]

Although Perdue did not respond to Ewart's harangue, the editors of the *Canadian Law Review* welcomed it as valid criticism of a judiciary increasingly consisting of men elevated to the bench as a reward for services rendered. It suggested that what made the employment of judges in extra-judicial matters reprehensible was the fact that such appointments were accepted entirely for monetary reasons. This, they argued, prostituted the bench and destroyed public confidence in its impartiality.[80]

Despite his silence during Ewart's commentary on the flaws of the judiciary, Perdue was seldom reluctant to engage in social commentary. For instance, he attributed an increase in criminal activity taking place in Winnipeg to deficiencies in the character of recent immigrants. When a grand jury empanelled in November 1905 returned a presentment laying the blame for crime on the doorstep of the federal government's department of immigration, Perdue agreed. The problem, he suggested, was that

> a great many foreigners had been induced to settle in Winnipeg, owing to the great advantages the city afforded of securing immediate employment at a high rate of wages, and when they got together in large numbers, as they had done in the north end, there was always danger of their lapsing into the condition from which they came ... and it might be a question whether it was not about time the government ceased, at all events, to discourage the immigration of certain nationalities.[81]

The 'north end' to which Perdue referred was the home of most of the city's eastern European immigrants, many of whom were Jewish.

Perdue was not easily intimidated by counsel. In one of his first assizes counsel for a defendant was R.A. Bonnar, one of Winnipeg's most flamboyant lawyers. When the Crown asked permission to call a witness who had been scheduled to testify the previous day, but had failed to show up, Bonnar immediately leapt to his feet and protested, suggesting that 'the request is so preposterous, it is hardly worth objecting to.' Perdue overruled the objection, sarcastically referring to Bonnar's defence as 'extraordinary.' Bonnar again protested, this time at what appeared to be the court's bias against the defence he was presenting on behalf of his client. He too turned sarcastic. 'I suppose I have the privilege of conducting the defence.' That was enough for Perdue. 'Yes, but I want you to understand that I do not intend to take any impertinent remarks from any counsel here, and certainly not from you. When you address this court you must address it respectfully.' Only after Bonnar withdrew his remarks and apologized did the trial continue.

Perdue's judgments suggested that he often injected into his decisions a sense of morality. One instance occurred during the trial of an action for alimony. The petitioner and respondent separated following the birth of the wife's child, delivered four months after they were married. The husband was neither the child's father nor aware that his bride was not a virgin on the day of their wedding. While making it clear that he felt that such cases should be settled out of court, Perdue carefully traced the applicable law through the statutes and cases of Manitoba to those of Ontario, and from there to the divorce and ecclesiastical courts of England. His judgment was succinct and persuasive. Despite finding in favour of the wife, he made it clear that he was morally offended by her conduct:

> The plaintiff in the case I am deciding inflicted on her husband one of the greatest wrongs a woman could do to a man. She humiliated him in the eyes of the world and made their marriage a subject for mockery. In such painful circumstances the wisest thing a man can do is to make the best arrangement he can with the unhappy woman who has done him the wrong, but who bears his name and is his wife.[82]

A second example involved the right of a lawyer to contract with a client to share in whatever was recovered in a court action. Perdue engaged in a considered and persuasive discussion of the law of maintenance and champerty before noting that, while most Canadian judges believed that both were part of the criminal law of England and therefore of Canada, he disagreed:

Perdue headstone. Perdue and many other judges appointed to the Court of Queen's Bench are buried in Winnipeg's St John's Cemetery. His simple headstone, like those of many of his colleagues, reflects the lack of pretention of many of the members of the province's highest trial bench. (Charles Roland Brawn)

> I am aware that expressions have been used by a high authority to the effect that the law of maintenance and champerty is in force throughout Canada as part of the criminal law of England. This, however, I would say, with great respect, was a mere *obiter dictum* in so far as Manitoba is concerned, and, as I have endeavored to show, the clause in the Dominion statute purporting to introduce that law differs widely from the other sections introducing the criminal law of England into other provinces.[83]

After explaining the basis for his belief, and holding that Manitoba lawyers had the legal right to enter into contingency agreements with their clients, he stated for the record his personal opinion. 'I can see nothing morally wrong in such a bargain between solicitor and client.[84]

Perdue sat as a puisne judge of the Court of Queen's Bench until 23 July 1906, when he was elevated to the newly created Court of Appeal. Twelve years later he succeeded H.M. Howell as chief justice. He was eighty years old in October 1929 when ill health forced him to retire. Although his resignation did not become effective until the end of the year, he spent his last three months in office on a leave of absence. For his twenty-five years on the bench he received an annual pension of $8000.

Perdue died of influenza on 16 January 1933.[85] Although kindly, courteous, affable, and mild-mannered, he was also considerably more:

> [E]ndowed in a very full measure with that intangible but invaluable quality known as the judicial temperament. In the courtroom he has displayed not only great learning and ability but also infinite tact and infinite patience, coupled with the necessary forcefulness to be at all times in complete control of every situation that developed and commanding respect, not because he was clothed with arbitrary powers which counsel and litigants feared would be used arbitrarily against them, but purely and simply because he conducted his court in such a manner as to merit the respect which was freely given.[86]

THOMAS GRAHAM MATHERS

Thomas Graham Mathers was born in Lucknow, Ontario on 16 April 1859. His Irish parents had emigrated to Canada shortly after they married, residing briefly in Toronto before moving to Lucknow.[87] Thomas was one of five brothers to leave Ontario for Manitoba. One sibling became the head of Winnipeg General Hospital's psychopathic ward, while the other four lived in Neepawa, a town located approximately 120 miles west of Winnipeg.

Mathers received his early education in Lucknow and Kincardine. His legal education, however, was taken in its entirety in Winnipeg. In 1883 he moved from Ontario to Portage la Prairie to edit the *The Manitoba Liberal*, a local newspaper. The following July he quit to become a student-at-law in the Winnipeg offices of Hagel & Davis. Before he was even entitled to practise the provincial government made him its right-of-way solicitor, a position he held until 1890.[88] As right-of-way solicitor Mathers was responsible to the Liberal administration of Thomas Greenway for handling all legal work associated with construction and operation of the Red River and Portage la Prairie railroad extensions.

After receiving his call to the Manitoba bar in 1890 Mathers resigned as government railway lawyer to practise with G.F. Munroe and G.H. West in the firm of Munroe, West & Mathers. That association lasted until January 1895, when he joined the Portage-Winnipeg firm headed by Joseph Martin. Martin, an Ontario native had arrived in Manitoba in 1882, and before entering politics practised law in Portage. When the Greenway government took power in 1888, he became the province's attorney general and its railway commissioner. In both capacities he lived up to his nickname, 'Fighting Joe.' He was seldom reluctant to use physical force to back up an argument and made little effort to hide his political partisanship or anti-French and anti-Catholic biases. After appointing Mathers his railway solicitor, Martin decided to lease the provincially controlled Red River Valley Railway to a Manitoba subsidiary of the Northern Pacific Railway, which agreed to assume responsibility for its completion and operation. His choice of an American company incensed the *Manitoba Free Press*, and it accused him of accepting a bribe. Although the libel suit he filed against the newspaper was thrown out of court, a royal commission of inquiry cleared him of any wrongdoing. In 1891 Martin was fired as attorney general and returned to private practice, where he was joined by Mathers. Two years later the former provincial cabinet minister was elected to the House of Commons. After losing his seat in the 1896 general election, Martin left the province to practise in British Columbia, and Mathers joined the firm headed by Hector Mansfield Howell, remaining with Howell (a future chief justice of Manitoba) until he went to the bench.

A year after he began practising with Martin, Mathers married twenty-one-year-old Jessie Waugh, daughter of the editor of the *Northwest*

Farmer. Richard Waugh was born in Scotland, where he apprenticed as a stonemason. Before emigrating to Winnipeg in 1882 he designed and built farmhouses and churches throughout Scotland. In Winnipeg he began writing for a living, and an interest in farming led to his co-founding the Manitoba Dairy Association. By the time Waugh retired, his knowledge of farming had brought him to the attention of much of the North American agricultural community. The elite of Winnipeg's political and social communities attended his funeral, and a painting of him hangs in Convocation Hall at the former Agricultural College of Manitoba. Mather's brother-in-law was Richard Deans Waugh, mayor of Winnipeg in 1912 and 1915 and the husband of Harriet Lillie Logan, whose father Alexander was one of the province's most honoured pioneer settlers and himself a four-time Winnipeg mayor.[89]

While in practice Mathers specialized in litigation, building up what the *Manitoba Free Press* referred to as 'the largest litigious business in the west.'[90] Between 1890 and 1905 sixty cases in which he appeared as counsel were reported. He won only slightly more often than he lost, except when representing corporations, when he won twice as often. Most of his clients, however, were individual plaintiffs. As competent as Mathers was, his last partner was even more so. When he joined Howell in 1899 Mathers's new partner was already widely regarded as one of the most dynamic counsel in Manitoba. The only lawyer with a reputation as large was James A.M. Aikins. The two were both senior partners in large and prestigious law firms and both possessed enormous egos. That was evident a year after Mathers and Howell became partners. When neither Howell nor Aikins could agree on who had been called to the bar first, thereby becoming the most senior lawyer in the province, they asked the Court of Queen's Bench to decide the issue. Although Howell had received his call in Ontario before Aikins, the court decided in favour of Aikins, since he was the first called in Manitoba.[91]

One way that Mathers attracted the attention of the public, and of potential clients, was through his involvement in politics. In 1890 he was elected president of the Liberal party's provincial organization, and the following year he became president of the Winnipeg Liberal Association. In 1893 he was one of the organizers and first president of the Young Men's Liberal Club, representing it at the convention that chose Wilfrid Laurier as leader of the Liberal Party of Canada. His first foray into elective politics occurred in 1897, when he won by a large margin to become alderman for Winnipeg's Ward 2. Thereafter, Mathers 'at once took a prominent position in the council and after serving one year he was unanimously elected chairman of finance and acting mayor.'[92] When his two-year term expired he sought the mayor's position full-time. His campaign against Horace Wilson was both colourless and uneventful. If the two did not treat each other as best friends, they at least regarded one another with respect. Although Mathers won four of the city's six wards, he was out-polled decisively in Winnipeg's two most heavily populated working-class districts and lost the election by seventy-two votes. When the results were announced Wilson told those assembled at the Leland Hotel that his opponent was 'a splendid specimen of a gentleman' and had acted like one throughout the campaign. As a result, he suggested, there had not been 'an ill word spoken.'[93]

Apart from law and politics Mathers was a passionate sports fan and an enthusiastic hunter and golfer. Before going to the bench he was an active member of Winnipeg's rowing club, a curler, and one of the founders of the exclusive St Charles Golf and Country Club. He was also a member of the very private and prestigious Manitoba Club. While a Winnipeg alderman he was instrumental in creating a board to manage city bicycle paths, and served as the body's first chair.

Mathers was appointed a justice of the King's Bench on 24 August 1905, succeeding the recently deceased Mr Justice Bain. Five years later he became the court's chief justice, a position he retained for seventeen years. In twenty-two years as a trial judge he presided over a number of famous cases and, despite his reluctance to break new legal ground, a number of his judgments have stood the test of time. Ironically, perhaps, two of his most notorious cases involved the same party, the czar of Russia. The first pitted the Russian ruler against a former treasurer of the department of the interior in the province of Turkestan. After embezzling over $160,000 in government funds, Ivan Proskouriakoff fled with his mistress to Japan, where he purchased more than $50,000 worth of goods. He then made his way, goods in hand, to Winnipeg, where he purchased several pieces of real property and a large number of chattels. After czarist officials located the fugitives, Russia filed a statement of claim in the Court of King's Bench and obtained an order attaching the fugitive's Manitoba assets.

What made the case so fascinating to Canadians was the exotic, even romantic, background of the defendant. Proskouriakoff, whose Winnipeg home became the rendezvous for some of Russia's most notorious outlaws,[94] was regarded as a helpless romantic who gave in to the temptation of his mistress, an attractive but dangerous and uncompromising nihilist. Over a period of two years the case proceeded through the courts, with decisions rendered by the Referee, King's Bench, the provincial Court of Appeal, and the Supreme Court of Canada. Mathers's involvement began in the spring of 1908, when the defendant moved to set aside an order of attachment obtained by the plaintiff.[95] Under its terms the sheriff seized the assets that the defendant left behind when he fled to Chicago, just days before a request for his arrest arrived from Russia. Mathers held that, because the defendant ceased to reside in Manitoba before the action was commenced, he had no authority to enforce against him a claim for money, unless Proskouriakoff voluntarily submitted to the jurisdiction of the court.

A month later the case again came before Mathers, this time by way of an application to set aside an order of the Referee allowing the plaintiff's statement of claim to be served substitutionally. In granting the application Mathers noted that the Referee had grounded his order on an affidavit which stated that the defendant was still a resident of Manitoba, although in hiding. He pointed out that the individual who gave the affidavit had also given one in an earlier proceeding, and in it he had sworn 'that the defendants had absconded from Manitoba for the purpose of defrauding their creditors.' Mathers said that he had no choice but to set aside the Referee's order, grounded as it was 'on the affidavit of a man whose conscience apparently so easily accommodates itself to the exigencies of the case.'[96] Two months after his second judgment was rendered, appeals from both decisions were dismissed by the provincial Court of Appeal.[97] An appeal to the Supreme Court of Canada was quashed four months later, and the following year the parties reached an out-of-court settlement.[98]

The second case involving the czar of Russia was even more exotic. The defendant this time was Savaa Fedorenko, a member of the Social Democratic Party, whose objectives were the overthrow of the Russian government and the abolition of private landholding. In January 1908 Fedorenko and a friend were spending the night in the village of Levkovka, in the district of Uman, when their presence came to the attention of the local constable. He and several watchmen immediately went to the home in which Fedorenko was staying. When the constable noticed that Fedorenko was dressed in expensive clothes, he suspected that the man was on an illegal mission and demanded that he submit to questioning at the village administrative office. Instead, the revolutionary pulled out a gun, shooting one of the watchmen before escaping. A year and a half later the Russian government learned that Fedorenko was living in Winnipeg and filed an application for his extradition. The issue before Mathers was whether the murder was committed in the furtherance of a political cause. If it was, Fedorenko could not be extradited. If it was not, he would be returned to Russia for trial.[99]

The hearing lasted more than two months. It was attended by Russian émigrés from all over the world, and Fedorenko's defence was funded by the Russian Freedom League. Although Mathers ultimately conceded that the accused was a member of a revolutionary party, and that at the time the offence occurred Russia was in a state of civil war, he held that the murder was not committed in furtherance of a revolution. Fedorenko was ordered extradited, but before the order could be carried out an application for *habeas corpus* was brought before Mr Justice Robson.[100] After being released and re-arrested, the Russian was eventually freed.

Although the two czar of Russia cases attracted a great deal of national and international attention, so too did a murder trial over which Mathers presided in 1914. In that case the accused had robbed a bank in a small town in southern Manitoba, killing the bank manager in the process. He escaped, was quickly captured, and escaped again when an associate smuggled a gun into his jail cell. The resulting manhunt was one of the largest in Winnipeg history. The trial itself was almost anticlimactic. The evidence proved conclusively that John Krafchenko was guilty, and he was duly convicted of murder and hanged. From a legal point of view, however, Mathers was forced to make a ruling that proved to be a source of considerable controversy within the legal community.[101] Until 1837 prisoners on trial for murder were not allowed to give evidence on their own behalf. To ensure that his or her story was heard by a jury, however, an accused was permitted to make an unsworn statement from the dock and to address the jury on his or her own behalf. In 1837 the *Prisoner's Counsel Act* gave an accused the right to be represented by a lawyer, but prisoners continued to be denied the right to give evidence in their own defence. Nearly a century of controversy was precipitated when a handful of judges held that the act did away with an accused's right to make an unsworn statement. The issue was further clouded by the passage of the *Canada Evidence Act* in 1893. Although the statute gave prisoners the right to testify on their own behalf, it was silent about whether they could refuse to testify, which would require that they be sworn, and instead make an unsworn statement.

Between 1893 and 1914 no Canadian court had ruled on the issue. Mathers, however, was not prepared to avoid the debate; and in denying Krafchenko's request to make an unsworn statement he held that '[t]he privilege [of making an unsworn statement] was granted to prisoners because they were debarred from giving evidence on oath, and for that reason alone. When the law was changed and the right accorded to them to tell their story on oath as any other witnesses, the reason for making an unsworn statement was removed.'[102] The ruling was criticized by the *Canada Law Journal* because Mathers had grounded it on the belief that England's *Evidence Act*, passed five years after the *Canada Evidence Act*, did away with the privilege by 'implication.' The author of the journal article suggested that Mathers had it wrong on two counts. First, no statute could be construed as taking away an individual's right unless it explicitly used words to that effect. To suggest that a right could be abrogated because of what was 'implied' in a statute was wrong at law. Second, the article suggested that Mathers seemed not to have realized that the privilege of making an unsworn statement had its origin in an accused's inability to have a counsel speak for him, not because he was unable to be called as a witness in his own defence. The only statute that could remove the privilege was the *Prisoner's Counsel Act*, not the *Evidence Act*, and the law had long been settled in favour of the prisoner on that point.[103]

Despite the criticism levelled at Mathers, his definition of 'reasonable doubt' in the same case earned him considerable praise and was adopted in courts throughout the country.[104]

> I have told you that you should not convict if you have a reasonable doubt of the prisoner's guilt. By the term 'reasonable doubt,' I do not mean a possible doubt, but an actual and substantial doubt. A juror may not create materials for doubt by resorting to trivial suppositions and remote conjecture as to a possible state of facts different from that established by the evidence. If, after a fair and impartial consideration of all the evidence in the case both for the Crown and for the defence, you have an abiding conviction of the guilt of the defendant and are fully satisfied to a moral certainty of the truth of the charge made against him, then you are satisfied beyond reasonable doubt; but, if the evidence has left you in that condition of mind that you cannot say you feel an abiding conviction to a moral certainty of the truth of the charge, then you have a reasonable doubt.[105]

Thomas Graham Mathers (1859–1927). Puisne judge 1905–10 and chief justice of the Court of King's Bench 1910–27. Mathers excelled as both a lawyer and a judge. The *Manitoba Free Press*, for instance, suggested that his was the largest litigation practice in western Canada, and his judicial definition of reasonable doubt was adopted by courts throughout Canada. Mathers played a significant role in drafting the first code of ethics adopted by the Canadian Bar Association. (Provincial Archives of Manitoba)

Mathers was involved in six commissions while on the bench: one established by the City of Winnipeg, two by the federal government and three by the province of Manitoba. His first experience as a commissioner occurred in 1908, when he sat on a three-person hospital commission charged with studying the operation of Winnipeg hospitals and with comparing the system in Manitoba to those elsewhere.[106] A second commission was established on 12 January 1914 to investigate Krafchenko's escape from the Winnipeg jail, and to determine whether suggestions that Krafchenko was head of a secret criminal organization were accurate. A month and a half after he started this inquiry Mathers reported that, other than the individuals already charged as a result of the escape, 'no other person whatsoever was cognizant of or privy to, or either directly or indirectly implicated in or connected with, any plot, plan or conspiracy to either assist in, or permit the escape of Krafchenko.'[107]

The third and fourth commissions on which Mathers sat were established to investigate charges of political corruption associated with the construction of government buildings.[108] In 1913 a Winnipeg company was awarded a contract to build a new provincial legislative building at a cost of just under $3 million. Before the work had started in earnest the provincial architect ordered a change from pile to caisson foundations, and from reinforced concrete to steel and concrete, thereby considerably increasing the cost of the project. By 1915 rumours of wrongdoing were rampant, and the provincial Liberals demanded that a royal commission be established to investigate them. When the Conservative government of Premier Rodmond Roblin failed to take action the province's lieutenant-governor gave Roblin the option of either starting an inquiry or submitting his resignation. The premier immediately appointed Mathers chair of a commission consisting of himself, King's Bench justice Daniel Alexander Macdonald, and Winnipeg police magistrate Hugh John Macdonald. The panel was officially known as the 'Royal Commission Appointed to Inquire into Certain Matters Relating to the New Parliament Buildings,' and hearings commenced on 27 April 1915. Within two weeks it reported that there was substance to the charges of corruption, and by the end of the summer the commissioners suggested that the premier, three members of his cabinet, the president of the Manitoba Conservative Association, and contractor Thomas Kelly had conspired to defraud the government. After the commission announced that Roblin was implicated in the wrongdoing, but well before anyone was actually charged, the premier and the leader of the opposition Liberals entered into an agreement whereby Roblin would resign, the Liberals would form a new government, the Mathers commission would be discontinued, and an investigation would be carried out by a government committee. The arrangements, however, were made without consulting Mathers. When it became apparent that he was not inclined to call off further hearings, Chief Justice Howell of the Court of Appeal was asked to intercede. The two met, but Mathers refused to give in.

Mathers's intransigence was a source of frustration to the new government of T.C. Norris, and was perceived as a threat by Kelly. After Mathers announced that commission hearings were going to resume, Kelly applied for a declaration that the inquiry was unconstitutional.[109] He argued that the Manitoba *Inquiries Act*, under which it was established, was *ultra vires*, and that the commission had no authority to compel witnesses to attend and to give evidence. Kelly's application was the first time the legality of the statute had been questioned, and his arguments were rejected at first instance and again on appeal.

Evidence turned up by the Mathers commission resulted in the arrest of Roblin and his three ministers, one of whom was the father of future King's Bench justice Percival Montague. None, however, was convicted. Walter Humphries Montague died and charges against the others were dropped after their first hearing ended in a mistrial. But the fact that the commission had uncovered actual wrong-doing did not deflect criticism of the way in which it went about collecting evidence. The *Winnipeg Telegram* was particularly upset:

> Before the Royal Commission no rules of evidence were observed. The Royal Commission rambled hither and thither, without restraint and without paying any respect to judicial procedure or precedent. One set of politicians set out to build up a case against their political enemies. No restrictions were placed upon them. In the Police Court one side was heard. When the case was called in the High Court, the Judge, the jury and the people of Manitoba generally will for the first time be given the opportunity to hear both sides. The facts – not merely hearsay, gossip, and suspicion – will then be brought out.[110]

Even before the political dust had settled more rumours of government corruption surfaced, this time in connection with construction of the new Law Courts building and Central Power House. Mathers was appointed a one-person commission to look into the charges, and on 5 May 1916 reported that, although contractors associated with the two projects had routinely made contributions to the Conservative party, he could find no evidence that the former government or any party member had been guilty of impropriety.

The remaining two commissions with which Mathers was associated were established by the federal government to investigate labour unrest. The first came into being on 26 June 1918 as a 'Commission to Enquire Into and Report Upon the Grave Friction and Unrest Existing Between Various Employers in the City of Winnipeg and Their Workmen.' It consisted of Mathers as chair and Fred G. Tipping, president of the Winnipeg Trades and Labour Council, and George Fisher, a Winnipeg alderman, as commissioners. Although the commission's inquiries were restricted to Manitoba, its creation was part of the federal government's response to growing labour unrest throughout the country.[111] Mathers opened hearings on 29 June and almost immediately local labour leaders committed a strategic blunder. In an effort to show that the refusal of employers to deal fairly with their employees was inconsistent with labour practices elsewhere in Canada, the Metal Trades Council tendered copies of labour contracts from other parts of the country. What these documents showed, however, was that Winnipeg workers were among the highest paid in the nation.

The commissioners submitted their report on 2 August. Although critical of the way that the Metal Trades Council had conducted wage negotiations with various employers, they suggested that employers, as a first step towards dissipating the cloud of suspicion that hovered over negotiators, abandon their objections to meeting with factory committees, and that the Council allow these committees to function without interference. The report was regarded by labour leaders as a thinly veiled attack on the Metal Trades Council, and its president used it to urge workers to continue to fight for union recognition.

Mathers's last governmental inquiry was the 'Commission to Inquire Into and Report Upon Industrial Relations in Canada.' Established two months before the Winnipeg General Strike, it consisted of Mathers as chair and Smeaton White, Charles Harrison, Frank Pauze, Thomas Moore, John W. Bruce, and Carl Riordan as commissioners. According to its terms of reference, the commission was to 'consider and make suggestions for securing a permanent improvement in the relations between employers and employees,' and 'to recommend means for ensuring that industrial conditions affecting relations between employers and employees shall be reviewed from time to time by those concerned, with a view to improving conditions in the future.'[112] The Mathers commission opened hearings in Victoria, British Columbia, twelve days after it was established[113] and before it handed in its final report it heard 486 witnesses in 70 sessions held in 28 communities. Among those who refused to appear were members of the executive of Winnipeg's Metal Trades Council. Hearings concluded on 13 June 1919 and a majority report was submitted sixteen days later. The inquiry concluded that labour unrest in Canada was caused by unemployment, the rising cost of living, long working days, lack of collective bargaining rights, a shortage of adequate housing, restrictions on freedom of speech and the press, and inequality in educational opportunities. Although commissioners agreed that labour unrest was a serious problem throughout the country, they concluded that worker protests were mainly due to political upheavals in Europe and to the uncertainty caused by the war. They were convinced, however, 'that the majority of workers did not believe in extreme ideas and would welcome cooperation and industrial harmony.'[114]

Apart from the attention he attracted by presiding over high-profile trials and commissions Thomas Mathers gained a considerable amount of attention within the national legal community as a result of his campaign for a code of ethics for lawyers. He first raised the issue in 1908 during a chambers motion in the Proskouriakoff case. When the lawyer for the Russian government submitted an affidavit based on comments made in a casual conversation by the defendant's lawyer, Mathers was alarmed at what appeared to him to be a lack of professional scruples. 'Without attempting to be more explicit or to prescribe any code of ethics for the regulation of the conduct of solicitors in such matters, it is sufficient to say that it does not appear that this alleged admission was obtained in a way that would justify its use.'[115] Ironically, despite Mathers's denial that he was advocating the implementation of a legal code of ethics, one newspaper headline read 'Judge Mathers ... Pleads for Code of Professional Ethics.'[116]

Mathers raised the issue of ethics on a number of succeeding occasions, including during an action brought by the Law Society against lawyer Percy Hagel who, two years later, was convicted of helping Krafchenko escape from jail.[117] Mathers believed that adoption of a standard of professional conduct was necessary, and his work in developing one was ultimately adopted by the Canadian Bar Association as its Canons of Legal Ethics. In a lengthy address made to the Manitoba Bar Association in 1920 Mathers discussed some of the principles according to which he believed lawyers should live. They should not regard law merely as a means by which to make money, because they have a larger calling. As veritable ministers of justice they are more than mere citizens, and as such should possess an ardent belief in the usefulness of law, in its respectability, and in its traditions. After all, he said, a lawyer whose mind is steeped in the history and customs of the legal profession is not likely to wander far from the path of rectitude. Mathers then gave his audience a list of some dos and don'ts that he believed would change the negative perception the public had of members of the bar. Lawyers should control their tempers, not for their own sake, but for the sake of other members of the profession and their clients. They should refrain from asserting any personal belief in the innocence or guilt of their clients, and whether a fact was or was not established by the evidence. Barristers should also feel an obligation to inform the court of any relevant decision they discovered, regardless of whether they believed it would hurt their client's case. And they should refrain from sitting in judgment of a client's actions, since a litigant's rights in law were those that the Court gave and that one was entitled to have so determined.

Among the duties that Mathers suggested a lawyer owed his client was to be informed of the real facts of a case and to avoid unnecessary litigation. Whenever possible lawyers should use their influence to negotiate a settlement, rather than force clients to bear the unnecessary expense of a trial. They should also treat opposing counsel and witnesses with respect. Nothing was ever gained, he said, by treating adverse parties unfairly. 'The best and most successful counsel are the most courteous to their opponents.'[118] And the best and most successful lawyers refuse to engage in arguments over fees.

> The lawyer who insists upon his strict legal right with respect to compensation under all circumstances will discover that he has adopted a poor method of attracting clients ... On the other hand generous treatment of clients, particularly if they are poor or in very bad circumstances, even the writing off of all fees is like casting your bread upon the waters; it will return after many days.'[119]

In his speech Mathers also referred to the quality of legal services received by those with few economic resources. He noted that the machinery of justice did not treat the poor with the same even-handedness as it did the more advantaged, particularly in criminal courts. 'I cannot say that the assignment of inexperienced fledglings to such a task has often resulted in any great benefit to the unfortunate accused.'[120] The profession, he suggested, owed a responsibility to provide experienced lawyers to criminal and civil clients alike.

Notwithstanding his ruling in the Krafchenko case and his influence in the creation of a legal code of ethics, Mathers was not a judicial activist, despite sitting during a period of rapid social and industrial change. A case in point was a 1924 action for nervous shock.[121] The plaintiff was a passenger in a street railway car who suffered a stroke after hearing a loud explosion-like sound. It was proved at trial that the explosive report was caused by the negligent operation of the streetcar, and in all probability the injuries sustained by the plaintiff were the direct result of the negligence of the defendant. At issue, therefore, was the question of remoteness. Since Great Britain's Judicial Committee of the Privy Council had established that nervous shock alone could not be regarded as the natural and reasonable result of an act of negligence, the plaintiff could succeed only if she were able to prove she suffered something more than nervous shock. Mathers acknowledged that the Privy Council's decision had come under considerable criticism from courts throughout England and Ireland, and that many judges refused to follow it. He also agreed with counsel for the plaintiff that the facts in the action before him were so unique that he could easily distinguish them from those in the case considered by the Privy Council. But he refused to do so, and he dismissed the action. The *Manitoba Bar News* criticized the decision, suggesting that Mathers was out of step with society. In arguing that the judgment 'is out of line with modern requirements' it said that Mathers had failed to appreciate that in a changing world 'law is not static. It is a flowing force which develops to meet changing conditions.'[122]

Although Mathers enjoyed a solid reputation as a judge he was frequently criticized by the Court of Appeal, particularly in the years leading up to his retirement. When he ruled that the Workmen's Compensation Board was a superior court, the Court of Appeal expressed amazement at how he could have arrived at such a conclusion. In overruling his decision it held that the Board is clearly nothing more than 'an administrative tribunal with certain ancillary judicial functions ... It has no controlling authority over any other Court which is a distinguishing characteristic of a Superior Court, nor is it subordinate to any other Court which is a distinguishing characteristic of an inferior Court.'[123] Mr Justice Fullerton was particularly perplexed by Mathers's interpretation of the law. After pointing out that the statute that brought the Board into existence had been in force since 1916, and that similar statutes had existed elsewhere for much longer, he said that he was unable to see any argument that could support the trial decision.

In overturning a decision rendered by Mathers just months before the trial judge's death, Mr Justice Trueman was even more critical. 'The learned Chief Justice states in his judgment that it is not alleged in the statement of defence that the statements were made fraudulently. This is incorrect.' He then went on to review Mathers's version of the facts, concluding, diplomatically, 'I look upon the matter quite differently.'[124]

Justice Mathers died in Rochester, Minnesota, just before midnight on 15 August 1927, a week after undergoing a duodenal operation. He was sixty-nine. His passing came as a surprise to members of the Manitoba legal profession and his fellow judges, despite the fact that for weeks it had been obvious that Mathers was in poor health.[125]

Justice Mathers was a towering presence in the Manitoba legal community. Fullerton described him as one of the most able trial judges in Canada. 'I have,' said Fullerton, 'never seen his superior.'[126] Others, however, regarded him with less fondness. His vanity bothered many, and both on and off the bench he was cold, arrogant, and humourless. When one of his judicial colleagues attempted to inject some humour into a judgment, Mathers called him into his office and gave him a thorough tongue-lashing, suggesting that the bench was no place for humour.[127]

John Allen was a lawyer in Manitoba's Department of the Attorney General when Mathers sat. One of Allen's friends was in London to argue a case before the Privy Council when he was startled to see Mathers, a fellow Manitoban, walking down a street in one of the world's largest cities. In an attempt to get the judge's attention he spontaneously called out 'Justice Mathers.' Without even knowing who had spoken Mathers turned and said, 'That's Chief Justice Mathers, please.'[128]

Mathers left an estate of $75,000, consisting of a variety of stocks, bonds, life insurance, cash, several mortgages, and an interest in a number of parcels of land.

DANIEL ALEXANDER MACDONALD

Daniel Alexander Macdonald was born on 17 August 1858 in Queen's County, near Charlottetown, Prince Edward Island. He was still a child when his Scottish father, Captain Alexander Hector Macdonald, was lost at sea with his entire crew when the *Isabella* went down in a gale.[129]

Macdonald received his early education in the schools of Queen's County before attending Prince of Wales College in Charlottetown. He subsequently became a law student there and was called to the bar of PEI in February 1883. He promptly left the Island for Manitoba and obtained his call two years later. Macdonald then spent a year practising with the Winnipeg firm of Ross, Killam & Haggart before moving sixty miles west to Portage la Prairie, where he became crown prosecutor for the Central Judicial District. In 1890 he joined W.J. Cooper in one of the town's six law firms. That association lasted only one year, however, and for the next nine Macdonald practised alone. Between 1901 and 1904 he and J.A. Hyndman were partners, and during his last two years at the bar Macdonald was again a solo practitioner.

Although he spent a considerable amount of time in criminal courtrooms as a crown prosecutor Macdonald made time for politics. For many years he was a trusted confidant of Liberal senator Robert Watson, and in his own right represented the Banner ward on the Portage town council. He was also nominated to run for the Liberals in the provincial constituency of Lakeside. Macdonald had no more luck winning election as a bencher, however, than he did as a provincial politician. In 1898 he was third in balloting in the Central Judicial District, earning six votes to the winner's thirty-three.[130] Three years later he was second with five votes and in 1904 second again, eighteen behind the winner. Three others, including future prime minister Arthur Meighen, each received one vote.[131]

While in practice Macdonald owned and operated a farm, and after his elevation to the bench he bought a considerable amount of property in Winnipeg. Among his other holdings was part ownership of a hunting lodge north of Portage la Prairie. Local newspapers made much of the fact that despite all his learning he and his three partners managed to build the lodge on land they did not even own. At first relatively unknown within the legal profession, Macdonald nevertheless succeeded in raising his profile through his involvement in a number of non-professional activities. He was an active member of the Anglican parish of St Luke, an enthusiastic golfer, hunter, billiard player, and curler, and a member of organizations like the Masonic Order and the Independent Order of Odd Fellows; and he held shares in private clubs like the Manitoba Club and the St Charles Golf and Country Club. For a time he was also chairman of the Winnipeg Foundation.

In 1883 Macdonald married Marie Helen St Luke Rogers, one of three daughters of David Rogers of Prince Edward Island. He was appointed to the Court of King's Bench on 23 July 1906, and made chief justice twenty-one years later.

While on the bench Macdonald served on two of the most controversial inquiries in Manitoba history. One was the Mathers commission established to investigate irregularities associated with construction of the provincial legislative buildings. The other, known as the Seven Sisters Commission, was created in response to allegations that members of Premier Bracken's government were involved in criminal activities over the awarding of a contract to build a large power plant. The suggestions of wrongdoing were made when the government decided against developing hydroelectric power on the Winnipeg River at public expense. Instead, it signed a contract to have the Winnipeg Electric Company develop the Seven Sisters Falls site on the understanding that the provincial government would purchase the power produced. The deal was so attractive that some governmental ministers, including the province's attorney general, purchased shares in the company. Premier Bracken appointed Macdonald and Justices Dysart and Kilgour to a three-person commission of inquiry. When their hearings ended Macdonald and Kilgour submitted a majority report exonerating the government. In his minority report Dysart argued that, although no evidence of wrong-doing could be found, the fact that the Winnipeg Electric Company had contributed to the election campaigns of a number of politicians deserved further investigation.

Macdonald submitted his resignation as chief justice on 28 October 1937, five months after the death of his wife, but he died before it became official. The Macdonalds were survived by daughters Annie Hester, Helen Winnifred, and Katie Macdonald, son Geoffrey Ernest, two grandsons, five granddaughters, and a great-grandson.

Most of Macdonald's contemporaries regarded him as a poor judge. Among his most severe critics was Joseph Thorson, a long-time lawyer, politician, academic, and, eventually, president of the Exchequer Court of Canada. Thorson suggested that Macdonald often had no idea of what was going on in court, and used as an example a motor-vehicle negligence trial over which the justice had presided. Macdonald seemed oblivious to proceedings until one counsel referred to the clutch of the car involved in the accident. In the middle of a witnesses's testimony Macdonald suddenly asked, 'What's a clutch?'[132] The *Manitoba Bar News*, however, was more sympathetic. It described him as possessing '[g]enerous instincts, a kindly disposition and a strong sense of natural justice.' He was, it suggested,

Daniel Alexander Macdonald (1858–1937). Puisne judge 1906–27, chief justice 1927–37. Although Macdonald was easy-going and always polite while on the bench, he was not regarded by his contemporaries as a good judge. His reputation suffered even more in the eight years before his retirement, owing to his declining health. (Provincial Archives of Manitoba)

> the soul of courtesy, not just when it pleased him, but at all times and under all circumstances. His last thought was ever of his own convenience. Counsel, litigants, witnesses – to all, he showed an even temper and an equal consideration. In his court, the newcomer at the Bar, not yet used to the sound of his own voice in the courtroom, was as assured of patient and considerate hearing as a veteran of the Bar.[133]

In terms of knowledge, however, the best it could say of Macdonald was that the justice possessed a perhaps barely adequate fund of black-letter law. Robert Blackwood Graham, a crown prosecutor before becoming a police magistrate, doubted even that assessment. He described Macdonald as a charming and courteous gentleman with only mediocre ability as either a lawyer or a judge. He noted that the justice was ill for many years before he retired and in a considerable understatement suggested that his illness did nothing to enhance his reputation. According to Graham, for at least eight years before his retirement Macdonald's memory had been so poor that he could neither follow nor understand the simplest evidence. He was, said Graham, a seventy-nine-year-old who looked ninety.[134]

Graham thought that the lack of respect felt by the legal profession for Macdonald was reflected in the number of lawyers who attended his funeral:

> I was a little surprised at the small turnout at the late Chief Justice's funeral. The profession was not well-represented as it should have been. Quite a number of the younger members of the society were there but the older ones were absent ... At the cemetery after the commitment service, everyone departed and the casket was yet above ground. The usual custom is that as the commitment service proceeds the casket is slowly lowered into the grave. I do not know why that custom was departed from. So although I attended the funeral, I do not know whether the Chief Justice is buried or not.[135]

The next day Graham learned that the mechanical device that was to have lowered Macdonald's casket into the ground had malfunctioned, and that after those attending the committal had left the cemetery, the casket was lowered into Macdonald's grave by hand.

Notwithstanding the low regard of his professional contemporaries, Macdonald won the affection if not the respect of the Board of the University of Manitoba, which in 1927 awarded him an honorary doctorate of laws.

5

The Emergence of a Provincial Elite, 1908–1920

Completion of the Canadian Pacific Railway in the mid-1880s opened Manitoba to large-scale development, a process that did not go unnoticed in the United States. In 1911 a special correspondent of the *Chicago Record Herald* visited Winnipeg and his impressions were published by the newspaper.

> All roads lead to Winnipeg. It is the focal point of the three transcontinental lines of Canada, and nobody, neither manufacturer, capitalist, farmer, mechanic, lawyer, doctor, merchant, priest nor laborer, can pass from one part of Canada to another without going through Winnipeg. It is a gateway through which all the commerce of the east and the west, and the north and the south must flow. No city, in America at least, has such absolute and complete command over the wholesale trade of so vast an area. It is destined to become one of the greatest commercial centres of the continent as well as a manufacturing community of great importance.[1]

The rapid growth in the population of Manitoba was reflected in the changes that were made to the province's court system. In 1908, for instance, the province created the Northern Judicial District, sitting in Minnedosa, a town located thirty miles north of Brandon. The new district was the province's fifth. Eight years later another was added. The Dauphin Judicial District was centred in Dauphin, a community located just above Riding Mountain National Park, approximately seventy-five miles north of Brandon.

In 1908 John Donald Cameron, a former attorney general of Manitoba and a leader of the provincial bar, was appointed to the Court of King's Bench. Within the year he was transferred to the Court of Appeal and his seat on the King's Bench taken by Thomas Llewellyn Metcalfe, a convivial man possessed of a well-developed sense of humour and, according to his critics, considerable bias.[2]

In 1910 two further changes affected Manitoba's judicial system, one of which reflected the sustained growth experienced by the province. The same year that Joseph Dubuc retired and was replaced by James Emile Pierre Prendergast, the court was enlarged from four to five judges. Filling the new seat was Hugh Amos Robson, the only person in Manitoba history to resign from and be reappointed to the King's Bench. During his first term Robson sat for only two years before resigning to become the first Public Utility Commissioner of Manitoba. He returned to the bench as a justice of the Manitoba Court of Appeal before he was reappointed to the King's Bench shortly before his death in 1944.

In 1914 yet more changes were made to the province's two highest courts. The first was geographic and involved extending their jurisdiction and the boundary of the province north to its present location. The second saw both the King's Bench and the Court of Appeal expanded, King's Bench from five to six members and the Court of Appeal from four to five justices. The move meant that one replacement and two new justices had to be appointed. Alexander Haggart went directly from the practice of law to the Court of Appeal, while John Philpot Curran and Alexander Casimir Galt were appointed to the King's Bench.

It was soon clear, however, that the appointment of Galt was not a good one. In 1916 he was involved in the first of the several controversies with which he was connected during his career on the bench, and which oddly enough had no formal conclusion. Shortly after Galt was appointed chair of a provincial commission of inquiry established to investigate allegations of wrong-doing associated with construction of the new provincial agricultural college, the editor of the *Winnipeg Saturday Post* wrote an editorial comparing the way in which Galt conducted commission hearings to the Spanish Inquisition. Galt took offence, cited the editor for contempt of court, fined him $500, and sentenced him to a month in jail. The Court of Appeal overturned Galt's decision on the basis that a judge sitting as a commissioner had no contempt powers. In an editorial published after his acquittal the editor rubbed salt into Galt's wounds. 'Since the Norris government set the precedent of employing judges to do the work that properly belongs to its campaign organization, the judiciary in this province, with a few honourable exceptions among its members, has gone steadily, step by step, into the bog of political debauchery.'[3] The Norris government promptly laid another charge of contempt against the editor; but before judgment was rendered the case was adjourned and never reconvened.

The disparity in salaries paid Manitoba judges compared to their Ontario counterparts continued to be a source of irritation to members of the provincial bar. In 1919 the annual salary of the chief justice of Manitoba's King's Bench was $7000, one thousand dollars more than the salaries of the five puisne justices. The Manitoba salaries were all one thousand dollars less than what the judges would have received had they sat on an Ontario bench, and exactly the same as Manitoba judges had received a decade and a half earlier.[4]

According to court statistics, Manitoba justices earned their pay. Between 1910 and 1926 more than 23,000 statements of claim were filed in Winnipeg's Court of King's Bench (an average of 1398 per year), approximately 150 more claims per year than were filed in the first decade of the twentieth century. The Court of Appeal was also busy. Over the same seventeen-year period (1910–26) it heard 2377 appeals, an average of 139 per year.

By the end of the First World War it was apparent that the costs of goods and services, unaccompanied as they were by a corresponding increase in wages, were beyond the means of many Winnipeggers. The resulting industrial unrest, culminating in the 1919 General Strike, substantially eroded Winnipeg's status as a city of economic growth and political stability. The fact that the strike was regarded by many as a revolution was the cause of considerable concern to city leaders. In an address to the Winnipeg Board of Trade delivered six years after the General Strike ended, one of the leaders of the provincial bar warned his audience about the continuing danger of too rapid social and political change.

> Our psychology has for some time been bad: we have been a city divided against itself, the north against the south, the south against the north, suspicion and want of confidence on both sides ... We must develop a militant opposition to all forms of mischievous agitation ... If we are to look to the outside world for capital for industrial purposes, we must be jealous of our fair name and do everything we can to avoid being classed as 'radical.'[5]

Travers Sweatman went on to suggest that the best way to achieve social and political peace was to ensure that people with 'communistic and half-baked social theories' were not elected to Winnipeg's city council, the provincial legislature, or parliament.[6] While the second judge appointed to Manitoba's Court of King's Bench in the twentieth century was indeed elected to the provincial legislature, he certainly was not ideologically left of centre.

JOHN DONALD CAMERON

Cameron was born on his father's farm in East Nissouri, Oxford County, Canada West, on 18 September 1858. His grandfather, a native of Glengarry, Scotland, had arrived in the region thirty-seven years earlier as one of its first pioneers. John's father, after whom he was named, was born there in 1821. When he turned twenty-one John senior was given the hundred-acre farm on which he and his wife were to raise John, George, Mary, Emma, and Jane.

John and Elizabeth Cameron resided in East Nissouri until their five children were of school age, and then the family moved to nearby Woodstock. There John was appointed governor of Oxford jail, an appointment he likely earned through his six years of service on township council, four years on county council, and the many terms he served as a school trustee. The appointment may also have been a much delayed reward for service rendered by his father, who led a contingent of East Nissourians against a group of rebels during the Rebellion of 1837. John's job as jail governor, however, almost ended prematurely when the local sheriff, under whom the governor served, dismissed him so that his position could be given to someone else. Cameron immediately took his letter of dismissal to the premier, who forced the sheriff to rescind the termination. To ensure that there was no recurrence Mowat changed the law to give the province's lieutenant-governor veto power over all staffing decisions made by sheriffs.[7]

The Camerons' hope that their children would receive a better education in Woodstock than in East Nissouri was satisfied, at least in the case of John Donald. Some time before their arrival the Woodstock Board of School Trustees built schools in both the eastern and western parts of town. Eight teachers taught more than 560 students in a community with a population of 2400. Before he ended up at the University of Toronto, John Donald Cameron's education took him to the Woodstock

Collegiate Institute, housed in a large brick building on Graham Street, and from there to the Canadian Literary Institute.

The Literary Institute was incorporated by an act of parliament in 1857. Although the original intent of its founders was to create a literary college, when that plan did not win the support of the Baptist church its organizers added theology to the curriculum and agreed to accept both female and male students. The school's final mandate was to provide young people with the opportunity to obtain an education under Christian influences in a residential setting. In 1860 the Canadian Literary Institute became the country's first co-educational college, and its curriculum included courses taught in public and high schools, and about half the courses taught at the University of Toronto. Students came from as far away as Texas, Michigan, Manitoba, and Quebec. Cameron was among the most gifted, graduating in 1876 with a double scholarship.

From the Literary Institute, renamed Woodstock College in 1883, Cameron entered the University of Toronto. He eventually became one of the school's outstanding scholars, and graduated with gold medals in Classics and Mental and Moral Sciences, and the Prince's Prize. The only student to rival his academic brilliance was Thomas Moss, a future chief justice of Ontario. Cameron continued to be an academic front-runner while a student-at-law. When called to the bar in 1882 he was one of the top students in his class, awarded a Silver Medal. Among his classmates were William Egerton Perdue, future federal minister of justice Sir Allen B. Aylesworth, and Sir Frederick Haultain, who served as premier of the North-West Territories before becoming chief justice of Saskatchewan.

Cameron was called to the bar of Ontario on 6 September 1882. A few months later he emigrated to Winnipeg, where he joined the practice of Hugh McMahon, who at the time was a Law Society bencher. The partnership ended a few years later when McMahon left for Ontario, where he eventually went to the bench. After McMahon's departure Cameron joined the firm of C.H. Allen and practised there until 1900. From then until he became a judge he was senior partner in Cameron & Phillips. Hugh Phillips was a tall, formal-looking lawyer. Like his partner, he had considerable experience in a courtroom and, like Cameron, he possessed a razor-sharp wit. In a criminal case opposite a veteran crown attorney Phillips decided to undermine his opponent's very strong presentation with a long series of specious objections, each followed by a lengthy explanation. When the crown attorney could no longer stand the interruptions, or the condescending way in which Phillips made them, he jumped to his feet to make an objection of his own. 'My learned friend objects to this and he objects to that! Well, I object to my learned friend's constant objections! There is no substance to them; he is simply trying to obstruct the proceedings! Furthermore, I object to his pompous manner! He acts as if only he knows any law. My learned friend is outrageously pompous.' Adjusting his glasses as he rose slowly to his feet, Phillips assumed his most condescending tone yet. 'My Lord, if it will expedite matters, I am quite willing to admit to the latter allegation.'[8]

From his days as a student in Woodstock through his career in Manitoba, J.D. (as Cameron was known to friends) was fascinated by politics According to a high school friend and university roommate, 'J.D. took the liveliest interest in political matters. He followed closely public affairs both Dominion and Local ... [and] with his strong radical views never failed to throw his cap into the ring, when the occasion offered for a political discussion.'[9] Chief Justice Purdue agreed. He felt that Cameron's temperament and abilities especially fitted him for a career in politics.[10]

Cameron was elected Liberal member for South Winnipeg in a by-election held on 13 January 1892. He defeated D.E. Sprague by 98 votes, but faced him again in a general election held six months later. This time he won by an even larger margin. A year after entering the legislature he joined the cabinet of Thomas Greenway as both provincial secretary and minister of municipal affairs. Almost immediately he became one of the province's principal negotiators in its dispute with the federal government over the Manitoba School question. After a compromise agreement was worked out by the two levels of government, Cameron was made responsible for ensuring that it was ratified by the provincial legislature.[11]

On 17 November 1896 Cameron resigned as provincial secretary to become the province's attorney general (he continued to serve as minister of municipal affairs). He was defeated in the general election held on 7 December 1899 but, although no longer a member of the legislature, he remained influential within the Liberal party. In 1906, for instance, he delivered a keynote speech on education to party members. In an 'elaborate address,' he urged them to demand that the government bring in a law making school attendance compulsory.[12]

During his career Cameron was appointed to two commissions. The first, established in 1896 to negotiate the terms of a final agreement to

John Donald Cameron (1858–1923). Puisne judge 1908–9, judge of the Court of Appeal 1909–23. Cameron is one of a handful of Manitoba judges who had outstanding careers at the bar, in politics, and on the bench. Justice Perdue attributed Cameron's success to a lifetime of study, reflected in articles he wrote after going to the bench. Cameron was much in demand as a speaker and his dynamic personality made him a powerful force in the seven years he was a member of the provincial legislature. (Provincial Legislature of Manitoba)

the Manitoba School Question, was officially referred to as 'Commissioners Appointed to Represent the Province of Manitoba at the Conference Held with the Representatives of the Dominion Government on the School Question.' Besides Cameron, the two-person body included the man he replaced as attorney general, Clifford Sifton. The second board of inquiry, the 'Royal Commission on the University of Manitoba,' which consisted of chairperson James A.M. Aikins and six commissioners, including Cameron, was established in 1907 to 'enquire into, and make recommendations upon, the government and finances of the university [of Manitoba], and particularly upon some 'less cumbersome' method of government than the University Council, the relations of the colleges and university, teaching in the university, the site, and all such other matters as they might think appropriate.'[13] After three years of hearings members submitted three very different reports. Cameron's was the first. He and W.A. McIntyre were unequivocal in their belief that the university should operate free of denominational control. A second report, submitted by three commissioners associated with the three religious colleges affiliated with the university, recommended that the university be given unlimited teaching powers, but that the religious colleges continue to possess degree-granting privileges for their theological programs. The last submission, by Aikins and the Reverend A.A. Cherrier, was ultimately adopted by the government. It suggested that the colleges should remain affiliated with the university and that there should be a separation of the body's financial and academic administrations.

Although Cameron was more active as a barrister than as a solicitor, he was able to attract a number of high-profile corporate clients, including the Grand Trunk Pacific Railway. Yet despite possessing an above-average reputation as a practitioner, he was unsuccessful in 60 per cent of his reported cases.

Cameron was appointed to the King's Bench on 21 January 1908, where he sat for just over a year before being elevated to the Court of Appeal. On both courts he was able to put aside the partisanship he had adopted while a member of the legislature. As a lawyer and a politician his views on state policy and political morality were definite, inflexible, and uncompromising. As a judge, however, he discarded his personal views when they came into conflict with what he considered to be the spirit of the issue under consideration.[14] Perdue felt that Cameron was able to do so because his life-long dedication to studying 'had amplified his capacity for clear and orderly reasoning; while his great memory for facts and principles retained them ready at hand for use and application. In conferences of the judges he was quick to discern the very crux of a case or to point out the fallacy in an argument.'[15]

> Cameron had a keen, analytical mind and was quick to seize on the core of an argument ... from all that was irrelevant, impertinent, or unnecessary. Then he dealt with the problem, viewing it from all sides, often with that hesitation to reach a conclusion common to keen minds, which are able to grasp all that is involved in conflicting arguments, of which weaker intellects are content to take one or other with less anxiety or apprehension of error. He would ponder for days upon a single point, and sometimes admit he had been unable to sleep as long as it remained unsettled in his mind. Then would come decision, and his mind, purged of conflict, was able to rest.[16]

Cameron's judgments suggest that his personality underwent a considerable change when he donned his robes. Outside court he was a racy raconteur with a keen sense of humour and a forceful, dynamic personality. On the bench he was a plodder, albeit with a keen appreciation for the written word. However much his judgments lacked colour, they were products of a judicial stylist who selected with care every word and phrase. He often spent days hunting for the source of certain words until he satisfied himself that they expressed the thought or sentiment he intended. Despite his love of language, he rarely adopted an academic tone or used unusual or 'learned' words. He once suggested that 'meticulous' should be used not more than once every two years.[17] He was also much opposed to *obiter dicta*, and urged his fellow judges to omit from their judgments extraneous comments.[18] When he went to the Court of Appeal, Cameron did not forget the difficulties faced by trial judges, especially in criminal cases, and was inclined to uphold the decisions of lower courts. 'When convinced that the trial judge had made a conscientious effort to give the accused a fair trial his sympathy was with the judge or magistrate, and he supported him if he could do so ... He was strongly of opinion that to support the trial judge was, as a rule, in the interest of a sound administration of justice and in accord with public policy.'[19]

Cameron was regarded by many as one of Manitoba's most literate and finest appellate judges.[20] Certainly England's Privy Council appeared to think well of his work. One of the first of his judgments to come before that body on appeal involved the company implicated in the legislative-building scandal. Its three shareholders were brothers, two of whom brought an action against the third for an order that secret profits earned with partnership money should be declared a partnership asset. In reversing the decision of the trial judge, a majority of the Court of Appeal held that, because the two plaintiffs were illiterate and had always trusted the defendant, the defendant had the right to do whatever he wanted with partnership funds. In a strongly worded dissent Cameron disagreed. While acknowledging that the plaintiffs had trusted their brother to make whatever decisions needed to be made on behalf of the business, that fact alone did not substantially alter the rights and obligations of the partners. In rejecting the opinion of Perdue and Richards in favour of that of Cameron, the Privy Council noted that Cameron's analysis left nothing to be desired, and 'it would serve no useful purpose to repeat the argument of Cameron, J.A. It is, in their Lordships' opinion, in every respect satisfactory and conclusive.'[21] Seven years later the Privy Council were again persuaded by a Cameron dissent, but this time they were more critical of the decision of the majority. The case involved a bank draft and allegations of wrong-doing on the part of an agent. The Court of Appeal, with the exception of Cameron, suggested that the issue was nothing more than a breach of contract, a view regarded by the Privy Council as wholly inadequate.[22]

The year before Cameron died the Privy Council was again asked to rule on an appeal in which he was the only member of the court to dissent. The case turned on the words 'against all loss' used in a consent judgment. Three members of the appeal court limited the way in which the words should be construed, while Cameron did not. In adopting his argument the Privy Council was at a loss to find any basis for the decision of the majority. 'Their Lordships agree with Cameron, J. A., and are unable to find ... any ground for limiting the words "all loss."'[23]

Apart from politics and law (including serving as a Law Society bencher between 1888 and 1898, the last six years of which he served as secretary), Cameron's abiding interest was literature. He was a voracious reader and kept himself fully informed about the topics of the day. He was particularly fond of the classics, however, and often quoted them to friends.[24] After he went to the bench he published two articles. Despite possessing a sparkling wit and a keen intellect he adopted in both a pedantic, plodding style devoid of either literary allusions or sweeping phrases. Cameron, for instance, viewed the legislature with considerable suspicion, something that should perhaps not come as a surprise, considering the many years he sat in it. In 'Codes and Codification,' published in 1917, he asserted his unwavering belief in the perfection of the common law.[25] He suggested that there have been only two significant systems of law: one that uses a code and the other the common law. His central argument was that codes were inherently unworkable:

> Words and facts are conditions precedent to ideas. Language is necessarily imperfect. No one person can say that the idea a certain word conveys to his mind is the same idea that is conveyed by it to the mind of another. How is any man to be certain that the idea presented to his mind by a section or definition of a code is that which was present in the mind of the man who drafted the section or the definition?[26]

The common law, on the other hand, was 'truly in accord with the laws of evolution. Can it be possible that there should arise any code which can have the effect of substituting another law for the law naturally and logically evolved in the progress of mankind?'[27]

In discussing the relative merits of codes and the common law Cameron offered his own view of how change in law was best effected. He agreed that law was founded on custom, and as such was slow to change, and that history had taught that it was wise to go slowly, particularly in matters of private law. But, he pointed out, the law did not stand still. It was a living force, and the change it brought about was both natural and logical. The key question was who should supervise the way in which change occurred? According to Cameron it should be the courts rather than the legislature, for only judges had the ability to set the standards governing the conduct of men.[28]

Cameron's second article, published the year before his death, was a short discussion about international treaties in relation to legislative power.[29] In the five years between publication of the two articles his writing style became even more plodding. He also acquired a tendency to rely on extended quotes and to repeat continually the same phrases. In neither work did he express an opinion of the substantive law, engage in legal analysis, or take a firm position on any issue. For example, he suggested that section 132 of the *British North America Act* was open to construction, but 'on the other hand, it can be argued ...' then again, 'From the one point of view ...' and lastly, 'From the other it might lie ...'

On 26 March 1923 Cameron was returning from a vacation in California when his train stopped briefly in St Paul, Minnesota. Breathing with effort and in obvious distress, he asked a porter to help him re-board Great Northern train no. 7. He barely made it to his seat when he collapsed and died from a heart attack. He was sixty-five and the fourth member of Manitoba's Court of Appeal to die in office in six years.

Cameron was tall, lanky, and slightly stoop-shouldered, with a high, domed head and large, prominent eyes. Frail health plagued him throughout his life and prevented him from participating in any activity that required physical exertion. On the surface he appeared cold and unemotional, even morose, but to those close to him he was a fascinating conversationalist and a warm friend. To them he was always the same, full of humour and ever ready to take part in a hoax or practical joke. Even political enemies sought his company. Sir Rodmond Roblin, a former premier and bitter political foe, regarded him as an exceptional and much-in-demand after-dinner speaker, and the province's raciest storyteller. Edith Rogers was one of the first women elected to a Canadian legislature and a close friend of Cameron's.[30] On their initial meeting both she and her husband were struck by the force of his personality, his intelligence, and his conviviality. 'We realized the depth of his intellectual powers, while his ready wit, his cordial disposition and his unvarying frankness always made him a most attractive and congenial companion.'[31]

The outpouring of emotion following Cameron's death cut across ideological divisions. He was unique, as Chief Justice Perdue pointed out a week after the death of his life-long friend: 'Apart from his learning and his manifold endowments as a judge, Mr. Justice Cameron's personal charm and companionship endeared him to all his associates on the bench. He was indeed to them a brother – not using that word as a mere term of judicial courtesy – but as the expression of affection, trust and confidence implied in the relationship of actual brotherhood.'[32]

Cameron was survived by his sister and two cousins, one of whom was Lady Mann, the wife of Sir Donald Mann, the railway magnate.

THOMAS LLEWELLYN METCALFE

The last judge appointed to the bench during the tenure of Chief Justice Dubuc was Thomas Llewellyn Metcalfe. He was born on 21 February 1870 in St Thomas, Ontario, where his father worked as a building contractor. Thomas was six when he, his parents, and his three brothers emigrated to Manitoba. They settled on a homestead twelve miles north of Portage la Prairie and remained there until 1887, when his father moved into town to manage the Portage Farmers' Elevator. He subsequently left that job to operate an oatmeal-manufacturing business with his son Charles. The enterprise prospered and the two sold their product throughout North America and Europe.[33] Metcalfe was educated in Portage, and it was there that he became a student-at-law in the office of Daniel Alexander Macdonald. His articles were subsequently assigned, in succession, to James Aikins, Smith Curtis, Peter Frances Georgen, Macdonald again, Thomas Cumberland, Hector Mansfield Howell, and finally Norman Phelps Buckingham of Boissevain. By the time his articles ended Metcalfe had served under seven lawyers in three communities. Of the seven, two became chief justices of the province and a third its lieutenant-governor.[34]

After receiving his call in 1894 Metcalfe practised with Robert Andrew Bonnar, one of the province's most colourful and successful criminal lawyers.[35] Unlike Bonnar, however, Metcalfe earned a reputation as a solicitor and a businessman, which might explain the various practices with which Metcalfe was associated. He and Bonnar, for example, maintained offices in both Portage and Winnipeg, and when they parted company after two years Metcalfe practised alone briefly before becoming a partner of E.E. Sharpe in Winnipeg and N.J. Buckingham in Killarney. After a year the Killarney firm was dissolved and Metcalfe was listed as a solo practitioner in that community. For the next two years Metcalfe & Sharpe operated an office in both locales. In 1902 they closed their Killarney office and opened one in Morris, a community just south of Winnipeg. From 1904 until going to the bench, however, Metcalfe practised only in Winnipeg. During his final four years at the bar he and Sharpe were joined by R.A. Stacpoole.

Although a solicitor Metcalfe still spent a considerable amount of time in courtrooms. Twenty-two of his cases were reported, and his results were statistically much better than those of judges who had specialized in litigation. He acted for individuals three times as often as he did for corporations, for plaintiffs twice as often as he did for defendants, and was successful two-thirds of the time. When acting for plaintiffs he was successful in twelve actions and unsuccessful only twice. Still, he was more closely identified with the business community than the courtroom and it was rumoured that he would retire from the bench at the conclusion of the Winnipeg General Strike trials to become chief counsel for the Dominion Bank of Canada.[36] Although it turned out that the rumour was untrue, there was some foundation for believing that it was a possibility. Two other Manitoba superior court justices had stepped down to practise corporate law. Hugh Amos Robson left the King's Bench to become chief counsel for the Union Bank of Canada, and Frank Phippen resigned from the Court of Appeal to join the Canadian Northern Railway.

Metcalfe was unsuccessful, however, at parlaying his solid legal reputation into success as a Law Society bencher. On the three occasions he sought election to convocation he received one, twelve, and sixteen votes.[37] Metcalfe's life-long interest in politics was likely inherited from his father, who served four years as councillor and two years as reeve of the Municipality of Portage la Prairie. Justice Metcalfe was a staunch Liberal, a popular stump speaker, and a member of the executive of the provincial constituency of Winnipeg Centre. In 1899 he ran in the city's municipal election, losing Ward Four by twenty-three out of more than twelve hundred votes cast.[38]

Unlike judges who kept themselves in the public eye through their involvement with charitable organizations or literary endeavours, Metcalfe's main interest was in sports. He was closely associated with the Victoria Lacrosse and the Winnipeg Canoe clubs; and he was a keen hockey fan who once followed his favourite team, the Winnipeg Victorias, all the way to their 1896 Stanley Cup triumph. He also played polo well enough to compete in tournaments and was an enthusiastic duck hunter and golfer. Apart from these activities he spent a considerable amount of time in one of the several clubs of which he was a member. They included the Commercial Club, the very exclusive Manitoba Club, and the St Charles Golf and Country Club, as well as Prince Rupert's Lodge No. 1, A.F. & A.M. The only legal body with which he involved himself was the Manitoba Law School, where he lectured in real property.

Metcalfe was appointed to two commissions while at the bar. The first was a ten-person body established in 1902 to revise and consolidate the public statutes of Canada. The work it produced was published five years later as the *Revised Statutes of Canada 1906*. The second was created in 1909 'To Inquire Into and Report Upon the Existing Requirements and Conditions of the Fisheries in the Provinces of Manitoba, Saskatchewan and Alberta.' The chair was Edward Prince, federal commissioner of fisheries, and the other two members Metcalfe and D.F. Reid of Selkirk. The body's mandate included investigating the past and the present state of the fisheries, the amount and type of nets and gear used, whether fishing restrictions were being observed, and whether whitefish hatcheries were effective. Apart from these practical concerns the commissioners also paid attention to the political aspects of the prairie fishing industry, which included determining whether prairie consumers were being adequately supplied with fish by the American companies that dominated the commercial marketplace, if domestic licences were being abused, and whether the numbers of fish of low economic but high sporting value, such as jackfish, were decreasing. Commission hearings opened in Manitoba in May, and after starting in Winnipeg the commissioners travelled to Dauphin, Gimli, Selkirk, and Portage la Prairie. By the time they were scheduled to get under way in Saskatchewan and Alberta, Metcalfe was appointed to the bench and his place on the commission was taken by fellow lawyer Jabez Bowen Hugg.[39]

Metcalfe was thirty-nine when he went to the King's Bench on 22 May 1909. His inability to control his deep-rooted sense of conviviality and good humour made him one of the province's least dignified judges. He found it almost impossible to sit still, and as he observed proceedings constantly ran his fingers through his hair, fidgeted, or threw a leg over the arm of his chair.[40]

Although Metcalfe is most remembered for the role he played in trying the leaders of the Winnipeg General Strike, a case that provides a better glimpse of the man beneath the robes was heard just months after he went to the bench.[41] It involved a pet racoon, a hotel patron, and an innocent watchmaker. Throughout his judgment it was obvious that Metcalfe enjoyed hearing the case. According to his summary of the facts the affair started when a resident of the Rural Municipality of Morden viciously beat a racoon kept chained by the son of a local hotel keeper. Some time after receiving the beating the racoon broke its chain and was let into the hotel's beverage room by a patron. Almost immediately 'it jumped on a chair and looked out of the window and otherwise becomingly conducted itself.' When the man who beat it entered the room, the racoon started towards him. As soon as it got near him the man tried to kick it, and in doing so

> over-reached himself and fell flat on his back on the floor. The opportunity appeared to be too good for the racoon to lose, and he thereupon attacked Hewitt, biting him severely in the fleshy part of the thigh, and holding on firmly. Hewitt, still on his back, wound his legs around the animal and grabbed him so as to prevent him getting any further hold. He called loudly for somebody to come with an axe and demolish the racoon,

> but those present hesitated to inflict the extreme penalty. Thereupon Hewitt expostulated loudly.[42]

If Metcalfe still had a sense of humour ten years later, it was not evident in his handling of one of the most contentious trials in Manitoba's history.[43] The background to the Winnipeg General Strike could be traced to a combination of labour unrest and opposition to the anti-communist policies adopted by the Canadian government following the end of the First World War. By the spring of 1919 it was obvious there was a legitimate basis for many of the complaints of union leaders, which included low wages, poor housing, and long hours of work. Things came to a head on 1 May, when Winnipeg metal workers went on strike after the Manitoba Bridge and Iron Company, Vulcan Iron Works, and Dominion Bridge and Iron refused to bargain collectively with the Metal Trades Council. Whether other unions should walk out in support of the striking metal workers was put to a vote by the Trades and Labour Council of Winnipeg, and a general strike was called for 15 May. Almost immediately nearly thirty thousand workers walked off their jobs, and public services, milk deliveries, and the operation of street cars and telephone and telegraph services were suspended. A Citizens' Committee of One Thousand, made up of the elite of Winnipeg's business and professional communities, was organized to combat what it perceived to be the work of enemy aliens and a few Anglo-Saxon malcontents.

Although Committee organizers argued that their principal aim was to keep public utilities operational, the actions of the special constables they hired made it clear that their real aim was breaking the strike. Things went from bad to worse when Winnipeg's city council, after voting to outlaw sympathetic strikes by civic employees, dismissed the entire police force and started swearing in special constables as permanent replacements. In June the federal government decided to play a more active role in ending the strike and amended the *Naturalization Act* to give it the authority to deport 'alien' strike leaders. Under a second amendment British-born protesters were included in the definition of alien and made subject to deportation. On 16 June the position of the strikers was undermined further when the three companies whose workers precipitated the labour conflict finally agreed to bargain collectively. When that did not bring an end to the unrest, however, the federal government charged eight strike leaders and four alleged Bolsheviks with seditious conspiracy and seditious libel, and ordered their arrest. Despite the fact that the labour leaders were immediately released on bail, union organizers called for a demonstration to be held on 21 June. When thousands of workers marched down Main Street, Winnipeg's mayor asked the North West Mounted Police to disperse the crowd. Things grew increasingly ugly, and the police were met with a hail of bricks.

Mayor Gray read the riot act from the steps of city hall and ordered the police into action. They promptly charged into the crowd with guns drawn, and in the ensuing melee one demonstrator was killed and numerous others were wounded. Four days later the Trades and Labour Council called the strike off. Two editors of the *Western Labour News* were arrested and charged with seditious libel, and on 3 July they and the twelve men charged earlier were remanded for a preliminary hearing. The four alleged Bolsheviks appeared before an Immigration Board of Inquiry. In the end one was deported to the United States for having illegally crossed the border three years earlier. Of the remaining ten accused, eight were remanded for trial on charges of seditious conspiracy, illegal combinations, and seditious libel. The editors were charged separately with seditious libel.

The first to be tried was R.B. Russell, whose trial before Metcalfe got under way on 26 November 1919. Although Russell was charged with six counts of seditious conspiracy, the real issue was whether the aim of strike leaders had been to overthrow constituted authority or to achieve improved conditions for workers. Jurors sat into the evening for twenty-three days and were frequent witnesses to bitter exchanges between opposing counsel. Metcalfe was both politically and socially a conservative, and throughout the trial he exhibited an obvious pro-prosecution bias that was reflected in his three-hour-and-twenty-minute charge to the jury. 'But if he was biassed, then so was most of the Manitoba bench and the majority of the legal profession.'[44] Russell was convicted and sentenced to two years in jail. The remaining labour leaders were also tried by Metcalfe. Since the evidence presented at their trial was essentially the same as that used to convict Russell, their verdict was, in all but one case, the same. The exception was A.A. Heaps, later a Member of Parliament, who was acquitted after acting as his own lawyer.

Metcalfe was elevated to the Court of Appeal on 3 October 1921 and was only fifty-two when he passed away six months later. After spending his last Saturday at the court house and Sunday at one of his clubs, Metcalfe took to bed and never left it. For two days he was attended by

Thomas Llewellyn Metcalfe (1870–1922). Puisne judge 1909–21, judge of the Court of Appeal October 1921–April 1922. Metcalfe was a sports enthusiast whose sense of humour and tendency to fidget while on the bench gave rise to his reputation as one of Manitoba's least dignified and serious justices. During the trials of the leaders of the 1919 Winnipeg General Strike, Metcalfe's social conservatism was made evident, and he was accused by some trial observers of displaying a pro-prosecution bias. (Provincial Archives of Manitoba)

two of his brothers and a number of friends, but around 1:00 a.m., Wednesday 2 April 1922, he became comatose, and shortly after noon on Thursday he died. Winnipeg papers were quick to attribute Metcalfe's death to the strain caused by the strike trials. There was probably some truth to that suggestion, since he had spent a month in hospital following the end of the trials, and ill health continued to plague him until his death. Officially, however, his death was attributed to a combination of high blood pressure and hardening of the arteries.

Following a Presbyterian service in Winnipeg Metcalfe's body, accompanied by fourteen friends and family members, was transported by train to Portage. There, in a driving rain, he was laid to rest in the family plot at Hillside cemetery. His seventy-eight-year-old mother had predeceased him by nine years and his father by one. Of his three brothers, George Albert had been a Winnipeg businessman before becoming provincial administrator of succession duties, William graduated from Manitoba Medical College in 1893 and became medical superintendent of the Portage General Hospital, and Charles worked with his father in their oatmeal business.

Metcalfe never married, and for most of his adult life resided alone in an apartment. For the last six years, however, he and a male friend lived together in a house just south of the Assiniboine River.[45] While some of his contemporaries remembered Metcalfe for his kindliness of character and catholic generosity, others spoke, in a tone not entirely complimentary, of how the depth of his learning came as such a revelation.

> His whimsical humour and jolly nature, even if at times stirred with biting sarcasm, had not led his associates to apprehend in him the close student he had been. Yet his friends at his home say that he was a constant student, an inveterate reader. He read far into the night hours in the leisure and seclusion of his own home; he read deeply in his chambers at the law courts.[46]

Joseph Thorson regarded Metcalfe as a renegade and a unique character, noting that although Metcalfe drank too much and was not morally above reproach, the justice was also a very likeable person and a good judge. Thorson's most severe criticism was that Metcalfe was biased, citing as an example Metcalfe's partisan handling of the strike trials. Still, like so many others, Thorson remembered Metcalfe as a very good lawyer with great personal charm.[47]

William Parker Fillmore was the head of one of Winnipeg's largest law firms, a life bencher, and president of the Law Society of Manitoba. He often appeared before Metcalfe and thought of him as bright and likeable and a good judge. Like Thorson, however, he was struck by Metcalfe's lack of subtlety. For example, Metcalfe made little effort to hide the lengthy affair he had with the wife of Alfred Joseph Andrews, a former mayor of Winnipeg and one of the city's most senior and respected lawyers.[48] Former Manitoba premier Douglas Campbell, a member of the legislature when Metcalfe sat, regarded him as a conscientious judge.[49]

Metcalfe left an estate valued at slightly more than $59,000. Among his assets was his home, title to one residential lot and a half-interest in a second, a half-interest in a mortgage, and interests in three residential properties. Among his other assets were a number of shares in Canada Traders, which had no value, and numerous Russian bonds, also of no value. He had, however, invested in a variety of stocks that had some value, owned seven life insurance policies with a cumulative value of $25,309, and kept both a savings and a current account. The balance of the former was $3234, and the latter $404.[50] As with most judges, careers at the bar and bench secured middle-class comfort but not upper-class riches.

JAMES EMILE PIERRE PRENDERGAST

Prendergast was born in Quebec City on 22 March 1858. The first of his family to settle in the region was his paternal grandfather, an Irish contractor. James's father was a barrister and coroner, but his influence on his son ended prematurely when he died while James was only sixteen and still a student at the Seminary of Quebec. That tragedy, however, did not prevent James from continuing his education. After graduating from both the Commercial Academy and the Quebec seminary he entered Laval University. While there Prendergast spent two years as French secretary to the Spanish consulate. At the time the consulate in Quebec handled most of Spain's North American legal affairs. The bulk of Prendergast's work was secretarial and consisted of commercial correspondence, a task he performed afternoons and evenings for $32 a month.

Prendergast graduated from Laval in 1878 with a Bachelor of Arts degree, and in 1881 received a degree in law. He was immediately called to the Quebec bar. Economically, however, times in Canada East were extremely difficult, particularly so in Quebec. The recently completed dredging of the St Lawrence River allowed ships to bypass the port of Quebec in favour of Montreal, throwing hundreds of stevedores out of work. The economy suffered a second blow when the troops that had been stationed in Quebec since the last quarter of the eighteenth century were transferred back to England. Compared to his native province, the west to Prendergast was a land of opportunity in an island of French culture. In the spring of 1882 he departed for Winnipeg, and on the first of April entered into an articling agreement with James Aikins. He also presented his academic credentials to officials at the recently established University of Manitoba, and on the strength of his Laval degrees was awarded, *ad eundem*, the first law degree granted by the institution. The following year he was called to the bar of Manitoba and promptly entered into partnership with Nicholas DuBois Beck. Their association lasted until Beck left for the North-west. After practising in Calgary and Edmonton, Beck became a justice of the Court of Queen's Bench of Alberta.

Following Beck's departure Prendergast practised alone until 1891, when he and J.T. Huggard established the firm of Prendergast & Huggard. Neither earned a large reputation at the bar, although much of Huggard's time was devoted to his duties with the fledgling *Western Law Times*. The firm persisted until 1895, however, when the two went their separate ways, Prendergast to practise alone for a year before entering partnership with A.J.H. Dubuc, one of the sons of Justice Joseph Dubuc. In 1897 he was appointed to the County Court bench. By his own admission his law practice was only moderately successful.[51] In a eulogy delivered shortly after his death by A.J. Andrews, Prendergast was described as 'pre-eminent as a criminal lawyer.'[52] That was likely not an accurate assessment. In a letter to his father former Manitoba premier Hugh John Macdonald mentioned that he had heard that Prendergast had just been appointed to examine the validity of the legislation dealing with the Manitoba School Question:

> Now I think it only fair that I should let you know that this will be a fatal mistake as Prendergast does not possess a single quality requisite to suit him to conduct important legal proceedings. I am told that he ... has but a small amount of brains, and knows absolutely no law. He has never conducted a case in the Supreme Court in his life either as counsel or solicitor and has no practice except a little in the County Court of the French parishes.[53]

James Emile Pierre Prendergast (1858–1945). Judge of the County Court for the Northern Division of the Eastern Judicial District of Manitoba 1897–1902, judge of the Supreme Court of the North-West Territories 1902–7, judge of the Court of King's Bench of Saskatchewan 1907–10, puisne judge of the Court of King's Bench of Manitoba 1910–22, judge of the Manitoba Court of Appeal 1922–30, chief justice of Manitoba 1930–44. Prendergast was a respected published poet and played an important role in the affairs of the Universities of Saskatchewan and Manitoba. Before going to the bench he was a prominent francophone politician and the unofficial spokesperson for the Catholic church. This picture was taken in 1885, the year he was first elected to the Manitoba legislature. (Provincial Archives of Manitoba)

There were two reasons why Prendergast was among the least accomplished lawyers to sit on a Manitoba bench. An admitted opponent, Manitoba premier Sir Rodmond Roblin described him as 'the laziest man in public life,' and noted that 'he did not like work any more than a schoolboy.'[54] A more likely explanation, however, was his involvement in politics, where he often took positions against prevailing majority views.

Prendergast's first exposure to politics was as a volunteer in the 1878 election campaign of Sir Wilfrid Laurier. His next came a few years later, when he was elected to the Roman Catholic section of the Manitoba board of education. In 1884 he took a small step towards entering public life by accepting appointment as clerk of the town of St Boniface, in which capacity he was charged with running the business affairs of the community, on an annual budget of $11,866.38. The following year he pursued a more active political role, running unopposed as a Liberal-Conservative in La Verendrye, the provincial seat vacated by L.A. Prud'homme when he was appointed to the County Court of St Boniface. A year later Prendergast retained his seat by seventeen votes. In 1888 he was asked to give up his 'safe' seat in favour of running in the more Protestant constituency of Woodlands. Although he won the election, his campaign against an Orange Order opponent was bitter and his victory narrow. His reward was a seat in the cabinet of Thomas Greenway, and on 19 January 1888 he became the government's provincial secretary. After a falling out with the premier Prendergast resigned from cabinet and refused to run in Woodlands again, preferring the more familiar turf of St Boniface. He was elected there as an independent in 1892 and 1896, a period during which he was also twice elected mayor of St Boniface. After the second campaign he left politics to rebuild his law practice, and a year later he went to the bench.[55]

Prendergast 'was a born politician, drinking delight of political battle with great gusto.' He had an unusual gift of eloquence and was a masterful speaker in both French and English. He seldom used notes, and as he spoke had the peculiar habit of continually running his fingers through his hair.[56] Despite his abilities as a politician, however, his influence was limited because of his close identification with the Catholic church.

Prendergast's resignation from Greenway's cabinet and the government's stated intention to withhold public funding of Catholic schools were both the result of a speech delivered at a Portage la Prairie meeting by Toronto ultra-Protestant Dalton McCarthy. An avowed francophobe and spokesperson for those who believed in 'One school, one flag, one language,' McCarthy toured the country, arguing:

> that the great danger which overshadowed Canada was the French national cry, this Bastard Nationality, not a nationality which will take us in as we have taken them in, but a nationality which begins and ends with the French race – which begins and ends with those who profess a Roman Catholic faith – and which now threatens the dismemberment of Canada ... Are we a free people? Is the Pope our ruler, or is Queen Victoria the ruler of this country? Do we govern ourselves by our own institutions, or are we subject to a foreign potentate in Rome? Why, we find the next thing is that the Pope distributes our money.[57]

In Portage McCarthy was hosted by the Loyal Orange Association of Central Manitoba. He urged his audience to unite in opposition to the province's separate school system and use of French as an official language. Attorney General Joseph Martin was in the audience, and as soon as McCarthy had finished speaking he announced that, although he had in the past been forced to put up with the 'disagreeable duty' of signing warrants and vouchers for public documents and statutes in both French and English, henceforth he would sign only documents printed solely in English. Within weeks the minister of public works announced the government's intention to abolish the province's dual system of education. When it was later announced that French would no longer be regarded as an official language, Prendergast had had enough. In August 1889 he resigned from cabinet and the government, and two months later the government stopped publishing the *Manitoba Gazette* in French. Prendergast immediately moved a resolution in the legislature condemning the decision. His motion was defeated by a vote of twenty-seven to six, and when the government introduced its language and school legislation both were passed by overwhelming margins. While the debate raged, however, Prendergast won the admiration of friend and foe alike with his eloquent defence of the rights of Manitoba's Catholic minority. He told the legislature that Catholics would never submit to the injustices that the government proposed to inflict upon them. Only when they had appealed to the court of last resort would they accept their fate. Then, and only then,

> the whole Catholic people of Manitoba would submit, sad, but resigned, conscious that they had contended for the most elementary principles of

> Christianity; and they would look for homes in other countries, where, perhaps, they would not find a more favourable condition of things, but where the principle will not have been laid down that all contracts may be ruthlessly trampled upon; that right means something only when it is in the hands of the majority; and that the most solemn privileges are mere trifles in the hands of politicians, to be used for party purposes.[58]

Prendergast spoke English with a fascinating French accent. A contemporary described his voice as one to which someone might listen with pleasure, and for hours, for the music that was in it.[59] In the legislature he was a courteous and thoughtful debater. In describing his conduct during debates on the Manitoba School question a reporter noted:

> [H]e grew in my estimation, not alone by the courtliness of his conduct throughout the hard battles of the days when the legislation was in process of enactment, but for his magnificent fight in defence of his ideals, both of inheritance and conscience. A more strenuous fight has never been put up in the annals of Manitoba's political history. And throughout it all, during nights and weeks of preparation, and those trying speeches, delivered in defence and attack, he was ever the personification of the gentleman, rising to statesmanlike heights, and discussing alone the issues of the hour.[60]

On 2 April 1897 Prendergast was appointed a County Court judge for the Northern Division of the Eastern Judicial District. He sat for five years before Prime Minister Laurier asked him to fill the vacancy on the Supreme Court of the North-West Territories caused by the death of Mr Justice Rouleau. At the time the Territories were divided into several vast, largely uninhabited regions, each presided over by a resident judge. Prendergast assumed responsibility for the Judicial District of Saskatchewan, and in February 1902 moved to Prince Albert, the area's principal city. Besides sitting in his home community he held court in Saskatoon, Battleford, and Rosthern, and four times a year sat with other district judges as a Court of Appeal. When the province of Saskatchewan was created in 1905, it did not immediately establish its own superior court. As a consequence, Prendergast sat for two more years before the Supreme Court of the North-West Territories was legislated out of existence and he was transferred to Regina.

One of the most controversial trials over which Prendergast presided was heard while he was a Territorial judge. Just days before voting was to begin in the 1905 Saskatchewan election, the returning officer for the district of Prince Albert ordered three new polls opened several hundred miles north of the city. After all of the southern votes were counted the Provincial Rights candidate had a majority of fifty-six. Ten days after the election, however, the three returning officers sent north to open the new polls returned with 151 ballots, all marked in favour of the Liberal candidate. An investigation was immediately launched, and it was discovered that none of the three officials had even reached their polling stations. A recount was ordered, and two of the officials were charged with election infractions. Both pled guilty and were fined $200, while the third deputy returning officer could not be found. On 17 February 1906 Prendergast presided over the recount, and in a decision severely criticized throughout the province, he held that even though he was aware that all 151 northern votes were forged, for purposes of his recount he was forced to regard them as properly cast. He argued that under the law he had no authority to look into the source of ballots, or to investigate whether they were genuine. His sole function was to count what was presented to him. The following month the returning officer, who had been charged with conspiracy to commit fraud, made his first appearance before Prendergast. The actual trial, however, did not get under way until June, when he was convicted by a jury. Sentencing was postponed to give his counsel time to argue before the full court that Prendergast had no authority to hear the case, since the offence was a political crime and outside his jurisdiction. Although the appeal court did not rule on that specific argument, it quashed the conviction on other grounds.[61]

Prendergast was appointed to the Court of King's Bench of Manitoba on 7 February 1910, his fourth judicial appointment in thirteen years. It was in Manitoba that he became involved in the two most sensational cases of his career. Both dealt with wrongdoing associated with the construction of the new legislative buildings, and the key player in each was Thomas Kelly. As the managing partner of the company charged with carrying out the construction, Kelly had established a close and allegedly criminal relationship with the provincial premier and three members of his cabinet. When the Mathers Commission announced that it had uncovered evidence that Kelly had been involved in a scheme of political kickbacks and overcharging, the contractor fled to the United States. Attempts to extradite him dragged on from 1915 until April 1916, when the Supreme Court of the United States ordered his extradition. Kelly's conspiracy to defraud trial opened two months after he was returned from Chicago. When Prendergast refused to grant an adjournment to allow Kelly's lawyers to review what had become a veritable mountain of evidence, they withdrew and Kelly acted on his own behalf. Thirty-nine witnesses were called, all by the Crown. Eleven days after it began, the trial ended with a jury convicting Kelly of defrauding the government of more than $1,200,000 in money, property, and securities. In July the Court of Appeal dismissed his appeal. The Supreme Court of Canada did likewise. The case was then remanded to Prendergast, who on 18 November 1916 sentenced Kelly to two and a half years in prison.

The following summer Prendergast presided over the trial of the ministers charged with conspiring with Kelly. From the perspective of the defence the most damaging of the forty-one witnesses called by the Crown was the provincial architect. He admitted that he and the accused had padded construction estimates to funnel money to the Conservative party, and that he had personally committed perjury, forgery, and theft and had falsified public documents. After hearing evidence throughout the summer Prendergast sent the case to the jury with a charge 'not unfavourable to the prisoners.'[62] The jury was unable to agree on a verdict, although its members voted nine to three in favour of convicting Premier Roblin, and eleven to one against his co-accused. A new trial was ordered, but because of the age and failing health of the former premier the government decided against further prosecution.[63]

While on the bench Prendergast was twice appointed a commissioner. On the first occasion the federal government asked him 'To Inquire Into and Report Upon Certain Alleged Fraudulent Practices and Irregularities in Connection with Public Auction Sales of School Lands in the Province of Manitoba.' His report was tabled in the House of Commons in April 1901, eight months after he opened hearings.[64] On the second occasion the provincial government appointed him to a royal commission to investigate charges of corruption in the Winnipeg city police 'with respect to Vice Protection.'[65]

Prendergast was a trial judge until 1 May 1922, when he was elevated to the Court of Appeal to fill the vacancy caused by Metcalfe's death. Eight years later he was sworn in as the province's chief justice, succeeding Perdue. Although ill health ultimately forced Prendergast to retire in 1944, he had ceased to be a force on the bench several years earlier,[66] and he became an example some Manitoba lawyers used for arguing that judges should be forced to retire at age seventy-five. In discussing Prendergast's pending retirement, one critic suggested that Prendergast should be replaced by a particular County Court judge, thereby improving the quality of both courts![67] Before stepping down Prendergast was asked what process he went through to reach a decision. He replied that he reviewed the evidence, determined who should win, and then applied the law in such a way as to bring about that result.[68]

When he retired Prendergast had been on the bench for forty-seven years and he was the only Canadian judge to have received patents for six judicial appointments. He was also one of the few judges, if not the only one, to move from a county court to become the chief justice of a province.[69] More than most who sat on Manitoba's Court of Queen's Bench, however, Prendergast is remembered with very mixed feelings. Many contemporaries had little good to say about him, before or after his appointment. To others, particularly French Catholics, he was a role model. Intensely proud of his heritage, he was for many years president of the St Jean Baptiste Society of Manitoba and served in a similar capacity in Saskatchewan. He was also the first president of the Société d'Éducation des Canadiens Français du Manitoba. In 1944 his service to the Church was acknowledged by Pope Pius XII, who made him a Commander of the Order of the Knights of St Gregory. The order is third in dignity after the Supreme Order of Christ and the Order of Pius IX, and the rank of commander is inferior only to the Grand Cross Knight of St Gregory.

Prendergast was a member of the senate of two universities. From 1895 to 1902 he sat on the council of the University of Manitoba, and six years later was appointed to a four-year term in the senate of the University of Saskatchewan. Laval University acknowledged his efforts on behalf of both the Catholic church and the advancement of education by awarding him an honorary doctor of laws degree.

Although a few Manitoba judges have engaged in artistic activities, none was as accomplished as Prendergast. Before his arrival in Manitoba he published two booklets of poems, both of which were well received by critics. He also worked part-time as a Quebec journalist and in Manitoba co-edited *Le Manitoba,* the first French-language newspaper published west of the Great Lakes. His poetry and involvement in literary circles earned him a seat in the prestigious Académie des Muses Santone, of Rouen, France. When not writing or painting he spent considerable time studying architecture.

On the bench Prendergast was never impatient, even with the

longest-winded of counsel. He had a special affection for young members of the bar, and his manner set at ease even the most shy and bashful among them. Experienced barristers also appreciated 'his unfailing patience, and above all, his consistent courtesy and kindness.'[70] On the way to and from his office and courtroom he never failed to acknowledge everyone he met, and whenever time permitted, he would stop for a short chat. Still, some harboured far less positive feelings about him. He was accused of being lazy[71] and of taking a year or two to write judgments.[72] In his last years on the bench he was obviously incapable of performing his obligations as a judge. As the authors of the leading history of the Manitoba legal profession note: 'The completion of so remarkable a judicial record ... should have been an occasion for warm congratulation, rather than embarrassed criticism. The need for some modification of the principle of life tenure for judges had become distressingly apparent.'[73] Fellow judges, however, had more tender feelings towards Prendergast. Thorson suggested that his family commitments[74] weighed heavily on Prendergast, and that he gave most of his salary to friends and relatives. As a consequence, said Thorson, Prendergast lived on next to nothing.[75] Probably the fairest assessment of his legacy was that, while his knowledge of the law was not profound, a humane outlook and good sense made him a sound trial judge.[76]

Prendergast was eighty-seven when he died of a heart attack on 18 April 1945, one year after he retired.[77]

HUGH AMOS ROBSON

There is little doubt that the judge with the largest legacy on and off the Manitoba bench was Hugh Amos Robson. Twice appointed a justice of King's Bench, the province's first Public Utilities commissioner, leader of the provincial Liberal party, chairman of the federal Board of Commerce, member of three royal commissions, bencher, founder of the Manitoba Law School, and an author, he was considered by some the most popular civil servant of his day.

Robson was born in Barrow-in-Furness, Lancashire, England, on 9 September 1871. Robert and Jane Robson emigrated to the North-West Territories in 1882 and three year later their son became a law student in the office of D.L. Scott, who had practised in Ontario for over a decade before moving to Regina the same year the Robsons arrived.

He became a crown prosecutor and was twice elected mayor. After the provinces of Alberta and Saskatchewan were carved out of the North-West Territories, he was appointed to the Alberta Supreme Court.

Robson was called to the bar of the North-West Territories in 1892 and for the next two years was a partner in Scott, Hamilton & Robson. When Scott left the firm Robson remained for two more years, then he too left to join the Territories' most dynamic politician,[78] Sir Frederick W.G. Haultain. He made Robson his associate deputy attorney general, an office Robson filled while still carrying on his private practice. Even before the appointment, however, Robson was well regarded by the legal community. The *Regina Leader Post* predicted that the new firm would do well. 'Mr. Haultain's training and experience, with Mr. Robson's ability and energy, should make a favourable and felicitous combination.'[79] As deputy attorney general Robson was responsible for everything from drafting legislation to supervising prosecutions. It was a demanding job, since the handful of lawyers who practised in the Territories did so only in the region's few populated areas. As a result, rural justices of the peace often worked unsupervised. Robson enjoyed telling an anecdote about one of them. When a resident found an Aboriginal using his boat to shoot ducks, he took the offender to the local magistrate and demanded that the Aboriginal be charged with theft. The accused admitted he took the boat, but the magistrate could not find in the *Criminal Code* a reference to an offence that exactly fit the crime. He first looked under 'boat,' but all the Code said was 'see ship.' When he located that section, he was told 'see piracy,' where he determined that the appropriate punishment was death. Satisfied, the justice sentenced the offender to be hanged. When word got back to officials in Regina they immediately wired Ottawa for instructions and received permission to release the bewildered duck hunter.[80]

On 30 June 1897 Robson married Fannie Laidlaw, a daughter of Vancouver resident John S. Laidlaw. Two years later he met someone else who would figure prominently in his life. While acting as Territorial prosecutor he was occasionally opposed by James Aikins, solicitor for the Canadian Pacific Railway. Aikins was much impressed by his young adversary and in 1899 convinced him to join his Winnipeg practice. Robson was a prodigious worker, and from his start as an assistant solicitor for the CPR quickly became Aikins's partner and the firm's busiest litigator.[81]

In the eleven years he practised with Aikins, fifty-two of Robson's cases were reported; he was successful in 60 per cent of them. He appeared in the Court of Appeal slightly more often than the King's Bench and usually acted for a defendant. Not surprisingly for a member of Manitoba's largest corporate law firm, 40 per cent of his cases involved corporate clients. Two interesting facts emerge from an analysis of Robson's activities as litigator. First, when acting for a defendant he was usually successful. By contrast, when acting for a plaintiff he was just as likely to be unsuccessful. Second, when he appeared in the Court of Appeal, he won twice as often as he lost. When appearing at trial, he lost as often as he won. These findings support a Manitoba study that examined 3500 statements of claim filed in Winnipeg's superior court between 1909 and 1939. Its results suggest that plaintiffs gained virtually no advantage by hiring an experienced litigator, whereas defendants substantially improved their chances by doing so. It also showed that, although corporations seldom sued, when they were sued they seldom lost.[82]

In 1908 Robson was appointed solicitor to the 'Commission to Investigate Taxation Conditions in the City of Winnipeg,' a body headed by Court of Appeal Justice Frank Phippen.[83] Two years later he represented the Alberta and Great Waterways Railway Company before an Alberta royal commission on which his former partner, D.L. Scott, sat. The commission's mandate included determining whether anyone connected to the Alberta government was involved in either the organization of the railway company or the contract entered into by the company and the provincial government.[84]

On 23 June 1910 Robson was appointed to the King's Bench. Among the first cases he heard was Russia's application to extradite Savaa Fedorenko. Chief Justice Mathers had already ordered that the revolutionary be extradited, and Robson's task was to determine if he should be released pending an appeal. The case attracted worldwide attention. Every day the court was packed with spectators as more and more evidence came out concerning the brutality of Russia's secret police. The hearing ended a week before Christmas. Robson was satisfied that, although the accused may have committed a murder, the charges against him were politically motivated and he ordered that Fedorenko be released.[85]

A year after he went to the bench Robson was appointed a commissioner to investigate allegations that members of the Winnipeg police force were accepting bribes from owners of houses of ill repute.[86] The accusations stemmed from an interview given various Toronto papers by the general secretary of the Moral and Social Reform Council of

Canada. After returning from a tour of western Canada, Reverend John Shearer said that he had been horrified to learn not only that there were a large number of houses of prostitution operating openly in Winnipeg, but that instead of closing them down and charging their owners and occupants, the police had actually prepared a set of rules by which the houses could operate. On 21 November 1910 Winnipeg city council passed a resolution establishing a commission to investigate Shearer's charges. Two days later Robson commenced hearings, and in less than sixty days submitted his report. He found that, although the charges were substantially true, and that houses of prostitution did flourish in a segregated section of the city, there was no evidence that any police officer had accepted a bribe. While no one disputed the accuracy of his report, the haste with which he carried out his work fuelled suggestions that the commission's real role was to divert attention away from the mayor and council during the municipal elections.[87]

Robson resigned from the Court of King's Bench in June 1912. When the provincial government privatized Manitoba's telephone system it hoped to provide better service at lower rates. Not only was that not achieved; the rates actually increased. In an attempt to bring spiralling telephone costs under control, the cabinet decided to create a public utilities commission, and it had come into being in April. The person chosen to run it was Brandon County Court judge T.D. Cumberland, a man of 'high character' and 'proven superiority to any considerations other than those of the public welfare.'[88] Within days of accepting the appointment, however, ill health forced Cumberland to resign. Premier Roblin asked Robson to fill the vacancy, and in the eyes of most Manitobans it was an inspired choice. 'In ability, in integrity, in every qualification requisite to the right discharge of those responsibilities and duties in the best interests of the public welfare and progress, Judge Robson is so eminently qualified that Manitoba can justly esteem itself specially fortunate among the Provinces of the Dominion in having such a man in such a position.'[89]

According to section 2(b) of *The Public Utilities Act*, every corporation having any connection to telephones or telegraphs was a public utility, as were railways, grain elevators, and companies engaged in producing or supplying water, gas, heat, light, or power. The Public Utility Commission was made a court of record, with the power to control and set rates, and it was given authority to investigate any matter within its jurisdiction.[90] Robson suggested that quite apart from the power given him by statute, it was his duty 'not only to protect the public from corporations, but also to protect corporations from themselves by preventing them from adopting a rapacious policy and by compelling them to make reasonable charges for public services.'[91] During his three years as commissioner he cured the ills of the provincial telephone company, shaped the legislation that created the Greater Winnipeg Water District, investigated the publicly owned hydro-electric system, settled a dispute between the City of Winnipeg and the Winnipeg Electric Railway to allow for the joint use of poles, issued an order allowing the Midland Railway to expropriate property to expand its line, and forbade the sale of electric power in St Boniface without the permission of that city's municipal officials. Under Robson's management the provincial telephone system not only accumulated nearly a quarter of a million dollars in its reserve fund, but revenues of the City of Winnipeg's hydro-electric system exceeded expenses by a million dollars a year.

Although Robson's accomplishments as public utility commissioner have been largely forgotten, the part he played in founding the Manitoba Law School has not. His involvement with the institution began in 1913, two years after the Law Society had organized a series of lectures intended to help prepare students for a career in law. He reorganized and improved the lectures and, with the Society's approval, began laying the groundwork for establishment of a law school. Within a year Robson and officials from the University of Manitoba and the Law Society developed a plan whereby the two bodies would jointly operate what became the Manitoba Law School, which would offer a three-year program of lectures to students-at-law. Modelled after Ontario's Osgoode Hall, the school was to be supervised by a board of trustees appointed by the two funding bodies. It officially opened its doors in October 1914 in space leased from the YMCA, its teaching staff consisting of a full-time recorder and seven part-time instructors. It was not until the following year, however, that the government amended *The Law Society Act* to ratify establishment of the school and to confirm that the agreement entered into by the Law Society and the University of Manitoba was within their legal competences.[92] When the new provincial Law Courts building was completed two years later, the law school became a tenant.

In 1915 Robson was asked to chair the legal education committee of the Canadian Bar Association. His mandate included investigating law-school admission requirements, the term and course of study most suited for use by law schools, the transfer of students from one province

Hugh Amos Robson (1871–1945). Puisne judge 1910–12, judge of the Manitoba Court of Appeal 1930–44, chief justice of the Court of King's Bench 1944–5. Robson was one of the most accomplished members of the Manitoba bar to be appointed to King's Bench, and the only judge in the province's history to resign from and then be reappointed to the bench. Robson was also a much respected lawyer and educator, politician, federal board chair, and civil servant. The faculty of law of the University of Manitoba resides in Robson Hall, named in his honour. (Provincial Archives of Manitoba)

to another, and the admission of students to the bar.[93] Among Robson's recommendations was that law students not be allowed to commence their studies before they were eighteen years old, and that they spend three uninterrupted years at a recognized law school, followed by one year of articles in a law office. In 1921 the Manitoba Law School became the first Canadian institution to adopt the new plan.

One of the biggest problems faced by Robson after the founding of the law school was locating casebooks and texts appropriate for its use. Three areas in which the need was particularly acute were company, corporate, and municipal law. He and J.B. Hugg set out to remedy the situation by compiling their own texts, and in 1916 they published *Cases on Company Law* and *Leading Cases on Public Corporations*.[94] Both were intended solely for the use of law students, some of whom helped assemble the material. The first book to appear, the casebook on corporations, was not an exceptional example of its type, and the authors acknowledged its shortcomings. 'Neither the limits assigned nor the time available permitted an exhaustive selection of cases.'[95] They explained their failure to offer any analysis or discussion with the disclaimer, 'The disquisitions of learned Judges are more illuminating than a text writer's epitomes.'[96]

Cases on Company Law consisted of twenty-five chapters organized around a series of conclusions, each followed by one or more cases that substantiated the accuracy of the statement. Some cases were lengthy expositions of the law, others less so. For example, the authors started their discussion of the sale of shares in chapter 3 with the heading 'Delay in Allotment of Shares.' The case comment that followed consisted of a citation of a leading case and the statement 'The Court gave judgment against the company on the ground that the allotment was not within a reasonable time after the application for shares.'[97] The material they covered under 'Subscription Under Seal for Shares. Issue and Allotment,' however, was more complete and included a lengthy statement of the facts and eight pages from a judgment of the Ontario Court of Appeal.[98]

While the first two books produced by Robson and Hugg were intended for the use of students, such was not the case with their third. *Municipal Manual* was a prodigious work and almost immediately became a standard treatise in use throughout the country. It offered lawyers a complete annotation of the Ontario *Municipal Act* together with commentary on sections similar to those found in statutes elsewhere. Only two texts produced by Manitoba judges have been its equal.[99]

Robson's association with the law school lasted the rest of his life. He was a lecturer, chairman of the Board of Trustees, and for two years the school's acting dean. Under his stewardship the Carnegie Foundation rated the institution as the best law school in Canada.[100] Even after he became a member of the Court of Appeal, Robson's passion for legal education did not wane. Beginning in 1939 he collected an assortment of appeal books, *facta*, written arguments, and transcripts of evidence that he lodged in the school's library as an aid to students.

Robson's reputation within the legal profession grew throughout his career. One area in which his expertise was recognized was company law. In 1915 he was asked to deliver a major paper on the subject at a meeting of the Canadian Bar Association.[101] In it he warned his audience that differences in the way the provinces treated corporate law and the incorporation of companies were the cause of uncertainty in the legal community, which he suggested could be avoided if the provinces agreed to abolish the existing charter system and adopt the English *Companies Act*.

Following accusations that the scandal-plagued Conservative government of Rodmond Roblin paid $50,000 to the incoming Norris administration as an inducement to terminate an on-going investigation into wrong-doing by the premier and three of his cabinet ministers, Robson was again appointed to a royal commission. Other members of the body established in 1915 included Chief Justice Perdue and Justice Alexander Casimir Galt. The three found evidence that the rumoured payment had been made, but determined that it represented settlement of a dispute over voting irregularities, and that it had nothing to do with the change of government.[102]

When Robson left the Public Utility Commission in 1915 to become general counsel, vice-president, and member of the board of directors of the Union Bank of Canada, he was described as 'the most popular public official that the province has ever known.'[103] He remained with the bank for ten years, but when it was absorbed by the Royal Bank of Canada he left to join the law firm of Wilson, Robson, Hamilton & Campbell. Hamilton was the same lawyer with whom Robson had articled and practised during the first years of his career. Two members of the Wilson firm were particularly special to Robson. Jean Robson, like her father, had articled with Hamilton before she joined his firm after receiving her call in 1924. The other person was the firm's senior partner, Charles Patrick Wilson, a lawyer of considerable skill and influence. For a quarter of a century he was a bencher, and between

1910 and 1916 either treasurer or president of the Law Society. He was retained as counsel in most of the important commercial and constitutional cases tried in Manitoba and regularly appeared before the Privy Council, the Supreme Court of Canada, the Exchequer Court, and the Board of Railway Commissioners. Just as the combination of Haultain and Robson had proved almost unbeatable at the beginning of Robson's career, the combination of Wilson & Robson proved equally so at the end.

Four years after resigning as public utility commissioner, Robson was again in the public spotlight. Before the general and central strike committees involved in the 1919 Winnipeg General Strike agreed to call off their protest, they extracted from the government of Manitoba its promise to establish a royal commission to investigate the circumstances surrounding the unrest. Two weeks after the strike ended the provincial government made Robson a commissioner 'To Enquire into and Report upon the Causes and Effects of the General Strike which Recently Existed in the City of Winnipeg for a Period of six Weeks, Including the Methods of Calling and Carrying on Such Strike.' Robson's 'remarkably astute' report was submitted exactly four months later.[104]

Although he had no involvement in the general strike itself, Robson did play a minor role in what amounted to a dress rehearsal. In 1918 Winnipeg civic officials were locked in a test of wills with unions representing electricians, waterworks employees, and teamsters. After workers struck a series of work stoppages virtually paralysed the city. When it became evident that there was no immediate solution in sight, a group of business and professional leaders formed the Citizens' Committee of One Hundred, which started bargaining with union leaders and, with the help of a mediator, worked out a settlement. The way in which the committee forced the city to back down encouraged union leaders to take a more extreme position the following year. The actions of Robson and the other members of the Citizens' Committee, instead of calming labour unrest, actually served 'to undermine the influence of moderate thought and to present the [labour] radicals with a powerful argument in favour of increased militancy.'[105]

Robson's commission sat for eleven days between 16 July and 10 September 1919. He concluded that the immediate cause of the strike was the refusal of employers in the iron industry to bargain with unions collectively. He also found that there were other significant but less immediate root causes. One was worker dissatisfaction with the conditions in which they laboured, a dissatisfaction exacerbated by a sense that with the war over there was no longer any need for employers to compromise. A second underlying cause was the discontent fomented by socialist leaders who co-opted the concerns of workers to further their own political agenda of 'Aggressive Socialism.'[106]

> There has for a long time past existed in Winnipeg an element which strongly advocated socialistic views. The group of men who have forced themselves to the front in that way directed their energies towards the conversion of their ideas of the working classes of Winnipeg ... [T]he motive of the radicals was not that of obtaining the right to a mode of collective bargaining for a group of workers, but that the purpose was to elevate Labour into a state of dictatorship.[107]

According to Robson, a great many workers either went out on strike, or stayed out, because of the intimidating presence of such radical socialists. Other contributory factors included the negative influence of the *Western Labour News*, a radical weekly newspaper that consciously fanned the flames of worker discontent, and the destabilizing efforts of the organizers of the One Big Union movement, whose aim was securing control of industry and eliminating the capitalist profit system. Robson believed that movement organizers were radical socialists, rather than craft unionists, who attempted to achieve their goals by dividing the community along class lines, turning workers against non-workers. In the end, however, he concluded that, although the editors of the *Western Labour News* and the One Big Union organizers may have been guilty of sedition, the majority of workers who went on strike were not:

> [It] is too much for me to say that the vast number of intelligent residents who went on Strike were seditious or that they were either dull enough or weak enough to allow themselves to be led by seditionaries. The men referred to may have dangerously inflamed certain minds, but the cause of the Strike, or of the exercise of mass action, was the specific grievances above referred to and the dissatisfied and unsettled condition of Labour.[108]

Although the Robson commission's report was almost completely ignored by officials from all three levels of government, one of the ways in which the federal government did respond to the Winnipeg General Strike was to establish a national Board of Commerce. Creation of the board represented Ottawa's most serious attempt to achieve economic security through state regulation,[109] and Robson became its first chair.

Consisting of three commissioners, the board was established as a court of record less than a month after the strike ended. Charged with administering *The Combines and Fair Prices Act*, it had the authority to prohibit mergers, the formation of monopolies, and the sale of necessities at prices higher than were reasonable or just. The three commissioners were not only given a mandate to determine what a fair price was, they could also require a company involved in the operation of a cold storage plant, packing house, mine, factory, cannery, or warehouse to prove that its profits were not excessive.[110]

The first three members of the board included Robson as chair and W.F. O'Connor and F.A. Acland as commissioners, although Acland was almost immediately replaced by James Murdock. The board opened hearings in Ottawa on 14 August 1919, and in December issued a series of official statements. Included was the declaration that it would restrict its investigations to those involving food, fuel, and clothing, and that when evidence of profiteering was found, criminal prosecutions would be initiated. The board also said that it would investigate all charges of an unreasonable accumulation of necessaries, hoarding food for an advance in price, and the cornering of food in order to raise prices.[111] After holding hearings in Toronto, Hamilton, Montreal, Halifax, Regina, Edmonton, and Ottawa, the commissioners issued an order setting out the maximum price that could be charged for ready-made suits and overcoats. It also restricted the gross profit of retailers of boots, shoes, and overshoes to $33^1/_3$ per cent, and the profit from the retail sale of pork products to 20 per cent.[112]

Reaction to the board's rulings was swift and critical. Retailers accused it of unnecessarily interfering with normal business activities, while farm groups criticized commissioners for not investigating the 300 per cent profits being made by cotton manufacturers, or the 74 per cent profits earned by wool producers. Six months after taking office even Robson was disillusioned, and on 23 February 1920 he resigned. In his official letter of resignation he referred to the impossibility of his moving to Ottawa and to the fact that his presence was required in Winnipeg. In another letter he sent the same day to the acting prime minister, however, he was more candid. He said that he found it frustrating that, although the government had asked the board to restrain excessive profit-taking by retailers, the government did not allow the board to apply the same rules to manufacturers. He recommended replacing the board with a federal body whose duties would include monitoring the level of profits made from the sale of all commodities.

His letter ended with the admission that in his view the government would never succeed in reducing prices by controlling profits. 'My short experience on the board of commerce in the administration of the Combines and Fair Prices act has led me to views which make it improper for me to hold a position on the board. The fact is that I am out of sympathy with the act.'[113] While most newspapers accepted at face value Robson's reasons for resigning, the Toronto *Globe* did not. It accused him of giving excuses rather than substantial reasons, and said that his letter of resignation was inherently inconsistent, and 'leaves much to be desired as a discussion of economic principles and of the practical problems facing the country.'[114] Other critics saw something more sinister in the resignation and suggested that Robson had been forced out of office after losing a battle for control with his vice-chair.[115] Shortly after Robson left, however, the remaining two board members also resigned.

During the decade between his brief tenure on the Board of Commerce and his return to the bench Robson was one of Winnipeg's busiest corporate lawyers. In the hours spent away from his office he was, among other things, a Law Society bencher (1918–25) and an advocate of change. In a 1922 speech to the Canadian Bar Association, Robson urged CBA members to embrace the concept of legal reform. While he did not consider himself someone likely to join 'the class of agitators seeking new things,'[116] he did believe that change was necessary. He warned, for instance, that unless legal principles and their administration were changed to take into account the needs of business, the commercial community would turn from lawyers to organizations like commercial arbitration societies. He suggested that pleadings and discoveries should be streamlined so that they could be resorted to more quickly and be more easily used to facilitate the settlement of actions. And he argued that when lawyers settled a dispute their compensation should be greater than it would have been had the issue gone to trial. There should, he said, be some better plan of remuneration 'so that lawyers will be encouraged to enter negotiations.'[117] Robson's other recommendations included the right of courts to proceed by way of stated cases, as was being done in England, and requiring that decisions of government that affected the rights of members of the public be approved by a court of law, rather than by civil servants.

In the fall of 1926 the leader of the Liberal Party of Manitoba, Tobias C. Norris, stepped down to accept a seat on the Board of Railway Commissioners. Between his resignation and the leadership convention held the following March party members were more concerned about whether they should join the Progressives of Premier John Bracken than about who should lead their own party. Most supported fusion, believing that over time the Liberals would absorb the Progressives. Although a few diehards found such a proposition distasteful, even they preferred a Progressive government to one led by the Conservatives. The debate over the future of the Liberal party continued until 20 March, a period during which no one acceptable to groups favouring and opposing fusion stepped forward. As a political adviser to Norris and as a party insider Robson was well known to Manitoba Liberals. Believing that he favoured cooperation with the Progressives, a group of Young Liberals urged Robson to let his name stand for party leader. Fifteen minutes before nominations closed, he agreed. He was an attractive candidate, and easily won the leadership, in no small part because of his past accomplishments. But delegates were also influenced by their conviction that he shared their views on the need for fusion.[118]

It was not until later that it became apparent that Robson was opposed to any kind of cooperation with the Progressives. When a provincial election was called weeks after his convention victory, he advised the country's Liberal prime minister that '[w]e have to open and continue this fight in an effort to place the Liberal Party in power. Understandings or entanglements will do infinite harm and we will not be led into them.'[119] In the end his intransigence forced the party to get rid of him as leader, but in the short run his candidates won seven seats to the Progressives' twenty-nine, the Conservatives' fifteen, Labour's three, and the election of a single independent. Robson won a Winnipeg seat in what would prove to be his only campaign. The Conservatives' fifteen seats were nine more than they had won in the previous election, and the thought of a resurgent Conservative party obsessed both Bracken and the federal Liberals. In an attempt to convince Robson of the need to reach some kind of accommodation with his Progressives the premier agreed to take the Liberal leader into his cabinet as attorney general. Although King enthusiastically supported the idea, Robson did not. In an effort to bring the matter to a head Bracken appealed to Robson personally:

> With regard to the present political situation in the Province, it seems to me opportune and desirable, from the point of view of the public interest, that the situation ought now to be considered carefully with the object of determining whether a greater measure of cooperation between our two

> groups cannot be worked out, upon terms honourable to both Parties and the Public interest ... I am willing to meet you personally to consider the whole matter; or, as an alternative, we might institute a joint committee of carefully chosen representatives of both Parties, to consider the possibilities of effecting an arrangement by which the Government of the Province might rest upon a basis of greater numerical strength in the House.[120]

The appeal did not change Robson's opposition to fusion, but he did agree to the appointment of a committee to at least investigate the possibility of some kind of merger arrangement. While negotiations were continuing he also agreed to support the government's legislative program. Late in 1929, however, he abruptly announced he would have nothing further to do with the Progressives. His decision to break off negotiations was probably based on the belief that the uncertainty associated with ongoing discussions could permanently divide the party, but its immediate effect was to alarm party insiders. Four members of Bracken's cabinet urged the federal Liberals to get rid of Robson by putting him back on the bench, or otherwise disposing of him politically.[121] During a private meeting with the prime minister Bracken reiterated his belief that the only way to prevent the Conservatives from taking control of the legislature was to replace Robson. King agreed, and within days announced Robson's appointment to the Court of Appeal. Robson resigned as leader of the provincial Liberals on 3 January 1930 and a week later gave up his seat in the legislature.

Robson's tenure as a politician had not been a success. While some believed that his refusal to negotiate with the Progressives was a sound political decision, others suggested that it was based solely on his strong personal dislike of Bracken and several members of the premier's cabinet. Robson particularly despised Attorney General William Major. A friend of the Liberal leader shared a drawing room with him during a train trip to Ottawa. Shortly before retiring for the evening the friend briefly left the room. When he returned he found Robson dressed in a long flannel nightgown, kneeling by his bed, praying aloud. His devotions took the form of a discussion about the problems of the day and his negative opinion of Major. When his prayer ended Robson arose, drank a tumbler full of water and whiskey, and without saying a word climbed into bed.[122]

Robson sat on the Court of Appeal for fourteen years before he was transferred to the Court of King's Bench as chief justice. According to a former dean of the Manitoba Law School, the move was necessitated after the antipathy that had grown between Robson and fellow justice W.H. Trueman began affecting the functioning of the Court of Appeal. Robson's strong negative feelings for Trueman, and Trueman's increasing senility, caused Robson to take positions opposite to those of Trueman, regardless of their merit. Members of the provincial bar were aware of the feud and of the effect it was beginning to have on all concerned. In a 1944 letter to a Liberal Member of Parliament written a week after the transfer, newly appointed Court of Appeal justice H.A. Bergman noted that 'Robson is very happy over his transfer. The Court of Appeal atmosphere and his feud with Trueman were beginning to get him down.'[123]

Robson died in the Winnipeg General Hospital at 5:40 a.m. on 9 July 1945, a month and a half after he was admitted with a serious illness. He was seventy-four years old. His death did not come as a complete surprise to family and friends. Thirteen years earlier he had collapsed on a Winnipeg street and nearly died of a heart attack.[124]

Robson was a Presbyterian, but most of his non-professional interests lay outside the church. He was an enthusiastic baseball fan, avid music lover, and an amateur historian. Throughout his life he kept a day-to-day record of events and experiences, including a first-hand account of the trial of Louis Riel. By 1944 his diary was several hundred pages long, and one of the abiding mysteries of the Manitoba legal profession is what happened to it following his death. Even without it, however, Robson left a scholarly legacy consisting of his three legal texts and four biographical articles published by the *Canadian Bar Review*.[125]

Robson was regarded by his contemporaries as an excellent lawyer and a good judge, and as a person was universally liked and respected.[126]

ALEXANDER CASIMIR GALT

Alexander Casimir Galt was the third relative of a father of Confederation to practise law in Winnipeg, following in the footsteps of Charles Tupper and Hugh John Macdonald. Born in Toronto on 15 March 1853 to a family of United Empire Loyalists, he was the grandson of the founder of the town of Guelph.

By the time his grandson was born, John Galt had earned an international reputation as author and a land developer. Although the son of a Scottish ship's captain, he became famous for his essays, poems, and works of both fiction and non-fiction. He even had the dubious distinction of attracting the attention of Sir Walter Scott, who referred to Galt's book of plays as the worst he had ever seen.[127] Galt's reputation, however, was considerably enhanced by his close relationship with Lord Byron and his friendship with members of the British aristocracy. In the early 1820s he became interested in the business opportunities to be had in North America and persuaded a group of London merchant bankers to become shareholders in the Canada Company. The company received its charter in 1826 and immediately purchased over a million acres of land in southern Ontario. Galt was hired to run its Canadian affairs and emigrated to Canada that year. The following spring he established Guelph, and later the town of Goderich.

John Galt was the father of three sons. The youngest became a father of Confederation, and the middle son was the father of Alexander Casimir Galt. Thomas Galt was born on 15 August 1815 in London. He spent two years in Canada while his father was with the Canada Company before returning permanently in 1833 as an eighteen-year-old immigrant. He spent six years with his father's former employer before quitting to enter the law office of William Henry Draper, the attorney general of Upper Canada. Galt received his call in 1845.[128] He was elected as a bencher in 1855, and appointed to the Court of Common Pleas fourteen years later.

The younger of Alexander Casimir Galt's two uncles was Alexander Tilloch Galt. In 1849 he was elected to the legislative assembly of Canada, but resigned the following year. Three years later he was re-elected, and in 1856 became one of the first to advocate the federal union of Britain's remaining North American colonies. As a member of the Macdonald-Cartier cabinet he attended the conferences in Charlottetown, Quebec, and Westminster that resulted in the creation of Canada.

Alexander Casimir Galt's most influential relative was probably his brother George Frederick. George was two years younger than Alexander and had no interest in law. He left school at fifteen to work in the tea industry, and in 1882 he and a cousin left Toronto for Winnipeg, where they established a tea importing and grocery company. Their business prospered and the two opened branches in Toronto, Calgary, Edmonton, Prince Albert, and Vancouver. His tea business, which became famous as the Blue Ribbon Tea Company, provided him with financial security, while his managerial ability and reputation for personal integrity resulted in his election to the boards of numerous companies.

George Galt was created a Knight of Grace of the Venerable Order of St John of Jerusalem. Though one was offered, he refused to accept a second knighthood for his work on the War-Purchasing Commission. He died in Winnipeg in 1928.[129]

Within such an achieving family, Alexander Casimir Galt spent his formative years in Galt, the town named after his grandfather (in 1973 it became part of the city of Cambridge, Ontario) and in Toronto. Before entering university he attended Dr Tassie's school in Galt and Bishop Hellmuth College in London, Ontario. His academic career at the University of Toronto was undistinguished, to put it kindly. He was last, or at least at the bottom of more than one third of his subjects.[130] After receiving his Bachelor of Arts degree in 1873 he was admitted to Osgoode Hall Law School and became a student in the offices of Sir Matthew Crooks Cameron. Cameron was one of the most dynamic lawyers of his time. He was a veteran member of the legislative assembly of Canada and, although an opponent of Confederation, agreed to enter the cabinet of Sandfield Macdonald as Ontario's first provincial secretary. After his party's defeat in 1871 he became its leader, but he resigned in 1878 to accept appointment to the Court of Queen's Bench. Six years later he became chief justice of Common Pleas court.

Before his articles were completed Galt left Cameron to finish his apprenticeship with Christopher Robinson, son of the former chief justice of Canada West and a leader of the 'Family Compact.' By the time Galt joined his office, Robinson was well known as a constitutional and international law specialist and had appeared as counsel in many of the country's most famous cases. After receiving his call in 1876 Galt joined the practice of Henry Edmons Caston. When the two parted company he practised alone briefly before spending two years with Toronto's mayor, A.R. Boswell. The partnership was dissolved in 1891, and for the next five years Galt again practised alone. He then left Toronto for Rossland, British Columbia, where he spent two years with P. Forin before once again becoming a solo practitioner. For a time his practice flourished, and he became solicitor for many of the area's largest mining companies. The region's economy collapsed in 1905, however, and he moved to Victoria, where he spent a year as a single practitioner before joining the Winnipeg firm of Tupper, Tupper, Minty & McTavish.

Galt was late providing the Law Society of Manitoba with the required notice of his intention to be called and was forced to write a special examination. He was asked three questions – 'What pleadings are allowed by the *King's Bench Act* and what is the principle adopted in framing our procedure as to pleadings?' 'How long a notice of trial is required?' and 'May a person be arrested for debt?' He was also asked to write a short essay on the *Real Property Act* 'dealing with its more important features,' and required to discuss 'the powers of a corporation to pass bylaws, i.e., where their powers should be exercised by bylaw, in whom the power to make bylaws is reposed.' The exam was marked by George Minty, who advised the Law Society on 27 June 1906 that his future partner had passed.

Compared to many of his contemporaries, Galt made little effort to raise his profile outside of the legal profession. Although a life-long Conservative, he never took an active part in politics. Instead, he devoted his attention to the affairs of All Saints' Anglican Church, where he was a devoted parishioner. Galt was also a member of several very exclusive clubs, including Sutton's of London, England, and Winnipeg's Manitoba Club. A year after arriving in Manitoba, Galt sought election to the Law Society. His eight votes placed him in a tie for nineteenth, 139 votes behind the winner.[131] Three years later he received three votes.[132] Despite a lack of success in bencher elections, however, Galt was well known within the profession as a scholar and a litigator. His twelve articles were not only the most ever published by a Manitoba judge, his approach was academically the most methodological. He consistently criticized members of both the bench and bar; and although his work often lacked depth and originality, he was not reticent about advocating new approaches to the law. On balance, however, most of his articles were extended case comments.

Galt published his first work eleven years after he was called, and twenty-six before going to the bench.[133] In it he noted that since 1792 the liability of common carriers was that of an insurer of goods. 'How is it then,' he asked, 'that in the absence of any statutory enactment extending the rights of carriers, our Reports show so many cases exonerating carriers from liability where the damage was caused by their negligence?'[134] In ten pages, after analysing more than a dozen cases, he provided an answer. More typical of his style, however, was his criticism of an 1890 Chancery decision published under the pseudonym Amicus Curiae.[135] He was probably wise not to have used his own name. The article is a vicious attack on the short-sightedness of judges, their unreserved acceptance of American authorities, and their failure to appreciate the consequences of their own decision. Throughout Galt used a series of nautical allusions, like 'currents of authority,' 'points of the compass,' 'circular storms,' 'legal mariner,' and 'conflicting winds,' before offering a trenchant analysis of the extent to which two Ontario courts misapplied the law of subrogation. After suggesting that Mr Justice Street misunderstood the legal principle upon which he grounded his decision, Galt argued that the court's judgment was not only wrong, but illogical. To illustrate, he showed how a subsequent court, applying Street's *ratio decidendi*, was forced to reach a decision not capable of being substantiated at law. Galt concluded by criticizing Justice Street for not thinking more about the practical implication of his ruling. 'We are reminded,' he noted, 'of the Mirage, in which objects beyond our horizon appear, by aerial magic, to be really in sight. In truth we see only images of objects, beautiful indeed and fantastic, but, alas, usually inverted.'[136] Galt was immediately attacked by the editors of the *Canada Law Journal*.[137] Although they found no fault with his reasoning, he was criticized for being more concerned about principles of law than 'the effectuating of substantial justice.' The editors suggested that he had become so caught up in judge-bashing that he had lost sight of the fact that his criticisms were based on a legal principle not yet argued before the court that he was attacking. When his critics offered their own analysis of the decision of which Galt was critical, however, they adopted both his reasoning and his conclusions.[138]

Galt responded to the criticism with a vigorous counter-attack,[139] accusing his critics of ignoring the consequences that would result if their position were adopted at law. The article presented Galt at his scholarly best. He reasoned aggressively and at the same time was thorough and persuasive. Throughout he illustrated how the conclusions reached by his critics were flawed by repeatedly asking 'if this view be correct, what then,' thereby emphasizing what he believed to be their misunderstanding of the law. The debate, however, seemed to have intellectually drained him. Thereafter he was far less critical, and rather than attacking he sought to educate. For example, in 'Set-off By Contributories,' he used a case decided in the Maritimes to discuss how an incomplete or inadequate report of a case could distort the way judges and lawyers view the law. The result of this misunderstanding, he suggested, was to occasionally thwart legislative efforts to bring about coherent change.[140]

Galt was practising alone in Toronto when he published the most superficial of his articles.[141] Instead of offering analysis and criticism he merely strung together a series of extended quotes around a case comment. Although he later reduced his reliance on quotation, he continued to discuss rather than analyse cases.[142] One of the most revealing of Galt's articles was 'Rights and Remedies in a Foreclosure Action.'[143] Largely grounded on an analysis of an 1893 decision of the Ontario Court of Appeal, it was a good example of the writing style Galt adopted on the bench. He became far less critical, and more diplomatic. Referring to the Chancellor's decision as a hasty examination of the evidence, and after suggesting that it would likely not be followed, he concluded by stating only that there was 'another and perhaps more persuasive way of looking at the matter.'[144]

In a number of his articles, however, Galt adopted the condescending style for which he became known on the bench.[145] His arrogance left him open to attack, and the *Canada Law Journal* was seldom reluctant to do so. In 1895 it directed readers to a case in which a principle of law argued by Galt had been discussed, noting that the court 'has decided the point adversely to the contention of Mr. Galt's article.' Rubbing it in a little more, the *Journal* suggested that '[i]n doing so it has, undoubtedly, followed the current of decision, both in this Province, and in England.'[146] This criticism says much about Galt's intellectual approach to law and perhaps his naivety. Few of his judicial colleagues had anything to say about substantive law and none were as innovative. As a lawyer he earned the respect of some while antagonizing most. The *Canada Law Journal* described the feelings of ambivalence the profession felt towards him. 'Mr. Galt's paper was a bold and ingenious attempt to establish that the law ought to be the other way; but we cannot say that we are disappointed at finding that the most recent deliverance of the court on this question adheres to what had been, previously, the established rule.'[147]

Shortly after the *Journal*'s comments appeared Galt left Toronto to practise in British Columbia. There he published two further papers.[148] Neither was methodologically or substantively different from his earlier efforts. More illuminating was his last work, published nine years after he went to the bench.[149] It was his shortest and his most arrogant. He suggested that although much had been written about appeals from Canadian courts to the Privy Council, most of what had been said amounted to arguments made by people unacquainted with the facts or with the law. Such cases, he argued, amounted 'to the blind leading the blind.'[150] In his view there was an overwhelming reason why such appeals should continue. British barristers were, he suggested, substantially more qualified than were their Canadian counterparts. Not only that, but '[t]he men who rise to the top of the Bar in England have arisen by their own ability and industry out of a population of forty-five millions ... Here in Canada we have a population of about nine millions; and some unkind critics say that our Judges are not always selected from the best available talent at the Bar.'[151] Only the uninformed, he believed, could fail to appreciate that the Privy Council was truly a 'splendid body of experts.'[152]

Apart from his scholarship, another way in which Galt attracted the attention of the legal profession was through his activities as a litigator. During the six years he practised in Winnipeg, twenty-eight of his cases were reported. He was successful slightly more often than not and generally appeared on appeals. The Court of Appeal, however, was frequently critical of his efforts and not reluctant to say so. On one occasion its criticism struck at the heart of his shortcomings as a lawyer. Galt refused to negotiate. Virtually every action went to trial and, if he failed there, to appeal. He frustrated clients and opposing counsel alike by routinely filing lengthy pleadings and raising issues that would later prove to have no relevance. On one occasion an irritated opponent applied to have portions of Galt's pleadings struck out as irrelevant. The application was granted by a referee and his decision was affirmed by a trial judge before it came before the Court of Appeal. Justice Phippen was incredulous that Galt had pursued with such vigour something other lawyers would have settled through negotiation. 'I think the plaintiff should have redrafted his pleading leaving out the useless and unnecessary portions and should not have come to this court.'[153]

Ironically, it was Galt's propensity for filing unnecessary pleadings that resulted in his appointment to the bench. One partner of the Tupper, Tupper, Minty & McTavish firm was James Stewart Tupper, Galt's brother-in-law. Tupper persuaded his associates to offer Galt a long-term contract to move from Victoria to Winnipeg; but almost immediately they regretted their decision. Galt's intransigence not only began alienating clients, it dramatically increased the firm's costs and made collecting fees much more difficult. The firm eventually saw Galt's appointment to the bench as the only way it could get rid of him without losing face. Their prayers were answered when Robert Rogers, the Conservative minister of the interior, persuaded Prime Minister Robert Borden to make Galt a judge. And so it was that on 24 October 1912 he replaced Hugh Robson as a puisne justice of the Court of King's Bench. His commission was the last made in Manitoba under the great seal of King Edward VII.

Alexander Casimir Galt (1853–1936). Puisne judge 1912–33. Galt was a much published though controversial trial judge who won little admiration from either Manitoba newspapers or members of the judiciary. His obsessive attention to detail made him difficult to get along with, and members of the bar were offended by his arrogance. Despite, or perhaps because of, these particular qualities he exhibited while at the bar, his law partners sought his appointment to the bench. (Provincial Archives of Manitoba)

Galt was regarded by his contemporaries as a poor trial judge, and over time the Court of Appeal grew increasingly critical of his decisions. His biggest problem was his inability to hide his personal biases, a problem that most often surfaced during criminal trials. In 1933 he presided over the trial of an accused charged with criminal negligence as a result of a motor vehicle accident. In his charge to the jury Galt noted:

> There is no denying it is a very serious case, a very serious case where any citizen is run down in Manitoba ... It was only last week a case very similar to this, a young lad run down and killed, and week by week, month by month, you see in the papers all these accidents that are happening all the time ... [T]he man should have stopped and he did not do that. He simply runs them down then and there ... Oh, no, he keeps straight along, scuttles along, although people are crying out 'stop.' Now, that is the kind of case and the kind of man you have to deal with today.[154]

On appeal Justice Trueman, considerably understating the effect that Galt's attitude likely had on the jury, said simply that 'this was a convicting charge that left nothing to be hoped for from the jury.'[155] That same year the same court heard another appeal grounded on Galt's apparent bias, and again it noted that '[t]he learned Judge's charge was very severe on the accused.'[156] In 1919 Joseph Thorson was junior to counsel representing two of the leaders of the Winnipeg General Strike. According to him, Galt's attitude was 'If you are not guilty, what are you doing in the box?' He believed that Galt's obvious prejudice against an accused often led juries to react with verdicts of not guilty and suggested that this was a factor in the 1919 acquittal of strike leader Frank Dixon.[157]

Galt's arrogance also attracted a good deal of attention from both the profession and the Court of Appeal. In an action over a real estate commission he refused to follow a decision of the Supreme Court of Canada because he could not understand its reasoning.[158] Because the case did not come before either court on appeal, neither the Court of Appeal nor the Supreme Court had an opportunity to respond to Galt's comments; but such was not the case when he decided that he was bound by the ruling of a judge of coordinate jurisdiction. The Court of Appeal overturned his decision, suggesting that it was made in the face of an overwhelming body of countervailing reason and authority. In a comment dripping with sarcasm, Justice Cameron noted that 'it is not the function of the Courts to make error perpetual.'[159] The longer Galt sat the more frustrated the Court of Appeal grew. Gratuitous criticisms became commonplace: 'With all respect for the learned Judge, I think this is begging the question ... I am unable to appreciate how ...'[160] and 'With the respect due to the learned Judge, it seems to me that it is manifest error ...'[161]

The notoriety he earned as a trial judge, however, paled in comparison to what he garnered as chair of a one-person royal commission.[162] On 14 July 1916 the Liberal government of T.C. Norris directed him to inquire into all matters pertaining to the construction of the Manitoba Agricultural College. The contract for work on the college, built on the west bank of the Red River a few miles south of Winnipeg, was let while Robert Rogers was the Conservative minister of public works. He was also one of the witnesses called by Galt to explain why the project cost so much more than had been projected. The aggressiveness of Hugh Phillipps, counsel for the crown, and the obvious animosity Galt felt towards Rogers, made the hearings a highly charged and much attended political event. The tension exploded during Rogers's final moments on the stand. All morning and afternoon he had been subjected to abusive and insulting questions, and when his testimony ended he received permission to make a statement.

Gesturing with his glasses as he walked towards Galt, Rogers held up to the commissioner a copy of the federal *Judges' Act*, which made it illegal for judges to engage in any occupation or to receive remuneration for anything other than judicial services. He explained that for a judge to accept anything other than a salary was unlawful and dishonest. Waiving aside the shouted demands of Phillipps and Galt that he stop talking, Rogers urged the commissioner to consult a dictionary for the definition of graft, which, he assured those in attendance, needed no royal commission to explain.

> Mr. Galt, in whose pockets the $100-a-day fees he had obtained for sitting as a 'commissioner' last year were still burning holes, sat for a second or two quite speechless. Then his rage got the better of him. His lantern jaws, which had relaxed during the recital of Mr. Rogers speech, came together with a snap. His usual anaemic face took on a decidedly purple tinge. His arms flung out in angry gesture. He was no longer a 'judge.' The judicial calm associated with the woolsack had completely deserted him. He was a man in a rage, and an impotent rage at that. Spluttering and stuttering, he

> attempted to defend himself. Like others caught in a like trap, he took refuge in the excuse, 'I'm not the only one.' ... Next , Mr. Galt turned on the personality of Mr. Rogers and insultingly enquired why he and not the Minister of Justice had undertaken to admonish the judges on their duty. To which Mr. Rogers, still smiling, replied that he was merely acting in his capacity as a citizen and not as a minister.
>
> Then it was that Mr. Galt's rage boiled over. After pretending for days to be sitting as an impartial investigator of certain facts, he frankly threw aside his assumption of impartiality and rendered on the spot a verdict against Mr. Rogers.
>
> 'You are involved,' fairly screamed Mr. Galt, his voice tremulous and his frame shaking as with palsy. 'You are involved, very deeply involved,' he repeated, shaking his fist, after Mr. Rogers had protested against the accusation. 'Thank you,' said the minister with a final smile, as he turned and left the room.[163]

Reports carried by the *Winnipeg Telegram* paled in comparison to an article published by the *Winnipeg Saturday Post* early on 23 September 1916, in which *Post* editor Knox Magee viciously attacked both Galt and the Norris government:

> The so-called Government we have picks its men for its purpose. Judge Galt, who is conducting the muckraking undertaking in regard to the Agricultural College, has had the dubious compliment paid to him of being selected twice by the perverters of British justice to act as a Royal Commissioner ... This summer he presided at a trial in a civil suit brought by a private individual against the *Winnipeg Telegram*. His charge to the jury on that occasion was so one-sided that the jury brought in a verdict against the *Telegram* which was the largest that has ever been recorded in a Canadian court in a similar case.
>
> At that time there was considerable speculation as to the judge who would be appointed to conduct this Agricultural College inquisition. The reports of the *Telegram* libel case had been printed but a very short time, before it was freely predicted in the streets that Judge Galt would preside on the fishing expedition that the Grit politicians of Manitoba had been announcing for a year that they would launch for the sole purpose of 'getting Rogers.' The predictions were justified. Judge Galt got the job – and from the moment that he obtained it he adopted an attitude of such obvious suspicion towards the simplest and most trivial statements made

> in evidence, that it was again freely and half-jocularly predicted in the streets that 'Galt will soak Rogers in any case.'
>
> Under the Norris regime, the Royal Commission has become the favorite weapon of political warfare. It has usurped the position of all regular processes. It ranks in the uses to which it has been put only with its ancient predecessor and model – the Spanish Inquisition. A partisan lawyer, hired with public money to misrepresent, is put up to ask all sorts of impertinent questions, to make all sort of deliberately false statements, to advance the meanest insinuations, to make the basest hints, without protest or without any rules of restraint.[164]

Within hours of the publication of the *Post* article Galt convened a Saturday sitting of his commission. Subpoenaed to appear before it were the editor, city news editor, and reporter for the *Winnipeg Telegram*, and Knox Magee of the *Post*. All four refused to apologize for what their papers had said about Galt and all were promptly held in contempt. Galt sentenced the *Telegram*'s editor to one month's imprisonment and imposed a $500 fine. The news editor received a sentence of two weeks in jail and a $100 fine, while the reporter who wrote the article was to be jailed for one month. Magee also received a one-month jail sentence and a fine of $500. Before the sentences could be executed, however, the newspapermen were released on a writ of *habeas corpus* by Mr Justice Haggart of the Court of Appeal. In his ruling Haggart noted that as a commissioner Galt did not possess the inherent and statutory powers of a Court of King's Bench judge. In fact, he said, Galt had no more power than any ordinary citizen commissioner had. The powers given a commissioner were limited by statute, and Galt knew, or should have known, that he had no authority to hold anyone in contempt.

An unrepentant Galt released the interim findings of his commission four months later and, in May, its final report.[165] After wading through six thousand typewritten pages of evidence he determined that the Crown had established the existence of fraudulent overcharges in the amount of $302,789.28. He also held that shortly after the site for the new Agricultural College was acquired a fraudulent conspiracy was entered into by Rogers and Thomas Kelly. One of its objects was siphoning funds from contractors working on the college to the Conservative's campaign fund. According to Galt, the conspirators were able to defraud the government because Rogers actively cultivated 'an atmosphere of laxity' that allowed contractors to submit false progress reports and estimates, secure in the knowledge that no one in government was going to check into their accuracy.

The federal government reacted to the report immediately. Rogers had left provincial politics to sit in the Commons as a Member of Parliament, and he was a highly respected and influential member of the federal cabinet. To undo the damage done to Rogers's reputation by Galt's report, the federal government appointed a royal commission to determine if the judge's comments or actions reflected upon or prejudicially affected the honour or integrity of Rogers.[166] Heading the commission were Sir Ezekiel McLeod, chief justice of New Brunswick, and Mr Justice Tellier, a retired judge of the superior court of Quebec. Even before it called its first witness, the commission was criticized by the *Manitoba Free Press*:

> What is the basis for the assumption that these Judges from the East are better qualified to draw inferences from a vast mass of evidence than the Judge on the ground, who saw the mountain of evidence built up piece by piece ... Is it their greater age, both gentlemen being well along in their seventies? Is it that, having both at former periods in their life [*sic*] had an active association with politics, it is deemed that they are better qualified to pass on a matter of this kind than a jurist who won his position solely on his merits as a lawyer? Or is this merely a new application of a principle, which has ofttimes been exemplified, that there is a native superiority in the man who remains East which qualifies him to approve in a spirit of condescension or reprove in a spirit of superiority the opinion, judgment, or action of the Western Canadian?[167]

The McLeod-Tellier commission met in Montreal daily between 11 and 12 June and between 28 June and 26 July 1917. It reviewed nine volumes of evidence, seven of which were of exhibits and two of legal arguments. Its findings were a full exoneration of Rogers and a stinging indictment of Galt. The commissioners found that, not only were his findings not supported by the evidence, many of Galt's statements were misleading and inaccurate and did not properly represent the facts. They also found that much of what Galt had to say amounted to a groundless personal attack on Rogers. The commissioners concluded by noting that the evidence heard by Galt could neither sustain nor support his findings and unfairly reflected upon the honour and integrity of the federal member. The *Montreal Gazette* regarded the report as a vindication of Rogers, and noted that 'Mr. Justice Galt showed that he lacked completely wisdom and equilibrium when he condemned to prison the editors of the *Telegram* who had dared criticize his conduct when he was investigating judge ... Judge Galt could come down from the bench without any harm being done to the judiciary of Manitoba.'[168]

Galt retired on 18 March 1933. He had not been a good judge. His aristocratic attitude and inability to place facts in perspective meant that 'there were certain things he couldn't see.'[169] He also made matters worse for himself, and those who appeared before him, by remaining on the bench long after he had become almost totally deaf.[170] Galt was an unrelenting stickler for detail. On one occasion, for example, he repeatedly refused to sign an order on the grounds it was drawn improperly. After trying and failing to persuade Galt to tell him what was wrong with the document, the lawyer involved returned with one draft after another. Finally, exasperated, he insisted on an explanation. It should be obvious, said Galt; the order contained a split infinitive.[171] Galt died at home on 29 July 1936.[172]

JOHN PHILPOT CURRAN

John Philpot Curran was born in Milan, Ohio, on 13 December 1858. His grandfather, a colonel in the English army, had emigrated to Canada from Newmarket, County Cork, Ireland in 1832. Curran's father was fourteen at the time and was raised successively on the colonel's military grant in London, Ontario, and then in Ohio. John Philpot Sr studied for the ministry at Gambier Theological College, and was ordained a deacon in 1856 and a priest three years later. He then returned to Canada, where between 1859 and 1886 he pastored in seven Anglican congregations, retiring as rector of Adelaide, Ontario.[173]

John Curran Jr attended schools in St Marys, Kincardine and Walkerton, all in Ontario, before entering the Stratford office of future justice John Idington and Charles J. Mickle. He was an undistinguished student and graduated twelfth in a class of twenty. After receiving his call in February 1881 he left the Idington firm for Manitoba, where he joined the Winnipeg practice of Biggs, Wood & Dawson, one of the city's busiest. That association did not last long, and before the year was out he joined A.M. Sutherland. The firm soon acquired a new senior partner when James Fisher, a Stratford lawyer and close friend of Robert Smith, joined. When the partnership was dissolved Curran and Henry Vivian formed an association that lasted until 1887. Curran then left the active practice of law to become law clerk to the legislature of Manitoba. A year later, however, the Norquay government was defeated in a provincial election and he lost his job. With few prospects, he was both angry and desperate. He demanded compensation from the Greenway administration, suggesting that had he known that his position was not permanent he would not have severed his connections to members of the business and professional community.[174] In reality Curran had no such connections. He was not considered a good lawyer and his reputation suffered further because of his alcoholism. Lacking an invitation to join someone's practice, he spent five months as office manager in the chambers of J.S. Kennedy before he moved to Neepawa. He practised there from June 1888 until 1890, when he relocated thirty miles south to Carberry. Curran, however, was neither successful nor lucky. Three years after settling into his new community his home, which contained his law office, was completely destroyed by fire. By the following spring he was destitute and was advised by the Law Society that he was in danger of being struck from its rolls because of non-payment of fees. He responded with an affidavit asking for time to pay, noting that the fire that destroyed his house also destroyed all his books of account, suit papers, client title deeds, notes, and vouchers for the payment of money. 'The scarcity of ready money at the present time renders it almost impossible for your petitioner to collect funds even from those who are willing to pay more than sufficient to supply the bare necessaries of life for your petitioner's wife and children.'[175]

Curran apparently realized that the chances of rebuilding his practice in Carberry were slim. Not only would it be difficult to do so without adequate financing, his reputation as a 'drunken bum' destroyed what little credibility he still possessed.[176] He therefore left for Minnedosa, an attractive community approximately equidistant from both Neepawa and Carberry. He practised alone for four years before obtaining an appointment in 1902 as District Registrar for the Neepawa Land Titles Office. In 1908 he moved to Brandon, where he joined the firm of G.R. Coldwell, minister of education in the Conservative government of Rodmond Roblin, and G.B. Coleman. Curran remained with that firm until he went to the bench five years later.

Although his career was undistinguished, Curran occasionally appeared as counsel in court. While with the Coldwell firm twelve of his cases were reported, and statistically he was as successful as many of his more accomplished contemporaries. His success rate was a commendable 66 per cent, one-third of his clients were corporations, and almost all his appearances were in the Court of Appeal. His reputation for dissolution, however, likely hurt him more in bencher elections than in the courtroom. On the two occasions he was nominated as a bencher he received a single vote, suggesting that in neither case did he even receive the support of his partners.[177]

Curran did, however, bring himself to the attention of potential clients through his involvement in the affairs of his church and in various fraternal organizations. He was an ardent member of the Anglican church and active in the affairs of every congregation of which he was a member. He was a frequent delegate to the General Synod of the Anglican church, and while on the bench he was a lay reader of his diocese and frequently conducted services. Congregations with which he was associated included All Saints, St Luke's, and Christ Church, the latter being one of the oldest Anglican congregations in Winnipeg. He was also a member of the Sons of England, a frequent guest speaker at both the St George's and St Andrew's societies, and a member of the Independent Order of Odd Fellows and the Ancient Order of United Workmen.

Curran was appointed to the Court of King's Bench on 24 October 1912, beginning a sixteen-year tenure that was marked by frequent controversy. Little more than a year after his elevation he presided over the sentencing of two of the men who helped John Krafchenko escape from the Winnipeg jail. One of the two was Percy Hagel, a lawyer and the son of one of the city's best-known barristers. In passing sentence Curran said that he thought the young lawyer would be out of prison within eighteen months, a fraction of the time his co-accused was to serve. His comments caused a storm of controversy. He was accused of bias and criticized in newspapers throughout the province. It was criticism he deeply resented. While presiding over the 1914 spring civil assizes, he could no longer hide his feelings. A recent *Winnipeg Tribune* editorial had particularly incensed him, and he told a startled courtroom that it was criticism that he was not going to ignore. 'So incorrect and so unfair to myself are some of these statements that I cannot in justice to myself and the position that I hold allow them to pass unnoticed, uncontradicted and without comment ... If reporters do not take the trouble to report verbatim what the judges say but paraphrase what judges do say, they are justly open to censure.'[178]

Curran's tirade did little to dispel the notion that he had acted inappropriately, and four years later he was again involved in a controversy. This time, however, the criticism was more heated and ended in

John Philpot Curran (1858–1928). Puisne judge 1912–28. Curran was one of the few judges appointed to Queen's Bench who were not successful while in practice. His reputation suffered even more because of his alcoholism, and for a time he was unable to pay his annual practising fee. While on the bench he was plagued by controversy and accusations of bias. (Provincial Archives of Manitoba)

a demand for his removal from the bench. In November 1917 a rural school teacher appeared before him charged with indecent assault and with having sexual relations with a girl under fourteen. The teacher was convicted of the indecent assault and sentenced to six months in jail. When Curran subtracted from the sentence the two and a half months that the accused had already spent in jail, the Winnipeg Council of Women was outraged. It promptly passed a resolution demanding his impeachment and called on the seventy other Canadian Councils of Women to support its action. The resolution noted that the maximum sentence for indecent assault was two years' imprisonment and a whipping. Curran's sentence was not only a fraction of that, it ignored the fact that the convicted teacher stood in a fiduciary relationship with the girl he assaulted. Members of the Council of Women were not only offended by Curran's sentence, they were upset by what they perceived to be his obvious bias in favour of the accused:

> [W]hereas the petit jury returned a verdict of guilty on the count of indecently assaulting this same girl, and, whereas, Section 292 of the criminal code states that the punishment for this offence is to be two years' imprisonment and whipping; and, whereas, Mr. Justice Curran, in sentencing Goodridge on January 14, 1918, gave him only six months' imprisonment and ordered that the two and a half months he (Goodridge) had been incarcerated should be included in the said six months; and, whereas, the accused stood in a fiduciary relationship to the victim of the assault; and, whereas, representatives from the leading women's organizations in Winnipeg attended the trial of Goodridge and were of the opinion that Mr. Justice Curran displayed a distinct bias in favor of Goodridge, and did all in his power to influence the jury in favor of the accused; and, whereas, Mr. Justice Curran has on several occasions displayed a similar lenient attitude toward other men accused of committing crimes on little girls and women; and, whereas, Mr. Justice Curran frequently displays an irritable temper in the court;
>
> 'Be [it] therefore resolved (1) that in our opinion the judge was lax in imposing the sentence he did, as we are of the opinion that if ever the maximum penalty of two years and whipping should be imposed it should have been on this occasion, when the guilty man was the trusted teacher of his victim; (2) that since Judge Curran is partial and since it is necessary in the interests of justice and morality that he should be impartial it is not therefore in the interests of justice that Mr. Justice Curran should continue on the bench.'[179]

The *Manitoba Free Press* not only reprinted the resolution in full, it listed the names of the women who attended the Goodridge trial and printed the comments made by each member of the Winnipeg organization. One of the women was Mrs A.A. Perry, who told the meeting that she met with Justice Curran during the trial and that she was horrified by his comments. He accused the victim of being a bad little girl with poor morals, and said that he could not help but notice that she had no religious convictions and that she had no idea of what it meant to sin.[180] Two days after publishing the resolution of the Council of Women, the *Free Press* printed an editorial defending Curran. Its defence, however, was lukewarm. It suggested that the issue between the judge and the women was merely one of opinion; and since he had only done what had seemed right to him at the time, Curran's independence as a superior court judge should protect him from any official sanction.

That controversy would surround Curran throughout his judicial career came as no surprise to members of the legal profession. Most regarded him as a second-rate lawyer and one of the province's weakest judges.[181] Others were offended by his antics on the bench. He typically spoke in a loud voice, almost yelling. Manitoba lawyers knew that this had nothing to do with any hearing problem. Curran was simply excitable and particularly so when testimony was coming from a police witness,[182] an attitude many attributed to his frequent run-ins with the police while he was drinking heavily during his brief tenure in Carberry.

As a Winnipeg Crown prosecutor Robert Blackwood Graham frequently appeared before Curran and often complained of the justice's pro-defence bias.[183] Most prosecutors did whatever they could to avoid his court. On one occasion Graham and a team of defence lawyers met to decide which judge should preside over a trial. The defence did not want the matter heard by Justice Adamson and Graham did not want it tried by Curran. When one of the defence team succeeded in having Curran assigned to the case Graham was livid. 'Just how this was accomplished is of no particular interest ... Suffice it to say that he thus succeeded in getting before the one judge who could be depended upon to acquit on very slight excuse.'[184]

Experienced lawyers like Graham had little respect for Curran's judicial abilities. On one occasion Curran complained that he could not follow Graham's reasoning. 'That is your Lordship's misfortune not my fault.' Curran sarcastically thanked Graham for the compliment. 'If your Lordship thinks my remark was intended for a compliment you are as mistaken in that as in your conception of the law of evidence.'[185] Although these exchanges were not unusual, the bias exhibited by Curran was not usually apparent in transcripts read by the Court of Appeal. As a result, few of his rulings were successfully appealed. On this occasion, said Graham, '[I] made up my mind that my only course was to force Curran to commit me for contempt in which case I could by habeas corpus proceedings get his conduct before another judge which would at least have the effect of causing the other judges to check him up.'[186] Curran, however, refused to be drawn in.

> This was the last straw. I said: 'My Lord there is nothing to be gained in proceeding with this case so long as your Lordship labours under the delusion that the presumption of innocence is irrebuttable and that any evidence which tends to show the guilt of the accused is ipso facto inadmissible. I regret my action in refusing to proceed for more reasons than one, but principally because through your Lordship's conduct and through no fault on the part of any one else the question of the guilt or innocence of the accused is left undecided. Your Lordship will acquit him, but he has never been tried and he goes out of the room with the black cloud of suspicion still over him.[187]

Graham noted in his diary that for a long time after the trial Curran refused to speak to him. Then one day, in a streetcar, '[he] sat down beside me and told me he was very dissatisfied with counsel employed by the Crown at the assizes and had urged them to appoint me to take all of the assize cases. I never knew what caused the change of heart.'[188]

While a judge Curran was a member of one commission. In 1916 he was appointed to a one-person inquiry 'to investigate into the Management and Supervision of the Gaol and Prison Farm of the Eastern Judicial District of Manitoba.'[189] In his report he suggested that the jail suffered from serious overcrowding, and he criticized officials for not separating into different areas those accused of a crime but not convicted, the insane, and ordinary prisoners. He also recommended that the province establish a single reformatory for the entire province, and that it purchase at least eight hundred acres within fifteen miles of Winnipeg so that prisoners could be provided with facilities for 'personal improvement and useful production.'[190]

Curran died on the morning of 9 January 1928 without regaining consciousness following exploratory surgery, a month before his daughter was to have been married. He left an estate valued at slightly more than $11,000.[191]

6

A Time of Transition, 1921–1938

In the 1920s both the government of Manitoba and the composition of the province's highest trial court underwent significant transformations. In early October 1921 Justice Metcalfe was raised from King's Bench to the Court of Appeal and his seat on the trial court was taken by Andrew Knox Dysart. The former Maritimer was one of the most literate and cultured judges to sit on a bench in Manitoba. Although some members of the Mantoba bar were less than enthusiastic about the appointment, largely because Dysart had little courtroom experience and had built only a modest practice, 'it is generally acknowledged that the presence of this tall, dignified gentleman on the Manitoba bench added significantly to its strength.'[1]

A month after Metcalfe's unexpected death on 2 April 1922, Justice Prendergast was raised from the King's Bench to the Court of Appeal and John Evans Adamson took the seat vacated by Prendergast. The appointment of the thirty-seven-year-old Adamson was the most controversial and vigorously contested in the history of the Manitoba judiciary. But despite the well-deserved nickname 'Blackjack,' by the time Adamson retired from the Court of Appeal he was widely regarded as a very able judge.

The change that affected the way politics was done in Manitoba after 1922 was substantially more significant than the changes to King's Bench. The sight of a former premier and two of his cabinet ministers in the prisoners' box, combined with suspicions about the ethics of the

Norris Liberals, profoundly disillusioned Manitobans; and voters turned their back on party politics and elected the non-partisan president of the province's Agricultural College, John Bracken, the staunchly Methodist leader of the United Farmers of Manitoba and its successor, the Progressives. He brought to government an unshakeable belief that the only way to fix the problems of the past was through a pragmatic rather than an ideological approach. Committed to balancing the province's budget in an era when few provinces had done so, Bracken's party held power for the next three decades.

Despite the commitment of the Bracken government to change the way politics was conducted in Manitoba in the 1920s and 1930s, there was no perceptible change in the federal judicial appointment process. Judicial appointments were still regarded as rewards for services rendered, at least in the opinion of the editors of the *Fortnightly Law Journal*, although they also acknowledged two other factors that influenced decisions about who went to the bench. Referring with approval to the comment of a leading Canadian lawyer, the editors suggested that 'in most judicial appointments the appointee owed his selection to the extent of seventy-five per cent to political considerations; fifteen per cent to religious affiliations, while ability and fitness measured up but ten per cent.'[2]

Regardless of whether they were appointed for political or other reasons, in the inter-war years Manitoba superior court judges were considerably less busy than they had been during the first two decades of the century. In Winnipeg, for instance, 9202 Statements of Claim were filed in the Court of King's Bench between 1927 and the end of the Second World War, an average of 484 per year, 900 a year fewer than had been filed between 1910 and 1926. Justices of the Court of Appeal, by contrast, were busier. They heard an average of 181 appeals per year between 1927 and 1945, compared to 139 a year during the previous decade and a half.

Between 1927 and 1929 the make-up of the King's Bench and Court of Appeal underwent a shake-up. In 1927 Chief Justice Mathers of the King's Bench died after surgery and was replaced by Justice Daniel Macdonald, whose seat was filled by James Frederick Kilgour, a prominent Brandon barrister. A few months later Justice Curran also died, and his seat was taken by William James Donovan. The cycle of change was completed in December 1929 when the Court of Appeal's W.E. Perdue retired. Prendergast replaced him as chief justice and the retirement vacancy was filled by Hugh Robson, who had stepped down from the King's Bench seventeen years earlier.

In 1931 Kilgour died of internal bleeding at age fifty-seven, and the following year his seat on the King's Bench went to the most prominent soldier in the court's history, Lieutenant General Percival John Montague. Two years later another well-known soldier joined the court, replacing the retired Justice Galt. Lieutenant Colonel Fawcett Gowler Taylor was also the recently retired leader of the resurgent provincial Conservative party. In 1937 the man Taylor defeated to enter the legislature was appointed chief justice of the Court of King's Bench. Ewen Alexander McPherson, like Taylor and several other members of the bench, was more politician than lawyer and had practised little law. Ironically, not only were Taylor and McPherson from the same community of Portage la Prairie, so too was Daniel Macdonald, the man McPherson replaced as chief justice. While Macdonald was kindly and well-intentioned, his abilities paled in comparison to those of another Maritimer, Andrew Knox Dysart.

ANDREW KNOX DYSART

Dysart was born on a farm in Cocagne, Kent County, New Brunswick, on 15 November 1875, one of a family of six sons and five daughters. Although Andrew Knox Dysart Sr and Henriette Miriam Cutler lived a life of relative simplicity near a small village on New Brunswick's Northumberland Strait, both came from prominent United Empire Loyalist stock. The father of Andrew Knox Sr had emigrated from Scotland when his Scottish regiment was disbanded following the Battle of Waterloo in 1814. He settled in Buctouche, New Brunswick, where he became a shipwright. Henriette's great-grandfather was Ebenezer Cutler, one of a number of Loyalists who fled Boston for Halifax in 1776. Her father, Robert, was prominent in New Brunswick politics both before and after Confederation. Between 1873 and 1878 he represented Kent County as a supporter of the Liberal government of Alexander Mackenzie. The same year that Cutler was elected to the House of Commons, Mackenzie appointed Dysart Sr a collector of customs, a position he held until he retired in 1910.

The Dysarts encouraged a diversity of opinion among their children. As a result, the family included Anglicans, Presbyterians, and Roman Catholics, Conservatives and Liberals, and Republicans and Democrats. Most were well educated. Four of the six Dysart sons became lawyers. Two eventually followed their brother Andrew to Manitoba, while a third remained in New Brunswick to become the province's premier and, later, a judge.

As a youth, Andrew Knox Jr wanted to be either an engineer or an architect, and his enjoyment of working with things mechanical remained with him all his life. He received his early education in local schools, and in 1897 entered St Joseph's University in Saint John. Three years later he graduated with a Bachelor of Arts degree, the top student in his class, and was elected valedictorian. Dysart financed his last two years at St Joseph's by teaching first-year students English and mathematics. After receiving his B.A. he worked as city editor for the *New Freeman*, a Saint John Catholic newspaper. His editorials 'were characteristic of the man. He won for himself a reputation for moderation, fairness, lucidity, and a style that showed evidence of a full knowledge of the placement of words.'[3] In 1901 he entered Harvard, graduating three years later with an honours degree in law. During a year of post-graduate study in constitutional law at Oxford his fascination with architecture grew, beginning a life-long obsession.

Dysart was called to the New Brunswick bar on 14 November 1905 but, before establishing himself in practice, he became one of those caught up in the mystique of western Canada. Although he knew little of Winnipeg, it became his destination because several New Brunswick lawyers had already moved there. Almost immediately he counted among his Manitoba friends Sir Rodmond Roblin, the province's Conservative premier, and several members of Roblin's cabinet. Dysart received his Manitoba call in June 1906 after he articled briefly with Tupper, Phippen and Tupper. He spent a year with Hugg & Kelley and another with G.A.S. Potts before practising for four years with Dysart & Wemyss.[4] During his last ten years at the bar he was a partner of his brothers Arthur and Harrison, specializing in commercial and company law. Andrew established only a modest practice, seldom appeared in court, and did not impress his contemporaries.[5] In a career that lasted fifteen years seven of his cases were reported, and he was usually unsuccessful.[6]

Two years after he was called to the Manitoba bar Dysart married Claire Helen Forrester.[7] The daughter of Charles H. Forrester was an alumnus of St Mary's Academy and Rupert's Land Ladies College. She was an accomplished artist and active in Winnipeg charities, including the Imperial Order of the Daughters of the Empire (I.O.D.E.) and St Joseph's orphanage.

Although he personally never sought elective office, Dysart's family name was well known in both Liberal and Conservative circles. His brother Allison spent five years as the Liberal premier of New Brunswick, and his maternal grandfather sat in the House of Commons during the tenure of Prime Minister Alexander Mackenzie. Andrew Dysart was a prominent member of the Conservative party, and between 1912 and 1921 he declined several invitations to contest an election. He was appointed to the King's Bench during the brief administration of Conservative prime minister Arthur Meighen, another native of Portage la Prairie.

Unlike most judges, who became involved in attention-attracting activities while at the bar, Dysart raised his profile after he went to the bench. In the years following his appointment he served on the executive of a number of non-profit organizations. He was president of the Winnipeg Canadian Club, vice-president and president of the Association of Canadian Clubs, chair of the Commission on Naturalization Ceremonies for Canada, committee chair of the Winnipeg branch of the National Council of Education, and in 1933 represented the Canadian Bar Association at the annual meeting of the American Bar Association, where he was elected an honorary member of the ABA. He also represented the University of Manitoba on the board of trustees of the Manitoba Law School, was vice-president and president of the Winnipeg Branch of the League of Nations Society, and served on the board of the Dafoe Foundation. The private clubs of which Dysart was a member included the St Charles Golf & Country Club, the Winnipeg Winter Club, the Manitoba Club and the Canadian Club.

In 1918, three years before Dysart was appointed to the bench, his wife became the first Winnipegger to die of the Spanish influenza, which swept much of the world following the end of the First World War. Her death occurred while she and her husband were on a trip celebrating their tenth wedding anniversary. Dysart's sister Ann promptly moved to Winnipeg to act as surrogate mother to her brother's children; Dysart never remarried.[8]

Dysart became a justice of the Court of King's Bench of Manitoba on 3 October 1921. He was not a judicial activist, and seldom broke new ground. An example involved an action for vehicular negligence brought against the Winnipeg Electric Company. Dysart held that the driver of a motor vehicle was obligated by statute to rebut the presumption that he or she was negligent if involved in a traffic accident. The Privy Council agreed and upheld his decision. Dysart's judgments were widely regarded for their legal scholarship, and they remain monuments to both

Andrew Knox Dysart (1875–1952). Puisne judge 1921–47, ad hoc judge of the Supreme Court of Canada 1935, judge of the Manitoba Court of Appeal 1947–52. Dysart was a respected lawyer, but by his own admission did not have a thriving practice. This photograph of his office was taken in 1912, four years after he was called to the bar of Manitoba. (Provincial Archives of Manitoba)

his personal values and his eloquence. An example is *Rex* v. *Oak Bluff School Division*,[9] in which he discussed the significance of education to society. Its aim, according to Dysart, was the development of character, strength, ability, and spirit. It was not

> intended to foster the pernicious system that would encourage each individual to get all he can from the 'state,' and give as little as possible in return. If this application succeeds, it will have a tendency to encourage children, not only to insist upon being clothed to go to school, to be carried to and from school, to be supplied with free books and teaching, but might also lead them to expect wages for the time spent at school.[10]

Dysart's sense of his judicial role stood in sharp contrast with that of judges like Thomas Wardlaw Taylor, who felt that it was no part of his job to do justice. In 1945 Dysart heard an action involving construction of the by-laws of a fraternal organization. He acknowledged a strict reading of the by-laws would appear to favour the plaintiff, but said he '[could not] believe that the society ever intended to strain at a gnat and swallow a camel – to withhold its benevolences from a needy housekeeper concubine in order to bestow them upon a faithless wife.'[11]

Dysart's judgments often evidenced both his sense of humour and fondness for Byron and Shakespeare. One of his best-known decisions involved a young woman, camping with a male friend, who was arrested during a moment of intimacy.[12] She brought an action against both the police officer who arrested her and the magistrate who sentenced her to six months' confinement. Dysart clearly felt that the defendants had been overzealous in their pursuit of justice. After receiving a complaint, the chief of police 'set out to find the offenders, and at four o'clock on a summer's afternoon, he found the tent, and in it, the plaintiff, recumbent on a bed – in extreme deshabille. On a adjoining bed lay her host, renewing his energy by "tired nature's sweet restorer – balmy sleep." To the indulgent eye of the law this scene was not offensive, but to the virtuous eye of Chief Rose it was highly reprehensible.' He suggested that the magistrate, although well-intentioned, was perhaps too willing to stretch his authority 'to embrace and to bring back to the straight and narrow path, an erring maiden whose venturesome feet may have carried her out upon the wide and easy way.'[13]

While not all of Dysart's decisions contained such literary allusions, many did. On one occasion he described a defendant's claim as 'conceived in dishonesty and ingratitude, and brought forth in naked technicality.'[14] In another case he was obviously unimpressed by the testimony of a witness: 'I cannot but think that his recent examination of the wall not only refreshed his recollection as to what he did ..., but so stimulated his imagination that it enabled him to "give to airy nothing a local habitation and a name," involving him at the same time in the unfortunate necessity of propounding a theory which if not absurd, is at least fantastic.'[15]

The case that attracted Dysart the most public attention involved the trial of a serial murderer. Earle Leonard Nelson was a drifter who had escaped from a California institution for the criminally insane. He killed at least eighteen women in the United States before fleeing to Canada. In June 1927 he arrived in Manitoba, passing himself off as a bible student. After murdering two Winnipeg women, Nelson was caught stealing a ride on the very train that carried a posse of police officers who had been dispatched to arrest him. He pled not guilty and his trial got under way in November. Newspapers all over North America carried daily accounts, and he was eventually found guilty and hanged. Despite the fate suffered by his client, Nelson's lawyer was impressed with Dysart's handling of the trial. 'To me, he was everything that a judge should be. He was learned, he was cultured, he was kindly and he was fair ... I do not know of any judge who was more impartial, more learned and more friendly than Mr. Justice Dysart.'[16]

Not everyone agreed with that assessment. While presiding over the trial of three men accused of killing an elderly woman, Dysart allowed into evidence statements picked up by a telephone transmitter placed in their cell. He justified his decision on the basis that if conversations overheard casually could be introduced, there was no reason those overheard through mechanical means should not be treated in a similar way. The *Fortnightly Law Journal* referred to the evidence as 'hopelessly inadmissible,' and suggested that Dysart had forgotten that 'the appearance of justice is often more important than its actual accomplishment, and the very fact that such a method of obtaining an unwitting confession is so fallibly open to abuse prevents even the appearance of justice in its use.'[17]

While a judge Dysart was a member of two federal and one provincial royal commissions.[18] His first appointment was in 1929, when he was named to the Seven Sisters inquiry headed by Chief Justice Daniel Macdonald. The three-person commission was asked to determine whether any member of the Bracken government, or anyone acting on their behalf, had entered into an illicit agreement with the Winnipeg

Electric Railway Company, which had been hired to develop the hydro-electric potential of the Seven Sisters River. Although Dysart wrote a minority report critical of the commission's refusal to press its investigation with more vigour, he agreed there was no evidence of wrong-doing.

Both federal royal commissions to which Dysart was appointed dealt with claims arising out of the federal government's administration of the natural resources of the North-West Territories. From its acquisition of the Northwest in 1870 until it created the provinces of Saskatchewan and Alberta in 1905 the federal government used the region's resources to subsidize railway construction and settlement. When the former territories entered confederation Ottawa retained control of their natural resources, and it was not until 1930 that it agreed to transfer ownership to the provinces. The federal government and the two provinces agreed that two commissions would be established to work out the details of the transfer. In December 1933 Dysart was named to head the Alberta commission, and seven months later was appointed chair of its Saskatchewan counterpart. Both reports were tabled in the House of Commons on 14 March 1935. Between 1924 and 1934 Dysart also chaired several boards of arbitration and conciliation. One involved a dispute between the Winnipeg Electric Company and its employees, and several others involved similar disputes between employees and the Winnipeg Electric Railway, Canadian National Railway, and Canadian Pacific Railway. During the same period Dysart chaired arbitrations involving a number of municipalities and one or more of their ratepayers.

Dysart was a practising Roman Catholic. Among his other affiliations was the University of Manitoba. In 1933 he was appointed vice-chair of the board of governors of the university, and the following year he became its chair. Ten years later he was elected chancellor of the university, following in the footsteps of Reverend Robert Machray, Anglican archbishop of Rupertsland, Reverend Samuel Matheson, another archbishop, and John Dafoe, the controversial editor of the *Manitoba Free Press*. Dysart served as chancellor for eight years, and the university acknowledged his efforts by awarding him an honorary doctorate of laws degree.

Despite the fact that Dysart was not regarded as a particularly talented lawyer, he was an outstanding judge. His abilities were recognized in 1935 when he was made an ad hoc member of the Supreme Court of Canada. For a time he was even regarded as a possible permanent member of the court, but considerations of geography and religion

Dysart was one of the few Canadian judges to have sat on a provincial trial court, court of appeal, and the Supreme Court of Canada. His judgments are considered among the most literate in Canadian history. Dysart's principal non-legal interest was woodworking, and in this 1939 photograph he is seen in his workshop. (Provincial Archives of Manitoba)

persuaded Prime Minister Bennett that Dysart's appointment would upset the court's delicate political balance.[19] During his tenure Dysart wrote six majority and three minority judgments.[20] On 11 September 1947 he was elevated to the Court of Appeal, filling the vacancy created by the retirement of Justice W.H. Trueman. The appointment made Dysart one of the few Manitoba judges to have sat on the Court of King's Bench, the provincial Court of Appeal, and the Supreme Court of Canada.

Dysart was six feet, three inches tall and possessed of a mass of silvery hair. He was a rather austere, laconic individual who treated everyone with the same degree of courtesy. Never accused of bias, either on or off the bench, his sympathetic manner put at ease junior counsel, while his intellect and power of concentration earned the respect of those more senior. He also had a natural dignity and was both cultured and well read. His leisure time was spent reading biographies, histories, poetry, and philosophy. He enjoyed walking and golf, and during his youth had been a rugby star; but the pastime he most enjoyed was woodworking. Often, when he had a judgment to write, he spent hours in his workshop sorting through his thoughts. When he died on 24 July 1952 while vacationing in Moncton, Dysart was seventy-seven and Manitoba's longest-serving judge.[21]

Neither of Dysart's enduring legacies have anything to do with law. One involved a gift to the University of Manitoba. Shortly after his death his family donated to the university his collection of manuscripts, rare books, and private press editions. The collection consisted of nine manuscripts and sixty books covering a period of six hundred years. Among the illuminated manuscripts were two antiphons, an early psalter, two official documents issued by Phillip II of Spain, and a fifteenth-century incunabulum edition of Caesar's *Commentaries*. Two-thirds of the collection dated from the fifteenth and sixteenth centuries.

Dysart's second legacy was a Winnipeg street located near the Faculty Law of the University of Manitoba named in his honour.

JOHN EVANS ADAMSON

The judicial career of John Evans Adamson was marked by a number of firsts. He was the first native Manitoban appointed to the King's Bench, one of the longest-serving superior court justices in Canada, and one of the least liked, and his appointment was by far the most controversial.

Adamson was born on his parents' farm on 9 September 1884. His father Alan was a native of Clifden, in Ireland's County Galway, where his grandfather was a clergyman. Adamson's Dublin-educated father emigrated to Canada in 1873, and seven years later married Julia M. Turriff, the daughter of a prominent Quebec businessman. Julia's father was a director of the Northern Bank and the Saskatchewan Valley and Manitoba Land Company. The Adamsons farmed south of Winnipeg until a rail line was run into southern Manitoba. Alan Adamson then quit farming and in 1883 entered the grain trade. Thirteen years later he became the secretary-treasurer of the Manitoba Grain Company. In 1900 he left Manitoba for the North-West Territories, settling in what is now Rosthern, Saskatchewan. There he became active in land sales and was instrumental in attracting to the region both American settlers and investment capital. His Canadian Territories Corporation was one of the largest land agencies in the west, and until 1914 it held the record for the value of its transactions.[22]

Until John Evans Adamson was fourteen he attended a one-room school about a mile and one half from his farm home. After high school he studied at Winnipeg's St John's College and the University of Manitoba. He graduated with a Bachelor and a Master of Arts degree, and with the governor general's silver medal in philosophy. Although he did not become a student member of the Law Society until 19 June 1907, Adamson had started clerking with Wellington Clifton Kelly a month earlier. He stayed with Kelly for nineteen months before his articles were assigned to Arthur Alexander Hobkirk, and from him to Hugh Amos Robson. Adamson was twenty-five when he was called to the bar on 13 June 1910. That event would have been delayed by four months had not the Law Society agreed to count as time served the term in 1909 when he studied at Toronto's Osgoode Hall law school.[23]

Adamson practised alone for a year before being joined by his brother. Christopher Arthur Adamson was also a graduate of St John's College, where he earned a Master of Arts degree. In 1907 he became the first Rhodes Scholar chosen from the new provinces of Alberta and Saskatchewan. Four years later, as a member of London's Inner Temple, he was called to the English bar. In September 1911 Christopher received his call in Manitoba, and he practised with his brother for three years before leaving the firm to become general manager of the Western Trust Company.[24]

From 1914 until he was appointed to the bench, John Adamson practised with Gordon Lindsay. After his partner went to the bench

Lindsay left Winnipeg and the practice of law for Toronto, where he became general manager of the Toronto General Trust Corporation. Lindsay and Adamson were both solicitors, and Adamson seldom appeared in court during his twelve years at the bar. He was, however, successful in five of his six reported cases. Of them, three dealt with procedural issues, two with election irregularities, and one with substantive law.

Although Adamson's single attempt to enter the political arena was unsuccessful, both his father and father-in-law were Members of Parliament. Of the two, the career of his father was the less distinguished. In 1904 Adamson Sr was elected as a Liberal in the Territories riding of Mackenzie. After winning election again later the same year, this time in Humboldt, he retired from politics. The political career of John Adamson's father-in-law was varied, lengthy, and distinguished. From 1884 until 1891 John Gillanders Turriff represented Moose Mountain District in the legislature of the North-West Territories. In the 1891 federal election he ran in Assiniboia East and was defeated by the federal minister of the interior. From 1898 to 1904 he was commissioner of dominion lands, but resigned to run in the federal general election, winning the riding of Assiniboia East. When the two Assiniboias were amalgamated he ran in the enlarged riding, and in 1908 was again successful. Three years later he won for a third time. In 1917 he ran successfully as an 'opposition' candidate, with the endorsement of Liberal opposition leader Sir Wilfrid Laurier. Turriff ended his political career in the senate.

Although John Adamson was never elected, he did have some political success. In 1911, the year before he married Mary Wilson Turriff, he was one of fifteen candidates vying for seven seats on the executive of the South Winnipeg Liberal association. He came in fifth, thirty-three votes behind the top vote-getter. His accomplishment had more significance, however, when weighed against the fact that Isaac Pitblado, one of Winnipeg's most influential lawyers, received only thirty-eight votes, and Stephen Elswood Richards, a future member of Manitoba's Court of Appeal, received just twenty-one.[25] In 1921 Adamson contested his only election, losing in the federal riding of Selkirk. Despite the loss, or perhaps because of it, he went to the bench the following year.

When news of Adamson's pending judicial appointment leaked in the spring of 1922, newspapers suggested that it was payment for political debts owed by the federal government to his father-in-law,

Senator Turriff. The leaders of the provincial bar were deeply offended that a thirty-seven-year-old lawyer with no experience was being forced on them, and on 28 April Law Society benchers and the executive of the Manitoba Bar Association met to adopt a joint resolution protesting the appointment. From the beginning of the meeting it was clear that those present were divided about how to proceed.[26] After Alfred J. Andrews presented a draft resolution the widely respected Isaac Campbell was the first to speak. There was, he suggested, a problem with the resolution. While the federal minister of justice may well have acted politically in appointing Adamson, there was no reason to believe that he was obligated to appoint someone recommended by the Manitoba bar. Esten Kenneth Williams, a future chief justice of the King's Bench, rejected Campbell's note of caution. He favoured protesting Adamson's elevation, despite the fact that previous political appointments had been made without consultation. D.H. Laird, a member of the board of supervisors of the Manitoba Law School and a member of the executive of the Bar Association, thought that such a course of action might offend those in positions of power. He argued that it would be ungracious and suggested that the matter be dealt with more diplomatically. Ultimately, however, the argument advanced by James Bowes Coyne (who, like many of those present, was to go to the bench himself) was adopted. 'Unless we make a protest [now] we can never hope for a favourable appointment except by accident.'[27] The meeting then resolved that:

> Whereas the foundation of the rights and liberties of our citizens depends upon the administration of justice by judges of the highest integrity and legal skill; and whereas experience has shown that this end cannot be achieved by appointments to the bench based upon political considerations;
>
> And whereas members of the legal profession are, from their intimate knowledge of one another, and of the work required of the judiciary, well qualified to recommend from among their members those to be appointed as judges; and whereas the ministers of justice for many years have expressed a willingness to receive from the benchers of the Law Society of Manitoba recommendations for vacant judgeships and have promised their consideration of same; and whereas recommendations were thereafter made by the benchers which met with the approval of the minister, but recently certain persons have been appointed without any opportunity

> having been given the benchers of making known to the government their views as to the fitness of such appointments, by both the past and present governments;
>
> Now, therefore, this meeting desires to express as strongly as possible its view that no appointment to the bench should be made for political reasons, and respectfully and earnestly urges upon the government that in future no judicial appointments within this province be made without consultation with the official representatives of the profession in the province, so as to insure that the appointee shall have the essential qualifications for the position, as well as the confidence of the bar and the public.[28]

Although the resolution was signed by the executives of the Law Society and the Bar Association, the matter did not end there. The organizations adopted a two-part strategy to persuade the federal government to rescind its decision to appoint Adamson. First, they appealed directly to the government. On 2 May they sent telegrams to Prime Minister Mackenzie King and to Minister of Justice Lomer Gouin, noting that according to a newspaper report, the government intended

> to appoint as judge of the Court of King's Bench of this province a member of the bar whom we consider wholly unfit for the position. It appears to us that such appointment if made will be solely as a reward for party faithfulness or service. We desire to register our most emphatic protest against the appointment believing as we do that it cannot but tend to destroy the confidence of the public in the judiciary of the province. We trust that we may have your assurance that the newspaper report is unfounded and that no such commission will issue.[29]

Ralph Maybank, one of a handful of influential and politically connected Winnipeg lawyers who went to the bench in the 1940s, believed that the storm of protest caused by rumours of Adamson's appointment would force King to back down.[30] Gouin quickly made it clear, however, that the protests had fallen on deaf ears. His response was a masterful example of political obfuscation. In a telegram to the president of the Law Society he said, 'I am unaware of the name mentioned in the newspaper reports you refer to. After full and mature consideration, the government has decided to appoint Mr. J. E. Adamson as judge of the court of King's Bench, and I desire to assure you that none of the reasons mentioned in your protest inspired the selection made.'[31]

The second part of the strategy was to circulate a protest petition among the province's lawyers. The effort revealed just how divided the provincial bar had become. On 4 May Coyne asked Frank Simpson, a fellow bencher and a Crown prosecutor in Dauphin, to obtain the signatures of members of the northern Manitoba bar. Simpson responded two days later. The meeting he called was attended by virtually every lawyer in the north, but the decision the group reached was not the one for which Coyne had hoped:

> The matter was very fully discussed and the meeting was unanimous in approval of the action taken upon the general principle that appointments to the Bench should not be made for political considerations only. The members of the local Bar felt, however, that they had no personal knowledge of the qualifications or lack of qualifications of Mr. Adamson, and consequently they would not be warranted in condemning his appointment.[32]

Coyne's law partner was similarly frustrated in his attempt to attract the support of members of the Winnipeg bar. On 9 May Robert Jacob, a senior partner in the firm of Jacob, Moore & Morton, wrote J.A. MacVicar:

> I have been informed this afternoon that my name appeared as endorsing the action of the officials of the Benchers and Bar Association in the wording of the telegram they had sent to the Premier in reference to the appointment of Mr. Adamson to the Bench and in which they stated that he was not a fit and proper person for the appointment, or words to that effect. If the information I received is correct, then I signed it without having knowledge of what I was appending my signature to ... I cannot endorse the wording of the telegram as I think it goes altogether too far in the circumstances. [If] I placed my signature, will you kindly see that it is erased.[33]

The reaction J.K. Sparling received when he asked lawyers to indicate their approval of the actions of the joint committee revealed how politically and professionally sensitive the issue had become. Three lawyers refused to sign Sparling's form because they had already written Adamson a letter of congratulation. Another wanted to remain neutral, while a fifth said that he could not sign because he had been one of the signatories on a petition supporting the appointment. A sixth refused to sign for what he referred to as 'good reasons.' Some lawyers, while certain they did not like the appointment, were unclear about why they did not want to sign the petition. W.R. Towers, for example, was 'incoherent,' while W.L. McLaws said only that he believed that it was 'better not to sign.'[34] Sparling presented his approval form to forty-five lawyers. Thirty-five signed, ten refused, one lawyer was away, and one was 'no use seeing.'[35]

While the efforts of protest leaders like Coyne and Sparling met resistance in Manitoba, they attracted the approval of lawyers elsewhere. The Law Society of British Columbia sent telegrams to the prime minister, the minister of justice, and Senator Hewitt Bestock, noting that its members had read 'with interest the action of the Manitoba Bar respecting the appointment of judges, and concur generally with Manitoba that judicial appointments should not be made as a reward for political services without regard to other qualifications.'[36] The protestors also received support from eastern Canada. On 11 May the solicitor for the City of Halifax wrote the president of the Law Society 'to extend to yourself and the Bar of Manitoba my warmest congratulations on their magnificent protest against the appointment of an unfit Politician to the Bench ... Here in the East, we have been dreadful sufferers from just such appointments. I used to be an enthusiastic Grit, and am still supposed to be a member of that Party, but I say with all conviction that if ever that Party made a proper appointment to the Bench, it was an accident.'[37]

The movement to prevent Adamson from going to the bench failed, but it was not forgotten, least of all by Adamson. Years later he kept near him a list of the lawyers who had opposed his appointment, and he took his revenge whenever one of their number appeared in his court.[38] And in an ironic twist of fate, twenty-one years later one of the leaders of the protest became the focus of criticism when he too was being considered for the bench. In the fall of 1943 word leaked that King, the same prime minister who had appointed Adamson, was considering appointing Coyne to the Manitoba bench. Ralph Maybank was among those most opposed to the move. Now a Member of Parliament, he was outspoken in his condemnation of Coyne. In a letter to the prime minister he said that he had heard that King was thinking of making Coyne a judge, and the possibility caused him a lot of concern. 'As long as I have known Mr. Coyne, which goes back a good many years by now, he has been on the receiving end with respect to favours; and rarely on the giving or contributing end. I think, in fact, he is about the most acquisitive man I have ever known.'[39]

On 1 May 1922 John Adamson finally received his reward, going to the King's Bench when Prendergast was elevated to the Court of Appeal. Throughout his career as a trial judge Adamson's relationship with many of the leaders of the bar was strained. In March 1928 one of the province's best-known lawyers was defence counsel in a drug case. Before closing, Robert Bonnar asked Adamson for an adjournment so he could receive instructions from his client about whether any further witnesses should be called. Adamson refused to grant it, and the two became embroiled in a heated argument. Bonnar accused the judge of calling him a liar, and when Adamson did not deny the accusation, Bonnar stormed out of the courtroom. Adamson told amazed onlookers that the absent lawyer could no longer appear before him until he apologized. When Bonnar reappeared to conclude his case, however, he refused to back down. 'I understood your lordship to call me a liar – at least the words you used gave me that impression – and because I prize my veracity, honour and honesty, I withdrew from the case.' Adamson was not mollified and insisted that the lawyer give a further explanation for his conduct. Bonnar refused, and the altercation between the two garnered headlines in Winnipeg newspapers. The issue was eventually resolved in private, and nothing further was said about it by either man.[40]

Soon after he went to the bench Adamson earned the nickname 'Blackjack' for the lack of sympathy he showed the criminally accused. An example was the murder trial of a Dauphin resident. The case involved 'a cruel, wicked murder,' and the accused was eventually convicted and executed. That fate satisfied Adamson, who throughout his judicial career was against 'molly-coddling' criminals, since he held little hope for their reformation. After he retired he acknowledged that his philosophy had always been to mete out harsh sentences for criminal wrong-doing in the belief that by so doing he would make young people aware of what would be in store for them should they engage in similar activities.[41]

During his tenure on King's Bench Adamson was regarded as an exceptionally weak judge. His pro-prosecution bias was regularly in evidence during criminal trials, where he routinely tormented the accused with questions if he felt that the Crown was not being aggressive enough.[42] James Wilson was not yet a judge when he first encountered Adamson. He suggested that 'Black-jack's' methodology was to give a charge that in the transcript would appear fair, while with inflection and gestures he made clear his real attitude.[43] This perhaps explains why few of Adamson's decisions were successfully appealed, and why those that made it to the Supreme Court of Canada were dismissed. Suggestions that Adamson lacked understanding, however, did not escape the notice of the Court of Appeal. When Adamson discharged a caveat because of a misdescription of a date, Justice Cameron acknowledged that the caveat contained a technical error but criticized Adamson's strict construction of the law. 'There was a mis-description in, or misdating of, the document referred to in the caveat ... but that is surely not sufficiently material to impair or destroy the rights of the bank. To be so meticulously strict would be to substantially affect the justice of the proceeding.'[44] Eight years later the Court was scathing in its criticism of Adamson's apparent bias. Justice Trueman noted that '[t]he learned Judge had no difficulty' in reaching his decision, but 'Strangely enough' had to ignore the existence of very material countervailing facts to do so. Rejecting Adamson's rationale for finding in favour of the defendant, Trueman said, 'This reasoning I am, with respect, unable to follow. A distinction is sought to be drawn by the learned Judge ... Clearly this is wrong.'[45]

Adamson was an enthusiastic fan of sports and an avid golfer. In 1934 he won the 'Hon. T. G. Murphy' silver trophy in the first annual open amateur golf championship at Riding Mountain National Park's Wasagaming Golf Course. He also won the longest-drive competition with three strokes totalling 720 yards (an average of 240 yards a stroke). He served as president of the Manitoba Golf Association and was a member of the St Charles Golf & Country Club, one of the most exclusive private golf clubs in the province. Adamson's appreciation of the finer points of golf stood him in good stead when he presided over an action brought by a plaintiff against a fellow golfer. The defendant's drive off the eighth tee was sliced badly, landing in the middle of the seventh fairway. When one of three golfers standing at the seventh tee asked him to play his second shot, the defendant did so, hitting the plaintiff. Although in plain sight, the plaintiff was given no warning and as a result of being struck by the ball lost an eye.[46] Adamson was highly critical of the defendant, and he took judicial notice that a golf ball driven at an unsuspecting golfer is not only hard and sometimes travels at a very high velocity, but is in some ways more dangerous than a bullet fired from a gun or a stone that is thrown:

> If it were to be found that it is a risk incidental to the game to have balls driven almost directly at one, it would, to say the least, interfere with the

> alleged pleasure and healthfulness of the game. The person playing a golf ball should be scrupulously careful not to hit anybody, and if he does, the onus of making an explanation showing the care and caution he took is much the same as though he had thrown a stone or fired a gun.[47]

Adamson was not a judicial trailblazer. When faced with an opportunity to make new law, he usually refused to do so. The Court of Appeal acknowledged his judicial conservatism in a case involving the accidental discharge of a gun by a twelve-year-old boy. At trial the suit was treated as a traditional action in negligence. Justice Dennistoun saw it differently, noting that it was obvious 'some points of law [arose] for decision, as to which it is difficult to find direct authority, but which may be discussed on principle, there being no dispute as to the facts.'[48] It was a discussion, however, in which Adamson refused to engage, and his judgment was reversed.

Despite a reluctance to break new ground, in 1937 Adamson became the first judge in Canada to set a value on human life.[49] His decision was applauded by the *Manitoba Bar News*, which noted that it 'should make an excellent foundation precedent in matters of this kind.'[50] One of the few occasions on which Adamson became an advocate of legal reform arose out of comments made in a divorce action. His description of what married couples had to go through to obtain a divorce, although an accurate assessment of the state of the law, was probably more a reflection of Adamson's moral outrage at being part of a fraud than judicial activism.

> If one does not actually know, there are good grounds for believing that a large percentage of the so-called 'hotel divorces' are collusive and connived at. A 'licensed operative,' after a remarkably small amount of watching, finds a man registered allegedly with his wife in a hotel. Usually he conveniently uses his own name. The operative then telephones the wife to meet him and together they go to the hotel and to the room. They invariably have no difficulty with either the hotel authorities or in getting into the room. Everything usually goes very smoothly. Undoubtedly many of these affairs are arranged and amount to divorce by consent if one of the parties is willing to commit adultery or engage in deceit and commit a fraud upon the Court.
>
> People do make mistakes in marriage and discover too late that they cannot live together, and so separate. Under the law as it is at present, such persons cannot be divorced and given a chance to start over again

> upon a respectable basis unless one of the spouses commits adultery, which, by some means, not only comes to the notice of the other spouse, but actual evidence of which also comes into the hands of the other spouse; or unless they manufacture a set of circumstances upon which the Court is asked to find that adultery has taken place. This means that respectable persons who neither commit adultery nor perpetrate a fraud upon the Court are without relief. The law gives relief to persons when one spouse commits adultery or engages in fraud; the law thus puts a premium on adultery and fraud. Is this in the national interest? Would it not be in the national interest to provide that upon separation for say two years or upwards, after a genuine attempt to live together as man and wife, a divorce be granted upon terms (perhaps) as should be considered just? To make an isolated act of adultery the sole and only cause for divorce is wrong in principle and vicious in practice.[51]

On 30 January 1948 Adamson was transferred from the King's Bench to the Court of Appeal to fill a spot created by the death of Justice H.A. Bergman. Seven years later Adamson became the province's chief justice. In the opinion of some, when he left the trial bench he became a changed man and a better judge. At the end of his career Adamson was regarded as a good, if not the best, judge on the Court of Appeal.[52] County Court judge Walter Lindal certainly was of that opinion. 'After Adamson was appointed Chief Justice he became a completely changed man. All the rancour disappeared and he seemed to grow in wisdom.'[53] Even his harshest critics agreed that his judicial temperament improved considerably when Adamson was elevated to the Court of Appeal, and particularly so when he became the court's chief justice.[54]

When Adamson left the bench it was with considerable reluctance. In 1960 the federal government amended section 99 of the *British North America Act* to force superior court judges to retire at seventy-five.[55] Historically they could sit as long as they chose, provided that they continued to be of good behaviour. The British House of Lords changed that on 6 December 1960 by amending the *BNA Act*. Of one hundred and seventy-two justices of a Canadian superior court, thirteen were forced to retire, including Adamson and four other chief justices. The longest serving of the group was eighty-year-old Chief Justice Albert Sevigny of Quebec. His forty-year tenure exceeded by one that of Adamson, who stepped down on 24 February 1961.

John Evans Adamson was seventy-seven when he died of a circulatory ailment on 22 December 1961.[56] He is remembered as the first

Manitoba-born lawyer to be appointed to the Court of King's Bench and the first to become its chief justice. When his wife gave birth to the couple's youngest daughter the then thirty-nine-year-old also became the second sitting King's Bench judge to become a father (Dubuc was the first). Apart from his interest in law and sports, Adamson was also a long-serving vestryman of St George's Anglican Church and a member of a number of Winnipeg clubs and organizations. Among them were the Masons, the Carleton Club, the Mobilization Board, the Selective Service Board, and the Electoral Boundaries Commission, the last three of which he chaired.

JAMES FREDERICK KILGOUR

Kilgour was born of Scottish ancestry in Hillsburg, Ontario on 22 January 1874. A year later his father John gave up his job as a storekeeper and moved with his wife Sophie and son to Guelph, where he became a long-serving district agent with the Mutual Life Assurance Company. Besides James the Kilgours were parents of daughters Edith and Annie and another son. David followed his father into the insurance business, eventually becoming president of the North American Life Assurance Company.

James Kilgour received his public and high school education in Guelph and at sixteen entered the University of Toronto. He was an above-average student and earned a spot on the university's honour list in both his first and third years.[57] After graduating in 1893 with a Bachelor of Arts degree he went on to earn a degree in law. As a student-in-law at Osgoode Hall he again excelled academically, standing sixth in a class of forty-five. He was also active in student affairs and was on the executive of the Osgoode Legal and Literary Society. One of his classmates was Clara Brett Martin, the first woman to practise law in Canada. Her entry into the profession, however, did not go as smoothly as that of her fellow students. Although the provincial legislature passed a law in 1895 allowing women to practise as barristers, by a vote of nine to six the benchers of the Law Society of Upper Canada 'decided not to consent to the Act' and refused to grant her membership. It took the personal intervention of the premier and an intensive lobbying effort by women's organizations before the Society reversed its decision.[58]

Although he did not remain after receiving his call, Kilgour articled with the Guelph firm headed by Donald and Hugh Guthrie, at the time one of Ontario's most influential. Donald was born in Scotland, emigrated to Canada in 1854, and studied law in the Toronto office of Premier Oliver Mowat. After receiving his call he moved to Guelph to practise with Senator A.J. Fergusson-Blair and future judge John J. Kingsmill. Donald was elected a bencher of the Law Society and sat at different times in the House of Commons and the legislature of Ontario. Hugh Guthrie had an even more illustrious political career than his father. He represented South Wellington in the House of Commons from 1900 to 1935, and served as solicitor general, minister of militia and defence, and minister of justice before retiring to become chief commissioner of the Board of Railway Commissioners.

James Kilgour received his call in 1896 and, until he moved to Winnipeg in 1901, practised alone in Fergus and Guelph. In Manitoba he worked in Winnipeg for two years before moving to Brandon, where he succeeded Clifford Sifton in the firm of Sifton, Philp & Cameron. He and A.E. Philp were later joined by R.L. Wardlaw and, in 1910, by A.G. Buckingham.[59] Kilgour had an extensive practice, and for 'a quarter of a century he was the outstanding lawyer of Brandon.'[60] He regularly appeared in court and with 'his keen incisive brain, ready wit and an unending fund of satire' was successful in two-thirds of thirty-three cases reported.[61] Neither his wit nor his satire helped him become a bencher, however. In 1907 he received only one vote in the Western Judicial District, four behind the second-place finisher, but 125 behind the winner.[62] Three years later his six votes placed him third out of eight,[63] and in 1916 his thirty-nine ballots were good only for fourth place.[64] He was finally elected eleven years later, when he became both a bencher and president of the Manitoba Bar Association.

Kilgour was a staunch Liberal whose political aspirations, like those of his father, were confined to local rather than provincial or federal politics. Unlike his father, however, who served three terms as a Guelph alderman, Kilgour's single election victory came as a school trustee.[65] Both before and after he went to the bench, Kilgour was active in a variety of non-professional organizations. He was a member of the board of deacons of Winnipeg's Westminister United Church, the president of Brandon's Children's Aid Society and the Canadian Club, and he sat on the executive of the Men's Canadian Club of Winnipeg and the Institute of International Affairs. In addition, he was also the provincial commissioner for the Manitoba Boy Scouts Association and a member of several private clubs, including the Manitoba Club, the Winter Club, and the St Charles Golf & Country Club.

Kilgour went to the Court of King's Bench on 10 September 1927, filling the vacancy created by the death of Chief Justice Mathers. When he died suddenly four years later, Kilgour was eulogized by the *Manitoba Free Press* as having 'displayed to the full the qualities of the great jurist: wide and accurate legal knowledge; a mind impartial and crystal clear; and the manner and bearing of the perfect judge.'[66] With the exception of the last comment, the assessment of the newspaper was not obviously accurate. During his abbreviated tenure on the bench only four of Kilgour's decisions were reported, by far the fewest of any of his colleagues. Eight appeals of his decisions were reported in the *Manitoba Reports*, however, and six were allowed. In discussing his trial judgments the Court of Appeal on only one occasion made an approving comment. In his first appeal Justice Trueman said, almost kindly, that 'On this evidence it is difficult to complain of the learned Judge's finding. It is a finding, nevertheless, that I cannot agree with.'[67] A year later Dennistoun was less diplomatic, complaining that because Kilgour had failed to supply the court 'with his reasons for judgment we must infer them from the facts.'[68] Dennistoun was not the only judge to criticize Kilgour. Fullerton, his harshest critic, suggested that after carefully reading one of Kilgour's decisions he was at a loss to know how the trial judge reached the conclusion he did, referring to the judgment as 'puzzling.'[69] And in a decision handed down shortly before he left the bench to become chief commissioner of the Board of Railway Commissioners, Fullerton accused Kilgour of making a finding that 'there is not a fragment of evidence in the whole case to justify.'[70]

Despite what some of the justices of the Court of Appeal might have thought of him, Kilgour at least had the confidence of the provincial government. In 1929 he was named to the three-person royal commission established to investigate possible wrongdoing connected to the Seven Sisters Falls power agreement.

Kilgour's most enduring claim to fame may well have been his connection to one of Canada's most famous war poets. In 1905 he married Geills McCrae, daughter of Lieutenant-Colonel David McCrae of Guelph, who had been born in Scotland and emigrated to Canada when he was four. After graduating from the Ontario Veterinary College as gold medalist McCrae gained prominence as an agricultural journalist and a member of the military. In the 1860s he organized a militia unit to repel Fenians crossing the border from the United States, and during the First World War, at sixty-nine, recruited and accompanied overseas the 43rd Battery. When permission to serve in active duty was denied, however,

The home of James Frederick Kilgour (1874–1931), puisne judge 1927–31. One of two judges appointed to Queen's Bench from the Brandon bar (the other was Curran), Kilgour was much respected as a lawyer and was elected a Law Society bencher and president of the Manitoba Bar Association. He was involved in a number of organizations and is remembered for his commitment to his family. This picture of his Brandon home suggests that Kilgour was one of the city's more successful lawyers. (Charles Roland Brawn)

he returned to Canada, leaving behind his son, who became famous for his poem 'In Flanders Field.'

James Kilgour died of internal bleeding on 27 November 1931 at age fifty-seven, having been admitted to the Winnipeg General Hospital several weeks earlier as a result of complications from an operation undergone a year earlier. He died on the thirtieth anniversary of his call to the Manitoba bar, leaving an estate of just under $72,000, most of which consisted of insurance and stocks and bonds.[71]

WILLIAM JAMES DONOVAN

William James Donovan was born in Ontario on 30 October 1875, the third of five children of Michael Donovan and Alice McDonald. The families of both were from Ireland, where his farmer-father was born.[72] William received his early education in Brockville before entering the University of Toronto in 1897. Academically, his years at university were marked by a series of highs and lows. His C+ average in his second year included a personal best of sixth in political science. The following year he passed nine courses with honours, but also failed one and received a C in two others. When he graduated with a Bachelor of Arts degree, however, he did so with honours, earning four firsts, one third, and two fifths.[73]

Following his 1900 graduation Donovan immediately left for Manitoba, where he enrolled in Winnipeg's Normal School. After a year of teacher training he taught briefly east of Winnipeg. In December 1901, however, he gave up teaching and entered into an articling agreement with Hugh Phillipps. Nine months later his articles were assigned to Horace Edgar Crawford, and a year after that to Henry Platt Grundy of the Campbell, Pitblado firm. He received his call in November 1904.[74] For the next two years Donovan practised alone until he and T.J. Murray became partners in Donovan & Murray. The two stayed together for only a year. Murray went on to earn a considerable reputation as a litigator, particularly for his role defending several leaders of the Winnipeg General Strike. Donovan spent another two years alone before being joined by A.M. Doyle. Their firm persisted until 1914, when it too was dissolved. Donovan was on his own briefly before spending seven years in practice with C.S. Scott. From 1922 until 1925 he was a partner of S.E. Nordquist, and during his last three years at the bar he practised alone.[75]

Although an authority on election legislation, Donovan specialized in commercial and corporate law. His clients included the Mason & Risch Piano Company and the Lewis Furniture Company. He took an active role in the management of a number of business ventures in which he had invested, and that activity, combined with his solicitor's practice, usually kept him out of court. Nevertheless, nine of his cases were reported, and he was successful in seven. Perhaps surprisingly, only two involved corporations. His reputation as a corporate lawyer, however, likely played a role in his selection to the only federal board on which he sat. In the spring of 1927 the Canadian National Railway was embroiled in a wage dispute with twenty thousand of its employees. When the Canadian Brotherhood of Railway Employees and the federal government agreed to have the dispute arbitrated, the federal minister of labour appointed Donovan chair of a three-person board of conciliation. Hearings opened in Montreal on 12 April, and eighteen days later the board recommended that employees be given a raise of four cents an hour. The union agreed to the recommendation but management did not, and a strike vote was called. Before the results were announced, an acceptable compromise was negotiated.[76]

When not working, golfing, bowling, or playing tennis, the Catholic Donovan spent his leisure time at the Carleton club. Those activities, however, still left him time for politics. He was a personal friend of Sir Wilfrid Laurier and served three years as secretary-treasurer of the Winnipeg Liberal Association before becoming the organization's president. He was also secretary, treasurer, and a member of the board of the Liberal Building Corporation. In 1922 he ran in his only election, finishing in a tie for twentieth place out of forty-three candidates seeking one of ten Winnipeg seats in the provincial legislature. He was thirty-seven votes behind W.H. Trueman, who was to become a justice of the Court of Appeal.[77]

Donovan was appointed to Manitoba's Court of King's Bench on 30 March 1928 and almost immediately became embroiled in a legal dispute that still ranks among the province's most controversial. Shortly after Donovan went to the bench a Winnipeg businessman died, leaving his estate of just under $2 million to his daughter, her husband, and a son who had predeceased him. After issuing a probate of the will, Surrogate Court judge Lewis St George Stubbs was informed unofficially that one of the witnesses to the will had not signed it in the presence of the testator. Stubbs immediately cancelled the grant of probate and demanded that the executors appear at a judicial hearing to investigate the truth of what he had heard. They refused, withdrew their application for probate, and applied for administration of the estate under *The Devolution of Estates Act*. Stubbs refused to act on their application, and insisted that the previously scheduled hearing proceed. When it ended he ruled that the will had been improperly witnessed, and in all likelihood the testator had lacked the capacity to know what he was signing. The daughter then asked Donovan for an order of *mandamus*, directing Stubbs to issue Letters of Administration. Donovan issued the writ, Stubbs appealed, and in 1930 the dispute was heard by the Court of Appeal. Although it agreed with the substance of Donovan's ruling, the court held that while he could order Stubbs to hear the application, Donovan had no authority to direct what the judge should decide after it was heard.[78]

Throughout his judicial career Donovan consistently ignored the social implications of his decisions. As a result, the Court of Appeal was regularly asked to determine whether in the exercise of his discretion Donovan had acted appropriately. An example involved an accused found guilty of having carnal knowledge of a feeble-minded woman. The accused allegedly signed a statement in which he confessed his guilt, and when the victim was unable to give evidence, it represented the Crown's entire case. At trial, defence counsel objected to the introduction of the confession and asked permission to introduce evidence that it had not been given voluntarily. Donovan refused to hear the evidence outside the presence of the jury, and the accused was convicted. In reviewing his decision the Court of Appeal criticized the way that Donovan had exercised his discretion and suggested that it had become routine for trial judges to hear testimony about the voluntariness of a statement without a jury being present.[79]

In 1937 the Court of Appeal again reviewed the way Donovan exercised his discretion. When Donovan ruled that whether a plaintiff had been injured as a result of the negligence of a defendant was too complicated a question for a jury to determine, the Court of Appeal disagreed. Although it held that a judge had the legal right to hear a negligence action without a jury, it noted that the discretion to do so existed only when a trial judge applied the right principle of law. In the case before them they saw nothing mysterious or unmanageable, and Mr. Justice Robson on behalf of a majority of the appeal court rejected Donovan's explanation for hearing the case alone. 'I respectfully think the reasons given are erroneous and that there has been nothing disclosed as a basis for the discretionary refusal of the application for the jury.'[80]

Another case in which the Court of Appeal was critical of Donovan involved a corespondent in a divorce action who agreed to testify about

The home of William James Donovan (1875–1949), puisne judge 1928–49. Donovan was one of a handful of Queen's Bench appointees who went to the bench after a career spent practising either alone or with one or two other lawyers. Although the size of their practice usually hampers small-firm lawyers' ability to specialize, such was not the case with Donovan. His house on Winnipeg's prestigious Harvard Avenue suggests that corporate law was good to the former Brockville, Ontario, native. (Charles Roland Brawn)

an act of adultery committed with the petitioner's wife. Donovan refused to hear the evidence on the basis that section 7 of *The Manitoba Evidence Act* said that no witness in a proceeding could be asked whether he or she had been guilty of adultery. The Court of Appeal held that he was not only wrong in law but insensitive to the social implications of his decision. Justice Trueman questioned how Donovan could have arrived at the conclusion he did, since '[h]e is aware that English cases have authoritatively determined that the section does not exclude the evidence if the witness is willing to give it.' He then went on to suggest that Donovan's 'misunderstanding' of the law showed 'a like want of appreciation' of a leading case, and 'a misappreciation' of the law generally.[81]

A further example of Donovan's disregard for the consequences of his use of discretion involved a petition brought by a married but separated woman who was living with a man who was the father of her illegitimate daughter. The woman's legal husband was also living in a common-law relationship and, like his wife, was the parent of a child born out of wedlock. Both parties wanted a divorce so that they could remarry and thereby remove from their respective child the stigma of being regarded as a bastard. Donovan refused the petition on the grounds that the adultery of the wife disentitled her to a divorce. In reversing his judgment the Court of Appeal pointed out how inappropriately he had exercised his discretion, suggesting that he ignored not only what was in the best interest of the parties and their children, but also the interests of the community at large.[82]

In 1940 Donovan was appointed to a commission established in response to accusations of negligence levied by Winnipeg alderman John Petley against the city's police department. The charges arose when a constable was killed during an aborted break-in at the offices of the Manitoba Motor League. Donovan chaired the inquiry, and he and two fellow commissioners were severely critical of Winnipeg councillors for not investigating Petley's charges before passing a motion alleging the existence of widespread criticism of the police force. Had they done so, council would have found out not only that the force was not being criticized, but that 'there was no reasonable nor probable cause or other justification for making the aforementioned charges or using them under the circumstances as a basis for granting by the council of the motion for inquiry.'[83]

Donovan died at home on 26 May 1949 from the effects of a heart attack suffered several weeks earlier. He was seventy-three.[84]

PERCIVAL JOHN MONTAGUE

Although a number of Manitoba judges had distinguished military careers, none served with more distinction that Percival John Montague. He was born on 10 November 1882 in Dunnville, a small community near Welland, in Haldimand County, Ontario. His paternal grandfather farmed in Middlesex County, and it was there that Percival's father Walter was born and raised. The Montague farm did sufficiently well to allow Walter to attend Woodstock College, Victoria University, and the Toronto School of Medicine. After graduating in 1882 he practised at Dunnville, where he and his wife, Angie Furry, raised a daughter and two sons, both of whom became lawyers and members of the military.[85]

Percival Montague was educated in Dunnville and Hamilton before he attended Upper Canada College, the University of Toronto, and Osgoode Hall Law School. He was an above-average student, although a little inconsistent. In the first year of his Bachelor of Arts program he failed to earn any honours, notwithstanding three A's, two B's, and two C's. In 1904, however, he not only graduated with honours, but took five first places, one third, and a fourth, all while a member of the university's Canadian champion football team.[86]

After the University of Toronto, Montague studied law at Osgoode Hall and became a student in the office of the Honourable William David McPherson, a future provincial secretary of Ontario. He was admitted to the Ontario bar in 1907 and then promptly left for Manitoba, where he almost immediately became a member of that province's Law Society. That same year he married Anne Isabel Fletcher, the daughter of the Reverend D.H. Fletcher. The Scotland-born minister had emigrated to Canada at age eighteen and nine years later was ordained a Presbyterian minister. In 1884 he was elected moderator of the synod of Hamilton and London, then in 1903 moderator of the general assembly. Queen's University and Knox College presented him with honorary doctorates for his work as a Hebrew scholar, and for his efforts on behalf of the church.[87]

Montague spent his entire legal career with the firm headed by Isaac Pitblado. On the death of Hugh John Macdonald he became Manitoba's official guardian responsible for protecting the civil rights of children and the mentally incompetent, although both before and after receiving the appointment he spent a considerable amount of time in court. His record was notable, however, in only two respects. Of thirty-six cases reported, he was successful in less than 40 per cent, making him one of least successful litigators to go to the bench. On the other hand, two-thirds of his clients were corporations, suggesting that he was one of the first lawyers to go to the Manitoba bench as a specialist in corporate litigation.

Although neither of Montague's two daughters went into law, both his brother and his nephew were lawyers. Furry Montague had a career in law and the military only slightly less illustrious than his older brother's. He graduated from the University of Toronto in 1906 with a degree in applied science, following his brother and father to Manitoba, where he spent most of his career with Sharp, Stacpoole, Elliott & Montague. During the First World War, Furry served on the staff of the Second Canadian Division and at the Canadian Military Headquarters in London. When Furry died in 1950 he was manager of the Winnipeg office of the London and Western Trusts Company. His son, George Hastings Montague, articled with the Pitblado firm before leaving the province to take his call in Ontario.[88]

During the First World War, Percival Montague entered the Canadian army as a captain. He was with the sixth Canadian Infantry Division when it shipped out to Europe in May 1915. Almost immediately he was promoted to assistant adjutant and quartermaster general of the Second Division, and shortly after arriving in Europe was appointed staff officer to General H.D.B. Ketchen. He was given command of Military Division 10 before serving in France on the staff of the Second Canadian Division. In 1917 he became its chief staff officer. When the war ended he was asked by General Sir Arthur Currie to organize the demobilization of the Canadian army corps in France. By the time he returned to Canada in 1919 he was a lieutenant colonel and had been mentioned in dispatches for distinguished conduct on the field five times. He received the Military Cross and the Distinguished Service Order, and was made a Companion of the Order of St Michael and St George.

Between 1920 and 1923 Montague commanded the Fort Garry Horse. When promoted to full colonel in 1928 he took over the Sixth Mounted Brigade and maintained his command for eight years. During that time he was one of Canada's most senior non-permanent military officers. In 1932 he was rewarded for his long service by being named honorary aide-de-camp to His Excellency Governor General Lord Bessborough.

He held that office until 1940. In 1935, three years after he went to the bench, Montague was appointed to the advisory board of Kingston's Royal Military College.

Although Percival Montague never became involved in politics, the same could not be said of his father, Walter Humphries Montague. In 1887 he was elected to the House of Commons for the riding of Haldimand, Ontario, and he entered the cabinet of Prime Minister Bowell as minister without portfolio on 21 December 1894. A year later he was made secretary of state.[89] When Bowell accused him of being part of a 'nest of traitors' conspiring against him, Montague and six of his colleagues resigned. Bowell became the only sitting prime minister in Canadian history to be forced out of office by his own cabinet. Following Bowell's resignation Sir Charles Tupper formed the government of Canada, and promptly made Montague his minister of agriculture. In the 1900 general election, however, Montague lost by 137 votes to Andrew Thorburn Thompson, and in 1908 he emigrated to Manitoba. Five years later, and without a seat in the legislature, the former Member of Parliament became minister of public works in the cabinet of Premier Rodmond Roblin.[90] His political career, and his life, ended prematurely and in disgrace when he, the premier, and two of his cabinet colleagues were arrested and charged with conspiracy to defraud the Crown by accepting bribes from the contractor hired to build the province's new legislative building. The four were committed to trial on 6 October 1915, but before it got under way Walter Montague died.[91]

Unlike his father-in-law, a prominent Presbyterian minister, Percival Montague was an Anglican. He was also a sportsman who enjoyed polo and shooting, and was a member of a number of clubs and organizations, including the Manitoba Club, the Winnipeg branch of the United Empire Loyalists, Delta Kappa Epsilon, and the Canadian Cavalry Association. In 1931 Montague was elected president of the Manitoba Bar Association, and after he went to the bench served as chair of the Manitoba section of the board of review under the federal *Farmers Creditors Act*.

Montague was appointed to the King's Bench on 11 March 1932 and almost immediately began making new law. For example, although the legality of holograph wills had been confirmed by statute, the question of attestation had never been settled by a Canadian court. In 1934 Montague became the first to decide with finality that a holograph will, bearing the signatures of witnesses, did not change the nature of the document. Before rendering his decision, however, he reviewed British,

Walter Humphries Montagne, the father of Percival John Montague (1882–1966). Puisne judge 1932–51, judge of Manitoba's Court of Appeal 1951–9. Percival Montague was the highest-ranking war veteran to sit on a Manitoba court. When appointed to King's Bench he was one of the most senior non-permanent military officers in Canada. Montague ended his military career as a highly decorated and much respected lieutenant-general. In contrast, his father, pictured in this photograph taken after he joined the provincial cabinet of Rodmond Roblin, died in 1915 while facing prosecution for embezzling public funds. (Provincial Archives of Manitoba)

American, and French authorities, and traced the applicable law back to the Romans. His treatment of the issue was applauded by the editors of the *Fortnightly Law Journal*, and his judgment was followed in 1983 by a court in Saskatchewan and by the Manitoba Court of Appeal in 1968, where it was also considered in a 1997 case.[92]

After making new law with regard to holograph wills, Montague did the same for negligence in the air. The case involved a fatal aeroplane accident in which a passenger died because of the negligence of the pilot. In 1937 Montague became the first judge in the British Commonwealth to consider what duty of care a pilot owed a non-paying passenger. He held that the law of negligence was applicable to aeroplane accidents in the same way that it was applicable to accidents on the ground, and that a loss of flying speed was prima facie evidence of negligence. His decision was followed by the Saskatchewan Court of Appeal as recently as 1989, and in both Nova Scotia and Ontario.[93] The third case in which he established a precedent dealt with another air accident, this time involving an air carrier. He held that, although a carrier was not an insurer of its passengers' safety, it could avoid liability only in the case of undiscoverable defects.[94]

Not all of Montague's attempts to make new law succeeded, however. When he ordered a defendant to pay the plaintiff's costs, despite dismissing the plaintiff's action, the Court of Appeal overturned his decision without even waiting for the trial transcripts. In doing so it acknowledged his efforts to adopt a new approach, but said that he had no authority for doing so:

> Does it follow that because the transaction showed the defendant to be a miscreant or in some fashion an odious person there was jurisdiction in the Court to order the defendant to pay the costs of the action to the unsuccessful plaintiff in order to mark the Court's condemnation of the defendant's conduct, not in connection with the trial of the action, but in connection with the transaction in question? The answer to that question seems fairly self-evident. The plaintiff having brought the defendant into Court and failed, there is no basis in law for ordering the defendant to pay the plaintiff the costs of an action he is shown to have had no right to bring.[95]

Although Montague was never regarded as biased, while hearing a negligence action prosecuted by a former partner, he might have created that impression. After listening intensely to the argument of counsel, he interrupted to ask, 'And which was our fellow's car?'[96]

With the outbreak of the Second World War, Montague returned to active duty in the military. His first posting was at the Canadian Military Headquarters in London, where he replaced General Crerar. From March 1939 until May 1946 he was in charge of administration and served as judge-advocate general. Montague was promoted to major general in 1940, and given the acting rank of lieutenant general while serving at Canadian headquarters. When he retired Montague was the highest ranking non-permanent officer in the Canadian Army.[97]

Montague received two honorary Doctor of Laws degrees in the 1940s. The first was bestowed on him in 1942 by the University of Manitoba, and the second in 1946 by the University of Toronto. Five years later he received yet another honour when he was raised from the King's Bench to the Court of Appeal, filling a vacancy created by the death of Justice S.E. Richards. He retired on 1 September 1959.

Montague was eighty-three when died on 11 June 1966, predeceased by his wife, who had died twenty-four years earlier.[98] His funeral was held at All Saints Anglican Church, across the street from the courthouse where he had sat for more than a quarter of a century. Those attending included the Right Honourable Vincent Massey, General A.G.L. McNaughton, commander of the Canadian army during much of the Second World War and minister of defence in the government of Prime Minister Mackenzie King, and the Honourable George Drew.

FAWCETT GOWLER TAYLOR

Taylor was born at Meadow Lea, Manitoba, on 29 April 1878, four years after his parents arrived from Peel County, Ontario. One of nine children, he attended public school in Winnipeg and was only sixteen when he became a student-at-law in the Winnipeg office of Nathaniel Hagel. Almost immediately, however, he moved to Portage la Prairie to article with William James Cooper, former law partner of Prime Minister Arthur Meighen.[99]

Taylor was called to the Manitoba bar in 1900 and practised alone for the next six years. He then spent two years with H.J. Cowan, two more alone, and twenty-one with J. Roy Colwill. Lawyers who practised briefly with Taylor & Colwill included H.D. Sparling, W. Carrie, G.L.

Newman, T.W.B. Hinch, and C.C. Sparling.[100] Although Taylor was for a time Crown prosecutor for the Central Judicial District, he still managed to attract a number of corporate clients, including life insurance and trust companies and several municipalities.[101] Fourteen of his cases were reported, and he was successful in eight.

Throughout his career Taylor enjoyed the fine things in life, which included the house he lived in. His home in Portage was one of three Canadian structures designed by the famous American architect Frank Lloyd Wright, although the house was built from a plan marketed to the general public. The two-and-a-half-storey brick building, built in 1913, had seventeen rooms and featured art-deco glass, a conservatory with a mosaic floor, a maid's bell in every room, and double walls built on a brick masonry foundation with steel supports resting on deep piles. It stood on a 150-by-140 foot lot that featured a curved driveway, a walled garden, and an unobstructed view of a lake and island park.

Taylor was closely associated with the military during his career at the bar. In 1910 he joined the 99th Manitoba Rangers as a captain, and the year after the First World War broke out he was promoted to major and attached to the 45th Battalion of the Canadian Expeditionary Force. Between August 1916 and October 1918 he served in France with the First Canadian Mounted Rifles. While there he was awarded the Distinguished Service Order and was mentioned in dispatches. In 1917 he was promoted to lieutenant colonel and assumed command of the First Manitoba Rangers, 46th Battalion, Canadian Expeditionary Force.

Taylor was one of a handful of Manitoba judges remembered more for their career in politics than in law. He served three terms as an alderman and three more as mayor of Portage la Prairie before running provincially against Liberal Ewen McPherson, a future chief justice of Manitoba. Taylor lost the 1915 election by 258 votes, but five years later defeated McPherson by almost the same margin. On 5 April 1922 Taylor was elected leader of the provincial Conservative party, and in an election held the same year defeated the sitting minister of public works. Taylor won re-election in 1927 and 1932, and in 1931 turned down an invitation to join the coalition government of Premier John Bracken.[102]

On and off the campaign trail Taylor was both formidable and dapper. Widely applauded for his war record and equally popular with urbanites and farmers, he routinely appeared in the legislature in morning dress, replete with black cutaway coat and serge trousers. His job as Conservative leader was often frustrating, however. The party was still tainted by the legislative building scandal, and more than once Taylor faced the embarrassment of speaking to nominating conventions that refused to nominate a candidate. By 1927, however, his efforts had begun to pay off and his party formed the official opposition.[103]

As a politician Taylor was not above making charges that he not only could not prove, but that had no foundation in fact. In a 1928 by-election he accused the Bracken government of accepting a bribe from the Winnipeg Electric Company to award the company a hydro monopoly on the Seven Sisters River. Throughout the campaign Taylor repeatedly told audiences what he had heard, what he suspected, and what he believed. In a meeting at Oak Lake he said that he had heard that the directors of the Winnipeg Electric Company had made individual donations to the government in the amount of $10,000 each, and he suspected that the stock of the company rose from $74 a share to $128 because of insider trading. He continually taunted the premier, wondering aloud how these things could happen without his knowledge, and demanding that a royal commission be established to investigate his charges. He made headlines throughout the province, especially after promising to resign if his accusations were proved incorrect. His rhetoric had an effect on the usually impassionate premier and were responsible for one of the most heated exchanges in the history of the legislature. After speaking for forty minutes about legislation his government was going to introduce, Bracken abruptly stopped: 'Suddenly, as the hands of the clock reached the hour of four, he turned fiercely upon Colonel Taylor. The whole tone of the speech changed. With his opening sentence he made a savage reference to the famous Oak Lake speech of the Conservative leader ... His dispassionate voice rang out a suddenly querulous note. Deep-seated anger was held back only by obvious effort.[104]

Taylor had branded him a thief, said the premier, and he was not going to put up with it. The Conservative leader immediately denied having done any such thing, and said that the charges he had made were against Bracken's government, not the premier. Two weeks later, however, Taylor was called to testify before the commission established to look into the affair, and was forced to admit that he had no evidence whatsoever to substantiate any of his charges. He rationalized his actions on the grounds that it had always been his policy to 'make political charges on less substantial grounds than if he was making allegations against a private individual.'[105] Ultimately, the commission found no evidence to justify Taylor's accusations.

Fawcett Gowler Taylor (1878–1940). Puisne judge 1933–40. Taylor is prominent among those appointed to Queen's Bench who spent much of their time pursuing outside interests. In Taylor's case it was the military and law. He took over as leader of the Manitoba Conservative party while it was still recovering from the scandal surrounding its former leader and provincial premier. Taylor was a highly entertaining speaker, and by his own admission something of a loose cannon. This picture was taken shortly before he went to the bench, when he was still a member of the legislature for Portage la Prairie. (Provincial Archives of Manitoba)

Taylor was still leader of the opposition when he went to the Manitoba Court of King's Bench. Two days after his appointment was announced he resigned from the Conservative party and gave up his seat in the legislature. Of his thirteen years in provincial politics, eleven were spent as Conservative leader. When Taylor was sworn in as a justice of the King's Bench on 13 April 1933 he had not actively practised law for nearly twenty years.[106] The year he went to the bench, however, he did double judicial duty after being made an ad hoc justice of the Pension Appeal Court in Ottawa. A year later he received a leave of absence from the government to serve as acting chair of the Canadian Pension Commission; in 1935 a special act of parliament was passed extending his term for an additional year. Taylor was still a member of the judiciary when he died unexpectedly on 2 January 1940.

The sixty-two-year-old judge had just returned from a New Year's reception at the official residence of the lieutenant governor when he suffered a heart attack. He was survived by his wife, Mabel Agnes Dykeman, and brothers Gardiner and Allan. His Portage funeral was attended by local politicians and a contingent from the Army and Navy Veteran's Association. After a prayer and benediction, a single hymn was sung before the funeral cortege, a mile in length, proceeded from the church to the Hillside cemetery.

EWEN ALEXANDER McPHERSON

Manitoba's ninth King's Bench chief justice was born in Worth County, Missouri, on 27 January 1878. His father had emigrated to Canada from Scotland in the 1850s, settling in Ayre, Ontario. He and his Canadian wife lived there until 1869, when they moved to Missouri. A year after Ewen was born his parents returned to Canada, settling in Portage la Prairie. Peter McPherson was a carpenter and spent most of his career in the employ of the city. Unlike his son, he took no interest in public affairs, devoting his spare time to the Methodist church.[107]

McPherson was educated in Portage la Prairie but left school at seventeen to spend three years working in a local clothing store. He then returned to high school and in 1898 was admitted to the Law Society as a student-at-law and articled clerk. The following month he entered into a formal articling agreement with Portage lawyer Stuart Robinson Wright. A year later his articles were assigned to Edward Anderson, who left the Anderson and Ormond firm before they were completed. McPherson remained until he received his call in 1903. On 24 October the following year he married Winnifred Finn. Born in Sterling, Ontario, she was the youngest of eleven children. The Finns had moved to Manitoba in 1882 when her father was transferred west by the Presbyterian church. After serving in a number of communities he spent his last ten years as chaplain at the Stony Mountain Penitentiary.

Between 1903 and 1906 McPherson practised with future Canadian prime minister Arthur Meighen. Meighen received his call the same year as McPherson and immediately rented two small rooms in the heart of the Portage business district. The two lawyers spent most of their time preparing wills, probating estates, drawing up real estate documents, and, when required, handling small civil and criminal trials. Although much of the work was routine, it was never boring. 'A cross-section of pioneer prairie life passed in and out of [their] office door: the proud and the humble, the belligerent and the contrite, the greedy, the desperate, the stupid, the hopeful, the downcast, farmers and labourers, merchants and tradesmen, English, Scots, French, Icelanders and "Hunkies."'[108]

In 1906 Daniel Alexander Macdonald left Portage to become a justice of the Court of King's Bench, and McPherson took over his firm. He practised alone for three years before being joined by A.C. Williams and E.P. Garland. Garland was replaced in 1913 by D.M. Ormond, but within a year both Ormond and Williams joined the Canadian Expeditionary Force. Williams was commissioned a lieutenant, and later promoted to major. After that, however, his luck ran out, and the year the war ended he was killed in action. Ormond, on the other hand, emerged as a brigadier general, became the superintendent of Canadian penitentiaries, and ended his career as librarian for the Supreme Court of Canada. When Williams and Ormond left for Europe, McPherson was joined by E.G. Porter and remained in practice with him until going to the bench. R.W. Webster joined the two in 1922, as did C.H. Diehl, although both stayed only a year.

Like Fawcett Taylor, McPherson was more politician than lawyer, and seldom appeared in court. In a career that spanned more than thirty years only six of his cases were reported, although to his credit he lost only once. He was equally successful in Law Society elections. Between 1916 and 1934 he won seven consecutive terms before being made a life bencher. In a letter sent to his children, the secretary of the Law Society commented about their late father's involvement with the Society, noting that '[e]ven after his appointment to the Bench he had, on many occasions, taken an active part in their [Benchers'] deliberations and was always keenly interested in the affairs of the Society.'[109]

McPherson spent virtually all of his professional life in politics, a career that might have been even longer had his attempt to run in the 1899 provincial election not been thwarted by a law requiring candidates to be at least twenty-one years of age. His first official campaign took place in 1910, when he ran for the provincial Liberals in the riding of Portage la Prairie. Despite being defeated by Hugh Armstrong, provincial treasurer in the Conservative cabinet of Rodmond Roblin, he was not deterred. Four years later he defeated the minister by seven votes and in 1915 he beat Fawcett Gowler Taylor. The two had been friends from childhood and Taylor proved to be both his political nemesis and a judicial colleague. In 1920 McPherson's career in provincial politics came to a temporary end. Defeated by Taylor, he left the legislature to return to his law practice. McPherson missed the cut-and-thrust of parliamentary debate, however, and in 1926 was easily persuaded to run in the federal riding of Portage la Prairie against the sitting member, his former partner Arthur Meighen.[110] He defeated the former prime minister by 428 votes, and regarded the four years he spent in Ottawa as the happiest of his life. His friendship with C.G. (Chubby) Power brought him immense satisfaction. The two became virtually inseparable and were widely regarded as among the most brilliant debaters in the House.[111] It was, however, a political relationship that did not last. In Portage the 1930 election was fought over the issue of New Zealand butter. Conservative W.H. Burns toured the constituency with a 'Canadian' cow in tow, lambasting his opponent for refusing to demand an end to butter imports. Burns's strategy paid off in a 142-vote victory, although, ironically, McPherson managed to win the farm vote.

In the ensuing two years McPherson was one of a number of Liberals approached about joining John Bracken's provincial coalition government. The underlying fear of both senior levels of government was that, unless some sort of political accommodation was made, the rejuvenated Conservatives under Taylor would take power. Beginning in February 1932 a committee of five Liberals and five Progressives met regularly to plot strategy. Out of these meetings came the idea of three Liberals joining the Bracken cabinet. Of the men discussed, the one regarded as having the best chance of becoming the next provincial premier was McPherson.[112] On 27 May 1932 he entered cabinet as provincial treasurer and municipal commissioner. An election was held three weeks later, but McPherson was defeated by Taylor. Bracken had realized that a victory over the Conservative leader was far from a sure thing, however, and had deferred voting in two ridings. McPherson took advantage of his second chance and returned to the legislature as the member for Rupertsland,[113] becoming provincial treasurer again. His job was hardly an enviable one. The depression was having a devastating effect on the province's economy, and the government begged Ottawa for help. Prime Minister Bennett not only refused to provide assistance, he told Bracken that if Manitoba's debt was not reduced to less than one million dollars, the federal government was going to appoint a financial controller.

McPherson became treasurer at very nearly the lowest point of the depression. He immediately reduced government expenditures, imposed a 2 per cent tax on salaries, and by year end had reduced the provincial deficit to less than half a million dollars. While his efforts may have saved the province from the embarrassment of having its financial affairs administered from Ottawa, they had a crippling effect on the fabric of society:

> They were bitter years, as worklessness became the accustomed mode of life of the unemployed, as every freight train had its row of transient unemployed, as the fires gleamed nightly in the 'jungles' where the wandering workless lived before moving on. On the farms equipment grew older year by year, houses and barns more weatherbeaten ... [and] towns became more rundown as year by year dust from the blowing fields swirled down their empty streets.[114]

When McPherson went to the bench on 23 November 1937 he became the eighth lawyer from Portage la Prairie to do so. The record of Portage is remarkable when compared to that of Brandon, a city more than twice its size, which could lay claim to just two members of the judiciary. Despite his lack of legal and judicial experience, McPherson's appointment made him the ninth chief justice of the Court of King's Bench. He acknowledged his lack of qualifications at a banquet given in his honour by the Blackstone Club, referring to himself as 'Exhibit "A" for identification.'[115] McPherson remained Chief Justice of Queen's Bench for seven years before replacing Prendergast on the Court of Appeal in 1944 and becoming the chief justice of Manitoba. Apart from hunting and philanthropy, McPherson maintained a low public profile during his tenure on the bench. Although he chaired a royal commission, established in 1949 to study the costs of hospitalization, he devoted most of his time to his job and his family. The seventy-six-year-old

Ewen Alexander McPherson (1878–1954). Chief justice of the Court of King's Bench 1937–44, chief justice of Manitoba 1944–54. McPherson, like Fawcett Gowler Taylor, resided in Portage la Prairie and spent virtually his entire adult life in politics. Although most of his political career was spent in the Manitoba legislature, McPherson served a single term in Ottawa after defeating Arthur Meighen, his one-time partner and former prime minister. Like Alexander Morris and Esten Kenneth Williams, McPherson had no previous judicial experience when he became chief justice of the Court of King's Bench. This photograph was taken in 1944, the year he became chief justice of Manitoba. (Provincial Archives of Manitoba)

judge was still a member of the Court of Appeal when he died of a heart attack on 18 November 1954 while celebrating his son's twenty-fifth wedding anniversary.

Despite the pressure of maintaining a dual career, as both a politician and a lawyer McPherson pursued a number of non-professional and non-political interests. He was a relatively active member of the United Church of Canada, and of the Ancient Free & Accepted Masons, the Independent Order of Odd Fellows, the Motor Club, the Manitoba Club, and the Portage la Prairie County Club, and as a Royal Arch Mason he was for a time the oldest past master of the 'Blue' Lodge. He also chaired the Portage Hospital Board, the Winnipeg Foundation, and, in 1946, the Manitoba Save-the-Children Fund. In 1948 he received an honorary Doctor of Laws degree from the University of Manitoba, and two months before his death was elected honorary president of the national Clan McPherson. Above everything else, however, McPherson enjoyed hunting. His fondest story was of bagging his limit of ducks for fifty-one consecutive shooting seasons.[116] He was not afraid, however, to poke fun at himself. He often spoke of how much he enjoyed an old pump-action shotgun he owned. One day, he said, 'I was standing in the marshes when five bluebills flying one behind the other came down the channel. I shot the first one and it dropped to the water. Then I shot the other four in the same manner. Just as the fifth duck hit the water, the bird I shot first got up. I shot at it with my sixth shell and missed. Then the rest of the "dead" bluebills got up and flew away.'[117]

McPherson died two years after the death of his wife Winnifred.[118]

7

A Most Political Bench, 1939–1950

The prosperity experienced by Manitobans following the Second World War was evident both at law and in society generally, as people 'elbowed each other for refrigerators, stoves, washers and furniture, cars and clothing.'[1] At law the number of Statements of Claim filed in Winnipeg's Court of Queen's Bench between 1946 and 1950 declined to only 194 per year, a decrease of almost 300 per year compared to claims filed during the preceding two decades. The Court of Appeal was also less busy, hearing an average of 110 appeals, almost 40 per cent fewer than heard annually between 1927 and 1945.

One thing that did not change, however, was the criteria for judicial appointments. In the 1940s four of the five men who went to the bench were well connected politically. The first was Attorney General William James Major, who replaced Taylor in 1941. His appointment, despite his lack of legal experience, was a source of little controversy compared to that which accompanied Robson's return to the Court of King's Bench. Although concerns over the advancing age and obvious infirmities of a number of members of the Court of Appeal were the subject of much discussion within the legal profession, the debate became public in February 1944 when the *Winnipeg Free Press* published details of a memorandum sent by leading members of the bar to the federal minister of justice. In it they set out in considerable detail why the government should immediately accept the resignation of Chief Justice Prendergast of the Court of Appeal, which had already been tendered. Following publication of the editorial the federal government moved to dispel criticism of the way in which it was handling judicial appointments in Manitoba by replacing Prendergast with McPherson, making Robson Chief Justice of the Court of King's Bench.[2]

In late 1946 Esten Kenneth Williams, a friend of Prime Minister Mackenzie King and one of the most distinguished scholars and practitioners in the history of the Manitoba bar, was appointed to King's Bench to replace Robson, who had died a year earlier. Williams brought a stern and intimidating presence to the court for witnesses and lawyers alike. He was a stickler for detail, in both procedure and dress, 'and junior counsel appearing before him were in constant fear of being caught out in some technical error, or being reprimanded for allowing a cigarette package to protrude from their pocket.'[3]

The last three justices appointed to the Court of King's Bench before 1950 were Arnold Munroe Campbell, Joseph Thomas Beaubien, and John Joseph Kelly. Campbell was a fourth-generation descendant of the Selkirk Settlers and a well-known backroom politician. He replaced Dysart on King's Bench in 1947 when Dysart was elevated to the Court of Appeal. The following year Beaubien, the brother of a former Member of Parliament, was appointed to fill the vacancy created when Adamson was transferred to the province's appellate court. 'Blackjack' was sent to the Court of Appeal in hopes his strong views might be moderated by those of his fellow justices. The last of the three was another decorated soldier and former law partner of Campbell. Kelly was appointed to King's Bench in August 1949 to fill the vacancy created by the death of Mr Justice Donovan. His tenure, however, was much shorter than that of fellow soldier William Major.

WILLIAM JAMES MAJOR

William James Major was the last Manitoba judge to emigrate to Canada from the United Kingdom. He was born in Shepton Mallet, Somerset, England, on 10 November 1881. At fourteen he entered the law office of Athelstan Rendall, Member of Parliament for the Thornbury Division of Gloucester, and a solicitor practising in Yeovil. Rendall was admitted to practice in 1894, and devoted most of his time to real estate development. Although a Liberal member of the Commons for seventeen years, he was regarded as an 'Advanced Radical' and was also a member of the Fabian party. Two years after leaving parliament he joined the

Labour party. While in the Commons he drafted the report of the Committee on Debtor's Imprisonment, sat on the Commons Panel and Selection Committee, and wrote articles on magistrates and divorce reform.[4]

During his tenure with Rendall, Major did conveyancing and attended in the county court. He also performed the ordinary duties of a student in a solicitor's office, including copying, engrossing, preparing simple drafts and accounts, and obtaining administration of probate and bills of costs. Along with handling office accounts, he was responsible for a wide range of contentious civil and criminal matters. On any given day he had under his supervision as many as two hundred cases in the local county court.[5]

At twenty Major and two friends tried to enlist in the British army in an attempt to fight in the Boer War. All were rejected on the basis that too many men from the Yeovil area had already joined. The three then quit their jobs and departed for Canada. On their arrival they went their separate ways, Major to work as a labourer on a farm near Kirkella, Saskatchewan. After helping with the fall's harvest he moved to Winnipeg, where he completed his high school education. By chance he also met Judge Alexander Dawson and entered his office as clerk. From 1901 until 1908 Major performed for Dawson & Graham many of the same duties he had carried out for Rendall, including conveyancing, minor court work, and supervising the firm's large loan business. Not only did he work days and read law evenings, Major was a serious if unaccomplished athlete, collecting 'an obviously broken nose, an athlete's heart and two broken shoulders playing outside left with the old Bisons and the Y.M.C.A. football team.'[6]

While clerking with Dawson, Major married Winnipeg native Sophie Kabel.[7] He also attended the University of Manitoba, graduating in 1909 to officially become a student-at-law under the tutelage of Dawson and Henry Nason. He was called to the bar on 9 June 1913, admitted as an attorney eleven days later, and for the next five years practised with Nason. From 1918 until appointed to the bench he was a member of Lawrence, Johnston & Major, although during the First World War he was called away to serve as a lieutenant in the infantry of the active militia.

Unlike McPherson, who actively sought involvement in politics, Major was recruited. When asked by Bracken to succeed R.W. Craig as the province's attorney general he did not even have a seat in the legislature. Craig's sudden resignation had, however, created a cabinet vacancy that the premier wanted filled immediately. That Major was his choice was kept a closely guarded secret right up until he was sworn in at 9:00 p.m. on 29 April 1927. Two months later Major ran in Winnipeg and entered the legislature as a Liberal-Progressive.[8] He was fifth in first counts in the ten-member constituency in which voting was conducted on the proportional representative principle. His only previous political experience had been as a worker in the campaigns of Donald A. Ross, member for St Clements, and as chief organizer for R.L. Richardson's campaign as a Union-Government candidate in the 1917 provincial election.

Although re-elected in 1932 and 1936, Major was considerably less popular than his controversial fellow member from Winnipeg, former county court judge Lewis St. George Stubbs. In 1936 just over 78,000 votes were cast in Winnipeg. Stubbs was the top vote-getter with 24,000. Major finished fourth with 5000.[9] He did, however, go on to spend his entire tenure in cabinet as the province's chief law enforcement officer, retiring as the longest-serving attorney general in the province's history.

Major's first task as attorney general was to modernize the province's liquor laws, which he did in 1928 by passing Manitoba's first *Liquor Control Act*. Designed to clear up the confusion created by an earlier statute, the *Moderation League Act*, the new law became a necessity as a result of a growing demand that the government allow beer to be sold by the glass. Major was also credited with establishing the Headingly Jail and with reorganizing the provincial magistrate system. His area of greatest influence, however, came as chair of the legislature's law-amendments committee. In that capacity he played a key role in determining what statutes were introduced or amended. While he headed the committee, civil marriages became a legal alternative to religious weddings, imprisonment for debt was abolished, and a modern *Highway Traffic Act* was introduced. But perhaps the largest undertaking he supervised was the revision and consolidation of the statutes of Manitoba, a mammoth effort carried out over several years.

Major's time in office was not scandal-free. In 1929 he and a cabinet colleague were accused of buying stock in the Winnipeg Electric Company shortly before the government awarded it a contract to develop a hydro-electric plant at Seven Sisters. On 22 February 1929 he was forced by public pressure to step down as attorney general until a commission appointed to review his conduct completed its investigation. His retirement was, however, short-lived. Calling his actions imprudent rather than illegal, the inquiry cleared him of wrong-doing and on 18 May he re-entered cabinet.

Major regularly spoke throughout the province about things both legal and non-legal. An example was the advice he gave a group about to be called to the bar:

> How to get clients ... [T]he more a lawyer appears before the public, the better are the chances of drawing clients to him. There are many ways in which this can be done. An active participation in the affairs of the Chambers of Commerce will bring one into contact with many captains of industry. An active participation in social service organizations and committees will give an entry into and actual contact with another class of citizen. Membership in Fraternal organizations and active participation therein will provide an excellent means of introduction to many worthwhile citizens ... Of course the field of politics has always been open to the lawyer and is followed by not a few members of the profession. I would hesitate to advise you to jump into [it] right at the start, for the time required to discharge the duties of alderman or legislator would greatly interfere with your studies and with the building up of your practice.[10]

Major was not reluctant to speak out on behalf of Manitoba's business community, and on more than one occasion he urged voters to spend rather than hoard their money:

> Now is the time to buy the many things you and your family need - shoes, clothing, furniture, household necessities, any one of the hundred and one things you require. Buy them now, and buy liberally ... Unlock your savings accounts ... People are not saving money; they are hoarding it ... What a difference between saving and hoarding! Saving is a sane way of preparing for a rainy day; but in many cases hoarding is just an open invitation, not for the rainy day, but for a long period of depression.[11]

On 14 March 1941 Major was appointed to fill the King's Bench seat formerly occupied by F.G. Taylor. Rumours that Major was about to be appointed to the bench circulated even before Taylor's untimely passing, and the appointment was regarded by many as a political reward. According to the diary of police magistrate and Law Society bencher Robert Graham: '*Free Press* yesterday evening announced the appointment of the Attorney General, W. J. Major, to fill the vacancy caused by the death of Judge Taylor. If this is official it means that Bracken has

William James Major (1881–1953). Puisne judge 1941–51. Major was the longest-serving attorney-general in Manitoba history when he resigned from the provincial cabinet of premier John Bracken to go to King's Bench. While a trial judge, Major made little effort to hide his opinion of those appearing in his court. His pro-prosecution bias was noticed by members of the Court of Appeal, and on one occasion an appeal court judge suggested that Major had not only ignored the case advanced by the defence, he manufactured one on his own. (Provincial Archives of Manitoba)

promised Mackenzie King the support of his government in the coming election in return for some favours of which Major's appointment is only one.'[12]

Graham did, however, give the appointment his qualified endorsement. 'Although Major has been out of active practice for over ten years and never had much court experience he will, if he works hard, make a good judge.'[13] A non-lawyer and political opponent gave the new judge a similar vote of confidence. 'I do not know the extent of your knowledge of law, but I do believe you understand men and the practical things of life, which combined constitutes a good background for the important duties you have assumed.'[14] Some, including a fellow judge, felt that Major's life would be far less stressful than it had been as a member of the legislature. Court of Appeal Justice R.M. Dennistoun suggested the former politician 'will greatly enjoy the leisure which forms a large part of a judge's life.'[15]

Major brought to the bench a firm set of beliefs. Speeches he made while in cabinet revealed his attitude towards many of the things with which he would have to deal as a judge. One was crime and criminals. While speaking about penitentiaries he noted that if provincial governments stopped whipping criminals for committing serious crimes, they would, in effect, be encouraging criminals to continue their activities. Those who committed crimes should not be molly-coddled. He suggested that there was already too much 'sentimental slobbering' over criminals and their mental attitude. 'We have criminologists, penologists, sociologists, Gov. Commissions & other agencies all contributing their ideas & views as to how to deal with criminals. Frankly I am always sceptical. Wherever these specialists & theorists & agencies exist there crime thrives abundantly.'[16] He suggested that Canada should follow Britain's example in the handling of criminals. The key, he argued, was to have a sure and certain system of criminal administration. Punishment must always be commensurate with the crime.

On the bench Major's attitude did not change. At the end of a trial involving a group of young men charged with rape, he was thunderstruck when the jury returned a verdict of not guilty. In his charge he had made it clear that the jury had no option but to find each guilty. After the foreman finished reading the verdict, obviously angry, he abruptly dismissed the panel. He could not, however, prevent himself from telling the departing jurors that if he had been charged with deciding the fate of the accused he would most certainly have reached a different decision. Then, his face flushed and his voice choking in anger, he told the youths to 'go back to your gang and tell them you pulled the wool over the eyes of a judge and jury of the Court of King's Bench. But before you go, listen to me, and mark my words well: If you ever appear here again, you are on the path to destruction!'[17]

Major seldom made any attempt to hide his opinion of those who appeared before him. During a murder trial, for instance, the last witness to see a cab driver alive was the only person to testify against the accused. Major did not believe a word she said, and he was incensed that she kept changing her version of what had transpired. In his charge he directed the jury to examine carefully the nature of the evidence given by the witness. 'As to her subsequent statements and as to her evidence given to you here on oath, these constitute, in my opinion, one of the most amazing feats of mental gymnastics ever displayed in a court of law, or elsewhere.'[18] One of the grounds of appeal was that his charge overwhelmingly favoured the Crown. The Court of Appeal sustained the trial verdict, but in doing so did not endorse Major's handling of the case. Chief Justice McPherson referred to his charge as fair, but only reasonably complete. In a dissenting judgment Donovan was critical of Major's conduct of the case, suggesting that his handling of circumstantial evidence was inadequate, and that his failure to clarify for the jury the significance of some of the evidence inappropriate. More important, he said that Major entirely ignored the case for the defence. Not only did he ignore it, said Donovan, he manufactured one all on his own, which he then put to the jury.[19]

Although a practising Anglican, Major devoted little time to the church. He chaired the Child Welfare Board of Winnipeg after acting as the vice-chair of its predecessor, and he was a member of the provincial executive of the Boy Scouts, the vice-chair of the Winnipeg Boy Scouts' Association, a director of Mount Carmel public health clinic, a patron of the Canadian Ukrainian Institute Prosvita, the Grand Master of the Masonic Order, and a member of the Supreme Council for Canada of the Scottish Rite of Free Masons. Other organizations to which he belonged included the Ancient Free & Accepted Masons, the Winnipeg Board of Trade, the Benevolent and Protective Order of Elks, Winnipeg Lodge No. 10, and the Niakawa, Carleton, and Rotary clubs. During the Second World War he was head of the Greater Winnipeg Co-Ordinating War Services Board, which supervised the work of organizations and agencies contributing to the welfare and entertainment of service men and women.

Major retired from the bench on 31 July 1951 and died two years later. His health had been a concern to his family even before his elevation and may have influenced his decision to retire from politics. In 1940 he was forced to take a two-and-a-half-month leave of absence from the legislature on the advice of his doctor. Bad health continued to plague him, however, and it was the cause of his early retirement from the bench. In the months preceding his death he suffered from the debilitating effects of a stroke.[20]

Major had a volatile temper and possessed what a contemporary referred to as one of the smallest, meanest minds in the judicial world.[21] Mr Justice J.W. Estey of the Supreme Court of Canada was one of the few who complimented his work as a judge. In a letter to Major he noted, 'I can say to you without any reservation that every comment I have ever heard by members of the bar in Manitoba as well as others has been most flattering with respect to your work as a judge.'[22] Another admirer was Chaplain Carruthers of the Department of Pensions and National Health. After watching one of Major's trials as a spectator, he wrote of his desire to 'most sincerely congratulate you on your masterly address to the jury in the Westgate case. It is sad work, I am sure, that you, in your position had to do, but I do feel that all are agreed that you were very wise and careful in what you said and the judgment you rendered. You did a responsible duty wisely and well.'[23]

ESTEN KENNETH WILLIAMS

Few men in the history of Canadian law have dominated a provincial bar in the manner of Esten Kenneth Williams. By the time he became Manitoba's eleventh Court of King's Bench chief justice Williams had profoundly influenced the province's legal profession as president of the Manitoba Law Society, chairman of the Board of Trustees of the Manitoba Law School, president of the Canadian Bar Association, and counsel to some of the most controversial royal commissions in the province's history. For nearly forty years he lectured at Manitoba's only law school, and one of his books became a standard text across Canada. For much of his career Williams chaired a federal or provincial bar association committee, was widely regarded as a counsel of national stature, and made hundreds of speeches to professional gatherings all over North America. It comes as no surprise, therefore, that he left his mark on the legal profession rather than the law.

More than the other men who made their way to the Queen's Bench,

Williams managed his career in a way most likely to bring him into contact with those with power and influence. He promoted himself through public speaking and became one of the province's best-known raconteurs. He also raised his profile through membership in professional organisations like the Law Society of Manitoba and the Canadian Bar Association. But most significantly, he kept himself in the public eye through his work on numerous royal commissions. On one of those, the federal government's 1946 espionage commission, he participated in one of the largest abrogations of human rights in the country's history.

Williams was born on 18 August 1889 in Parkhill, Ontario, the eldest son of Esten Williams and Edith H.H. Goodman. He was the fifth of six generations, excepting his father, of lawyers. His great-grandfather was the Honourable Rowland Williams, the first judge appointed in the county of Middlesex following the rebellion of 1837. Before that the judicial patriarch of the Williams family had practised in Spanish Town, Jamaica. He and partner Colonel J.S. Bernard emigrated to England shortly after the British government abolished slavery in Jamaica, but their stay was brief and both soon left for Upper Canada. Bernard opened a law office in Brockville before relocating to Kingston. It was there that he accepted as a student the man destined to be Canada's first prime minister, John A. Macdonald. Williams parted company with Bernard shortly after the two arrived in North America and established his own practice in London. He ended his career as a judge of the county of Middlesex and the Huron Tract.[24]

Both grandfathers of Esten Kenneth were distinguished lawyers. On his maternal side Lieutenant Colonel Kenneth Goodman, K.C., practised law at New Hamburg, Ontario, from 1860 to 1870 and at Parkhill, Ontario, from 1870 to 1924.[25] His paternal grandfather, the Honourable George Williams, was for many years the local master in chancery at Chatham, Ontario. Although his son Esten, E.K.'s father and namesake, was not a lawyer, he did have a close connection with the law. When he left Ontario, Esten Sr settled in Leduc, Alberta, where he became a local magistrate.

Williams's mother was the daughter of Goodman and Annie Hainer. Educated at Dufferin House in Toronto, Edith Helen Henrietta and Williams's father married on 3 October 1888. At the time Esten Sr was a clerk in Ontario's Department of Education. The couple were the parents of three daughters and two sons. They resided in Toronto until 1912, then moved briefly to Winnipeg before settling in Leduc. Edith was seventy when she died there in 1938. Esten Sr had been a police magistrate for the northern portion of Alberta for more than twenty years when he retired to British Columbia.[26] He died in Vancouver in August 1949 at the age of eighty-two.

E.K. Williams attended public school in Ontario before entering Osgoode Hall Law School. He spent his entire period under articles in Toronto with John Dawson Montgomery and Robert Alexander Montgomery, and was called to the bar on 19 May 1911. He ranked seventh in a class of forty-two.[27] One of his lecturers at Osgoode was John King, father of Prime Minister William Lyon Mackenzie King. Williams practised briefly with Montgomery, Fleury & Montgomery but within a year left the province for Winnipeg. Thirty-one years later John Dawson Montgomery still regretted his departure. 'It was a raw day for me when you quit me.'[28] On 15 February 1912 Williams was admitted to the Law Society of Manitoba. He practised with T.R. Ferguson until early 1914, when the firm was reconstituted as Ross & Williams. Nine months later it expanded to become Ross, Williams, O'Grady & Layton. When G.F. O'Grady re-entered the partnership following his return from active service in the First World War, the firm became Williams & O'Grady. On 31 March 1915 Williams took time off from his already busy practice to marry Mary Matheson in a quiet weekday ceremony.[29] Williams soon left O'Grady, however, to join Sir James Aikins in Aikins, Loftus, Aikins, Williams, Fisher & Bridgman. He remained there until 1940, when he became counsel for Hough, Campbell, Ferguson, Dilts & Baker. When appointed chief justice of the Court of King's Bench he was senior partner in Williams, Dilts, Baker, Laidlaw, Shepard & Hamilton.

Throughout his legal career Williams's principal form of recreation was reading and writing. As both lawyer and judge his distaste for physical exercise was as well known as his scholarship.[30] In 1914 he published the first of his two books. *Manitoba King's Bench Act* reflected his overwhelming interest in the intricacies of law, and it consisted of two parts subdivided into a number of short sections.[31] The first part was 367 pages long, with a preface, reference table, table of cases, an annotation of the *King's Bench Act* and Rules, a general index, and an index of forms. The second consisted of the *Court of Appeal Act* and *Court of King's Bench Act* with a general index. In his preface Williams wrote of his motives for writing the book. First, he said that Manitoba practitioners were making such frequent use of Holmested & Langston's edition of the *Ontario Judicature Act* that he believed a similar edition, more focused on Manitoba and western Canadian decisions, would be useful. Second, he thought that the most recent revision of Ontario rules, adopted in 1913, required a key to facilitate its use in Manitoba. To that end he included in his work a reference table in which he provided opposite each Manitoba rule the number of the corresponding Ontario rule.

Part of the value of Williams's book is its completeness. He made extensive comments on virtually the entire *King's Bench Act* and throughout described ways in which Ontario and Manitoba rules differed. He not only summarized leading cases from Manitoba, Ontario, Alberta, Saskatchewan, and British Columbia, he discussed in detail 'elemental points' useful to both law students and lawyers unfamiliar with court procedure. Although not a scholarly work, it is one of the earliest examples of its kind in Manitoba.

Between the publication of his first and second books Williams was the editor of the *Western Law Reporter* (1915–16) and the *Digest of Canadian Case Law* (1916–20). It was his second book, however, which established his reputation as a legal scholar. *Notes on The Canadian Law of Landlord and Tenant as Applied to Corporeal Hereditaments* was published in 1922 to overwhelming acclaim.[32] In its twelve hundred pages he discussed the law of landlord and tenant to 1920, commented on leading cases, and referred to a number of articles in which either case law or a provincial statute was discussed. The work was, and remains, impressive for both its breadth and depth. According to Williams, the book was designed to provide law students and solicitors practising where libraries were poor or non-existent with a statement of the general principles of the law of landlord and tenant. His methodology was to make a statement of the law and then provide a full report of the facts of the leading cases. As with all his scholarship, Williams relied heavily on extended quotes. Although this tended to make the work a little disconnected, the book's superior structure more than made up for it. Sixteen chapters contained between four and nineteen 'articles' in which Williams discussed rules and practice. These he supplemented with a ninety-page table of cases, a thirty-three-page table of statutes, four appendices, and a seventy-nine-page index.

The Canadian Law of Landlord and Tenant quickly became a standard Canadian text. According to Carswell, one of Canada's largest publisher of legal texts, its appearance was timely. In a notice to the profession, the publisher pointed out that

> [t]here has been no purely Canadian Textbook on the Law of Landlord and Tenant since 1904. Since then two new provinces have come into being. A large body of case law has been developed, creating an urgent need of a comprehensive textbook thoroughly revised and brought down to date. Williams' Landlord and Tenant cites over 3,000 cases. It is believed that all of the law and statute law, down to date of publication, May, 1922, is here available to the profession. There are nearly 1100 pages of text, aside from appendices and tables of cases.[33]

During Williams's lifetime Carswell published three editions of the book. A fifth was released as recently as 1983 as *Williams and Rhodes Canadian Law of Landlord and Tenant*.

In addition to his two books Williams published nineteen articles. Eleven reproduced speeches, and all but two appeared before he went to the bench. The first, published in 1923, was the substance of a speech given to the Manitoba Bar Association.[34] He made substantial use of case law and English and European treatises to support his discussion of the law of domicile as it related to the province of Manitoba. As was typical of most of his work, the article contained as much history as law. Williams typically wound a single argument around a series of extended quotes,[35] but at the core of his scholarship was a romanticized, almost ahistorical, view of the law and the legal profession. Articles like 'The Lawyer's Wife,'[36] 'The Unalterable Law,'[37] and 'Whither?'[38] were little more than emotional statements describing how lawyers felt about themselves.

Williams's topics were usually antiquarian. He rarely commented on the current state of the law or how it impacted society. His beliefs were spiritual rather than intellectual, and he seldom made evident a social consciousness. Three articles were brief biographies or tributes to a judge or lawyer,[39] two were about items of clothing associated with the court (robes and white gloves),[40] one was a brief practice note,[41] and one an overview of Manitoba legal history.[42] Only in his thirty-four-page article on legal education did he engage in analysis and criticism.[43]

Apart from his scholarship one of Williams most enduring interests was the Manitoba Law School. Between 1914 and 1933 he gave a regular series of lectures. While attendance at the school varied from year to year, by 1919 it stood at one hundred and two. When it moved from its initial location in Winnipeg's downtown YMCA to its own building on Kennedy Street, Williams stayed on as one of fourteen lecturers. His classes began the moment he entered the room, with Williams calling the roll as he walked in. By the time he reached the front of the room he was already lecturing at a rapid pace, and he finished his last sentence as he walked out the door. Williams was a brilliant and eloquent speaker who took obvious delight in his words, often grinning when he found a particularly appropriate way to express an argument.[44] He was, however, a tough examiner. At a meeting held in 1920 the benchers were asked to deal with a petition from students unhappy with an examination set by the jurist.[45] The Law Society investigated the complaint, but took no action when it determined that not all students shared the same feeling as those who signed the petition.[46] The controversy did little to change Williams's style. Five months later the benchers fielded another complaint, this time concerning his examination on pleading and discovery.[47]

While Williams may have overworked his own students, he believed that an overly vigorous approach to teaching was not always appropriate. In October 1924 the *Winnipeg Tribune* described one of his speeches under the headline 'Homework Condemned as Sin Against Childhood.' Williams suggested that the curriculum in schools was too heavy, and that 'more attention should be paid to fundamental subjects. Leave the child to get the frills himself if he desires them after he has gained a thorough knowledge of the main subjects ... The number of subjects taught should be cut down.'[48]

After he gave up his duties as a regular lecturer at the Manitoba Law School, Williams maintained his connection to the school for a further twenty-one years through a series of special lectures. He became a member of its board of trustees in 1938 and board chair in 1947. Although initially opposed to the Law School becoming part of the University of Manitoba, Williams eventually warmed to the idea. He even cooperated in developing a three-year academic curriculum, to be followed by a bar admission course administered by the Law Society. These developments brought legal education in Manitoba into line with that of other Canadian provinces. The role he played in the growth of the University of Manitoba's law school was acknowledged in September 1969 when the law library of the newly created faculty of law was named in his honour.

Although Williams described himself as an independent Conservative, he seldom involved himself in partisan politics. One of the few times he did was in November 1921, when he spoke on behalf of Brigadier General Hugh M. 'Teddy' Dyer, Independent candidate for

Table 1 What Williams spoke about

Topics	1921–9	1930–4	1935–9	1940–6	Total
Legal profession	10	6	5	11	32
Substantive law	6	4	0	1	11
Politics	9	4	4	6	23
Insurance	0	3	3	2	8
Education and religion	0	3	5	5	13
History and literature	1	5	10	3	19
War effort	0	0	1	17	18
Unknown topic	1	3	7	9	20
Totals	27	28	35	54	144

the federal riding of Marquette. He was, however, very active in church matters. In 1922 he accepted appointment to the vestry of St Luke's Anglican Church and the following year to the church's advisory board. When he became a member of the congregation of St George's Anglican Church he promptly became a vestryman, and was one of its representatives at meetings held to discuss church union. He also participated in the 1928 conference organized by the United church, the Church of Christ, and the Baptist church. In 1933 Williams preached an evening sermon at St Columba's Church in Montreal. Eleven years later he was elected rector's warden for St George's.

Williams's library consisted of more than 10,000 books, and he made extensive use of them in preparing the hundreds of speeches that made him one of Manitoba's most popular raconteurs. A brilliant conversationalist, he impressed audiences with his free and informal style of speaking.[49] A Winnipeg newspaper described one of his speeches as an address both scholarly and full of beautiful imagery, and the *Vancouver Province* referred to him as a clear and thoughtful speaker with a trained and perceptive mind.[50]

During the twenty-five years preceding his judicial appointment Williams gave over 144 speeches.[51] In table 1 they have been categorized according to their subject matter, the year they were delivered, and the audience to whom he spoke. To better measure change over time, the data are also subdivided into four periods, beginning in 1921, when he had already become a leader of the Manitoba bar, and ending with his elevation to the bench. Some of the findings come as no surprise. For example, all eighteen of his speeches on war were delivered between 1939 and 1945. Nor was it unexpected that he would speak about insurance after he became solicitor for many of the country's largest insurers, or that he spoke about education and religion after he achieved a position of prominence within both the United Church and the Manitoba Law School. Nevertheless, the findings are revealing.

The data suggested that Williams was interested in the legal profession throughout his career. Initially that interest was more antiquarian than academic. For example, in 1924 he spoke about the 'Romance of the Legal Profession,'[52] 'A Few Humorous Tilts Between the Bench and Bar,'[53] and the 'History of the Inns of Court.'[54] By the late 1930s, however, the subject of his speeches had become more appropriate for a leader of the national bar. He spoke of the 'Need for Lawyers to Continue Reading,'[55] 'The Unalterable Law,'[56] and 'The Lawyer in the Changing World.'[57] His most reflective addresses were speeches delivered shortly after his appointment, entitled 'Today and Tomorrow,'[58] and 'Whither?'[59]

Williams's speeches about the legal profession rarely included a discussion of substantive law. Even as he became more reflective generally, he continued to speak about 'The Lawyer's Wife,'[60] and 'A Day in Court.'[61] The only real difference between his first and last speech, separated as they were by twenty-five years, was their titles. He did, however, speak about substantive law at least eleven times. Six were speeches delivered in the 1920s, when he discussed topics like 'Stare Decisis' and 'Domicil.' In the first years of the 1930s he focused on the 'Right of Privacy'[62] and 'The Trials of a Rules Revision Committee,'[63] and in his last speech on law, delivered to the inaugural meeting of the Manitoba Medico-Legal Society, he spoke of legal procedure.[64]

It may have been that Williams avoided a more substantial approach to his topics because of potential conflicts with issues that he was litigating. A more speculative conclusion, however, is that he refrained from discussing the law because he had little to say. His interests were romantic and historical, rather than philosophical or pragmatic. He was a talented lawyer but not an intellectual. His speeches identified what he thought his audiences wanted to hear, being a sort of raconteur for hire, and there was no evidence that he had an agenda of his own. In few of his speeches does he describe a personal philosophy or belief system. His limited formal education may have made him reluctant to state a view likely to be criticized by the media or the academic community.

Regardless of what a lawyer talks about, a speech can attract the attention of potential clients or it can enhance the speaker's status within the legal profession. Neither likely motivated Williams. By the

Table 2 To whom Williams spoke

Audiences	1921–9	1930–4	1935–9	1940–6
Lawyer groups	11	7	6	12
Client organizations	0	2	3	1
Clubs and fraternal groups	13	11	9	12
Professional groups	2	4	5	9
Rallies	0	0	6	10
Schools and conferences	1	3	7	10
Totals	27	27	36	54

time he gave his first speech he had already attracted a stable of corporate clients and was among the profession's elite. His two books were widely regarded as outstanding professional contributions, and by 1919 his advice was sought by both federal and provincial governments. It was unlikely, therefore, that he chose his audiences on the basis of what they could do for him. Table 2 offers a breakdown of his audiences.

Williams usually spoke to lawyers and members of social organizations. As president of bodies such as the Law Society of Manitoba and the Canadian Bar Association he received numerous invitations to speak. More revealing were the speeches he gave to groups likely less impressed by his status as a lawyer. As already mentioned, he told them what they wanted to hear. To Jewish organizations he spoke about 'The Jew and the Teuton,'[65] to Winnipeg's St David's Society he talked about Wales,[66] with the Dickens Fellowship Society he discussed 'Why I Read Dickens,'[67] members of the Polish Club heard about 'The Struggle of Poland,'[68] and his address to the Caledonian Club was about 'Hadrian's Wall.'[69] The topic that most fascinated Williams, however, was politics. He spoke of it more often and to more groups than any other subject except the legal profession, although he rarely spoke about politics to an audience of lawyers. Table 3 gives a breakdown of his speeches by topic and the type of group to which he spoke.

In reflecting on the data in table 3 one should keep in mind that Williams gained his professional reputation as a litigator and as a member of the executive of a number of professional organizations. To most of the bar, many of whom were elected politicians, the political opinions of another lawyer were irrelevant. As a result, Williams usually discussed politics when he addressed schools, clubs, and fraternal organizations. To members of these groups he spoke of 'Canada's National Problems,'[70] 'Canada's Nationality and What It Involves,'[71] 'Ca-

Table 3 What Williams spoke about and to whom

Topics	Bar associations	Professional groups	Schools and conferences	Clubs and fraternal groups
Legal profession	23	0	0	5
Law	6	4	0	1
Politics	0	0	7	15
History and literature	1	3	1	12
Totals	30	7	8	33

nadian Nationalism and What It Signifies'[72] and the 'Americanization of Canada.'[73]

By the time he went to the bench Williams had refined his speaking skills to an art form. After his address to the American Life Convention in the fall of 1945 he received a number of letters from members of his audience. One was from the manager and general counsel of the convention, who was effusive in his praise. Referring to Williams's speech as masterful, he noted that '[e]very speaker can sense the reaction of his audience and consequently you know the superb way in which your address was received.'[74] Another letter was from a member of the convention audience, who asked permission to read Williams's 'Canada and the United States – a Study in Similarities and Contrasts,' to a literary club in Tarrytown, New York.[75] The general manager of the Canada Life Assurance Company, who had also heard his convention address, told Williams in November that the 'highlight of the meeting, to me, was unquestionably your interesting and brilliant address. All of us were proud to have you as the spokesman for the Canadians in that large group. I feel sure your remarks will add considerably to the prestige of Canada and Canadians among all who heard, or who will eventually read, your remarks.'[76]

Three months later Williams's speech to a Canadian gathering generated a similar response. A meeting organizer thanked him for his 'sensational' speech and quoted from a letter he had received from a Montreal member of his organization: 'When you think that the man [Williams] spoke without the aid of the loud-speakers and without notes and that his speech was straight forward from beginning to end, I cannot understand why he has not been in greater demand as a public speaker across Canada and also below the Southern Boundary.'[77]

Apart from speech-making Williams also maintained a high degree of public and professional visibility through his participation in the

Canadian Bar Association, the Law Society of Manitoba, and a variety of non-profit organizations. From 1918 until he went to the bench he continuously chaired one or more committees of the CBA, was a long-time member of the Association's editorial board, was the convenor of its committee on comparative provincial legislation and law reform from 1922 to 1932, and between 1933 and 1938 he chaired the insurance section. For much of that time he was also a member of the special committee on 'Legal Problems of International Organization for the Maintenance of Peace,' and became committee chair in the year in which he went to the bench. Williams was the honorary secretary of the Canadian Bar Association between 1932 and 1934, a national vice-president in 1944, and the following year he succeeded F. Philippe Brais as CBA president. In appreciation of his work on its behalf the Canadian Bar Association made Williams a life member, and in 1937 he became an honorary member of the American Bar Association.

Williams was just as active with the Law Society of Manitoba. Elected a bencher in 1931, 1934, 1937, 1940, and 1943, he became a life bencher in 1946. He was the Society's secretary in 1937, two years later its treasurer, and two years after that its president. Prominent among the non-legal organizations with which he was involved was the University of Manitoba, on whose senate he sat from 1936 to 1942. He was also president of the Winnipeg branch of the United Nations Society in Canada, the chair of the Manitoba Advisory Board of the Canadian Broadcasting Corporation, and sat on the board of the Manitoba Cancer Relief and Research Institute, the Winnipeg branch of the Canadian Institute of International Affairs, the Winnipeg General Hospital, Ravenscourt School for Boys, and the Winnipeg Orchestral Club. Other boards on which Williams sat included those of the National Trust Company and the Midland Railway Company.

In speeches both before and after his elevation to the bench Williams often dealt with the role of religion in history. The 'goal of history, however dimly sensed in human terms, is the Kingdom of God, an aspiration which redeems history from being a futile tragedy of blood.'[78] He also discussed how important religion and the Anglican church were to him. In an address to the St Andrew's Society he spoke of the benefits he derived from having deep religious values, and of the need to put spiritual things first.[79] In another speech he said he was convinced that the church was the salvation not only of 'workers,' but of everyone and everything else.[80] Williams's activities on behalf of his church became so well known that in a newspaper advertisement promoting a lecture he was to deliver in Minneapolis he was described as a 'widely-known Winnipeg lawyer and Anglican layman.'[81]

The status of Williams as a member of Manitoba's legal elite was acknowledged in 1923 when the province's attorney general made him 'one of His Majesty's Counsel learned in the law for the Province of Manitoba.' Thirteen years later he was made King's Counsel for the province of Alberta in recognition of his long association with the Canadian Bar Association. Williams also received two honorary doctorates of law, the first from Laval University (1947) and the second from the University of Manitoba (1953).

Williams's belief in individualism was evident in nearly all of his public speeches. So, too, was his belief that governments have no business interfering in the lives of their citizens. In a 1927 address he suggested: 'We must do to parliament what we have done to the king: curb its power. The interest of the party has come to supersede the interest of the country at large, and that is an evil we must cure.'[82] In a speech delivered later the same year he returned to the role of government in society. Law-making, he suggested, had become such a vice that Canadians groaned beneath the burden of laws.[83] Seven years later he received thunderous applause when he said that the government should keep its regulatory hands off the life insurance industry. It was better, he argued, for individuals to learn not to rely on the government for assistance in times of stress or old age.[84] In the midst of the Great Depression he spoke of the same topic: 'It will be a sad and unfortunate day for this country if sturdy and self-reliant individualism is not permitted to go hand in hand with reasonable and proper social legislation.'[85]

Williams's service on a number of royal commissions and boards of inquiry solidified his reputation as one of the country's best-known lawyers. Whether he served as a commission member or as legal counsel, it was work he described as the most enjoyable of his career.[86] One of the first commissions with which he was associated, consisting of Manitoba King's Bench justices Macdonald, Dysart, and Kilgour, was established in 1929 to investigate charges of improprieties in the awarding of a provincial governmental power contract. As commission counsel Williams was paid $5658.83.

In 1931 Manitoba Premier John Bracken appointed Williams a royal commissioner to investigate charges made against the Manitoba Pool Elevator Company by James Murray, manager of the Alberta-Pacific Grain Company. Murray charged Manitoba Pool with depriving its farmer-shareholders of large sums of money through an organized system of false billing. The one-person inquiry opened on 25 March, and three months later Williams announced that three of the four accusations against Manitoba Pool had been proved. He determined that Manitoba Pool Elevators not only had the most expensive elevator system ever constructed in western Canada, but had foisted onto its members elevators that should never have been built. He also found that the company had adopted a system of overages and underages as a means of cheating members out of thousands of dollars in payments. According to Williams, the system was put into place by Pool officials to hide losses resulting from corporate mismanagement. His third finding was that Manitoba Pool had refused to provide members with its financial statements, thus preventing them from learning just how inefficient the company really was. Murray's fourth charge was that many Pool elevators would not be able to meet their expenses if the farmers delivering grain to them received the same amount for their product as they could have obtained at non-Pool elevators. Williams found this charge not proven.

When not practising law or involved in commission work, Williams was an outspoken defender of the status quo. A 1935 magazine biography described him as a reactionary, a reputation likely earned because of his well-known association with Canada's political and corporate elite. According to the article, men like Williams were rarely willing to entrust the conduct of their personal affairs to those who expect and hope for the dawn of a new day.[87] The article's author was not far off the mark. In a 1939 convocation address delivered at United College, Williams warned his audience against the tendency 'to step aside and follow new leaders and strange gods.'[88]

Perhaps because of his belief in the need to preserve the status quo, Williams was outraged at the selfishness and thoughtlessness of some members of society. In 1935, for example, he bemoaned the fact that for centuries the fundamental law of mankind was the survival of the fittest, rather than 'loving thy neighbour.'[89] He suggested that survival should no longer depend upon one's ability to acquire power. Instead, the value of both individuals and nations should be based on a willingness to serve others in a selfless way.[90] He saw no contradiction in his corollary argument that serving was not the same as helping others. He believed that one of the chief obstacles to progress was self-pity, and suggested that for democracy to survive it must deserve to survive. That point would be reached, he said, when people ceased to expect the help of the state. 'I have never yet met a man of normal mentality who has never had a chance.'[91] Williams also believed that nations too should put aside selfishness and intolerance, and suggested that it was essential for world peace that people everywhere be more tolerant of each other. After all, he said, 'Nations manifest on a larger stage the same characteristics as individuals.'[92]

Williams took advantage of his many appearances on speakers' podiums to refine his skill at networking. The author of a brief 1935 biography noted: '[He] greets his friends with the most engaging smile and his handshake suggests a caress. How he accosts his clients we cannot say, we have never been in that category. But we imagine that he never shakes a tree which bears desirable fruit roughly enough to impair the chances of a harvest.'[93] Williams was not someone easily ignored. His career-focused skills, his self-confidence, and his moralistic view of the world earned him a national reputation as lawyer, author, legal insider, and public speaker, as was acknowledged in a magazine sketch published in 1936:

> Our subject is a lawyer and a great one too. Not content with winning leadership among the shock troops of the Bar he has spent many hours browsing around the withered grass and leaves of legal textbooks, cases and precedents. These he has crystallized into books which have been sold to and read by others not so well equipped by disposition or training for labourious research ... [He] is often found when men foregather and his name is frequently mentioned as addressing various gatherings on various subjects. Apparently he is generous almost to prodigality in the distribution of his intellectual wealth. It may be, of course, that he is not entirely unselfish in his activities. Such exertions, like virtue, bring their own reward and the most conspicuous flowers in the garden attract the greatest swarm of bees.
>
> Our subject is an excellent after dinner speaker. At times he forsakes the well-beaten highway of prose to wander among the flowers of posey. A man who can write prosy law books and quote copiously from the poets, can justly lay claim to versatility.
>
> Such is E.K. Williams, capable court lawyer, authoritative legal writer, after-dinner speaker and orator, and very prominent citizen.[94]

Williams was a member of Manitoba's legal elite during a time when it was not fashionable for large law firms to hire Jewish lawyers. Despite this, he was a staunch supporter of the Jewish cause. In 1931 he spoke to the Menorah Society of the University of Manitoba about 'The

Legacy of Israel,' and in 1934 was among the first prominent Manitobans to speak out against the spread of fascism and the growing persecution of Jews in Germany.[95] Two years later Williams gave a lecture on a local Winnipeg radio station, 'My Neighbour, the Jew,'[96] and in 1940 he delivered a series of speeches warning Manitobans about the threat Hitler posed to the survival of European Jews.[97] Shortly after Canada declared war on Germany he sent a letter, with a cheque attached, to a well-known leader of Winnipeg's Jewish community, describing the cheque as his way of expressing 'in some tangible form, however slight, my deep sympathy for the people to whom we all owe so much, amongst whom I number some of my most valued friends, and who once again are undergoing a persecution, which fills all decent people with inexpressible horror and disgust.' The letter was reprinted, in full, in the *Western Jewish News*.[98]

After the war Williams campaigned to have Samuel Freedman become the first Jewish lawyer appointed to the Court of King's Bench. When the campaign succeeded in 1952, many within the Manitoba legal community believed it was a direct result of his influence. One such believer was Freedman's brother Max: 'I am aware of your recommendations which resulted in Sam's appointment. I hope he will be able to sustain the traditions of a court which has been so greatly ennobled by your scholarship and leadership. My kindest regards and utmost thanks.'[99] Despite Williams's very visible support for the cause of Jews, however, he was a member of Manitoba's two most prestigious clubs, neither of which admitted Jews as members.[100]

Williams was also an advocate of a bicultural Canada. Toronto's *Globe & Mail* described him as a lifelong advocate of bilingualism who believed that a knowledge of both official languages made for better Canadianism.[101] An editorial published by Montreal's *Le Canada* in January 1945 described him as a Canadian who recognized what national unity called for.[102] Twenty years earlier Williams had made it clear that if Canada was to remain strong and united, western Canadians in particular had to start trying to understand the viewpoint of French Canadians.[103] His opinions were given added legitimacy by the fact that he was a non-francophone westerner who both wrote and spoke flawless French.[104]

Williams repeatedly compared Canada to the United States. At the 1945 annual meeting of American life insurance underwriters he spoke about 'A Study in Similarities and Contrasts.' He noted that Canada approached problem solving in a way quite different to that of the

United States, largely because of the differences between Canada's two founding races. English Canadians, he suggested, thought of things inductively, with a Baconian-like mind, which produced the common law. French Canadians, by contrast, used a deductive or Aristotelian approach, which produced the codes of the civil law.[105] Williams then went on to describe differences between the constitutions of Canada and the United States. 'We have decided upon a constitution which is only partly written and preferred, what we considered the more flexible English system, where the law of the constitution is largely the Common Law ... We did not adopt your system of checks and balances by which your Supreme Court, in interpreting your Bill of Rights may declare laws passed by the elected representatives of the people to be unconstitutional.'[106] To assert that judicial review did not exist in Canada might have been what American insurance executives wanted to hear, but it certainly did not define constitutional realities north of their border.

When Williams compared Canada and the United States he often spoke about the criminal law, the legal profession, and tolerance. He believed that because criminal law and procedure were federal matters, and therefore uniform throughout the country, the Canadian court system was much simpler than its American counterpart. He also believed that Canada's legal profession had an advantage over its American counterparts. In Canada, lawyers in each province were obligated by law to become members of statutory bodies that had control over their education, admission to practice, and discipline.[107] In a speech made after his elevation to the bench, however, he suggested that what really distinguished Canada from the United States was tolerance. '[What] we in Canada have been able to achieve has been achieved by unremitting efforts at mutual tolerance by men of good will of all groups.'[108] Eleven years later he still spoke of the same issue, noting that Canada had no John Birch Society or evidence of McCarthyism.[109]

Despite his belief in the need for tolerance and understanding, Williams at times displayed neither quality. In a 1942 speech he said that his personal view was that communists had no place in Canadian society. We should, he suggested, place the mark of beasts on them and put them where they belonged.[110] Four years later his work as counsel to the Taschereau-Kellock espionage commission made evident just how intolerant he could be. The commission not only denied to those merely suspected of wrong-doing access to legal counsel, it intimidated them into making statements that they were not required at law to make, and then used what they said to obtain convictions. By 1952 Williams may even have forgotten that he once said that everyone was fundamentally and permanently influenced by their own life experiences. Judges, he now suggested, were the impartial and fearless protectors of the law because they alone had the capacity to resist being influenced by their cultural and religious backgrounds.[111]

Williams was firm in his belief that Canadian courts should remain unsullied by American influences. The purity of the Canadian judicial system, he said, was an inducement for many Americans to emigrate to this country. 'In our judicial and legal systems there is not the slightest trace of American influence, which incidentally is one of the main reasons a number of people have moved from the United States to Canada. They knew that in Canada there were laws and a legal system that could be relied upon.'[112]

Like others with ambition, Williams was prepared to advance his career by cultivating a relationship with someone in a position of influence. An example was the dialogue he established with the man who appointed him to the bench. In February 1945 he sent Prime Minister Mackenzie King an unsolicited package containing a commonplace book owned by Williams's brother-in-law, Robert Murray Gourlay.[113] In the book was a copy of a letter written by Robert Gourlay, the famous Upper Canadian reformer, to King's grandfather, William Lyon Mackenzie. Although Williams had no direct connection to the letterbook, he sent it to the prime minister in his own name. On 15 February 1945 King returned the book, thanking Williams for the kindness he had shown in sending it, ending his note, 'With kindest personal regards, Believe me.'[114]

A week later Williams wrote a second letter, informing King that he had once been a student in a class to which King's father lectured on evidence.[115] 'Perhaps I might be permitted to mention that one of the things that always drew me to your father was that in appearance he greatly resembled my own grandfather.' With that reference Williams shifted the focus of his relationship with the prime minister from the Gourlay letterbook to the relationship he had with the prime minister's father. The two men immediately began communicating as intimate friends. Prime Minister King noted that the on-going correspondence between the two of them was an 'additional link in our friendship which it serves to afford.'[116] King soon was sharing with Williams that awareness of the spiritual for which the prime minister has been remembered. He directed Williams's attention to a letter in the Gourlay book in which reference was made 'to the greater insight into spiritual truths which men come to have through withdrawing themselves to a certain extent from the world.'[117] Williams was quick to respond, noting that he was 'enjoying the correspondence very much and particularly appreciate it when I know how tremendously busy you are and what vitally important matters you are dealing with all the time.'[118] Two other letters were exchanged between the two, the first from Williams to King,[119] and the second from King to Williams, sent five months before King appointed Williams to the Manitoba bench.[120]

The most controversial commission with which Williams was associated was established at the end of the Second World War, just as Western democracies were becoming increasingly anxious about the threat posed by communism. The circumstances leading to establishment of the inquiry had all the drama of a spy novel. Early in the morning of 15 February 1946 squads of Royal Canadian Mounted Police officers barged into the homes of eleven men and two women. All were officials in either the armed forces or civil service, and all were arrested without being charged. Late that afternoon Prime Minister Mackenzie King announced to the Canadian nation that his government had ordered the raids after it learned that a foreign power had been receiving unauthorized confidential information. Shortly after the arrests were carried out the police made a startling announcement: Fred Rose, the Labour-Progressive Member of Parliament for Montreal-Cartier, had been arrested and charged with spying for Russia. A total of twenty-two people were detained on suspicion that they had supplied secret information to a foreign government. All were denied access to legal counsel.

The commission of inquiry established by the federal government was chaired by two Supreme Court of Canada justices, Robert Taschereau and R.L. Kellock. Williams was one of three lawyers appointed as commission counsel. The others were Gerald Fauteux of Montreal (later Chief Justice of Canada) and D.W. Mundell of the Department of Justice. Williams, however, was the most influential of the three.[121] In July the commission's 733-page report immediately became a 'must-read.'[122] In Great Britain alone more than 4000 copies were sold, making it the most widely circulated document of its kind ever issued by a Commonwealth government.[123] Following release of the report two more arrests were made, two suspected foreign agents disappeared, and eighteen officials in the Russian embassy returned to Russia, including Ambassador Georges Zaroubin.

Prosecutions of those arrested began even before the commission released its findings. On 4 March 1946 the first of three interim reports was tabled in the House of Commons. Four individuals were accused of having passed, directly or indirectly, secret and confidential information to representatives of the Russian government. Two were arrested and convicted before the final report was made public.[124] Shortly after a Second Interim Report was issued four more individuals were charged with spying.[125] The last five accused were named in the commission's Third Interim Report, released on 29 March 1946.[126] Not named was Fred Rose. The Polish native, born in 1907, became a Canadian citizen in 1926 and a year later joined the Communist Party of Canada. In 1943 he was the only Labour-Progressive Member of Parliament. Rose went to trial a month and a half after his arrest and was convicted and sentenced to six years in prison. Eight others were also found guilty. One was fined, and the rest received sentences ranging from two and a half to six years.[127]

Throughout its proceedings the commission adopted unprecedented methods of detaining and questioning those arrested. Among the first to criticize its procedures was M.J. Coldwell, leader of the CCF. Four days after the First Interim Report was released he complained that

> [under] Order-in-Council No. 6444 suspected persons have been held for days without proper charge, without access to counsel, and have been forbidden communication, except by letter, with their relatives or friends. This was bad enough in wartime; it is intolerable in peacetime. The war was fought to destroy states which made such police activities a general practice. To say that it was necessary to resort to totalitarian methods in order to secure evidence is no valid excuse for abrogating the elementary principles of Canadian justice.[128]

The author of a 1946 *Canadian Bar Review* article was equally critical. He accused the commission of acting simultaneously as investigator, judge, and counsel for the Crown.[129] The Civil Liberties Committe of the CBA was so appalled at the actions of Williams and other commission members that it presented a motion to the twenty-eighth annual meeting of the organization. In it the committee affirmed its unequivocal support for the rule of law and its strong disapproval of the actions of the federal government, which it suggested amounted to an abrogation of the freedoms enjoyed by Canadians. The motion was a particular source of embarrassment to Williams, not just because he was the person most often singled out for criticism, but because he was the CBA's president.[130] Louis St George Stubbs, a former county court judge, member of Manitoba's legislature, and prominent social activist, was outspoken in his criticism of Williams. He noted that the commission counsel was a well-known anti-communist and Rose an easy victim of the fervour whipped up by the espionage commission. As 'a Jew, a Communist, and an M.P. from Quebec, [he was] in short an ideal victim for the big shots.'[131] Stubbs was probably accurate in suggesting that Williams's work on behalf of the espionage inquiry and in the prosecutions that followed was motivated by ideology. In 1942, during a widely reported speech, he he had made his position clear, blaming Canadian communists for hampering the country's war efforts. 'It is about time our own Quislings were named by somebody. Who are they? The obvious ones are the communists. They have been disloyal to Canada from the start of the war to June 22, 1940.'[132]

By the time Williams went to the bench the furor caused by the work of the commission had largely been extinguished. In an editorial discussing his part in the hearings the *Winnipeg Free Press* assumed the role of a Williams apologist:

> [W]hatever else may be felt about the advice tendered by Mr. Williams there never has been, and is not now, any doubt about the sincerity of his judgment. Moreover, it should be recalled that this advice was given under the initial shock of the revelations; when the exact dimensions of the espionage ring were matters of conjecture and speculation; and when the threat to the safety of the state embodied in these spy activities was pictured as being more formidable than the event proved.[133]

That 'event,' as the editorialist referred to the commission, was ranked as the world's second most important story in 1946, right after the Nuremberg war crimes trials.[134]

Williams was sworn in as chief justice of Manitoba's Court of King's Bench by Lieutenant-Governor R.F. McWilliams at eleven o'clock in the morning on 10 December 1946. Before his appointment was announced there had been speculation that he might receive an even higher honour. In October the Vancouver *Daily Province* ran an article under the headline 'E. K. Williams May Enter Supreme Court.' It noted that Williams had long been regarded as having the right of first refusal to fill the vacant position of chief justice of Manitoba's Court of Appeal, and the paper speculated that he would either go to the Supreme Court of Canada or become the chair of the soon-to-be-created Income Tax Appeal Board.[135] When Williams went to the bench a *Winnipeg Free Press* editorial described him as a man whose mind moved in broad horizons, with a profound interest in history and literature. He was, it suggested, also a man of rare courtesy and even temper.[136] While the paper may have been right about the first part of its assessment, it was off the mark in the second. Williams ran his court as he practised law, with a firm hand, and he was quick to show his irritation. If a court were to sit at a certain time, one minute before the allotted time he entered the room. If counsel was late, he was told in no uncertain terms that he had just used his last chance. Williams's standards were enforced both on and off the bench. 'No one appeared in his office unless properly dressed with a coat and tie and instructions were given to the messengers not to allow any infringement of this order.'[137]

Speculation about Williams's future did not end with his appointment as chief justice. In 1954 a Winnipeg newspaper suggested that he was being mentioned as a replacement for Ewen McPherson, the former chief justice of the Court of Appeal.[138] Others in the running were rumoured to include the federal minister of justice, Stuart Garson, and Court of Appeal justices Adamson and Kilgour. A follow-up article predicted that the next chief justice of Manitoba would be either Williams or Adamson. In the end, Adamson received the appointment.[139]

While on the bench Williams often spoke of his belief that law was a gentleman's profession and an occupation in which there was no excuse for deviating from the highest standards.[140] He believed that the fundamental obligation of lawyers was waging a battle between right and wrong, between law and chaos.[141] In that struggle lawyers had only one thing for which to strive: reputation. A good name, he suggested, was worth more than riches, and the satisfaction that came from a duty well done was the great impelling motive actuating all who sought to climb the hill of success.[142] In the opinion of Williams, success in the law came only to those who continued as students and maintained the tradition of the profession.[143]

Williams also frequently spoke of how difficult it was for judges to arrive at the truth during a trial. Their biggest problem, he suggested, was 'false-swearing,' which he speculated occurred more often in criminal than in civil cases. While most witnesses tried to tell the truth, those inclined to embellish were usually deterred from doing so by their respect for the oath they had taken, and the possibility that they could be charged with perjury. The other thing that encouraged witnesses to tell the truth was the knowledge they would be subjected to cross-examination by opposing counsel and, on occasion, interrogation by the judge.[144] Williams believed that most judges understood that different witnesses were bound to see events from different perspectives, and that this often obscured the value of what was said by even the most educated witnesses. 'Judges understand and appreciate these difficulties and have to take them into consideration in weighing the evidence. My own experience leads me to the conclusion that, in cases such as this, there is little to choose between the abilities of the best-educated and the uneducated witness to see clearly, to recollect clearly, and to relate intelligently.'[145]

Williams regarded two cases as the most interesting of his judicial career. One, tried in 1960, was known as the 'sugar combines case.' It was the first combines prosecution heard in Manitoba, and by the time it ended it had produced over 3400 pages of evidence and a 130-page judgment. The other case was more unusual than legally significant, and involved a lawsuit filed against both a physician and the University of Manitoba's Faculty of Medicine. The plaintiff sued for damages because the physician did not permit him to be present in the delivery room when his wife gave birth to the couple's child. Representing himself, he argued that as a husband he had a special right under the laws and customs of Manitoba to be present when his wife gave birth. He also maintained that the part of his marriage vow which provided that he and his wife should share 'all the joys and sorrows of their natural life together' included the right to share childbirth. Although Williams dismissed the claim on the grounds that a physician must be in complete control of a delivery room at all times, he regarded the case as the strangest that he had ever tried.[146] Two weeks after Williams rendered his decision the plaintiff appealed. In his factum, prepared without legal assistance, he cited four grounds of appeal, the first of which was 'surprise,' a ground that had never previously been argued in a Manitoba court. Both the province's Court of Appeal and the Supreme Court of Canada were unimpressed, and both dismissed the appeal.

Williams's opinions did not change appreciably after he went to the bench. In an article written shortly before he retired a Winnipeg newspaper noted that some judges were inclined to move in advance of the law, and through their judgments make new law. Not so Williams. The 'chief justice holds firmly to the belief that the making of the law is the business of legislators. The Court's business is to interpret and administer.'[147] Although this formalistic approach was not uncommon in mid-twentieth-century Canada, attitudes were changing, especially among those appointed to the bench after Williams retired in 1962.[148]

In a newspaper article discussing Canadian prime ministers Borden and Laurier, Williams said of Borden, 'It may be easy to point to errors he committed, to inconsistencies from time to time in some views he held and some policies he followed; that is, he was human. But we are not concerned with these things if it can be said that in the fundamentals his policy over the years was consistent and vision pure.'[149] With his sense of history, Williams may have been speaking of himself. The eighty-one-year-old chief justice died of a heart attack in 1970 while visiting his son in Dunsberg, England. His death came fourteen years after he had suffered an earlier attack. Manitoba's late former chief justice was buried in Surrey, England.[150]

Possessed of a full head of hair, piercing blue eyes, and an immaculately manicured Van Dyke beard, E.K. Williams was physically distinctive, despite being only five feet nine inches tall, weighing only 123 pounds, and being slight almost to the point of 'attenuation.'[151] His slightness, however, was due to poor health rather than an improper diet. In 1911 he was so ill that his doctors gave him only six months to live.[152] But Williams always had a strong sense of personal dignity, something that did not fail him after he left the bench. An example was his fondness for honorifics. Before his retirement became official he was determined to retain the title 'Honourable,' and his petition to Canada's secretary of state to do so was granted.[153]

Williams was also a stern and humourless man, not easily approached.[154] Some, like Chief Justice Bora Laskin of the Supreme Court of Canada, remembered him for his scholarship, successful practice, and professional leadership.[155] Others, however, thought of him in less glowing terms. Some never forgave him for the espionage commission, suggesting that it was his advice to Prime Minister King that resulted in the use of the extraordinary legal procedures that produced such a deep schism in public opinion over the government's arbitrary infringement of personal freedoms.[156] It is perhaps ironic that 'in his constant concern for proper form Williams sometimes lost sight of substance, and that his influence tended to deflect the legal profession's attention from the goal of "substantial justice."'[157]

ARNOLD MUNROE CAMPBELL

Arnold Munroe Campbell was born on 15 July 1892 in East Kildonan, Manitoba, a fourth-generation descendent of the original Selkirk Settlers. He attended elementary and high school in Winnipeg, and in 1915 graduated from the University of Manitoba with a Bachelor of Arts degree. In August of that year he signed articles of clerkship with Edward Spice of Hudson, Ormond, Spice & Symington. Two years later he enlisted in the Canadian army as a gunner in the 76th Battery of the Canadian Field Artillery. He was discharged in 1919 as a lieutenant, a year after the Manitoba Law School awarded him a Bachelor of Laws degree in absentia. In December Campbell was admitted to the bar as a solicitor, and on 7 January 1920 he was called as a barrister.

Although Campbell remained with the Hudson firm following his call, within a year he left to practice with W.L. McLaws and G.A. Axford. Between 1922 and 1935 he and James C. Berg were partners in a largely solicitor's practice located in Winnipeg's venerable Paris Building. Campbell spent his last twelve years at the bar with John Joseph Kelly. Both, however, were more comfortable in a political scrum than a courtroom. In a career that spanned a quarter of a century, only seven of Campbell's cases were reported. Six involved trials, and he was successful twice. That three of his seven clients were corporations is suggestive of the real focus of his practice. Among those he served as solicitor was the Royal Norwegian Consulate.

A lack of experience did not mean that Campbell was intimidated by the court process. In 1943 his attempt to introduce prohibited evidence through a legal loophole almost succeeded. The case involved an undefended divorce action in which the only evidence of adultery was an admission made during the respondent's examination for discovery. Campbell was aware that, although courts in western Canada refused to order discovery relating to adultery, once discovery had taken place they usually treated the evidence given as admissible. When Campbell could not persuade his client's wife to testify at trial, he had her examined for discovery. At the subsequent divorce hearing he attempted to introduce her discovery statements. Justice Dysart agreed that technically they should be admitted, but he refused to grant a decree *nisi* on the grounds that trials of divorce suits should be conducted in 'open' court, and not in pre-trial discoveries. 'I hold that discovery evidence, even where obtained freely and willingly after proper warning, is not sufficient evidence in proof of adultery. I do not hold that the evidence is inadmissible, but I do hold that it is not the best evidence.'[158] Campbell's efforts were both novel and sophisticated for a lawyer with little courtroom experience.[159]

Perhaps because he did not attract the kind of exposure that trials give barristers, Campbell sought attention elsewhere. He became part of a six-person committee involved in writing the diary of Harold Lex, excerpts of which appeared every Saturday in both Winnipeg newspapers. Lex was a fictional young man 'of discerning mind, deep human insights, and practical common sense' employed in a law office. His work brought him in touch with a variety of people and many interesting experiences. The Manitoba Bar Association used Lex's daily diary entries, offered 'with philosophic sadness over the follies of man,' to illustrate the ways in which members of the bar could serve the public.[160] One example involved a will:

> Today I assisted my principal on another case involving a will which had been drawn by an elderly gentleman named Matt, on a printed form he had obtained from a stationer's store. One friend suggested getting a lawyer but Matt said 'this form will do.'
>
> The will was drawn to read 'to each of the children of my nephew ... at the date of issue, $500.00.
>
> After Matt's death, his executor puzzled over the words 'at date of issue.' Did they mean at the date of the will or the date of the birth of each child, or the date of probate of the will? The executor had to apply to the court to interpret the will.
>
> The costs of the court application had to be paid out of the estate and was many times the small fee a lawyer would have charged for a simple will like Matt's.[161]

The 'Diary of Harold Lex, law student' was so popular that it received an award from Canadian newspaper advertisers as the country's most unique and original institutional publicity campaign. Others applauding the efforts of Campbell's committee included the law societies of Alberta and Saskatchewan, the Ontario section of the Canadian Bar Association, and the advertising department of Toronto's *Globe & Mail*.[162]

Campbell also attracted the attention of his peers and members of the public in a number of other ways. In 1936, for example, he was appointed commissioner under the *Inquiries Act* to investigate charges of political partisanship levied against federal civil servants in Manitoba; and four years later he replaced C.S. Booth on a board of review established under *The Farmers' Creditors Arrangement Act*. Between 1944 and his appointment to the bench he was a bencher, chair of the Law Society's committee on unauthorized practice, president of the Manitoba Bar Association, the Blackstone Club, and the Lord Selkirk Association of Rupert's Land, and lectured in agency and partnership law at the Manitoba Law School. He was also a member of the Ancient Free & Accepted Masons, an 18th Degree Scottish rite-holder, an active member of the United Church of Canada, an enthusiastic golfer and shooter, and a Liberal. Campbell's backroom influence was sufficiently significant that few political appointments were made in Winnipeg without his input. Although he never sought elective office, he served on a number of executives, including that of the Manitoba Liberal Association.

Campbell went to the Court of King's Bench on 11 September 1947. His judicial career was uneventful and free of scandal, but things were perhaps a little more relaxed when Campbell tried an action in which a family member appeared as counsel. In 1948 his son represented the petitioner in an uncontested divorce. The client shared with both his judge and his lawyer the same family name. After hearing the evidence Justice Campbell turned to his son and asked whether, as a member of the Campbell clan, he had any explanation for what had brought about the divorce. 'Perhaps,' said his son, 'as the senior member you can explain, my Lord.'[163]

He regularly spoke to law students, as in 1951 when he emphasized a lawyer's two principal responsibilities.[164] The first was the duty to protect oneself from clients. Movies and biographies of famous lawyers, he suggested, created the impression that lawyers lacked ethics and would do anything to advance a client's cause. He warned his audience not to allow themselves to come under the sway of clients who ask them to do unconscionable things. But Campbell also acknowledged that lawyers owed a duty to clients. For instance, a good lawyer either made or saved their clients money. And he shared his thoughts about what judges look for in the lawyers who appeared before them. Judges, he said, respected lawyers who were discreet and easy-going, who argued objectively and impersonally, who assisted the court in reaching a just decision, who spoke no more than was necessary, who did not encumber the court with the force of their personality, and who were neither excessively verbose nor overly subtle. The difficulty faced by the profession, he suggested, was that many clients thought that the best lawyers were those who were outspoken, overbearing, and opinionated. In the end, however, the great lawyer was fair-minded and

Arnold Munroe Campbell (1892–1963). Puisne judge 1947–63. Campbell enjoyed a very successful career at the bar and became one of the province's most influential non-elected politicians. Between 1944, when this picture was taken, and his appointment to the bench three years later, Campbell was a Law Society bencher, president of the Manitoba Bar Association, and a lecturer at the Manitoba Law School. (Provincial Archives of Manitoba)

perceived to be so by others, and was sufficiently generous to never appear mean.

However well intentioned his comments, Campbell's opinion of a lawyer's lawyer was not shared by legal historian Roy St. George Stubbs. In a stinging attack Stubbs accused the justice of having lowered 'the coinage of an expressive phrase by his inference that the lawyer's lawyer lives in the clouds of contemplation and cannot come down to earth to do equal battle with his more practical brethren on the active battle fronts of the profession.' He suggested that Campbell was, like the 'uninitiated,' of the view that it was the whistle rather than the engine that pulled the train, and that he had only a surface knowledge of what he was talking about.[165]

Campbell was seventy-one and the most senior puisne judge on the Queen's Bench when he died on 13 February 1963 while undergoing a heart operation.[166] Justice Ralph Maybank was presiding over a jury trial when informed about the death. The two men had been close friends for fifty years, and Maybank was visibly upset as he described to the jury what had just happened:

> In the days not long before the operation he exhibited his usual bravery in the way he met affairs in life. As already intimated, Judge Campbell knew for a long time that this operation was coming and he knew that it was extremely serious. It was an operation in which it was expected he would be on the table for a couple of hours. He had a heart condition about which he knew and about which he often, but casually, spoke. It never disturbed or dismayed him. He talked to me quite blithely about what the doctors were going to do to him and what his chances were, and he laconically remarked that it was a fifty-fifty chance. He said, 'If I come off the table it will be right in two or three months and if I don't there won't be any need to worry about anything as far as I am concerned'; and he chuckled as he said it. He exhibited at those times I thought the bravery that he had always shown in life's problems and incidents.[167]

JOSEPH THOMAS BEAUBIEN

Beaubien was born at St Jean Baptiste, Manitoba, on 19 March 1886. Although his ancestors arrived in Canada in the first years of the sixteenth century, the first to come west was his father, who had been an advocate in Victoriaville when Wilfrid Laurier practised in the same

Quebec town. When Aimé Beaubien arrived in Manitoba in 1880, however, he put aside law to farm. In time he combined that occupation with his duties as municipal clerk for the district of Youville.

Joseph Beaubien had one sister and four brothers, one of whom was probably responsible for his appointment to the bench. Arthur Lucien was the politician in the family. Although born in Quebec seven years before Joseph, like his brother he was educated in Manitoba. His political career started at the municipal level in 1921 when he was elected reeve of the Rural Municipality of Montcalm. In December of the same year he was also elected the National-Progressive Member of Parliament for Provencher. Re-elected in 1925, 1926, 1930, and 1935, he was a member of the Liberal party when he went to the Senate in 1940.[168]

Joseph Beaubien attended school in St Jean before being admitted to St Boniface College, where he earned a Bachelor of Arts degree in 1910. After graduating he entered into an articling agreement with his brother Louis Philippe. His articles were assigned to Louis Alfred Delormé a year later, then transferred back to Louis Phillipe. He finished his clerkship under Fredrerick Joseph Gustin McArthur and was called to the bar on 9 June 1913.[169] Following his call Beaubien spent a year with McArthur and then practised on his own until 1930, when he and Leon H. Benard became partners. The firm survived for ten years before being dissolved. Beaubien then worked alone until joined by W.J.B. Grierson and A.M. Monnin in 1946. Grierson left law the following year, and Beaubien went to the bench in January 1948. Although regarded as a general practitioner rather than a barrister or specialist, Beaubien was in court often enough to have seventeen cases reported. Of that number only three involved trials. His overall success rate of slightly more than 70 per cent was the highest of any member of the judiciary.

Despite his older brother Arthur's high profile and success as a Liberal politician, Beaubien was a Conservative. Rather than politics, his main interests were religious, artistic, and cultural. He was a strong supporter of the Roman Catholic church, an enthusiastic patron of the arts, and the first director of the Winnipeg Symphony Orchestra. He was also president of La Pensée Françoise, the founder of Winnipeg's first French-language radio station, an active member of the French Canadian Education Association, a member of the executive of the Manitoba Bar Association, the chair of the Advisory Committee of St Boniface Sanitarium Board, and a member of the Rhodes Scholarship Appointment Committee for Manitoba. Clubs in which he held a membership included the Manitoba Club and the Southwood Country Club.

Beaubien's 1948 appointment was delayed almost two years because of political infighting. When word leaked out in August 1946 that he and E.K. Williams, both Conservatives, were about to be appointed to the bench by a Liberal government, Manitoba Liberals virtually exploded in fury. Member of Parliament Ralph Maybank wrote C. Rhodes Smith, the provincial minister of labour, to share with him the concern of Liberal Members of Parliament. 'I think we have to approach this from the viewpoint that we are trying to avoid the appointment of Tories. In order to do that, we must settle on any Liberals at all. I repeat: – any Liberals at all.'[170] Maybank was not alone in advocating that strategy. A month earlier he had received a letter from Arnold Campbell, who claimed to speak for the majority of the executive of the Manitoba Bar Association when he said, 'While it is agreed that good men must be put into Court, it is objectionable to appoint any Tory at any time.'[171] The same day that Maybank wrote to Smith Maybank's law partner reported on the progress that was being made to stop the Beaubien and Williams appointments:

> Rhodes [Smith], Arnold [Campbell], Cecil [Philp; all future judges] and I had lunch today, and after some plain talking they finally got down to something concrete. I told them there was absolutely no use being indefinite – and that they all had to agree of a slate which would be a final solution and present it as a unanimous choice. The alternative is either a concrete proposal or complete defeat ... The idea was to propose the very strongest alternative to the Williams-Beaubien set-up, and everyone get behind it - regardless of what each felt about the individuals proposed.[172]

Although Maybank, like his fellow Manitoba Liberals, had nothing personally against Beaubien, 'the man is a Tory and ... while this is too bad it is a fact which finally, irrevocably, definitely, disqualifies him.'[173] In fact, being a Tory did not disqualify him. A year and a half after starting the 'stop-Beaubien' movement, Maybank said that it was time to admit defeat:

> It has been made clear that the French cannot be held off anyway with regard to a judicial appointment ... The French boys ... say that politically they cannot get along unless one of their own is put on the bench ... Politically Beaubien may be objectionable to those who know politics but with the generality of French people in Manitoba he is not known as a Conservative. Most people simply think of him as the brother of the

> Senator and consequently conclude that he is probably Liberal also ... This means that Beaubien has to be the choice ... The upshot of it all is that considering the fact that Ilsley [federal minister of justice] will have to yield anyway and that there is a political disadvantage to our French friends if a French judge is not appointed, I felt I had to agree not to stand in the way.[174]

With his efforts to block Beaubien's appointment dead in the water, Maybank became a supporter. Less than a week after the appointment was announced, Maybank accepted the thanks of a French Canadian member of the Manitoba legislature who wrote to thank him for the active part he played 'in the recent nomination of our good friend Mr. T. Beaubien, K.C.'[175] Even Beaubien acknowledged Maybank's efforts, although his letter of thanks could be interpreted as sarcasm:

> I know definitely what you have done for me, and I certainly wish you to know that I do know. The reward for your kind and generous action will be forthcoming to you, in the fact that I shall do my best to fulfil my position with dignity and effectiveness, and that my compatriots of this Province and in fact all over Canada, will forever be grateful to you for the honor which you were greatly instrumental in conferring upon them, by consenting to the appointment of one of their own to such a high office.[176]

Maybank was blunt in his acknowledgment of Beaubien's letter. While conceding that the battle was over, even in defeat he could not resist firing a parting shot. '[For] a long time, as I know you are aware, I opposed your appointment ... I changed my position out of regard for your compatriots for whom, as you know, I have a profound affection.'[177] Beaubien, however, insisted on having the last word. In another letter that appears tinged with sarcasm, he said that Maybank's attitude was 'just what I knew it to be and I appreciate your frankness as exhibited in your said letter ... The decks are completely clear and I am now preparing to enter upon my new career.'[178]

Regardless of how much he may have wanted to go to the bench, Beaubien's efforts to bring about his own appointment were more subtle than those of his former partner. In 1949 Benard told Maybank that St Boniface County Court Judge Roy was rumoured to be about to retire. 'I think I should be seriously considered for this vacancy.' In case Maybank had any doubts, Benard pointed out: 'I can assure you that I am well fitted for this appointment.'[179]

When he went to the King's Bench on 30 January 1948 Beaubien became the fourth French Canadian judge named to province's highest trial court. He was elevated to the Court of Appeal on 1 October 1952 and was seventy-one when he died of a heart attack on 26 March 1957 while vacationing in Tucson, Arizona.[180]

JOHN JOSEPH KELLY

John Joseph Kelly was born on 20 October 1898 on a farm near Thornhill, a small community south of Winnipeg. He attended several rural schools before entering high school in Morden, but managed only a summer term at the University of Manitoba before his education was cut short by the First World War. Enlisting in 1915 just after his seventeenth birthday, he joined the Canadian Expeditionary Force as a private and was sent overseas the following spring with the Winnipeg Rifles. In France he was transferred to the army's Eighth Battalion, and fought there and in Belgium, participating in the battles of the Somme, Vimy Ridge, and Hill 70. During the Somme confrontation he was wounded so badly that the army's medical staff decided not to amputate his legs, the only operation that could save his life. Kelly recovered, however, and was wounded a second time (during the battle for Hill 70). He was invalided to England, and returned to Canada in 1918, still a private.

Kelly promptly entered the Manitoba Law School. After graduating he became a student of Edward Anderson for two months, before finishing his articles with David Campbell. Kelly received his call in 1922 and practised with Campbell until his partner died ten years later. He then spent four years alone before being joined by Arnold Campbell.[181] Kelly's clients included the International Railway Union and several other international labour organizations. Many of his individual clients were relatives, often widows, of union members.[182] His practice frequently took him to court, usually the Court of Appeal, and he was successful in two-thirds of seventeen cases reported. Although he did not have a high profile within the profession, Kelly was well known and respected because of his war record.

In August 1940 Kelly rejoined the Canadian army, this time as a lieutenant. Initially attached to Military District 10 headquarters, he was transferred in 1941 to the headquarters staff of the Fourth Canadian Armoured Division. The following June he was shipped overseas to serve as assistant judge advocate general at the Canadian military headquarters in London. He was discharged as a lieutenant colonel the year before the war ended.

In 1946 Kelly took part in one of the most sensational court martials ever held in Winnipeg. His client, Corporal John Hugh Harvey, had served in the medical division of the British Army, and while a prisoner of war he allegedly committed a variety of crimes. After the cessation of hostilities he was charged with thirty offences, including manslaughter, collaborating with an enemy, and ill treatment of fellow prisoners. All the offences were alleged to have taken place while Harvey was held in Japan's Oeyama prison camp. The most serious charge he faced was the murder of private John Unger Friesen of the Winnipeg Grenadiers.[183]

By the time he went to the bench, in 1949, Kelly had a high profile quite apart from law and the military. He was politically active and for a time served as secretary of the South Winnipeg Liberal Association. He was also president of the Blackstone Club, the Laurier Club, and the Crescentwood–River Heights branch of the Canadian Legion. He succeeded C. Rhodes Smith as president of the Manitoba and Northwest Ontario command of the Canadian Legion. In addition, he sat on the board of the Manitoba Canteen Fund and was a member of St Andrews Church, the Canukeena Club, the Mason's Ionic lodge, and the Ancient Free & Accepted Masons. He also served as vice-chair of the Manitoba Power Commission. Kelly's principal recreational interests were golf and socializing at the Carlton, Manitoba, and Winter clubs. His non-professional profile, together with the status associated with lecturing at the Manitoba Law School, likely contributed to his success in bencher elections between 1937 and 1949. The last two years he sat in convocation as secretary of the Law Society.

Kelly went to the bench on 10 August 1949, filling the vacancy created by the death of Justice Donovan. He was still a member of the Queen's Bench and only fifty-three years old when he died of a heart attack on 2 April 1952.[184] Kelly is remembered for his sincerity and disregard for ritual, and as an indefatigable worker.[185]

Conclusion

The Introduction suggested that three arguments run through this book's thirty-three biographies. The first holds that judicial appointments represent the culmination of an on-going process of socialization. As the biographies illustrate, the legal profession is a community within other communities. Its members are trained similarly, define their roles similarly, share similar values and interests, are governed by the same code of ethics, and speak a common professional language. Regardless of the social background of members, these factors work to ensure the homogeneity of the legal profession.[1]

While they were not all of a piece, the first thirty-three judges of Manitoba's Queen's Bench shared remarkably similar beliefs, in part because they were products of multiple interactions among members of a group who shared the same life experiences. That is not to say, however, that every aspect of this process of socialization had the same effect on each member of the group, or that all influences to which these judges were exposed produced lasting results. Nevertheless, one of the arguments implicit in this history is that encounters in the practice of law socialize lawyers similarly because they are vehicles by which values are transmitted. As Griffith pointed out in his examination of the English bench, years in practice invariably remove aberrations in outlook.[2]

The second argument advanced is that being connected to a person of influence is a key criterion in the judicial appointment process. This history suggests that for many of those appointed to the Queen's Bench being connected to a member of a social, political, or business elite was as important as winning a seat in a legislature. Member of Parliament Ralph Maybank bitterly complained to the prime minister of one such group of Manitoba insiders.

> For some little time there has been a group in Winnipeg who have pretty well settled all appointments that were to be made; all appointments, at any rate, of a major sort. Coyne has been a member of this group. It is jocularly referred to as the Sanhedrin. This group of academicians has not given advice and direction, speaking generally, which has resulted in success. I should just like to ask you if it isn't about time that you sought advice with respect to Manitoba from people who look to and can speak for the future, rather than from those who have, perhaps, a splendid past?[3]

Members of groups like the 'Sanhedrin' were not the only insiders whose opinions influenced judicial appointments. A letter from Member of Parliament G.W. Allan to Isaac Pitblado, a titan of the Manitoba bar, accurately reflected the influence of a handful of elite lawyers. 'My single objective is to have appointments made out of names submitted by you!'[4] And referring to one of Winnipeg's more senior solicitors, a recently arrived lawyer wrote that one 'friend like Mr. Hoskin is worth about forty thousand relations.'[5]

The advantage of being associated with someone politically connected would appear obvious, since a well-placed benefactor can significantly advance the career of a lawyer. A federal Member of Parliament involved in the judicial appointment process was referring to two of Winnipeg's most senior lawyers when he noted, '[M]y confidence in such lawyers as Mr. Pitblado or his partner Mr. Hoskin, was such that if one of them told me he knew a lawyer whose name was being considered [for a judicial appointment] and felt that he had the required qualifications, I would not feel it necessary to seek information on that score from any other quarter.'[6]

These biographies suggest that while two-thirds of Manitoba's first judges had an association with someone politically connected, as the bar aged that number declined, and the number of judges connected through someone with whom they articled increased. More important than articling relationships, though, were those made through a law partner. The relationship between law partners was more mature, longer lasting, and more equal than the relationship between an articling clerk and his senior. About a third of Manitoba's first Queen's Bench judges practised with one or more politically connected partners. The remainder established connections outside law offices. For instance, McKeagney, Dubuc, and Prendergast owed both their electoral successes and judicial appointments to the influence of the Catholic church. Some influential patrons were connected to neither a law office nor a church. Edmund Burke Wood's success in law was as much linked with the work he did for railroad interests as was his success in politics. Other judges had close friendships with someone prominent. In the case of Thomas Wardlaw Taylor it was a provincial premier, and for William Donovan and Esten Kenneth Williams it was a prime minister.

These biographies provide insights into how relationships were established with individuals who could advance a lawyer's career. Involvement in both professional and non-professional organizations, for instance, benefited lawyers in two ways. It was an effective method for becoming known and demonstrating professional skill, and it provided access to community leaders who had the potential to facilitate the development of additional contacts.[7]

Cultivating a professional and non-professional profile simultaneously is particularly important to lawyers, since they derive their prestige from a combination of professional skills, from participation in public activities, and through an association with prestigious persons and institutions. It is not uncommon for a lawyer to be highly regarded by colleagues in his professional capacity, yet remain virtually unknown to the general public. Conversely, lawyers who develop a profile in business, community affairs, or politics may be well known to the public, yet be without standing within the profession.[8]

This history argues that whether consciously or unconsciously, non-litigating members of the Manitoba bar seemed to recognize their lack of professional stature and sought to build a reputation through non-professional activities. This was done through involvement in politics, civic or educational organizations, the military, or the arts. Most lawyers were active in several organizations at the same time.

The data also indicate that the number of activities in which judges were involved before their appointments was evenly divided between the professional and non-professional. The particular avenue to prominence a judge took depended on a number of factors, the most important of which were family background and connection to someone of influence. Lawyers denied appointments, commission memberships, or election to professional bodies, and lacking a large reputation, used the influence of others to earn a seat on the bench. Those without an appropriate background or affiliation with a patron were required to prove their worth at the bar, thereby opening doors that would otherwise have remained closed. Although practitioners typically divided their time between professional and non-professional activities, an analysis of the activities that attracted to them the most attention suggests that connections were as vital in determining who went to the bench as merit.

It is possible to trace the evolution of the Manitoba bar through an examination of how judicial appointees brought themselves to the attention of others. For the first men appointed to the Queen's Bench prominence was more likely to come from non-professional than professional activities, and their appointments were rewards for service other than in law. That was not surprising. While the rudimentary legal institutions of a new province were unlikely to attract the leaders of the eastern bar, they offered members of the profession's second echelon what may have been their best, perhaps only, chance to become a judge.

This changed after 1884, when, it becomes evident, most of those going to the bench had an above-average professional reputation. Again, this comes as no surprise. As the domination of the Manitoba bar by eastern trained lawyers was coming to an end, but before an indigenous elite had taken their place, an opportunity for lawyers lacking connections or social status presented itself. Men like Perdue, Mathers, and Metcalfe were all sons of farmers, and Bain, Cameron, Robson, and Curran the children or grandchildren of immigrants. Most used their professional reputation to compensate for a lack of connections, and were thereby able to join an elite from which they would otherwise have been excluded.

By the 1930s, however, an indigenous group had taken control of the profession, and lawyers with connections but no professional standing once again started going to the bench in large numbers. While these findings do not suggest that judges who gained prominence through non-professional activities were less competent than those with a higher legal profile, for most of Manitoba's first seventy-eight years a reputation earned outside of law was as highly regarded by those making judicial appointments as professional stature.

The last of the three arguments referred to in the Introduction was that the Manitoba bar underwent a transformation between 1885 and 1922, and that its evolution reflected changes in the criteria for judicial appointments. An example was age. Walker and Hulbary suggest that in the United States the ideal appointment age is the mid- to late fifties, a time when stable political values have become evident, a public record established, and the likelihood of a relatively lengthy tenure remains. Less desirable are younger practitioners, because their values and attitudes have not yet solidified.[9] This history suggests that the Manitoba legal profession went through a three-stage maturing process before the age of judicial appointees stabilized at the ideal described by Walker and Hulbary. As political institutions in Manitoba matured and the profession aged, those selected for the bench were increasingly lawyers who had paid their dues, professionally and politically. In the 1870s the province's judges had not been members of the nascent provincial bar before their elevation, and the political IOUs they acquired had been earned elsewhere. From that point on, however, it was debts owed locals rather than outsiders that became the criterion for appointment.

Because judicial appointments have traditionally been rewards for services rendered, in established bars they come relatively late in a lawyer's career, since it is only then that candidates have accumulated sufficient years of service to merit a reward. For a time in Manitoba that was not the case. Before 1885 the provincial bar was not sufficiently mature for there to be a significant number of elder statesmen to whom the party in power was indebted. As a consequence, judicial appointments went to the relatively young, and half of those going to the bench did so in their late thirties or early forties. By the end of the nineteenth century the influence of the new leaders of the Manitoba bar had grown, but they were neither as professionally mature nor as experienced as the men they replaced. Between 1885 and 1922, however, the average age of those going to the bench had increased to forty-nine, suggesting that the bar was beginning to age. By 1922 the maturation process was complete, and those appointed thereafter were in their fifties or sixties, with several decades of proven service behind them.

The transformation of the Manitoba bar can also be seen in the changing significance of professional merit. Before 1884, for example, one half of those appointed had a solid if not outstanding reputation. That number increased slightly between 1885 and 1929, but fell to 20 per cent for the last appointed. These findings, however, do not suggest that the competence of judges actually declined. In fact, the opposite was likely true. Although the Canadian legal profession never divided into barristers and solicitors as in England, until the first decade of the twentieth century Canadian judges were usually chosen from among those active as barristers. As the profession grew more specialized an increasing number of skilled and ambitious lawyers left the courtroom for the boardroom. So many, in fact, that solicitors eventually formed the pool from which a majority of judicial candidates were selected. Mr Justice Trueman of the Manitoba Court of Appeal discussed this change in a 1930 address to the Manitoba Bar Association:

> Two or three decades ago the best legal minds devoted themselves to litigation ... In the past few years there has been a considerable falling off of important litigation, and men who, if former conditions had continued, would have sought eminence and a career in Court work have devoted themselves to a marked extent to solicitor's work. This change has been facilitated by the advent of corporation work. When big business made the discovery that it could secure unlimited capital through the sale of stocks, and was no longer dependent on capital supplied by creditors or banks or bond issues, organization and expansion on an unparalleled scale brought to lawyers a source of business that has given the profession earning power and an outlook unknown in the days when litigation was its chief means of support ... One result of this change is that the men who would be leaders in Court work are seldom in Court.[10]

A careful reading of the biographies of the first thirty-three judges appointed to Manitoba's Court of Queen's Bench suggests a number of other conclusions about the province's highest trial court. Suggestions that lawyers are actually politicians at heart, that a law office is merely a staging platform for a political career, and that the bench is a retirement benefit for faithful hacks no longer able to endure the demands of the political arena are not, however, accurate.[11]

One shortcoming of studies that lead to these kinds of conclusions is their focus on elective politics. The assumption implicit in them is that participation in the electoral process is the most accurate way of measuring political commitment.[12] These biographies argue that assessment is wrong, and that political affiliation does not come close to exhausting the kinds of politically useful connections typically involved in judicial appointments.[13] A holistic analysis of political involvement suggests that many judges previously regarded as nonpolitical were in fact behind-the-scenes supporters of the government party, or closely connected to someone who was.

Notwithstanding this fact, most who sat on the Queen's Bench were sincere, practical men who became involved with politics for the same reason that they participated in other nonprofessional bodies. There is no evidence that, apart from a small minority, their involvement was entirely self-motivated. These biographies do suggest, however, that because many judges spent so much time engaged in activities not connected to law, there was reason to question how much law they practised and, by extension, how much law they knew at the time of their appointment. Most justices of the Supreme Court of the United States, for example, practised only minimally.[14] Canadian historians Snell and Vaughan reached much the same conclusion about the justices of Canada's Supreme Court. Referring to twelve appointments to the Supreme Court of Canada made by the Laurier government between 1901 and 1911, they found that the appointees had all spent little time practising and displayed no special commitment to law.[15]

Undermining these conclusions is the fact that there is simply no way to determine the extent to which time practising is related to legal ability. This history, a more detailed biographical study of the judiciary than those of Hulbary and Walker or Snell and Vaughan, suggests that lawyers practising full-time were no more likely to be regarded as good judges than those who spent their career pursuing other endeavours. It also suggests that, although Manitoba's first judges were more politicians than lawyers, the law they practised was impressive. With the exception of McKeagney, Betournay, and Curran, the province's Queen's Bench judges were regarded as outstanding lawyers and as respected members of the profession. While many did indeed devote as much of their time to non-legal interests as they did to the practice of law, there is no evidence that they were not competent lawyers. Even the concerns expressed about the province's most controversial appointment centred on Adamson's age and inexperience rather than his ability.

One thing that makes it difficult to assess the extent to which someone's experience in practice qualifies him for the bench is the fact that what lawyers do behind the closed doors of their offices is largely unknown. Some spend days sitting, 'feet elevated Yankee fashion,' waiting for clients to appear.[16] Others spend their time in courtrooms, while still others devote their days to preparing wills, probating estates, drawing real estate documents, and, when required, handling civil and criminal trials.

The data relating to the relative courtroom success of the men who went to the Queen's Bench suggest that even relatively inexperienced lawyers were as successful as experienced counsel; and the argument that it is possible to determine a lawyer's ability by examining his or her success in reported cases may be untenable. Lawyers do not always litigate to win. Cases often go to trial to determine not whether a plaintiff should succeed but the extent to which a defendant should lose. Applying the narrow criterion of wins and losses makes it appear that some counsel are winners, and others losers, when the opposite may be true.

The debate over how best to determine legal ability was waged in Manitoba as early as 1884, when the *Manitoba Law Journal* discussed it in the context of the appointment of Queen's Counsels:

> But in so doubtful a matter as legal ability, who can decide? What is the criterion? Is it success? That comes sometimes without learning. Is it learning? That may exist without success. Is it both learning and success? Then what degree of each? Twenty briefs at an assize, with fifteen wins to five losses? There is no gauge, and from the leaders to the duffers the graduation is so insensible that there must always be great difference of opinion as to the proper order of merit.[17]

What these biographies make evident is that by the end of the nineteenth century lawyers like Bain and Richards were increasingly content to build a reputation in a boardroom rather than a courtroom. This tendency was referred to in an anecdote published in 1889 by the *Canada Law Journal*. Entering the office of a recent Queen's Counsel appointee, a junior begged his more experienced associate to take over conduct of a case set for trial in County Court. Asked if the case was particularly difficult, the junior responded that it was not. Asked if he was likely to win, the Q.C. was assured that he was. Puzzled, he asked why if these things were true the junior did not take the trial himself. 'Well, the fact is, I don't care to ruin my chances of a silk gown by appearing in court.'[18]

How the men who went to the Queen's Bench before 1950 managed their careers had a substantial impact on their appointments. While not everything they did was self-serving, there is evidence that much was. When Court of Appeal Justice Dennistoun described his career to his son in a letter written in 1928, he could have been speaking for many of his contemporaries. Peel Dennistoun practised law in Manitoba for six years before moving to California. His father was concerned by the move, and wrote offering advice. After noting that words of wisdom offered by the old to the young are 'often, nay usually, considered antiquated and unpractical,' Justice Dennistoun explained how he had managed his own career. He first went into politics and the military, won election to town council, joined the Masons, and took up curling and shooting, all before leaving Ontario for Manitoba. In Winnipeg he joined all the important social and golf clubs, including the Manitoba, Carleton, Adenae, Conservative, and St Charles Country Clubs. Dennistoun concluded by noting that 'these things were to help in working into the knowledge and acquaintance of the community so that I might have more & more clients.'[19]

The biographies that make up this history suggest that two-thirds of the lawyers appointed to the Court of Queen's Bench before 1950 were born and raised outside the province (it was not until 1922 that a Manitoba-born lawyer became a member of the judiciary). The experiences of the first twenty-one men who went to the bench were sufficiently different from those of the last twelve, however, that it is impossible to make a single composite sketch of the group.

Early Manitoba judges were born and raised in Ontario, their fathers were upper-middle-class professionals, they married at twenty-eight, had more than four children, and were Anglicans. Later appointed judges were born elsewhere but educated in Manitoba, their fathers as likely to be middle-class professionals as working-class farmers, they married at twenty-six, had fewer than four children, and were as often members of the United as the Anglican church.

Neither group of judges were involved in the affairs of a cultural organization, but members of the first appointed were active in a religious organization, had a university degree, were better connected politically than socially, and as likely to die in office as to retire. Later appointed judges were as involved in educational associations as their predecessors, were more active in sports than the affairs of a church, had a university degree, were better connected socially than politically, were members of a fraternal organization or private club, were ten years older than earlier appointed judges when promoted, and were likely to die in office after sitting for nine years.

Regardless of where they were born, raised, and educated and where they practised before their appointments to the bench, it was fortunate for Manitoba's first judges that the repercussions from 'bad' decisions was different than during the time of King Alfred, who is said to have hanged in one year forty-four judges who had made an error in applying the law:

He hanged Cole because he judged Ive to death when he was a madman.

He hanged Athulf because he caused Copping to be hanged before the age of one-and-twenty.

He hanged Markes because he judged During to death by twelve men who were not sworn.

He hanged Athelstan because he judged Herbert to death for an offence not mortal.[20]

Appendix 1
Judicial Appointments, by Date, Manitoba Court of Queen's Bench, 1870–1950

Judge	Date appointed	Date left Queen's Bench	Tenure in years
Morris Alexander	21 July 1872	1 December 1872	1
James McKeagney	7 October 1872	14 September 1879	7
Louis Betourney	31 October 1872	30 October 1879	7
E.B. Wood	11 March 1874	7 October 1882	8
Joseph Dubuc	13 November 1879	15 November 1909	30
J.A. Miller	20 October 1880	31 December 1882	2
Lewis Wallbridge	12 December 1882	20 October 1887	5
T.W. Taylor	5 January 1883	31 March 1899	4
Robert Smith	27 June 1884	19 January 1885	½
Albert C. Killam	3 February 1885	23 July 1903	8
John Farquhar Bain	15 November 1887	12 May 1905	18
A.E. Richards	1 May 1899	23 July 1906	7
William E. Perdue	25 August 1903	30 December 1929	26
Thomas G. Mathers	24 August 1905	15 August 1927	22
Daniel Alexander Macdonald	23 July 1906	28 October 1937	31
John D. Cameron	21 January 1908	26 March 1923	15
Thomas L. Metcalfe	22 May 1909	2 April 1922	13
J.E.P. Prendergast	7 February 1910	18 March 1944	34
Hugh A. Robson	23 June 1910	May 1912	2
Alexander C. Galt	24 October 1912	18 March 1933	21
John P. Curran	24 October 1912	9 January 1928	16
Aalexander K. Dysart	3 October 1921	24 July 1952	31
J.E. Adamson	1 May 1922	1 March 1961	39
J.F. Kilgour	8 September 1927	27 November 1931	4
William J. Donovan	30 March 1928	26 May 1949	21
P.J. Montague	11 March 1932	1 September 1959	27
F.G. Taylor	28 March 1933	2 January 1940	7
E.A. McPherson	23 November 1937	18 November 1954	17
William J. Major	14 March 1941	31 July 1951	10
Hugh A. Robson	18 March 1944	9 July 1945	1
E.K. Williams	10 December 1946	1 January 1962	16
A.M. Campbell	11 September 1947	13 February 1963	16
J.T. Beaubien	30 January 1948	26 March 1957	9
J.J. Kelly	10 August 1949	2 April 1952	3

Appendix 2
Judicial Appointments, Alphabetical, Manitoba Court of Queen's Bench, 1870–1950

Name	Born	Appointed	Retired	Died
Adamson, John Evans	09-09-1884	01-05-1922	01-03-1961	22-12-1961
Bain, John Farquhar	unknown	15-11-1887	12-05-1905	12-05-1905
Beaubien, Joseph Thomas	19-03-1886	30-01-1948	26-03-1957	26-03-1957
Betournay, Lewis	13-11-1825	31-10-1872	30-10-1879	30-10-1879
Cameron, John Donald	18-08-1858	21-01-1908	26-03-1923	26-02-1923
Campbell, Arnold Munroe	15-07-1892	11-09-1947	13-02-1963	13-02-1963
Curran, John Philpot	13-12-1958	24-10-1912	09-01-1928	09-01-1928
Donovan, William James	30-09-1875	30-03-1928	26-05-1949	26-05-1949
Dubuc, Joseph	26-12-1840	13-11-1879	15-11-1909	07-01-1914
Dysart, Andrew Knox	15-11-1875	03-10-1921	24-07-1952	24-07-1952
Galt, Alexander Casmir	15-03-1853	24-10-1912	18-03-1933	28-07-1936
Killam, Albert Clements	18-09-1849	03-02-1885	23-07-1903	01-03-1908
Kelly, John Joseph	28-10-1898	10-08-1949	02-04-1952	02-04-1952
Kilgour, James Frederick	22-01-1874	08-09-1927	27-11-1931	27-11-1931
Macdonald, Daniel Alexander	17-08-1878	23-07-1906	28-10-1937	28-10-1937
Major, William James	10-11-1881	14-03-1941	31-07-1951	13-08-1953
Mathers, Thomas Graham	16-04-1859	24-08-1905	16-08-1927	16-08-1927
McKeagney, James Charles	1815	07-10-1872	14-09-1879	14-09-1879
McPherson, Ewen Alexander	27-01-1878	23-11-1937	18-11-1954	18-11-1954
Metcalfe, Thomas Llewellyn	21-02-1870	22-05-1909	02-04-1922	02-04-1922

Appendix 2 (*concluded*)

Name	Born	Appointed	Retired	Died
Miller, James Andrews	29-07-1839	20-10-1880	31-12-1882	01-11-1886
Montague, Percival John	10-11-1882	11-03-1932	01-09-1959	11-06-1966
Morris, Alexander	17-03-1826	21-07-1872	01-12-1872	28-10-1889
Perdue, William Edgerton	20-06-1850	25-08-1903	30-12-1929	16-01-1933
Prendergast, James Emile Pierre	22-03-1858	03-07-1910	18-03-1944	18-04-1945
Richards, Albert Elswood	18-07-1848	01-05-1899	23-07-1906	27-05-1917
Robson, Hugh Amos	09-09-1871	23-06-1910	May 1912	09-07-1945
second appointment		18-03-1944	09-07-1945	
Smith, Robert	19-06-1839	27-06-1884	19-01-1885	19-01-1885
Taylor, Fawcett Gowler	29-04-1878	28-03-1933	02-01-1940	02-01-1940
Taylor, Thomas Wardlaw	25-03-1833	05-01-1883	22-10-1887	02-03-1917
Wallbridge, Lewis	27-11-1816	12-12-1882	20-10-1887	20-10-1887
Williams, Esten Kenneth	18-08-1889	10-12-1946	01-01-1962	April 1970
Wood, Edmund Burke	13-03-1820	11-03-1874	07-10-1882	07-10-1882

Appendix 3
Reasons for Departure, Justices of the Manitoba Court of Queen's Bench, 1870–1950

	Departed	Reason
Morris	01-12-1872	Lieut-Gov. Man.
McKeagney	14-09-1879	Died
Betournay	30-10-1879	Died
Wood	07-10-1882	Died
Dubuc	15-11-1909	Retired
Miller	31-12-1882	Retired
Wallbridge	20-10-1887	Died
Taylor, T.W.	31-03-1899	Retired
Smith	19-01-1885	Died
Killam	08-08-1903	Supreme Court
Bain	12-05-1905	Died
Richards	23-07-1906	Court of Appeal
Perdue	23-07-1906	Court of Appeal
Mathers	15-08-1927	Died
Macdonald	28-10-1937	Retired
Cameron	27-04-1909	Court of Appeal
Metcalfe	03-10-1921	Court of Appeal
Prendergast	01-05-1922	Court of Appeal
Robson	May 1912	Retired
Galt	18-03-1933	Retired
Curran	09-01-1928	Died
Dysart	11-09-1947	Court of Appeal
Adamson	30-01-1948	Court of Appeal
Kilgour	27-11-1931	Died
Donovan	26-05-1949	Died
Montague	01-03-1951	Court of Appeal
Taylor, F.G.	02-01-1940	Died
McPherson	18-03-1944	Court of Appeal
Major	31-07-1951	Retired
Robson	09-07-1945	Died
Williams	01-01-1962	Retired
Campbell	13-02-1963	Died
Beaubien	27-08-1952	Court of Appeal
Kelly	02-04-1952	Died

Appendix 4
Date Appointed, Manitoba Court of Appeal, 1906–1950

Judge	Date appointed	Date left Queen's bench	Tenure in years
Howell, Hector M.	23 July 1906	7 April 1918	12
Richards, A.E.	23 July 1906	27 May 1917	11
Perdue, William E.	23 July 1906	25 May 1918	12
Phippen, F.H.	23 July 1906	15 April 1909	3
Cameron, John D.	27 April 1909	26 March 1923	14
Haggart, A.	3 April 1912	1 November 1920	8
Fullerton, C.P.	20 July 1917	13 August 1931	14
Dennistoun, R.M.	2 July 1918	30 October 1946	28
Metcalfe, Thomas L.	3 October 1921	2 April 1922	1
Prendergast, J.E.P.	1 May 1922	30 December 1929	7
Trueman, W.H.	14 April 1923	1 January 1947	23
Robson, Hugh Amos	31 December 1929	18 March 1944	14
Richards, S.E	11 March 1932	17 October 1950	18
Bergman, H.A.	18 March 1944	20 January 1948	4
Coyne, J.B.	10 December 1946	31 August 1959	12
Dysart, Alexander K.	11 September 1947	24 July 1952	5
Adamson, John E.	30 January 1948	13 January 1955	6
Beaubien, Joseph T.	27 August 1952	26 March 1957	5

Appendix 5
Chief Justices of Manitoba, 1870–1950

Judge	Date appointed	Date left Queen's bench	Tenure in years
A. Court of Queen's Bench			
Alexander Morris	21 July 1872	1 December 1972	0.5
E.B. Wood	11 March 1874	7 October 1882	8
Lewis Wallbridge	12 December 1882	20 October 1887	5
Thomas W. Taylor	22 October 1887	31 March 1899	12
A.C. Killam	15 April 1899	8 August 1903	4
Joseph Dubuc	8 August 1903	15 November 1909	6
T.G. Mathers	7 February 1910	15 August 1927	17
D.A. Macdonald	8 September 1927	28 October 1937	10
E.A. McPherson	23 November 1937	18 March 1944	7
Hugh Amos Robson	18 March 1944	9 July 1945	1
E.K. Williams	10 December 1946	1 January1962	16
B. Court of Appeal			
H.M.Howell	23 July 1906	7 April 1918	12
W.E. Perdue	25 May 1918	30 December 1929	11
J.E.P. Prendergast	30 December 1929	18 March 1944	15
E.A. McPherson	18 March 1944	18 November 1954	10
J.E. Adamson	13 January 1955	1 March 1961	6

Notes

Introduction

1 Richard A. Willie, '"A Proper Ideal During Action": Fraternity, Leadership and Lifestyle in Winnipeg Lawyers' Professional Culture, 1878–1900' (1992) 27 J. Can. Studies 58 at 59 & 60.
2 *Ibid.* at 61.
3 (1892) 3 Western Law Times 10.
4 *Ibid.*
5 *Supra* note 1 at 63.
6 R.F.V. Heuston, *Lives of the Lord Chancellors 1885–1940* (Oxford: Alden Press, 1964) and *Lives of the Lord Chancellors 1940–1970* (Oxford: Clarendon Press, 1987).
7 Robert Stevens, *Law and Politics: The House of Lords as a Judicial Body, 1800–1976* (Chapel Hill: University of North Carolina Press, 1978).
8 Daniel Duman, *The Judicial Bench in England 1727–1875, The Reshaping of a Professional Elite* (London: Royal Historical Society, 1982).
9 David B. Read, *The Lives of the Judges of Upper Canada and Ontario, From 1791 to the present time* (Toronto: Rowsell & Hutchison, 1888).
10 Joseph Wilson Lawrence, *The Judges of New Brunswick and Their Times* (Fredericton: Acadiensis Press, 1983).
11 *Ibid.* at ix.
12 A.W. Patrick Buchanan, Q.C., *The Bench and Bar of Lower Canada Down to 1850* (Montreal: Burton's, 1925).

13 William John Klein, *Judicial Recruitment in Manitoba, Ontario, and Quebec 1905–1970* (Ph.D. thesis, Department of Sociology, University of Toronto, 1975) [unpublished].
14 Robert L. Fraser, ed., *Provincial Justice: Upper Canadian Legal Portraits from the Dictionary of Canadian Biography* (Toronto: Osgoode Society, 1992).
15 Hon. David R. Verchere, *A Progression of Judges: A History of the Supreme Court of British Columbia* (Vancouver: UBC Press, 1988).
16 Ian Bushnell, *The Captive Court: A Study of the Supreme Court of Canada* (Montreal: McGill-Queen's University Press, 1992).
17 Ian Bushnell, *The Federal Court of Canada, A History, 1875–1982* (Toronto: Osgoode Society, 1997).
18 James G. Snell & Frederick Vaughan, *The Supreme Court of Canada, History of the Institution* (Toronto: Osgoode Society, 1985).
19 Paul Weiler, *In the Last Resort: A Critical Study of The Supreme Court of Canada* (Toronto: Carswell, 1974).
20 George Adams & Paul J. Cavalluzzo, 'The Supreme Court of Canada, A Biographical Study' (1969) 7 Osgoode Hall L.J. 61.
21 Clara Greco, 'The Superior Court Judiciary of Nova Scotia, 1754–1900: A Collective Biography' in Philip Girard & Jim Phillips, eds., *Essays in the History of Canadian Law*, vol. 3, *Nova Scotia* (Toronto: Osgoode Society, 1990) at 42.
22 *Supra* note 20 at 62.
23 Louis A. Knafla & Richard Klumpenhouwer, *Lords of the Western Bench: A Biographical History of the Supreme and District Courts of Alberta, 1876–1990* (Edmonton: Legal Archives Society of Alberta, 1997).
24 R. Blake Brown & Susan S. Jones, 'A Collective Biography of the Supreme Court Judiciary of Nova Scotia, 1900–2000' in Philip Girard, Jim Phillips, & Barry Cahill, eds., *The Supreme Court of Nova Scotia, 1754–2004: From Imperial Bastion to Provincial Oracle* (Toronto: Osgoode Society, 2004) 204.
25 *Ibid.* at 224.
26 *Supra* note 23 at 1.
27 John Palmerston Robertson, *A Political Manual of the Province of Manitoba and the North-west Territories* (Winnipeg: Call Printing, 1887).
28 Henry J. Morgan, *The Canadian Legal Directory: A Guide to the Bench and Bar of the Dominion of Canada* (Toronto: Carswell, 1878).
29 Rev. Thomas Wardlaw Taylor, Jr, *A Sketch of the Life of Sir Thomas Wardlaw Taylor* [unpublished], Thomas Wardlaw Taylor AVF file, PAM; Margaret Charteris-Thomson, *The Colonial Ancestry of the Honourable Sir Thomas Wardlaw Taylor Kt.B. Chief Justice of the Province of Manitoba – 1887–1899* (London: Dumfries, 1937); Edouard Le P. Lecompte, *Sir Joseph Dubuc*

(1840–1914), Un Grand Chrétien (Montreal: Imprimerie du Messager, 1923); Sister M.M. McAlduff, *Joseph Dubuc, Role and Views of a French Canadian in Manitoba 1870–1914* (M.A. thesis, University of Ottawa, 1967) [unpublished]; Lewis St. George Stubbs, *A Majority of One: The Life and Times of Lewis St. George Stubbs* (Winnipeg: Queenston House, 1983); Richard Armstrong, 'The Hon. Edmund Burk Wood, Late Chief Justice of Manitoba' (1895) 1 *The Barrister* 114; Roy St. George Stubbs, 'Hon. Edmund Burke Wood' (1958) 13 Hist. Sc. Soc. Man. 27; Roy St. George Stubbs, 'Chief Justice Jacques Emile Pierre Prendergast' in *Lawyers and Laymen of Western Canada* (Toronto: Ryerson Press, 1939) 100, 'Andrew Knox Dysart' in *Prairie Portraits* (Toronto: McClelland & Stewart, 1954) 119, 'Chief Justice Wallbridge' (1937) 10 Man. Bar N. 481, and 'The Chief Justice of Manitoba' [John Adamson] (1960) 32:2 & 3 Man. Bar N. 29; L.A. Prud'Homme, 'Sir Joseph Dubuc' (1914) Revue Canadienne 386 & 506; J. Ragnar Johnson, 'Honourable W.E. Perdue, an Appreciation of an Eminent Jurist' (1933) 11 Can. Bar Rev. 199; A.J. Andrews, 'Jurist and Gentleman' (1945) 17 Man. Bar N. 31; Hon. John T. Haig, 'Mr. Justice Fawcett Gowler Taylor, D.S.O., K.C.' (1940) 12 Man. Bar N. 44; Gerald O. Jewers, 'Chief Justice E.K. Williams' (1961) 33 Man. Bar N. 145; Dale Gibson, 'Unobtrusive Justice' (1974) 12 Osgoode Hall L.J. 339 and 'Manifest Destiny: A Biographical Sketch of Chief Justice Brian Dickson' (1991) 20 Man. L.J. 268.

30 Dale & Lee Gibson, *Substantial Justice: Law and Lawyers in Manitoba 1670–1970* (Winnipeg: Peguis, 1972).

31 Richard A. Willie, *'These Legal Gentlemen': Lawyers in Manitoba: 1839–1900* (Winnipeg: Legal Research Institute of the University of Manitoba, 1994).

32 W. Wesley Pue, '"Trajectories of Professionalism": Legal Professionalism after Abel' (1990) 19 Man. L.J. 384; 'Becoming "Ethical": Lawyers' Professional Ethics in Early Twentieth Century Canada' (1991) 20 Man. L.J. 227; *Lawyers and the Constitution of Political Society: Containing Radicalism and Maintaining Order in Prairie Canada, 1900–1930* (Winnipeg: Canadian Legal History Project Working Paper, 1993); 'In Pursuit of Better Myth: Lawyers' Histories and Histories of Lawyers' (1995) 33 Alta. L. Rev. 730; 'Common Law Education in Canada's Age of Light, Soap and Water' (1996) 23 Man. L.J. 654; 'Foxes, Henhouses, Unfathomable Mysteries, and the Sufferance of the People: A Review of Regulating Professions and Occupations' (1996–7) 24 Man. L.J. 283; '"The Disquisitions of Learned Judges": Making Manitoba Lawyers, 1885–1931' in G. Blaine Baker & Jim Phillips, eds., *Essays in the History of Canadian Law*, vol. 8, *In Honour of R.C.B. Risk* (Toronto: Osgoode Society, 1999) 512; and 'British Masculinities, Canadian Lawyers: Canadian Legal Education, 1900–1930' in Rob McQueen & W.

Wesley Pue, eds., *Misplaced Traditions, British Lawyers, Colonial Peoples* (Leichhardt, NSW: Federation Press, 1999) 80.

33 'Disquisitions' at 535. The practitioners who migrated west following Manitoba's entry into Confederation were from the beginning regarded as members of the province's middle class. But although their claims to status were grounded on the occupational authority of the legal profession transmitted to Canada by lawyers trained in England, by the end of the nineteenth century Manitoba lawyers lived in an increasingly industrial world, and traditional values were gradually giving way to a culture of professionalism based on education, professional associations, and informal codes of ethics. Andrew Holman argues that the emergence of this new capitalist order gave to legal work a new social utility and pushed lawyers to professionalize. See Andrew C. Holman, *A Sense of Their Duty: Middle-Class Formation in Victorian Ontario Towns* (Montreal: McGill-Queen's University Press, 2000) c. 2.

34 'Disquisitions' at 541.

35 Edmund Henry Oliver, *The Canadian North-West, Its Early Development and Legislative Records*: *Minutes of the Councils of the Red River Colony and the Northern Department of Rupert's Land*, vol. 1 (Ottawa: Government Printing Bureau, 1914) at 135; also (1690) 2 W. & M., c. 23.

36 43 George II, c. 138.

37 *Supra* note 30 at 5.

38 *Ibid.* at 3.

39 1 & 2 George IV, c. 66: *An Act for regulating the Fur Trade, and establishing a Criminal and Civil Jurisdiction within certain parts of North America.*

40 *Supra* note 30 at 125.

41 *Ibid.* at 41.

42 *Ibid.* at 48.

43 31–32 Victoria, c. 105.

44 S.C. 1869, c. 31.

45 *Ibid.* at ss. 27 and 28.

46 *Ibid.* at s. 91.

47 S.M. 1875, c. 9, s. 4. This was, however, consistent with the British practice at the time.

48 S.C. 1869, c. 32.

49 S.M. 1872, c. 3, s. 37.

50 S.M. 1876, c. 4, s. 7.

51 S.M. 1872, c. 3.

52 S.M. 1875, c. 41.

53 R.S.M. 1891, c. 93, s. 737.

54 S.M. 1879, c. 1.
55 S.M. 1881, c. 28.
56 *Ibid.*
57 S.M. 1882, c. 33, ss. 6 and 7.
58 S.M. 1887, c. 9.
59 S.M. 1874, c. 38.
60 They also had an inherent jurisdiction to correct and supervise other courts in the province. In addition, they could preside over courts in the North-West Territories and act as stipendiary magistrates: S.M. 1872, c. 3.
61 S.M. 1886, c. 14.
62 *Ibid.* at ss. 9 and 11.
63 S.M. 1895, c. 6.
64 *Supra* note 30 at 198.
65 S.M. 1871, c. 2, s. 47.
66 S.M. 1872, c. 3, s. 13.
67 S.M. 1874, c. 12.
68 C.S.M. 1880, c. 31, s. 18.
69 S.M. 1883, c. 23, s. 3.
70 S.M. 1883, c. 20.
71 S.M. 1886, c. 34, s. 10.
72 S.M. 1887, c. 9, s. 117.
73 S.M. 1895, c. 6, s. 45, ss. 2.
74 S.M. 1896, c. 3, s. 315.
75 S.M. 1906, c. 18.
76 *Ibid.* at s. 2, ss. 1.
77 *Ibid.* at s. 6.
78 R.S.M. 1902, c. 40, s. 23.
79 R.S.M. 1913, c. 46, s. 10.

Chapter 1

1 Tuesday, 23 August 1870: W.J. Healy, *Winnipeg's Early Days* (Winnipeg: Stovel, 1927) at 11.
2 *Ibid.* at 12.
3 *Ibid.*, quoting Alexander Begg & Walter R. Nursey, *Ten Years in Winnipeg* (Winnipeg: Time, 1879) at 14.
4 Gerald Friesen, *The Canadian Prairies, A History* (Toronto: University of Toronto Press, 1987) at 201 & 202. See also W.L. Morton, *Manitoba, A History* (Toronto: University of Toronto Press, 1957).
5 33 Victoria, c. 3.

6 For an overview of the establishment of Manitoba's court system see Dale & Lee Gibson, *Substantial Justice: Law and Lawyers in Manitoba 1670–1970* (Winnipeg: Peguis, 1972).
7 *Manitoba Gazette*, 6 October 1870.
8 Roy St. George Stubbs, *Four Recorders of Rupert's Land* (Winnipeg: Peguis, 1967) at 71.
9 M.S. Donnelly, 'The Story of the Manitoba Legislature' (1957) 12 Hist. & Sc. Soc. Man. 29 at 32.
10 Joseph Dubuc and John Bain went to the bench from the bar of Manitoba. Admitted on 9 May 1871 were Marc Amable Girard and James Ross. The remaining five to be examined by Girard and Ross, all of whom were admitted on 29 June 1871, included Joseph Royal, David Mair Walker, Henri J. McConville, Thomas Bunn, and Felix Chernier. Alexander Morris was admitted on 1 October 1872, James Charles McKeagney on 6 November 1872, Louis Betournay on 12 December 1872, and Edmund Burke Wood on 9 June 1874. Wood was the thirty-first lawyer called to the bar of Manitoba.
11 *Supra* note 6 at 78–9. The *Manitoba Directory*, however, suggests that such appointments continued to be made by the lieutenant-governor until at least 1877: *Manitoba Directory, 1877–78* at 104.
12 Letter from Archibald to Macdonald, 24 February 1872, Macdonald Papers, MG 26A, at 78146, NAC.
13 *Ibid.*, letter from Morris to Macdonald, 10 October 1872 at 113840.
14 Information about Morris's ancestors was obtained from material contained in the William Morris Papers, Archives of Queen's University, Kingston, Ontario.
15 Details about the life of Alexander Morris (1752–1809) can be found in H.J. Bridgman's biography of William Morris. See 'Morris, William' in Francess G. Halpenny & Jean Hamelin, eds., *Dictionary of Canadian Biography*, vol. 8 (Toronto: University of Toronto Press, 1985) 638.
16 Janet Morris was the daughter of Alexander Land, a native of Paisley, Scotland. The four children born to her and William Morris Sr were Alexander (1782–1851), William (1786–1858), Margaret, who in 1824 married Daniel Jones, of Maitland (1792–1828), and James (1798–1865).
17 Susan Code, *A Matter of Honour, and Other Tales of Early Perth* (Burnstown, Ont.: General Store Publishing House, 1996) at 86.
18 *Supra* note 15 at 639.
19 For a more complete account of Morris's involvement in education, see Bridgeman, *supra* note 15.

20 *Ibid.* at 641.
21 Hilda Neatby, *Queen's University*, vol. 1, *1841–1917* (Montreal: McGill-Queen's University Press, 1978) at 43.
22 McMartin was called to the bar in 1823.
23 Alexander Morris Papers, Archives of Queen's University, Collection 2138, box 8, file 134, Articles of Apprenticeship, p. 4.
24 *Ibid.*: Certificate of James Williamson, College Registrar, dated 6 January 1849.
25 *Ibid.*: Notes of Alexander Morris, M.P.P. for East Toronto, dated 16 December (year unknown).
26 Margaret Cline was born in 1832 and died in 1908. The children born to her and Alexander included Arthur Henry, Christine van Koughnet (1854–1922), Robert Cochran (d. 1917), Elizabeth Cochran (1856–1907), Margaret Cline (1857–80), Ann Eva (b. 1859), William (1860–1936), Alexander Cline (1861–1934), Alfred van Koughnet (1868–73), Emily Murney (1868–82), and Edmund Montague (1871–1913).
27 *Montreal Empire*, 29 October 1889, 5.
28 Most of the information extant concerning the Torrance-Morris law firm is contained in G. Blaine Baker's article "Law Practice and Statecraft in Mid-Nineteenth-Century Montreal: The Torrance-Morris Firm, 1848 to 1868" in Carol Wilton, ed., *Essays in the History of Canadian Law*, vol. 4, *Beyond the Law: Lawyers and Business in Canada, 1830 to 1930* (Toronto: Osgoode Society, 1990) 45.
29 *Ibid.* at 58.
30 Lila Staples, 'The Honourable Alexander Morris: The Man; His Work' in (1925–8) Can. Hist. Assoc. His. Papers 91 at 93.
31 Alexander Morris, *The Railway Clauses Consolidation Acts of Canada, 14 & 15 Victoriae, Chapter 51, and 16 Victoriae, Chapter 169, with an Alphabetical and Analytical Index Thereto* (Montreal: Lovell, 1853).
32 Alexander Morris, *Analytical Index to the Act 20th Victoriae, Cap. XLIV., amending the Judicature Acts of Lower Canada* (Montreal: Lovell, 1857).
33 The Hon. Alexander Morris, P.C., *The Treaties of Canada with The Indians of Manitoba and the North-West Territories* (Toronto: Willing & Williamson, 1880).
34 *Ibid.* at 11.
35 *Supra* note 23.
36 *Ibid.*
37 Jean Friesen, "Alexander Morris" in Francess G. Halpenny & Jean Hamelin, eds., *Dictionary of Candian Biography*, vol. 11 (Toronto: University of Toronto Press, 1982) 608 at 610.

38 *Ibid.*
39 W.L. Morton, *The Critical Years: The Union of British North America 1857–1873* (Toronto: McClelland & Stewart, 1968) at 147.
40 *Ibid.* at 96.
41 *Supra* note 37 at 611. Morris was said to have had a sensitive and nervous disposition.
42 *Ibid.* at 610.
43 Morris was sworn in on 1 July 1872.
44 *Supra* note 6 at 97.
45 *Supra* note 12. Letter from Morris to Macdonald, 10 October 1872, at 113840.
46 *Supra* note 37 at 610.
47 (1872) 8 Can. L.J. 262.
48 *Surpa* note 12. Letter from Morris to Macdonald, 5 November 1872, at 113883.
49 *Supra* note 9 at 32.
50 Doug Owram, *Promise of Eden: The Canadian Expansionist Movement and the Idea of the West, 1856–1900* (Toronto: University of Toronto Press, 1980) at 55.
51 Letter from Morris to Laird, 4 December 1873, Alexander Morris Papers, MG 12, B2, PAM.
52 *Supra* note 37 at 612.
53 John Andrew Kerr, 'The Indian Treaties of 1876' in (1937) 17 Dalhousie Rev. 189.
54 *Supra* note 4, *Canadian Prairies* at 143.
55 *Ibid.* at 144.
56 *Supra* note 12. Letter from Morris to Macdonald, 20 September 1873.
57 *Ibid.* Letter from Morris to Dorion, 10 December 1873.
58 Letter from Morris to Laird, 25 November 1873, Lieutenant-Governor's Collection 1872–7, MG 12, B1 at 570, PAM.
59 *Ibid.* Letter from Morris to Mackenzie, 27 November 1874.
60 Alan F.J. Artibise, ed., *Gateway City: Documents on the City of Winnipeg 1873–1913* (Winnipeg: Manitoba Record Society, 1979) at 58.
61 *Supra* note 3 at 75.
62 The source for most of the details regarding the role Alexander Morris played in creating the University of Manitoba can be found in W.L. Morton's *One University: A History of the University of Manitoba 1877–1952* (Toronto: McClelland & Stewart, 1957) and Jean Friesen's biography of Morris, *supra* note 37.
63 *Ibid.* Morton at 23.

64 *Supra* note 37 at 613.
65 *Ibid.* at 613.
66 *Supra* note 61 at 193.
67 *Ibid.* at 194.
68 The election was held on 26 September 1878.
69 *Supra* note 61 at 196–7.
70 *Manitoba Free Press*, 15 July 1909.
71 *Supra* note 37 at 614.

Chapter 2

1 Alan F.J. Artibise, 'An Urban Economy: Patterns of Economic Change in Winnipeg, 1873–1971' (1976) 2 Prairie Forum 163 at 164.
2 Alan F.J. Artibise, *Winnipeg, a Social History of Urban Growth 1874–1914* (Montreal: McGill-Queen's University Press, 1975) at 23 and W.L. Morton, *Manitoba, A History* (Toronto: University of Toronto Press, 1957) at 171.
3 *Supra* note 1 at 165.
4 Charles M. Studness, 'Economic Opportunity and the Westward Migration of Canadians during the Late Nineteenth Century' (1964) 30 Canadian Journal of Economics and Political Science 570 at 571.
5 McKeagney was sworn in as a member of the Manitoba bar on 6 November 1872 and Betournay on 12 December.
6 *Manitoba Gazette*, 31 December 1872, 26 May 1873, 30 August 1873, and 16 October 1873.
7 Dale & Lee Gibson, *Substantial Justice: Law and Lawyers in Manitoba 1670–1970* (Winnipeg: Peguis, 1972) at 118. *Judgments in the Queen's Bench, Manitoba* (Winnipeg: *The Nor'wester*, 1875) is the first law report published in western Canada.
8 Gerald Friesen, *The Canadian Prairies, A History* (Toronto: University of Toronto Press, 1987) at 134–5.
9 *Ibid.* at 137. Fewer than 2000 white settlers lived surrounded by 35,000 Indians and 10,000 Metis.
10 Alexander Begg & Walter R. Nursey, *Ten Years in Winnipeg* (Winnipeg: Times, 1879) at 111 and 106.
11 *Ibid.* at 135.
12 Lieutenant-Governor's Collection, 1872–7, MG 12, B1 at 1073, PAM.
13 M.S. Donnelly, 'The Story of the Manitoba Legislature' (1957) 12 Hist. & Sc. Soc. Man. 29 at 32.
14 William J. Healy, *Winnipeg's Early Days, A Short Historical Sketch* (Winnipeg: Stovel, 1927) at 26.

15 Alexander Begg, *History of the North-West* (Toronto: Hunter, Rose, 1895) at 392–3; also W.L. Morton, *supra* note 2, for a more detailed discussion.
16 *Supra* note 14 at 21.
17 *Supra* note 10 at 149.
18 The Battle of Culloden was fought on 16 April 1746 near Inverness, Scotland. It marked the end of the Jacobite Rebellion against Britain's Hanoverian monarchy.
19 For a summary of Irish immigration to Nova Scotia, see Douglas F. Campbell, *Banked Fires: The Ethnics of Nova Scotia* (Port Credit, NS: Scribblers' Press, 1978) c. 5.
20 Henry McKeagney was born on 15 June 1796 at Clogher, Ireland. He received tonsure at Quebec on 1 June 1821 and was ordained on 30 September that year. Patrick McKeagney was born in Ireland in 1809 and ordained in 1832. A good description of the career of the Fathers McKeagney, which includes a discussion of the career of their cousin Michael, can be found in Rev. Angus Anthony Johnston, *A History of the Catholic Church in Eastern Nova Scotia*, vol. 1, *1611–1827* (Antigonish, NS: St Francis Xavier University Press, 1960) and vol. 2, *1827–1880* (1971).
21 *Ibid.*, vol. 2 at 49.
22 *Supra* 20, vol. 1 at 357.
23 Michael died on 21 July 1847 after becoming infected with the disease that took the life of the parishioner to whom he had administered the last rites the previous evening.
24 *Supra* note 20, vol. 1 at 470 & 472.
25 G.C. Campbell, *The History of Nova Scotia* (Toronto: Ryerson Press, 1948) at 236–7.
26 *Supra* note 19 at 99.
27 Beamish Murdoch, *Epitome of the Laws of Nova Scotia*, vol. 1 (Halifax: Joseph Howe, 1832) at 5.
28 Philip Girard, 'The Roots of a Professional Renaissance: Lawyers in Nova Scotia 1850–1910' (1991) 21 Man. L.J. 148 at 167.
29 *Statutes of Nova Scotia* 1811, c. 3.
30 Bernard F. Miller, 'The Legal Profession in Late Victorian Nova Scotia' (1988) 8:2 N.S. Hist. Rev. 57.
31 *Supra* note 27 at 13. Other books recommended include *Selwyn's Nisi Prius, Tidd's Practice, Newland's Chancery Practice, Toller on Executors, Adams on Ejectment, Comyn's Landlord and Tenant, Saunders' Reports, Roberts on Wills, Sugden on Vendors, Roberts on Frauds, Leach's Crown Law*, and *Archbold's Criminal Pleading and Evidence.*

32 D.G. Bell, 'Paths to the Law in the Maritimes, 1810–1825: The Bliss Brothers and Their Circle' (1988) 8:2 N.S. Hist. Rev. 6 at 13.
33 *Supra* note 30 at 62.
34 McKeagney was called as a barrister on 30 October 1838.
35 *Supra* note 20, vol. 1 at 116.
36 Statistics for those called to the bar can be found in Girard, *supra* note 28 at 154. Data for those practising in Cape Breton and Sydney is located in the various almanacs for the period.
37 C.B. Fergusson, ed., *The Diary of Adolphus Gaetz, 1855–1873* (Halifax: Public Archives of Nova Scotia, 1965) at 58.
38 *Ibid.*
39 *Ibid.* at 92.
40 (1855) 1 Upper Canada Law Journal 11.
41 *Supra* note 32 at 6.
42 For a brief discussion of the efforts involved in repealing the *Test Act* see Terrence M. Punch, 'The Irish Catholic, Halifax's First Minority Group' (1980) 10:1 N.S. Hist. Quart. 23 and *Banked Fires*, supra note 19.
43 *Supra* note 20, vol. 1 at 126–7.
44 McKeagney was made a registrar of probate and surrogate in the Court of Vice-Admiralty on 8 November 1842. He became a judge of probate on 20 June 1848 and held that position until 1867, when he became a Member of Parliament.
45 For a description of the authority and responsibilities imposed on judges of probate see Fazley K. Siddiq, 'Nineteenth-Century Wealth Transfers in Nova Scotia: The Administration of Probate' (1989) 9:2 N.S. Hist. Rev. 35.
46 Phyllis Wagg offers a good discussion of the role played by courts of probate in 'The Bias of Probate: Using Deeds to Transfer Estates in Nineteenth-Century Nova Scotia' (1990) 10:1 N.S. Hist. Rev. 74.
47 J. Murray Beck, 'The Nomination of Candidates in Nova Scotia' (1957) 36 Dal. Rev. 361 at 362.
48 C.B. Fergusson's *A Directory of the Members of the Legislative Assembly of Nova Scotia 1758–1958* (Halifax: Public Archives of Nova Scotia, 1958) contains a summary of McKeagney's provincial political career, including the dates of elections and the dates when legislatures were convened and dissolved.
49 McKeagney was a member, without portfolio, of Nova Scotia's Executive Council between 29 January and 26 July 1851.
50 *Supra* note 37 at 49 & 73.
51 *Ibid.* at 50.

52 McKeagney was appointed to the Land Board in June 1848, to the Board of School Commissioners on 25 June 1864, and as Harbour Master for the port of Sydney in 1865.

53 Shirley B. Elliott, *The Legislative Assembly of Nova Scotia 1758–1983, A Biographical Directory* (Halifax: Province of Nova Scotia, 1984) at 137.

54 A detailed history of the Nova Scotia militia can be found in Joseph Plimsoll Edwards, 'The Militia of Nova Scotia, 1749–1867' (1913) 17 N.S. Hist. Soc. 63.

55 Delphin Andrew Muise, *Elections and Constituencies: Federal Politics in Nova Scotia, 1867–1878* (Ph.D. thesis, University of Western Ontario, 1971) [unpublished] at 199.

56 J. Murray Beck, *Joseph Howe*, vol. 2, *The Briton Becomes Canadian 1848–1873* (Montreal: McGill-Queen's University Press, 1983) at 264.

57 Letter from Macdonald to Morris, 24 October 1872, Macdonald Papers, MG 26A, Letterbook 19 at 16, NAC.

58 Letter from Macdonald to Howe, 12 January 1869, in Sir Joseph Pope, *Correspondence of Sir John A. Macdonald* (Toronto: Oxford University Press, 1921) at 85.

59 *Ibid*. Letter from Gilbert McMicken to Macdonald, 8 February 1873, Letterbook 17 at 110,796. See *supra* note 7 for additional comments about McKeagney.

60 *Ibid*. Letter from Morris to Macdonald, 16 January 1873, at 113,998.

61 *Statutes of Manitoba*, c. 3, s. 5, assented to on 21 February 1872.

62 For a discussion of this incident see *supra* note 7 at 102 and (1873) 9 Can. L.J. 279.

63 *Substantial Justice*, *supra* note 7 contains a brief account of the trial and death of Gordon. For a more detailed description of Gordon see J.L. Johnston, 'Lord Gordon Gordon' (1952) 7 Hist. & Sci. Soc. Man. 7.

64 McKeagney is referred to several times in Phyllis R. Blakely, 'William Alexander Henry, a Father of Confederation from Nova Scotia' (1968) 36 N.S. Hist. Soc. 96.

65 McKeagney's second wife was Eliza Hearne, the only daughter of Sydney's Peter A. Hearne.

66 Pierre Betournay (1698–1750) was the husband of Marie Deshaies. In George Stanley, 'Betournay, Louis' in Marc La Terreur, ed., *Dictionary of Canadian Biography*, vol. 10 (Toronto: University of Toronto Press, 1972) 58 Pierre is referred to as Adrien Betourne.

67 Betournay's parents, Pierre Betournay (1770–1825) and Archange Vincent, were married in Longueuil in 1805. Pierre died on 28 July 1825.

68 For a brief summary of Beaudry's life and career see Jean-Jacques

Lefebvre's biography of him in Marc La Terreur, ed., *Dictionary of Canadian Biography*, vol. 10 (Toronto: University of Toronto Press, 1972) 37.

69 Letter from Macdonald to Morris, 8 November 1872, Letterook 19 at 149–50.

70 For a discussion of the role played by de Plainval in Manitoba see *Substantial Justice, supra* note 7.

71 *The Manitoba Gazette*, 24 September 1873, 2.

72 *Supra* note 12. Despatch to the Secretary of State, 26 June 1875, and letter written on behalf of Getz to Lieutenant-Governor Alexander Morris, 20 August 1875, items 1032 and 1044.

73 *Supra* note 57 at 14014. Letter from Morris to John A. Macdonald, 25 January 1873.

74 Undated letter from Gilbert McMicken to John A. Macdonald, McMicken Papers, PAM.

75 *Supra* note 57 at 164071-2. Letter from N.F. Davin to John A. Macdonald, 22 February 1879.

76 Jean-Jacques Lefebvre, 'Louis Betournay (1825–1879) Premier Juge Canadien-Français d'une Cour Supérieure dans L'Ouest Canadien.'

77 Betournay's Law Society member file contains a summary of the incident. It cites as a source an article that it said appeared in the *Manitoba Free Press* on 3 August 1879. See Archive of Manitoba Legal-Judicial History, file P 1212, PAM.

78 Details of Betournay's funeral can be found in an article that appeared on the front page of the *Manitoba Free Press* on 3 November 1879.

79 *Supra* note 66, Stanley.

80 *Manitoba Free Press*, 31 October 1879, 2.

81 Despite dying young Betournay lived long enough to establish one of the first legal dynasties in the history of his adopted province. His son Louis Napoleon articled with J. Stanley Hough and was twenty-seven when entered on the rolls of the Law Society as a clerk. Ernest Louis, the son of Louis Napoleon, followed in the footsteps of his father and grandfather, and was called to the bar in 1915. He died of a cerebral haemorrhage in 1957 while practising in St Boniface. His sons Louis Noel Robert and Maurice Paul were the fourth generation to practise in Manitoba. Paul, the last of the family to do so, graduated from the University of Manitoba with a Bachelor of Arts degree in 1949 and was called five years later. He practised with Monnin, Grafton & Deniset and Marcoux, Dureault & Betournay before joining the federal department of justice in Ottawa.

82 Despite the prominence he achieved as a lawyer, politician, and jurist, little has been written about Wood's family background. What we do

know comes largely from newspaper articles and: Richard Armstrong, 'The Hon. Edmund Burk Wood, Late Chief Justice of Manitoba' (1895) 1 The Barrister 114; Roy St George Stubbs, 'Hon. Edmund Burke Wood' (1962) 34 Man. Bar N. 109; F. Douglas Reville, *History of the County of Brant*, vol. 1 (Brantford: Hurley, 1920); and J.D. Livermore, 'Edmund Burke Wood' in Francess G. Halpenny, ed., *Dictionary of Canadian Biography*, vol. 11 (Toronto: University of Toronto Press, 1982) 934. From these sources it is known that his mother's name was Charlotte and one of his grandmothers was a daughter of the Hon. H. Hatch, of New Brunswick, and sister of H.H. Hatch, Recorder of Wills and Deeds for St Andrew's, New Brunswick.

83 A brief summary of Wood's early career can be found in Livermore's biography of him, *ibid.*, and an obituary in the *Brantford Evening Telegram*, 9 October 1882, at 1.

84 Frank N. Weiler, 'Birth of The Buffalo and Brantford Railway' (1955) 47 Ont. Hist. Soc. 81.

85 *Supra* note 82, Reville, vol. 1 at 286.

86 *Ibid.* Armstrong at 115.

87 Edmund Burke Wood Papers, Brantford County Museum and Archives.

88 *Studer* v. *The Buffalo and Lake Huron Railway Co.* (1867), 25 U.C.Q.B. 160 at 164.

89 *Manitoba Free Press*, 9 October 1882, 4.

90 Sir John Willison, *Reminiscences Political and Personal* (Toronto: McClelland & Stewart, 1919) at 14.

91 *Supra* note 7 at 117.

92 C.B. Sissons, *Egerton Ryerson, His Life and Letters*, vol. 2 (Toronto: Clarke, Irwin, 1947) at 554.

93 James Cleland Hamilton, *Osgoode Hall, Reminiscences of the Bench and Bar* (Toronto: Carswell, 1904) at 79.

94 For a discussion of the role Wood played in the fall of the Sandfield Macdonald government see Joseph Schull, *Edward Blake, The Man of the Other Way (1833–1881)* (Toronto: Macmillan, 1975); Bruce W. Hodgins, *John Sandfield Macdonald 1812–1872* (Toronto: University of Toronto Press, 1971); and Livermore, *supra* note 82.

95 J.D. Livermore, 'The Ontario Election of 1871: a Case Study in the Transfer of Political Power' (1979) 71 Ont. Hist. 39 at 46.

96 *Supra* note 10 at 143.

97 *Ibid.* at 98.

98 *Manitoba Free Press*, 27 October 1874, 2.

99 *Supra* note 82, Livermore.

100 *Manitoba Free Press*, 28 January 1875, 2.

101 Morris Papers, MG10 F2 at 17, PAM.
102 *Ibid.*
103 *Manitoba Free Press*, 15 February 1875, 2.
104 *Supra* note 101. Letter from Mackenzie to Morris, 3 December 1875.
105 *Manitoba Free Press*, 9 February 1875, 2.
106 *Ibid.*, 19 August 1875, 2.
107 *Ibid.*, 23 August 1875, 2.
108 *Supra* note 101. Letter from David Young to Morris, 5 November 1879.
109 Roy St George Stubbs, 'Hon. Edmund Burke Wood' (1958) 13 Hist. & Sci. Soc. Man. 27 at 42.
110 *Supra* note 12. Despatch from Morris to the Secretary of State, 29 June 1876, Letterbook 'M,' no. 36.
111 *Supra* note 7, *Substantial Justice* at 127.
112 (1880) 1 W.L.T. 14.
113 The issue of Metis land sales has been the subject of much debate. See, for example, D.N. Sprague, 'Government Lawlessness in the Administration of Manitoba Land Claims, 1870–1887' (1980) 10 Man. L.J. 415 and *Canadian Prairies, supra* note 8 at 198.
114 *Schultz* v. *Wood* (1882), 6 S.C.R. 585 at 596.
115 *Boultbee* v. *Shore*, [1882] Temp. Wood 376 at 380 and 383.
116 Arthur Chiel, *Jewish Experiences in Early Manitoba* (Winnipeg: Manitoba Jewish Publications, 1955) at 17 and 20.
117 *Petitions and Reply to the Charges Preferred against the Hon. E.B. Wood, C.J., Province of Manitoba* (Ottawa: Maclean, Roger, 1882).
118 *Globe*, 7 March 1881, 4.
119 *Manitoba Free Press*, 10 March 1881.
120 *Ibid.*, 2 October 1882, 2.
121 *Ibid.*, 9 October 1882, 5.
122 *Brantford Evening Telegram*, 9 October 1882, 1.
123 *Supra*, note 82, Reville, at 112.
124 *Farmer* v. *Livingston*, [1879] Temp. Wood 233 (Q.B.).
125 (1874) 10 Can. L.J. 31.
126 *Supra* note 90 at 20.

Chapter 3

1 Dale & Lee Gibson, *Substantial Justice: Law and Lawyers in Manitoba 1670–1970* (Winnipeg: Peguis, 1972) at 137.
2 Letter from A.C. Campbell to Sir John A. Macdonald, 8 October 1880, Macdonald Papers, MG 26A at 81765, PAM.

3 (1880) 16 Can. L.J. 285.
4 S.M. 1879, c. 28.
5 S.C. 1881, c. 14; also *Substantial Justice, supra* note 1 at 134 and W.L. Morton, *Manitoba, A History* (Toronto: University of Toronto Press, 1957).
6 Both changes were part of S.M. 1881, c. 28.
7 (1884) 18 Can. L.J. 235.
8 Minutes of the Law Society of Manitoba, 27 May 1882, Archive of Manitoba Legal-Judicial History, PAM.
9 Wallbridge was appointed in December 1882 and Taylor on 5 January 1883.
10 S.C. 1883, c. 54.
11 *Supra* note 1 at 146.
12 *Ibid.* at 146.
13 *Ibid.* at 147.
14 (1884) 1 Man. L.J. 185.
15 Hartwell Bowfield, ed., *The Letters of Charles John Brydges 1879–1882* (Winnipeg: Hudson's Bay Record Society, 1977) at lxxvi.
16 Alexander Begg, *History of the North-West* (Toronto: Hunter, Rose, 1895) at 393.
17 George F.G. Stanley, *Louis Riel* (Toronto: Ryerson, 1963) at 24.
18 Historic Resources Branch of the Province of Manitoba, *The Honourable Joseph Dubuc, K.S.M.G.* (Winnipeg: Historic Resources Branch, 1981) at 1.
19 William H. Kerr, "The Bench and Bar of Quebec" (1873) 9 Can. L.J. 86.
20 *Supra* note 1.
21 *Supra* note 5, Morton, at 145.
22 M.M. McAlduff, *Joseph Dubuc, Role and Views of a French Canadian in Manitoba 1870–1914* (M.A. thesis, University of Ottawa, 1967) [unpublished] at 17.
23 George Woodcock, *Faces from History, Canadian Profiles & Portraits* (Edmonton: Hurtig, 1978) at 106.
24 Letter from Riel to Dubuc, 21 October 1870, Joseph Dubuc Papers, MG 14, B26, PAM.
25 *Supra* note 2. Letter from Archibald to Macdonald, 26 May 1871, at 77897.
26 Manitoba Biographical Scrapbooks, Legislative Library of the Province of Manitoba, scrapbook 5 at 106.
27 *Ibid.*, scrapbook 3 at 17.
28 *Manitoba Free Press*, 8 October 1909.
29 John H. O'Donnell, *Manitoba As I Saw It* (Toronto: Musson, 1909) at 61.
30 *Supra* note 22 at 102.
31 *Le Metis*, 22 September 1873, 2.
32 For example, see the pamphlet published by Thomas P. Foran, *Trial of*

Ambrose Lepine at Winnipeg for the Wilful Murder of Thomas Scott. Question of Jurisdiction (Montreal: Lovell Printing, 1874).

33 *Supra* note 22 at 329.

34 Richard A. Willie, *'These Legal Gentlemen': Lawyers in Manitoba, 1870–1890* (Winnipeg: Legal Institute of the University of Manitoba, 1994) at 83.

35 Maggie Siggins, *Louis Riel: A Life of Revolution* (Toronto: Harper Collins, 1994) at 264.

36 H. Douglas Kemp, 'Land Grants under the Manitoba Act' (1954) 3:9 Hist. & Sc. Soc. Man. 33 at 47.

37 A.I. Silver, 'French Canada and the Prairie Frontier, 1870–1890' (1969) 50 Can. Hist. Rev. 11.

38 *Journals of the Legislature of Manitoba*, 22 and 23 March 1871, at 25 and 27.

39 *Supra* note 22 at 167.

40 Unattributed newspaper article, Colin Inkster Papers, MG 14, B30, box 2, scrapbook at 8, PAM.

41 *Supra* note 24. Joseph Dubuc, *Mémoires d'un Manitobain* (unpublished autobiography, 1913) at 579.

42 According to the 1881 Manitoba census, Joseph Henault, Marie Girard, and Marguerite Sausugret were residing with the Dubucs and their six children, two of whom were born after Dubuc went to the bench.

43 *Supra* note 22 at 240.

44 *Manitoba Free Press*, 2 December 1879, 1.

45 (1880) 16 Can. L.J. 1.

46 *Supra* note 34 at 99, referring to testimony Archibald gave to the committee on 23 November 1881. See also GR174, 19 November 1881, PAM.

47 (1885), 2 Man. L.J. 113; *Maddill* v. *Kelly* (1884), 1 Man. L.J. 280.

48 *Supra* note 22 at 244.

49 *Wood* v. *Wood* (1885), 2 Man. L.J. 198 (Q.B.).

50 *Supra* note 35 at 212–13.

51 *Supra* note 22 beginning at 268.

52 *Supra* note 2. Letter from Aikins to John A. Macdonald, 31 October 1887, at 77503.

53 Taylor was sworn in as chief justice on 22 October 1887, Killam on 15 April 1899, and Dubuc on 8 August 1903.

54 *Manitoba Free Press*, 24 August 1903.

55 *Tribune*, 15 January 1914.

56 Dubuc and his wife were the parents of eleven children, many of whom became socially or professionally prominent. Gustave, for example, practised in Pincher Creek, Alberta, before earning a reputation as one of New York's finest surgeons. Of more significance to the Manitoba bar,

however, was the fact that Dubuc established the province's second legal dynasty. His oldest son, Alexandre Joseph Henri, was called to the bar in 1895 and practised with J.E.P. Prendergast, a future justice of the Queen's Bench. He became Belgium's counsel for Winnipeg and represented many of the city's largest financial institutions. Alexandre was just as prominent socially, especially after his marriage to the daughter of Montreal barrister Auguste Couillard de l'Épinay, head of one of the oldest families in Canada. Three other sons also went into law. Lucien practised in Edmonton before going to the bench, first as a judge of the District Court of Peace River and subsequently as a member of the same court in Edmonton. Albert practised with his brother Alexandre and sat as a magistrate for ten years before emigrating briefly to France and, eventually, Quebec. A fourth son, Antonin, became a lawyer in Los Angeles, California. All of Dubuc's sons earned Bachelor of Arts degrees from St Boniface College, and each of his daughters was educated at a convent school in Montreal. A grandson, Paul, attended Edmonton College, Montreal College, and the University of Laval before he too went into law.

57 The Miller family were Episcopalians of Scottish ancestry. Following the death of Miller's father, John, his widow Mary moved to St Catharines.
58 *Winnipeg Sun*, 1 November 1886.
59 Junius, *St. Catharines A to Z* (St. Catharines: St Catharines and Lincoln Historical Society, 1967) at 1856.
60 Miller was elected a bencher on 15 May 1876 and served until 26 October 1880.
61 *Supra* note 34 at 134.
62 *Manitoba Free Press*, 30 October 1880, 4.
63 *Supra* note 3.
64 *Manitoba Free Press*, 25 October 1880, 2.
65 *Supra* note 1 at 137.
66 *Manitoba Free Press*, 27 October 1881, 1 and, 6 November 1882, 8.
67 *Manitoba Free Press*, 17 November 1881, 2.
68 *Manitoba Free Press*, 3 November 1882, 8.
69 Rev. Thomas Wardlaw Taylor Jr, *A Sketch of the Life of Sir Thomas Wardlaw Taylor* [unpublished biography], Thomas Wardlaw Taylor AVF file, diary entry for 9 October 1882 at 209–10, PAM.
70 *Ibid.*, entry for 17 October 1882 at 210.
71 *Ibid.*, entry for 18 October 1882 at 211.
72 45 Victoria, c. 1, s. 5.
73 *Re The Hon. James A. Miller* (1886), 3 Man. R. 367.

74 *Winnipeg Sun*, 1 November 1886.
75 James Andrew Miller Papers, St Catharines Museum and Archives, Ontario.
76 *Manitoba Free Press*, 9 January 1883, 4.
77 *Manitoba Free Press*, 9 January 1883, 2.
78 *Regina v. Biggs* (1885), 2 Man. R. 18.
79 S.J.R. Noel, *Patrons, Clients, Brokers: Ontario Society and Politics*, 1791–1896 (Toronto: University of Toronto Press, 1990) at 258.
80 *Winnipeg Sun*, 1 November 1886.
81 William Canniff, *History of the Settlement of Upper Canada, (Ontario) with Special Reference to the Bay of Quinte* (Toronto: Dudley & Burns, 1869) at 576.
82 A good biography of the Wallbridge family can be found in Rolph and Clark, eds., *Pioneer Life on the Bay of Quinte* (Toronto: Rolph & Clark, 1904) at 894.
83 (1937) 10 Man. Bar N. 481.
84 For a description of the Baldwin firm and its offices see J.C. Hamilton's *Osgoode Hall, Reminiscences of the Bench and Bar* (Toronto: Carswell, 1904) at 148–9.
85 Nick & Helma Mika, *Belleville, Friendly City* (Belleville: Mika Publishing, 1973) and William Henry Smith, *Canada: Past, Present and Future*, vol. 2 (Belleville: Mika Publishing, 1973) at 56.
86 Letter from William Wallbridge to Marianne Howard, 24 January 1838, Wallbridge Family Papers, MS 93, Provincial Archives of Ontario.
87 G. Blaine Baker, 'Legal Education in Upper Canada 1785–1889: The Law Society as Educator' in David H. Flaherty, ed., *Essays in the History of Canadian Law*, vol. 2 (Toronto: Osgoode Society, 1983) 49 at 99 and 136.
88 *Ibid.* at 98.
89 (1887) 23 Can. L.J. 361.
90 Clare A. Dale, *'Whose Servant I Am': Speakers of the Assemblies of the Provinces of Upper Canada, Canada and Ontario, 1792–1992* (Toronto: Ontario Legislative Library, 1992) at 132.
91 Bruce W. Hodgin's biography of Wallbridge in the *Dictionary of Canadian Biography* contains a good overview of his career in politics. See 'Lewis Wallbridge' in Francess G. Halpenny & Jean Hamelin, eds., *Dictionary of Canadian Biography*, vol. 11 (Toronto: University of Toronto Press, 1982) 908.
92 [Toronto] *Globe*, 13 October 1882, 1 and 14 October 1882, 9.
93 J.K. Johnson & P.B. Waite, 'Sir John Alexander Macdonald' in Francess G. Halpenny, ed., *Dictionary of Canadian Biography*, vol. 12 (Toronto: University of Toronto Press, 1990) 606.

94 (1882) 18 Can. L.J. 429.
95 (1890) 1 West. L.T. 63.
96 *Manitoba Free Press*, 21 October 1887, 4.
97 Margaret Charteris-Thomson, *The Colonial Ancestry of The Honourable Sir Thomas Wardlaw Taylor, Kt.B. Chief Justice of the Province of Manitoba – 1887–1899* (London: Courier Press, 1937) contains a detailed description of both the Taylor and Wardlaw families.
98 *Supra* note 69 at 27.
99 *Ibid.* at 37.
100 *Ibid.* at 60.
101 *Ibid.* at 78.
102 *Ibid.* at 146.
103 *Ibid.* at 138.
104 *Ibid.* at 161.
105 *Ibid.* at 171–2, quoting an unattributed newspaper editorial, 11 September 1866.
106 *Ibid.* at 181–2.
107 *Ibid.* at 182–4.
108 *Ibid.* at 191.
109 (1883) 19 Can. L.J. 21.
110 Thomas Wardlaw Taylor, Esq., M.A., *Orders of the Court of Chancery for Upper Canada, With Notes* (Toronto: Roswell, 1860).
111 *Ibid.* at 47.
112 T. Wardlaw Taylor, M.A. & G.M. Rae, *General Orders of the Court of Chancery, of 6th February, 1865, With Notes and Forms* (Toronto: Rollo & Adam, 1865).
113 *Ibid.*
114 Thomas Wardlaw Taylor, M.A., *The Investigation of Titles to Estates in Fee Simple* (Toronto: Adam, Stevenson, 1869). A second edition was published by Toronto's Willing & Williamson in 1873.
115 *Ibid.* at iv.
116 *Ibid.* at 55.
117 Thomas Wardlaw Taylor, M.A., *Commentaries on Equity Jurisprudence Founded on Story* (Toronto: Willing & Williamson, 1875).
118 *Ibid.* at 28.
119 Thomas Wardlaw Taylor, *The Public Statutes Relating to the Presbyterian Church in Canada: Acts and Resolutions of the General Assembly, and By-laws for the Government of the Colleges and Schemes of the Church* (Toronto: Willing & Williamson, 1879). A second edition was published by Hart, of Winnipeg, in 1897.

120 Thomas Wardlaw Taylor, Q.C., & John S. Ewart, *The Judicature Act and Rules 1881, and Other Statutes and Orders Relating to the Practice of the Supreme Court of Judicature for Ontario, With Notes* (Toronto: Carswell, 1881).
121 *Supra* note 69 at 220.
122 *Ibid.* at 233–4.
123 *Ibid.* at 225–7.
124 Taylor became chief justice on 22 October 1887 and retired 31 March 1899.
125 *Winnipeg Free Press*, 24 April 1965.
126 *Supra* note 69 at 173.
127 *Ibid.* at 231.
128 Ibid. at 232.
129 *Ibid.* at 253–4.
130 *Ibid.* at 262.
131 The Taylors had seven children, one of whom followed his father into law. In 1886 Thomas Wardlaw Taylor Jr graduated from the University of Manitoba and became a student-at-law in the office of James Albert Manning Aikins. After completing articles and receiving his call he went on to become a Presbyterian minister and clerk of the General Assembly of the Presbyterian Church in Canada. Two of Taylor's daughters married university professors, two sons became civil engineers, and a third was a captain when killed in action during the First World War. The couple's youngest child was a housewife. All were raised, for a time at least, in the home their father built in what was to become Winnipeg's most exclusive residential area. Although their house bore the number '229' Wellington Crescent, for ten years it was the only home on what was nothing more than a wagon trail through the bush. Winnipeg's last tribute to the chief justice was naming Wardlaw Street in his honour.
132 The first Thomas Smith about whom something is known married Dorothy Wilson. They had only one child, also named Thomas. He married Ann Bewely, of Gil Crux House. They had two children, William and Thomas. William died a bachelor, while Thomas married Isabella Sproule, daughter of Captain Sproule of the Royal Navy. Her mother, Eleanor, was the daughter of James Grayson, a privateer under letters of marque in England's war against Napoleon.
133 Several Smith family histories, together with genealogies, can be found in the Stratford Perth Archives.
134 *Canty* v. *Clark* (1879), 44 U.C.Q.B. 222 (H.C.), followed by *Merriam* v. *Portage la Prairie (Town) Parks Board*, [1912] 1 W.W.R. 1082 (Man. C.A.) and *Davidson* v. *Francis* (1902), 14 Man. R. 141 (Man. C.A.).

135 *Regina* v. *Smith et al.* (1878), 43 U.C.Q.B. 369.
136 Roy Bayne MacInnes, 'Justice Robert Smith Won Admiration Both as Lawyer and Judge' in the *Stratford Herald-Beacon*, 18 June 1938.
137 (1884) 1 Man. L.J. 112 and (1884) 20 Can. L.J. 217.
138 Burritt was sworn in on 24 January 1853, but ten months later exchanged jurisdictions with Charles Robinson, the recently appointed county court judge for the County of Lambton. On 17 October 1853 Robinson moved to Perth and Burritt took his place in Lambton. That lasted only until 16 April 1855, when they again switched offices.
139 Adelaide Leitch, *Floodtides of Fortune: The Story of Stratford and the Progress of the City through Two Centuries* (Stratford: City of Stratford, 1980) c. 17; and William Evans, ed., *The Directory of Stratford for 1880–81* (Stratford, 1880) at 7.
140 For a brief history of the County Court of Perth see Leitch, *ibid.* at c. 7.
141 *Manitoba Free Press*, 20 January 1885, quoting an article that had appeared in a Stratford paper.
142 *Supra* note 136.
143 *Supra* note 2. Letter from S.R. Hesson to Macdonald, 30 November 1882.
144 *Ibid.* Letter from Campbell to Macdonald, 5 June 1884.
145 (1885) 2 Man. L.J. 1, discussing Smith's decision in *Re Stanbro* (1885), 2 Man. R. 1.
146 *Armstrong* v. *Portage, Westbourne and North Western Railway Co.* (1884), 1 Man. R. 344 at 346.
147 *Brimstone* v. *Smith* (1884), 1 Man. R. 302 at 305.
148 *Supra* note 146 at 346.
149 *Stratford Beacon*, 30 January 1885, 1.
150 The Smith Papers in the Stratford Perth Archives and the Lizars Collection at the University of Western Ontario both contain information about Smith's estate.
151 Much has been written about Robert Home Smith, but probably the most complete biography is James H. Gunn's 'The Lawyer as Entrepreneur: Robert Home Smith in Early-Twentieth-Century Toronto' in Carol Wilton, ed., *Essays in the History of Canadian Law*, vol. 4, *Beyond the Law – Lawyers and Business in Canada, 1830 to 1930* (Toronto: Osgoode Society, 1994) 235.
152 Robina & Kathleen Macfarlane Lizars, *In the Days of the Canada Company: The Story of the Settlement of the Huron Tract and a View of the Social Life of the Period 1825–1850* (Toronto: William Briggs, 1896).
153 Robina & Kathleen Macfarlane Lizars, *Humours of '37 Grave, Gay and Grime: Rebellion Times in the Canadas* (Toronto: William Briggs, 1897) at 1.

154 Robina & Kathleen Macfarlane Lizars, *Committed to His Charge: A Canadian Chronicle* (Toronto: George N. Morang, 1900).
155 *Ibid.*
156 *Toronto Globe,* 20 October 1900 and 24 October 1900.
157 *Canadian Churchman,* 22 November 1900 and *The Westminister,* 3 November 1900. The Lizars Collection at the University of Western Ontario contains a number of scrapbooks of reviews of all of the sister's books.
158 Kathleen Macfarlane Lizars, *The Valley of the Humber, 1615–1913* (Toronto: McClelland & Stewart, 1913).
159 Etobicoke Historical Society, eds., *The Story of Etobicoke* (Etobicoke: Etobicoke Historical Society, 1950) at 33 and *supra* note 150 at 238.

Chapter 4

1 (1884) 4 Can. L.T. 234.
2 *Manitoba Free Press,* 23 January 1885, 2.
3 (February 1885) 5 Can. L.T. 64.
4 Gerald Friesen, *The Canadian Prairies, A History* (Toronto: University of Toronto Press, 1987) c. 8; and W.L. Morton, *Manitoba, A History* (Toronto: University of Toronto Press, 1957).
5 *Ibid.* Morton at 211.
6 *Supra* note 4, Friesen at 207–10 and Morton, c. 9.
7 *Ibid.* Morton at 274.
8 *Ibid.* at 229.
9 *Ibid.* at 232–3.
10 Richard A. Willie, *'These Legal Gentlemen': Lawyers in Manitoba: 1839–1900* (Winnipeg: Legal Research Institute of the University of Manitoba, 1994) at 167.
11 *Ibid.* at 255.
12 Letter to the Editor, *Manitoba Free Press,* 6 March & 13 February 1891.
13 *Supra* note 10 at 204.
14 Dale & Lee Gibson, *Substantial Justice: Law and Lawyers in Manitoba 1670–1970* (Winnipeg: Peguis, 1972) c. 4.
15 S.M. 1890, c. 2, s. 37; also *ibid.*, Gibson, 166.
16 S.M. 1904, c. 41. Known as the southern district, its courts sat at Morden, a small community located south and west of Winnipeg near the Canada–United States border.
17 Winnipeg's population was approximately 10,000 fewer than that of Hamilton, the nation's fifth largest city.
18 *Manitoba Free Press,* 17 January 1908.

19 K.G. Pryke, 'Thomas Killam' in Francess G. Halpenny, ed., *Dictionary of Canadian Biography*, vol. 9 (Toronto: University of Toronto Press, 1976) 425.
20 George S. Brown, *Yarmouth, Nova Scotia: A Sequel to Campbell's History* (Boston: Rand Avery, 1888).
21 Robert M. Stamp, 'Adam Crooks' in Francess G. Halpenny & Jean Hamelin, eds., *Dictionary of Canadian Biography*, vol. 11 (Toronto: University of Toronto Press, 1982) 220.
22 Killam was admitted to the Law Society of Upper Canada on 28 August 1876 and called 5 February 1877. He was called in Manitoba on 15 February 1879.
23 David Burley, 'Arthur Wellington Ross' in Ramsay Cook, ed., *Dictionary of Canadian Biography*, vol. 13 (Toronto: University of Toronto Press, 1994) 898 and Ross, Ross & Killam, eds., *Important to Intending Settlers in Manitoba* (Winnipeg: Ross, Ross & Killam, 1879).
24 *Manitoba Free Press*, 24 January 1883, 4.
25 (1903) 2 Can. L. Rev. 656.
26 Telegram from Norquay to Macdonald, Macdonald Papers, MG 26A at 10099, PAM.
27 *Manitoba Free Press*, 31 January 1885, 2.
28 *Canadian Pacific Railway Company* v. *Municipality of Cornwallis* (1890), 7 Man. R. 1; *Gibbons* v. *Metcalfe*, [1905] 1 W.W.R. 139 (Man. C.A.); and *The Queen* v. *Riel* (1886), 2 Man. R. 321 (C.A.).
29 *Real Estate Loan Co.* v. *Molesworth* (1886), 3 Man. R. 116 at 132.
30 The Manitoba Court of Appeal was not established until 1906.
31 *McKenzie* v. *Fletcher* (1897), 11 Man. R. 540.
32 *Ibid.* at 545.
33 *Winnipeg and Hudson's Bay Co.* v. *Mann* (1890), 6 Man. R. 409.
34 *Ibid.* at 416.
35 *Re Logan Trusts* (1885), 3 Man. R. 49 at 54.
36 *Supra* note 10 at 130.
37 *Wellbrand* v. *Moore* (1885), 2 Man. R. 193 at 195.
38 *Regina* v. *Vrooman* (1886), 3 Man. R. 509 at 513.
39 (1890) 1 W.L.T. at 190 and *Mulvihill* v. *Lachance* (1890), 7 Man. R. 189 at 191.
40 *Boultbee* v. *Shore*, [1882] Temp. Wood 376 (Q.B.).
41 *Supra* note 29 at 136–7.
42 *Supra* note 25.
43 (1895) 6:8 W.L.T. 76.
44 (1895) 6:9 W.L.T. 81.
45 (1903) 30 Can. L.J. 497.
46 *The Railway Act*, 1903, C. 58, s. 8 and J. Castell Hopkins, *The Canadian*

Annual Review of Public Affairs 1903 (Toronto: Annual Review Publishing Co., 1904) at 430.

47 He and his wife, the youngest of three daughters born to Windsor contractor Robert A. Whyte and Mary Ann Whyte, were married for thirty-one years. They had two children. Their daughter Gladys predeceased her father by two years, while their son George Knight Killam was a member of a Winnipeg law firm at the time of his father's death. During the First World War George was attached to the headquarters of the Canadian Expeditionary Force in France, and for a time was on the staff of General Currie. After being wounded in 1918, he was awarded the Distinguished Service Order and promoted to major.

48 *Manitoba Free Press*, 2 March 1908, 1.

49 References to the Reverend William Bain in the *Presbyterian Record* and the archives of the United Church of Canada reflect the problem of relying on secondary sources. Bain is variously described as coming to Canada in 1834 or 1838 and as having died on 27 and 29 October 1889. See the *Presbyterian Record*, vol. 14, no. 12 (December 1889) 326 and records of the General Assembly of the Presbyterian Church in Canada, A & P 1890, appendix no. 27, p. I.

50 S.M. 1871, c. 10.

51 *Supra* note 26. Letter from Alexander Morris to John A. Macdonald, 5 December 1872, at 113933.

52 *Supra* note 10 at 89, quoting the *Manitoban News-Letter*, 3 June 1871.

53 The best discussion of the intimate relationship between Bain & Blanchard, particularly Blanchard, and the Hudson's Bay Company is contained in the two volumes of correspondence of the Company's Winnipeg land agent, Charles Brydges. See Hartwell Bowsfield, ed., *The Letters of Charles John Brydges 1879–1882* (Winnipeg: Hudson's Bay Record Society, 1977) and *The Letters of Charles John Brydges 1883–1889* (Winnipeg: Hudson's Bay Record Society, 1981).

54 *Supra* note 10 at 158.

55 *Ibid.* at 152–3.

56 *Supra* note 53, *1883–1889* at 110–11.

57 *Manitoba Free Press*, 9 March 1886, 4 and 10 March 1886, 4.

58 *Ibid.*, 7 November 1887, 4, quoting an article in a recent edition of the *Montreal Herald*.

59 *Re J.B., An Attorney* (1889), 6 Man. R. 19 at 27–8.

60 Sir William Buell Richards was Chief Justice of the Supreme Court of Canada from 8 October 1875 to 9 January 1879. His brother Albert Norton Richards was the Lieutenant-Governor of British Columbia, and a second

brother, Albert Elswood's father, was a prominent Ontario politician. His son was Stephen Elswood Richards.

61 The contest became heated when Gowan questioned the loyalty of his opponent's family during the rebellion of 1837.

62 Russ Disotell, *Brockville, the River City* (Toronto: Natural Heritage, 1997) 78.

63 Diaries of Robert Blackwood Graham, vol. 2 at 166–7, Robert Blackwood Graham Papers, PAM, MG 14 C109.

64 In 1880 Richards married Harriet Edith Henderson, the fourth daughter of a prominent Kingston lawyer. The couple had three sons and two daughters. One son became a member of the Manitoba Court of Appeal, another practised law in Winnipeg, while a third managed Edmonton's Northern Crown Bank. Both daughters married. The sixty-nine-year-old Richards was survived by his wife, children and mother.

65 Besides William Egerton, the Perdues were the parents of Henry, Thomas, John, and Mary. A detailed biography of each is located in the Bull Collection at the Brampton Public Library, MS 515, Reel 57.

66 The Perdue siblings included James, Thomas, Henry, William, Michael, and Prudence.

67 Details about the Perdue family's involvement in farming and exhibiting can be found in the Bull Collection, *supra* note 65.

68 Perdue and his teaching career are mentioned in Hilda Kirkwood, 'History of Education, a Most Interesting Story' in C.V. Charters, ed., *Brampton's 100th Anniversary as an Incorporated Town 1873–1973* (Brampton: Charters Publishing, 1973) 67 and in the Ferguson Papers, copies of which are located in the Brampton Public Library.

69 Perdue often spoke about his first interview with George Brown: *Winnipeg Free Press*, 18 January 1933, 4.

70 J. Ragnar Johnson, "Honourable W.E. Perdue, an Appreciation of an Eminent Jurist" (1933) 11 Can. Bar Rev. 199 at 200.

71 (1882) 2 Can. L.T. 428.

72 (1884) 1 Man. L.J. 175.

73 The men referred to are H.M. Howell, Hugh John Macdonald, Sir James Aikins, and Albert Elswood Richards. See Law Society of Manitoba, Minute Book 6, page 48 in Archive of Manitoba Legal-Judicial History, PAM.

74 *Re Nicholson & The Railway Commissioner* (1890), 6 Man. R. 419 at 423.

75 Mowbray Macdonnell Perdue articled with Robert Maxwell Dennistoun (later Chief Justice of Manitoba) between 5 October 1909 and 1 May 1912 and with Albert Blellock Hudson (later a justice of the Supreme Court of Canada) between 1 May 1912 and 5 October 1914.

76 (1903) 2 Canadian L. Rev. 667.

77 *Ibid.* at 668.

78 *Ibid.*
79 *Ibid.*
80 *Ibid.* at 668–9.
81 *Manitoba Free Press*, 24 November 1905, 2.
82 *A.* v. *A.* (1905), 15 Man. R. 483.
83 *Thomson* v. *Wishart* (1910), 19 Man. R. 340 at 348.
84 *Ibid.* at 349.
85 Perdue and his wife Mary were married on 9 January 1885. She was born in 1858 to Hugh James Macdonnell, Q.C., and Olivia Fairbanks, both of whose families were United Empire Loyalists. Robert Perdue was a lieutenant when he was killed in action. For details of the legal career of Mowbray Macdonnell Perdue, see the Archive of Manitoba Legal-Judicial History, Law Society of Manitoba member file P 1310, PAM. The couple's third son was Charles Egerton Perdue. Their daughter, Alice, married and resided in Winnipeg.
86 Comments of H.A. Bergman in (1930) 2:5 Man. Bar N. 4.
87 Christopher Mathers was born in the Town of Portadown, County Armagh, and his wife, Rachel Graham, in the Town of Inniskillen, County Fermanagh.
88 Mathers was appointed government railway solicitor in 1888.
89 Alan F.J. Artibise, *Winnipeg, a Social History of Urban Growth 1874–1914* (Montreal: McGill-Queen's University Press, 1975) at 31.
90 *Manitoba Free Press*, 23 August 1905, 1.
91 *In the Matter of Her Majesty's Counsel* (1892), 8 Man. R. 155.
92 *Manitoba Free Press*, 23 August 1905, 1.
93 *Manitoba Free Press*, 13 December 1899, 2.
94 Winnipeg newspaper (June 1909), Law Society of Manitoba scrapbook, Archive of Manitoba Legal-Judicial History, PAM.
95 *Emperor of Russia* v. *Proskouriakoff* (1907), 7 West. L.R. 766.
96 *Emperor of Russia* v. *Proskouriakoff* (1908), 8 West. L.R. 10 at 11.
97 *Ibid.* 461.
98 *Emperor of Russia* v. *Proskouriakoff* (1910), 42 S.C.R. 226.
99 *Re Fedorenko (No. 1)* (1910), 20 Man. R. 221.
100 *Re Fedorenko (No. 2)* (1910), 20 Man. R. 224.
101 *Rex* v. *Krafchenko* (1914), 24 Man. R. 652.
102 *Ibid.* at 659.
103 Charles Percy Plaxton, 'Has an Accused Person the Right to Make a Statement at His Trial without Being Sworn or Subject to Cross-Examination?' (1916) 52 Can. L.J. 10 at 17.
104 Murray Peden, *Hearken to the Evidence* (Stittsville, Ont.: Canada's Wings, 1983) at 16.

105 *Supra* note 101 at 670–1.
106 The commission consisted of Mathers, Dr J.R. Jones, and G.R. Crowe.
107 J. Castell Hopkins, ed., *The Canadian Annual Review of Public Affairs 1914* (Toronto: Annual Review Publishing Co., 1915) at 579. The commission consisted of Mathers as commissioner and his former partner, Edward Anderson, as prosecutor.
108 One of the most complete discussions of the background to the establishment of the commissions can be found in Morton, *supra* note 4.
109 *Kelly* v. *Mathers et al.* (1915), 25 Man. R. 580.
110 *Winnipeg Telegram*, 9 October 1915, quoted in J. Castell Hopkins, ed., *The Canadian Annual Review of Public Affairs 1915* (Toronto: Annual Review Publishing Co., 1916) at 639.
111 For an overview of the work of both commissions see David Jay Bercuson, *Confrontation at Winnipeg* (Montreal: McGill-Queen's University Press, 1974) c. 5.
112 Sue Buchanan, *Canadian Federal and Provincial Royal Commissions* (Vancouver: University of British Columbia Library, 1968). See also Lise Maillet, *Provincial Royal Commissions and Commissions of Inquiry, 1867–1982: A Selective Bibliography* (Ottawa: National Library of Canada, 1986); James Murray Whalen, ed., *Records of Federal Royal Commissions (RG 33)*, 2 vols. (Ottawa: National Archives of Canada, 1990, 1994); and George Fletcher Henderson, *Federal Royal Commissions in Canada 1867–1966, a Checklist* (Toronto: University of Toronto Press, 1967) at 94 and 97.
113 The commission was established on 4 April 1919 and its members appointed five days later.
114 *Supra* note 112, Buchanan at 236.
115 *Supra* note 96 at 12.
116 *Supra* note 94, Winnipeg newspaper, 15 April 1908.
117 *Re P.E.H.* (1912), 22 Man. R. 746.
118 B.E. Chaffey, *Legal Ethics, Address by The Hon. T.G. Mathers, Chief Justice of The Court of King's Bench, Manitoba* (Winnipeg: Law Society of Manitoba, 1920) at 22.
119 *Ibid.* at 29.
120 *Ibid.* at 11.
121 *Penman et al.* v. *Winnipeg Electric Railway Company (No. 2)*, [1925] 1 W.W.R. 156.
122 Wallace Johnson, 'Damages for Nervous Shock' (1939) 11:7 Man. Bar N. 49 at 50–1.
123 *Kowhanko* v. *The J.H. Tremblay Company, Limited et al.* (1919), 30 Man. R. 198 at 244–5.

124 *Grain Claims Bureau, Limited* v. *Canadian Surety Company* (1928), 37 Man. R. 235 at 244–5.

125 The Matherses were the parents of Marguerite and Francis Graham. Although little is known about Marguerite, Francis was born in 1894 and educated in Ontario at the Tuckwell School, Trinity College, and the Uni-versity of Toronto. When the First World War started he was a third-year arts student, but he soon left school to join the Canadian armed forces. On 19 February 1916 he was posted to France, where he served as a lieu-tenant with the Cameron Highlanders. He was wounded in action on three separate occasions before being transferred to the Royal Flying Corps. He trained in England as an observer and then returned to France, where he served until February 1918. The war ended shortly after he finished pilot training in Canada. While serving overseas he was granted his Bach-elor of Arts degree *in absentia* by the University of Toronto. When the war ended he became a student-at-law in Manitoba, and in 1920 was called to the provincial bar. A year later he became an assistant to Attorney General Thomas H. Johnson, but he soon returned to private practice and joined the firm of Green & Mathers. In 1929 he left to work with B.V. Rich-ardson, who specialized in estate analysis, business insurance, succession duties, and income tax. Among the firm's largest clients was the Canada Life Insurance Company. Thomas Graham Mathers, the son of Francis, was also a lawyer. He practised law for a time before entering the business world and in 1984 he was made a vice-president of Spar Aero-space.

126 *Manitoba Free Press*, 17 August 1927, 5.

127 Law Society of Manitoba member file of Thomas Graham Mathers, file P 1288, Archive of Manitoba Legal-Judicial History, PAM.

128 *Supra* note 104 at 17 and 18.

129 Macdonald's mother was Mary McRae.

130 *Supra* note 73, Law Society of Manitoba Minute Book 6, p. 49.

131 *Ibid.* at 202.

132 *Supra* note 127, Law Society of Manitoba member file P 1283.

133 (1937) 10 Man. Bar N. 474.

134 Diaries of Robert Blackwood Graham, MG 14 C109, microfiche 329, roll 4, p. 104–5, PAM.

135 *Ibid.* at 106 and 108, entry for 1 November 1937.

Chapter 5

1 Margaret McWilliams, *Manitoba Milestones* (Toronto: J.M. Dent, 1928) at 179–80.

2 Dale & Lee Gibson, *Substantial Justice: Law and Lawyers in Manitoba 1670–1970* (Winnipeg: Peguis, 1972) at 200.
3 *Ibid.* at 226.
4 (1919) 39 Can. L.T. 28 at 29–30.
5 Speech by Travers Sweatman in Alan F.J. Artibise, 'An Urban Economy: Patterns of Economic Change in Winnipeg, 1873–1971' (1976) 2 Prairie Forum 163 at 178.
6 *Ibid.*
7 John Cameron Sr died after falling down his basement stairs on 15 August 1908. His wife, Elizabeth Ross, born in 1825, had died on 10 April 1899. The oldest of their five children was Mary, born in 1857. John was born two years later, and Emma, Jane, and George thereafter. George died on 17 March 1891 and Emma, at age twenty-three, on 30 October 1879. Much of the information about the Cameron family is in the John Cameron Family file located in the Local History Collection of the Woodstock Public Library. Additional information was obtained from census reports and various issues of the *Woodstock Sentinel-Review*.
8 The anecdote is related by Dale Gibson in 'An Anecdotal Sample' in Cameron Harvey, ed., *The Law Society of Manitoba 1877–1977* (Winnipeg: Peguis Publishers, 1977) 191 at 205.
9 E.R. Cameron in (1923) May *University of Toronto Monthly* 398.
10 (1923) 1 Can. Bar Rev. 298.
11 Cameron was re-elected in the general election on 23 July 1892. He was then re-elected in a by-election on 20 January 1893, before being defeated in a general election on 7 December 1899. He served as provincial secretary from 10 January 1893 to 17 November 1896, as minister of municipal affairs from 13 January 1893 until 6 January 1900, and as attorney general from 17 November 1896 until the Greenway government resigned on 6 January 1900.
12 J. Castell Hopkins, ed., *The Canadian Annual Review of Public Affairs for 1906* (Toronto: Annual Review Publishing Co., 1907) at 444.
13 W.L. Morton, *One University: A History of the University of Manitoba 1877–1952* (Toronto: McClelland & Stewart, 1957) at 75.
14 (1923) 1 Can. Bar Rev. 873 at 875.
15 (1923) 1 Can. Bar Rev. 298 at 299.
16 *Supra* note 14 at 873–4.
17 *Ibid.* at 875.
18 *Ibid.*
19 *Ibid.*
20 *Supra* note 2 at 200 and 239.

21 *Kelly* v. *Kelly* (1923), 23 W.L.R. 953 at 957.
22 *The British America Elevator Company Limited* v. *Bank of British North America*, [1919] 2 W.W.R. 748 at 751.
23 *Attorney-General for Manitoba* v. *Kelly*, [1922] 1 A.C. 268 at 279.
24 *Supra* note 15 at 299.
25 John Donald Cameron, 'Codes and Codification' (1917) 37 Can. L.T. 177.
26 *Ibid.* at 188.
27 *Ibid.* at 192.
28 *Ibid.* at 192 and 195.
29 John Donald Cameron, 'International Treaties in Relation to Legislative Powers' (1922) 42 Can. L.T. 10.
30 On 29 June 1920 Rogers became the first woman elected to the Legislative Assembly of Manitoba. She was re-elected on 18 July 1922 and 28 June 1927, but did not run in the election of 16 June 1932. Rogers was a Liberal from Winnipeg.
31 Manitoba newspaper, 27 March 1923, Law Society of Manitoba scrapbook, Archive of Manitoba Legal-Judicial History, PAM.
32 *Supra* note 15 at 299.
33 Thomas Llewellyn Metcalfe's father, Thomas Hatton Metcalfe, was born in Little York (Toronto) on 4 November 1836 and died shortly before his son at the age of eighty-two. He was of English descent. His mother, Eliza Hatton, was born in County Wicklow, Ireland, and died in the family home at Portage in 1914 when she was seventy-eight. The couple farmed in the Rural Municipality of Oakland before moving to Portage la Prairie. They had four children: Thomas, William, Charles, and George.
34 Macdonald and Howell became chief justice of Manitoba and Aikins the province's lieutenant-governor.
35 For details about Bonnar see Roy St George Stubbs, 'Robert Andrew Bonnar, K.C.' (1937) 10 Man. Bar N. 497.
36 *Manitoba Free Press*, 12 March 1920.
37 Law Society of Manitoba Minute Book 6, pp. 124 and 202, and Minute Book 7, p. 69, Archive of Manitoba Legal-Judicial History, PAM.
38 For mention of his father's political career, see J.H. Metcalfe's *The Tread of the Pioneers* (Portage la Prairie: Portage la Prairie and District Old Timers' Association, 1932) at 196. Metcalfe's career is described in the *Manitoba Free Press*, 10 October 1899, 5; 6 December 1899, 6; and 13 December 1899, 2.
39 For a brief summary of the work and mandate of the fisheries commission see J. Castell Hopkins, ed., *The Canadian Annual Review of Public Affairs 1909* (Toronto: Annual Review Publishing Co., 1910) at 479.

40 *Manitoba Free Press*, 4 January 1929.
41 *Andrew* v. *Kilgour* (1909), 19 Man. R. 545.
42 *Ibid.* at 546–7.
43 Most accounts of the strike discuss its background and Metcalfe's role in the trials that followed its conclusion. The accounts used in the present discussion include W.L. Morton, *Manitoba: A History* (Toronto: University of Toronto Press, 1957); Donald Avery, 'The Radical Alien and the Winnipeg General Strike' in J.M. Bumsted, ed., *Interpreting Canada's Past*, vol. 2, *After Confederation* (Toronto: Oxford University Press, 1986) 222; Desmond H. Brown, 'The Craftsmanship of Bias: Sedition and the Winnipeg Strike Trial 1919' (1984) 14 Man. L.J. 1; and Jack Walker, with Duncan Fraser, *The Great Canadian Sedition Trials: The Courts and the Winnipeg General Strike 1919–1920* (Winnipeg: Legal Research Institute of the University of Manitoba and the Canadian Legal History Project, 2004).
44 *Ibid.* Brown at 32.
45 Metcalfe's friend was Dr W.H. Reid.
46 *Manitoba Free Press*, 3 April 1922, 1 at 2.
47 J.S. Walker Oral Histories, tape 24, side 1, PAM.
48 *Ibid.* Tape 26, side 2.
49 *Ibid.* Tape 22, side 2.
50 Last Will and Testament of Thomas Llewellyn Metcalfe, PAM.
51 For a description of Prendergast and his career see Roy St George Stubbs, *Lawyers and Laymen of Western Canada* (Toronto: Ryerson, 1939) 100. Much of the detail presented by the author was supplied by Prendergast personally.
52 A.J. Andrews, 'Jurist and Gentleman' (1945) 17 Man. Bar N. 31.
53 Letter from Hugh John Macdonald to Sir John A. Macdonald (4 May 1890) in Sir John A. Macdonald Papers at 253293, NAC.
54 *Supra* note 51 at 105.
55 Prendergast was elected by acclamation in a by-election held on 24 August 1885. He was re-elected in La Verendrye in a general election held on 9 December 1886 and in Woodlands in a general election held on 11 July 1888. He was then re-elected in St Boniface in general elections held on 23 July 1892 and 15 January 1896. Prendergast resigned as provincial secretary on 31 August 1889.
56 *Supra* note 51 at 104 and 106.
57 Virginia R. Robson, ed., *Debates about Canada's Future 1868–1896* (Toronto: Ontario Institute for Studies in Education, 1977) at 101.
58 Alexander Begg, *History of the North-West*, vol. 3 (Toronto: Hunter, Rose, 1895) at 335.

59 Undated Winnipeg newspaper column entitled 'I First Saw' in a scrapbook located in the Herbert Walker Papers, MG 16 B7, PAM.

60 *Ibid.*

61 For more information about the role Prendergast played in the controversy, see J. Castell Hopkins, ed., *The Canadian Annual Review of Public Affairs for 1906* (Toronto: Annual Review Publishing Co., 1907) at 466–8; *Re Prince Albert City Provincial Election. Strachan* v. *Lamont* (1906), 3 W.L.R. 571 (Q.B.) 4 W.L.R. 411 (C.A.); and *Rex* v. *Sinclair* (1906), 4 W.L.R. 374.

62 J. Castell Hopkins, ed., *The Canadian Annual Review of Public Affairs for 1916* (Toronto: Annual Review Publishing Co., 1917) at 667.

63 *Ibid.* at 667 and *supra* note 51 at 119.

64 George Fletcher Henderson, *Federal Royal Commissions in Canada 1867–1966, a Checklist* (Toronto: University of Toronto Press, 1967) at 42.

65 Lise Maillet, *Provincial Royal Commissions and Commissions of Inquiry, 1867–1982: A Selective Bibliography* (Ottawa: National Library of Canada, 1986) at 123.

66 Prendergast was appointed chief justice on 10 January 1930, and retired 18 March 1944.

67 William Parker Fillmore, Q.C., 'The Lighter Side of the Law' (1973) 39 Man. Bar N. 114 at 118.

68 *Supra* note 51 at 120.

69 *Winnipeg Free Press*, 1 April 1944.

70 (1944) 16 Man. Bar N. 25.

71 1971 taped interview with Provincial Judge Ian Dubienski, File A2404, PAM. Dubienski practised law when Prendergast was on the bench and regarded him as lazy.

72 Mark Shinbane, Law Society of Manitoba, in Archive of Manitoba Legal-Judicial History, PAM.

73 *Supra* note 2 at 282.

74 Prendergast married Olivina, daughter of Joliette, Quebec's François Mondar, on 29 July 1886. The two had four sons and seven daughters.

75 James Emile Pierre Prendergast member file, Law Society of Manitoba, Archive of Manitoba Legal-Judicial History, PAM.

76 *Supra* note 2 at 201.

77 Prendergast died in the St Boniface General Hospital at 3:25 a.m. on 18 April 1945.

78 Haultain also became the first chief justice of Saskatchewan.

79 *Regina Leader Post*, 6 August 1896, quoted in Lee Gibson, *A Proud Heritage, The First Hundred Years of Aikins, MacAulay and Thorvaldson* (Winnipeg: Aikins, MacAulay and Thorvaldson, 1993) at 53–4.

80 *Supra* note 67 at 119.

81 Robson joined the Aikins firm in 1899.

82 Dale Brawn, *Manitoba Litigants and Their Law Suits, 1909–1939: Quantitative Patterns and Results* (LL.M. thesis, University of Manitoba, 1995) [unpublished]. Corporate defendants seldom lose because they are more likely to settle out of court than are individual defendants, who often have little to induce a plaintiff to discontinue an action.

83 J. Castell Hopkins, ed., *The Canadian Annual Review of Public Affairs for 1908* (Toronto: Annual Review Publishing Co., 1909) at 457.

84 J. Castell Hopkins, ed., *The Canadian Annual Review of Public Affairs for 1910* (Toronto: Annual Review Publishing Co., 1911) at 512–13.

85 *Re Fedorenko* (No. 2) (1910), 20 Man. R. 224.

86 *Supra* note 65 at 120.

87 'Report of Royal Commission on Charges Re Vice and Of Graft Against the Police' in Alan F.J. Artibise, ed., *Gateway City: Documents on the City of Winnipeg 1873–1913* (Winnipeg: Manitoba Record Society, 1979) c. 10; and Alan F.J. Artibise, *Winnipeg, a Social History of Urban Growth 1874–1914* (Montreal: McGill-Queen's University Press, 1975) at 260–1.

88 *Manitoba Free Press*, 24 May 1912, 4.

89 *Ibid.*

90 *The Public Utilities Act*, S.M. 1912, c. 66.

91 J. Castell Hopkins, ed., *The Canadian Annual Review of Public Affairs for 1914* (Toronto: Annual Review Publishing Co., 1915) at 578.

92 *An Act to amend 'The Law Society Act,'* S.M. 1915, c. 37, s. 8 (2).

93 C. Ian Kyer & Jerome E. Bickenbach, *The Fiercest Debate: Cecil A. Wright, the Benchers, and Legal Education in Ontario 1923–1957* (Toronto: Osgoode Society, 1987) at 62–3.

94 Hugh Amos Robson & J.B. Hugg, *Cases on Company Law* (Toronto: Carswell, 1916) and *Leading Cases on Public Corporations* (Toronto: Carswell, 1916).

95 *Ibid. Leading Cases*, Preface.

96 *Ibid.* at 9.

97 *Ibid.* at 30.

98 *Ibid.* at 33.

99 Hugh Amos Robson & J.B. Hugg, *Municipal Manual, Being a Complete Annotation of the Ontario Municipal Act and Commentary on Certain Analogous Sections of the Municipal Acts of the Other Provinces* (Toronto: Carswell, 1920). The only other works by judges of comparable quality and reputation were Thomas Wardlaw Taylor's *Investigation of Titles to Estates in Fee Simple* (Toronto: Adam, Stevenson & Co., 1869) and Esten

K. Williams, *Notes on The Canadian Law of Landlord and Tenant as Applied to Corporeal Hereditaments* (Toronto: Carswell, 1922).

100 *Supra* note 2 at 249.

101 Hugh Amos Robson, 'Company Law' (1916) 36 Can. L.T. 861.

102 J. Castell Hopkins, ed., *The Canadian Annual Review of Public Affairs for 1915* (Toronto: Annual Review Publishing Co., 1916) at 627–30.

103 *Manitoba Free Press*, 3 September 1915, 2.

104 Kenneth McNaught & David J. Bercuson, *The Winnipeg Strike: 1919* (Don Mills, Ont.: Longman Canada, 1974) 101.

105 *Ibid.* at 16.

106 *Royal Commission Report of H. A. Robson, K.C. Commissioner* (Winnipeg: King's Printer, 1919) at 4–5.

107 *Ibid.* at 9–10.

108 *Ibid.* at 13.

109 Tom Traves, *The State and Enterprise: Canadian Manufacturers and the Federal Government, 1917–1931* (Toronto: University of Toronto Press, 1979) c. 4.

110 *The Board of Commerce Act*, S.C. 1919, c. 37 and *The Combines and Fair Prices Act, 1919*, S.M. 1919, c. 45.

111 J. Castell Hopkins, ed., *The Canadian Annual Review of Public Affairs for 1919* (Toronto: Annual Review Publishing Co., 1920) at 335.

112 *Ibid.* at 335–6.

113 *Manitoba Free Press*, 3 March 1920, 1 and the [Toronto] *Globe*, 3 March 920, 1.

114 *Globe*, 4 March 1920, 6.

115 Robert James McFall, 'Regulation of Business in Canada' (1922) 37 Pol. Sc. Quart. 177 at 207.

116 Hugh Amos Robson, speech to Canadian Bar Association, (1922) 7 Can. Bar Assoc. Proc. 240 at 241.

117 *Ibid.* at 244.

118 For a summary of Robson's views about fusion, and a description of his political career, see John Kendle, *John Bracken, A Political Biography* (Toronto: University of Toronto Press, 1979).

119 Letter from Robson to Prime Minister Mackenzie King, 5 April 1927, in Mackenzie King Papers, box 147, series J1, item 125552, NAC.

120 Letter from Bracken to Robson, 6 March 1929, in John Bracken Papers, MG 13 I1, BP, file Coalition 1929–36, folder 1929, box 4, PAM.

121 *Supra* note 118 at 105.

122 Hugh Amos Robson member file, Law Society of Manitoba, file P 1319, interview of Mark Shinbane, Archive of Manitoba Legal-Judicial History, PAM.

123 *Ibid*. Letter from H.A. Bergman to Ralph Maybank, 28 March 1944. Robson was appointed to the Manitoba Court of Appeal on 31 December 1929, and transferred to the Court of King's Bench on 18 March 1944

124 (1932) 2 Fortnightly L.J. 120.

125 'The Honourable Sir James Albert Manning Aikins, K.C.' (1929) 7 Can. Bar Rev. 266; 'Edward Ludlow Wetmore' (1944) 22 Can. Bar Rev. 442; 'Sir Frederick Haultain' (1944) 22 Can. Bar Rev. 643; and 'Hon. Horace Thomas McGuire' (1945) 23 Can. Bar Rev. 139.

126 Robson was survived by his wife, four daughters, two sons, two sisters and three grandchildren. Fannie Robson's interest in public affairs very nearly equalled that of her husband. At the time of her death in 1950 she was the honorary president of the provincial missionary society of the Presbyterian church and of the Ladies Aid Society of the First Presbyterian Church. She was also an alumnus of the Canadian Club, the Women's Music Club, and the women's auxiliary of the Canadian National Institute for the Blind, and during the First World War was a volunteer visitor for the Manitoba Patriotic Fund and active supporter of the work of the Red Cross. One of the Robson's sons followed in his father's footsteps. Hugh Laidlaw Robson earned a B.A. and LL.B. from the University of Manitoba, articled with C.P. Wilson, and after receiving his Ontario call in 1930 became legal counsel to the Imperial Bank of Canada. Ten years later he joined the Canadian Bankers Association, retiring in 1968. His sister Jean was both a lawyer and the wife of the dean of the Manitoba Law School. Jean Robson succeeded in establishing her own identity within the legal profession. She was an active member of the Canada Welfare Council, and the author of a brochure entitled 'Welfare Legislation in Canada.' In it she reproduced federal and provincial laws relating to unemployment, public health, juvenile delinquency, and domestic relations and other laws connected to welfare legislation. Her work brought her into contact with Ottawa's Charlotte Whitten and the two became close friends. During the Second World War another of Robson's daughters, Kathleen, served in the Royal Navy at Lowestoft, England, as a first officer with the Women's Royal Naval Service.

127 Roger Hall & Nick Whistler, 'John Galt' in Francess G. Halpenny & Jean Hamelin, eds., *Dictionary of Canadian Biography*, vol. 7 (Toronto: University of Toronto Press, 1988) 335 at 336.

128 G.A.G., 'Sir Thomas Galt (1815–1901)' in Charles G.D. Roberts & Arthur L. Tunnell, eds., *A Standard Dictionary of Canadian Biography* (Toronto: Trans-Canada Press, 1934) 209 at 210.

129 G.A.G., 'George Frederick Galt' in Charles G.D. Roberts & Arthur L.

Tunnell, eds., *A Standard Dictionary of Canadian Biography* (Toronto: Trans-Canada Press, 1934) at 208.

130 Archives of the University of Toronto, file A73-0026/112(69).

131 Law Society of Manitoba Minute Book 7 at 70, Archive of Manitoba Legal-Judicial History, PAM.

132 *Ibid.* Minute Book 8 at 45.

133 'Common Carriers of Ontario' (1886) 22 Can. L.J. 293, 314.

134 *Ibid.* at 293.

135 'The Principle of Subrogation' (1891) 11 Can. L.T. 9.

136 *Ibid.* at 19.

137 'Priorities Under Registry Act' (1891) 27 Can. L.J. 98.

138 'Editorial Review, Notice by Registration' (1891) 11 Can. L.T. 23 at 26.

139 'The Principle of Subrogation: A Reply' (1891) 11 Can. L.T. 89.

140 'Set-off By Contributories' (1891) 11 Can. L. Times 264.

141 'The Power of Sale Without Notice' (1893) 13 Can. L.T. 36.

142 'Mortgagees' Rights Under the Statute of Limitations' (1893) 13 Can. L.T. 85.

143 'Rights and Remedies in a Foreclosure Action' (1893) 29 Can. L.J. 312.

144 *Ibid.* at 320.

145 *Supra* note 142 for example.

146 (1895) 31 Can. L.J. 523.

147 *Ibid.* at 524.

148 'Liabilities of Trade Unions and Their Members' (1903) 2 Can. L. Rev. 627 and 'Right of a Third Party Under a Contract Inter Alios' (1905) 4 Can. L. Rev. 364.

149 'Appeals to the Privy Council' (1921) 41 Can. L.T. 168.

150 *Ibid.* at 168.

151 *Ibid.* at 170.

152 *Ibid.* at 172.

153 *Theo. Noel Co.* v. *Vitae Ore Co.* (1908), 17 Man. R. 319 at 328.

154 *Rex* v. *Gudmondson* (1933), 41 Man. R. 87 (C.A.).

155 *Ibid.* at 94.

156 *Rex* v. *Duguay* (1933), 41 Man. R. 211 at 212 (C.A.).

157 Alexander Casimir Galt member file, Law Society of Manitoba, file P 1249, Archive of Manitoba Legal-Judicial History, PAM.

158 *Complin* v. *Beggs* (1913), 24 Man. R. 596 at 618.

159 *In Re Fenton Estate* (1921), 30 Man. R. 246 at 257 (C.A.).

160 *Newton & Company* v. *Wolvin et al* (1930), 39 Man. R. 285 at 298 (C.A.).

161 (1927) 36 Man. R. 482.

162 A year before he presided over the Agricultural College Commission Galt was one of three judges appointed commissioners to investigate

charges levied by Conservative politicians that the Norris government had ac-cepted $50,000 in bribes when it took office, an accusation the commission concluded was groundless.

163 *Winnipeg Telegram*, 22 September 1916.

164 *Winnipeg Post*, 23 September 1916.

165 The interim report was released on 26 January 1917 and the final report on 25 May 1917.

166 The 'Commission to Inquire Into Reports of Mr. Justice Galt of Manitoba Against the Honourable Robert Rogers, Minister of Public Works,' was established on 6 June 1917.

167 *Manitoba Free Press*, 8 June 1917.

168 *Montreal Gazette*, 1 August 1917.

169 Interview with Joseph Thorson in Jack S. Walker Oral Histories, Tape 24, PAM.

170 *Ibid.* interview with William Parker Fillmore, Tape 26, side 2.

171 *Supra* note 157. Anecdote of Mark Shinbane.

172 In 1885 Galt had married Ella Grace Vivian of Toronto. The two had four sons and two daughters. One son was a lieutenant when killed in active duty during the First World War, and his daughter Cecily was awarded the Mons Star and the Royal Red Cross (second class) for her efforts as a Nursing Sister. Cecily was a graduate of the Montreal General Hospital and had joined the war effort the day war was declared, and by November 1914 was already stationed in France. Galt was survived by two sons, a daughter, three sisters, and two brothers.

173 Curran's father served in Southampton (1859–66), St Mary's (1866–70), Walkerton (1870–4), the diocese of North Carolina (1874–6), Stratford (1876–82), and Huntingford (1882–4) and from 1884 to 1886 was the rector of Adelaide. For a brief summary of his career, see *Crockford's Clerical Directory* for 1891.

174 Richard A. Willie, *'These Legal Gentlemen': Lawyers in Manitoba: 1839–1900* (Winnipeg: Legal Research Institute of the University of Manitoba, 1994) at 173–4.

175 John Philpot Curran member file, Law Society of Manitoba, file P 123, Affidavit of John Philpot Curran dated 28 May 1894, Archive of Manitoba Legal-Judicial History, PAM.

176 *Ibid.* Interview with Joseph Thorson.

177 In 1907 and 1910 he was last. The winner on the second occasion, with 144 votes, was his partner, G.R. Coldwell. See Law Society of Manitoba Minute Book 7, p. 71 and Minute Book 8, p. 46, Archive of Manitoba Legal-Judicial History, PAM.

178 *Manitoba Free Press*, 1 April 1914.
179 *Manitoba Free Press*, 26 January 1918, 4.
180 *Ibid.*
181 *Supra* note 175.
182 *Ibid.* Recollections of Billy Perkins and Joseph Thorson.
183 Robert Blackwood Graham Papers, MG 14 C109, diary at 165–4, PAM.
184 *Ibid.* at 166.
185 *Ibid.* at 169.
186 *Ibid.*
187 *Ibid.* at 170.
188 *Ibid.* at 174.
189 *Supra* note 65.
190 *Supra* note 62 at 650
191 Despite his many shortcomings there was no evidence to suggest that Curran did not have a reasonably content family life. In 1883 he married Emily Grant Hayden, the daughter of a prominent post office official. The couple were parents of Sarah Helen, Hayden, John Philpot Jr, Robert Emmett, Veysie, and Lionel Edward. The latter two sons were twins.

Chapter 6

1 Dale & Lee Gibson, *Substantial Justice: Law and Lawyers in Manitoba 1670–1970* (Winnipeg: Peguis, 1972) at 238.
2 (1933) 2 Fortnightly L.J. 194.
3 Undated newspaper column 'I First Saw,' Herbert Walter scrapbook, MG 16 B7, PAM.
4 Dysart was admitted on 25 June 1906 and called 26 November 1906.
5 Much of the information available about Dysart comes from Roy St George Stubbs's biography of him in *Prairie Portraits* (Toronto: McClelland & Stewart, 1954) 119.
6 Of his seven cases four were heard by the Court of Appeal. He was successful three times.
7 The Dysarts were married on 2 September 1908.
8 Claire Dysart was thirty-one when she died.
9 *Rex* v. *Oak Bluff School Division* (1937), 45 Man. R. 409.
10 *Ibid.* at 417.
11 *Supra* note 5 at 129. Quote from *Blanchett* v. *Hansell et al* (1945), 45 Man. R. 1.
12 Dysart's decision is described in Louis Blom-Cooper, ed., *The Language of the Law: An Anthology of Legal Prose* (New York: Macmillan, 1965) at 349.
13 *Mitchell* v. *Martin and Rose*, [1925] 1 W.W.R. 500 at 501.

14 *Supra* note 5 at 131.
15 *O'Leary et al.* v. *Smith* (1924), 34 Man. R. 386 at 389.
16 *Supra* note 5 at 136.
17 (1939) 8 Fortnightly L.J. 209.
18 George Fletcher Henderson, *Federal Royal Commissions in Canada 1867–1966, A Checklist* (Toronto: University of Toronto Press, 1967) at 124 and 126; James Murray Whalen, ed., *Records of Federal Royal Commissions (RG 33)*, vol. 1 (Ottawa: National Archives of Canada, 1944) at 115–19; and Lise Maillet, *Provincial Royal Commissions and Commissions of Inquiry, 1867–1982: A Selective Bibliography* (Ottawa: National Library of Canada, 1986) at 125.
19 *Supra* note 5 at 137.
20 His majority decisions included *Humphrey Motors Limited* v. *Joseph Ells*, [1935] S.C.R. 249; *Century Indemnity Company* v. *Northwestern Utilities Limited*, [1935] S.C.R. 291; *Robert W. Maguire* v. *Northland Drug Company, Limited*, [1935] S.C.R. 412; *Ross Mason* v. *His Majesty The King*, [1935] S.C.R. 513; *General Dairies, Limited* v. *Maritime Electric Company, Limited*, [1935] S.C.R. 519; and *J.P. McLaughlin* v. *Isaac W.C. Solloway and Harvey Mills*, [1936] S.C.R. 127. Dysart's minority judgments included *Carl Schwartzenhauer* v. *His Majesty The King*, [1935] S.C.R. 367; *Yetta Weiss and Morris Weiss* v. *The State Life Insurance Company*, [1935] S.C.R. 461; and *The Southern Canada Power Company Ltd.* v. *His Majesty The King*, S.C.R. 4.
21 The Dysarts were the parents of two sons, Knox and Forrester, and a daughter Cecelia. Knox became a prominent lawyer in his own right and eventually joined the legal department of the Canadian National Railway.
22 Alan was born on 1 August 1857 and died on 4 April 1928. His father, the Reverend John Evans Adamson, was married to Harriet A. Adamson. The father of Alan's wife Julia was Robert Turriff.
23 Adamson was admitted to the Law Society at a bencher meeting held on 19 June 1907 (Minute Book 7, p. 80). He articled with Kelly from 1 May 1907 to 24 November 1908; with Hobkirk from 3 December 1908 to 29 March 1909; and with Robson from 29 March 1909 until he was called in 1910.
24 Christopher Arthur Adamson was born on 17 April 1887 and died 6 May 1940. He was called to the Manitoba bar on 27 September 1911 and became managing director of the Western Trust Company in 1916.
25 Finkelstein Papers, MG 14, C77, PAM.
26 Minutes of a joint meeting of Law Society benchers and the executive of the Manitoba Bar Association held on 28 April 1922, in John Evans Adamson member file, Law Society of Manitoba, file P 1201, archive of Manitoba Legal-Judicial History, PAM.

27 *Ibid.* at 2.
28 *Winnipeg Tribune*, 5 May 1922, 1.
29 *Ibid.*
30 Ralph Maybank Papers, MG 14 B35, PAM.
31 *Supra* note 26.
32 *Ibid.* Letter from Frank Simpson to James Coyne, 6 May 1922, PAM.
33 *Ibid.* Letter from Robert Jacob to J. A. MacVicar, 9 May 1922, PAM.
34 *Supra* note 30.
35 *Ibid.* Letter from J.K. Sparling to Col. H. J. Riley, 13 May 1922, PAM.
36 *Manitoba Free Press*, 10 May 1922.
37 *Supra* note 30. Letter from F.H. Bell to W. Redford Mulock, 11 May 1922, PAM.
38 *Ibid.* Interview with Mark Shinbane. See also comments of County Court judge Walter J. Lindal in Walter J. Lindal Papers, MG 14 B78, box 3, PAM.
39 *Supra* note 31, box 4, file 78.
40 *Supra* note 26 Winnipeg newspaper, 15 March 1928.
41 *Winnipeg Free Press*, 14 June 1960.
42 *Supra* note 26. Interview with Shinbane.
43 *Ibid.* Interview with James Wilson.
44 *Union Bank of Canada* v. *Turner* (1922), 32 Man. R. 435 at 436 (C.A.).
45 *Black* v. *Stebnicki* (1930), 39 Man. R. 123 at 128–9 (C.A.).
46 *Ratcliffe* v. *Whitehead*, [1933] 3 W.W.R. 447 (Man. Q.B.).
47 *Ibid.* at 448.
48 *Wasney* v. *Jurazsky* (1933), 41 Man. R. 46 at 50 (C.A.).
49 *Winnipeg Tribune*, 6 March 1961.
50 (1938) 10 Man. Bar N. 533 at 535, referring to *Stebbe* v. *Laird*, [1938] 1 W.W.R. 173 (Man. Q.B.).
51 *Thomas* v. *Thomas* (1946), 53 Man. R. 210 at 211–12.
52 *Supra* note 43.
53 *Supra* note 38 Lindal Papers.
54 *Supra* note 26. Interview with Joseph Thorson, Adamson file.
55 *An Amendment to the British North America Act, 1867*, S.C. 1960, vol. 1, Prefix to Statutes, at 5.
56 Adamson was survived by four daughters, eight grandchildren, and four great-grandchildren. An only son, Alan, died in infancy. The father of his wife Mary was John Gillanders Turriff, the son of Robert Turriff and Jane Gillanders. John was born in Little Metis, Quebec, on 14 December 1855. He married Mary's mother, Eva Louise Josephine Bartlette Buchanan, on 1 October 1884. Mary died in 1973. The Adamsons' daughters were Mrs S.G. Pugh and Mrs John M. Hunt of Winnipeg, Mrs T.N. Dickson of

Ottawa, and Mrs M.O. Bidwell of Chicago. Mrs Hunt's husband was appointed to the Court of Queen's Bench in 1966.

57 John W. Kilgour was thirty-four when he, his thirty-one-year-old wife, and James moved to Guelph, where the rest of their children were born. David joined the actuarial department of North American Life when he was twenty-two. Eleven years later he became the company's official actuary and an active member of the British Institute of Actuaries and the Actuarial Society of America. He was for many years the honorary secretary of the Canadian Life Insurance Officers Association, and was the organization's president in 1923. In 1928 he was appointed general manager of North American Life. Three years later he became a member of its board of directors, and in 1930 the company's president.

58 For reference to Kilgour's academic performance and Clara Brett Martin's difficulties in gaining admission to the Law Society, see (1896) 2 Barrister 209. For mention of Kilgour's involvement in student affairs, see (1895) 1 Barrister 478. *The Barrister* was the official organ of the Osgoode Legal and Literary Society

59 By the time Kilgour went to the bench, the firm of Kilgour, Laidlaw & Buckingham had become Kilgour, Foster & McQuarrie.

60 *Manitoba Free Press*, 28 November 1931, 11.

61 *Manitoba Free Press*, 28 November 1931, 4.

62 Law Society Minute Book 7, p. 71, Archive of Manitoba Legal-Judicial History, PAM.

63 Law Society Minute Book 8, p. 46, *ibid.*

64 Law Society Minute Book 10, p. 96, *ibid.*

65 John Kilgour's tenure on Guelph's municipal council is described in Leo A. Johnson's *History of Guelph 1827–1927* (Guelph: Guelph Historical Society, 1977) at 367. For James Kilgour see *Manitoba Free Press*, 28 November 1931, 4.

66 *Supra* note 61.

67 *Zeidel* v. *Winnipeg Electric Company* (1928), 37 Man. R. 412 at 427.

68 *In Re Lobel* (1929), 38 Man. R. 48 at 50.

69 *Jones* v. *McClean et al.* (1931), 39 Man. R. 321 at 330.

70 *Heake* v. *City Securities Company* (1931), 39 Man. R. 399 at 402.

71 Geills and James Kilgour were the parents of Margaret, Katherine, John, and David. David was born in Brandon on Boxing Day 1912. To a remarkable extent his career mirrored that of his namesake and uncle. He was one year older than his uncle when he too joined an insurance company, in his case, the Great West Life Assurance Company, and seven years younger when he became his employer's general manager. David was

president of Great West Life from 1959 to 1971, the chair of the Canada Committee of the Hudson's Bay Company, and a governor of the University of Manitoba. He was sixty-one when he died in 1973. Margaret also had a successful career, earning a Master's degree from the University of Toronto before joining the editorial department of the *Winnipeg Free Press*.

72 Their children included John, Thomas, Mary, a second daughter, and Dennis. Michael's mother also resided with the family.

73 William James Donovan file, Archives of the University of Toronto, file A73- 0026/086(58).

74 Donovan articled with Phillipps from 2 December 1901 to 2 September 1902; with Horace Edgar Crawford from 2 September 1902 to 19 August 1903; and with Henry Platt Grundy from 19 August 1903 to 31 October 1904.

75 According to what law lists are available, Donovan practised alone from 1904 to 1906; was with T.J. Murray from 1906–7; alone for 1910 and 1911; with A.M. Doyle from 1912–14; with C.S. Scott 1915–22; with S.E. Nordquist 1922–25; and alone from 1925 until 1928.

76 J. Castel Hopkins, ed., *The Canadian Annual Review of Public Affairs for 1926–7* (Toronto: Annual Review Publishing Co., 1928) at 195 and for 1927–8 at 197.

77 Donovan's political activities are discussed in the *Toronto Star*, 10 April 1928, and the [Toronto] *Globe* (27 May 1949). The results of the 1922 election can be found in the 20, 21, and 22 July issues of the *Manitoba Free Press*.

78 *In Re Macdonald Estate (No. 1)* (1930), 38 Man. R. 446. For a brief discussion of the controversy see *Substantial Justice, supra* note 1 at 260–1.

79 *Rex* v. *Baschuk* (1931), 39 Man. R. 554 (C.A.).

80 *McMillan* v. *Harrison*, [1937] 1 W.W.R. 237 (Man. C.A.) at 243.

81 *Woodstock* v. *Woodstock* (1942), 49 Man. R. 113 (C.A.). at 115, 116–17.

82 *Robertson* v. *Robertson* (1945), 53 Man. R. 27 (C.A.) at 32.

83 *Supra* note 18, Maillet at 127; also *supra* note 1 at 279, and *Winnipeg Free Press*, 1 October 1940, 1.

84 Donovan was survived by his wife, three daughters, two sons, two sisters, a brother, and five grandchildren. Donovan married Margaret Mary, daughter of Winnipeg's D.F. Allman, on 28 August 1907. Their daughters were Wilhemina, Evelyn Imelda, and Alice. Their sons were Daniel James and John Emmet. His sisters were Mrs R. Hamilton of Elgin, Ontario, and Mrs C. Hamilton of Kingston. His brother, Dennis, lived in Lansdowne, Ontario, at the time of his death.

85 Percival Montague's paternal grandfather was Joseph Montague. His father Walter Mumphries was born on 21 November 1858 in Adelaide Township, and on 19 March 1879 married Barbara Ellen Angelina Furry. Percival was

two years older than his brother Fergeson and seven years older than his sister Pearl.

86 For a description of Montague's academic work at the University of Toronto, see his file in the Archives of the University, A73-0026/331(42).

87 Lyle Dalgleish, 'Donald Hugh Fletcher' in Thomas Melville Bailey, ed., *Dictionary of Hamilton Biography*, vol. 2, *1876–1924* (Hamilton: Griffin, 1991) at 49.

88 See (1950) 22:3 Man. Bar N. 58 for the obituary of Furry Ferguson (Ray) Montague. Other information can be found in the Archives of the Law Society of Manitoba, PAM, file P 1300, and the Archives of the University of Toronto. Information about GeorgeHastings Montague can be found in his Law Society of Manitoba file, Archive of Manitoba Legal-Judicial History, PAM.

89 Walter Montague won the 22 February 1887 general election by a single vote over Charles W. Coulter, the sitting MP. His election was voided and he won the ensuing by-election held on 12 November 1887 by 17 votes. He lost a by-election held on 30 January 1889 to Coulter by 46 votes, but defeated him by 227 votes in another by-election held on 20 February 1890. Montague was re-elected in the 1891 general election (by 78 votes) and in a by-election held on 17 April 1895 (by 594 votes). In the 1896 general election his constituency became known as Haldimand-Monck, and Montague won by 713 votes. He was defeated in the 1900 general election by Andrew Thompson and left federal politics permanently.

90 Montague was appointed minister of public works on 4 November 1913. He was elected the member for Kildonan–St Andrews in a by-election held on 29 November 1913, and was re-elected in the general election held on 10 July 1914. He resigned on 12 May 1915, and was not a candidate in the general election held on 6 August 1915.

91 W.L. Morton discusses the controversy and Montague's part in it in *Manitoba: A History* (Toronto: University of Toronto Press, 1957). Whether or not the jury actually split eleven to one in favour of conviction has never been proved.

92 *In Re Eames Estate* (1934), 42 Man. R. 474 (Man. Q.B.). The case was followed by the Saskatchewan Surrogate Court in *Wagenhoffer* v. *Wagenhoffer Estate* (1983), 26 Sask. R. 30 and by the Manitoba Court of Appeal in *Re Tachibana* (1968), 63 W.W.R. 99. It was also considered by the Manitoba Court of Appeal in *George* v. *Daily* (1997), 15 E.T.R. (2d) 1.

93 *McInnerny et al.* v. *McDougall*, [1937] 3 W.W.R. 625 (Man. Q.B.). Among the courts following it are the Saskatchewan Court of Appeal in *Johnson Estate* v. *Pischke*, [1989] 3 W.W.R. 207, the Nova Scotia Trial Division in

Stephens v. *Gittens* (1974), 15 N.S.R. (2d) 63, and the Ontario High Court in *McWilliam* v. *Thunder Bay Flying Club*, [1950] O.W.N. 696.

94 *Galer* v. *Wings*, [1938] 3 W.W.R. 481 (Man. Q.B.).

95 *Gislason* v. *Gislason*, [1935] 2 W.W.R. 282 (Man. C.A.) at 284.

96 Dale Gibson, 'Anecdotal Sampler' in Cameron Harvey, ed., *The Law Society of Manitoba 1877–1977* (Winnipeg: Peguis, 1977) 191 at 208.

97 Montague's file in the Archives of the University of Toronto, *supra* note 86, contains much information about his military career. A much briefer description can be found in (1944) 16:6 Man. Bar N. 99.

98 Montague was survived by his daughters Eleanor and Nancy.

99 Taylor's father William was born in Lincolnshire, England, in 1835. In 1860 he marriedMarietta Jane Plummer of Brampton. The two were the parents of sons Eli, a United Church minister, Allan Reid, a medical doctor in Wisconsin, Gardiner, Matthew, John, W.R., James, and Fawcett.

100 According to various law lists, Taylor was alone between 1900 and 1906, with Cowan in 1907 and 1908, alone between 1909 and 1911, and with Colwill from 1912 to 1933. H.D. Sparling and Carrie were members of the firm in 1922, Newman in 1924, Hinch in 1925, and C.C. Sparling in 1929.

101 (1940) 12:5 Man. Bar N. 44.

102 Taylor was defeated on 6 August 1915, then elected in general elections held on 29 June 1920, and re-elected on 18 July 1922, 28 June 1927, and 16 June 1932. He resigned from office in 1933.

103 Bracken's Progressives won 29 seats, the Conservatives 15, the Liberals 7, Labour 3, and a single independent was elected.

104 *Manitoba Free Press*, 16 February 1929, 13.

105 *Manitoba Free Press*, 1 March 1929, 1.

106 *Supra* note 101.

107 Joseph H. Metcalfe's *The Tread of the Pioneers* (Toronto: Ryerson Press, 1932) at 186–7, provides a good description of the McPherson family. Peter McPherson was born in Fort William, Inverness-shire, Scotland, in 1837. He was living in Ayre, Ontario, when he married Ellen Wallace. The couple had five children, including John (an employee of the Canadian National Railway), Peter (an employee of Canadian Pacific Railway), Ella, Ewen Alexander, and Ernest, who became the Indian agent for the Selkirk District in Manitoba.

108 Roger Graham, *Arthur Meighen*, vol. 1, *The Door of Opportunity* (Toronto: Clarke, Irwin, 1960) at 36.

109 Letter from G.P.R. Tallin to the children of McPherson, 4 July 1955, in

McPherson member file, Law Society of Manitoba, file P 1296, Archive of Manitoba Legal-Judicial History, PAM.

110 Meighen had been elected in Portage in 1908, 1911, 1917, 1921, and 1925.

111 *Winnipeg Free Press*, 19 November 1954, 25.

112 The best description of the relationship between the Liberal and Progressive parties is John Kendle's *John Bracken: A Political Biography* (Toronto: University of Toronto Press, 1979).

113 McPherson was defeated by Hugh Armstrong on 11 July 1910, was elected on 10 July 1914, re-elected 6 August 1915, defeated on 29 June 1920 and 16 June 1932, and elected on 16 July 1932.

114 *Supra* note 91 at 426.

115 (1938) 10 Man. Bar N. 517.

116 *Supra* note 111.

117 *Winnipeg Free Press*, 12 October 1953.

118 McPherson was survived by his daughter Peggy and sons Donovan Ewen, Wallace Alexander, and Glenn Willoughy. Wallace and Glen were both called to the Bar of Manitoba.

Chapter 7

1 Alan F.J. Artibise, 'An Urban Economy: Patterns of Economic Change in Winnipeg, 1873–1972' (1976) 2 Prairie Forum 163 at 181.

2 Dale & Lee Gibson, *Substantial Justice: Law and Lawyers in Manitoba 1670–1970* (Winnipeg: Peguis, 1972) at 282.

3 *Ibid.* at 287.

4 Major's parents were Job and Emily Major. Information about Athelstan Rendall was obtained from Michael Stenton & Stephen Lees, eds., *Who's Who of British Members of Parliament*, vol. 3, *1919–1945* (Sussex: Harvester Press, 1976) at 300.

5 Major worked for Rendall between 1895 and 1901. A description of his responsibilities was obtained from an affidavit Rendall filed (16 March 1901) in support of Major's application to join the Law Society of Manitoba. See William James Major member file, Law Society of Manitoba, file P 1286, Archive of Manitoba Legal-Judicial History, PAM.

6 *Winnipeg Tribune*, 7 August 1948.

7 The Majors were married on 12 October 1904.

8 Major was elected in a general election held on 28 June 1927 and was re-elected on 16 June 1932 and 27 July 1936. He was appointed attorney general on 29 April 1927 and served until 22 February 1927, when he stepped down briefly to await the outcome of a commission of inquiry

looking into charges that he had misconducted himself. He was reappointed attorney general on 18 May 1929, and served until 1 April 1941, when he resigned to go to the bench. Major also became the minister of telephones and telegraphs on 31 December 1929, resigning on 1 April 1941. He became municipal commissioner on 21 September 1936 and stepped down on 22 November 1939, and was minister of dominion–provincial relations from 4 November 1940 until 1 April 1941.

9 Stubbs actually received 24,671 votes compared to Major's 5155.

10 William James Major Papers, MG 14 B34, Box 1, 'Speeches' file, PAM.

11 *Ibid.* Speech to the Retail Merchants Association of Manitoba.

12 Diary of Robert Graham, MG 14 C109, vol. 5, p. 247, entry for 30 January 1940, PAM.

13 *Ibid.*

14 *Supra* note 10, letter from Captain Wilson to Major, PAM.

15 *Ibid.* Letter from Dennistoun to Major, July, 1940.

16 *Supra* note 10.

17 Murray Peden, *Hearken to the Evidence* (Stittsville, Ont.: Canada's Wings, 1983) at 56–7.

18 *Ibid.* at 45.

19 *Ibid.* at 48–50.

20 Major died on 13 August 1953. He was survived by his wife and daughters Helen and Vera.

21 For reference to his temper, see *supra* note 17 at 56. For reference to his mind, see oral interview with Joseph Thorson in Major file, *supra* note 5.

22 *Supra* note 10. Letter from Justice J.W. Estey to Major.

23 *Ibid.* Letter from Chaplain Carruthers to Major.

24 Esten Kenneth Williams Papers, MG 14, B39, box 1, PAM.

25 *Ibid.* Letter from Williams to Mackenzie King, 22 February 1945.

26 *Winnipeg Free Press*, 9 January 1932.

27 *Ibid.*

28 *Ibid.* Telegram from J.D. Montgomery to Williams, 3 September 1942.

29 The ceremony was presided over by Reverend F.W. Goodeve, vicar of Vancouver's St Margaret's Church. Mary was the only daughter of former Parkhill resident Neil Matheson.

30 *Supra* note 24. Comments of Les Rutherford, *Winnipeg Tribune* courts reporter.

31 *Manitoba King's Bench Act, an Annotation of the King's Bench Act, and the Rules Made Thereunder* (Toronto: Carswell, 1914).

32 *Notes on The Canadian Law of Landlord and Tenant as Applied to Corporeal Hereditaments* (Toronto: Carswell, 1922).

33 *Supra* note 24.
34 'Domicil' (1923) 1 Can. Bar Rev. 243.
35 'Stare Decisis' (1926) 4 Can. Bar Rev. 289.
36 (1937) 62 Rep. ABA 453, speech to 1937 annual meeting.
37 (1939) 17 Can. Bar Rev. 551, speech to 1939 annual meeting of the Law Society of Saskatchewan.
38 (1947) 33 ABA Journ. 10, speech to 1946 annual meeting.
39 'The Editorship. Vale Caesar Atque Ave' (1946) 24 Can. Bar Rev. 1; 'Foreword' in Roy St George Stubbs, *Sir George Jessel, Master of the Rolls* (Winnipeg: self-published, 1951); and 'Alfred Erskine Hoskin' (1960) 32 Man. Bar N. 65.
40 'Judicial Robes' (1949) 21:1 Man. Bar N. 117 and 'Maiden Assizes and White Gloves' (1950) 22 Man. Bar N. 106.
41 'Practice Note: Applications Under the Lunacy Act' (1958) 30:4 Man. Bar N. 77.
42 'Aspects of the Legal History of Manitoba' (1949) Hist. & Sc. Soc. Man. 48.
43 'Legal Education in Manitoba' (1950) 28 Can. Bar Rev. 759, 880.
44 E.K. Williams member file, Law Society of Manitoba, Archive of Manitoba Legal-Judicial History, PAM.
45 Law Society of Manitoba Minute Book 10 at 222, Archive of Manitoba Legal-Judicial History, PAM.
46 *Ibid.* at 244.
47 *Ibid.* at 252.
48 *Winnipeg Tribune*, 10 October 1924.
49 *Supra* note 24, Box 1, unattributed newspaper article, 27 March 1951, and [The] *Manitoban*, 7 March 1930.
50 *Winnipeg Tribune*, 2 March 1935; *Vancouver Province*, 13 December 1945.
51 Information about speeches given by Williams was obtained from references in newspapers, the *Manitoba Bar News*, Canadian and American legal journals, and the Williams and Maybank papers. It is likely that these references represent only a portion of the total number of speeches he gave. The only texts available can be found in the Williams and Maybank papers (*infra* note 79). Whenever a text is referred to, it has been cited to the appropriate collection.
52 *Winnipeg Tribune*, 8 January 1924, speech to the Winnipeg Law Students' Society.
53 *Winnipeg Tribune*, 31 March 1927, speech to the Blackstone Club.
54 *Winnipeg Free Press*, 3 March 1928, speeches to the Caledonian and Lions clubs.
55 *Supra* note 24, 1938 address to the Manitoba Bar Association.
56 (1939) 17 Can. Bar Rev. 551, address to the Law Society of Saskatchewan.

57 *Winnipeg Tribune*, 4 November 1940, speech to the Western Bar Association.
58 (1946) 24 Can. Bar Rev. 647, address to the annual meeting of the Canadian Bar Association.
59 *Supra* note 38.
60 *Supra* note 36.
61 *Supra* note 24, 1949 address to the Manitoba Bar Association.
62 *Ibid.*, 1931 address to the Caledonian Club.
63 *Ibid.*, 1934 address to the Manitoba Bar Association.
64 *The Doctor, the Lawyer, and the Judge* (Toronto: CCH Canadian, 1952).
65 *Supra* note 24, 1939 address to the Young Mens' Hebrew Association.
66 *Ibid.* In 1933 he spoke about 'Ancient and Modern Wales,' and in 1944 of 'The Courage of the Welsh.'
67 *Ibid.* 1938 address.
68 *Winnipeg Free Press*, 21 September 1942.
69 *Winnipeg Tribune*, 3 April 1936.
70 *Winnipeg Free Press*, 3 September 1924, address to the Kinsmen Club.
71 *Winnipeg Free Press*, 18 September 1924, address to the Lions Club.
72 *Winnipeg Tribune*, 31 March 1927, speech to the Rotary Club.
73 *Supra* note 24, 1930 speech to the Kiwanis Club.
74 *Ibid.* Letter from Robert L. Hogg to Williams, 5 November 1945.
75 *Ibid.* Letter to Williams, 7 November 1945.
76 *Ibid.* Letter from R. Leighton to Williams, 8 November 1945.
77 *Ibid.* Letter from W. Ferguson to Williams, 13 February 1946.
78 *Winnipeg Tribune*, 22 April 1947.
79 Ralph Maybank Papers, MG 14, B35, Williams' speech file, speech no. 39 at 3, PAM.
80 *Winnipeg Free Press*, 14 February 1934.
81 *Winnipeg Free Press*, 25 March 1941.
82 *Winnipeg Free Press*, 31 March 1927.
83 *Winnipeg Tribune*, 3 August 1927.
84 *Winnipeg Free Press*, 26 May 1934.
85 *Winnipeg Tribune*, 19 June 1936.
86 *Supra* note 24, *Winnipeg Free Press*, 25 November 1961.
87 *Wilton's Review*, 'The Picture Gallery,' 25 May 1935.
88 *Winnipeg Free Press*, 20 March 1939.
89 *Winnipeg Tribune*, 27 September 1935.
90 *Supra* note 79, 1945 speech at Macalester College, St Paul, Minnesota.
91 *Winnipeg Free Press*, 25 July 1933.
92 *Winnipeg Tribune*, 17 March 1934.
93 *Supra* note 87.

94 *Ibid.*
95 The Williams Papers contain unattributed newspaper clippings that refer to an address to the Griffons Club, during which he spoke of the persecution of German Jews, and to a speech to the Rotary Club during which he offered 'Some Observations on the Spread of Fascism.'
96 CKY radio address, 20 February 1936, the text of which could not be located.
97 The Williams Papers contain unattributed newspaper clippings that refer to 1940 addresses to the Shaaron Zionist Club during which he discussed 'What is Democracy,' to a speech to the Griffons Club concerning 'War,' and to dozens of Victory Loan and war rallies during which he discussed the plight of European Jews.
98 *Western Jewish News*, 4 January 1940.
99 *Supra* note 24, box 4, telegram, 11 April 1952.
100 Manitoba Club and the St Charles Golf & Country Club.
101 [Toronto] *Globe & Mail*, 22 April 1961.
102 *Winnipeg Tribune*, 17 January 1945.
103 *Winnipeg Free Press*, 31 May 1926.
104 *Winnipeg Tribune*, 19 September 1945.
105 *Supra* note 24, 1945 speech to a meeting of American insurance underwriters.
106 *Ibid.* at 13–14.
107 *Ibid.* at 14.
108 *Supra* note 10, 1951 speech at St Louis, Missouri, Kiwanis convention.
109 *Ibid.* Speech delivered 18 October 1962.
110 *Winnipeg Free Press*, 16 February 1942.
111 *Supra* note 79.
112 *Supra* note 24, box 1, 1930 article.
113 *Ibid.* References to the Gourlay letterbook can be found in much of the early correspondence between Williams and King.
114 *Ibid.* Letter from King to Williams, 15 February 1945.
115 *Ibid.* Letter from Williams to King, 22 February 1945.
116 *Ibid.* Letter from King to Williams, 4 March 1945.
117 *Ibid.*
118 *Ibid.* Letter from Williams to King, 8 March 1945.
119 *Ibid.* Letter from Williams to King, 31 March 1945.
120 *Ibid.* Letter from King to Williams, 30 July 1945.
121 *Winnipeg Free Press*, 16 February 1946.
122 *The Report of the Royal Commission Appointed under Order in Council P.C. 411 of February 5, 1946*, Ottawa: King's Printer, 1946.

123 *Canadian Press*, 29 April 1948.
124 Named in the First Interim Report were Emma Woikin, Gordon Lunan, Edward Wilfred Mazerall, all of whom worked for the federal government, and Kathleen Mary Willsher, who was an employee of the British government. Woikin pleaded guilty during her first appearance in court, while Mazerall was convicted after his April trial.
125 The four included Dr Raymond Boyer, assistant professor of chemistry at McGill University, Harold Samuel Gerson, Squadron Leader Matt Simons Nightingale, and Dr David Shugar, also of McGill.
126 Those named were Eric Adams, Israel Halperin, Durnford Smith, J.S. Benning, and Squadron Leader F.W. Poland.
127 In its final report the commission named fourteen public officials or persons in positions of trust who disclosed confidential information to Russia. Eight others were accused of helping procure a false Canadian passport for a Russian agent, and three were described as being prepared to take part in subversive activities had they been asked to do so. Among its other conclusions was the allegation that there existed in Canada a fifth column directed by Russian agents, several spy rings, and an organization devoted to the procurement of false Canadian passports for use by foreign agents in Canada and elsewhere. For his work on behalf of the commission Williams received $16,500.
128 *Toronto Daily Star*, 8 March 1946, 1.
129 M.H. Fyfe, 'Some Legal Aspects of the Report of the Royal Commission on Espionage' (1946) 24 Can. Bar Rev. 777.
130 'Report of the Civil Liberties Committee of the Canadian Bar Association' (1946) 28 Can. Bar Assoc. Proceedings 141.
131 *Supra* note 24, Winnipeg newspaper clipping, 13 September 1946.
132 *Winnipeg Free Press*, 16 February 1940.
133 *Winnipeg Free Press*, 11 December 1946.
134 *Winnipeg Tribune*, 2 January 1947.
135 [Vancouver] *Daily Province*, 10 October 1946.
136 *Winnipeg Free Press*, 11 December 1946.
137 Comments of Les Rutherford, Williams AVF file, PAM.
138 *Supra* note 24, Winnipeg newspaper clipping, 30 December 1954.
139 *Winnipeg Tribune*, 6 January 1955.
140 *Ibid.*
141 *Kansas City Star*, 1 October 1947.
142 *Winnipeg Tribune*, 13 May 1931.
143 *Winnipeg Free Press*, 13 May 1931.
144 *Supra* note 79, 'The Search for Truth' at 10.

145 *Ibid.* at 14.
146 *Winnipeg Free Press*, 12 April 1961.
147 *Supra* note 24, Box 1, unattributed newspaper clipping.
148 Williams's retirement became official on 1 January 1962.
149 *Supra* note 24, newspaper clipping, November, 1938.
150 *Ibid.* Box 4. Williams was survived by his wife Mary and son. Rowland Hugh Williams was born on 24 November 1926 and followed his father into law. He was called to the Manitoba bar in 1949 and practised with his father's old firm before leaving to become a solicitor in London, England.
151 *Supra* note 87.
152 *Winnipeg Tribune*, 11 December 1946.
153 *Supra* note 24. Letter from the Secretary of State for Canada to Williams, 13 December 1961.
154 *Supra* note 2 at 198 and note 17 at 4.
155 'A Judge and His Constituencies' (1976) 1 Man. L.J. 1.
156 *Winnipeg Free Press*, 16 December 1961, 33.
157 *Supra* note 2 at 315.
158 *Robinson* v. *Robinson and Schmitke* (1943), 50 Man. R. 223 (Q.B.). at 226.
159 In *Carey* v. *Carey* (1943), 50 Man. R. 263, Court of King's Bench Chief Justice McPherson suggested the *Robinson* case settled the question of whether discovery evidence concerning adultery was admissible at trial.
160 (1944) 16:3 Man. Bar N. 45.
161 *Supra* note 2 at 278.
162 *Ibid.* at 277.
163 Interview with Lorne Campbell, 29 June 1999.
164 *Winnipeg Free Press*, 19 November 1951.
165 Roy St. George Stubbs, 'What Is the "Lawyer's Lawyer"?' (1951) 23 Man. Bar N. 103 at 103–4.
166 Campbell was survived by his wife, two sons, a daughter, a sister, and eight grandchildren. Campbell's parents, Neil and Barbara Campbell, predeceased him. He and Petrina Flora Isobel Wilson, the daughter of Robert Wilson, were married on 26 December 1917, and were the parents of A. Lorne Campbell, A. Barrie Campbell, and Barbara Elizabeth. Lorne followed his father into law, and was senior partner in one of western Canada's largest firms when elected president of the Canadian Bar Association. Barrie was an engineer.
167 (1963) 35:1 Man. Bar N. 10 at 11.
168 Beaubien's mother was Codelia Hamel. His sister was Mrs S. Paradia and his brothers J.A., Louis Phillipe, Eugene, and Arthur Lucien Beaubien.

169 Beaubien began articling on 3 June 1910. His articles were assigned to Delorme on 1 September 1911, back to Louis Beaubien on 5 February 1912, and to McArthur on 3 March 1912.
170 *Supra* note 79. Letter from Ralph Maybank to C. Rhodes Smith, 19 August 1946, in box 4, file 78.
171 *Ibid.* Letter from Arnold Campbell to Ralph Maybank, 11 July 1946.
172 *Ibid.* Letter from Irving Keith to Ralph Maybank, 19 August 1946.
173 *Ibid.* Letter from Ralph Maybank to Irving Keith, 17 February 1947.
174 *Ibid.* Letter from Ralph Maybank to Cecil Philp and Irving Keith, 17 December 1947.
175 *Ibid.* Letter from Sauver Marcoux to Ralph Maybank, 6 February 1948.
176 *Ibid.* Letter from Joseph Beaubien to Ralph Maybank, 7 February 1948.
177 *Ibid.* Letter from Ralph Maybank to Joseph Beaubien, 12 February 1948.
178 *Ibid.* Letter from Joseph Beaubien to Ralph Maybank, 17 February 1948.
179 *Ibid.* Letter from Leon Benard to Ralph Maybank, 22 November 1948. Benard got his appointment in 1960.
180 Beaubien was survived by his wife Marie, son Leon, brothers Arthur, Louis Phillippe, Eugene, and J.A., and sister Mrs S. Paradis.
181 Kelly's parents were Daniel Joughin Kelly and Asenath Hoskins. He was called to the bar on 22 December 1922.
182 *Hniden* v. *Herr* (1931), 40 Man. R. 108. See also *Winnipeg Free Press*, 3 April 1952, 21.
183 *Winnipeg Free Press*, 4 March 1946.
184 Kelly was married on 4 October 1924. He was survived by his wife Violet and daughters Maureen and Joan Both his daughters became teachers.
185 *Winnipeg Free Press*, 3 April 1952, 21.

Conclusion

1 See Joel F. Handler, *The Lawyer and His Community: The Practicing Bar in a Middle-Sized City* (Madison: University of Wisconsin Press, 1967) c. 1.
2 J.A.G. Griffith, *The Politics of the Judiciary*, 5th ed. (London: Fontana Press, 1997) at 338.
3 Letter from Ralph Maybank to Prime Minister Mackenzie King, 1 November 1943, Maybank Papers, MG 14, B35, PAM.
4 Letter from G.W. Allan to Isaac Pitblado, 14 May 1918, Judicial Appointments 1917–22, file P 1495, Archive of Manitoba Legal-Judicial History, AM.
5 Richard W. Willie, *'These Legal Gentlemen': Lawyers in Manitoba: 1839–1900* (Winnipeg: Legal Research Institute of the University of Manitoba, 1994) at 121–2.

6 *Supra* note 3. Letter from Currah to Maybank, 14 November 1942.
7 David Stager with Harry Arthurs, *Lawyers in Canada* (Toronto: University of Toronto Press, 1990) at 312.
8 Harry W. Arthurs, Richard Wiesman & Frederick H. Zemans, 'Canadian Lawyers, a Peculiar Professionalism' in Richard L. Abel & Philip S.C. Lewis, eds., *Lawyers in Society*, vol. 1, *The Common Law* (Berkeley: University of California Press, 1988) 123 at 157.
9 Thomas G. Walker & William E. Hulbary, 'Selection of Capable Justices: Factors to Consider' in Albert P. Blaustein & Roy M. Mersky, eds., *The First One Hundred Justices: Statistical Studies on the Supreme Court of the United States* (Hamden, Conn.: Archon Books, 1978) 52 at 67.
10 Mr Justice Trueman, 'Judicial Appointments' (1930) 8 Can. Bar Rev. 1 at 4.
11 *Supra* note 5 at 4.
12 William John Klein, *Judicial Recruitment in Manitoba, Ontario, and Quebec 1905–1970* (Ph.D. thesis, Department of Sociology, University of Toronto, 1975) [unpublished] at 262.
13 Dennis Olsen, *The State Elite* (Toronto: McClelland & Stewart, 1980) at 49–50.
14 *Supra* note 9 at 65.
15 James G. Snell & Frederick Vaughan, *The Supreme Court of Canada, History of the Institution* (Toronto: Osgoode Society, 1985) at 92.
16 Alexander Begg & Walter R. Nursey, *Ten Years in Winnipeg* (Winnipeg: Times, 1879) at 73.
17 (1884) 1 Man. L.J. 177 at 178.
18 (1889) 26 Can. L.J. 1.
19 Dennistoun Papers, MG 14, B 24, box 3, file 15, PAM.
20 'Judicial Murder' (1927) 5 Can. Bar Rev. 329.

Bibliographies

Introduction and Conclusion

Adams, George, and Paul J. Cavalluzzo. 'The Supreme Court of Canada, A Biographical Study,' (1969) 7 Osgoode Hall L.J. 61.

Andrews, A.J. 'Jurist and Gentleman.' (1945) 17 Man. Bar N. 31.

Armstrong, Richard. 'The Hon. Edmund Burk Wood, Late Chief Justice of Manitoba.' (1895) 1 *The Barrister* 114.

Arthurs, Harry W., Richard Wiesman, and Frederick H. Zemans. 'Canadian Lawyers, A Peculiar Professionalism.' In Richard L. Abel and Philip S.C. Lewis, eds., *Lawyers in Society*, vol. 1, *The Common Law* 123. Berkeley: University of California Press, 1988.

Begg, Alexander, and Walter R. Nursey. *Ten Years in Winnipeg* at 73. Winnipeg: Times, 1879.

Brown, R. Blake, and Susan S. Jones. 'A Collective Biography of the Supreme Court Judiciary of Nova Scotia, 1900–2000.' In Philip Girard, Jim Phillips, and Barry Cahill, eds., *The Supreme Court of Nova Scotia, 1754–2004: From Imperial Bastion to Provincial Oracle* 204. Toronto: Osgoode Society, 2004.

Buchanan, A.W. Patrick, Q.C. *The Bench and Bar of Lower Canada Down to 1850.* Montreal: Burton's, 1925.

Bushnell, Ian. *The Captive Court: A Study of the Supreme Court of Canada.* Montreal: McGill-Queen's University Press, 1992.

The Federal Court of Canada, A History, 1875–1982. Toronto: Osgoode Society, 1997.

Charteris-Thomson, Margaret. *The Colonial Ancestry of the Honourable Sir Thomas Wardlaw Taylor Kt.B. Chief Justice of the Province of Manitoba – 1887–1899*. London: Dumfries, 1937.

Duman, Daniel. *The Judicial Bench in England 1727–1875, The Reshaping of a Professional Elite*. London: Royal Historical Society, 1982.

Fraser, Robert L., ed. *Provincial Justice: Upper Canadian Legal Portraits from the Dictionary of Canadian Biography*. Toronto: Osgoode Society, 1992.

Gibson, Dale. 'Unobtrusive Justice.' (1974) 12 Osgoode Hall L.J. 339.

– 'Manifest Destiny: A Biographical Sketch of Chief Justice Brian Dickson.' (1991) 20 Man. L.J. 268.

Gibson, Dale, and Lee Gibson. *Substantial Justice: Law and Lawyers in Manitoba 1670–1970*. Winnipeg: Peguis, 1972.

Greco, Clara. 'The Superior Court Judiciary of Nova Scotia, 1754–1900: A Collective Biography.' In Philip Girard and Jim Phillips, eds., *Essays in the History of Canadian Law*, vol. 3, *Nova Scotia* 42. Toronto: Osgoode Society, 1990.

Griffith, J.A.G. *The Politics of the Judiciary*, 5th ed. London: Fontana Press, 1997.

Haig, Hon. John T. 'Mr. Justice Fawcett Gowler Taylor, D.S.O., K.C.' (1940) 12 Man. Bar N. 44.

Handler, Joel F. *The Lawyer and His Community: The Practicing Bar in a Middle-Sized City* c. 1. Madison: University of Wisconsin Press, 1967.

Heuston, R.F.V. *Lives of the Lord Chancellors 1885–1940*. Oxford: Alden Press, 1964.

– *Lives of the Lord Chancellors 1940–1970*. Oxford: Clarendon Press, 1987.

Holman, Andrew C. *A Sense of Their Duty: Middle-Class Formation in Victorian Ontario Towns*. Montreal: McGill-Queen's University Press, 2000.

Jewars, Gerald O. 'Chief Justice E.K. Williams.' (1961) 33 Man. Bar N. 145.

Johnson, J. Ragnar. 'Honourable W.E. Perdue, an Appreciation of an Eminent Jurist.' (1933) 11 Can. Bar Rev. 199.

'Judicial Murder.' (1927) 5 Can. Bar Rev. 329.

Klein, William John, *Judicial Recruitment in Manitoba, Ontario, and Quebec 1905–1970*. Ph.D. thesis, Department of Sociology, University of Toronto, 1975 [unpublished].

Knafla, Louis A., and Richard Klumpenhouwer. *Lords of the Western Bench: A Biographical History of the Supreme and District Courts of Alberta, 1876–1990*. Edmonton: Legal Archives Society of Alberta, 1997.

Lawrence, Joseph William. *The Judges of New Brunswick and Their Times*. Fredericton: Acadiensis Press, 1983.

Lecompte, Edouard Le P. *Sir Joseph Dubuc (1840–1914), Un Grand Chrétien*. Montreal: Imprimerie du Messager, 1923.

McAlduff, Sister M.M., *Joseph Dubuc, Role and Views of a French Canadian in Manitoba 1870–1914*. M.A. thesis, University of Ottawa, 1967 [unpublished].

Morgan, Henry J. *The Canadian Legal Directory: A Guide to the Bench and Bar of the Dominion of Canada*. Toronto: Carswell, 1878.

Oliver, Edmund Henry. *The Canadian North-West, Its Early Development and Legislative Records: Minutes of the Councils of the Red River Colony and the Northern Department of Rupert's Land*, vol. 1, at 135. Ottawa: Government Printing Bureau, 1914.

Olsen, Dennis. *The State Elite*. Toronto: McClelland & Stewart, 1980.

Prud'Homme, L.A. 'Sir Joseph Dubuc.' (1914) Revue Canadienne 386 and 506.

Pue, W. Wesley. '"Trajectories of Professionalism": Legal Professionalism after Abel.' (1990) 19 Man. L.J. 384.

– 'Becoming "Ethical": Lawyers' Professional Ethics in Early Twentieth Century Canada.' (1991) 20 Man. L.J. 227.

– *Lawyers and the Constitution of Political Society: Containing Radicalism and Maintaining Order in Prairie Canada, 1900–1930* (Winnipeg: Canadian Legal History Project Working Paper, 1993).

– 'In Pursuit of Better Myth: Lawyers' Histories and Histories of Lawyers.' (1995) 33 Alta. L. Rev. 730.

– 'Common Law Education in Canada's Age of Light, Soap and Water.' (1996) 23 Man. L.J. 654.

– 'Foxes, Henhouses, Unfathomable Mysteries, and the Sufferance of the People: A Review of Regulating Professions and Occupations.' (1996–97) 24 Man. L.J. 283.

– '"The Disquisitions of Learned Judges": Making Manitoba Lawyers, 1885–1931.' In G. Blaine Baker and Jim Phillips, eds., *Essays in the History of Canadian Law*, vol. 8, *In Honour of R.C.B. Risk* 512. Toronto: Osgoode Society, 1999.

– 'British Masculinities, Canadian Lawyers: Canadian Legal Education, 1900–1930.' In Rob McQueen and W. Wesley Pue, eds., *Misplaced Traditions, British Lawyers, Colonial Peoples* 80. Leichhardt, NSW: Federation Press, 1999.

Read, David B. *The Lives of the Judges of Upper Canada and Ontario, From 1791 to the present time*. Toronto: Rowsell & Hutchison, 1888.

Robertson, John Palmerston. *A Political Manual of the Province of Manitoba and the North-west Territories*. Winnipeg: Call Printing, 1887.

Snell, James G., and Frederick Vaughan. *The Supreme Court of Canada, History of the Institution*. Toronto: Osgoode Society, 1985.

Stager, David, with Harry Arthurs. *Lawyers in Canada* at 312. Toronto: University of Toronto Press, 1990.

Stevens, Robert. *Law and Politics, The House of Lords as a Judicial Body, 1800–1976*. Chapel Hill: University of North Carolina Press, 1978.
Stubbs, Lewis St. George. *A Majority of One: The Life and Times of Lewis* St. George *Stubbs*. Winnipeg: Queenston House, 1983.
Stubbs, Roy St. George. 'Chief Justice Wallbridge.' (1937) 10 Man. Bar N. 481.
– 'Chief Justice Jacques Emile Pierre Prendergast.' In *Lawyers and Laymen of Western Canada* 100. Toronto: Ryerson Press, 1939.
– 'Andrew Knox Dysart.' In *Prairie Portraits* 119. Toronto: McClelland & Stewart, 1954.
– 'Hon. Edmund Burke Wood.' (1958) 13 Hist. Sc. Soc. Man. 27.
– 'The Chief Justice of Manitoba' [John Admason] (1960) 32:2 and 3 Man. Bar N. 29.
Taylor, Rev. Thomas Wardlaw Jr. *A Sketch of the Life of Sir Thomas Wardlaw Taylor*. Unpublished. Thomas Wardlaw Taylor AVF file, PAM.
Verchere, Hon. David R. *A Progression of Judges: A History of the Supreme Court of British Columbia*. Vancouver: UBC Press, 1988.
Walker, Thomas G., and William E. Hulbary. 'Selection of Capable Justices. Factors to Consider.' In Albert P. Blaustein & Roy M. Mersky, eds., *The First One Hundred Justices: Statistical Studies on the Supreme Court of the United States*. Hamden, Conn.: Archon Books, 1978.
Weiler, Paul. *In the Last Resort: A Critical Study of the Supreme Court of Canada*. Toronto: Carswell, 1974.
Willie, Richard A. '"A Proper Ideal during Action": Fraternity, Leadership and Lifestyle in Winnipeg Lawyers' Professional Culture, 1878–1900.' (1992) 27 J. Can. Studies 58.
– *'These Legal Gentlemen': Lawyers in Manitoba: 1839–1900*. Winnipeg: Legal Research Institute of the University of Manitoba, 1994.

BIOGRAPHICAL

John Evans Adamson

PRIMARY SOURCES

Adamson, John Evans, Papers, Archives of the Law Society of Manitoba, file P 1201, PAM.
– Papers, Legal-Judicial Collection, file P 1495, PAM.
Finkelstein Papers, MG 14, C 77, microfilm M110, PAM.
Graham, Robert Blackwood, Papers, MG 14, C 109, microfilm M328, vol. 4 at 105, PAM.

Law Society, Minute Books 7 at 80 and 11 at 58, Archives of the Law Society of Manitoba, PAM.
Lindal, Walter J., Papers, MG 14, B 78, box 3, PAM.
Maybank, Ralph, Papers, MG 14, B 35, box 4, file 78, PAM.

A.R. Williams Machinery Company of Winnipeg, Limited v. *Winnipeg Storage, Limited* (1927), 37 Man. R. 187 (C.A.).
Black v. *Stebnicki* (1930), 39 Man. R. 123 (C.A.).
Brendzij et al. v. *Hajdij et al.* (1927), 36 Man. R. 300 (C.A.).
Murphy v. *Robertson et al.* (1941), 49 Man. R. 182 (Q.B.).
Portage Milling & Transfer Company v. *Grand Trunk Pacific Railway et al.* (1923), 33 Man. R. 91 (Q.B.).
Ratcliffe v. *Whitehead*, [1933] 3 W.W.R. 447 (Q.B.).
Stebbe v. *Laird*, [1938] 1 W.W.R. 173 (Q.B.).
Thomas v. *Thomas* (1945), 53 Man. R. 210 (Q.B.).
Union Bank of Canada v. *Turner* (1922), 32 Man. R. 435 (C.A.).
Wasney v. *Jurazsky* (1933), 41 Man. R. 46 (C.A.).

SECONDARY SOURCES

Adamson, John Evans. 'Judicial Sentences.' (1933) 11 Can. Bar Rev. 681.
Gibson, Dale. 'An Anecdotal Sampler.' In Cameron Harvey, ed., *The Law Society of Manitoba 1877–1977* at 201. Winnipeg: Peguis, 1977.
Greene, B.M., ed. 'Christopher Arthur Adamson.' In *Who's Who in Canada, 1923–1924* 1212. Toronto: International Press, 1924.
– 'John Evans Adamson' in *Who's Who in Canada, 1943–44* (Toronto: International Press, 1944) 524.
Johnson, J.K., ed. *The Canadian Directory of Parliament 1867–1967* at 2. Ottawa: Public Archives of Canada, 1968.
Perrault. *The Canadian Parliament* at 145, 241. Montreal: Perrault Printing, 1906.
Read, Frederick. 'Damages for Loss of Expectation of Life.' (1938) 10 Man. Bar N. 533.
Schultz, Mr Justice Ivan. 'Remarks on the Occasion of the Retirement from the Bench of Chief Justice Adamson' (1961) 33:1 Man. Bar N. 26.
Stubbs, Roy St. George. 'The Chief Justice of Manitoba.' (1960) 32 Man. Bar N.29.

(1933) 11 Can. Bar Rev. 681.
(1934) 3 Fortnightly L.J. 195.
(1934) 7 Man. Bar N. 52.
(1938) 10 Man. Bar N. 533.
'Christopher Arthur Adamson.' (1940) 12 Man. Bar N. 96.

'Mr. Justice Adamson Urges Changes in Divorce Laws.' (1945) 17 Man. Bar N. 64.
'Judicial Vacancies Filled' (1948) 20:1 Man. Bar N. 5.
(1960) 32 Man. Bar N. 30.
(1961) 33 Man. Bar N. 1, 27.

Manitoba Free Press, 29 January 1907, 13; 10 May 1922.
Newspaper, unknown. 'Judge Announces Lawyer Barred from His Court Pending an Explanation.' 15 March 1928, Archives of Law Society of Manitoba, scrapbook of newspaper clippings, PAM.
Winnipeg Free Press, 14 June 1960; 27 January 1961; 22 December 1961, 1; 23 December 1961, 34.

John Farqhuar Bain

PRIMARY SOURCES

Baker, George W., Papers, MG 14, B2, scrapbook, PAM.
Census of Canada West, 1861.
Census of Manitoba, 1891, Ward 2, sub-district 4 at 31.
Census of Ontario, 1871, 1881.
Census of the North-West Territories, 1901.
United Church of Canada, Archives, Presbyterian Record, vol. 14, no.12 (Dec. 1889) at 326.

Bain v. *McDonald* (1873), 32 U.C.Q.B. 190.
Re J.B., An Attorney (1889), 6 Man. R. 19 (C.A.).
Re Nicholson & The Railway Commissioner (1891), 7 Man. R. 400 (Q.B.).
Reg. v. *Galbraith* (1889), 6 Man. R. 14 (Q.B.).
Regina v. *Burke* (1889), 6 Man. R. 121 (C.A.).
Regina v. *Great West Laundry Company* (1900), 13 Man. R. 66 (Q.B.).
Rowland v. *Martin* (1890), 7 Man. R. 160.
St. Germain v. *Charette* (1900), 13 Man. R. 63 (Q.B.).
West v. *Lynch* (1888), 5 Man. R. 167 (Q.B.).
Wilton v. *Murray* (1897), 12 Man. R. 35 (Q.B.).

SECONDARY SOURCES

Begg, Alexander, and Walter R. Nursey. *Ten Years in Winnipeg*. Winnipeg: Times, 1879.
Benham, Mary Lile. *The Manitoba Club 100 Years 1874–1974* at 69. Winnipeg: Manitoba Club, 1974.

Bowsfield, Hartwell, ed. *The Letters of Charles John Brydges 1879–1882*. Winnipeg: Hudson's Bay Record Society, 1977.
– *The Letters of Charles John Brydges 1883–1889*. Winnipeg: Hudson's Bay Record Society, 1981.
Bryce, George. 'The Illustrated History of Winnipeg.' In *Manitoba Free Press*, 27 May 1905, at 1.
Gibson, Dale, and Lee Gibson. *Substantial Justice: Law and Lawyers in Manitoba 1670–1970*. Winnipeg: Peguis, 1972.
Hardy, H.R., ed. *Ontario, Manitoba and North-West Legal Directory* at 137. Toronto: Carswell, 1883.
Harvey, Cameron, ed. *The Law Society of Manitoba 1877–1977*. Winnipeg: Peguis, 1977.
Henderson, George Fletcher. *Federal Royal Commissions in Canada 1867–1966, A Checklist* at 6. Toronto: University of Toronto Press, 1967.
Henderson, James, ed. *Henderson's Directory of the City of Winnipeg*. Winnipeg: James Henderson, 1883.
LaRiviere & Gauvin, eds., *Manitoba Directory for 1876*. St Boniface: LaRiviere & Gauvin, 1876).
McDonald, Donna. *Lord Strathcona: A Biography of Donald Alexander Smith* at 343. Toronto: Dundurn, 1996.
Morgan, Henry J., ed. *The Canada Legal Directory: A Guide to the Bench and Bar of the Dominion of Canada*. Toronto: Carswell, 1878.
Robertson, John Palmerston, ed. *A Political Manual of the Province of Manitoba and the North-West Territories* at 143. Winnipeg: Call, 1887.
Rordans & Nicholls, eds. *The Ontario Law List and Solicitor's Agency Book*, 8th ed. Toronto: Rordans & Nicholls, 1876.
Willie, Richard A. *'These Legal Gentlemen': Lawyers in Manitoba: 1839–1900*. Winnipeg: Legal Research Institute of the University of Manitoba, 1994.
Wilson, Alan. '"In a Business Way": C.J. Brydges and the Hudson's Bay Company, 1879–1889.' In Carl Berger and Ramsay Cooks, eds., *The West and the Nation: Essays in Honour of W.L. Morton* 114 at 125–31. Toronto: McClelland & Stewart, 1976.

(1871) 7 Can. L.J. 60.
(1884) 1 Man. L.J. 96.
(1891) 2 W.L. Times 149.
'Obituary.' (1894) 5 W.L. Times 144.

Manitoba Free Press, 3 August 1874, 4; 4 August 1874, 2; 12 August 1880, 1; 9 March 1886, 1, 4; 10 March 1886, 4; 7 November 1887, 4; 16 November

1887, 2, 4; 19 November 1888, 1; 5 November 1894, 7; 8 November 1894, 2, 6; 4 August 1903, 9; 13 May 1905, 29.
Newspaper, unknown. 'Manitoba Bench Loses a Member,' 12 May 1904. Archives of Law Society of Manitoba, scrapbook of newspaper clippings, PAM.

Joseph Thomas Beaubien

PRIMARY SOURCES

Beaubien, Joseph Thomas, Papers, Archives of the Law Society of Manitoba, file P 1209, PAM.

Shebaylo v. *Crown Trust and Guarantee Co.* (1948), 56 Man. R.124 (Q.B.).

SECONDARY SOURCES

Beaubien, Mr. Justice. 'Address to the Graduating Class, Manitoba Law School.' (1952) 24:3 Man. Bar N. 30.
Graham, Roger. *Arthur Meighen*. Vol. 2, *And Fortune Fled* at 372. Toronto: Clarke, Irwin, 1963.
Greene, B.M., ed. 'Hon. Arthur Lucien Beaubien.' In *Who's Who in Canada, 1943–44* 974. Toronto: International Press, 1944.
Johnson, J.K., ed. *The Canadian Directory of Parliament 1867–1967* at 27. Ottawa: Public Archives of Canada, 1968.

'Judicial Vacancies Filled' (1948) 20:1 Man. Bar N. 5.
(1952) 24:3 Man. Bar N. 30.

Winnipeg Free Press, 26 March 1957, 5; 29 March 1957, 17.

Louis Betournay

PRIMARY SOURCES

Betournay, Ernest Louis, Papers, Archives of the Law Society of Manitoba, file P 1212, PAM.
Betournay, George Albert, Papers, Archives of the Law Society of Manitoba, file P 1212, PAM.
Betournay, Louis, Papers, Archives of the Law Society of Manitoba, file P 1212, PAM.
Betournay, Louis Napoleon, Papers, Archives of the Law Society of Manitoba, file P 1212, PAM.

Betournay, Louis Noel Robert, Papers, Archives of the Law Society of Manitoba, file P 1212, PAM.
Betournay, Maurice Paul, Papers, Archives of the Law Society of Manitoba, file P 1212, PAM.
Macdonald, John A. Papers, MG 26A, NAC.

Breden v. *Lyon et al.* (1876), Temp. Wood 50 (Q.B.).
Clarke v. *The Mayor and Council of the City of Winnipeg* (1876), Temp. Wood 56 (Q.B.).
Young v. *Smith* (1880), 4 S.C.R. 494.

SECONDARY SOURCES

Bonenfant, J.-C. 'Sir George-Étienne Cartier.' In Marc La Terreur, ed. *Dictionary of Canadian Biography*, vol. 10, 142. Toronto: University of Toronto Press, 1972.
Gibson, Dale, and Lee Gibson. *Substantial Justice: Law and Lawyers in Manitoba 1670–1970*. Winnipeg: Peguis, 1972.
Lefebvre, Jean-Jacques. 'Louis Betournay (1825–1879) Premier Juge Canadien-Français d'Une Cour Supérieure Dans L'Ouest Canadien.' In *Voyage-éclair: Dans l'ouest Canadien et Americain*. Montreal: Éditions B.D. Simpson, 1948.
– 'Beaudry (Baudry), Joseph-Ubalde.' In Marc La Terreur, ed., *Dictionary of Canadian Biography*, vol. 10, 37. Toronto: University of Toronto Press, 1972.
Maillet, Lise, *Provincial Royal Commissions and Commissions of Inquiry, 1867–1982: A Selective Bibliography* at 117. Ottawa: National Library of Canada, 1986.
Manitoba Library Association. *Pioneers and Early Citizens of Manitoba.* Winnipeg: Peguis, 1971.
McAlduff, Sister M.M. *Joseph Dubuc, Role and Views of a French Canadian in Manitoba 1870–1914*. M.A. thesis, University of Ottawa, 1967 [unpublished].
McDonald, Donna. *Lord Strathcona, A Biography of Donald Alexander Smith* at 293. Toronto: Dundurn, 1996.
Monet, Jacques. 'Sir Louis-Hippolyte La Fontaine.' In Francess G. Halpenny, ed., *Dictionary of Canadian Biography*, vol. 9, 440. Toronto: University of Toronto Press, 1976.
Morgan, Henry James. *The Canadian Legal Directory: A Guide to the Bench and Bar of the Dominion of Canada* at 202. Toronto: Morgan, 1878.
Robertson, John Palmerston, ed. *A Political Manual of the Province of Manitoba and the North- West Territories* at 142. Winnipeg: Call, 1887.
Stanley, George F.G. *Louis Riel* at 193–4, 210. Toronto: Ryerson, 1963.
Stanley, George F.G. 'Betournay, Louis.' In Marc La Terreur, ed., *Dictionary of Canadian Biography*, vol. 10, 58. University of Toronto Press: Toronto, 1972.

Sweeny, Alastair, *George-Étienne Cartier, A Biography*. Toronto: McClelland & Stewart, 1976.

Willie, Richard A. *'These Legal Gentlemen': Lawyers in Manitoba: 1839–1900*. Winnipeg: Legal Research Institute of the University of Manitoba, 1994.

Willson, Beckles, *The Life of Lord Strathcona and Mount Royal* at 396–7. Boston: Houghton Mifflin, 1915.

Young, Brian. *George-Etienne Cartier, Montreal Bourgeois*. Montreal: McGill-Queen's University Press, 1981.

Manitoba Free Press, 14 July 1879. 1; 31 October 1879, 2; 3 November 1879, 1.

Manitoba Gazette, 24 September 1873, 2.

Ottawa Daily Free Press, 4 Nov. 1879.

Winnipeg Free Press, 10 January 1990, 1.

John Donald Cameron

PRIMARY SOURCES

Cameron, John, Family Papers, Local History Collection, Woodstock Public Library.

Cameron, John Donald, Papers, Archives of the Law Society of Manitoba, file P 1221, PAM.

– Papers, Archives of the University of Toronto, file A73-0026/048(93).

Census of Ontario, 1871.

Index to the 1871 Census of Ontario, Oxford County. Toronto: Ontario Genealogical Society, 1991.

Attorney-General for Manitoba v. *Kelly*, [1922] 1 A.C. 268 (Privy Council).

The British American Elevator Company Limited v. *Bank of British North America*, [1919] 2 W.W.R. 748 (Privy Council).

Frank v. *Beswick et al.* (1880), 44 U.C.Q.B. 1.

Kelly v. *Kelly* (1913), 23 W.L.R. 953 (Privy Council).

Imperial Brewers Ltd. v. *Gelin* (1908), 18 Man. R. 283 (Q.B.).

Muldowan v. *German Canadian Land Co.* (1909), 19 Man. R. 667 (Q.B.).

Re McGregor (1909), 18 Man. R. 432 (Q.B.).

Rex v. *Russell et al.* (1919), 29 Man. R. 511 (C.A.).

SECONDARY SOURCES

Cameron, John Donald. 'The Disallowance of Provincial Legislation by the Federal Government.' In *Manitoba Free Press*, 17 November 1884.

– 'Codes and Codification.' (1917) 37 Can. L. Times 177.

– 'International Treaties in Relation to Legislative Powers.' (1922) 42 Can. L. Times 10.

Canadian Literary Institute. *Annual Catalogue of the Canadian Literary Institute for 1874–'75*. Toronto: Dudley & Burns, 1874.

– *Directory of the Studies, Terms, &c. of the Canadian Literary Institute for the Years 1877–8*. Woodstock: Sentinel Steam, 1877.

Gibson, Dale, and Lee Gibson. *Substantial Justice: Law and Lawyers in Manitoba 1670–1970*. Winnipeg: Peguis, 1972.

Hamilton, John Cleland. *Osgoode Hall, Reminiscences of the Bench and Bar* at 183. Toronto: Carswell, 1904.

Hodgins, George. *The Establishment of Schools and Colleges in Ontario, 1792–1910*. Toronto: L.K. Cameron, 1910.

Hopkins, J. Castell, ed. *The Canadian Annual Review of Public Affairs 1906–1907*. Toronto: Annual Review Publishing.

Maillet, Lise. *Provincial Royal Commissions and Commissions of Inquiry, 1867–1982: A Selective Bibliography*. Ottawa: National Library of Canada, 1986.

Morgan, Henry James, ed. *Canadian Men and Women of the Time*, 2nd ed., at 187. Toronto: Briggs, 1912.

Morton, W.L. *One University: A History of the University of Manitoba 1877–1952* at 75–81. Toronto: McClelland & Stewart, 1957.

Perdue, Hon. W.E. 'The Late Mr. Justice Cameron,' (1923) 1 Can. Bar Rev. 298.

[Woodstock] *Sentinel-Review*, 22 February 1908, 1; 21 August 1908, 1; 22 August 1908, 1; 2 August 1909, 1.

(1923) 1 Can. Bar Rev. 193.
'The Late Mr. Justice Cameron' (1923) Can. Bar Rev. 299, 873.
(1882) 18 Can. L.J. 356.
(1917) 37 Can. L. Times 177.
(1922) 42 Can. L. Times 10.
(1935) 7 Man. Bar N. 145.

Arnold Munroe Campbell

PRIMARY SOURCES

Campbell, Arnold Munroe, Papers, Archives of the Law Society of Manitoba, PAM.

Agar v. *Rural Municipality of East St. Paul* (1935), 43 Man. R. 114 (Q.B.).
Carey v. *Carey* (1943), 50 Man. R. 263 (Q.B.).
Davies v. *Commissioner of Excise* (1942), 50 Man. R. 220 (Q.B.).

Frankel et al. v. *Gillis* (1942), 50 Man. R. 380 (Q.B.).
In re Lawther Estate (1947), 55 Man. R. 142 (Q.B.).
In Re Winnipeg Silver Fox Company Limited Assessment Appeal (1940), 48 Man. R. 229 (Q.B.).
Robinson v. *Robinson and Schmitke* (1943), 50 Man. R. 223 (Q.B.).
St. Vital Investments, Limited v. *Halldorson and Clements* (1920), 30 Man. R. 573 (C.A.).

SECONDARY SOURCES

Campbell, Arnold Munroe. 'Hon. Stuart Sinclair Garson, K.C., M.L.A., LL.B.: An Appreciation by a Classmate.' (1943) 15:1 Man. Bar N. 1.
Campbell, Mr. Justice A.M. 'A Lawyer's Duties.' In *Winnipeg Free Press*, 19 November 1951.
– 'Address to the Graduating Class, 1951.' (1951) 23 Man. Bar N. 77.
– 'Address of Mr. Justice Campbell to the Gentlemen Called to the Bar on September 20, 1961.' (1961) 33 Man. Bar N. 151.
Gibson, Dale. 'Anecdotal Sampler.' In Cameron Harvey, ed., *The Law Society of Manitoba 1877–1977* at 218. Winnipeg: Peguis, 1977.
Greene, B.M., ed. 'Hon. Arnold Munroe Campbell.' In *Who's Who in Canada, 1947–48* 614. Toronto: International Press, 1948.
Stubbs, Roy St. George, 'What Is the "Lawyer's Lawyer"?' (1951) 23 Man. Bar N. 103.

(1936) 5 Fortnightly L.J. 236.
(1944) 16:3 Man. Bar N. 45, 64.
(1947) 19:5 Man. Bar N. 86.
(1951) 23 Man. Bar N. 7.
'Mr. Justice Campbell.' (1963) 35 Man. Bar N. 10.

Winnipeg Free Press, 19 November 1951; 13 February 1963, 16; 14 February 1963, 33.

John Philpot Curran

PRIMARY SOURCES

Curran Family Papers, Stratford Perth Archives.
Curran, John Philpot, Estate, Records of the Surrogate Court of Manitoba, PAM.
Curran, John Philpot, Papers, Archives of the Law Society of Manitoba, file P 123, PAM.

Curran Papers, Archives of the Anglican Church of Canada, Proceedings of the Synod of the Anglican Church of Canada, [undated] at 21.
Graham, Robert Blackwood, Papers, MG 14, C 109 at 165–74, PAM.
Law Society, Minute Books 7 and 8, Archives of the Law Society of Manitoba, PAM.

Curran v. *Carey* (1887), 4 Man. R. 450 (Q.B.).
Curran v. *The Rural Municipality of North Norfolk* (1892), 8 Man. R. 256 (Q.B.).
North West Battery, Ltd. v. *Hargrave* (1913), 23 Man. R. 923 (Q.B.).
Pickering v. *Grand Trunk Pacific Ry. Co.* (1913), 23 Man.R. 723 (C.A.).
Rex v. *Hagel and Westlake* (1914), 24 Man. R. 19 (Q.B.).
Rex v. *Kooten* (1925), 35 Man. R. 461 (Q.B.).
Rex et rel. Sovereen v. *Edwards* (1912), 22 Man. R. 790 (Q.B.).
Spencer v. *Spencer* (1913), 23 Man. R. 461 (Q.B.).

SECONDARY SOURCES

Bryce, George, *A History of Manitoba: Its Resources and People* at 597. Toronto: Canada History, 1906.
Crockford's Clerical Directory. London: 1891.
Maillet, Lise. *Provincial Royal Commissions and Commissions of Inquiry, 1867–1982: A Selective Bibliography*. Ottawa: National Library of Canada, 1986.
Manitoba Free Press. 'Demand Removal of Mr. Justice Curran.' In *Manitoba Free Press*, 18 January 1918.
Morley, Marjorie. *Royal Commissions and Commissions of Inquiry Under 'The Evidence Act' in Manitoba* at 3. Winnipeg: Provincial Library of Manitoba 1979.
Willie, Richard A. *'These Legal Gentlemen': Lawyers in Manitoba: 1839–1900* at 173–5. Winnipeg: Legal Research Institute of the University of Manitoba, 1994.

(1881) 17 Can. L.J. 90.
(1937) 10 Man. Bar N. 501.

Manitoba Free Press, 25 December 1888; 26 December 1901; 23 October 1912; 25 January 1918; 26 January 1918, 4; 10 January 1928, 5; 13 January 1928, 8.

William James Donovan

PRIMARY SOURCES

Donovan, William James, Papers, Archives of the Law Society of Manitoba, file P 1238, PAM.

– Papers, Archives of the University of Toronto, file A73-0026/086(58).
Census of Ontario, 1881, District 110, South Leeds, Sub-district Lansdowne & Leeds, Front, Division 2 at 22.

Brown v. *Keele*, [1934] 2 W.W.R. 570 (Man. C.A.).
Cutler v. *Law Society of Manitoba* (1930), 39 Man. R. 209 (Q.B.).
In re Macdonald Estate; Rex v. *Surrogate Court Judge (No. 1)* (1929), 38 Man. R. 446 (C.A.).
Kizlyk v. *Canadian Pacific Railway* (1943), 51 Man. R. 33 (C.A.).
McMillan v. *Harrison*, [1937] 1 W.W.R. 237 (Man. C.A.).
Rex v. *Baschuk* (1931), 39 Man. R. 554 (C.A.).
Robertson v. *Robertson* (1946), 53 Man. R. 27 (C.A.).
W. v. *W.* (1934), 42 Man. R. 578 (C.A.).
Woodcock v. *Woodcock and Roeder* (1942), 49 Man. R. 113 (C.A.).

SECONDARY SOURCES

Gibson, Dale, and Lee Gibson, *Substantial Justice: Law and Lawyers in Manitoba 1670–1970*. Winnipeg: Peguis, 1972.
Greene, B.M., ed. 'Hon. Justice William James Donovan.' In *Who's Who in Canada, 1943–44* 452. Toronto: International Press, 1944.
Maillet, Lise. *Provincial Royal Commissions and Commissions of Inquiry, 1867–1982: A Selective Bibliography* at 127. Ottawa: National Library of Canada, 1986.
(1932) 1 Fortnightly L.J. 194.
(1937) 6 Fortnightly L.J. 244.

Manitoba Free Press, 20 July 1922, 1; 21 July 1922, 1; 22 July 1922, 1; 1 October 1940, 1; 26 May 1949, 1; 27 May 1949, 9.

Joseph Dubuc

PRIMARY SOURCES

Census of Manitoba, 1881.
Dubuc, Albert, Papers, Archives of the Law Society of Manitoba, file P 1239, PAM.
Dubuc, Alexandre Joseph Henri, Papers, Archives of the Law Society of Manitoba, file P 1239, PAM.
Dubuc, Antonin, Papers, Archives of the Law Society of Manitoba, file P 1239, PAM.
Dubuc, Lucien, Papers, Archives of the Law Society of Manitoba, file P 1239, PAM.

Dubuc, Joseph, Papers, MG 14, B26, PAM.
Dubuc, Paul A., Papers, Archives of the Law Society of Manitoba, file P 1239, PAM.
Inkster, Colin, Papers, MG 14, B30, box 2, scrapbook, PAM.
Macdonald, John A., Papers, MG 26A, PAM.
Manitoba Biographical Scrapbooks, Legislative Library of Manitoba, books 3 and 5.
Parliamentary Debates, 5th Session, 6 June 1872.

Canadian Bank of Commerce v. *Adamson* (1884), 1 Man. L.J. 3 (Q.B.).
Herb v. *Lawrence* (1890), 7 Man. R. 222 (C.A.).
Maddill v. *Kelly* (1884), 1 Man. L.J. 280 (Q.B.).
Re George A. Stanbro (1884), 1 Man. R. 263 (C.A.).
Re G.A. Stanbro (1884), 1 Man. R. 325 (C.A.).
Re G.A. Stanbro (1885), 2 Man. R. 1 (Q.B.).
Rex. v. *Wasyl Kapij, et al.* (1905), 15 Man. R. 110 (C.A.).
Wood v. *Wood* (1884), 1 Man. R. 317 (Q.B.).

SECONDARY SOURCES

Begg, Alexander, and Walter R. Nursey. *Ten Years in Winnipeg*. Winnipeg: Times, 1879.
Buchanan, A.W. Patrick. *The Bench and Bar of Lower Canada Down to 1850*. Montreal: Burton's, 1925.
Canada Law Journal. 'Judicial Appointments.' (1920) 56 Can. L.J. 401.
Cote, N. Omer, ed. *Political Appointments, Parliaments and the Judicial Bench in the Dominion of Canada 1867 to 1895*. Ottawa: Thoburn, 1896.
– *Political Appointments, Parliaments and the Judicial Bench in the Dominion of Canada 1896 to 1917*. Ottawa: Loew-Martin Company, 1917.
Donnelly, M.S. 'The Story of the Manitoba Legislature.' (1957) 12 Hist. & Sc. Soc. Man. 29 at 30–3.
Foran, Thomas P. *Trial of Ambrose Lepine at Winnipeg for the Wilful Murder of Thomas Scott: Question of Jurisdiction*. Montreal: Lovell, 1874.
Friesen, Gerald. *The Canadian Prairies, A History* at 196. Toronto: University of Toronto Press, 1987.
Henderson, George Fletcher. *Federal Royal Commissions in Canada 1867–1966, A Checklist* at 6, 13, 105. Toronto: University of Toronto Press, 1967.
Historic Resources Branch of the Province of Manitoba. *The Honourable Joseph Dubuc, K.S.M.G.* Winnipeg: Historic Resources Branch, 1981.
Kemp, H. Douglas. 'Land Grants under the Manitoba Act.' (1954) 3 Hist. & Sc. Soc. Man. 33.
Kerr, William H. 'The Bench and Bar of Quebec.' (1873) 9 Can. L. Times 86.

Knafla, Louis, and Richard Klumpenhouwer. 'Lucien Dubuc.' In *Lords of the Western Bench: A Biographical History of the Supreme and District Courts of Alberta, 1876–1990* 37. Edmonton: Legal Archives Society of Alberta, 1997.
Lecompte, Le P. Edouard. *Sir Joseph Dubuc (1840–1914), Un Grand Chrétien.* Montreal: Imprimerie du Messager, 1923.
McAlduff, Sister Maureen M. *Joseph Dubuc, Role and Views of a French Canadian in Manitoba 1870–1914.* M.A. thesis, University of Ottawa, 1966 [unpublished].
Milligan, F.A. 'The Establishment of Manitoba's First Provincial Government.' (1950) 5 Hist. & Sci. Soc. Man. 5 at 8, 14.
Morton, W.L. *Manitoba, A History.* Toronto: University of Toronto Press, 1957.
O'Donnell, John H. *Manitoba As I Saw It* at 61. Toronto: Musson, 1909.
Prud'Homme, L.A. 'Sir Joseph Dubuc.' (1914) Revue Canadienne 386, 506.
Rich, E.E. *London Correspondence Inward from Eden Colvile 1849–1852.* London: Hudson's Bay Record Society, 1956.
Ritchot, Rev. N.-J. 'The Journal of Rev. N.-J. Ritchot March 24 to May 28, 1870.' In W.L. Morton, ed., *Manitoba: The Birth of a Province* 131 at 155. Winnipeg: Manitoba Record Society, 1965.
Robertson, John Palmerston, ed. *A Political Manual of the Province of Manitoba and the North-West Territories* at 163. Winnipeg: Call, 1887.
Roscoe, Alexander Allan. *The Manitoba Act in Transition, 1870–1896: The Transformation of Manitoba's French-Canadian Politico-Cultural Institutions.* M.A. thesis, University of Manitoba, 1968 [unpublished].
Siggins, Maggie, *Riel: A Life of Revolution.* Toronto: HarperCollins, 1994.
Stanley, George F.G. *Louis Riel.* Toronto: Ryerson, 1963.
Wallace, W. Stewart, ed. *The Macmillan Dictionary of Canadian Biography* 225. Toronto: Macmillan, 1926.
Western Law Times. 'Private Prosecutors.' (1890) 1 W.L. Times 164.
Willie, Richard A. *'These Legal Gentlemen': Lawyers in Manitoba: 1839–1900.* Winnipeg: Legal Research Institute of the University of Manitoba, 1994.
Woodcock, George. *Faces from History: Canadian Profiles & Portraits* at 106. Edmonton: Hurtig, 1978.

(1873) 9 Can. L.J. 86 at 87.
(1884) 1 Man. L.J. 78.
(1885) 2 Man. L.J. 113.
– (1932) 1 Fortnightly L.J. 228.
(1934) 3 Fortnightly L.J. 283.
(1939) 8 Fortnightly L.J. 332.

Manitoba Free Press, 15 February 1874, 2; 16 October 1874, 2; 8 October 1909, 6; 14 January 1914, 4; 16 January 1914, 11.

Manitoba Gazette, 24 September 1872, 1; 1 October 1872, 2.
Newspaper, unknown. 'Sudden Death of Sir Joseph Dubuc.' (January 1914), Archives of the Law Society of Manitoba, scrapbook of newspaper clippings, PAM.

Andrew Knox Dysart

PRIMARY SOURCES

Dysart, Andrew Knox, Papers, Archives of the Law Society of Manitoba, file P 1241, PAM.
Dysart, Arthur Long, Papers, Archives of the Law Society of Manitoba, file P 1241, PAM.
Dysart, George Augustus Harrison, Papers, Archives of the Law Society of Manitoba, file P 1241, PAM.

Blanchett v. *Hansell et al.* (1944), 52 Man. R. 1 (Q.B.).
Century Indemnity Company v. *Northwestern Utilities Limited*, [1935] S.C.R. 291.
Cook v. *Westgate* (1944), 51 Man. R. 227 (C.A.).
Dominion Royalty Corporation Ltd. (1930) and Dominion Royalty Corporation Ltd. (1934) v. *W.C. Goffatt*, [1935] S.C.R. 565.
General Dairies, Limited v. *Maritime Electric Company, Limited*, [1935] S.C.R. 519.
Hague v. *Cancer Relief and Research Institute* (1939), 47 Man. R. 325 (Q.B.).
Humprehy Motors Limited v. *Joseph Ells*, [1935] S.C.R. 249.
In Re Hole Estate (1948), 56 Man. R. 295 (Q.B.).
In the Matter of the Estate of Herbert Carlyle Hammond, Deceased, [1935] S.C.R. 550.
Maguire v. *Northland Drug Company, Limited*, [1935] S.C.R. 412.
Markadonis v. *His Majesty the King*, [1935] S.C.R. 657.
Mason v. *His Majesty the King*, [1935] S.C.R. 513.
McLaughlin v. *Isaac W.C. Solloway and Harvey Mills*, [1936] S.C.R. 127.
McLean v. *McLean* (1941), 49 Man. R.143 (Q.B.).
Minister of Finance of British Columbia v. *His Majesty the King (at the Prosecution of Andler et al.)*, [1935] S.C.R. 278.
Mitchell v. *Martin and Rose*, [1925] 1 W.W.R. 500 (Man. Q.B.).
O'Leary et al. v. *Smith* (1924), 34 Man. R. 386 (Q.B.).
Peggy Sage Inc. and Northam-Warren Limited v. *Siegel Kahn Company of Canada Limited*, [1935] S.C.R. 539.
Rex ex rel Kowalski v. *Oak Bluff School Division* (1937), 45 Man. R. 409.
Rex v. *Westgate* (1928), 38 Man. R. 34 (C.A.).
Royal Trust Company v. *Toronto Transportation Commission*, [1935] S.C.R. 671.
Sampson v. *The King*, [1935] S.C.R. 634.

Schwartzenhauer v. *His Majesty the King*, [1935] S.C.R. 367.
Schweyer Electric and Manufacturing Company v. *New York Central Railroad Company*, [1935] S.C.R. 665.
Shoprite Stores et al. v. *Robert W. Gardiner*, [1935] S.C.R. 637.
Sing et al. v. *His Majesty the King*, [1935] S.C.R. 635.
Smith v. *Wesley College* (1923), 33 Man. R. 477 (Q.B.).
Southern Canada Power Company Ltd. v. *His Majesty the King*, [1936] S.C.R. 4.
St. John and the Vancouver Stock and Bond Company Limited v. *George L. Fraser*, [1935] S.C.R. 441.
Swartz Bros. Limited v. *August Wills*, [1935] S.C.R. 628.
T.C. Glennie v. *McD. & C. Holdings Limited*, [1935] S.C.R. 257.
The St. Vincent De Paul Children's Aid Society of Toronto v. *Spence*, [1935] S.C.R. 652.
The Toronto General Trusts Corporation v. *The Corporation of the City of Ottawa*, [1935] S.C.R. 531.
Toronto Transportation Company v. *The Corporation of the Village of Swansea*, [1935] S.C.R. 455.
Weiss and Morris Weiss v. *The State Life Insurance Company*, [1935] S.C.R. 461.
William Stott and Sarah Stott v. *Ellis A. Heninger*, [1935] S.C.R. 408.
Williams v. *Stewart & Cameron, Limited* (1923), 33 Man. R. 436 (C.A.).
Winnipeg Electric Company v. *Jacob Geel*, [1932] A.C. 690 (Privy Council).

SECONDARY SOURCES

Dysart, Andrew Knox. 'Go Forth in Faith, Hope and Charity.' (1944) 16 Man. Bar N. 31.
Ferns, H.S. *Reading from Left to Right: One Man's Political History* at 259–63, 289. Toronto: University of Toronto Press, 1983.
Gibson, Dale, and Lee Gibson. *Substantial Justice: Law and Lawyers in Manitoba 1670–1970*. Winnipeg: Peguis, 1972.
Greene, B.M., ed. 'Hon. Andrew Knox Dysart.' In *Who's Who in Canada, 1943–44* 1299. Toronto: International Press, 1944.
Henderson, George Fletcher, *Federal Royal Commissions in Canada 1867–1966, a Checklist* at 124, 126. Toronto: University of Toronto Press, 1967.
Kealey, Dr T. Herman. 'The Brewers Benefaction.' (1992 autumn) Univ. Man. Alumni J. 4.
Maillet, Lise. *Provincial Royal Commissions and Commissions of Inquiry, 1867–1982: A Selective Bibliography* at 125. Ottawa: National Library of Canada, 1986.
Manitoba Bar News. 'On Judgments.' (1940) 12 Man. Bar N. 75.
– 'Judicial Vacancies Filled.' (1947) 19 Man. Bar N. 85.

– 'Obituary.' (1949) 21 Man. Bar N. 56.
– 'Obituary.' (1952) 24 Man. Bar N. 52.
Morton, W.L. *One University: A History of the University of Manitoba 1877–1957* at 163–5. Toronto: McClelland & Stewart, 1957.
– *Manitoba, a History* at 404–5. Toronto: University of Toronto Press, 1957.
Stubbs, Roy St. George. 'Andrew Knox Dysart.' In *Prairie Portraits* 119. Toronto: McClelland & Stewart, 1954.
– 'Mr. Justice Dysart.' (1954) 32 Can. Bar Rev. 161.
Tulloch, Judith. 'Thomas Cutler.' In Francess G. Halpenny and Jean Hamelin, eds., *Dictionary of Canadian Biography*, vol. 7, 223. Toronto: University of Toronto Press, 1988.
Whalen, James Murray, ed. *Records of Federal Royal Commissions (RG 33)*, vol. 1, at 115–119. Ottawa: National Archives of Canada, 1990.

(1933) 2 Fortnightly L.J. 346.
(1933) 3 Fortnightly L.J. 12.
(1937) 6 Fortnightly L.J. 212, 229.
(1938) 7 Fortnightly L.J. 212, 219.
(1939) 8 Fortnightly L.J. 209, 260–1, 267.
(1940) 9 Fortnightly L.J. 267, 276.

Manitoba Free Press, 19 January 1933, 19.
Winnipeg Free Press, 25 July 1952, 1, 13; 26 July 1952, 6; 28 July 1952, 1; 29 July 1952, 3.

Alexander Casimir Galt

PRIMARY SOURCES

Galt, Alexander Casimir, Papers, Archives of the Law Society of Manitoba, file P 1249, PAM.
Galt, Alexander Casimir, Papers, Archives of the University of Toronto, file A73-0026/112(69).
Manning, R.A.C., Papers, MG 14, B 36, PAM.

Bridges v. *The Real Estate, Loan and Debenture Co.* (1885), 21 Can. L.J. 161 (Chancery).
Chase et al. v. *Starr* (1923), 33 Man. R. 26 (Q.B.).
Clarke v. *The Union Fire Insurance Company* (1883), 19 Can. L.J. 363 (Masters).
Complin v. *Beggs* (1913), 24 Man. R. 596 (Q.B.).
Goodbun v. McRae (1927), 36 Man. R. 483 (C.A.).
Kelley v. *Holley* (1912), 22 Man. R. 601 (Q.B.).

Hart v. *Wishard Langan Co., Ltd.* (1909), 18 Man. R. 376 (C.A.).
Hubbard v. *The Union Fire Insurance Company* (1880), 44 U.C.Q.B. 391.
In Re The Prudential Life Insurance Company (1920), 30 Man. R. 468 (Q.B.).
In Re Fenton Estate (1921), 30 Man. R. 246 (C.A.).
In Re Skaleski (1927), 36 Man. R. 221 (C.A.).
McLean v. *Garland* (1883), 19 Can. L.J. 35 (Com. Pleas).
McLean v. *Smith* (1884), 20 Can. L.J. 31.
McLeod v. *Krusko* (1931), 1 Fortnightly L.J. 7 (Q.B.).
Muttlebury v. *King* (1880), 44 U.C.Q.B. 355.
Newton v. *Newton* (1924), 34 Man. R. 190 (C.A.).
Newton & Company v. *Wolvin et al.* (1930), 39 Man. R. 285 (C.A.).
Northwood v. *Rennie* (1878), 14 Can L.J. 215 (Com. Pleas).
Pescovitch v. *Western Canada Flour Mills Co., Ltd.* (1914), 24 Man. R. 783.
Powell v. Maddock (1915), 25 Man. R. 730 (Q.B.).
Re Edward Beck (1916), 27 Man. R. 288 (C.A.).
Re Jos. Chamryk (1914), 25 Man. R. 50 (Q.B.).
Re Meek v. *Scoble* (1884), 20 Can. L.J. 15 (Com. Pleas).
Rex v. *Gudmondson* (1933), 41 Man R. 87 (C.A.).
Rex v. *Duguay* (1933), 41 Man. R. 211 (C.A.).
Theo. Noel Co. v. *Vitae Ore Co.* (1907), 17 Man. R. 319 (C.A.).
Union Fire Insurance Company v. *Lyman* (1882), 46 U.C.Q.B. 453 and 471.

SECONDARY SOURCES

Barrister, The. 'Wit and Humor.' (1894) 1 Barrister 13.
– 'Sir Thomas Galt, KC.M.G., As a Lawyer.' (1895) 1 Barrister 185.
– 'Law School, Part II.' (1895) 1 Barrister 213.
Bowsfield, Hartwell, ed. *The Letters of Charles John Brydges 1883–1889* at xxxii, 172. Winnipeg: Hudson's Bay Record Society, 1981.
Canada Law Journal. 'Priorities Under Registry Act.' (1891) 27 Can. L.J. 98.
– 'Sir Thomas Galt.' (1894) 30 Can. L.J. 488.
– Editorial (1895) 31 Can. L.J. 523.
Canada Law Times. 'Editorial Review, Notice by Registration' (1891) 11 Can. L. Times 23.
Chadwick, Edward Marion, 'Galt.' In *Ontario Families*, vol. 1, 138. Lambertville, NJ: Hunterdon House, 1970.
Coulson, Cary F. *A Source Book of Royal Commissions and Other Major Government Inquiries in Canadian Education, 1787–1978*. Toronto: University of Toronto Press, 1981.
Den Otter, A.A. *Civilizing the West: The Galts and the Development of Western Canada* at 8–9. Edmonton: University of Alberta Press, 1982.

G.A.G. 'George Frederick Galt.' In Charles G.D. Roberts and Arthur L. Tunnell, eds., *A Standard Dictionary of Canadian Biography* 208. Toronto: Trans-Canada Press, 1934.

– 'Sir Thomas Galt.' In Charles G.D. Roberts and Arthur L. Tunnell, eds., *A Standard Dictionary of Canadian Biography* 209. Toronto: Trans-Canada Press, 1934.

Galt, Alexander Casimir. 'Common Carriers in Ontario.' (1886) 22 Can. L.J. 293, 314.

– 'The Principle of Subrogration' (1891) 11 Can. L. Times 9.

– 'The Principle of Subrogation: A Reply.' (1891) 11 Can. L. Times 89.

– 'Set-off By Contributories.' (1891) 11 Can. L. Times 264.

– 'Power of Sale Without Notice.' (1893) 13 Can. L. Times 36.

– 'Mortgagees' Rights Under the Statute of Limitations.' (1893) 13 Can. L. Times 85.

– 'Rights and Remedies in a Foreclosure Action.' (1893) 29 Can. L.J. 312.

– 'Title by Estoppel.' (1894) 14 Can. L. Times 121.

– 'Mortgagee v. Purchaser Subject to Mortgage.' (1894) 30 Can. L.J. 490.

– 'Liabilities of Trade Unions and Their Members.' (1903) 2 Can. L. Rev. 627.

– 'Right of a Third Party Under a Contract Inter Alios.' (1905) 4 Can. L. Rev. 364.

– 'Appeals to the Privy Council.' (1921) 41 Can. L. Times 168.

– 'Obiter Dicta.' (1930) 3:2 Man. Bar N. 4.

Goulson, Carlyn Floyd. *A Source Book of Royal Commissions and Other Major Governmental Inquiries in Canadian Education, 1787–1978* at 208. Toronto: University of Toronto Press, 1981

Greene, B.M., ed., 'Hon. Alexander Casimir Galt.' In *Who's Who in Canada, 1923–1924* 494. Toronto: International Press, 1924.

Hall, Roger, and Nick Whistler. 'John Galt.' In Francess G. Halpenny and Jean Hamelin, eds., *Dictionary of Canadian Biography*, vol. 7, 335. Toronto: University of Toronto Press, 1988.

Henderson, George Fletcher. *Federal Royal Commissions in Canada 1867–1966* at 88. Toronto: University of Toronto Press, 1967.

Maillet, Lise. *Provincial Royal Commissions and Commissions of Inquiry, 1867–1982: A Selective Bibliography* at 122. Ottawa: National Library of Canada, 1986.

Morley, Marjorie. *Royal Commissions and Commissions of Inquiry Under 'The Evidence Act' in Manitoba* at 3. Winnipeg: Provincial Library of Manitoba.

Stubbs, Roy St. George. 'Knox Magee and the Judges, When the Bench Was Compromised.' In *Winnipeg Free Press* 27. 22 November 1962.

Wallace, W. Stewart, ed. *The Macmillan Dictionary of Canadian Biography*, 3rd ed., 256. Toronto: Macmillan, 1963.

(1869) 5 Can. L.J. 142.
(1891) 27 Can. L.J. 98.
(1894) 30 Can. L.J. 488.
(1895) 31 Can. L.J. 461, 523.
(1896) 32 Can. L.J. 604.
(1912) 48 Can. L.J. 639.
(1917) 53 Can. L.J. 41.
(1891) 11 Can. L. Times 23.
(1933) 3 Fortnightly L.J. 37.

Manitoba Free Press, 26 February 1912, 5; 23 October 1912; 1 September 1915, 8.
Manitoba Free Press, 29 May 1917, 9.
Winnipeg Free Press, 30 July 1936, 1; 31 July 1936, 1.

John Joseph Kelly

PRIMARY SOURCES

Hniden v. *Herr* (1931), 40 Man. R. 108 (C.A.).

SECONDARY SOURCES

Kelly, John Joseph. 'Limitation of Strict Liability Under Rylands vs. Fletcher.' (1946) 18:1 Man. Bar N. 1.
Manitoba Bar News. 'Our Newest Judges.' (1949) 21 Man. Bar N. 71.
– 'Obituary.' (1952) 24 Man. Bar N. 17.
Peden, Murray. *Hearken to the Evidence* at 52–5. Stittsville, Ont.: Canada's Wings, 1983.

Winnipeg Free Press, 2 April 1952, 27; 3 April 1952, 21; 4 April 1952, 38.

James Frederick Kilgour

PRIMARY SOURCES

Kilgour, David Errett, Papers, Archives of the University of Toronto, file A73-0026/200(86).
Kilgour, David William, Papers, Archives of the Law Society of Manitoba, file P 1273, PAM.
Kilgour, James Frederick, Papers, Archives of the Law Society of Manitoba, file P 1273, PAM.
– Papers, Archives of the University of Toronto, file A73-0026/200(94).
Census of Ontario, 1871, 1881.

Kilgour v. *White* (1923), 33 Man. R. 398 (Q.B.).
Heake v. *City Securities Company* (1931), 39 Man. R. 399 (C.A.).
In Re Lobel (1929), 38 Man. R. 48 (C.A.).
In Re Somerset Estate (1928), 40 Man. R. 566 (Q.B.).
In Re Thacker Estate (1930), 39 Man. R. 375 (Q.B.).
Jones v. *McClean et al.* (1931), 39 Man. R. 321 (C.A.).
McPherson v. *Furlong* (1928), 37 Man. R. 508 (Q.B.).
Ross v. *Ross* (1930), 39 Man. R. 364 (Q.B.).
Zeidel v. *Winnipeg Electric Company* (1928), 37 Man. R. 412 (C.A.).

SECONDARY SOURCES

American Biographical Publishing Company, ed. *The Canadian Biographical Dictionary and Portrait Gallery of Eminent and Self-Made Men*, Ontario volume, 98. Toronto: American Biographical, 1880.

Barrister, The. 'Osgoode Legal and Literary Society.' (1895) 1 Barrister 478.

– 'Osgoode Hall Notes.' (1896) 2 Barrister 209.

Bloomfield, Elizabeth. *Inventory of Primary and Archival Sources: Guelph and Wellington County to 1940*. Guelph: Guelph Regional Project, 1989.

Bloomfield, Elizabeth, and Gilbert A. Stetler. *Guelph and Wellington County, a Bibliography of Settlement and Development Since 1800*. Guelph: Guelph Regional Project, 1988.

Johnson, Leo A. *History of Guelph 1827–1927*. Guelph: Guelph Historical Society, 1977.

Maillet, Lise. *Provincial Royal Commissions and Commissions of Inquiry, 1867–1982: A Selective Bibliography* at 125. Ottawa: National Library of Canada, 1986.

Rose, George Maclean, ed. *A Cyclopedia of Canadian Biography* 50. Toronto: Rose, 1888.

Wallace, W. Stewart, ed. *The Macmillan Dictionary of Canadian Biography*, 4th ed., at 321, 411. Toronto: Macmillan, 1978.

(1931) 4:4 Man. Bar N. 12.

Manitoba Free Press, 28 November 1931, 4, 11; 30 November 1931, 10; 1 December 1931, 16.

Albert Clements Killam

PRIMARY SOURCES

Killam, Albert Clements, Papers, Archives of the Law Society of Upper Canada, file 12690.

– Papers, Archives of the University of Toronto, file A73-0026/201(04).
Killam, George Knight, Papers, Archives of the Law Society of Manitoba, file P 1273, PAM.
Census of Manitoba, 1891, Ward 1, page 34.
The Railway Act, S.C. 1903, C. 58, s. 8.
The Railway Act, R.S.C. 1906, C. 37, s. 10.

Barrett v. *The City of Winnipeg* (1891), 7 Man. R. 273 (C.A.).
Beemer v. *Inkster* (1886), 3 Man. R. 534 (Q.B.).
Bertrand v. *Canadian Rubber Co.* (1897), 12 Man. R. 27 (Q.B.).
Grey v. *Manitoba & N.W. Ry. Co.*, [1897] A.C. 254 (Privy Council).
Kirchoffer v. *Clement* (1897), 11 Man. R. 460 (C.A.).
Liquor Prohibition Appeal 1895, [1896] A.C. 348 (Privy Council).
McKenzie v. *Fletcher* (1897), 11 Man. R. 540 (Q.B.).
Mulligan v. *Hubbard* (1888), 5 Man. R. 225 (C.A.).
Mulvihill v. *Lachance* (1890), 7 Man. R. 189 (C.A.).
Queen v. *Riel* (1886), 2 Man. R. 321 (C.A.).
Re Logan Trusts (1886), 3 Man. R. 49 (Q.B.).
Real Estate Loan Co. v. *Molesworth* (1886), 3 Man. R. 116 (Q.B.).
Regina v. *Cloutier* (1898), 12 Man. R. 183 (C.A.).
Regina v. *Herrell* (1898), 12 Man. R. 198 (C.A.).
Regina v. *Vrooman* (1886), 3 Man. R. 509 (Q.B.).
Rex v. *Young* (1902), 14 Man. R. 58 (Q.B.).
Smith v. *Strange* (1885), 2 Man. R. 101 (C.A.).
Wellband v. *Moore* (1885), 2 Man. R. 193 (Q.B.).
Winnipeg and Hudson's Bay Co. v. *Mann* (1890), 6 Man. R. 409 (Q.B.).

SECONDARY SOURCES

Barrister, The. 'The Manitoba School Case: The Privy Council Decisions.' (1895) 1 Barrister 145.
Begg, Alexander, and Walter R. Nursey, *Ten Years in Winnipeg*. Winnipeg: Times, 1879.
Benham, Mary Lile. *The Manitoba Club 100 Years 1874–1974* at 69. Winnipeg: Manitoba Club, 1974.
Bowsfield, Hartwell, ed. *The Letters of Charles John Brydges 1879–1882*. Winnipeg: Hudson's Bay Record Society, 1977.
– *The Letters of Charles John Brydges 1883–1889* at 106, 246, 272. Winnipeg: Hudson's Bay Record Society, 1981.
Brown, George S. *Yarmouth, Nova Scotia: A Sequel to Campbell's History*. Boston: Rand Avery, 1888.

Burley, David G. 'Arthur Wellington Ross.' In Ramsay Cook, ed., *Dictionary of Canadian Biography*, vol. 13, 898. Toronto: University of Toronto Press, 1994.

Bushnell, Ian. *The Captive Court: A Study of the Supreme Court of Canada*. Montreal: McGill-Queen's University Press, 1992.

Canada Law Journal. (1873) 9 Can. L.J. 335.

– (1877) 13 Can. L.J. 59.

– 'Queen's Counsel.' (1884) 1 Can. L.J. 96.

– Case Comment. (1900) 36 Can. L.J. 614.

– Case Comment. (1901) 37 Can. L.J. 217.

– Editorial. (1903) 39 Can. L.J. 497.

– 'Hon. Mr. Justice Killam.' (1908) 44 Can. L.J. 129.

– Railway Commission. (1908) 44 Can. L.J. 172.

Canadian Law Review. 'Judicial Appointments.' (1903) 2 Can. L.R. 656.

Charlton, ed. *Charlton & Co.'s General Directory of Windsor, Sandwich & Amherstburg for 1875–6*. (London, Ont.: Charlton, 1875).

Cruikshank, Ken. *Close Ties: Railways, Government, and the Board of Railway Commissioners, 1851–1933*. Montreal: McGill-Queen's University Press, 1991.

Elliott, Bruce, ed. *Index to the 1871 Census of Ontario, Essex-Kent*. Toronto: Ontario Genealogical Society, 1989.

Fisher & Taylor, eds. *Toronto Directory, For 1875*. Toronto: Fisher & Taylor, 1875.

Gibson, Dale & Lee Gibson, *Substantial Justice: Law and Lawyers in Manitoba 1670–1970*. Winnipeg: Peguis, 1972.

Gibson, Lee. 'Albert Clements Killam.' In Mary P. Bentley, ed., *Dictionary of Canadian Biography*, vol. 13, 542. Toronto: University of Toronto Press, 1994.

Harvey, Cameron, ed. *The Law Society of Manitoba 1877–1977* at 274, 284. Winnipeg: Peguis, 1977.

Hibbitts, Bernard J. *A Change of Mind: The Supreme Court of Canada and the Board of Railway Commissioners, 1903–1939*. LL.M. thesis, University of Toronto, 1986 [unpublished].

Hopkins, J. Castell, ed., *The Canadian Annual Review of Public Affairs 1903* at 237, 364, 430–1, 478. Toronto: Annual Review Publishing Co., 1904.

Hutchinson, Thomas, ed. *Hutchinson's Nova Scotia Directory, for 1864–65*. Halifax: Muir, 1864.

– *Hutchinson's Nova Scotia Directory for 1866–67*. Halifax: McAlpine, 1865.

Johnson, J.K., ed. *The Canadian Directory of Parliament 1867–1967* at 304. Ottawa: Public Archives of Canada, 1968.

Lawson, J. Murray, *Record of the Shipping of Yarmouth, N.S.* Yarmouth: Lawson, 1876.

Lefroy, A.H.F. 'Manitoba Liquor Act Case.' (1901) 37 Can. L.J. 217.

Maillet, Lise. *Provincial Royal Commissions and Commissions of Inquiry, 1867–1982: A Selective Bibliography* at 118. Ottawa: National Library of Canada, 1986.
Manitoba Bar News. 'Hon. Mr. Justice Killam.' (1892) 3 Man. Bar N. 122.
Marble, Allan Everett. *Nova Scotians at Home and Abroad* at 232. Windsor, NS: Lancelot, 1977.
McWilliams, Margaret. *Manitoba Milestones*. Toronto: J.M. Dent, 1928.
Pryke, K.G. 'Thomas Killam.' In Francess G. Halpenny, ed., *Dictionary of Canadian Biography*, vol. 9, 425. Toronto: University of Toronto Press, 1976.
Rordans & Nicholls, eds. *The Ontario Law List and Solicitor's Agency Book*, 8th ed. Toronto: Rordans & Nicholls, 1876.
Rose, George Maclean, ed. 'Albert Clement Killam.' In *A Cyclopedia of Canadian Biography* 398. Toronto: Rose, 1888.
Ross, Arthur Wellington. *Speeches on the Canadian Pacific Railway and the Canadian North West*. Montreal: Gazette Printing, 1884.
Ross, Ross & Killam, eds. *Important to Intending Settlers in Manitoba*. Winnipeg: Ross, Ross & Killam, 1879.
Snell, James G. 'The West and the Supreme Court of Canada.' (1985) 14 Man. L.J. 287 at 293.
Snell, James G., and Frederick Vaughan. *The Supreme Court of Canada, History of the Institution* Toronto: Osgoode Society, 1985.
Stamp, Robert M. 'Adam Crooks.' In Francess G. Halpenny & Jean Hamelin, eds. *Dictionary of Canadian Biography*, vol. 11, 220. Toronto: University of Toronto Press, 1982.
Western Law Times. 'Timely Expressions.' (1890) 1 W.L. Times 189.
– 'Student Lectures' (1890) 1 W.L. Times 235.
– 'The Privy Council and the School Case.' (1892) 3 W.L. Times 81.
– 'The Supreme Court Vacancies.' (1895) W.L. Times 75.
Willie, Richard A. *'These Legal Gentlemen': Lawyers in Manitoba: 1838–1900*. Winnipeg: Legal Research Institute of the University of Manitoba, 1994.

Manitoba Free Press, 29 October 1880, 1; 24 January 1883, 4; 31 January 1885, 2; 24 July 1903, 1; 2 March 1908, 1, 4; 3 March 1908, 10; 6 March 1908, 5.
[Toronto] *Globe*, 7 March 1908.

(1895) 1 Barrister 472.
(1878) 14 Can. L.J. 242.
(1905) 41 Can. L.J. 205.
(1908) 44 Can. L.J. 209.
(1884) 1 Man. L.J. 96.
(1892) 3 W.L. Times 122.
(1895) 6 W.L. Times 81.

Daniel Alexander Macdonald

PRIMARY SOURCES

Macdonald, Daniel Alexander, Papers, Archives of the Law Society of Manitoba, file P 1283, PAM.

Grand Lodge, A.O.U.W. v. *Supreme Lodge, A.O.U.W.* (1907), 17 Man. R. 360 (Q.B.).
In re Thiessen (1923), 34 Man. R. 125 (C.A.).
Nagy v. *Manitoba Free Press Co.* (1907), 16 Man. R. 619 (C.A.).
Patton v. *Pioneer Navigation & Sand Co.* (1908), 21 Man. R. 405 (Q.B.).
Rex v. *Fidler* (1921), 31 Man. R. 358 (C.A.).

SECONDARY SOURCES

Canada Law Journal. Case Comment. (1917) 53 Can. L.J. 21 at 32.
Gibson, Dale, and Lee Gibson, *Substantial Justice: Law and Lawyers in Manitoba 1670–1970.* Winnipeg: Peguis, 1972.
Manitoba Bar News. 'To Chief Justice D.A. Macdonald on the Occasion of His Retirement.' (1937) 10 Man. Bar N. 474.
Maillet, Lise. *Provincial Royal Commissions and Commissions of Inquiry, 1867–1982: A Selective Bibliography* at 125, 131. Ottawa: National Library of Canada, 1986.
Parker, Dr C.W., ed. 'Hon. Daniel Alexander Macdonald.' In *Who's Who And Why, 1914* 562. Toronto: International Press, 1914.

Winnipeg Free Press, 29 October 1937, 5; 30 October 1937, 5; 1 November 1937, 2.

(1932) 2 Fortnightly L.J. 20.

William James Major

PRIMARY SOURCES

Major, William James, file, Archives of the Law Society of Manitoba, file P 1286, PAM.

Sawka and Sawka v. Torbiak (1941), 49 Man. R. 153 (Q.B.).
L. v. *L. and N.* (1944), 52 Man. R. 243 (Q.B.).
McLaughlin v. *McLaughlin* (1945), 53 Man. R. 125 (Q.B.).
Rex v. *Stewart* (1946), 54 Man. R. 324 (Q.B.).

SECONDARY SOURCES

Jackson, James A. *The Centennial History of Manitoba* at 208. Toronto: McClelland & Stewart, 1970.

Kendle, John. *John Bracken: A Political Biography*. Toronto: University of Toronto Press, 1979.
Major, Hon. Mr Justice. 'The Place of the Lawyer.' (1950) 22 Man. Bar N. 44.
Manitoba Bar News. 'Obituary.' (1953) 25 Man. Bar N. 50.
Morton, W.L. *Manitoba: A History*. Toronto: University of Toronto Press, 1957.
Parker, Dr C.W., ed. 'Hon. William James Major.' In *Who's Who in Canada, 1943–44* 782. Toronto: International Press, 1944.
Peden, Murray. *Hearken to the Evidence*. Stittsville, Ont.: Canada's Wings, 1983.
Stenton, Michael, and Stephen Lees, eds. 'Athelstan Rendall.' In *Who's Who of British Members of Parliament*, vol. 3, *1919–1945* 300. Sussex: Harvester, 1976.

(1950) 22 Man. Bar N. 44.

Winnipeg Free Press, 13 September 1946, 1; 19 May 1951; 4 August 1951; 14 August 1953, 1.

Thomas Graham Mathers

PRIMARY SOURCES

Law Society, Minute Book 6, Archives of the Law Society of Manitoba, PAM.
Mathers, Francis Graham, Papers, Archives of the Law Society of Manitoba, file P 1288, PAM.
Mathers, Thomas Graham, Papers, Archives of the Law Society of Manitoba, file P 1288, PAM.
Census of Manitoba, 1891.
National Industrial Conference of Dominion and Provincial Governments with Representative Employers and Labour Men, on the subjects of Industrial Relations and Labour Laws, and for the consideration of the Labour Features of the Treaty of Peace at 235. Ottawa: King's Printer, 1919.
Report of a Commission Appointed under Order-in-Council (P.C. 670) to Enquire into Industrial Relations in Canada, Together with a Minority Report and Supplementary Report. Ottawa: The Commission, 1919.

Ashmore et al. v. *Trans-Canada Finance Corporation Limited*, [1930] 1 W.W.R. 537 (Q.B.).
Brett v. *Foorsen* (1907), 17 Man. R. 241 (Q.B.).
Brown v. *Fox* (1921), 31 Man. R. 365 (Q.B.).
Canada Permanent Mortgage Corporation v. *School District of East Selkirk* (1907), 16 Man. R. 618 (Q.B.).
Emperor of Russia v. *Proskouriakoff*, [1907] 7 W.L.R. 766.
Emperor of Russia v. *Proskouriakoff*, [1908] 8 W.L.R. 10 and 461.
Emperor of Russia v. *Proskouriakoff* (1908), 18 Man. R. 56.

Emperor of Russia v. *Proskouriakoff* (1908), 17–18 Man. R. 143.
Emperor of Russia v. *Proskouriakoff* (1908), 42 S.C.R. 226.
Grain Claims Bureau, Limited v. *Canadian Surety Company* (1928), 37 Man. R. 235 (C.A.).
Hunter v. *Trans-Canada Finance Corporation et al.*, [1929] 3 W.W.R. 503 (Q.B.).
In the Matter of Her Majesty's Counsel (1892), 8 Man. R. 155 (Q.B.).
Kelly v. *Mathers et al.* (1915), 25 Man. R. 580 (C.A.).
Kowhanko v. *The J.H. Tremblay Company, Limited et al.* (1919), 30 Man. R. 198 (C.A.).
Penman v. *Winnipeg Electric Railway Company*, [1924] 1 W.W.R. 1087 (Q.B.).
Penman et al. v. *Winnipeg Electric Railway Company*, [1924] 2 W.W.R. 260 (Q.B.) and 587 (C.A.).
Penman et al. v. *Winnipeg Electric Railway Company (No. 2)*, [1925] 1 W.W.R. 156 (Q.B.).
Re Fedorenko (No. 1) (1910), 20 Man. R. 221.
Re P.E.H. (1912), 22 Man. R. 746 (Q.B.).
Rex v. *Alamazoff* (1919), 30 Man. R. 143 (Q.B.).
Rex v. *Hagel and Westlake* (1914), 24 Man. R. 19 (Q.B.).
Rex v. *Krafchenko* (1914), 24 Man. R. 652 (Q.B.), 22 C.C.C. 277.
Sanderson v. *Heap* (1909), 19 Man. R. 122 (Q.B.).

SECONDARY SOURCES

Avery, Donald. 'The Radical Alien and the Winnipeg General Strike.' In J.M. Bumsted, ed., *Interpreting Canada's Past*, vol. 2, *After Confederation* 222. Toronto: Oxford University Press, 1986.
Bercuson, David Jay. *Confrontation at Winnipeg*. Montreal: McGill-Queen's University Press, 1974.
Brown, Robert Craig, and Ramsay Cook. *Canada 1896–1921, A Nation Transformed* at 310–15, 324. Toronto: McClelland & Stewart, 1974.
Buchanan, Sue. *Canadian Federal and Provincial Royal Commissions*. Vancouver: University of British Columbia Library, 1968.
Canadian Annual Review. *Canadian Annual Review for 1919*. Toronto: University of Toronto Press.
Chaffey, B.E., ed. *Legal Ethics, Address by The Hon. T.G. Mathers, Chief Justice of The Court of King's Bench, Manitoba*. Winnipeg: Law Society of Manitoba, 1920.
– *A Summary of The Law of Divorce, by The Hon. T.G. Mathers, Chief Justice of The Court of King's Bench, Manitoba*. Winnipeg: Law Society of Manitoba, 1920.
Collier, Anne. *A History of Portage la Prairie and Surrounding District*. Altona, Man.: Friesen, 1969.
Courtney, John Childs. *Canadian Royal Commissions of Inquiry, 1946 to 1962: An*

Investigation of an Executive Instrument of Inquiry. Ph.D. thesis, Political Science, Duke University, 1964 [unpublished].
Coyne, J.B. 'Judges and Royal Commissions.' (1917) 37 Can. L. Times 416.
Gibson, Dale, and Lee Gibson. *Substantial Justice: Law and Lawyers in Manitoba 1670–1970*. Winnipeg: Peguis, 1972.
Greene, B.M., ed. 'Richard Deans Waugh.' In *Who's Who In Canada, 1923–24* 228. Toronto: International Press, 1924.
– 'Hon. T.G. Mathers.' In *Who's Who In Canada, 1923–24* 480. Toronto: International Press, 1924.
Henderson, George Fletcher, *Federal Royal Commissions in Canada 1867–1966, A Checklist*. Toronto: University of Toronto Press, 1967.
Jackson, James A.. *The Centennial History of Manitoba* at 186–9. Toronto: McClelland & Stewart, 1970.
Johnson, Wallace. 'Damage for Nervous Shock.' (1939) 11:7 Man. Bar N. 49.
Locke, Philip C. 'Lien Notes.' (1930) 2:8 Man. Bar N. 1.
Maillet, Lise. *Provincial Royal Commissions and Commissions of Inquiry, 1867–1982: A Selective Bibliography*. Ottawa: National Library of Canada, 1986.
Manitoba Bar News. (1937) 10 Man. Bar N. 498.
Manitoba Free Press. 'Judge Mathers Succeeds Dubuc.' In *Manitoba Free Press*, 8 February 1910, 1.
Mathers, Mr Justice. 'Divorce.' Archives of Law Society of Manitoba, lectures, 1919–20, PAM.
– 'Legal Ethics.' (1920) 5 Can. Bar Assoc. Proc. 268.
– 'Legal Ethics.' (1920) 40 Can. L.T. 809, 925.
– 'Address of Hon. Chief Justice Mathers to the Saskatchewan Bar Association, July, 1923.' (1923) 8 Can. Bar Assoc. Proc. 304.
Maxwell, James Douglas. *Royal Commissions and Social Change in Canada 1867–1966*. Ph.D. thesis, Political Science, Cornell University, 1969 [unpublished].
Metcalfe, J.H., ed. *The Tread of the Pioneers*. Portage la Prairie: Portage la Prairie and District Old Timers' Association, 1932.
Miller, Henry. 'Richard Waugh.' In Ramsay Cook and Jean Hamelin, eds., *Dictionary of Canadian Biography*, vol. 13, 1077. Toronto: University of Toronto Press, 1994.
Morton, W.L., *Manitoba, A History*. Toronto: University of Toronto Press, 1957.
Peden, Murray. *Hearken to the Evidence*. Stittsville, Ont.: Canada's Wings, 1983.
Plaxton, Charles Percy. 'Has an Accused the Right to Make a Statement at His Trial without Being Sworn or Subject to Cross-Examination.' (1916) 52 Can. L.J. 10.
Pope, Sir Joseph. *Correspondence of Sir John Macdonald* at 430. Toronto: Oxford University Press, 1921.

Pross, A. Paul, Christie Innis, and John A. Yogis. *Commissions of Inquiry*. Toronto: Carswell, 1990.
Snell, James G., and Frederick Vaughan. *The Supreme Court of Canada: History of the Institution*. Toronto: Osgoode Society, 1985.
Whalen, James Murray, ed. *Records of Federal Royal Commissions (RG 33)*, vol. 1. Ottawa: National Archives of Canada, 1990.
– *Records of Federal Royal Commissions (RG 33)*, vol. 2. Ottawa: National Archives of Canada, 1994.
(1920) 5 Can. Bar Assoc. Proc. 268.
(1923) 8 Can. Bar Assoc. Proc. 304.
(1900) 36 Can. L.J. 363.
(1916) 52 Can. L.J. 10.
(1917) 53 Can. L.J. 41.
(1920) 40 Can. L. Times 809, 925.
(1930) 2:8 Man. Bar N. 1.
(1939) 11:7 Man. Bar N. 49.

Manitoba Free Press, 10 October 1899, 1; 6 December 1899, 6; 9 December 1899, 6; 13 December 1899, 2; 23 August 1905, 1; 13 January 1914, 1; 11 August 1921, 5; 17 August 1927, 5; 19 August 1927, 6.

James Charles McKeagney

PRIMARY SOURCES

Macdonald, John A., Papers, MG 26A, vol. 25 (C 1496) at 9448, 47030–40, 47069–72, 47124–6, 47357–8, 47401–3, 157564–7, and Letterbooks 12 and 20, NAC.

Provincial Archives of Nova Scotia:
- McKeagney, James, Papers, RG 1, vols. 175, #95, #261, #491–60, #514, #515; 176, #28; 176 1/4, #9; 200, #307; 202, #371; 268, #25.
- Biography Collection, RG 3, vol. 1, #198; 2, #222, #271;
- Biography Collection, RG 5, Series P, vols. 4, 5; 8, #57; 11; Series D, vol. 10.
- Biography Collection, MG 100, vol. 200, #21.
- Biography Collection, Novascotian, 24 February 1868, 3.

Estate of Alexander McDonald (1853), 2 N.S.R. 123 at 125.
Regina v. *Biggs* (1885), 2 Man. R. 18 (Q.B.).
Re Rockwood Election, W.J. Brandrith, Petitioner, v. *S.J. Jackson, Respondent* (1885), 2 Man. R. 129 (C.A.).

SECONDARY SOURCES

Armstrong, C.H.A. *The Honourable Society of Osgoode Hall* at 32–5. Toronto: Clarke, Irwin, 1952.

Barristers' Society. *The Supreme Court of Nova Scotia and Its Judges 1754–1978*. Halifax: Nova Scotia Barristers' Society, 1978.

Beck, J. Murray. 'The Nomination of Candidates in Nova Scotia.' (1957) 36 Dal. Rev. 361.

– *Joseph Howe*, vol. 2, *The Briton Becomes Canadian 1848–1873*. Montreal: McGill-Queen's University Press, 1983.

– *Politics of Nova Scotia*, vol. 1, *1710–1896* at 144. Tantallon, N.S.: Four East Publication, 1985.

Belcher, C.H. *Belcher's Farmer's Almanack*. Halifax: C.H. Belcher, 1837, 1838, 1852, 1868, 1869, 1872.

Bell, D.G. 'Paths to the Law in the Maritimes, 1810–1825: The Bliss Brothers and Their Circle.' (1988) 8:2 N.S. Hist. Rev. 6.

Blakeley, Phyllis R. 'William Alexander Henry, a Father of Confederation from Nova Scotia.' (1968) 36 Collections N.S. Hist. Soc. 96.

Cahill, Barry. 'The Origin and Evolution of the Attorney and Solicitor in the Legal Profession of Nova Scotia.' (1991) 14 Dalhousie L.J. 277.

Calkin, John B. *A History and Geography of Nova Scotia*. Halifax: MacKinlay, 1878.

Campbell, Douglas F., ed. *Banked Fires: The Ethnics of Nova Scotia* c. 5. Port Credit, NS: Scribblers,' 1978.

Campbell, G.C. *The History of Nova Scotia*. Toronto: Ryerson Press, 1948.

Canada Law Journal. 'Judges in Manitoba' (1873) 9 Can. L.J. 279.

Cruickshank, Jim. 'The Chancery Court of Nova Scotia: Jurisdiction and Procedure 1751–1855.' (1992) 1 Dal. J.Leg. Stud. 27.

Cunnabell, W., *Cunnabell's Nova Scotia Almanac*. Halifax: W. Cunnabell, 1842, 1844.

Cuthbertson, Brian, *Johnny Bluenose at the Polls: Epic Nova Scotian Election Battles, 1758–1848*. Halifax: Formac, 1994.

Edwards, Joseph Plimsoll. 'The Militia of Nova Scotia, 1749–1867.' (1913) 17 Coll. N.S. Hist. Soc. 63.

Elliott, Shirley B., ed. *The Legislative Assembly of Nova Scotia 1758–1983* at 137. Halifax: Province of Nova Scotia, 1984.

Fergusson, C.B., ed. *A Directory of the Members of the Legislative Assembly of Nova Scotia 1758–1958*. Halifax: Public Archives of Nova Scotia, 1958.

– *The Diary of Adolphus Gaetz 1855–1873*. Halifax: Public Archives of Nova Scotia, 1965.

Gibson, Dale, and Lee Gibson. *Substantial Justice: Law and Lawyers in Manitoba 1670–1970*. Winnipeg: Peguis, 1972.

Girard, Philip. 'The Roots of a Professional Renaissance: Lawyers in Nova Scotia 1850–1910.' (1991) 21 Man. L.J. 148.

Healy, W.J. *Women of Red River*. Winnipeg: Russell, Lang, 1923.

Hill, Rev. George W. *Nova Scotia and Nova Scotians*. Halifax: James Bowes, 1858.

Hutchinson, Thomas. *Hutchinson's Nova Scotia Directory 1864–65*. Halifax: Muir, 1864.

– *Hutchnson's Nova Scotia Directory 1866*. Halifax: Muir, 1866.

Johnson, J.K., ed. *The Canadian Directory of Parliament 1867–1967* at 417. Ottawa: Public Archives of Canada, 1968.

Johnston, Rev. Angus Anthony. *A History of the Catholic Church in Eastern Nova Scotia*, vol. 1, *1611–1827*. Antigonish, NS: St. Francis Xavier University Press, 1960.

– *A History of the Catholic Church in Eastern Nova Scotia*, vol. 2, *1827–1880*. Antigonish, NS: St Francis Xavier University Press, 1971.

Johnston, J.L. 'Lord Gordon Gordon.' (1952) 7 Hist. & Sci. Soc. Man. 7.

MacKenzie, A.A. *The Irish in Cape Breton*. Antigonish, N.S.: Formac, 1979.

MacKinnon, J.G. *Old Sydney* at 77. Belleville, Ont.: Mika, 1973.

MacLean, Raymond, ed. *History of Antigonish*. Halifax: Casket, 1976.

Martell, J.S. *Immigration to and Emigration from Nova Scotia 1815–1838*. Halifax: Public Archives of Nova Scotia, 1942.

McAlpine, David. *McAlpine's Nova Scotia Directory 1868–69*. Halifax: McAlpine, 1868.

Miller, Bernard F. 'The Legal Profession in Late Victorian Nova Scotia.' (1988) 8:2 NS Hist. Rev. 57.

Morgan, Henry James, ed. *The Canadian Parliamentary Companion*, 5th ed. at 129. Montreal: Montreal Printing, 1869.

– *The Canadian Legal Directory: A Guide to the Bench and Bar of the Dominion of Canada* at 238. Toronto: Carswell, 1878.

Morgan, Robert. 'Separatism in Cape Breton 1820–45.' In Kenneth Donovan, ed., *Cape Breton at 200: Historical Essays in Honour of the Island's Bicentennial 1785–1985* 41. Sydney: University College of Cape Breton Press, 1985.

Muise, Delphin A. 'The Federal Election of 1867 in Nova Scotia: An Economic Interpretation.' (1968) 36 Coll. Nova Scotia Hist. Soc. 327.

– *Elections and Constituencies: Federal Politics in Nova Scotia, 1867–1878* Ph.D. thesis, University of Western Ontario, 1971 [unpublished].

Murdoch, Beamish. *Epitome of the Laws of Nova Scotia*, vol. 1. Halifax: Joseph Howe, 1832.

– *Epitome of the Laws of Nova Scotia*, vol. 3. Halifax: Joseph Howe, 1833.

– *Epitome of the Laws of Nova Scotia*, vol. 4. Halifax: Joseph Howe, 1833.

Nova Scotia Barristers' Society. *The Supreme Court of Nova Scotia and Its Judges 1754–1978*. Halifax: Nova Scotia Barristers' Society, 1978.

Outram, Joseph. *The Counties of Nova Scotia, Condition and Capabilities.* Halifax: Grant, 1867.
Pope, Sir Joseph. *Correspondence of Sir John A. Macdonald* at 56–9, 82–5. Toronto: Oxford University Press, 1921.
Pryke, K.G. 'McKeagney, James Charles.' In Marc La Terreur, ed., *Dictionary of Canadian Biography*, vol. 10, 475. Toronto: University of Toronto Press, 1972.
– *Nova Scotia and Confederation 1864–74* at 70. Toronto: University of Toronto Press, 1979.
Punch, Terrence M. 'The Irish Catholic, Halifax's First Minority Group.' (1980) 10:1 NS Hist. Q. 23.
Roberts, Sir G.D., and Arthur L. Tunnell, eds. 'Thomas Louis Connolly.' In *A Standard Dictionary of Canadian Biography*, vol. 2, 67. Toronto: Trans-Canada Press, 1938.
Robertson, John Palmerston, ed. *A Political Manual of the Province of Manitoba and the North-West Territories* at 151. Winnipeg: Call, 1887.
Siddiq, Fazley K. 'Nineteenth-Century Wealth Transfers in Nova Scotia: The Administration of Probate.' (1989) 9:2 N.S. Hist. Rev. 35.
Smith, Thomas B. *Backward Glances.* Halifax: James Bowes, 1898.
Stone, Arthur J. 'The Admiralty Court in Colonial Nova Scotia.' (1994) 17 Dal. L.J. 363.
Trombley, K. Fay. *Thomas Louis Connolly [1815–1876], The Man and His Place in Secular and Ecclesiastical History.* Leuven: Katholieke Universiteit Leuven, 1983.
Wagg, Phyllis. 'The Bias of Probate: Using Deeds to Transfer Estates in Nineteenth-Century Nova Scotia.' (1990) 10:1 N.S. Hist. Rev. 74.
Whidden, D.G. *The History of the Town of Antigonish* at 101–3. Wolfville, N.S., 1934.
Willie, Richard A. *'These Legal Gentlemen': Lawyers in Manitoba: 1839–1900.* Winnipeg: Legal Research Institute of the University of Manitoba, 1994.

(1933) 2 Fortnightly L.J. 138.

Manitoba Free Press, 15 August 1879, 1; 19 August 1879, 1; 16 September 1879, 2; 17 November 1879, 1.

Ewen Alexander McPherson

PRIMARY SOURCES

Macvicar, Helen, Papers, MG 9, A 62, item 25, files 1–29, PAM.
McPherson, Ewen Alexander, Papers, Archives of the Law Society of Manitoba, file P 1296, PAM.

SECONDARY SOURCES

Flanagan, Kathryn M., and Katherine J. Miller, eds. *Canadian Parliamentary Guide*. Toronto: Info Globe, 1991.
Graham, Roger. *Arthur Meighen*. Vol. 1, *The Door of Opportunity*. Toronto: Clarke, Irwin, 1960.
Greene, B.M., ed. 'Hon. Ewen Alexander McPherson.' In *Who's Who in Canada, 1943–44* 328. Toronto: International Press, 1944.
Harvey, Cameron, ed. *The Law Society of Manitoba 1877–1977* at 278. Winnipeg: Peguis, 1977.
Johnson, J.K., ed. *The Canadian Directory of Parliament 1867–1967* at 437. Ottawa: Public Archives of Canada, 1968.
Kendle, John. *John Bracken: A Political Biography*. Toronto: University of Toronto Press, 1979.
Maillet, Lise. *Provincial Royal Commissions and Commissions of Inquiry, 1867–1982: A Selective Bibliography* at 128. Ottawa: National Library of Canada, 1986.
Manitoba Bar News. (1935) 8 Man. Bar N. 198.
– 'Chief Justice McPherson.' (1937) 10:4 Man. Bar N. 509.
– 'Chief Justice McPherson.' (1938) 10:5 Man. Bar N. 517.
Metcalfe, Joseph H., ed. *The Tread of the Pioneers* at 186–7. Toronto: Ryerson, 1932.

(1933) 2 Fortnightly L.J. 341.
(1937) 7 Fortnightly L.J. 146.

Christian Guardian, 18 December 1907, 32.
Manitoba Free Press, 14 July 1906; 13 June 1914.
Winnipeg Free Press, 18 November 1954, 1; 19 November 1954, 1, 25; 20 November 1954.

Thomas Llewellyn Metcalfe

PRIMARY SOURCES

Law Society of Manitoba, Archives, Minute Books 6 and 7, PAM.
Macvicar, Helen, Papers, MG 9, A 62, file 30-51, item 32, PAM.
Metcalfe, Thomas Llewellyn, Last Will and Testament, Metcalfe file, PAM.
Walker, J.S., Oral Histories, PAM.

Andrew v. *Kilgour* (1910), 19 Man. R. 545 (Q.B.).
Rex v. *Alamazoff*, [1919] 3 W.W.R. 28 (Q.B.).
Rex v. *Russell et al.*, [1919] 3 W.W.R. 306 (Q.B.).

Rex v. *Russell*, [1920] 1 W.W.R. 164 (C.A.) and 624 (C.A.).
Rex v. *Schoppelrei*, [1919] 3 W.W.R. 322 (C.A.).
Rose v. *Clark* (1911), 21 Man. R. 635 (Q.B.).
Vulcan Iron Works v. *Winnipeg Lodge No. 174* (1911), 21 Man. R. 473 (C.A.).

SECONDARY SOURCES

Avery, Donald. 'The Radical Alien and the Winnipeg General Strike.' In J.M. Bumsted, ed., *Interpreting Canada's Past*, vol. 2, *After Confederation* 222. Toronto: Oxford University Press, 1986.

Benham, Mary Lile. *The Manitoba Club 100 Years 1874–1974*. Winnipeg: Manitoba Club, 1974.

Brown, Desmond H. 'The Craftsmanship of Bias: Sedition and the Winnipeg Strike Trial 1919.' (1984) 14 Man. L.J. 1.

Brown, Robert Craig, and Ramsay Cook. *Canada 1896–1921, A Nation Transformed*. Toronto: McClelland & Stewart, 1974.

Canada Law Journal. (1903) 39 Can. L.J. 1.

Friesen, Gerald. *The Canadian Prairies: A History* at 360–63. Toronto: University of Toronto Press, 1987.

Gibson, Dale, and Lee Gibson, *Substantial Justice: Law and Lawyers in Manitoba 1670–1970*. Winnipeg: Peguis, 1972.

Hopkins, J. Castell, ed. *The Canadian Annual Review of Public Affairs 1909*. Toronto: Annual Review, 1902.

Maillet, Lise. *Provincial Royal Commissions and Commissions of Inquiry, 1867–1982: A Selective Bibliography*. Ottawa: National Library of Canada, 1986.

Manitoba Free Press. 'Mr. Justice Metcalfe Is Martyr to Duties.' *Manitoba Free Press*, 3 April 1923.

Metcalfe, J.H., ed. *The Tread of the Pioneers*. Portage la Prairie: Portage la Prairie and District Old Timers' Association, 1932.

Morton, W.L. *Manitoba: A History*. Toronto: University of Toronto Press, 1957.

Parker, Dr C.W., ed. 'Hon. Thomas Llewellyn Metcalfe.' in *Who's Who and Why, 1914* 669. Toronto: International Press, 1914.

Stubbs, Roy St. George. 'Robert Andrew Bonnar, K.C.' (1937) 10 Man. Bar N. 497.

(1903) 39 Can. L.J. 1.

Manitoba Free Press, 10 October 1899, 5; 6 December 1899, 6; 13 December 1899, 2; 12 March 1920; 3 April 1922, 1; 4 April 1922, 3; 5 April 1922, 9; 6 April 1922, 3; 4 January 1929.

James Andrews Miller

PRIMARY SOURCES

Macdonald, John A., Papers, MG 26A at 9607–8, PAO.

Manitoba Biographical Scrapbooks, vol. B1 at 5, Legislative Library, Province of Manitoba.

Miller, James Andrews, Papers, Archives of the Law Society of Manitoba, file P 1378 (A692), PAM.

– Papers, Archives of the Law Society of Upper Canada, file 4736.

– Papers, Archives of the University of Toronto, 1914 Register at 117.

– Papers, St Catharines Museum and Archives.

Taylor, Thomas Wardlaw. Biography [unpublished]. Thomas Wardlaw Taylor AVF at 209–11, PAM.

Banting v. *The Niagara District Mutual Fire Assurance Company* (1867), 25 U.C.Q.B. 431.

Bender v. *The Canada Southern R.W. Co.* (1876), 37 U.C.Q.B. 25.

Bigger v. *Howie* (1881), 23 U.C.Q.B. 399.

Chaffey v. *Schooley* (1877), 40 U.C.Q.B. 165.

Cross v. *Currie* (1879), 43 U.C.Q.B. 599.

Darby v. *The Corporation of the Township of Crowland* (1877), 38 U.C.Q.B. 338.

Fitzgerald v. *The Gore District Mutual Fire Insurance Company* (1871), 30 U.C.Q.B. 97.

Frazee et al. v. *McFarland et al.* (1879), 43 U.C.Q.B. 281.

Freehold Loan and Savings Company v. *Bank of Commerce* (1880), 44 U.C.Q.B. 284.

Greaves v. *The Niagara District Mutual Fire Insurance Company* (1867), 25 U.C.Q.B. 127.

Hersee v. *White el al.* (1879), 29 U.C.Q.B. 232.

In Re Foster and The Great Western R.W. Co. (1873), 32 U.C.Q.B. 162.

In Re Heyden, An Insolvent (1879), 29 U.C.Q.B. 262.

In the Matter of the Niagara High School Board and the Corporation of the Township of Niagara (1877), 39 U.C.Q.B. 362.

In Re the Niagara High School Board and the Township of Niagara, and the Reeve, &c., of the said Township (1876), 37 U.C.Q.B. 529.

In Re the Sheriff of the County of Lincoln and the Treasurer and The Corporation of the County of Lincoln (1875), 34 U.C.Q.B. 1.

McCarthy v. *Phelps and Hellems* (1871), 30 U.C.Q.B. 57.

McLean and the Corporation of the Town of St. Catharines (1869), 27 U.C.Q.B. 603.

McLean v. *McLellan* (1879), 29 U.C.Q.B. 548.

Montgomery, Richard and Hannah v. *James S. Graham and William Hobson* (1872), 31 U.C.Q.B. 57.
Newman v. *Niagara District Mutual Ins. Co.* (1867), 25 U.C.Q.B. 435.
Ontario Salt Company, Plaintiffs in the Court below, Respondents, and *Patrick Larkin, Defendant in the Court below, Appellant* (1876), 36 U.C.Q.B. 486.
Owens v. *The Quebec Bank* (1871), 30 U.C.Q.B. 382.
Re The Hon. James A. Miller (1886), 3 Man. R. 367.
Regina v. *Biggs* (1885), 2 Man. R. 18.
Regina v. *Patrick Breen* (1876), 36 U.C.Q.B. 84.
Rykert, John Charles, Petitioner, v. *Neelon, Sylvester, Respondent,* (1883) Hodgins Reports of the Decisions of the Judges for the Trial of Election Petitions In Ontario 391.

SECONDARY SOURCES

Brant Union, ed. *Gazetteer and Business Directory of Lincoln and Welland Counties for 1879* at 136. Brantford: Brant Union, 1878.
Canada Law Journal. 'Judges Returning to the Bar.' (1872) 8 Can. L.J. 291.
– (1883) 19 Can. L.J. 1.
Evans, William W., ed. *St. Catharines Directory for 1881–82* at 143. Toronto: William W. Evans, 1881.
Fisher & Taylor, eds. *St. Catharines Directory for 1874* at 74. Toronto: Fisher & Taylor, 1875.
– *St. Catharines Directory for 1875–6* at 35. Toronto:Fisher & Taylor, 1875.
– *St. Catharines Directory for 1877–78* at 58. Toronto: Fisher & Taylor, 1877.
Friesen, Gerald. *The Canadian Prairies, A History* at 212. Toronto: University of Toronto Press, 1987.
Fuller, O.L., ed. *Fuller's St. Catharines Directory for 1863–64* at 63. St Catharines: O.L. Fuller, 1863.
Gibson, Dale, and Lee Gibson. *Substantial Justice: Law and Lawyers in Manitoba 1670–1970*. Winnipeg: Peguis, 1972.
Gibson, Lee. 'Miller, James Andrews.' In Frances G. Halpenny and Jean Hamelin, eds., *Dictionary of Canadian Biography*, vol. 11, 593. Toronto: University of Toronto Press, 1982.
Henderson, George Fletcher. *Federal Royal Commissions in Canada 1867–1966, A Checklist* at 13. Toronto: University of Toronto Press, 1967.
Leavenworth, E.S., ed. *Directory of St. Catharines, Thorold, Merriton, and Port Dalhousie, for 1877–78* at 58. St. Catharines: Leavenworth, 1877.
Lovell, John, ed. *Lovell's Province of Ontario Directory for 1871* at 771. Montreal: Lovell, 1871.

Mackay, Robert W.S., ed. *The Canada Directory for 1851* at 5. Montreal: Lovell, 1851.
Manitoba Library Association, ed. *Pioneers and Early Citizens of Manitoba.* Winnipeg: Peguis, 1971.
Mitchell & Co., ed. *Mitchell & Co.'s General Directory for the Town of St. Catharines, and Gazetteer of the Counties of Lincoln and Welland for 1865* at 50. Toronto: Mitchell, 1865.
Ontario Genealogical Society, ed. *Index to the 1871 Census of Ontario for Lincoln, Welland, Niagara* at 177. Toronto: Ontario Genealogical Society, 1987.
Noel, S.J.R. *Patrons, Clients, Brokers: Ontario Society and Politics, 1791–1896* at 257–8. Toronto: University of Toronto Press, 1990.
Robertson & Cook, eds. *The Province of Ontario Gazetteer and Directory for 1869* at 421. Toronto: Robertson & Cook, 1869.
Robertson, John Palmerston, ed. *A Political Manual of the Province of Manitoba and the North-West Territories* at 150. Winnipeg: Call, 1887.
St Catharines and Lincoln Historical Society, ed. *Junius, St. Catharines A to Z* c. 'M.' St Catharines: St Catharines and Lincoln Historical Society, 1967.
Willie, Richard A. *'These Legal Gentlemen': Lawyers in Manitoba: 1839–1900.* Winnipeg: Legal Research Institute of the University of Manitoba, 1994.

(1880) 16 Can. L.J. 285.

Manitoba Free Press, 25 October 1880, 2; 29 October 1880, 4; 30 October 1880, 4; 6 November 1880, 1; 27 October 1881, 1; 17 November 1881, 2; 3 November 1882, 8; 6 November 1882, 8; 1 January 1883, 8; 3 January 1883; 9 January 1883, 2; 9 January 1883, 4; 16 January 1883, 4; 16 January 1883, 8; 13 September 1883, 4; 13 September 1883, 5; 29 September 1883, 4; 2 November 1886, 2, 4; 4 November 1886, 4.
[St Catharines] *Daily Standard,* 9 May 1904, 1.
[Toronto] *Globe,* 17 October 1882, 1; 18 October 1882, 3; 21 October 1882, 8.
Winnipeg Sun, 1 November 1886.

Percival John Montague

PRIMARY SOURCES

Census of Ontario, 1891, District 94, Monck, Sub-Dis. Dunnsville, Village, Div. 2 at 30.
Montague, Furry Ferguson, Papers, Archives of the Law Society of Manitoba, file P 1300, PAM.

Montague, George Hastings, Papers, Archives of the Law Society of Manitoba, file P 1300, PAM.
Montague, Percival John, Papers, Archives of the Law Society of Manitoba, file P 1300, PAM.
– Papers, Archives of the University of Toronto, file A73-0026/331(42).
– Papers, MG 14, B 40, PAM.

Galer v. *Wings*, [1938] 3 W.W.R. 481 (Q.B.).
Gislason v. *Gislason*, [1935] 2 W.W.R. 282 (C.A.).
In re Eames Estate (1934), 42 Man. R. 474 (Q.B.).
McInnerny v. *McDougall*, [1937] 3 W.W.R. 625 (Q.B.).

SECONDARY SOURCES

Dalgleish, Lyle. 'Donald Hugh Fletcher.' In Thomas Melville Bailey, ed., *Dictionary of Hamilton Biography*, vol. 2, *1876–1924* 49. Hamilton: W.C. Griffin, 1991.
Flanagan, Kathryn M., and Katherine J. Miller, eds. *Canadian Parliamentary Guide*. Toronto: Info Globe, 1991.
Gibson, Dale. 'Anecdotal Sampler.' In Cameron Harvey, ed. *The Law Society of Manitoba 1877–1977* at 208. Winnipeg: Peguis, 1977.
Gibson, Dale, and Lee Gibson. *Substantial Justice: Law and Lawyers in Manitoba 1670–1970*. Winnipeg: Peguis, 1972.
Johnson, J.K., ed. *The Canadian Directory of Parliament 1867–1967* at 372. Ottawa: Public Archives of Canada, 1968.
Kemp, A.F., F.W. Farries, and Halkett, eds. *Hand-Book of the Presbyterian Church in Canada, 1883* at 194. Ottawa: Presbyterian Church in Canada, 1883.
Manitoba Bar News. 'Early Judges of Manitoba.' (1932) 5:4 Man. Bar N. 4.
– 'Lt.-Gen. P.J. Montague Appointed Chief of Staff.' (1944) 16 Man. Bar N. 99.
– 'News of the Profession.' (1945) 17 Man. Bar N. 22.
– 'Obituary.' (1950) 22 Man. Bar N. 58.
– 'Our Newest Judges.' (1951) 23 Man. Bar N. 12.
Montague, P.J. 'Early Judges of Manitoba.' (1932) 5:4 Man. Bar N. 4.
Montague, P.J., et al. 'Hands Off the Court of Appeal.' (1932) 4:6 Man. Bar N. 9.
– 'More About the Court of Appeal.' (1932) 4:7 Man. Bar N. 1.
Morton, W.L. *Manitoba: A History*. Toronto: University of Toronto Press, 1957.
Presbyterian Church in Canada at 584. General Assembly A. & P., 1913.
Wallace, W. Stewart, ed. 'Walter Humphries Montague.' In *The Macmillan Dictionary of Canadian Biography*, 3rd ed., 286. Toronto: Macmillan, 1963.
Wallace, W. Stewart, ed., and updated by W.A. McKay, 'Percival John

Montague.' The Macmillan Dictionary of Canadian Biography, 4th ed (Toronto: Macmillan, 1978 at 585).
(1934) 4 Fortnightly L.J. 131.
(1935) 5 Fortnightly L.J. 52.

Alexander Morris

PRIMARY SOURCES

Morris, Alexander, Papers, Archives of Queen's University, Collection 2138, box 8, files 131, 133, 134, and 138.
– Papers, PAM.
– Papers, MS 535, PAO.
Morris, Edmund, Papers, MG 30, D 6, NAC.
Morris, William John, Papers (1872), MG 29, C 8, NAC.
Morris, William, Papers (1802–53), MG 24, B 8, NAC.

SECONDARY SOURCES

Artibise, Alan F.J., 'An Urban Economy: Patterns of Economic Change in Winnipeg, 1873–1971' (1976) 2 Prairie Forum 163 at 164.
Artibise, Alan F.J., ed. *Gateway City: Documents of the City of Winnipeg 1873–1913*. Winnipeg: Manitoba Record Society, 1979.
Babion, R.G. *Alexander Morris: His Place in Canadian History*. M.A. Thesis, Queen's University, 1945 [unpublished].
Baker, G. Blaine. 'Law Practice and Statecraft in Mid-Nineteenth-Century Montreal: The Torrance-Morris Firm, 1848 to 1968.' In Carol Wilton, ed., *Essays in the History of Canadian Law*, vol. 4, *Beyond the Law: Lawyers and Business in Canada, 1830 to 1930* 45. Toronto: Osgoode Society, 1990.
Begg, Alexander, and Walter R. Nursey. *Ten Years in Winnipeg*. Winnipeg: Times, 1879.
Boultbee, W.M. 'Edmund Morris, Painter.' (1908) 31 *Canadian Magazine* 121.
Bowles, R.S. 'Adams George Archibald First Lieutenant-Governor of Manitoba.' (1968–9) 25 Hist. & Sc. Soc. Man. 75.
Bowsfield, Hartwell, ed., *The Letters of Charles John Brydges 1879–1882*. Winnipeg: Hudson's Bay Record Society, 1877.
– *The Letters of Charles John Brydges 1883–1889*. Winnipeg: Hudson's Bay Record Society, 1981.
Bridgman, H.J. *Three Scots Presbyterians in Upper Canada: A Study in Emigration, Nationalism and Religion*. Ph.D. thesis, Queen's University, 1978 [unpublished].

– 'Morris, William.' In Francess G. Halpenny and Jean Hamelin, eds., *Dictionary of Canadian Biography*, vol. 8, 638. Toronto: University of Toronto Press, 1985.

Canada Law Journal. 'Queen's Counsel.' (1876) 12 Can. L.J. 103.

Canadian Illustrated News. Vol. 1 (22 January 1878) at 177.

Careless, J.S.M. *Brown of the Globe*, vol. 2, *Statesman of Confederation 1860–1880* at 130. Toronto: Macmillan, 1963.

– 'The Development of the Winnipeg Business Community, 1870–1890.' (1970) 8 Trans. Royal Soc. Can. 239.

Code, Susan. *A Matter of Honour and Other Tales of Early Perth*. Burnstown, Ont.: General Store, 1996.

Cote, N. Omer, ed. *Political Appointments, Parliaments and the Judicial Bench in the Dominion of Canada 1867 to 1895*. Ottawa: Thoburn, 1896.

Den Otter, A.A. *Civilizing the West: The Galts and the Development of Western Canada*. Edmonton: University of Alberta Press, 1982.

Donnelly, M.S. 'The Story of the Manitoba Legislature.' (1957) 12 Hist. & Sc. Soc. Man. 29 at 33–5.

Evening Telegram. 'Art Collectors Are Lucky – Small Pieces.' In [Toronto] *Evening Telegram*, 21 June 1928, 37.

Fitz-Gibbon, Mary. *The Diaries of Edmund Montague Morris, Western Journeys 1907–1910*. Toronto: Royal Ontario Museum, 1985.

Friesen, Gerald. *The Canadian Prairies: A History* at 143–5. Toronto: University of Toronto Press, 1987.

Friesen, Jean. 'Alexander Morris.' In Francess G. Halpenny and Jean Hamelin, eds., *Dictionary of Candian Biography*, vol. 11, 608. Toronto: University of Toronto Press, 1982.

Gibson, Dale, and Lee Gibson, *Substantial Justice: Law and Lawyers in Manitoba 1670–1970*. Winnipeg: Peguis, 1972.

Globe. 'Body of E.M. Morris Found in River.' In [Toronto] *Globe*, 26 August 1913, 7.

Hodgins, Bruce Willard. *The Political Career of John Sandfield Macdonald to the Fall of His Administration in March 1864: A Study in Canadian Politics*, Ph.D. thesis, Duke University, 1965 [unpublished] at 124.

– 'VanKoughnet, Philip.' In Marc La Terreur, ed., *Dictionary of Canadian Biography*, vol. 10, 693. Toronto: University of Toronto Press, 1972.

Kerr, John Andrew. 'The Indian Treaties of 1876.' In (1937) 17 Dalhousie Rev. 189.

Manitoba Bar News. 'Practice Rules Prior to 1895.' (1930) 2:6 Man. Bar N. 1.

McGill, Jean S. 'The Indian Portraits of Edmund Morris.' (Summer 1979) The Beaver 34.

– 'Edmund Morris among the Saskatchewan Indians and the Fort Qu'Appelle Monument.' (1982) 35 Sask. Hist. 101.
– *Edmund Morris Frontier Artist*. Toronto: Dundurn, 1984.
– 'Morris, Edmund Montague.' In Ramsay Cook, ed., *Dictionary of Canadian Biography*, vol. 14, 769. Toronto: University of Toronto Press, 1998.
Milligan, F.A. *The Lieutenant-Governorship in Manitoba, 1870–1882*. M.A. thesis, University of Manitoba, 1950) [unpublished].
Morgan, Henry J., ed. *The Canadian Legal Directory: A Guide to the Bench and Bar of the Dominion of Canada* 126. Toronto: Carswell, 1878.
Morris, Alexander. *The Railway Clauses Consolidation Acts of Canada, 14 & 15 Victoriae, Chapter 51, and 16 Victoriae, Chapter 169, with an Alphabetical and Analytical Index Thereto*. Montreal: Lovell, 1853.
– *Canada and Her Resources*. Montreal: Lovell, 1855.
– *Analytical Index to the Act 20th Victoriae, Cap. XLIV., amending the Judicature Acts of Lower Canada* (Montreal: Lovell, 1857).
Morris, The Hon. Alexander. *Nova Britannia; or, Our New Canadian Dominion Foreshadowed*. Toronto: Hunter, Rose, 1858.
– First Address to a Manitoba Court (1872) 8 Can. L.J. 262.
– *The Treaties of Canada with The Indians of Manitoba and the North-West Territories*. Toronto: Willing & Williamson, 1880.
Morris, Edmund. 'Old Lords of the Soil.' In [Toronto] *News*, 9 May 1907, 13.
– *Portraits of the Aborigines of Canada and Notes on the Tribes*. Toronto: self-published, 1909.
– 'An Ancient Indian Fort.' (1911) 36 *Canadian Magazine* 256.
– 'L't-Col. Irvine and the North-West Mounted Police.' (1911) 37 *Canadian Magazine* 493.
– *The Diaries of Edmund Montague Morris, Western Journies 1907–1910*. Toronto: Royal Ontario Museum, 1985.
Morris, James Lewis. *Indians of Ontario*. Toronto: Department of Lands and Forests,1943.
Morris, William. *The Accountant's Guide for Elementary Schools in Canada*. Quebec: self-published, 1833.
– *The correspondence of the Hon. William Morris with the Colonial Office, as the delegate, from the Presbyterian body in Canada*. Niagara-on-the-Lake: Examiner, 1837.
– *A letter on the subject of the clergy reserves, addressed to the Very Rev. Principal MacFarlan and the Rev. Dr. Burns, D.D.* Toronto: British Colonist, 1838.
– *Reply of William Morris, member of the Legislative Council of Upper Canada to six letters addressed to him by John Strachan, D.D., Archdeacon of York*. Toronto: Scotsman, 1838.

– *Facts and Particulars relating to the case of Morris vs. Cameron recently tried at Brockville*. Montreal: Montreal Gazette, 1845.
Morton, W.L. *One University: A History of the University of Manitoba 1877–1957*. Toronto: McClelland & Stewart, 1957.
– *Manitoba: A History*. Toronto: University of Toronto Press, 1957.
– *The Critical Years, The Union of British North America 1857–1873*. Toronto: McClelland & Stewart, 1968.
Neatby, Hilda. 'The Honourable William Morris, 1786–1858.' In (1972) 20 Historic Kingston 65.
– *Queen's University*, vol. 1, *1841–1917*. Montreal: McGill-Queen's University Press, 1978.
Owram, Doug. *Promise of Eden: The Canadian Expansionist Movement and the Idea of the West, 1856–1900*. Toronto: University of Toronto Press, 1980.
Pope, Sir Joseph. *Correspondence of Sir John Macdonald*. Toronto: Oxford University Press, 1921.
Rordans, J. *The Upper Canada Law List 1860–61*. Toronto: Rordans, 1860.
Saturday Night. 'Art Notes.' In [Toronto] *Saturday Night* 9:16 (7 March 1896) 9.
– 'Art.' In [Toronto] *Saturday Night* 9:49 (24 October 1896) 9 and 10:6 (26 December 1896) 9.
Siggins, Maggie. *Riel: A Life of Revolution* at 217. Toronto: Harper, 1994.
Simmins, Geoffrey, and Michael Parke-Taylor. *Edmund Morris 'Kyaiyii' 1871–1913*. Regina: Norman Mackenzie Art Gallery, 1984.
Staples, Lila. 'The Honourable Alexander Morris: The Man; His Work.' In (1925–8) Can. Hist. Assoc. Hist. Papers 91.
Strachan, John, *Letters to the Honourable William Morris, being strictures on the correspondence of that gentleman with the Colonial Office, as a delegate from the Presbyterian body in Canada*. Coburg, Ont.: Chatterton, 1838.
Wallace, W. Stewart, ed. 'Morris, Alexander.' In *The Macmillan Dictionary of Canadian Biography*, 3rd ed., 528. Toronto: Macmillan, 1963.
– 'Morris, Edmund Montague.' In *Macmillan Dictionary* 529.
– 'Morris, James.' In *Macmillan Dictionary* 529.
– 'Morris, James Lewis.' In *Macmillan Dictionary* 530.
– 'Morris, William.' In *Macmillan Dictionary* 530.
Willie, Richard A. *'The Legal Gentlemen': Lawyers in Manitoba 1839–1900*. Winnipeg: Legal Research Institute of the University of Manitoba, 1994.

(1887) 10 Legal N. 14.
(1891) 2:1 Man. Bar N. 25.

Manitoba Daily Free Press, 29 October 1889, 1.
Montreal Empire, 29 October 1889, 5.
Montreal Mail, November 1889, 11.

Montreal Star, 29 October 1889, 1.
Toronto News, 9 May 1907, 13.

Although Morris gave hundreds of speeches during his career, he retained copies or accounts of only twenty. Those twenty, contained in *Nova Britannia*, include:

1 Nova Britannia; or, The Consolidation of the British North American Provinces Into the Dominion of Canada [read before the Mercantile Library Association of Montreal, 18 March, 1858.
2 The Hudson's Bay and Pacific Territories [read before the Mercantile Library Association of Montreal and, later, before the Mechanics' Institute of Hemmingford, winter of 1858].
3 Speech in Canadian Assembly, 28 March 1862, during debate on the speech from the throne, at 93.
4 Undated speech, 23 February 1865, during confederation debate, at 101.
5 Speech at Perth, Ontario, 1 July 1867, at 126.
6 Speech, 5 December 1867, during debate on whether Canada should acquire the North West Territories, at 134.
7 Speech to constituents of Perth, in November 1869, after his appointment as federal Minister of Inland Revenue was confirmed by his election by acclamation, at 142.
8 Farewell address to constituents, on his retirement from politics, 9 July 1872, at 148.
9 Reply to invitation by leading constituents in South Lanark that reception be held, 29 July 1872, at 150.
10 Charge as Chief Justice of Manitoba to first grand jury convened in Manitoba, October 1872, at 152.
11 Address to annual dinner of Selkirk St Andrew's Society, at 156.
12 Reply to address from Manitoba College, 20 December 1872, at 158.
13 Reply to address from Kildonan, at 161.
14 Reply to address from Marquette, at 164.
15 Reply to address from Lisgar, at 166.
16 Reply to address from loyal Metis of Provencher and Lisgar, at 167.
17 Address to council of the North-West Territories, 23 November 1875, at 168.
18 Reply to address of half-breeds following conclusion of Qu'Appelle Treaty, 16 September 1874, at 173.
19 Account of proceedings connected with signing Qu'Appelle Treaty, 7 September 1876, at 175.
20 Address at banquet held in Winnipeg in honour of Lord Dufferin, 29 September 1877, at 183.

William Egerton Perdue

PRIMARY SOURCES

Census of Manitoba, 1891, Ward 2A, page 45.
Law Society, Archives, Minute Book 6, PAM.
Perdue Family Papers, Perkins Bull Collection, Brampton Public Library, MS 515, reel 57.
Perdue, Mowbray Macdonnell, Papers, Archives of the Law Society of Manitoba, file P 1310, PAM.
Perdue, William Egerton, Papers, Archives of the Law Society of Manitoba, file P 1310, PAM.
– Papers, Archives of the University of Toronto, file A73-0026/361(38).

A. v. *A.* (1905), 15 Man. R. 483 (Q.B.).
Alloway v. *The Rural Municipality of St. Andrews* (1906), 16 Man. R. 255.
Drinkwater v. *Clarridge* (1881), 17 Can. L.J. 227.
McCracken v. *Creswick* (1881), 17 Can. L.J. 227.
Re Nicolson & The Railway Commissioner (1890), 6 Man. R. 419 (C.A.).

SECONDARY SOURCES

Canada Law Review. (1903) 2 Can. L. Rev. 667.
Greene, B.M., ed. 'Hon. William Egerton Perdue.' In *Who's Who In Canada, 1923–1924* 154. Toronto: International Press, 1924.
Kirkwood, Hilda. 'History of Education, a Most Interesting Story.' In C.V. Charters, ed., *Brampton's 100th Anniversary as an Incorporated Town 1873–1973* 67. Brampton: Charters, 1973.
Hamilton, James Cleland. *Osgoode Hall, Reminiscences of the Bench and Bar* at 8–9. Toronto: Carswell, 1904.
Hardy, H.R., ed. *Ontario, Manitoba and North-West Legal Directory*. Toronto: Carswell, 1883.
Harvey, Cameron, ed. *The Law Society of Manitoba 1877–1977* at 277, 280, 284. Winnipeg: Peguis, 1977.
Hodgins, William E., ed. *The Ontario Legal Directory. A Complete Law List for the Province of Ontario*. Toronto: Roswell & Hutchison, 1879.
Johnson, J. Ragnar. 'Honourable W.E. Perdue, an Appreciation of an Eminent Jurist.' (1933) 11 Can. Bar Rev. 199.
Loverseed, Hilga V. *Brampton, an Illustrated History* at 84. Burlington: Windsor, 1987.
Maillet, Lise. *Provincial Royal Commissions and Commissions of Inquiry, 1867–*

1982: A Selective Bibliography at 131. Ottawa: National Library of Canada, 1986.

Manitoba Bar News. 'Honourable William Egerton Perdue.' (1903) 2:5 Man. Bar N. 4.

– 'Editorial.' (1937) 9 Man. Bar N. 386.

Manitoba Free Press. 'Grand Jury Presentment.' In *Manitoba Free Press*, 23 November 1905.

Manitoba Law Journal. 'Winnipeg Legal Club.' (1884) 1 Man. L.J. 175.

Perdue, William Egerton. 'Fusion of Law and Equity in Manitoba.' (1882) 2 Can. L. Times 428.

Riddell, William Renwick. *The Legal Profession in Upper Canada in Its Early Periods*. Toronto: Law Society of Upper Canada, 1916.

Rordans, J., ed. *The Ontario Law List and Solicitors' Agency Book*, 9th ed. Toronto: Rordans, 1882.

Rordans & Nicholls, eds. *The Ontario Law List and Solicitor's Agency Book*, 8th ed. Toronto: Rordans & Nicholls, 1876.

Winnipeg Legal Club, ed. *Constitution of the Winnipeg Legal Club*. Winnipeg: McIntyre, 1884.

(1933) 11 Man. Bar N. 199.

(1935) 7 Man. Bar N. 85.

(1884) 1 Man. L.J. 175.

[Brampton] *Conservator*, 23 January 1885, 3.

Brampton Times, 30 October 1868, 3.

Manitoba Free Press, 10 October 1899, 5; 24 August 1903, 9; 9 September 1903, 12; 24 November 1905, 2; 18 January 1933, 4, 11; 19 January 1933, 13; 20 January 1933, 15; 8 July 1940, 16.

James Emile Pierre Prendergast

PRIMARY SOURCES

The Manitoba School Question: Speech delivered by Hon. James E.P. Prendergast, member for Woodlands, in the Legislative Assembly of Manitoba, on the 10th and 12th days of March, A.D. 1890. Winnipeg: E.J. Dermody, 1893.

Prendergast, James E.P. *Soir d'Automne*. Quebec: P.-G. Delisle, 1881.

McColl v. *Canadian Pacific Railway Company and Attorney-General for Manitoba*, [1923] A.C. 126 (Privy Council).

Re Prince Albert City Provincial Election. *Strachan* v. *Lamont* (1906), 4 W.L.R. 411 (C.A.).

– 3 W.L.R. 571 (Q.B.).
Re St. Boniface Election (1892), 8 Man. R. 474 (Q.B.).
Re Wasney v. *Jurazsky*, [1933] 1 W.W.R. 155 (C.A.), 1 D.L.R. 616 (Q.B.).
Rex v. *Kelly* (1916), 27 Man. R. 105 (C.A.).
Rex v. *Sinclair* (1906), 4 W.L.R. 374 (C.A.).
Rex v. *Thomas Kelly*, [1916] 10 W.W.R. 1345 (Q.B.).

SECONDARY SOURCES

Andrews, A.J. 'Jurist and Gentleman.' (1945) 17 Man. Bar N. 31.
Begg, Alexander. *History of the North-West*, vol. 3, at 301, 326–39. Toronto: Hunter, Rose, 1895.
Canada Law Journal. (1902) 38 Can. L.J. 137.
Fillmore, William Parker, Q.C. 'The Lighter Side of the Law.' (1973) 39 Man. Bar N. 114 at 118.
Gibson, Dale, and Lee Gibson. *Substantial Justice: Law and Lawyers in Manitoba 1670–1970*. Winnipeg: Peguis, 1972.
Henderson, George Fletcher. *Federal Royal Commissions in Canada 1867–1966, a Checklist* at 42. Toronto: University of Toronto Press, 1967.
Hopkins, J. Castell, ed. *The Canadian Annual Review of Public Affairs for 1906*. Toronto: Annual Review Publishing Co., 1907.
– *The Canadian Annual Review of Public Affairs for 1916*. Toronto: Annual Review Publishing Co., 1917.
Maillet, Lise. *Provincial Royal Commissions and Commissions of Inquiry, 1867–1982: A Selective Bibliography* at 123. Ottawa: National Library of Canada, 1986.
Manitoba Bar News. 'Prendergast Appointed Chief Justice.' (1930) 2:5 Man. Bar N. 5.
– 'Early Alumni.' (1930) 2:9 Man. Bar N. 4.
– 'Hon. J.E.P. Prendergast.' (1944) 16 Man. Bar N. 25.
McCarthy, D'Alton. In Virginia R. Robeson, ed., *Debates about Canada's Future 1868–1896* at 100. Toronto: Ontario Institute for Studies in Education, 1977.
Morton, W.L. *Manitoba: A History*. Toronto: University of Toronto Press, 1957.
Parker, Dr C.W., ed. 'Hon. James Emile Pierre Prendergast.' In *Who's Who and Why, 1914* 764. Toronto: International Press, 1914.
Robertson, John Palmerston, ed. *A Political Manual of the Province of Manitoba and the North- West Territories* at 67. Winnipeg: Call, 1887.
Stubbs, Roy St. George. 'James Emile Prendergast.' In *Lawyers and Laymen of Western Canada* 100. Toronto: Ryerson, 1939.

(1923) 1 Can. Bar Rev. 260.

Manitoba Free Press, 8 February 1910, 1; 18 April 1945, 1; 21 April 1945, 11.

Albert Elswood Richards

PRIMARY SOURCES

Richards, Albert Elswood, Papers, Archives of the University of Toronto.

British Canadian Loan & Agency Co. v. *Farmer* (1904), 15 Man. R. 593 (Q.B.).
Brown v. *Hoare* (1905), 16 Man. R. 314 (Q.B.).
Coffin v. *Danard and Richards* (1866), 24 U.C.Q.B. 267.
In Re Sutherland, Landlord, and Portigal, Tenant (1899), 12 Man. R. 543 (Q.B.).
Kellett v. *Canadian Pacific Railway Co.* (1906), 16 Man. R. 391 (Q.B.).
Queen v. *Sparham and Greaves* (1875), 25 U.C.C.P. 143.
Rex. v. *Duggan* (1906), 16 Man. R. 440 (C.A.).
Rex. v. *Osberg* (1905), 15 Man. R. 147 (Q.B.).
Tait v. *Canadian Pacific Railway Co. et al.* (1906), 16 Man. R. 391 (Q.B.).
Vulcan Iron Works v. *Winnipeg Lodge, No. 122, International Association of Machinists, & Others* (1906), 16 Man. R. 207 (Q.B.).

SECONDARY SOURCES

Canada Law Journal. (1871) 7 Can. L.J. 147.
– (1874) 10 Can. L.J. 32.
– (1875) 11 Can. L.J. 266.
– 'Sir William Buell Richards.' (1889) 25 Can. L.J. 194.
– 'Hon. Stephen Richards, Q.C.' (1894) 30 Can. L.J. 612.
Disotell, Russ. *Brockville, the River City*. Toronto: Natural Heritage, 1997.
Harvey, Cameron, ed. *The Law Society of Manitoba 1877–1977*. Winnipeg: Peguis, 1977.
Johnson, J.K., ed. *The Canadian Parliament 1867–1967* at 489. Ottawa: Public Archives of Canada, 1968.
MacPherson, Ian. 'Sir William Buell Richards.' in Francess G. Halpenny & Jean Hamelin, eds., *Dictionary of Canadian Biography*, vol. 11, 730. Toronto: University of Toronto Press, 1982.
Manitoba Bar News. 'Obituary.' (1950) 22 Man. Bar N. 92.
Manitoba Free Press. 'Judge Richards Dies on Sunday.' In *Manitoba Free Press*, 28 May 1917, 1.
Morgan, Henry James, ed. *The Canadian Men and Women of the Time: A Handbook of Canadian Biography of Living Characters* at 938. Toronto: William Briggs, 1912.

Siggins, Maggie. *Riel: A Life of Revolution* at 100, 108–9. Toronto: HarperCollins, 1994.
Snell, James G., and Frederick Vaughan. *The Supreme Court of Canada: History of the Institution* at 12. Toronto: Osgoode Society, 1985.
Wallace, W. Stewart. 'Political History.' In Adam Shortt & Arthur G. Doughty, eds., *Canada and Its Provinces*, vol. 17, 103. Toronto: Constable, 1914.
Wallace, W. Stewart, ed. 'Albert Norton Richards.' In *The Macmillan Dictionary of Canadian Biography*, 3rd ed., 337. Toronto: Macmillan, 1963.
– 'Sir William Buell Richards.' In *The Macmillan Dictionary of Canadian Biography*, 3rd ed., 337. Toronto: Macmillan, 1963.
Winnipeg Tribune. 'Fellow Jurists Pay Tribute to Judge Richards.' In *Winnipeg Tribune*, 28 May 1917.

Manitoba Free Press, 29 May 1917, 5.

Hugh Amos Robson

PRIMARY SOURCES

An Act Respecting Public Utilities, to create a Public Utility Commission and to prescribe its Powers and Duties, S.M. 1912, c. 66.
An Act to amend 'The Law Society Act,' S.M. 1915, c. 37, s. 8.
Report of the Royal Commission to Enquire Into and Report Upon the Causes and Effects of the General Strike Which Recently Existed in the City of Winnipeg for a Period of Six Weeks, Including the Methods of Calling and Carrying On Such Strike. Winnipeg: King's Printer, 1919.
Report of Royal Commission on Charges Re Vice and Of Graft Against the Police.' In Alan F.J. Artibise, ed., *Gateway City: Documents on the City of Winnipeg 1873–1913* 207. Winnipeg: Manitoba Record Society, 1979.
The Board of Commerce Act, S.C. 1919, c. 37.
The Combines and Fair Prices Act, S.C. 1919, c. 45.

Law Society, Archives, Minute Books 6 and 8, PAM.
Maybank, Ralph, Papers, MG 14, B 35, PAM.
Robson, Hugh Amos, Papers, Archives of the Law Society of Manitoba, file P 1319, PAM.
Robson, Hugh Laidlaw, Papers, Archives of the Law Society of Manitoba, file P 1319, PAM.
Robson, Jean Hay Robson, Papers, Archives of the Law Society of Manitoba, file P 1319, PAM.

Wolfe v. *McArthur* (1908), 18 Man. R. 30 (Q.B.).
In Re Macdonald Estate (1933), 41 Man. R. 418 (Q.B.).
Re Fedorenko (No. 2) (1910), 20 Man. R. 224 (Q.B.).

SECONDARY SOURCES

Artibise, Alan F.J. *Winnipeg, a Social History of Urban Growth 1874–1914* at 261. Montreal: McGill-Queen's University Press, 1975.

Canada Law Journal. 'Judges Returning to Practice.' (1905) 41 Can. L.J. 806.

– 'The Board of Commerce.' (1919) 55 Can. L.J. 285.

– 'The Board of Commerce for Canada.' (1920) 56 Can. L.J. 95, 173.

Fillmore, William Parker, Q.C. 'The Lighter Side of the Law.' (1973) 39 Man. Bar N. 114 at 118.

Gibson, Dale, and Lee Gibson. *Substantial Justice: Law and Lawyers in Manitoba 1670–1970*. Winnipeg: Peguis, 1972.

Gibson, Lee. *A Proud Heritage: The First Hundred Years of Aikins, MacAulay and Thorvaldson*. Winnipeg: Aikins, MacAulay and Thorvaldson, 1993.

Greene, B.M., ed. 'Hugh Amos Robson.' In *Who's Who In Canada, 1923–1924* 202. Toronto: International Press, 1924.

Harvey, Cameron, ed. *The Law Society of Manitoba 1877–1977*. Winnipeg: Peguis, 1977.

Hopkins, J. Castell, ed. *The Canadian Annual Review of Public Affairs, 1908, 1910, 1914, 1915, and 1919*. Toronto: Annual Review Publishing Co., 1909–20.

Kendle, John. *John Bracken, a Political Biography*. Toronto: University of Toronto Press, 1979.

Kyer, C. Ian, and Jerome E. Bickenbach. *The Fiercest Debate: Cecil A. Wright, the Benchers, and Legal Education in Ontario 1923–1957*. Toronto: Osgoode Society, 1987.

Maillet, Lise. *Provincial Royal Commissions and Commissions of Inquiry, 1867–1982: A Selective Bibliography*. Ottawa: National Library of Canada, 1986.

Manitoba Bar News. 'H.A. Robson Elevated to Bench.' (1930) 2:5 Man. Bar N. 3.

– (1940) 13:1 Man. Bar N. 2, 25.

– 'Chief Justice Robson Dies.' (1945) 17 Man. Bar N. 61.

– (1954) 26:5 Man. Bar N. 79.

Manitoba Reports. (1933) 41 Man. R. 418.

Masters, D.C. *The Winnipeg General Strike*. Toronto: University of Toronto Press, 1950.

McFall, Robert James. 'Regulation of Business in Canada.' (1922) 37 Pol. Sci. Q. 177 at 205.

McNaught, Kenneth, and David J. Bercuson. *The Winnipeg Strike: 1919*. Don Mills, Ont.: Longman Canada, 1974.
Micay, Archie R. '*Rex* vs. *Andrusiak and Barnett*.' (1940) 13 Man. Bar N. 25.
Morton, W.L. *Manitoba, A History*. Toronto: University of Toronto Press, 1957.
Robson, Hugh Amos. 'Company Law.' (1916) 36 Can. L. Times 861.
– (1922) 7 Can. Bar Assoc. Proc. 240.
– 'The Honourable Sir James Albert Manning Aikins, K.C.' (1929) 7 Can. Bar Rev. 266.
– 'Edward Ludlow Wetmore.' (1944) 22 Can. Bar Rev. 442.
– 'Sir Frederick Haultain.' (1944) 22 Can. Bar Rev. 643.
– 'Hon. Horace Thomas McGuire.' (1945) 23 Can. Bar Rev. 139.
Robson, H.A., and J.B. Hugg. *Cases on Company Law*. Toronto: Carswell, 1916.
– *Leading Cases on Public Corporations*. Toronto: Carswell, 1916.
– *Municipal Manual, Being a Complete Annotation of the Ontario Municipal Act and Commentary on Certain Analogous Sections of the Municipal Acts of the Other Provinces*. Toronto: Carswell, 1920.
Traves, Tom. *The State and Enterprise: Canadian Manufacturers and the Federal Government, 1917–1931* c. 4. Toronto: University of Toronto Press, 1979.
Winnipeg Free Press. 'Robson Is Appointed to Court of Appeal.' In *Winnipeg Free Press*, 1 January 1930.

(1925) 3 Can. Bar Rev. 510.
(1936) 14 Can. Bar Rev. 497.
(1910) 30 Can. L. Times 701.
(1931) 1 Fortnightly L.J. 56.
(1932) 2 Fortnightly L.J. 120.
(1973) 39 Man. Bar N. 118.

[Toronto] *Globe*, 3 March 1920, 1; 4 March 1920, 6.
Manitoba Free Press, 24 May 1912, 2, 4; 3 September 1915, 2; 3 March 1920, 1, 13; 1 January 1930.
Winnipeg Free Press, 9 July 1945, 1; 2 January 1930.

Robert Smith

PRIMARY SOURCES

Census of Ontario, 1881.

County Marriage Register of Ontario, Canada, 1858–1869, vol. 17, *Perth County*, 115.
Index to the 1871 Census of Ontario, Perth County at 45, 169. Toronto: Ontario Genealogical Society, 1991.

Lizars Collection, J.J. Talman Regional Collection, D.B. Weldon Library, University of Western Ontario, B4306–4307.
Lizars Family Papers, Stratford Perth Archives.
Register of the University of Toronto for the Year 1914 at 240. Toronto: University Press, 1914.
Smith, Robert Home, Papers, Archives of the University of Toronto, file A73-0026/429(87).
Smith, Robert, Papers, Archives of the University of Toronto, file A73-006/429(87).
– Papers, Stratford Perth Archives.

Adams v. *Corcoran* (1876), 12 Can. L.J. 178.
Armstrong v. *Portage, Westbourne & North Western Railway Co.* (1884), 1 Man. R. 344 (C.A.).
Brimstone v. *Smith* (1884), 1 Man. R. 302 (Q.B.).
Canty v. *Clark* (1880), 44 U.C.Q.B. 222.
Canty v. *Clarke et al.* (1880), 44 U.C.Q.B. 505.
Conn v. *Merchants' Bank* (1880), 16 Can. L.J. 31.
Cummins v. *Trustees of the Congregational Church* (1887), 4 Man. R. 374 (C.A..).
Edgar v. *Newell* (1866), 24 U.C.Q.B. 215.
Farrow v. *Tobin* (1884), 20 Can. L.J. 264.
Lizars and McFarlane v. *Dawson* (1873), 32 U.C.Q.B. 237.
McHardy v. *Corp. of the Township of Ellice and Township of Downie* (1876), 37 U.C.Q.B. 580.
McHardy v. *Corporations of the Townships of Ellice & Downie* (1877), 39 U.C.Q.B. 546.
McQuade v. *Lizars and McPherson* (1877), 39 U.C.Q.B. 215.
Montreal City & District Savings Bank v. *Corporation of Perth* (1881), 17 Can. L.J. 169, 272.
Re Lloyd & Corporation of the Township of Elderslie (1880), 44 U.C.Q.B. 235.
Re Stanbro, G.A. (1884), 2 Man. R. 1 (C.A.).
Regina v. *Corporation of the County of Perth* (1884), 20 Can. L.J. 249.
Regina v. *Smith et al.* (1879), 43 U.C.Q.B. 369.
Stratford and Huron R.W. Co., In re v. *Corp. of County of Perth* (1877), 38 U.C.Q.B. 112.
Widder v. *Buffalo and Lake Huron R.W. Co.* (1869), 27 U.C.Q.B. 425.

SECONDARY SOURCES

Canada Law Journal. Obituary (1885) 21 Can. L.J. 65.
Chadwick, Edward Marion. 'Lizars.' In *Ontarian Families*, vol. 2, 136. Lambertville, NJ: Hunterdon House, 1970.

– 'Smith.' In *Ontarian Families*, vol. 2, 132. Lambertville, NJ: Hunterdon House, 1970.

Ebbs-Camavan. 'Manitoba's First Premier and Attorney-General Henry Joseph Clark, Q.C.' [unpublished paper: Osgoode Hall Law School Library].

Etobicoke Historical Society, ed. *The Story of Etobicoke* at 33. (Etobicoke: Etobicoke Historical Society, 1950.

Evans, William W. *Stratford Directory for 1880–81*. Toronto: Hill & Weir, 1880.

Gunn, James H. 'The Lawyer as Entrepreneur: Robert Home Smith in Early-Twentieth-Century Toronto.' In Carol Wilton, ed., *Essays in the History of Canadian Law*, vol. 4, *Beyond the Law – Lawyers and Business in Canada, 1830 to 1930* 235. Toronto: Osgoode Society, 1994.

Hill, Robert B. *Manitoba: History of Its Early Settlement, Development and Resources* at 753. Toronto: William Biggs, 1890.

Hodgins, J. George. *Schools and Colleges in Ontario,1792–1910*. Toronto: L.K. Cameron, 1910.

Irwin, W.H., ed. *City of Stratford and County of Perth Directory & Gazetteer for 1885–8*. Stratford: Stratford Advertiser, 1885.

Johnston, William. *History of the County of Perth from 1825 to 1902*. Stratford: W.M. O'Beirne, 1903.

Leitch, Adelaide. *Floodtides of Fortune: The Story of Stratford and the Progress of the City through Two Centuries*. Stratford, Ont.: City of Stratford, 1980.

Lizars, Robina, and Kathlene MacFarlane Lizars. *In The Days of the Canada Company: The Story of the Settlement of the Huron Tract and a View of the Social Life of the Period 1825–1850*. Toronto: William Briggs, 1896.

– *Humours of '37 Grave, Gay and Grime: Rebellion Times in the Canadas*. Toronto: William Briggs, 1897.

– *Committed to His Charge, A Canadian Chronicle*. Toronto: George N. Morang, 1900.

MacInnes, Roy Bayne. 'Justice Robert Smith Won Admiration Both as Lawyer and Judge.' In *Stratford Beacon-Herald* 12. 18 September 1938.

Manitoba Law Journal. 'Mr. Justice Smith.' (1884) 1 Man. L.J. 112.

– 'Judicial Knowledge.' (1885) 2 Man. L.J. 1.

– 'Mr. Justice Smith.' (1885) 2 Man. L.J. 31.

Robertson, John Palmerston, ed. *A Political Manual of the Province of Manitoba and the North-West Territories* at 155. Winnipeg: Call, 1887.

Wallace, W. Stewart, ed. 'Lizars, Robina.' In *The Macmillan Dictionary of Canadian Biography*, 3rd ed., 417. Toronto: Macmillan, 1963.

Wallace, W. Stewart, ed. 'Smith, Robert.' In *The Macmillan Dictionary of Canadian Biography*, 3rd ed., 701. Toronto: Macmillan, 1963.

(1881) 17 Can. L.J. 313.

(1884) 20 Can. L.J. 217.
(1885) 2 Man. L.J. 11.

Manitoba Free Press, 20 January 1885, 2, 4.
Stratford Beacon, 19 June 1863, 3; 28 July 1876, 5; 20 June 1884, 1; 23 January 1885, 1; 30 January 1885, 1; 7 May 1924.
Stratford Herald, 27 August 1918, 4.

Fawcett Gowler Taylor

PRIMARY SOURCES

Taylor, Fawcett Gowler, Papers, Archives of the Law Society of Manitoba, file P 1338, PAM.

Rex v. *Nahirniak* (1931), 39 Man. R. 509 (C.A.).

SECONDARY SOURCES

Greene, B.M., ed. 'Lieutenant-Colonel the Honourable Mr. Justice Fawcett Gowler Taylor.' In *Who's Who in Canada, 1934–35* 1566. Toronto: International Press, 1935.
Haig, Hon. John T. 'Mr. Justice Fawcett Gowler Taylor, D.S.O., K.C.' (1940) 12 Man. Bar N. 44.
Kendle, John. *John Bracken: A Political Biography* at 40. Toronto: University of Toronto Press, 1979.
McManus, John. 'Home with a Pedigree.' In *Winnipeg Free Press*, 8 February 1986, 69.
Metcalfe, J.H., ed. *The Tread of the Pioneers* at 247. Portage la Prairie: Portage la Prairie & District Old Timers' Association, 1932.
Morton, W.L. *Manitoba: A History*. Toronto: University of Toronto Press, 1957.

(1931) 1 Fortnightly L.J. 44.
(1933) 3 Fortnightly L.J.121.

Manitoba Free Press, 18 July 1922, 13; 19 July 1922, 6; 4 October 1928, 1; 30 October 1928, 1; 31 October 1928, 1; 16 February 1929, 1, 13; 1 March 1929, 1.
Winnipeg Free Press, 2 January 1940, 1; 5 January 1940, 1, 3, 9.

Thomas Wardlaw Taylor

PRIMARY SOURCES

Census of Manitoba, 1891, Ward 1, page 31.

Taylor, Thomas Wardlaw, Papers, Archives of the Law Society of Upper Canada.
- Papers, Archives of the University of Toronto, file A73-0026/463(28).
- Papers, MG 30, E 484, PAM.
Taylor, Rev. Thomas Wardlaw Jr., *A Sketch of the Life of Sir Thomas Wardlaw Taylor* [unpublished biography], Thomas Wardlaw Taylor AVF file, PAM.

Blair v. *Smith* (1883), 1 Man. R. 5 (Q.B.).
Farmers and Traders Loan Co. v. *Conklin* (1884), 1 Man. R. 181 (Q.B.).
Herb v. *Lawrence* (1890), 7 Man. R. 222 (C.A.).
McIlroy v. *Davis* (1884), 1 Man. R. 53 (Q.B.).
Miller v. *McCuaig* (1890), 6 Man. R. 539 (Q.B.).
Plummer Wagon Co. v. *Wilson* (1886), 3 Man. R. 68 (Q.B).
Queen v. *Riel* (1885), 2 Man. R. 321 (C.A.).
Rankin v. *McKenzie* (1886), 3 Man. R. 554 (Q.B.).
Re Lewis (1888), 5 Man. R. 55 (Q.B.).
Re George A. Stanbro (1884), 1 Man. R. 263 (Q.B.).
Re G.A. Stanbro (1884), 1 Man. R. 325 (C.A.).
Rex v. *Stewart* (1890), 6 Man. R. 257 (C.A.).
Sutherland v. *Schultz* (1883), 1 Man. R. 13 (Q.B.).
Winnipeg & Hudson's Bay Railway Co. v. *Mann* (1890), 7 Man. R. 81 (Q.B.).
Wishart v. *McManus* (1884), 1 Man. R. 213 (C.A.).

SECONDARY SOURCES

Blackwell, John D. 'William Hume Blake and the Judicature Acts of 1849: The Process of Legal Reform at Mid-Century in Upper Canada.' In David H. Flaherty, ed., *Essays in the History of Canadian Law*, vol. 1, 132. Toronto: Osgoode Society, 1981.
Canada Law Journal. (1873) 9 Can. L.J. 4.
- Review of [T.W. Taylor,] *The Investigation of Titles to Estates in Fee Simple* (1873) 9 Can. L.J. 240.
- Review of [T.W. Taylor,] *Commentaries on Equity Jurisprudence, Founded on Story* (1875) 11 Can. L.J.176.
- 'Examination Questions.' (1878) 14 Can. L.J. 30.
- 'Diary for October.' (1882) 18 Can. L.J. 353.
- 'Diary for January.' (1883) 19 Can. L.J. 1–2.
- 'Diary for February.' (1883) 19 Can. L.J. 41.
- 'Mr. Justice Taylor and the Ontario Bar.' (1883) 19 Can. L.J. 42.
- Case Comment *R.* v. *Fant* (1887) 23 Can. L.J. 421.
- 'The Torrens Act in Manitoba.' (1888) 24 Can. L.J. 610.

– (1908) 44 Can. L.J. 88.
– 'The Late Sir Thomas Wardlaw Taylor.' (1917) 53 Can. L.J. 124.
Canada Law Times. 'Sir Thomas Taylor.' (1899) 19 Can. L. Times 46.
Canada Presbyterian. 'The Late Dr. John Taylor.' (1880) 8 *Canada Presbyterian* 888.
Charteris-Thomson, Margaret. *The Colonial Ancestry of the Honourable Sir Thomas Wardlaw Taylor Kt.B. Chief Justice of the Province of Manitoba – 1887–1899*. London: Dumfries, 1937.
Gibson, Dale, and Lee Gibson. *Substantial Justice: Law and Lawyers in Manitoba 1670–1970*. Winnipeg: Peguis, 1972.
Globe. 'News of the Day.' In [Toronto] *Globe*, 14 October 1882, 2.
Hamilton, John Cleland. *Osgoode Hall, Reminiscences of the Bench and Bar* at 63, 185. Toronto: Carswell, 1904.
Henderson, George Fletcher. *Royal Commissions in Canada 1867–1966, a Checklist* at 18. Toronto: University of Toronto Press, 1967.
Maillet, Lise. *Provincial Royal Commissions and Commissions of Inquiry, 1867–1982: A Selective Bibliography* at 117. Ottawa: National Library of Canada, 1986.
Manitoba Bar News. 'The Chief Justice's Portrait.' (1891) 2 Man. Bar N. 187.
– 'Note on Child's Evidence.' (1938) 10:5 Man. Bar N. 513.
– 'Obituaries.' (1953) 25 Man. Bar N. 15.
Manitoba Free Press. 'Sir Thomas Taylor Dies at Hamilton.' In *Manitoba Free Press*, 3 March 1917, 24.
Manitoba Law Journal. 'Rows in Court.' (1884) 1 Man. L.J. 70.
Morgan, Henry James, ed. 'Hon. Sir Thomas Wardlaw Taylor.' In *The Canadian Men and Women of the Time: A Handbook of Canadian Biography of Living Characters*, 2nd ed., 1088. Toronto: Briggs, 1912.
Taylor, Thomas Wardlaw. *Orders of the Court of Chancery for Upper Canada, With Notes*. Toronto: Roswell, 1860.
– *The Investigation of Titles to Estates in Fee Simple*. Toronto: Adam, Stevenson, 1869; 2nd edition Toronto: Willing & Williamson, 1873.
– *Commentaries on Equity Jurisprudence Founded on Story*. Toronto: Willing & Williamson, 1875.
– *The Public Statutes Relating to the Presbyterian Church in Canada: Acts and Resolutions of the General Assembly, and By-laws for the Government of the Colleges and Schemes of the Church*. Toronto: Willing & Williamson, 1879; 2nd edition Winnipeg: Hart, 1897.
– *Historical Sketch of Saint James Square Presbyterian Congregation, Toronto, 1853–1903*. Toronto: Brown-Searle, 1903.
Taylor, Thomas Wardlaw, and John S. Ewart. *The Judicature Act and Rules*

1881, and Other Statutes and Orders Relating to the Practice of the Supreme Court of Judicature for Ontario, With Notes. Toronto: Carswell, 1881.

Taylor, T. Wardlaw, and G.M. Rae. *General Orders of the Court of Chancery, of 6th February, 1865, With Notes and Forms*. Toronto: Rollo & Adam, 1865.

Taylor, Thomas Wardlaw, Jr. *The Individual and the State, An Essay on Justice*. Ph.D. dissertation, Cornell University, 1895.

United Presbyterian. 'The Late Dr. John Taylor.' (January 1881) *United Presbyterian* 26.

Wallace, W. Stewart, ed. 'Sir Thomas Wardlaw Taylor.' In *The Macmillan Dictionary of Canadian Biography*, 3rd ed., 821. Toronto: Macmillan, 1963.

Western Law Times. 'Is This Justice?' (1890) 1 W.L. Times. 101.

– 'Miscarriages of Justice.' (1894) 5 W.L. Times 69.

– 'Michaelmas Term.' (1890) 1 W.L. Times 198.

Willie, Richard A. 'Sir Thomas Wardlaw Taylor.' In Ramsay Cook and Jean Hamelin, eds., *Dictionary of Canadian Biography*, vol. 14, 990. Toronto: University of Toronto Press, 1998.

(1869) 5 Can. L.J. 27.

(1870) 6 Can. L.J. 29, 54.

(1879) 15 Can. L.J. 61.

(1881) 17 Can. L.J. 248, 357.

(1882) 18 Can. L.J. 353.

(1883) 19 Can. L.J. 1, 21, 41, 42.

(1890) 1 West. L. Times 198.

Hamilton Spectator, 3 March 1917, 1; 7 March 1917, 19.

Manitoba Free Press, 17 May 1884, 4.

Winnipeg Free Press, 24 April 1965, 23.

Lewis Wallbridge

PRIMARY SOURCES

Journals of the Legislative Assembly of Manitoba, 1886 at 189–95.

Wallbridge, Campbell Miller, Papers, University of Toronto Archives, file A73-0026/493(35).

– Family, Papers, MG 26A, NAC.

– Family Papers, MS 93, PAO.

Wallbridge, Francis George, Papers, University of Toronto Archives, file A73-0026/493(36).

Wallbridge, Lewis, Diary [unpublished], MG 29, E 119, PAM.

– Papers, Archives of the Law Society of Upper Canada, file 4874.
– Papers, MG 24, B 124, NAC.

Bartels, Francis v. *Bartels, Esther, Isabel Bartels, Andrew Bartels, and James Burt* (1878), 42 U.C.Q.B. 22.
Blanchard v. *Snider* (1870), 28 U.C.Q.B. 210.
Campbell et al. v. *Fox* (1868), 26 U.C.Q.B. 631.
Canniff v. *Bogert*, 7 U.C.C.P. 81.
Chambers v. *Dollar and Stevenson* (1870), 29 U.C.Q.B. 599.
Chambers v. *Unger*, 25 U.C.C.P. 180.
Dafoe v. *The Johnstown District Mutual Insurance Co.*, 7 U.C.C.P. 55.
Fairman v. *White* (1866), 24 U.C.Q.B. 123.
Grant v. *O'Hare (a)* (1882), 46 U.C.Q.B. 277.
Grass v. *Allan et al.* (1868), 26 U.C.Q.B. 123.
Henderson v. *Vermilyea and S. Gonsoles* (1869), 27 U.C.Q.B. 544.
Hicks v. *Snider et al.* (1880), 44 U.C.Q.B. 486.
Hooper v. *Coombs* (1887), 4 Man. R. 35 (Q.B.).
Hutchinson v. *Calder* (1884), 1 Man. R. 46.
Jackson et ux. v. *Yeomans* (1870), 28 U.C.Q.B. 307.
Jones v. *Grand Trunk R.W. Co.* (1881), 45 U.C.Q.B. 193.
Loucks v. *Wallbridge* (1872), 31 U.C.Q.B. 32.
McFarlane v. *Martin and Another*, 3 U.C.C.P. 64.
McMahon v. *Grover*, 3 U.C.C.P. 65.
McPhail v. *Clements* (1884), 1 Man. R. 165 (Q.B.).
Moody (Sheriff) v. *Bull et al.*, 7 U.C.C.P. 15.
Murphy v. *Healey* (1871), 30 U.C.Q.B. 192.
Mykel v. *Doyle* (1881), 45 U.C.Q.B. 65.
North West Navigation Co. v. *Walker* (1886), 3 Man. R. 25 (Q.B.).
Orr, William v. *Samuel Orr* (1872), 31 U.C.Q.B. 13.
Pritchard v. *Hanover* (1884),1 Man. R. 72 (Q.B.).
Queen v. *Connor* (1885), 2 Man. R. 235 (C.A.).
Queen v. *Riel* (1885), 2 Man. R. 321 (C.A.).
Regina v. *Blackstone* (1887), 4 Man. R. 296 (Q.B.).
Regina v. *Leveque* (1886), 3 Man. R. 582 (C.A.).
Reynolds v. *Corporation of Ontario* (1879), 15 Can. L.J. 193.
Rupert, Thomas and Josephine v. *Johnston, James; James Moore and Antoinette Smith Prinyer* (1877), 40 U.C.Q.B. 11.
Ruttan et al. v. *Smith* (1875), 35 U.C.Q.B. 165.
Trickey v. *Seeley et al.* (1872), 31 U.C.Q.B. 214.
Wallbridge v. *Jones* (1874), 33 U.C.Q.B. 613.

Wesley, Elisha v. *Wills, Thomas* (1875), Reports of the Decisions of the Judges for the Trial of Election Petitions in Ontario 211.
West v. *MacInness* (1881), 23 U.C.Q.B. 357.

SECONDARY SOURCES

Albert College, ed. *Albert College, University Calender for the year 1877*. Belleville: Daily Ontario Steam Printing, 1876.
American Biographical Publishing Co., ed. 'Hon. Lewis Wallbridge, Q.C.' In *The Canadian Biographical Dictionary and Portrait Gallery of Eminent and Self-Made Men*, vol. 1, 85. Toronto: American Biographical Publishing Company, 1880.
Baker, G. Blaine. 'Legal Education in Upper Canada 1785–1889: The Law Society as Educator.' In David Flaherty, ed., *Essays in the History of Canadian Law*, vol. 2, 49 at 99, 136. Toronto: Osgoode Society, 1983.
Bowell, Mackenzie, ed. *Directory of the County of Hastings for 1860–61*. Belleville: Intelligencer, 1860.
– *Directory of the County of Hastings for 1864–65*. Belleville: Intelligencer, 1865.
– *Directory of the County of Hastings for 1868–69*. Belleville: Intelligencer, 1869.
Boyce, Betsy Dewar. *The Rebels of Hastings*. Toronto: University of Toronto Press, 1992.
Boyce, Gerald E. *Historic Hastings*. Belleville: Ontario Intelligencer, 1967.
Burwash, Nathanael. *The History of Victoria College*. Toronto: Victoria College Press, 1927.
Canada Law Journal. (1882) 18 Can. L.J. 429.
– 'Hon. Lewis Wallbridge, Chief Justice of Manitoba.' (1887) 23 Can. L.J. 361.
– (1902) 38 Can. L.J. 614.
Canniff, William. *History of the Settlement of Upper Canada with Special Reference to The Bay of Quinte*. Toronto: Dudley & Burns, 1869.
Careless, J.M.S. *Brown of The Globe*, vol. 2, *Statesman of Confederation 1860–1880* at 99, 381. Toronto: Macmillan, 1963.
Cote, J.O., ed. *Political Appointments and Elections in the Province of Canada from 1841 to 1865*. Ottawa: G.E. Desbarats, 1866.
Cote, Narceisse Omer. *Political Appointments, Parliaments and the Judicial Bench in the Dominion of Canada, 1867 to 1895*. Ottawa: Thoburn, 1896.
Dale, Clare A. *'Whose Servant I Am': Speakers of the Assemblies of the Province of Upper Canada, Canada and Ontario, 1792–1992* at 131. Toronto: Legislative Library, 1992.
Gibson, Dale, and Lee Gibson. *Substantial Justice: Law and Lawyers in Manitoba 1670–1970*. Winnipeg: Peguis, 1972.

Globe. 'News of the Day.' In [Toronto] *Globe*, 10 October 1882, 1; 13 October 1882, 1.

Haines, Max. 'The Last Duel,' In *Winnipeg Sun*, 24 April 1988, 19.

Hamilton, James Cleland. *Osgoode Hall, Reminiscences of the Bench and Bar* at 148–150. Toronto: Carswell, 1904.

Hodgins, Bruce W. *The Political Career of John Sandfield Macdonald to the Fall of His Administration in March 1864: A Study in Canadian Politics*. Ph.D. thesis, Duke University, 1965 [unpublished].

– 'Lewis Wallbridge' in Francess G. Halpenny & Jean Hamelin, eds., *Dictionary of Canadian Biography*, vol. 11, 908. Toronto: University of Toronto Press, 1982.

Hodgins, Thomas. *Reports of the Decisions of the Judges for the Trial of Election Petitions in Ontario* at 211. Toronto: Carswell, 1883.

Intelligencer Printing, ed. *Directory of the County of Hastings for 1879–80*. Belleville: Intelligencer, 1879.

Maillet, Lise. *Provincial Royal Commissions and Commissions of Inquiry, 1867–1982: A Selective Bibliography* at 117. Ottawa: National Library of Canada, 1986.

Manitoba Bar News. 'Chief Justice Wallbridge.' (1937) 10 Man. Bar N. 481.

Manitoba Law Journal. 'More Judges.' (1884) 1 Man. L.J. 16.

Mika, Nick, and Helma Mika. *Belleville, Friendly City*. Belleville: Mika, 1973.

Robertson, John Palmerston. *A Political Manual of the Province of Manitoba and the North-west Territories* at 44. Winnipeg: Call, 1887.

Rolph & Clark, eds. *Pioneer Life on the Bay of Quinte* at 894. Toronto: Rolph & Clark, 1904.

Rose, George Maclean, ed. *Cyclopaedia of Canadian Biography* at 374. Toronto: Rose, 1888.

Sissons, Charles Bruce. *Egerton Ryerson, His Life and Letters*, vol. 2, at 448. Toronto: Clarke, Irwin, 1947.

– *A History of Victoria University* at 124. Toronto: University of Toronto Press, 1952.

Smith, William Henry. *Canada, Past, Present and Future*, vol. 2, at 56. Toronto: Mavclear, 1851.

Stubbs, Roy St. George. 'Chief Justice Wallbridge.' (1937) 10 Man. Bar N. 481.

Wallace, W. Stewart, ed. *The Macmillan Dictionary of Canadian Biography*, 4th ed., 870. Toronto: Macmillan, 1978.

Western Law Times. 'Portrait of Chief Justice Wallbridge.' (1890) 1 W.L. Times 166.

Willie, Richard A. *'These Legal Gentlemen': Lawyers in Manitoba: 1839–1900*. Winnipeg: Legal Research Institute of the University of Manitoba, 1994.

(1931) 1 Fortnightly L.J. 117.
(1855) 1 U.C.L.J. 220.
(1856) 2 U.C.L.J. 72.
(1857) 3 U.C.L.J. 194.

[Kingston] *Daily British Whig*, 14 August 1863.
[Toronto] *Globe*, 14 October 1882, 9; 17 October 1882, 1; 18 October 1882, 1, 2, 3; 21 October 1882, 8.
[Belleville] *Hastings Chronicle*, 1857, 1861, 1867.
[Belleville] *Intelligencer*, 1880, 21/22/23 etc. October 1887.
[Belleville] *Weekly Intelligencer*, 27 October 1887, 2.
Manitoba Free Press, 21 October 1887, 2, 4; 22 October 1887, 4.

Esten Kenneth Williams

PRIMARY SOURCES

Documents relating to the proceedings of the Royal Commission established by Order in Council P.C. 411 of February 5th, 1946 (Ottawa: King's Printer, 1946).
The Report of the Royal Commission Appointed under Order in Council P.C. 411 of February 5, 1946 (Ottawa: King's Printer, 1946).

Maybank, Ralph, Papers, MG 14, B 35, PAM.
Williams, Esten Kenneth, Papers, MG 14, B 39, PAM.

Bairner v. *Hedges* (1947), 54 Man. R. 489 (Q.B.).
Boyer v. *The King* (1947), 7 C.R. 165 (Que. K.B., Appeal).
Bradley v. *The Queen*, [1957] 6 D.L.R. (2d) 385 (Man. Q.B.).
Fryer v. *Fryer* (1948), 55 Man. R. 523 (Q.B.).
Gray et al. v. *Lafleche et al.* (1949), 57 Man. R. 396 (Q.B.).
In Re Demery Halland v. *Standard Trust Company* (1924), 34 Man. R. 534.
In Re The Estate of Williams James Ferguson, Deceased (1944), 51 Man. R. 301 (C.A.).
In Re Estate of William James Ferguson, Deceased (No. 2) (1945), 52 Man. R. 140 (C.A.).
In Re Nanton Estate (1948), 56 Man. R. 71 at 85 (Q.B.).
In Re The Testator's Family Maintenance Act in re La Fleur Estate (1948), 56 Man. R. 44 (Q.B.).
In Re The Winnipeg Charter; City of Winnipeg v. *The T. Eaton Company Limited* (1945), 52 Man. R. 69 (C.A.).
M. v. *M.* (1955), 62 Man. R. 537 (Q.B.).
Malanik and *Her Majesty The Queen (No. 3)*, [1952] 2 S.C.R. 335.
McLeod and More v. *Sweezey* (1944), 51 Man. R. 129 (C.A.).

Miller et al. v. *Aikins* (1928), 38 Man. R. 18.
North American Accident Insurance Co. v. *Newton* (1919), 45 D.L.R. 247 (S.C.C.).
The North Canadian Trust Co. v. *Smith* (1947), 55 Man. R. 122 (C.A.).
Northern Shirt Co. v. *Chester E. Clark* (1918), 38 D.L.R. 1 (Exchequer).
Provincial Treasurer of Manitoba v. *Wm. Wrigley Junior Co. Ltd.* (1946), 53 Man. R. 213 (C.A.).
R. v. *Deacon* (1948), 56 Man. R. 1 (C.A.).
Regina v. *Jourdain and Kudyba* (1958), 25 W.W.R. 160 (Man. Q.B.).
Rex v. *Bodnarchuk*, [1949] 2 W.W.R. 161 (Man. Q.B.).
Rex v. *Emma Woikin* (1946), 1 C.R. 224 (Ont. Cty. Ct.).
Rex v. *Gerson*, [1947] O.R. 715 (C.A.).
Rex v. *Lunan*, [1947] O.R. 201 (C.A.).
Rex v. *Malanik*, [1951] 1 W.W.R. 561 (Man. Q.B.).
Rex v. *Malanik (No. 2)*, [1951] 3 W.W.R. 577 (Man. Q.B.).
Rex v. *Mazerall*, [1946] O.R. 511 (H.C.) and 762 (C.A.).
Rex v. *Rose* (1947), 3 C.R. 277 (Que. K.B., Appeal).
Rex v. *Smith* (1947), 4 C.R. 98 (Ont. C.A.).
Rex v. *Vescio*, [1948] 2 W.W.R. 161 (Man. Q.B.).
Safeway Stores Ltd. v. *Harris* (1948), 56 Man. R. 146 (C.A.).
Vescio v. *The King*, [1949] 1 D.L.R. 721 (Man. Q.B.).

SECONDARY SOURCES

American Bar Association. 'The Honorable Esten Kenneth Williams' (1947) 33 ABA Journal 71.
Armstrong, H.R. 'Two Women, Two Men Aided Soviet-Ottawa.' In *Toronto Daily Star*, 4 March 1946, 1.
Barrister. (1894) 1 Barrister 48.
– (1895) 1 Barrister 395.
– 'Judicial Robes.' (1897) 3 Barrister 160.
Bothwell, Robert, and J.L. Granatstein, eds. *The Gouzenko Transcripts*. Ottawa: Deneau, 1981.
Canada Bar Review. 'Canada's Nominees for the International Court of Justice.' (1946) 24 Can. Bar Rev. 55.
Canada Law Review. 'Legal Education in Ontario, Part II.' (1905) 4 Can. L. Rev. 192.
Canadian Bar Association. 'Report of the Civil Liberties Committee of the Canadian Bar Association' (1946) 28 Can. Bar Assoc. Proc. 141.
Fyfe, M.H. 'Some Legal Aspects of the Report on the Royal Commission on Espionage.' (1946) 24 Can. Bar Rev. 777.
Gibson, Dale. 'Anecdotal Sampler.' In Cameron Harvey, ed., *The Law Society of Manitoba 1877–1977* at 208, 221. Winnipeg: Peguis, 1977.

Gibson, Dale, and Lee Gibson. *Substantial Justice: Law and Lawyers in Manitoba 1670–1970*. Winnipeg: Peguis, 1972.

Gibson, Lee. *A Proud Heritage: The First Hundred Years of Aikins, MacAulay and Thorvaldson*. Winnipeg: Aikins, MacAulay and Thorvaldson, 1993.

Greene, B.M., ed. 'Williams, The Honourable Esten Kenneth, LL.D.' In *Who's Who In Canada* 37. Toronto: International Press Limited, 1962.

Hamilton, John Cleland. *Osgoode Hall, Reminiscences of the Bench and Bar* at 138–39. Toronto: Carswell, 1904.

Henderson, George Fletcher. *Federal Royal Commissions in Canada 1867–1966, a Checklist* at 148. Toronto: University of Toronto Press, 1967.

Huband, Charles R. 'A New Problem in Adoption.' (1958) 30 Man. Bar N. 97.

Jewers, Gerald O. 'Chief Justice E.K. Williams.' (1961) 33 Man. Bar N. 145.

Kendle, John. *John Bracken: A Political Biography* at 122–3. Toronto: University of Toronto Press, 1979.

Laskin, Bora. 'A Judge and His Constituencies.' (1976) 1 Man. L.J. 1 at 1.

MacTavish, D.K. Review of Williams, *Notes on The Canadian Law of Landlord and Tenant* (1934) 12 Can. Bar Rev. 118.

Maillet, Lise. *Provincial Royal Commissions and Commissions of Inquiry, 1867–1982: A Selective Bibliography*. Ottawa: National Library of Canada, 1986.

Manitoba Bar News. 'Revision of Statutes.' (1930) 3:2 Man. Bar N. 4.

– 'Some New Legislation.' (1931) 3:9 Man. Bar N. 1.

– 'News of the Profession.' (1931) 3:8 Man. Bar N. 8.

– 'Attorney General Entertains.' (1931) 3:10 Man. Bar N. 4.

– 'Rules of the Court of Appeal.' (1934) 6:9 Man. Bar N. 8.

– (1937) 10 Man. Bar N. 505.

– 'Revision Committee's Report.' (1939) 12:4 Man. Bar N. 31.

– 'The New King's Bench Rules.' (1940) 12:5 Man. Bar N. 48.

– 'Tallin Succeeds Laidlaw as Dean.' (1945) 17:3 Man. Bar N. 39.

– 'The President of the Canadian Bar Association.' (1945) 17 Man. Bar N. 81.

– 'Mr. E.K. Williams, K.C.' and 'Convention Afterthoughts.' (1946) 18 Man. Bar N. 58 and 71.

– 'The New Judges.' (1947) 19:1 Man. Bar N. 2.

– 'Law In Action.' (1954) 26 Man. Bar N. 50.

– (1954) 26 Man. Bar N. 81.

– (1959) 31 Man. Bar N. 21.

– 'Nos Disparus.' (1970) 38 Man. Bar N. 108.

McCaffrey, D'Arcy. 'Interview with Chief Justice Samuel Freedman.' (1970) 38 Man. Bar N. 180 at 187

Moon, Barbara. 'The Gouzenko Spy Case.' In Pierre Berton, ed. *Historic Headlines: A Century of Canadian News Dramas* 96. Toronto: McClelland & Stewart, 1967.

Morton, W.L. *Manitoba: A History* at 422. Toronto: University of Toronto Press, 1957.
Peden, Murray. *Hearken to the Evidence* at 4–5, 36–43, 88–91. Stittsville, Ont.: Canada's Wings Inc., 1983.
Saxe, John Godfrey. 'A Ministry of Justice or Law Revision Commission.' (1925) 3 N.Y.L. Rev. 98.
Snell, James G., and Frederick Vaughan. *The Supreme Court of Canada, History of the Institution* at 158. Toronto: Osgoode Society, 1985.
Whalen, James Murray, ed. *Records of Federal Royal Commissions (RG 33)*, vol. 2 Ottawa: National Archives of Canada, 1994.
Williams, Esten K. *Manitoba King's Bench Act, an Annotation of the King's Bench Act, and the Rules Made Thereunder*. Toronto: Carswell, 1914.
– *Notes on The Canadian Law of Landlord and Tenant as Applied to Corporeal Hereditaments*. Toronto: Carswell, 1922.
2nd edition, Toronto: Carswell, 1934.
3rd edition, *Notes on The Canadian Law of Landlord and Tenant*. Toronto: Carswell, 1957.
4th edition, with two new chapters, F.W. Rhodes, ed. *Williams' The Canadian Law of Landlord and Tenant*. Toronto: Carswell, 1973.
5th edition, *Williams and Rhodes Canadian Law of Landlord and Tenant*. Toronto: Carswell, 1983.
– 'The Editorship. Vale Caesar Atque Ave.' (1946) 24 Can. Bar Rev. 1.
– 'Aspects of the Legal History of Manitoba.' (1949) 4 Hist. & Sci. Soc. Man. 48.
– 'Judicial Robes.' (1949) 21:1 Man. Bar N. 117.
– 'Legal Education in Manitoba.' (1950) 28 Can. Bar Rev. 759, 880.
– 'Maiden Assizes and White Gloves.' (1950) 22 Man. Bar N. 106.
– 'Forword.' In Roy St. George Stubbs, *Sir George Jessel, Master of the Rolls*. Winnipeg: self-published, 1951.
– 'Practice Note: Applications Under the Lunacy Act.' (1958) 30:4 Man. Bar N. 77.
– 'Alfred Erskine Hoskin.' (1960) 32 Man. Bar N. 65.
Williams, Rowland, with assistance of Dale Gibson. 'The Plight of the Unlicensed Foreign Corporation' (1957) 29 Man. Bar N. 126.

SPEECHES OF E.K. WILLIAMS REPRINTED AS ARTICLES

'Domicil.' (1923) 1 Can. Bar Rev. 243.
'Stare Decisis.' (1926) 4 Can. Bar Rev. 289.
'Some Developments of the Law Relating to Voluntary Unincorporated Associations.' (1928) 6 Can. Bar Rev. 16, (1927) 12 Can. Bar Assoc. Proc. 184.
'The Lawyer's Wife.' (1937) 62 Reports of the ABA 453.

'The Unalterable Law.' (1939) 17 Can. Bar Rev. 551.
'The Lawyer in the Changing World.' (1940) 13 Man. Bar N. 34.
'A Study of Some of the Recent Developments Affecting Insurance.' (1943) 21 Can. Bar Rev. 547, (1943) 26 Can. Bar Assoc. Proc. 190.
'The Canadian Lawyer: A Startling Paradox.' (1945) 23 Can. Bar Rev. 169.
'Today and Tomorrow.' (1946) 24 Can. Bar Rev. 647, 28 Can. Bar Assoc. Proc. 79.
'Whither?' (1947) 33 ABA Journal 10, 81.
The Doctor, the Lawyer, and the Judge. Toronto: CCH, 1952.

(1919) 55 Can. L.J. 74.
(1962) 34:2 Man. Bar N. 54.

Toronto Daily Star, 8 March 1946, 1; 14 March 1946, 1; 15 March 1946, 1; 15 March 1946, 1; 16 March 1946, 1; 26 March 1946, 1; 29 March 1946, 1; 30 March 1946, 1, 2.
Winnipeg Free Press, 19 January 1933, 1; 21 January 1933, 7; 30 April 1970, 11; 1 May 1970, 29.

Edmund Burke Wood

PRIMARY SOURCES

Census of Manitoba, 1881.
Journals of the 3rd Session of the 4th Parliament of Canada, Session 1880–81.
Journals of the 4th Session of the 4th Parliament of Canada, Session 1882.
Journals of the Senate of Canada, Third Session of the Fourth Parliament (1880–81).
Manitoba. *Report on Commission of Inquiry into Administration of Justice as to Infant Lands and Estates*. Winnipeg: Government of Manitoba, 1881. In GR 174, Box 19, PAM.
Petitions and Reply to the Charges Preferred against Hon. E.B. Wood, C.J., Province of Manitoba. Ottawa: Government of Canada, 1882.
Cunningham, Robert, Papers, MG 14, B16, PAM.
Greenway, Thomas, Papers, MG 13, B1 (GR 1662), PAM.
Wood, Edmund Burke, file, Law Society of Upper Canada, file 4895.
Wood, Edmund Burke, Papers, MG 10, F2, PAM.
Wood, Edmund Burke. *Speech of the Hon. E.B. Wood, Treasurer of the Province of Ontario Delivered on the 15th December 1868 in the Legislative Assembly of Ontario*. Toronto: Hunter, Rose, 1869.
– *Speech of the Hon. E.B. Wood, Treasurer of the Province of Ontario: Delivered on the 10th December, 1869, in the Legislative Assembly of Ontario*. Toronto: Hunter, Rose, 1869.

– *Arguments of Hon. E.B. Wood, Before the Arbitrators under the British North America Act of 1867*. Toronto: Hunter, Rose, 1870.
– *Mr. Wood's Argument before the Provincial Arbitrators on the Modes Proposed for the Apportionment of the Excess of Debt and Division of Assets between Ontario and Quebec*. Toronto: Hunter, Rose, 1870.
– *Report of the Royal Commission to Inquire into and concerning any Complaints of Ill-treatment or Extortion Practiced upon Visitors at Niagara Falls*. Brantford: The Commissioner, 1872.
– *Speech of the Hon. E.B. Wood, in the House of Commons, on the Pacific scandal*. Ottawa: 1873.
Wood, Edmund M., Papers, Archives of the Law Society of Manitoba, file P 1350, PAM.

Allan v. *McKay* (1877), Temp. Wood 111 (Q.B.).
Bank of Montreal v. *Cornish* (1878), Temp. Wood 272 (Q.B.).
Belyea v. *Muir et al.* (1871), 7 Can. L.J. 83 (Q.B.).
Biggs v. *Wood* (1885), 2 Man. L.J. 272 (C.A.).
Black v. *Kennedy* (1877), Temp. Wood 144 (Q.B.).
Bose v. *Morris* (1881), Temp. Wood 368 (Q.B.).
Bouchette v. *Anderson* (1876), Temp. Wood 64 (Q.B.).
Boultbee v. *Shore* (1882), Temp. Wood 376 (Q.B.).
Breden v. *Lyon* (1876), Temp. Wood 50 (C.A.).
City of Winnipeg v. *Cauchon* (1881), Temp. Wood 350 (Q.B.).
Clarke v. *The City of Winnipeg* v. *Clarke* (1876), Temp. Wood 56 (C.A.).
Clarke v. *Murray* (1877), Temp. Wood 119 (Q.B.).
Comber v. *LeMay* (1876), Temp. Wood 35 (Q.B.).
Corporation of the County of Welland, The v. *The Buffalo and Lake Huron Railway Company* (1872), 31 U.C.Q.B. 539.
Craig v. *The Great Western Railway Company* (1866), 24 U.C.Q.B. 504.
Farmer v. *Livingston* (1879), Temp. Wood 233 (Q.B.).
Farmer v. *Livingstone* (1881), 5 S.C.R. 221.
Farmer v. *Livingstone* (1884), 8 S.C.R. 140.
Fitch v. *Murray* (1876), Temp. Wood 74 (Q.B.).
Follansby v. *McArthur* (1875), Temp. Wood 4 (Q.B.).
Hoskins v. *Barber* (1879), Temp. Wood 264 (Q.B.).
Hudson Bay Co. v. *Attorney-General of Manitoba* (1878), Temp. Wood 209 (Q.B.).
Jones v. *Jenkins* (1867), 25 U.C.Q.B. 151.
Lacerte v. *Hargrave* (1881), Temp. Wood 343 (Q.B.).
Lewis v. *Wood* (1885), 2 Man. R. 73 (Q.B.).
Margaret Christie, Administratix of Robert Christie v. *Clark* (1869), 27 U.C.Q.B. 21.
McKenney v. *Spence et al.* (1875), Temp. Wood 11 (Q.B.).

McLean et al. v. *The Buffalo and Lake Huron Railway Company* (1866), 23 U.C.Q.B. 448.
McLean et al. v. *The Buffalo and Lake Huron Railway Company* (1866), 24 U.C.Q.B. 270.
McMicken v. *Clarke* (1877), Temp. Wood 157 (Q.B.).
Mercer v. *McLean* (1876), Temp. Wood 95 (C.A.).
Merritt v. *Rossiter* (1875), Temp. Wood 1 (Q.B.).
Monitor Plough Works, The v. *Allen* (1877), Temp. Wood 165 (Q.B.).
Murdoch v. *The Manitoba South Western Colonization Railway Company* (1881), Temp. Wood 334 (Q.B.).
Nelson v. *Gurney* (1877), Temp. Wood 173 (Q.B.).
Ontario Bank v. *Miner* (1877), Temp. Wood 167 (Q.B.).
Osler, In re (1877), Temp. Wood 205 (Cty.Ct.).
Queen, The v. *Dease* (1875), Carey's Manitoba Reports 1 (Q.B.).
Queen, The v. *Schultz* (1875), Carey's Manitoba Reports 32 (Q.B.).
Regina v. *Anderson* (1877), Temp. Wood 177 (Q.B.).
Regina v. *Biggs* (1885), 2 Man. L.J. 18 (Q.B.).
Regina v. *Rowe* (1880), Temp. Wood 309 (Cty.Ct.).
Re McMichael and The Corporation of the Township of Townsend (1874), 33 U.C.Q.B. 158.
Schultz v. *Wood* (1882), 6 S.C.R. 585.
Simpson v. *Ellis* (1876), Temp. Wood 31 (Q.B.).
Studer v. *The Buffalo and Lake Huron Railway Co.* (1867), 25 U.C.Q.B. 160.
Thibeaudeau, In re (1877), Temp. Wood 149 (Q.B.).
Trottier v. *The Red River Transportation Company* (1879), Temp. Wood 255 (Q.B.).
Tucker v. *Young* (1877), Temp. Wood 186 (Q.B.).
Widder v. *The Buffalo and Lake Huron Railway Company* (1866), 24 U.C.Q.B. 520.
Williamson v. *Gore District Mutual Ins. Co.* (1868), 26 U.C.Q.B. 145.
Wilson v. *The City of Winnipeg* (1887), 4 Man. R. 193 (C.A.).
Wood v. *Schultz* (1881), 17 Can. L.J. 451 (Q.B.).
Wood v. *Wood* (1885), 2 Man. L.J. 198 (Q.B.).
Young v. *Smith* (1880), 4 S.C.R. 494.

SECONDARY SOURCES

Armour, E.D., ed. *Reports of Cases Argued and Determined in the Court of Queen's Bench in Manitoba Both at Law and in Equity during the Time of Chief Justice Wood from 1875 to 1883*. Toronto: Carswell, 1884 [cited as Temp. Wood].
Armstrong, Richard. 'The Hon. Edmund Burk Wood, Late Chief Justice of Manitoba' (1895) 1 Barrister 114.

Begg, Alexander. *Ten Years in Winnipeg*. Winnipeg: Times, 1879.

– *History of The North-West*, vol. 2, at 135–44. Toronto: Hunter, Rose, 1894.

Berton, Pierre. *Niagara, A History of the Falls*. Toronto: McClelland & Stewart, 1992.

Biggar, C.R.W. *Sir Oliver Mowat, A Biographical Sketch*, vols. 1 and 2. Toronto: Warwick Bros. & Rutter, 1905.

Bumsted, J.M. *The Red River Rebellion* at 238–41. Winnipeg: Watson & Dwyer, 1996.

Canada Law Journal. 'The Outlawry of Louis Riel' (1875) 11 Can. L.J. 105.

Carey, Daniel, ed. *Carey's Manitoba Reports*. Calgary: Burroughs & Co., 1918.

Charteris-Thomson, Margaret. *The Colonial Ancestry of The Honourable Sir Thomas Wardlaw Taylor, Kt.B. Chief Justice of the Province of Manitoba – 1887–1899* (London: Courier Press, 1937).

Chiel, Arthur. *Jewish Experiences in Early Manitoba* at 13–20. Winnipeg: Manitoba Jewish Publications, 1955.

Cooke, Britton B. 'Famous Canadian Trials' (1915) 45 *Canadian Magazine* 57.

Elliott, George B., and Frederick Thomas Brokovski. *Preliminary Investigation and Trial of Ambroise D. Lepine for the Murder of Thomas Scott: Being a Full Report of the Proceedings in This Case before the Magistrates' Court and the Several Courts of Queen's Bench in the Province of Manitoba*. Montreal: Burland-Desbarats, 1875.

Ens, Gerhard. 'Metis Lands in Manitoba' (1983) 5 Man. Hist. 2.

Foran, Thomas P. *Trial of Ambrose Lepine at Winnipeg for the Wilful Murder of Thomas Scott: Question of Jurisdiction*. Montreal: Lovell, 1874.

Friesen, Gerald. *The Canadian Prairies, A History* at 198–99. Toronto: University of Toronto Press, 1987.

Gibson, Dale, and Lee Gibson. *Substantial Justice: Law and Lawyers in Manitoba 1670–1970*. Winnipeg: Peguis, 1972.

Globe. 'Chief Justice Wood.' In [Toronto] *Globe*, 11 October 1882, 3.

– 'Stricken in Harness.' In [Toronto] *Globe*, 14 October 1882, 10.

– 'The Late Chief Justice Wood.' In [Toronto] *Globe*, 16 October 1882, 2.

Hamilton, James Cleland. *Osgoode Hall, Reminiscences of the Bench and Bar* at 79, 102–04. Toronto: Carswell, 1904.

Henderson, George Fletcher. *Federal Royal Commissions in Canada 1867–1966, a Checklist* at 10. Toronto: University of Toronto Press, 1967.

Hodgins, Bruce W. *John Sandfield Macdonald* at 88–97, 107–09, 115. Toronto: University of Toronto Press, 1971

Johnson, J.K., ed. *The Canadian Directory of Parliament 1867–1967* at 607. Ottawa: Public Archives of Canada, 1968.

Johnston, C.M. *Brant County, A History 1784–1945* at 48–49. Toronto: Oxford University Press, 1967.

Livermore, J.D. 'The Ontario Election of 1871: A Case Study of the Transfer of Political Power.' (1979) 71 Ont. Hist. 39.

– 'Edmund Burke Wood.' In Francess G. Halpenny, ed., *Dictionary of Canadian Biography*, vol. 11, 934. Toronto: University of Toronto Press, 1982.

Livingston, William Guy. *Farmer vs. Livingston, An Appeal by W.G. Livingston to the Members of the House of Parliament at Ottawa* [self-published].

Manitoba Law Journal. Letter to the Editor. (1884) 1 Man. L.J. 79.

McAlduff, Sister Maureen M. *Joseph Dubuc, Role and Views of a French Canadian in Manitoba 1870–1914*. M.A. thesis, University of Ottawa, 1967 [unpublished].

McDonald, Donna. *Lord Strathcona, a Biography of Donald Alexander Smith.* Toronto: Dundurn, 1996.

Morgan, Henry James. *The Canadian Legal Directory: A Guide to the Bench and Bar of the Dominion of Canada* 269. Toronto: Carswell, 1878.

Murder of the Mail Carrier. In Edmund Burke Wood Papers, Brant County Museum and Archives.

Noel, S.J.R. *Patrons, Clients, Brokers: Ontario Society and Politics, 1791–1896.* Toronto: University of Toronto Press, 1990).

O'Donnell, John H. *Manitoba As I Saw It* at 101–03. Toronto: Musson, 1909.

Reville, F. Douglas. *History of the County of Brant*, vol. 1. Brantford: Hurley, 1920.

Robertson, John Palmerston. *A Political Manual of the Province of Manitoba and the North-West Territories* at 88, 161. Winnipeg: Call Printing, 1887.

Schull, Joseph. *Edward Blake, The Man of the Other Way* at 74–81. (1833–1881) Toronto: Macmillan, 1975.

Siggins, Maggie. *Riel: A Life of Revolution* at 238–241. Toronto: Harper Collins, 1994.

Sissons, C.B. *Egerton Ryerson, His Life and Letters*, vol. 2, at 554, 564–9, 594. Toronto: Clarke, Irwin, 1947.

Sprague, D.N. 'Government Lawlessness in the Administration of Manitoba Land Claims, 1870–1887.' (1980) 10 Man. L.J. 415.

Stanley, George F.G. *Louis Riel.* Toronto: Ryerson, 1963.

Stubbs, Roy St. George. 'Hon. Edmund Burke Wood.' (1958) 13 Hist. & Sc. Soc. Man. 27.

– 'Hon. Edmund Burke Wood.' (1962) 34 Man. Bar N. 109.

Walker, Frank N. 'Birth of the Buffalo and Brantford Railway.' (1955) 47 Ont. Hist. Soc. 81.

Wallace, W. Stewart. 'Political History.' In Adam Shortt and Arthur G.

Doughty, eds., *Canada and Its Provinces*, vol. 17, 103. Toronto: Constable, 1914.

Wallace, W. Stewart, ed. *The Macmillan Dictionary of Canadian Biography* at 901. Toronto: Macmillan, 1926.

Warner, Beers, ed. *The History of the County of Brant, Ontario*. Toronto: Warner, Beers, 1883.

Western Law Times. 'A Legal Incident' (1890) 1 W.L. Times 14.

Willie, Richard A. *'These Legal Gentlemen': Lawyers in Manitoba: 1839–1900*. Winnipeg: Legal Research Institute of the University of Manitoba, 1994).

Willison, Sir John. *Reminiscences Political and Personal*. Toronto: McClelland & Stewart, 1919.

Wood, Chief Justice Edmund Burke. 'Inaugural Address – 1879.' (1959) 14 Hist. & Sci. Soc. Man. 6.

(1874) 10 Can. L.J. 31, 93.

(1880) 16 Can. L.J. 308.

(1882) 2 Can. L. Times 529.

(1880) 1 Man. Bar N. 14.

Brantford Telegram, 9 October 1882, 1.

Globe, 7 March 1881, 4.

Globe (11 October 1882) 3.

Globe (14 October 1882) 10.

Globe (16 October 1882) 2.

Manitoba Free Press, 18 July 1874, 3; 10 October 1874, 3; 27 October 1874, 2; 13 November 1874, 2; 14 January 1875, 4; 28 January 1875, 2; 3 February 1875, 2; 9 February 1875, 2; 13 February 1875, 2; 15 February 1875, 2, 4; 16 February 1875, 2; 17 February 1875, 2; 19 August 1875, 2; 20 August 1875, 2, 3; 23 August 1875, 2, 4; 8 December 1875, 2; 7 January 1876, 3; 8 July 1879, 1; 6 September 1879, 1; 9 September 1879, 1; 13 January 1880, 1; 17 Janauary 1880, 1; 27 January 1880, 1; 13 August 1880, 1; 10 March 1881, 2; 12 March 1881, 1; 15 March 1881, 2; 21 March 1881, 2; 27 October 1881, 1; 17 November 1881, 2; 2 October 1882, 2; 9 October 1882, 2, 4, 5; 10 October 1882, 1, 8; 11 October 1882, 2; 16 October 1882, 8; 1 September 1884, 4; 2 September 1884, 4; 8 September 1884, 4; 9 September 1884, 4; 10 September 1884, 4; 22 March 1886, 4; 1 November 1930, 31.

The Nor' Wester, 2 November 1874.

Winnipeg Daily Times, 8 September 1884; 9 September 1884; 11 September 1884.

Index

PUBLICATIONS OF THE OSGOODE SOCIETY FOR CANADIAN LEGAL HISTORY

1981 David H. Flaherty, ed., *Essays in the History of Canadian Law: Volume I*

1982 Marion MacRae and Anthony Adamson, *Cornerstones of Order: Courthouses and Town Halls of Ontario, 1784–1914*

1983 David H. Flaherty, ed., *Essays in the History of Canadian Law: Volume II*

1984 Patrick Brode, *Sir John Beverley Robinson: Bone and Sinew of the Compact*
David Williams, *Duff: A Life in the Law*

1985 James Snell and Frederick Vaughan, *The Supreme Court of Canada: History of the Institution*

1986 Paul Romney, *Mr Attorney: The Attorney General for Ontario in Court, Cabinet, and Legislature, 1791–1899*
Martin Friedland, *The Case of Valentine Shortis: A True Story of Crime and Politics in Canada*

1987 C. Ian Kyer and Jerome Bickenbach, *The Fiercest Debate: Cecil A. Wright, the Benchers, and Legal Education in Ontario, 1923–1957*

1988 Robert Sharpe, *The Last Day, the Last Hour: The Currie Libel Trial*
John D. Arnup, *Middleton: The Beloved Judge*

1989 Desmond Brown, *The Genesis of the Canadian Criminal Code of 1892*
Patrick Brode, *The Odyssey of John Anderson*

1990 Philip Girard and Jim Phillips, eds., *Essays in the History of Canadian Law: Volume III – Nova Scotia*
Carol Wilton, ed., *Essays in the History of Canadian Law: Volume IV – Beyond the Law: Lawyers and Business in Canada, 1830–1930*

1991 Constance Backhouse, *Petticoats and Prejudice: Women and Law in Nineteenth-Century Canada*

1992 Brendan O'Brien, *Speedy Justice: The Tragic Last Voyage of His Majesty's Vessel Speedy*
Robert Fraser, ed., *Provincial Justice: Upper Canadian Legal Portraits from the Dictionary of Canadian Biography*

1993 Greg Marquis, *Policing Canada's Century: A History of the Canadian Association of Chiefs of Police*
F. Murray Greenwood, *Legacies of Fear: Law and Politics in Quebec in the Era of the French Revolution*

1994 Patrick Boyer, *A Passion for Justice: The Legacy of James Chalmers McRuer*
Charles Pullen, *The Life and Times of Arthur Maloney: The Last of the Tribunes*
Jim Phillips, Tina Loo, and Susan Lewthwaite, eds., *Essays in the History of Canadian Law: Volume V – Crime and Criminal Justice*
Brian Young, *The Politics of Codification: The Lower Canadian Civil Code of 1866*

1995 David Williams, *Just Lawyers: Seven Portraits*

Hamar Foster and John McLaren, eds., *Essays in the History of Canadian Law: Volume VI – British Columbia and the Yukon*
W.H. Morrow, ed., *Northern Justice: The Memoirs of Mr Justice William G. Morrow*
Beverley Boissery, *A Deep Sense of Wrong: The Treason, Trials, and Transportation to New South Wales of Lower Canadian Rebels after the 1838 Rebellion*

1996 Carol Wilton, ed., *Essays in the History of Canadian Law: Volume VII – Inside the Law: Canadian Law Firms in Historical Perspective*
William Kaplan, *Bad Judgment: The Case of Mr Justice Leo A. Landreville*
F. Murray Greenwood and Barry Wright, eds., *Canadian State Trials: Volume I – Law, Politics, and Security Measures, 1608–1837*

1997 James W. St.G. Walker, *'Race,' Rights, and the Law in the Supreme Court of Canada: Historical Case Studies*
Lori Chambers, *Married Women and Property Law in Victorian Ontario*
Patrick Brode, *Casual Slaughters and Accidental Judgments: Canadian War Crimes and Prosecutions, 1944–1948*
Ian Bushnell, *A History of the Federal Court of Canada, 1875–1992*

1998 Sidney Harring, *White Man's Law: Native People in Nineteenth-Century Canadian Jurisprudence*
Peter Oliver, *'Terror to Evil-Doers': Prisons and Punishments in Nineteenth-Century Ontario*

1999 Constance Backhouse, *Colour-Coded: A Legal History of Racism in Canada, 1900–1950*
G. Blaine Baker and Jim Phillips, eds., *Essays in the History of Canadian Law: Volume VIII – In Honour of R.C.B. Risk*
Richard W. Pound, *Chief Justice W.R. Jackett: By the Law of the Land*
David Vanek, *Fulfilment: Memoirs of a Criminal Court Judge*

2000 Barry Cahill, *The Thousandth Man: A Biography of James McGregor Stewart*
A.B. McKillop, *The Spinster and the Prophet: Florence Deeks, H.G. Wells, and the Mystery of the Purloined Past*
Beverley Boissery and F. Murray Greenwood, *Uncertain Justice: Canadian Women and Capital Punishment*
Bruce Ziff, *Unforeseen Legacies: Reuben Wells Leonard and the Leonard Foundation Trust*

2001 Ellen Anderson, *Judging Bertha Wilson: Law as Large as Life*
Judy Fudge and Eric Tucker, *Labour before the Law: The Regulation of Workers' Collective Action in Canada, 1900–1948*
Laurel Sefton MacDowell, *Renegade Lawyer: The Life of J.L. Cohen*

2002 John T. Saywell, *The Lawmakers: Judicial Power and the Shaping of Canadian Federalism*
Patrick Brode, *Courted and Abandoned: Seduction in Canadian Law*
David Murray, *Colonial Justice: Justice, Morality, and Crime in the Niagara District, 1791–1849*

F. Murray Greenwood and Barry Wright, *Canadian State Trials, Volume II: Rebellion and Invasion in the Canadas, 1837–1839*

2003 Robert Sharpe and Kent Roach, *Brian Dickson: A Judge's Journey*
Jerry Bannister, *The Rule of the Admirals: Law, Custom, and Naval Government in Newfoundland, 1699–1832*
George Finlayson, *John J. Robinette, Peerless Mentor: An Appreciation*
Peter Oliver, *The Conventional Man: The Diaries of Ontario Chief Justice Robert A. Harrison, 1856–1878*

2004 Philip Girard, Jim Phillips, and Barry Cahill, *The Supreme Court of Nova Scotia, 1754–2004: From Imperial Bastion to Provincial Oracle*
Frederick Vaughan, *Aggressive in Pursuit: The Life of Justice Emmett Hall*
John D. Honsberger, *Osgoode Hall: An Illustrated History*
Constance Backhouse and Nancy Backhouse, *The Heiress versus the Establishment: Mrs Campbell's Campaign for Legal Justice*

2005 Philip Girard, *Bora Laskin: Bringing Law to Life*
Christopher English, *Essays in the History of Canadian Law: Volume IX – Two Islands: Newfoundland and Prince Edward Island*
Fred Kaufman, *Searching for Justice: An Autobiography*

2006 Donald Fyson, *Magistrates, Police, and People: Everyday Criminal Justice in Quebec and Lower Canada, 1764–1837*
Dale Brawn, *The Court of Queen's Bench of Manitoba, 1870–1950: A Biographical History*
Richard Risk, *A History of Canadian Legal Thought*, ed. G. Blaine Baker and Jim Phillips